2

THE PHILOSOPHY OF
JOHN DEWEY

THE LIBRARY OF LIVING PHILOSOPHERS

PAUL ARTHUR, *Editor*

Already Published:

THE PHILOSOPHY OF JOHN DEWEY (1939)

THE PHILOSOPHY OF GEORGE SANTAYANA (1940)

THE PHILOSOPHY OF ALFRED NORTH WHITEHEAD (1941)

THE PHILOSOPHY OF G. E. MOORE (1942)

THE PHILOSOPHY OF BERTRAND RUSSELL (1944)

THE PHILOSOPHY OF ERNST CASSIRER (1949)

ALBERT EINSTEIN: PHILOSOPHER-SCIENTIST (1949)

THE PHILOSOPHY OF SARVEPALLI RADHAKRISHNAN (1952)

THE PHILOSOPHY OF KARL JASPERS (1957)

THE PHILOSOPHY OF C. D. BROAD (1959)

THE PHILOSOPHY OF RUDOLF CARNAP (1963)

THE PHILOSOPHY OF MARTIN BUBER (1967)

THE PHILOSOPHY OF C. I. LEWIS (1968)

In Preparation:

THE PHILOSOPHY OF KARL R. POPPER

THE PHILOSOPHY OF GABRIEL MARCEL

THE PHILOSOPHY OF BRAND BLANSHARD

Other volumes to be announced later

THE

PHILOSOPHY

OF

JOHN DEWEY

EDITED BY

PAUL ARTHUR SCHILPP

NORTHWESTERN UNIVERSITY &
SOUTHERN ILLINOIS UNIVERSITY

LA SALLE, ILLINOIS • OPEN COURT • ESTABLISHED 1887

THE PHILOSOPHY OF JOHN DEWEY

Printed in the United States of America

GENERAL INTRODUCTION

TO

"THE LIBRARY OF LIVING PHILOSOPHERS"

ACCORDING to the late F. C. S. Schiller, the greatest obstacle to fruitful discussion in philosophy is "the curious etiquette which apparently taboos the asking of questions about a philosopher's meaning while he is alive." The "interminable controversies which fill the histories of philosophy," he goes on to say, "could have been ended at once by asking the living philosophers a few searching questions."

Perhaps the confident optimism of this last remark goes too far. Living thinkers have often been asked "a few searching questions," but their answers have not stopped "interminable controversies" about their real meaning. It is none the less true that there would be far greater clarity of understanding than is now often the case, if more such searching questions had been directed to great men while they were still alive.

This, at any rate, is the basic thought behind the present undertaking. The volumes of *The Library of Living Philosophers* can in no sense take the place of the original writings of great thinkers. Students who would know the philosophies of such men as John Dewey, Henri Bergson, Alfred North Whitehead, George Santayana, Benedetto Croce, Bertrand Russell, Léon Brunschvicg, Ernst Cassirer, Martin Heidegger, *et al.*, will still need to read the writings of these men. There is no substitute for first-hand contact with the original thought of the philosopher himself. Least of all does this *Library* pretend to be such a substitute. The *Library* in fact, will spare neither effort nor expense in offering to the student the best possible guide to the published writings of a given thinker. We shall attempt to meet this aim by providing at the end of each volume in our series a complete bibliography of the published work of the philosopher in question. Nor should one overlook the fact that the

vii

essays in each volume cannot but finally lead to this same goal. The interpretative and critical discussions of the various phases of a great thinker's work and, most of all, the reply of the thinker himself, are bound to lead the reader to his work and thereby to the philosopher himself.

At the same time, there is no blinking the fact that different experts find different things in the writings of the same philosopher. This is as true of the appreciative interpreter and grateful disciple as it is of the critical opponent. Nor can it be denied that such differences of reading and of interpretation on the part of other experts often leave the neophyte aghast before the whole maze of widely varying and even opposing interpretations. Who is right and whose interpretation shall he accept? When the doctors disagree among themselves, what is the poor student to do? If, finally, in desperation, he decides that all of the interpreters are probably wrong and that the only thing for him to do is to go back to the original writings of the philosopher himself and then make his own decision—uninfluenced (as if this were possible!) by the interpretation of any one else—the result is not that he has actually come to the meaning of the original philosopher himself, but rather that he has set up one more interpretation, which may differ to a greater or lesser degree from the interpretations already existing. It is clear that in this direction lies chaos, just the kind of chaos which Schiller has so graphically and inimitably described.[1]

It is strange that until now no way of escaping this difficulty has been seriously considered. It has not occurred to students of philosophy that one effective way of partially meeting the problem is to put these varying interpretations and critiques before the philosopher while he is still alive and to ask him to act at one and the same time as both defendant and judge. If the world's great living philosophers can be induced to coöperate in an enterprise whereby their own work can at least partially be saved from becoming merely "desiccated lecture-fodder," which on the one hand "provides innocuous sustenance for ruminant professors," and, on the other hand, gives an opportunity to such ruminants and their understudies to "speculate safely,

---

[1] In his essay on "Must Philosophers Disagree?" in the volume by the same title (Macmillan, London, 1934), from which the above quotations were taken.

endlessly, and fruitlessly, about what a philosopher may have meant, nay must have meant," (Schiller), they will have taken a long step toward making their intentions clearly comprehensible.

With this in mind *The Library of Living Philosophers* expects to publish at more or less regular intervals a volume on each of the greater among the world's living philosophers. In each case it will be the purpose of the editors of *The Library* to bring together in the volume the interpretations and criticisms of a wide range of that particular thinker's scholarly contemporaries, each of whom will be given a free hand to discuss the particular phase of the thinker's work which has been assigned to him. All contributed essays will finally be submitted to the philosopher with whose work and thought they are concerned, for his careful perusal and reply. And, although it would be expecting too much to imagine that the philosopher's reply will be able to stop all differences of interpretation and of critique, this should at least serve the purpose of stopping certain of the grosser and more general kinds of misinterpretations. If no further gain than this were to come from the present and projected volumes of this *Library*, it would still seem to be fully justified.

In carrying out this principal purpose of the *Library*, the editor announces that each volume will conform to the following pattern:

First, a series of expository and critical articles written by the leading exponents and opponents of the philosopher's thought;

Second, the reply to the critics and commentators by the philosopher himself;

Third, an intellectual autobiography of the thinker whenever this can be secured; in any case an authoritative and authorized biography; and

Fourth, a bibliography of the writings of the philosopher to provide a ready instrument to give access to his writings and thought.

Future volumes in this series will appear in as rapid succession as is feasible in view of the scholarly nature of this *Library*. The editor hopes to publish at least one new volume each year.

It is a real pleasure, finally, to make grateful acknowledgment for the financial assistance which this project has already received. Without such help the work on this *Library* could never have been undertaken. This volume (and at least one further volume in this series) was made possible in part by funds granted by the Carnegie Corporation of New York. Additional financial assistance came from the Alumni Foundation Fund of the College of Liberal Arts of Northwestern University. To these donors the editor desires to express his sincere gratitude. The Carnegie Corporation and the Northwestern University Alumni Foundation are not in any sense the authors, owners, publishers, or proprietors of this *Library* and they are therefore not to be understood as approving by virtue of their grants any of the statements made in this or in any succeeding volume.

PAUL ARTHUR SCHILPP
Editor

TABLE OF CONTENTS

PREFACE

THIS VOLUME on *The Philosophy of John Dewey* was intended as a tribute to one of the greatest living Americans, John Dewey, on his eightieth birthday, October 20, 1939. At the same time it is not at all what the Germans mean by a *Festschrift,* for in no *Festschrift* could one find severe criticism of or a reply from the recipient of the tribute. It is in doing precisely these last two things that we believe the unique and significant value of this book lies. Within the covers of this unusual kind of birthday gift the reader will find both pertinent criticism of the work and thought of John Dewey and the reply by the master himself. This is, indeed, something new in philosophical literature.

Here, too, the reader will find a biography written by Professor Dewey's three daughters on the basis of facts directly available to them and, indeed, with some help from Dr. Dewey himself. It is not only the editor who owes to Miss Jane M. Dewey, to Mrs. Granville M. Smith (Evelyn Dewey), and to Mrs. W. C. Brandauer (Lucy A. Dewey), and to Professor Dewey himself a permanent debt of gratitude. Rather he knows that he is herein voicing the appreciation also of all who are interested in philosophy, in education, or in the lives of great men.

The work on this volume was indeed a labor of love. At the same time its successful consummation was far from certain at the outset. Where would the editor have been if philosophers and educators from far and near had not been willing, at almost a moment's notice, to lay down other important work in order to participate in the present undertaking? The answer is all too obvious. Next to the personal privilege of coming somewhat closer to John Dewey the man, the greatest reward in this undertaking has been the magnificent way in which thinkers in Europe and America have readily given of their time and efforts in order to make this book possible. There is no adequate fashion in which the editor can express his heartfelt gratitude to them all. The gratitude of thousands of readers in our own generation and in times to come will be their lasting reward for having helped to point up and clarify the issues in Dewey's philosophy and for having given Dewey himself the opportunity to make his reply.

The reader must know that this volume could never even have been undertaken, much less been brought to a successful completion, without the kind coöperation and continuous helpfulness of Professor Dewey himself. For, since the *Reply by the Philosopher Himself* is precisely the major unique feature of all the volumes in this *Library*, no such volume as this could have been planned unless Professor Dewey had been willing to make such a reply. In the midst of all his other work, this involved no small sacrifice on Professor Dewey's part. At the same time it must be clearly understood that Professor Dewey himself had nothing whatever to do with the selection of the contributors. That responsibility is wholly the editor's.

Finally, as the "first reader" not merely of the contributed essays but also of Professor Dewey's "Reply," I cannot, in retrospect upon the completion of the first volume in our new *Library*, forbear making a brief remark. I would warn the reader, at this very beginning of his reading, that, in the two-way discussion between Professor Dewey and his commentators and critics contained between these covers, he will *not* find that the discussion issues in perfect harmony or complete agreement on the part of the philosophers concerned. Any reader who expects such an outcome from the following pages is doomed to certain disappointment. What he will find, however, is a decided clearing of atmosphere, a specific and continuous pointing out of misunderstandings and misinterpretations, and therefore an unquestionable clarifying of major issues. With reference to the still existing differences one might well bear in mind Bertrand Russell's telling comment, in his essay herein contained, that it is "hard to imagine any arguments on either side which do not beg the question; on fundamental issues perhaps this is unavoidable." In other words, philosophers, after all, "*must* disagree," if for no other reason but the fact that (1) they are philosophers, and (2) each one has lived a life of his own leading inevitably to an interpretation of his own. At the same time, even this first volume offers conclusive evidence that it is possible for the minds of philosophers to "meet;"—if not on precisely the same ground, at any rate for purposes of significant and fruitful discussion.

P. A. S.

DEPARTMENT OF PHILOSOPHY
NORTHWESTERN UNIVERSITY
EVANSTON, ILLINOIS
August 1939

ACKNOWLEDGMENTS

GRATEFUL ACKNOWLEDGMENT is hereby made to the publishers of all of Professor Dewey's books as well as to the editors and publishers of philosophical and educational journals and magazines for their kind permission to quote from the works of Professor Dewey as well as for their courtesy in not insisting upon a detailed enumeration of the books and articles quoted.

PREFATORY NOTE ADDED
IN 1971

The editor wishes to express his appreciation to the new publishers of the Library—The Open Court Publishing Company—for undertaking to keep all of the volumes of the Library permanently in print; to the Advisory Board of the Library, for their help in planning future volumes (the present membership of the board is listed below); and to the National Endowment for the Humanities, Washington, D. C., for generous grants for the years 1967-1969.

Paul A. Schilpp

Department of Philosophy
Southern Illinois University
Carbondale, Illinois

BIOGRAPHY OF JOHN DEWEY

BIOGRAPHY OF JOHN DEWEY

EDITED BY JANE M. DEWEY*

BURLINGTON, Vermont, is one of those New England towns which are not very different today from what they were in 1860. Then, as now, it was the commercial and cultural center of the state. French Canadians have since come in to help build its industries; its charm has been discovered by wealthy persons from large cities who have built summer residences in and around it; the automobile has enabled many of the better-to-do inhabitants to move from the city to its surroundings where they have built houses of colonial type in spacious grounds. But it remains essentially the same town of settled New England character, with the same beauty of location, set on a hill rising from Lake Champlain. At the top of the hill is a plain from which the Adirondacks are seen across the lake to the west while the Green Mountains bound the view across green fields to the east.

In this town John Dewey was born on October 20, 1859, the third of four sons of a middle class couple. The first son died in infancy but Davis Rich Dewey, a year and a half older than John, and Charles Miner Dewey, as much younger, grew up and attended the nearby public school with John. To this school went almost all the boys and girls of the town, from all kinds of homes, well-to-do and poor, old American and immigrant. The few who attended private schools were regarded as "sissies" or "stuck-up" by the majority. For, in spite of the especial prestige of the few first families, life was democratic—not consciously, but in that deeper sense in which equality and absence of class distinctions are taken for granted.

It would be difficult to say what hereditary influences were

* This biography was written by the daughters of its subject from material which he furnished. In the emphasis on varied influences and in the philosophical portions it may be regarded as an autobiography, but its subject is not responsible for the form nor for all the details.

3

important in forming the Dewey boys. But if we consider cultural rather than biological heredity there is no doubt of the importance of the pioneer background in their lives. Their father, Archibald Sprague Dewey, was born in northern Vermont in 1811. Late in life he married Lucina Rich, nearly twenty years younger than he, and he was nearly fifty years old when his sons were born. Pioneer days did not seem far off to these boys for, as late marriages were the rule in his family, only four generations separated Archibald from Thomas Dewey, who settled in Massachusetts between 1630 and 1633. Archibald's father was born before the revolution; one of his uncles was said in the family to have been killed during the Revolutionary War by Tories disguised as Indians. Archibald told his sons of hearing the gunfire of boats during a battle on Lake Champlain in the war of 1812.

There are various traditions in different branches of the family about the Deweys before Thomas came to this country. A member of the family who had been collecting genealogical material about Deweys in this country for many years was enabled to publish it by the boost given the family name by the exploits of Admiral Dewey, which made many Deweys wish to know how they were related to "Cousin George." As expected in a published genealogy, the book provides progenitors of royal blood. This origin, however, is all on the female side; the Dewey origin remains plebeian. The probability is that the family came from Flanders with the weavers who introduced fine weaving into England and bore the name de Wei, "of the meadow." Family tradition states that the parents or grandparents of Thomas Dewey left Flanders to escape the persecutions of the Duke of Alva. Certainly Thomas and his descendants were yeoman stock, farmers, wheelwrights, joiners, blacksmiths. Thomas Dewey witnessed documents with his mark; his sons signed their names; but none of his descendants in the line to which Archibald belonged had a college education until Davis and John, living near the University of Vermont, were enabled by low tuition and some help from scholarships to attend.

Thomas Dewey was one of the settlers of Dorchester, Massachusetts, named for the English town from which many of them came. It is probable that they had much the same reasons for leaving Dorsetshire that led the *Mayflower* passengers to leave Devonshire about a dozen years earlier. Dorchester, now one end of the subway system of Boston, was for a time the most populous town in New England. Possibly Thomas found it too crowded for the combination of farming and a trade by which most of the settlers made a living. At all events, as early as October 1635, he started, with a number of fellow immigrants, on a new, hard, journey to Windsor, Connecticut. In Windsor his six children were born and received a rudimentary education. Their descendants spread out around the Connecticut River valley. John Dewey's great-grandfather, Martin, was born in Westfield, Massachusetts, in 1716 and lived there until he was unchurched for marrying his deceased wife's sister.

John's father, Archibald, came of a farmer's family but moved to Burlington and engaged in the grocery business. He served as quartermaster of a Vermont cavalry regiment for four years of the Civil War. With only a little schooling, which he supplemented by reading, his literary tastes were distinctly classical. He read Shakespeare and Milton, not for culture, but because of his enjoyment of their words and turns of speech. He often quoted Milton while he worked, rolling with delight the unusual and euphonious phrases. He had lost his taste for Carlyle before his boys were growing up, but enjoyed Charles Lamb and Thackeray. Through an associate he had learned the Scottish dialect and he took delight in reciting long passages from Burns to his children, finding satisfaction in Burns's type of humor. He disliked Emerson and Hawthorne, probably because of intellectual conversatism and a regard for conventional theology. He had, himself, the gift of picturesque speech which he admired in others and used it to compose advertisements which obtained local fame at a time when writing copy was not recognized as an art. One was: "Hams and cigars, smoked and unsmoked;" and he advertised a brand of cigars as "A good excuse for a bad habit." He had an extraordinary memory for details and often told his sons what he had been doing at the same date in his boyhood or when he was at war. His energy was seldom directed toward advancing himself financially and he was said to sell more goods and collect fewer bills than any other merchant in town.

Lucina Artemesia Rich, his wife, came from Shoreham, Vermont, of a family supposed to have settled in this country at about the same time as the Deweys. The Riches were a more prosperous family; Lucina's grandfather was a congressman in Washington and her brothers graduated from college. Her father, Davis Rich, was known in the surrounding country as "Squire" Rich and served as a lay judge, locally known as a "side" judge, in the Addison County court. His reputation for fairness and understanding caused his neighbors in the township to bring their controversies to him for arbitration. Lucina, when a young woman, visited an uncle in Ohio who was, like all the Rich family, an active Universalist. The uncle wrote her father in Shoreham that she was attending revival meetings in the neighborhood, and he feared that unless her father intervened she would become a "Partialist." His forebodings were fulfilled and she became a member of the Congregational Church.

Her disposition was more intense and she had more missionary zeal than her easy-going husband, so that she was stricter with the boys and had more ambition for them. It was largely due to her influence that the boys broke with family tradition and obtained a college education; when their father was asked what his boys were going to do he usually replied that he hoped at least one of them would become a mechanic. The tastes of both parents contributed to giving the boys a wider range of good reading material than was customary for those of their financial circumstances. A public library founded while the boys were still in school and the University library widened the range of books at their disposal. They spent their own hard-earned money on a set of Chambers' Encyclopedia and on a set of the Waverley novels at a book auction and the latter, at least, they read.

In spite of the difference in age and temperament between Lucina and her husband their marriage was a successful one. The life of the boys was simple and healthful but somewhat isolated from the current of life about them. John and Davis were book-worms and John was bashful, with the tendency to self-consciousness which so often accompanies that trait. A cousin, John Parker Rich, less than two years older than John, was almost another brother to him. While Archibald Dewey was in the army, John Rich, still very young, lost his mother and Lucina took charge of the Rich household. Their close friends and companions were the two older Buckham boys, distant cousins on the Rich side and sons of the president of the University of Vermont. Summer vacations were often spent on their grandfather Rich's farm, where the comfortable residence was only a few steps from the country general store. Nearby, on a branch of the Lamoille River called Lemon Fair, stood a sawmill and gristmill erected by members of the Rich family, where the boys spent many hours of curiosity and contentment. At other times they visited John Rich's father near St. Albans, Vermont. He managed a haypressing establishment and lime kilns, which were also sources of enjoyment, drawing the boys from books. School was boredom, but, as they learned fairly easily, not much tax upon their energies. They were younger than other boys in their grades, though not markedly precocious, and took little interest in games. However, they were unconscious of any unhappy differences between themselves and their mates, satisfied with their own company in work and play. From a present-day point of view, too much moralistic emotional pressure was exerted by the religious atmosphere, evangelical rather than puritanic, which surrounded them. But, in addition to the escape into the outdoors open to all small town boys, more positive broadening influences were not lacking. Their mother, weary of the long separation from her husband brought about by his service in the Union army, moved the family to his headquarters in northern Virginia for the last winter of the war. This was an almost heroic move for a woman of those days and the privations in this devastated district made a deep impression on the boys, young as they were.

The money the boys spent at the book auction they earned by taking a carrier route for the daily afternoon paper published in Burlington and by tallying lumber brought in from Canada to the yards near the lake. While the family was not in very straitened circumstances, its needs were such that the boys took part as a matter of course in household activities. On their relatives' farms they helped with the work boys can do. Vermont was then, as now, a temperance stronghold, with the speakeasy problems usual in a prohibition community. Deploring the bad influence of the numerous "blind pigs," Archibald Dewey sought to offset them as far as he could by conducting with strict legality and great respectability the licensed medical liquor dispensary for the town. His sympathetic stories about this branch of the business gave the boys an early glimpse of a side of life their more stiff-necked maternal relatives preferred to ignore.

The unusual natural beauties of the surroundings were not consciously appreciated but were somehow absorbed. John and Davis tramped through the Adirondacks and to Mt. Mansfield. They outfitted Lake Champlain rowboats with a tent, blankets, and cooking utensils and explored the lake from end to end. On similar trips they rowed into Lake George or, with the help of a lumber wagon hired to carry the rowboat, descended the river and canal that connects Lake Champlain with the St. Lawrence and rowed up another river in French Canada to a beautiful inland lake. This Canadian venture was called a fishing trip but, according to their Indian guide, "la lune était trop faible;" in any case they caught few fish. Their usual companions on the boating trips were James and John Buckham. James Buckham had an extraordinary sensitiveness to all natural things and spent all his spare time in the woods. As he grew older he carried a gun, but this was only an excuse for the many hours he spent in watching animals and growing things in the country. On their trips into Canada the boys added to the French they had picked up in Burlington so that they read French novels before they studied French in school, novels of the most innocuous type, borrowed from a New England public library.

John Dewey was, as a young boy, particularly bashful in the presence of girls. As he grew older he and his brothers naturally became members of a group which included both boys and

girls of his neighborhood and this shyness wore off. One summer was spent camping at the foot of Mt. Mansfield in a
group of eight or ten young girls and boys, with his mother
taking charge. Two of these companions are still living in
Burlington, Cornelia Underwood and her sister Violet, now
Mrs. Edward Hoyt.

That his boyhood surroundings played a large part in forming John Dewey's educational theories is clear. As a boy and
young man he saw almost all his associates assuming a share
in household activities and responsibilities. Young people were
brought into intimate contact with a whole round of simple
industrial and agricultural occupations. On the other hand
school was a bore, not only to his companions, but to Davis and
himself, who were interested in reading almost anything except their school books, and its tiresomeness was mitigated only
by the occasional teacher who encouraged conversation on outside topics. By the time he reached manhood and became a
teacher himself, the growth of cities and the extension of the
work done by machines had interfered with the invaluable supplements to school education provided by active occupational responsibilities and intimate personal contacts with
people in all walks of life, which occurred spontaneously in
his boyhood. By this time also, reading matter, instead of being
sparse and difficult of access, was plentiful, cheap, and almost
forced on everyone. This had removed the significance which
formal schooling in the three R's possessed in the mainly agrar-
ian republic in which he grew up. The realization that the
most important parts of his own education until he entered
college were obtained outside the school-room played a large
rôle in his educational work, in which such importance is attached, both in theory and in practice, to occupational activities
as the most effective approaches to genuine learning and to
personal intellectual discipline. His comments on the stupidity
of the ordinary school recitation are undoubtedly due in no
small measure to the memory of the occasional pleasant class
hours spent with the teachers who wandered a little from the
prescribed curriculum.

When John Dewey was fifteen he graduated from high

school. At this time the family lived in a house which still
stands on Prospect Street, near the University of Vermont. His
brother Davis had entered college the year before and John
Rich was ready to enter with his cousin. Davis lost a year because of ill health and the three boys graduated from college
together in 1879.

The University was small at the time; the colleges of engineering and agriculture, the first professional schools, had
opened only a dozen years earlier. Eighteen students graduated
in 1879. All students who took Greek, as did the Dewey boys,
came in contact with the entire faculty of eight, except the professor of engineering. All studies were required. The first two
years were given to Greek, Latin, ancient history, analytic geometry and calculus. In the junior year the natural sciences came
to the fore. Professor G. H. Perkins taught geology, using
Dana's text, and zoology, by lectures and demonstrations. He
ordered his presentation of material on the theory of evolution.
Included in his lectures on the development of animal life
were scholarly accounts of the ideas of several of the early
church fathers, showing that they did not hold to a literal seven
day period of creation at the immediate fiat of the Creator. In
spite of the orthodox environment (the professor was a member
of the Congregational Church) the emphasis on evolution
aroused little, if any, visible resentment. The course in physiology taught the same year used the text written by T. H.
Huxley. From this book John Dewey derived an impressive
picture of the unity of the living creature. This aroused in him
that intellectual curiosity for a wide outlook on things which
interests a youth in philosophic study.

The University library subscribed to English periodicals
which were discussing the new ideas which centered about the
theory of evolution. The *Fortnightly* represented the more
radical wing of scientific thought; the *Contemporary Review*
was a moderate organ of more traditional views; whereas the
Nineteenth Century steered a middle course. It was at this
time that joint discussions of a single topic, known as "symposia,"
originated; at this time that Tyndall and Huxley exerted their
greatest influence. Students were interested in biology more

from curiosity about the theory of evolution than from considerations of a technical nature. These periodicals discussed far more than this particular subject, however, for the controversy about evolution was but the forefront of the rising interest in the relation between the natural sciences and traditional beliefs. English periodicals which reflected the new ferment were the chief intellectual stimulus of John Dewey at this time and affected him more deeply than his regular courses in philosophy.

The senior year was given to introducing students into the larger intellectual world as a sort of "finishing" process, and featured philosophy. Professor H. A. P. Torrey gave lectures on psychology, a course based on Noah Porter's *Intellectual Philosophy,* and a shorter course in Butler's *Analogy.* Seniors read Plato's *Republic* and acquired some knowledge of British empiricism from Bain's relatively innocuous *Rhetoric.* President Buckham gave courses in political economy, international law and Guizot's *History of Civilization.* He was a remarkable teacher. With an orderly and logical mind he combined powers of clear expression. A man of positive convictions, he refrained from attempting to force them on his students and his teaching method was Socratic rather than dogmatic. The only contact students who were not called up for discipline had with him before their senior year was when he met freshmen once a week, nominally to discuss elementary moral questions, but really to make the students' acquaintance. The moral topics considered made little permanent impression on the future philosopher but he was abidingly influenced by one incident of the classroom. On this occasion President Buckham attempted to secure from any member of the class a statement of the general subject of the chapter assigned for that week's discussion. None could give it. After this at least one of the students made a point of making sure what he was going to read about before losing himself in the details of any topic of intellectual import.

The philosophic teaching of Professor Torrey was, like most philosophy taught in American colleges at this time, based upon the writings of the Scotch school. The idealistic-realistic controversy was not acute, and little was being written or said about Bishop Berkeley. The influence of the Scotch philosophers was due to their insistence upon intuitions, which formed, before the introduction of German spiritualistic idealism, the chief intellectual bulwark of moral and religious beliefs against the dissolving effect of English empiricism. The rather dry bones of Scotch thought were somewhat enlivened by ideas and topics which persisted from the teachings of the Reverend Professor James Marsh, one of the first Americans to disregard the dangerous reputation of the German philosophers sufficiently to study and teach them. Their ideas were largely presented as reflected through Coleridge, but even in this form were regarded with suspicion by the orthodox. The ideas that institutions of society carried in themselves a spiritual significance and that the Bible was inspired because it was inspiring were considered dangerous even in the diluted form in which Torrey presented them. Marsh, as his *Remains* shows, had a speculative mind and it is probable that some of his writings first directed the attention of Emerson to German thought and to Coleridge as its interpreter.

These studies helped to fix the direction of Dewey's intellectual interests, if they did not settle his career at the time. His philosophical reading was extended by articles of Frederick Harrison in the *Fortnightly*, which drew his attention to Comte and caused him to study Harriet Martineau's condensation of Comte's *Positive Philosophy*. Neither the idea of three stages of the evolution of society nor Comte's construction of a new religion interested him especially, but what was said about the disorganization of existing social life and the necessity of finding a social function for science remained a permanent influence in his thought, although in his own philosophy emphasis is placed upon the method of science rather than upon organization of its conclusions. Reading Comte and his English expositors first awakened in Dewey his characteristic interest in the interaction of social conditions with the development of thought in science and in philosophy. When Dewey was in the university each senior and junior student was required to prepare a speech for presentation; the best orators were selected to deliver theirs at a public exhibition. The title of one which he prepared but did not deliver, "The Limits of Political Economy," discloses Comte's influence who subordinated political economy to sociology.

Dewey learned easily and always received fairly good grades. The studies of the senior year aroused him to such an extent that his record for that year is as high as has been obtained by any student of the college. He joined a local fraternity, Delta Psi, in his sophomore year and was made a member of Phi Beta Kappa upon graduation.

The summer following graduation was one of anxiety. Like many other young graduates uncertain about their life career he wanted a teaching position. His youth and inexperience made it difficult for him to find the job which his economic condition made it important for him to have, and when schools opened in the autumn he still had nothing. Then he received a telegram from a cousin, Clara Wilson, who was principal of the High school in South Oil City, Pennsylvania, informing him of a vacancy there. For two years he taught a little of everything, Latin, algebra, natural science from Steele's *Fourteen Weeks*. The first year he was paid forty dollars a month. At the end of the period his cousin resigned to marry and he also left, returning to Burlington. During part of the following winter he taught in a village school in the neighboring town of Charlotte. In Burlington he read some of the classics in the history of philosophy under the direction of Professor Torrey. Mr. Torrey took him for long walks in the woods and spoke more directly of his own views than he had in the classroom, disclosing a mind which under more favorable circumstances might have attained distinction. Among the journals in the college library was *Speculative Philosophy*, edited by W. T. Harris, who, while superintendent of schools in St. Louis, had come in contact with a group of German exiles of 1848 who were ardent students of German thought, especially of Schelling and Hegel. Dr. Harris's Journal, appearing somewhat irregularly, was for many years the only distinctively philosophical magazine in the United States and it became an organ for this group. Dewey's mind was now turned toward the teaching of philosophy as a career. He wrote an essay which he sent in fear and trembling to Dr. Harris, asking him whether its author should go professionally into philosophy. After some time Dr. Harris wrote that the essay showed a philosophical mind of high rank. He published the essay in the issue of the *Journal* dated April 1882 (but appearing later) under the title "The Metaphysical Assumptions of Materialism." Dr. Harris's encouragement decided the new author to continue his studies and led him to write two other articles which were published by Dr. Harris. In their author's mature opinion all three articles are more notable for schematic logical form than for substance.

Encouraged by Professor Torrey and by Dr. Harris, he borrowed five hundred dollars from an aunt and started for Baltimore in the fall of 1882 to attend The Johns Hopkins University. This move proved to be a permanent break with his boyhood surroundings. John Rich had gone into his father's business in Vermont, Charles Dewey also entered the business world and during most of his life was on the west coast where his brother did not see him often. James Buckham, who had shown a poetic interest in nature as a boy, was for a time one of the editors of the old and famous *Youth's Companion* but died before his talents came to full maturity. John Buckham is now a professor in the Pacific School of Religion, an interdenominational (though originally Congregational) Theological Seminary in Berkeley, California. Davis Dewey came to Johns Hopkins after several years of very successful high school teaching, at the beginning of John's second year. After receiving his doctorate in political economy he went to the Massachusetts Institute of Technology to take charge of courses in statistics and economics which had been organized by General Walker, then president of the Institute. Davis remained Walker's close associate as long as the latter lived and developed the course of study in engineering administration which is the Institute's equivalent of the schools of business now established at many large universities. His Course XV was the first, or one of the first, experiments in this field, and has proved one of the most successful. The fact that the courses were intended for engineering students put an emphasis upon the practical rather than the speculative aspects of economics which was thoroughly congenial with his preferences. He has been very active in the American Statistical Society, editing their publications and serving as delegate at international meetings. Although he retired from active teaching some years ago he is still, at eighty, editor of the "American Economic Review."

Davis' years at Johns Hopkins were for John a grateful renewal of the close intimacy of school and college days, strengthening the friendship which has bound the two brothers to one another through the half century which has elapsed since. Although Davis Dewey is more conservative in his social and political opinions than his younger brother, the resemblance, physical and mental, between them is strong. Both have an unusual power of hard, disinterested work and of detached objective judgment. Both also have extraordinarily pleasant dispositions with the ability to laugh at much that would otherwise irritate them.

When John Dewey went to The Johns Hopkins University it had been open for some years for graduate study. President Gilman had gathered there a fine band of scholars and teachers with the intention of enabling graduate students, who had been going to Germany to prepare for a life of scholarship, to find what they wanted nearer home. A few students living nearby were permitted to take the last two years of undergraduate work but every emphasis was placed upon the graduate school. President Gilman constantly urged upon the students the feasibility and importance of original research. The very possibility of students' doing anything new, anything original, was a novel and exciting idea to most of these young men. They must have been aware that there were people in the world doing intellectual things which had not been done before, but their previous education had never suggested to them that they might be of this happy band. The atmosphere of the new university was thus exceedingly stimulating, an experience in itself that could hardly be duplicated later. Many of the students felt that it was bliss to be alive and in such surroundings. The seminar was then practically unheard of in American colleges but was the center of intellectual life at Hopkins. President Gilman's occasional enthusiastic talks in which he told of the intellectual and professional success of students who had gone forth from the university were ably seconded by Herbert Adams of the department of history and political science under whom Dewey took a "minor." Students were few enough to be in intimate contact with each other and with the faculty. Among John Dewey's close associates, besides his brother Davis, were Yager of Connecticut, later governor of Porto Rico, Arthur Kimball, a roommate for a time, and later professor of physics at Amherst, Harry Osborn, who taught biology at Hamlin College near St. Paul and whom Dewey saw frequently during the year he taught at the University of Minnesota, Frederic S. Lee in physiology, and Joseph Jastrow and James McKeen Cattell in psychology. Cattell was not only a close friend but the active agency in bringing Dewey to Columbia after his resignation from Chicago in 1904. Such friendships were an invaluable supplement to the education obtained in class rooms and in the Pratt Library.

President Gilman met graduate students individually and gave them friendly encouragement and advice. He was not favorably inclined to the study of philosophy, partly because of his recollection of the philosophy taught him as an undergraduate and partly because it afforded few positions, most institutions having clergymen to teach philosophical subjects. He suggested to Dewey that he change to some other field but was unable to turn the enthusiastically budding philosopher from his path. Dr. Gilman did not lose his friendly interest because his advice was not heeded; when Dewey was called to the president's office after obtaining the doctorate he received not only an excellent personal warning against his seclusive and bookish habits but an offer of a loan to enable him to continue his studies in Europe.

In Dewey's major department Professor George S. Morris of the University of Michigan taught the first half year and Dr. G. Stanley Hall, who had recently returned from prolonged study in Germany, the second half. Contact with these two men, especially with Professor Morris, left a deep impress on the mind of this student. Morris was one of the few teachers of philosophy in the United States who was not a clergyman, he had translated Ueberweg's *History of Philosophy* into English and had a rich historic background upon which he drew in all his teaching. A man of intense intellectual enthusiasms, he put emotional loyalty as well as intellectual understanding into all his teaching. He had reacted strongly against the religious orthodoxy of a puritanic New England upbringing and, for a time, had been intellectually a disciple of Mill, Bain and other British empiricists. In Germany he came under the influence of Trendelenburg and made for himself a synthesis of Hegelian idealism and Aristotelianism somewhat of the type presented in a little book by Wallace. He corresponded with Caird and other Oxford Hegelians of the period.

In Dewey's sketch "From Absolutism to Experimentalism," in the second volume of *Contemporary American Philosophy*, he gives an account of the appeal the philosophy of Hegel had for him and of the reason for that appeal. The singular and sensitive purity, the whole-souled and single-minded personality of his teacher undoubtedly contributed, but the effect of this appeal is understandable only if the New England background of the pupil is kept in mind. He had nominally accepted the religious teachings in which he was brought up and had joined the White Street Congregational Church in Burlington at an early age. He had tried, without being aware of the effort this required of him, to believe in the doctrines of the church, but his belief was never whole-hearted enough to satisfy his emotional need. From the idealism of Hegel, as interpreted by Morris, he obtained in his late adolescence that fusion of emotions and intellect for which he had sought unsuccessfully in his boyhood religious experience. In the sketch referred to he says that his acquaintance with Hegel "left a permanent deposit in his thinking." The following statement as to the nature of this deposit is his.

"Hegel's idea of cultural institutions as an 'objective mind' upon which individuals were dependent in the formation of their mental life fell in with the influence of Comte and of Condorcet and Bacon. The metaphysical idea that an absolute mind is manifested in social institutions dropped out; the idea, upon an empirical basis, of the power exercised by cultural environment in shaping the ideas, beliefs, and intellectual attitudes of individuals remained. It was a factor in producing my belief that the not uncommon assumption in both psychology and philosophy of a ready-made mind over against a physical world as an object has no empirical support. It was a factor in producing my belief that the only possible psychology, as distinct from a biological account of behavior, is a social psychology. With respect to more technically philosophical matters, the Hegelian emphasis upon continuity and the function of conflict persisted on empirical grounds after my earlier confidence in dialectic had given way to scepticism. There was a period extending into my earlier years at Chicago when, in connection with a seminar in Hegel's Logic I tried reinterpreting his categories in terms of 'readjustment' and 'reconstruction.' Gradually I came to realize that what the principles actually stood for could be better understood and stated when completely emancipated from Hegelian garb."

The influence of Professor Morris was undoubtedly one source of Dewey's later interest in logical theory. Morris was given to contrasting what he called "real" logic, and associated with Aristotle and Hegel, with formal logic of which he had a low opinion. Dewey, in his years of association with Morris in Ann Arbor, developed the idea that there was an intermediate kind of logic that was neither merely formal nor a logic of inherent "truth" of the constitution of things; a logic of the processes by which knowledge is reached. Mill's logic seemed to him an effort in this direction, but an effort that was disastrously blocked and deflected by Mill's uncritical acceptance of a sensationalistic and particularistic psychology. In some of the earlier volumes of Muirhead's *Library of Philosophy* there is announced for publication *"Principles of Instrumental Logic,* by John Dewey, Ph.D., Professor of Philosophy in the University of Michigan."* That book was never published. Perhaps an echo of the idea is found in Dewey's later "instrumentalism," but at the time the title was submitted it meant a theory of thought viewed as the means or instrumentality of *attaining* knowledge, as distinguished from the theory of the truths about the structure of the universe of which reason was in possession, or "real" logic. Dewey found that the development of his ideas on the subject led him entirely away from the doctrines associated with "real" logic into a group of problems of experience and the relation of knowledge to experience that occupied his time and intellectual energy for many years to come.

Association with Morris was immensely fruitful in the evolution of Dewey in varied ways. When Morris returned to Michigan at the end of the first semester he gave Dewey his undergraduate class in the history of philosophy to teach for the remainder of the year. This gave confidence in the presence of others to the student, who until then had felt it only in writing. The following year Morris was influential in securing for Dewey a fellowship enabling him to continue his studies without increasing his debt. The summer of 1884, following his studies at Hopkins, was almost a repetition of his first summer out of college and the new doctor was beginning to doubt the wisdom of his choice of profession when Professor Morris wrote him offering an instructorship in philosophy at the University of Michigan. The offer was very gladly accepted, at a salary of nine hundred dollars.

President James B. Angell of Michigan University had preceded Buckham at the University of Vermont. At this time he was engaged in the processes by which a great state university was to achieve leadership and creative scholarship. To all who taught under him Angell remains the ideal college president, one who increased the stature of his institution by fostering a truly democratic atmosphere for students and faculty and encouraging the freedom and individual responsibility that are necessary for creative education. His personal charm and geniality created a general atmosphere of friendliness to newcomers and to students. Professors made a point of calling even on young instructors. Instructors attended the weekly faculty meeting, a highly educative process for them. This immediate acceptance as an adult responsible member of the faculty and the fact that the institution was the natural culmination of the coeducational state education system made a deep impression on Dewey, starting the chain of ideas which later comprised his educational theory. His boyhood surroundings, although not marked by genuine industrial and financial democracy, created in him an unconscious but vital faith in democracy which was here brought to consciousness to form the foundation of much of his philosophical writing.

During his first winter in Ann Arbor, Dewey lived with another new instructor, Homer Kingsley, in a boarding house in which two "coeds" had rooms. One of these, Alice Chipman, was a few months older than the young philosophy instructor she was to marry two years later, in July 1886. A native of Michigan, she had been teaching school for several years to earn the money to complete her education. Her family background had the same pioneer sources as Dewey's. Her father, a cabinet maker, moved from Vermont to Michigan as a boy. She and her sister were orphaned very young and brought up by their maternal grandparents, Frederick and Evalina Riggs. Mr. Riggs came to the state from upper New York as agent for the Hudson Bay Company. One of the very early settlers, he surveyed the first road through the northern part of the state, managed Indian trading posts, and later took up farming in the wilderness. The two grandchildren, Alice and Esther, grew up in a household where memories of pioneering days were strong and the spirit of adventure was a living force. While a fur trader Grandfather Riggs had been initiated into the Chippewa tribe and he learned their language so that an Indian could not tell by his voice that he was a white man. Indians visited him all his life and he was a champion of their vanishing rights. He was a member of that faction of the democratic party which extended its aversion to war to the war between the states. He was a temperamental dissenter from established conventions; a freethinker who gave money toward the erection of every church in his village of Fenton; an opponent of war who drew heavily on what he had accumulated to buy substitutes for friends and relatives who were drafted. He suffered from asthma and spent some years in the new West seeking a better climate, part of the time in Dodge City, where he served as judge in a Volunteer Court which condemned to death a frontiersman who had shot his victims in the back. Among other ventures, he found in Colorado a gold mine which was too far from any center to be profitable. His rich experience and responsive and original mind more than compensated for the scantiness of his schooling. One of his remarks has been quoted more than once by Dewey, "Some day these things will be found out, and not only found out but *known.*" His granddaughters received plenty of loyal affection but not as much material help in realizing their ambitions as the family resources justified, for the grandparents put their extreme individualism into practice in the home and confined their training largely to "do whatever you think right." Of doubtful comfort to the young, this advice certainly fostered intellectual independence and self-reliance in a strong character, such as Alice Chipman's. Her influence on a young man from conservative Burlington was stimulating and exciting. She possessed the qualities her grandparents believed in without the mold of their beliefs and had added to them a lively desire for an education that would enlarge her horizon. She had a brilliant mind which cut through sham and pretense to the essence of a situation; a sensitive nature combined with indomitable courage and energy, and a loyalty to the intellectual integrity of the individual which made her spend herself with unusual generosity for all those with whom she came in contact. Awakened by her grandparents to a critical attitude toward social conditions and injustices, she was undoubtedly largely responsible for the early widening of Dewey's philosophic interests from the commentative and classical to the field of contemporary life. Above all, things which had previously been matters of theory acquired through his contact with her a vital and direct human significance. Whatever skill Dewey acquired in so-called "intuitive" judgment of situations and persons he attributes to her. She had a deeply religious nature but had never accepted any church dogma. Her husband acquired from her the belief that a religious attitude was indigenous in natural experience, and that theology and ecclesiastic institutions had benumbed rather than promoted it.

The years of Dewey's association with Morris in Ann Arbor were those in which his philosophical position was closest to German objective idealism. This was the period of greatest influence of German upon English thought. Important English and Scotch philosophical writings were highly critical of traditional British philosophy. They appealed to German thought to offset the disintegrative and dissolvent effect of extreme British individualism on religion and all phases of social life and theory by a philosophy of "organic" relations. Edward Caird's critical exposition of Kant revised in a Hegelian sense Kant's philosophy. Caird's skillful liberation of the function of negation from entanglement in the Hegelian dialectic especially influenced Dewey. He had previously worked through T. H. Green's criticism of Locke and Hume and his *Prolegomena to Ethics*. Two articles in *Mind* and parts of his *Psychology* show Dewey's position at this time. In addition to the work in "instrumental" logic two further influences were gradually undermining the dominant position of German thought in his mind. One was the systematic study of ethics which he undertook when courses in this subject were assigned him to teach. Two small works published locally for the use of his classes show the continuing change in his position which his ethical studies brought about. The first of these, *Outlines of a Critical Theory of Ethics*, published in 1891, shows his concern with the function of intelligence in concrete direction of human action, individual and social, in distinction from the once-for-all operation of reason in constituting the scheme of things which is set forth by rationalistic idealism. The second book, *The Study of Ethics*, printed in 1894 when the edition of the first was exhausted, is based upon the idea that intelligence is "mediation" of native impulses with respect to the consequences of their operation, an idea which contains the germ of his later "instrumental" pragmatism and cannot be harmonized with the idealistic view of mind as inherently constitutive.

The other influence, his psychological studies, is already seen in this basic idea of the second syllabus of moral theory. G. Stanley Hall's discursive lectures on psychological topics, experimental and theoretical, had left him with the belief that the relation between psychology and philosophy was an intimate one, but one which must be worked out on the basis of the new experimental psychology. Experiment was overthrowing the older "rational" psychology traditionally associated with philosophy, and probably an ambition to help bring about an alliance of the new psychology with philosophy was directing Dewey's intellectual activity to a greater extent than he realized. Certainly the ethical studies had a psychological foundation. William James's *Principles of Psychology* was much the greatest single influence in changing the direction of Dewey's philosophical thinking. The marked increase in the prominence of the psychological approach in the second ethical syllabus may be attributed to the appearance of this book shortly after the first one was written.

James's influence on Dewey's theory of knowledge was exercised not by the *Pragmatism*, which appeared after Dewey's theory had been formed, but by chapters in the *Principles of Psychology* dealing with conception, discrimination and comparison, and reasoning. Dewey has frequently recommended these chapters to students as a better introduction to the essentials of a pragmatic theory of knowledge than the *Pragmatism*. The nature of James's influence may be learned from Dewey's autobiographical sketch previously referred to. That article states that there are two unreconciled strains in James's *Principles,* one of them derived from the traditional view of psychology as the theory of "consciousness," the other from the much more objective psychological theory which is founded on biology. It is of the latter that Dewey writes: "It worked its way more and more into all my ideas and acted as a ferment to transform old beliefs." In the period we are discussing the difference between the two strains was not so clear to him as it became later and his language was colored by ideas which he was abandoning. This has led to some misinterpretation of his philosophy, almost inevitable in the case of a theory based on newly established or not quite accepted knowledge, which has led others to give it a more "subjective" meaning than he does himself. In republishing in 1916 the logical essays written in 1901 he says that "the essays in their psychological phases are written from the standpoint of what is now termed a behavioristic psychology," although antedating the use of that expression.

Dewey's teaching at the University of Michigan was interrupted for one year when he accepted a professorship at the University of Minnesota. During that year his revered teacher

Professor Morris died and Dewey was invited to return to Ann Arbor to take charge of the department. Professor R. M. Wenley, who succeeded Dewey at Michigan, has written a life of Morris which is a valuable document in an important phase of the development of philosophy in the United States. In the last chapter he reprints passages written by Dewey after Morris's death which set forth in more detail than is possible here the nature of Dewey's debt to his teacher and associate. On the personal as well as the professional side of Dewey's life Morris's death was a great loss. The Morrises had opened their house to the young instructor and later to his wife and their kindness and hospitality were the focal point of the Deweys' social life.

The Deweys named their third child, born in Ann Arbor in 1893, Morris. This child was the most intellectually advanced in nature of their six sons and daughters and joined with a kind of inherent maturity an extraordinarily attractive disposition. His death of diphtheria in Milan, Italy, at the age of two and a half, was a blow from which neither of his parents ever fully recovered. One of their fellow travellers on the voyage to England remarked on the last day of the voyage: "If that boy grows up what he is now there will be a new religion in the world." The exaggeration of the remark conveys an idea of the impression little Morris made upon others and the quality of the loss experienced by his family.

Dr. Hough, the second member of the Ann Arbor department while Dewey was in Minneapolis, was called to Minnesota when Dewey returned to Ann Arbor. James Hayden Tufts was called to take Hough's place at Michigan. Tufts is an Amherst graduate who received his doctorate at Berlin and established himself as a scholar through his translation of Windelband's *History of Philosophy*. Of New England descent, as solid and rugged in character as its mountains, he formed with Dewey, in the short time he was at Ann Arbor, a personal and intellectual friendship which has continued through the years. When the University of Chicago opened, Tufts accepted a position there and this led to Dewey's being called to Chicago in 1894. Their association in Chicago bore fruit in the *Ethics*, published in 1908 and, in a new edition in 1932, an evidence of their intellectual connection which renders further comment superfluous.

When Tufts left Michigan it was necessary to add two teachers of philosophy to care for the increasing number of students. Alfred H. Lloyd and George H. Mead were chosen. Both had studied at Harvard University, Lloyd having just received his doctorate, while Mead was called from Berlin before he had completed his dissertation. Personal and intellectual association with these two men and their families meant much to the Dewey family. Lloyd had an original mind, gifted in unusual insights which he expressed in a language so individual that he could not be identified with any particular philosophical school. This limited the influence of his writings but possibly intensified his power to stimulate originality and independence in his associates and students. His transparent candor and unswerving fairness, with his intellectual gifts, procured for him a distinguished position in the faculty. At the time of his death he had been for many years Dean of Graduate Students.

Mead and his family were close neighbors of the Deweys in Ann Arbor and after both families moved to Chicago they lived in the same apartment house. The older children of the two families are nearly of an age and close family friendships were quickly established, the Deweys visiting the Castle home in Honolulu from which Mrs. Mead had come. The Meads remained the closest friends of the Deweys, even after the removal of the Deweys to New York, until their deaths.

Since Mead published little during his lifetime, his influence on Dewey was the product of conversations carried on over a period of years and its extent has been underestimated. At Mead's funeral exercises in 1931 Dewey said that Mead had a seminal mind of the first order, a view publicly endorsed by Whitehead after he had read some of Mead's posthumously published work. Mead's scholarship, especially in the natural sciences, was much greater than Dewey's. In the years of his association with Dewey, Mead's principal interest was the bearing of biological theories upon scientific psychology. The psychologists and philosophers who, up to that time, had recognized any connection between psychological phenomena and the human body had found the physical basis of mind in the brain alone, or at most in the nervous system isolated from the whole organism, and thus from the relations of the organism to its environment. Mead, on the contrary, started from the idea of the organism acting and reacting in an environment; in this view the nervous system, brain included, is an organ for regulating the relations of the organism as a whole with objective conditions of life. Psychological phenomena, including processes of thought and knowledge, must then be described from this point of view. Mead had also developed an original theory of the *psychical* as the state occurring when previously established relations of organism and environment break down and new relations have not yet been built up; and, through inclusion of relations of human beings with one another, a theory of the origin and nature of selves. Dewey did not attempt a development of these special ideas, but he took them over from Mead and made them a part of his subsequent philosophy, so that, from the nineties on, the influence of Mead ranked with that of James. Mead was continuously reworking his ideas so that most of his work was published only after his death. Shortly before his death he gave the Carus lectures before the American Philosophical Association but he was unable to make his notes ready for publication. Former students and colleagues edited his manuscripts and lecture notes taken by students, and four volumes of Mead's work appeared. One of his graduate students said after Mead's death that for many years articles and even books would continue to be published of which the first author was George Mead.

During the last years of his stay in Michigan, John Dewey's parents came to live with him. While his father was hurt at his sons' recreance to the Republican Party, associated in his mind with the preservation of the union, and his mother at their defection from the religious teachings of their boyhood, both were sufficiently liberal in their views and had sufficient confidence in their children to keep the family relation a close one.

Two strong links bound the University of Michigan to the state school system of which it formed a part. The first chair of education in the country was established there, occupied first by Payne and then by Hinsdale; the high schools of the state were visited by members of the university faculty, who reported on the preparation for college work of their students. Dewey's interest in general education was stimulated by the visits which he made and he was a member of the Schoolmasters Club of Michigan, designed to bring secondary and college education nearer together by its conferences and committees. His interest in psychology led him to a study of the learning process and in his later years at Ann Arbor he spoke frequently at Teachers' Institutes and Conventions on such topics as "attention," "memory," "imagination," and "thinking," all in relation to teaching and study. He had at this time three small children, Frederick Archibald, born in 1887, Evelyn, born in 1890 in Minneapolis, and Morris. His observation of them gave a practical emphasis to what he had learned from James of the importance of native tendencies and caused him to attach great importance to proper development in the early years. With Professor McLellan of the University of Toronto, who wrote the portion dealing with practical applications, he published two books for teachers in training. His belief in the social function of philosophy, strengthened by an emotional dissatisfaction with pure theorizing, made him feel the need of practical experience to check and develop purely theoretical ideas. He had come to the conviction that existing educational methods, especially in the elementary schools, were not in harmony with the psychological principles of normal development. This inspired a desire for an experimental school which should combine psychological principles of learning with the principle of coöperative association which he derived from his moral studies. At the same time it should release his children from the intellectual boredom of his own school days. Philosophy was to find its social application and test in direct educational experience in the school.

When, in 1894, he received an offer from the University of Chicago, one of the factors leading to its acceptance was the inclusion of Pedagogy in the department with Philosophy and Psychology. After a few years he found a group of parents interested in procuring for their children a different kind of education from any available in Chicago. With their aid, financial as well as moral, an elementary school was started under the auspices of this department, of which he was head. Later named

"The Laboratory School," it was popularly known as the "Dewey School." The University allowed one thousand dollars in free tuition to teachers in the school, but gave no further financial aid. For the seven and a half years of its existence friends and patrons contributed more to the support of this school than did the University.

The school was not a practice or progressive school as the terms are used today. Its general relation to the department of pedagogy was that which laboratories in the physical sciences bear to instruction in these subjects. Mayhew and Edwards,[1] who were teachers in the school, give a full and authoritative account of its work which makes it unnecessary to discuss it here.

The most widely read and influential of Dewey's writings, *School and Society*, which has been translated into a dozen European and Oriental languages, consists of talks given to raise money for the Laboratory School. Two series of educational monographs, published by the University of Chicago Press and by Houghton Mifflin Company are joint products of the work of the school and of association with a group of educationalists of the state of Illinois. In *Contemporary American Philosophy* Dewey says that after his movement from idealism to his naturalistic and pragmatic experimentalism personal contacts had, on the whole, more influence in directing his thought than the books he read. Contacts formed through the school are among the most important of the many formed in Chicago. The friendly conflict of different schools of educational thought of these years may be said to mark the beginnings of the "progressive" movement which is remaking the educational system of the United States. Francis W. Parker, later principal of the Cook County Teachers Training School in Chicago, marked by his work in Quincy, Massachusetts, the beginning of a new educational movement in the public schools. He was also active in forming a Child Study Association. DeGarmos and the McMurrys after working with Rein in Germany, introduced Herbartian methods into the United States. W. T. Harris was the active promoter of an educational philosophy that drew, with marked originality, upon Hegel.

[1] K. C. Mayhew and A. C. Edwards, *The Dewey School*, D. Appleton-Century Co. (1936).

A more intimate personal contact was Dewey's friendship with Ella Flagg Young, during the early years of his stay in Chicago a District Superintendent of City Schools. To her and to his wife he attributes the greatest influence in educational matters of those years. He regards Mrs. Young as the wisest person in school matters with whom he has come in contact in any way. She had begun as a grade teacher, made her way through teaching in high schools to high administrative positions. She was the first woman to be superintendent of the school system of any large American city and the first to be President of the National Educational Association. She habitually and systematically thought out the implications of her actual experience. Her respect for the moral and intellectual personality of the individual, two things she did not separate, developed through her own experience into an insistence upon respect by teachers for the integrity of the mental processes of students and a constant protest against school administration from above which had an enormous influence upon school methods, first in Chicago and then throughout the country. Contact with her supplemented Dewey's educational ideas where his own experience was lacking in matters of practical administration, crystallizing his ideas of democracy in the school and, by extension, in life.

Another influence in Dewey's life deriving from residence in Chicago rather than from his professional position was his interest in Hull House. Hull House was a social settlement in more sense than one. It was a place in which all sorts of people of all beliefs and non-beliefs met on a common footing. The Deweys were regular visitors and formed warm personal friendships with its residents, especially with Jane Addams. They found contact with many types of persons there the most interesting and stimulating part of their non-professional life. One of Miss Addams' main convictions was that the associations formed through Hull House were as important for those from homes more privileged in economic status and cultural opportunities as for the poorer residents of the district around the House. There was no question in her mind of "seeing how the other half lives" but only of joint learning how to live together; learning especially that democracy is a way of life, the truly moral and human way of life, not a political institutional device.

Dewey became a trustee of the settlement when it became necessary to incorporate it, a step which Jane Addams avoided as long as possible because of her fear of institutionalizing its life. Dewey's faith in democracy as a guiding force in education took on both a sharper and a deeper meaning because of Hull House and Jane Addams.

Close association was interrupted when the Deweys left Chicago but there was never a breach in their mutual esteem and affection. At the time of the war Miss Addams remained true to her Quaker antecedents and her Tolstoyan policy of non-resistance (which had stood her in good stead during the early days when Hull House was the object of hostility and she herself of personal insults). Dewey felt that our entrance into the war was the lesser of two evils and this difference was a source of pain on both sides. Their later relations were cordial; Jane Addams was a speaker at the celebration of Dewey's seventieth birthday in New York City in 1929 and Dewey spoke both at a more recent anniversary celebration at Hull House and at a memorial meeting held near New York after death brought to a close the personal career of one of the most remarkable women of her day. Dewey attributes much of the enthusiasm of his support of every cause that enlarged the freedom of activity of women to his knowledge of the character and intelligence of his wife, of Ella Flagg Young, and of Jane Addams.

During the years Dewey was in Chicago he spent his vacations in the Adirondacks. While still in Ann Arbor the family went one summer to the camp and summer school conducted by Thomas Davidson at Glenmore at the foot of Mount Hurricane, virtually a successor to the Concord School of Philosophy. The following summer they built a cabin not far from Davidson's property and here their summers were spent for many years. Their property was separated from Glenmore by a small stream, called Gulf Brook because of the deep channel it had dug for itself, and Davidson remarked that the Deweys had chosen to live "across the gulf," a recognition on his part that they did not agree wholly with his ideas of devoting the summer school to inculcating moral discipline in those who attended it. He was a brilliant, scholarly and highly independent man.

One of William James' essays is a striking memorial to him; all who came close to him felt his influence. His winters were spent in New York City where he organized clubs of young men who would otherwise have been without intellectual opportunities and, by his teaching, encouragement, and financial aid, started many of them on professional careers.

At Hurricane Dewey was brought into close relations with a number of stimulating minds. W. T. Harris had a cottage there; Bakewell of Yale, Hyslop and Jones of Columbia were regular visitors; Gardiner of Smith came often. Felix Adler was a summer resident of the other end of Keene Valley and occasional visits back and forth occurred; William James visited at Hurricane for a few days almost every summer and Dewey first became personally acquainted there with the man who had so profoundly influenced his thought. James R. Angell, son of President Angell of Michigan and a colleague at Chicago, was at Glenmore regularly.

John Dewey's call to Chicago as head of the department of philosophy, psychology and pedagogy was not only a recognition of his already established place in American philosophy but made a great change in the type of teaching to which his time was given. At Michigan most of his classes were undergraduate, and the change to graduate work at Chicago not only released him from much of the routine of large classes but gave him the opportunity, particularly important in view of his rapidly developing individual position, of working out his own ideas with students able to make real contributions to their presentation. The greater emphasis on graduate work throughout the institution led to a stimulation of original work in the entire faculty and he found himself surrounded by a faculty of eminent men in a productive atmosphere. The closest and most influential contacts within the University were those continuing from Michigan, with Mead and Tufts; but two other names should be mentioned. Addison Moore was one of the very able graduate students in philosophy and continued in the department on the instructing staff. The most aggressive pragmatist of the group, he was prevented by continued ill health and premature death from full realization of his abilities. Angell was a member of the department in psychology. He had been an undergraduate at Michigan and studied under Dewey. After graduation he studied at Harvard under James, Royce and the brilliant band of teachers there. He taught for a while at Minnesota, then came to Chicago. Although psychology was then becoming an experimental laboratory subject and was no longer a dependent branch of philosophy, the two subjects were much more closely connected than they are considered at present, a fact splendidly manifest in the career of Angell's teacher, James. Angell became one of those most active in promoting *functional* psychology, the chief rival of the *analytic* school of which Titchener at Cornell was the acknowledged leader. This movement played a part in developing the logical theories of Dewey and in making a bridge from his logical to his moral theory.

For a number of years Dewey gave during the three winter quarters courses entitled, "psychological ethics," "the logic of ethics," and "social ethics." The first of those courses was a further development of the principles set forth in his *Study* published in Ann Arbor: it developed moral theory in terms of an interplay of impulses, habits, desires, emotions, and ideas. The material of this course provided the background of *Human Nature and Conduct,* which he published many years later. The course in "the logic of ethics" gave an analysis of the categories of end, standard, principle, and obligation, in terms of distinctive functions of resolution of practical problems arising from a conflict of incompatible desires and purposes. Dewey also conducted regularly a seminar for candidates for the doctorate which had some logical theme as the focus of study. Owing to the prestige of idealistic theories at this time the logical writings of Bradley and Bosanquet, then quite recent, received special attention, with the older logics of Mill, Venn, and Jevons. Lotze's logic was chosen for analysis in one seminar because the importance attached by its author to empirical and scientific theories made it one of the least extreme in exposition of idealistic logical theories. The Decennial of the founding of the University was celebrated by the publication by the University of Chicago Press of a series of monographs representing all departments. Among the publications was a volume by graduate students in philosophy called *Studies in Logical Theory*, with a series of introductory essays giving an analysis of Lotze's logical theory by Dewey. The volume would probably have attracted little attention even among university teachers of philosophy had it not received a cordial greeting from William James, whose review hailed the birth of a "Chicago School" of thought, working along lines sympathetic to his pragmatism. This secured for it a certain recognition, for the most part hostile. Dewey's contribution marks a final and complete break with his early Hegelian idealism and launches his instrumental theory of reflective thought.

Another of these publications was a monograph by Dewey, *The Scientific Conditions of a Theory of Morality*, which gives in schematic outline his first published endeavor to set forth the principles of a unified logic of scientific enquiry and moral judgment. This attracted no attention and has never been republished; but in a study of his development it marks a crucial change of position.

How We Think and *Democracy and Education*, written after Dewey was at Columbia University, are direct fruits of his Chicago experience. His own work and his contacts with others led to a fusion in them of his educational and philosophical ideas; he expresses, in *Democracy and Education*, the opinion that philosophy itself is "the general theory of education," taking education in a sense broad enough to include all the factors that serve to shape the disposition, emotional, intellectual, and active, of the individuals who constitute society.

During the last years of Dewey's stay in Chicago there was increasing friction between him and the president of the University on matters connected with the administration of the Laboratory School. The Chicago Institute, a training school for teachers which had a practice school for children, had been founded to continue the work of Francis Parker free from the political influences which hindered it in the Cook County institution. In 1901 this Institute was joined with the University. As the department of which Dewey was head did not undertake the training of teachers for other than university and normal school positions in the philosophy and psychology of education there was no conflict on this side. But, while Dewey was away for a short time lecturing, the president agreed to merge the Laboratory School with the school connected with the former Institute, now the University's school of education. This merger made no provision either for maintaining the type of work done in the Laboratory School nor for the corps of teachers who had given devoted service against obstacles due to the scarcity of funds. When the trustees of the Institute learned that Dewey had not been consulted when the contract joining the Institute to the University was drawn and was unaware that his school had been virtually abandoned, they volunteered adjustments. The parents and friends who had given the school its financial support were organized into what was probably the first active Parents and Teachers Association in the country. They protested the abandonment of the school vigorously and raised a fund to guarantee its continuance. Educators all over the country wrote the University administration urging its support. Francis Parker was at this time seriously ill and his illness was the leading reason for the transfer of the Institute to the University. A temporary solution of the difficulties was worked out and while it was in force Colonel Parker's death led to the merger of the two schools under a school of education directed by Dewey. The attitude of the president remained so indifferent or hostile to the unendowed school, however, that Dewey resigned in 1904. His resignation was followed by that of Ella Flagg Young as professor of education.

At the time of his resignation Dewey had no position in view. After he had taken the decisive step he wrote to William James and to his old friend J. McKeen Cattell of the Department of Philosophy and Psychology at Columbia University, informing them of it. Through the efforts of Cattell he was offered a position at Columbia University, including, as means of increasing the salary offered, two hours a week of work at Teachers College.

The Deweys decided to spend the interval in Europe. Three children had been born to them in Chicago, Gordon Chipman (named after his mother's father), Lucy Alice, and Jane Mary (named after Jane Addams and her close friend, Mary Smith).

They took their five children with them, but tragedy again accompanied their European trip. Gordon contracted typhoid fever on the ship in which they sailed from Montreal to Liverpool. After a serious illness in a Liverpool hospital he appeared to have recovered; but on a trip to Ireland he had a relapse and died. Gordon, only eight, had made many friends. He was a mature personality, without precocity, at the age of six. A memorial meeting was held at Hull House when news of his death was received. Miss Addams made the leading address, which was published much later in a volume of similar addresses; this evidence of the affection and warm appreciation Gordon aroused outside his immediate family testifies to the loss which they experienced. The blow to Mrs. Dewey was so serious that she never fully recovered her former energy. Nevertheless, with characteristic courage, she took the other children to the continent to learn foreign languages. Dewey, who had gone to Columbia to teach in the fall, rejoined his family in June at Venice. A happy outcome of the Italian stay was the adoption of Sabino, an Italian boy of about the same age as the one recently lost. His unflagging gayety, courage through a severe illness, energy, and capacity for making friends brought comfort to the bereaved family of which he remains a beloved member. It is interesting that the adopted child is the one who has carried on the parents' practical work in elementary education, as a teacher in progressive schools and as designer and manufacturer of educational equipment for constructive activities and scientific experimentation. The oldest daughter, Evelyn, after visiting a number of schools, wrote *Schools of Tomorrow* with her father, and *New Schools for Old*, a book dealing with rural education. She was connected for some time with the Bureau of Educational Experiments, engaged in working out methods of educational testing and statistical formulation of the results. Later she edited a complete report of investigations of infant development.

Dewey found himself at Columbia in a new philosophical atmosphere. By 1905 the realistic movement was in the forefront of philosophy. It was ably represented at Columbia by Woodbridge, a thorough classical and Aristotelian scholar, and an original and stimulating teacher of the history of philosophy.

Woodbridge accepted and taught naturalistic metaphysics of the Aristotelian type. Contact with him made Dewey aware of the possibility and value of a type of metaphysical theory which did not profess to rest upon principles not empirically verifiable. The result of new contacts is seen especially in *Experience and Nature,* the first series of lectures given before the American Philosophical Association on the Carus Foundation. Woodbridge and Dewey agreed in acceptance of pluralism, in opposition to absolutism and to a theory of knowing which made subject and object its end-terms; they had a common disbelief in theories of immediate knowledge. These points were so joined with points of difference as to make their intellectual association of peculiar importance in further developing Dewey's thought. The period, up to about 1915, was one of warm critical controversy of monistic and dualistic realists with one another (Woodbridge holding a different position without taking an active public part in the controversy) and of all realists with idealists. James repeated his lectures on *Pragmatism* at Columbia by invitation of the Department of Philosophy and during the following years developed his "radical empiricism." The new intellectual conditions in which Dewey found himself, including the teaching of graduate students to whom his point of view was quite foreign, led to a rethinking of all his philosophic ideas. The result is seen in *Reconstruction in Philosophy,* lectures delivered at the Imperial University in Tokyo, in *Experience and Nature,* and in *The Quest for Certainty,* lectures given at Edinburgh in 1929 on the Gifford Foundation. Almost all of Dewey's books published after he came to New York developed from lectures given on various foundations. This is true of *Human Nature and Conduct, The Public and Its Problems, German Philosophy and Politics, Liberalism and Social Action, Art as Experience,* as well as those named above. In addition to books, voluminous contributions to philosophical periodicals, especially *The Journal of Philosophy,* edited and published at Columbia, record his philosophical positions of recent years.

His personal contacts were numerous. Montague, a Columbia colleague, developed a theory of monistic realism on the basis of his knowledge of and deep interest in modern physical theories. The resulting theory of perception and knowledge is based upon an original and highly ingenious hylozoistic theory of nature. Montague and Dewey came closer together in their ideas on social subjects than upon technical philosophical ones. Friendship between the two families has always been close and Montague was the chief speaker at the funeral exercises of Mrs. Dewey, who died, after long illness, in 1927, of arteriosclerosis and heart trouble.

Other associates who influenced Dewey for shorter or longer periods, both positively and by criticisms of his positions, were Lovejoy, Tawney, Sheldon, Harold Chapman Brown, and, as students became members of the faculties of Columbia and neighboring institutions, Bush, Schneider, Randall, Edman, Kilpatrick, Goodsell, Childs, Eastman, Hook, Ratner and others. Association with Hook and Ratner remained close after they left Columbia, as both remained in New York; each has been connected with Dewey's recently published work. Ratner collected and edited a volume of Dewey's articles on topics of the day and published a volume of selections from his philosophical writings, *Intelligence in the Modern World*, prefaced by an interpretative introduction. Hook has worked through the manuscripts of all of Dewey's recent volumes before their publication and helped their rewriting by many suggestions.

Around 1915, Dr. Albert C. Barnes of Merion, Pennsylvania, was led to join a seminar of Dewey's by the similarity of the ideas he had worked out personally to those expressed in *Democracy and Education*. A close friendship resulted from their acquaintance in this seminar. Barnes, best known for his unrivalled collection of modern paintings, is a scientist and student. He wished his collection to be used for educational ends which only art could serve and had interested himself in methods of art education. His personal experience had developed a method of discriminating observation by which a deeper appreciation of works of art and of experience in general was effected. Contact with The Barnes Foundation gave definite philosophic form to Dewey's previously rather scattered ideas of the arts. Barnes dedicates *Art in Painting* to Dewey and Dewey dedicates *Art as Experience* to Barnes; the two books are evidence of their intellectual collaboration.

There exists in New York City a Philosophic Club of twelve

to eighteen members from institutions in New York and as far
from it as Yale and the University of Pennsylvania, which has
met monthly for many years. It would be difficult to bring together a greater variety of philosophical points of view, expressed in frank mutual criticism, than are and have been found
in this club. In it Dewey found stimulating contact with such
men as McGiffert, Thomas Hall, Adams Brown, and Lyman,
of Union Theological Seminary; Felix Adler of the Ethical
Culture Society; Henry Rutgers Marshall, the architect and
writer on æsthetics and psychology; Bakewell, Sheldon, Fite,
Singer, Cohen, deLaguna, and, for brief periods, Fullerton and
Kemp-Smith, in addition to many previously mentioned. Its
discussions kept him constantly aware of the wide variety of
views held by men of equal sincerity and intellectual capacity.

Dewey's ventures in the political field bring his social philosophy to the fore in this period. He began giving courses in
political philosophy while teaching at Ann Arbor. In these lectures he discussed, largely from the historical point of view,
theories of "natural right," utilitarianism, the British school of
jurisprudence, and the idealistic school. The most noteworthy
feature of the course was that in the department of philosophy
the topics of sovereignty, the nature of legal and political rights
and duties, and the history of political thought, in terms of
Hobbes, Locke, and Rousseau, were discussed. A criticism of
Austin's theory of sovereignty, published in the *Political Science
Quarterly*, and a lecture on "The Ethics of Democracy," published by the Philosophical Union of the University, show
Dewey's social thought at this period. The latter combines a
criticism of the quantitative individualistic theory of political
democracy with a definitely moral interpretation in terms of
"liberty, equality, fraternity." The most significant statement
in the address from a present-day point of view is that political
democracy is impossible without economic and industrial democracy, but this statement should not be taken to have its
present meaning. Its immediate source was probably Henry
Carter Adams, a colleague in political economy, who frequently
pointed out the desirability and probability of a development in
economic life parallel to that which had taken place in politics,
from absolutism and oligarchy to popular representation.

For a time Dewey's political philosophy developed as a line of thought independent of his technical philosophical interests. It was inevitable that these currents should gradually fuse in the mind of a man who believed that the influence of the social scene on philosophy should be not merely the unavoidable unconscious one but that of furnishing a testing ground for the correctness of philosophic theory. This fusion was aided by courses given at Chicago and at Columbia on social and political philosophy. In his earlier years Dewey shared the faith then rather common that American democracy in its normal evolution would in time do away with the serious injustices of the economic field. He was thus able to support Bryan for president, in spite of disagreement on the silver question and many other points of the populist movement; partly on anti-imperialist grounds, but largely because he saw in the movement signs of a democratic revival.

Residence in New York City completed the change already begun in Chicago in his social convictions. The frontier atmosphere of Chicago tended to keep alive the naïve middle-western faith in the manifest destiny of democracy, in spite of the rawness of much of the city's life. In New York, the center of the financial interests of the country, it was impossible to ignore the acute conflict existing between political and social democracy and irresponsible finance capitalism. In 1912 Dewey actively supported the "Bull Moose" campaign, in spite of his distrust of Theodore Roosevelt's military and imperialistic tendencies. He joined also in the La Follette campaign of 1924. His long and active support of the woman suffrage cause was based on the belief that the enfranchisement of women was a necessary part of political democracy. He was the first president of The Peoples Lobby, conducted at Washington by its energetic secretary, Ben C. Marsh, and was chairman for a number of years of The League for Independent Political Action.

He interested himself in a number of ways in the democratic administration of schools and universities. He was a charter member of the first Teachers Union in New York City, withdrawing with regret when that union was used for promoting a particular political opinion rather than for educational purposes. The motto of the teachers' unions, "Education for Democracy and Democracy in Education," is obviously taken from his works. With his friends Cattell and Lovejoy he was active in founding the American Association of University Professors and he served as its first president.

Dewey's trips abroad played a decided part in the evolution of his social and political views. The most influential was to Japan and China. He had become acquainted with Dr. Yegiro Ono when the latter was a student of political economy in Ann Arbor. Dr. Ono attained a distinguished position in banking in Japan and was in New York on business after Dewey moved there. Their friendship was renewed and Dr. Ono, with a professor at the Tokyo Imperial University, arranged that Dewey should be invited to lecture at that university during sabbatical leave in 1918-19. The first half of that winter Dewey lectured at the University of California and from there he went to Japan. In Tokyo Mr. and Mrs. Dewey visited the I. Nitobes, who hospitably opened their charming home to them for the period of the lectures. Mrs. Nitobe was an American of Quaker descent and the months at the Nitobe home, with the university connection, brought the Deweys into close contact with the liberal culture of Japan, including its comparatively small feminist movement. The liberal movement in that country probably reached its height at about this time, due to the success of the Allies in the war. It was even possible for Dewey to be invited to lecture on democracy. The close affiliation of Japanese thought and action with German and the tendency of the ablest men to go into the army were, however, apparent even then.

While in Japan, Dewey was visited by former students from China, including Chancellor Chiang Mon-Lin of the National University of Peking, who invited him to lecture in China for a year under the auspices of a newly formed Chinese Society. Dewey obtained leave of absence from Columbia and sailed for China on a visit which was to lengthen to two years.

What was later to be a well organized student movement was beginning to take form in 1919. In fact, the Chancellor, who had accompanied the Deweys to Hangchow after they landed at Shanghai, returned suddenly to Peking because university students had been arrested for vigorous demonstrations against the Cabinet, which they considered pro-Japanese. From the start of their visit the Deweys saw the power of the student and teaching class in China and the potentialities of public opinion acting in non-political channels. For the student strike aroused so much public sympathy that when the government offered to release the students they refused to leave until they received a formal apology from the Cabinet. The fact that the leadership of the movement to modernize China, by ridding it of Japanese control and turning the nominal republic into genuinely democratic channels, lay in educational circles gave the Deweys an extraordinary opportunity to know at first hand the forces at work. Dewey was especially fortunate in his interpreters, advisors and guides. Chief among them was Dr. Hu Shih, now Ambassador from China to the United States. Hu Shih had taken a doctorate at Columbia and returned to China to take a leading part in the "literary revolution," a movement to substitute the spoken language for classic Chinese, which was understood only by professional scholars. The movement spread with a rapidity which surprised its initiators and served alike to form a wider educational basis, as textbooks were written in a language with which pupils were familiar, and to disseminate modern ideas among the literate public.

Besides lecturing in the National Universities at Peking and at Nanking (where Dr. W. T. Tao, also a former Columbia student, was dean) the Deweys visited almost every capital of the Pacific coast provinces from Mukden to Canton and a number of capitals of interior provinces. His lectures were attended not only by students and teachers but by other representatives of the educated classes and were reported fully in the local newspapers. In many cases they were recorded by a stenographer and published in pamphlets which had a wide circulation. Mrs. Dewey also lectured and she was made an honorary Dean of Women at Nanking. Coeducation was just beginning in China and the Deweys were at Nanking for the summer session at which women were, for the first time, admitted to classes on the same footing with men. Mrs. Dewey's encouragement of the feminist movement in Chinese education was commemorated recently when, with traditional ceremonies, a delegation of Chinese students presented a scroll honoring her services to her family in New York. This recognition, a cherished memory of the family, recalls the warmth with which the Chinese received the Deweys at a time when democratic and national ideals were spreading rapidly in their country. The Deweys were the first foreign lecturers under specifically Chinese auspices and were accepted into such close association with Chinese as to become familiar with their point of view on internal and international problems.

Whatever the influence of Dewey upon China, his stay there had a deep and enduring influence upon him. He left feeling affection and admiration not only for the scholars with whom he had been intimately associated but for the Chinese people as a whole. China remains the country nearest his heart after his own. The change from the United States to an environment of the oldest culture in the world struggling to adjust itself to new conditions was so great as to act as a rebirth of intellectual enthusiasms. It provided a living proof of the value of social education as a means of progress. His visits to Turkey in 1924 and to Mexico in 1926 confirmed his belief in the power and necessity of education to secure revolutionary changes to the benefit of the individual, so that they cannot become mere alterations in the external form of a nation's culture.

In Russia his chief contacts were with educationalists; his time there was too short for investigation of economic and political fields. His experience in other countries had taught him to be distrustful of the ability and desire of officials and politicians to give an honest statement of conditions. His membership in a visiting group of American educators brought him into relations with remarkable Russian men and women, teachers and students, who were ardently convinced of the necessary place of education with a social aim and coöperative methods in making secure the purposes of the revolution. They were enthusiastically engaged in building a new and better world. Their interest in the economic and political aspects of the revolution came from their belief that these would serve to liberate the powers of all individuals. The impression he derived from these associations was so unlike the beliefs current in the United States that he wrote a series of articles very sympathetic in tone with the U. S. S. R., which led to his being described as a "Bolshevik" and a "red" in the conservative press.

His Russian trip took place in 1928, when the earlier "freedom" of pupils to dictate to teachers and educational authorities had been curbed and before the later scholastic regimentation was established. Although there was much political propaganda in the schools, there was also in the better ones a genuine promotion of personal judgment and voluntary coöperation. The reports which came to him after the high-pressure five year plan was put into effect of the increasing regimentation of the schools and of their use as tools for limited ends were a great disappointment to Dewey. After the Moscow trials of the old Bolsheviks he concluded that the clash of what appeared to be creeds of political sects, which he had believed to be similar to those of sects in the formation of Christian dogma, had a deeper meaning; events in Russia were interpretable as the effects of any dogmatic social theory, in contrast to democratic liberalism.

His visit to Russia was short but it had a sequel which greatly extended his knowledge of affairs in the Soviet Union. He was invited to be a member of the Commission of Inquiry into the Charges Against Leon Trotsky at the Moscow Trial. While he believed in the right of every accused person to a hearing, this belief did not of itself lead him to accept. Upon the personal side he felt that it was an opportunity to carry on his own practical education in the principles of social action, in this case as illustrated in the theory of violent class conflict and class dictatorship. The immediate result for him was the study not only of all the official reports on the Moscow trials but of the translated writings of Lenin and other revolutionary leaders. This convinced him that the method of violent revolution and dictatorship was by its very nature ineffective in producing the ends sought, no matter which particular set of leaders, illustrated in this case by Trotskyites and Stalinists, came into power. In his own phrase, "to be asked to choose between Bolshevism and Fascism is to be asked to choose between the G. P. U. and the Gestapo." The public result of the inquiry was the publication of two volumes, one a verbatim report of the hearings held at

Trotsky's home in Mexico City, the other an analysis of the evidence on both sides and a statement of The Commission's findings which was published under the title *Not Guilty*. In left wing literary circles he was now denounced indifferently as a Trotskyite or as a reactionary and a section of the conservative press welcomed him into a fold in which he has never belonged. All of his political activities are explainable by a belief in what was called "Americanism" before that term was associated by war propaganda with "jingoism" and by economic reactionaries with a *laissez faire* financial and industrial policy. This belief is now more commonly known as "liberalism" but, in explaining Dewey's activities, this word must be taken in its old-fashioned American sense.

Of the interaction of public activities and technical philosophy he states: "I have usually, if not always, held an idea first in its abstract form, often as a matter chiefly of logical or dialectic consistency or of the power of words to suggest ideas. Some personal experience, through contact with individuals, groups, or (as in visits to foreign countries) peoples, was necessary to give the idea concrete significance. There are no ideas which are original in substance, but a common substance is given a new expression when it operates through the medium of individual temperament and the peculiar, unique, incidents of an individual life. When, to take an example, I formed the idea that the 'mind' of an individual, the set of beliefs expressed in his behavior, is due to interaction of social conditions with his native constitution, my share in the life of family and other groups gave the idea concrete personal significance. Again the idea that lay back of my educational undertaking was a rather abstract one of the relation of knowledge and action. My school work translated this into a much more vital form. I reached fairly early in the growth of my ideas a belief in the intimate and indissoluble connection of means used and ends reached. I doubt if the force of the idea in the theory of social action would have come home to me without my experience in social and political movements, culminating in events associated with my membership in the Trotsky Inquiry Commission. My theories of mind-body, of the coördination of the active elements of the self and of the place of ideas in inhibition and control of overt action required contact with the work of F. M. Alexander and in later years his brother, A. R., to transform them into realities. My ideas tend, because of my temperament, to take a schematic form in which logical consistency is a dominant consideration, but I have been fortunate in a variety of contacts that has put substance into these forms. The fruits of responsiveness in these matters have confirmed ideas first aroused on more technical grounds of philosophical study. My belief in the office of intelligence as a continuously reconstructive agency is at least a faithful report of my own life and experience."

I

Joseph Ratner

DEWEY'S CONCEPTION OF PHILOSOPHY

DEWEY'S CONCEPTION OF PHILOSOPHY

IN HIS opening contribution to *Studies in Logical Theory*, Dewey outlined a conception of philosophy which, from the vantage point of the present time, we can see he has been working on and working out ever since. It has not, however, been a development proceeding on a smooth and unbroken line. It has not been an unperturbed and undeviating unfoldment of an ideally preformed idea, nourished and sustained by an environment ideally preformed for it. Rather has the development been of a more natural, even of a more human sort. Its historic career is marked by crises, by phases of change—and some of them of major importance. Hence in our discussion we shall, to some extent, follow the historic route.

I

Philosophy, as described in the essay referred to ("The Relationship of Thought and Its Subject-Matter") has three areas of inquiry. For the sake of convenience, these may be provisionally represented in the form of three concentric circles. The first area, bounded by the innermost circle, is occupied by reflective thought, by logic, or what Dewey now calls inquiry. In the second area are the typical modes of human experience, such as the practical or utilitarian, the esthetic, religious, socio-ethical, scientific. Philosophic inquiry here concerns itself with analyzing what these modes of experience are and, particularly, with discovering their interrelations, how one leads into and emerges out of the other, how the practical or utilitarian develops, perhaps, into the scientific, the scientific into the esthetic or vice versa or whatever the case may be discovered to be. The third area is that of the socio-cultural world, society in its organized and institutional form, the world which generates what we commonly and quite accurately call "social questions." Of the myriad possible questions that can be found here for philosophy to study and answer, Dewey singled out the following as representative samples: "the value of research for social progress; the bearing of psychology upon educational procedure; the mutual relations of fine and industrial art; the question of the extent and nature of specialization in science in comparison with the claims of applied science; the adjustment of religious aspirations to scientific statements; the justification of a refined culture for a few in face of economic insufficiency for the mass, the relation of organization to individuality."[1]

Today, at any rate, there is nothing new in this conception of the subject-matter of philosophy, taken distributively. To what extent Dewey's own work has contributed to making our contemporary range of philosophic interest and work legitimate, familiar and accepted we need not stop to inquire. But the significance of Dewey's conception is not to be found in the mere extension of the range, significant as that undoubtedly was and is. It is to be found in the idea of the interrelation of the three areas: that they are functional distinctions, discriminable divisions within one inclusive field of experience, the boundary lines being neither fixed nor impermeable, marking off, but not insulating any one from any of the rest.

The fundamental idea then is that the primary subject-matter of philosophic inquiry is a continuously interconnected field of experience. But philosophy, especially in the modern epoch and as an academic pursuit, does not receive its subject-matter in its primary form. It receives it, instead, in derivative forms of various orders of remoteness and complication. It gets bundles of highly intellectualized and generalized problems. Each bundle is outfitted with its own tag: epistemology, ethics, logic, esthetics, social philosophy and whatnot. Philosophy is an enterprise of reflective thought and not only should but can only deal with problems in a reflective or intellectual way. But when each bundle of intellectualized problems is treated as if it constituted a separate and distinct substantive realm, as being the original and primary subject-matter of inquiry, philosophy, instead of prospering as a reflective enterprise, degenerates into a

---

[1] Reprinted in *Essays in Experimental Logic*, 99.

mere dialectical process of untying each bundle in some way and tying it up again in another.

To recur to our three concentric circles for a moment. The contents of those circles, as described above, were all intellectualized contents, that is, problems already given an intellectual form. This is as true of the "social questions" which are the contents of the outer circle as it is of the contents located in the others. "The relation of organization to individuality, the justification of a refined culture for a few in face of economic insufficiency for the mass, the value of research for social progress" and so on, are, with respect to their intellectual form, on a par with any other intellectual problems conceived or conceivable. However, no one of ordinary commonsense would confuse these "social questions," or intellectualized problems, with the actual social conditions that raise those questions or that *are* those problems. And certainly no one of commonsense would substitute the former for the latter, treating the social questions as self-sufficient in themselves, as being the primary and original subject-matter and pushing the social conditions completely to one side as irrelevant, if not even non-existent.

Whether any philosopher ever succeeded in making a complete substitution of the sort indicated, in any field whatsoever, is more than doubtful. Indeed, it is certain that none ever did. Such a feat is beyond the powers even of a philosopher, no matter how "idealistically" or "intellectualistically" he may be constitutioned or conditioned. However, the temptation to make the substitution is omnipresent in the intellectual class, and the one to which philosophers most frequently and recurrently fall. In the degree that the substitution is made, to that degree does philosophy become a vain dispute and an arid verbal jugglery. The stress falls on *substitution* and in the sense indicated. Reflective inquiry, philosophic or otherwise, can handle an actual condition that *is* a problem only by transforming it into an intellectual form. But such a transformation, when understood and handled as such, is what Dewey calls a surrogate for the actual problem, not a substitute for it. An architect engaged on the problem of remodelling a house uses a blueprint. The blueprint is an intellectualized form of the actual house, a surrogate for it. An architect does not *substitute* his blueprint for the house; he does not consider the blueprint as constituting the original and primary subject-matter of his inquiry; and he does not think that he changes the house when he changes the blueprint—although changing the blueprint may be all that he professionally contributes towards the consummation of that final end.

Let us suppose there is an architect's office, full of blueprints of various orders and descriptions, rolled up in different sets. Now put a philosopher in that office, bolt the door and shutter the windows and what can he do? It all depends upon what the philosopher experienced before he was imprisoned. If he can read the blueprints and has an active and fertile mind, there is no telling what he will be able to do with them, what strange new blueprint or system of blueprints he will be able to fashion out of the blueprints before him. But suppose the philosopher who was sealed in the office was grabbed out of the transcendental blue and was transported and imprisoned so quickly he had no time to have any earthly experience on the way? What could he do with the blueprints? Barring miracles, whatever he did would be a purely transcendental doing, having no relation whatever to the earthly blueprints, what they stand for and where they came from, what they are surrogates of and what they are used for. Our transcendental philosopher would be bottled up in the architect's office much as the mind is still supposed by some to be bottled up in the brain or some part of the brain.

Pictorial analogies or illustrations when taken too literally or when pressed too far are bound to be misleading. However, if in the foregoing illustration the appropriate substitutions are made, the result is a fair picture of the kind of situation in philosophy against which Dewey fundamentally protested in *Studies in Logical Theory* and which his own conception of the nature of philosophic inquiry was designed to correct.

II

The problem of unbolting the door and unshuttering the windows of the philosopher's study is the problem of establishing continuous, functional connection between philosophic inquiry and all other activities of human beings, including among the latter of course other activities of inquiry, such as the scientific.

How can this be done? Poised as an abstract problem at large and this problem itself becomes a dialectical one of the insoluble variety, on the order of the problem of determining whether an "inside" mind can know an "outside" world. If we start off with the mind at large as being "inside" and the world at large as being "outside," the dialectical operation can be pursued indefinitely without ever effecting any connection, let alone a functional connection, between the two. In the course of the dialectic, the mind and the world may exchange positions, recurrently yielding what superficially may seem to be the amazing result of getting the world "inside" and the mind "outside." But such consequence, should it prove unduly unpleasant to contemplate, can always be reversed by carrying the dialectic one round further. Similarly, if we start off with philosophy at large and seek by dialectic to connect it with the common world of human experience and affairs at large. In fact, the two problems are variants of the same.

The only way in which the connection can be shown to be —for it *is* and does not have to be made—is by giving up the futile task of abstractedly considering "problems in general" and approaching all problems empirically, as a series of specific, concrete problems. Does this beg the question? Dewey has formulated his answer in a great variety of ways, sometimes more clearly and sometimes less. The fundamental idea recurring in all his answers is that this does not beg the question: the only thing it begs is the empirical method and this only at the outset. Thenceforward, the method proves itself by its works.

Of course, the contemporary philosopher in "begging" the adoption of the empirical method for use in philosophy is not asking philosophers to start out on a completely blind hunch. The scientists have been empirical in their procedure for quite some time now, and it is agreed on all hands that it is a good procedure, that, to put it in the vernacular, it produces the goods. The "appeal to example" is as significant in the intellectual as in the moral life. It has at least a quasi-logical force. One scientist does something in a certain way, getting certain results, and that way becomes an "example" for other scientists to follow; not slavishly and blindly, of course, but nevertheless something to follow. There is a logical presumption in its favor —in so far forth. Likewise when it is a case of adopting a method used in one field for use in another field. Of course, the *justification* of a method comes through the fruits of its use where it is used. It is not and cannot be justified by pointing to its fruitfulness elsewhere or whence it was taken. Arguments for adopting empirical method in philosophy because the scientists use that method are, therefore, at the outset, always of the nature of "begging;" they are, in the good sense of the term, hortatory. This of course applies equally to any method *to be* adopted for use in *any* field, or any part of any field.

That a method justifies itself by the goods it produces where it is used is a principle that cuts both ways. It operates to cut a method out as well as to cut a method in. Cutting a method out that is deeply entrenched is no simple, automatic or instantaneous affair. It is accomplished only progressively, only in the course of actually reconstructing the field by the operative use of the new method.

The adoption of the empirical method for use in philosophy may be considered to be in the nature of an initial attitude or standpoint taken towards the work, that is, the assumption of the empirical attitude is of the nature of an overt act whereby the philosopher identifies himself as one human being among other human beings, as one worker among other workers, or what amounts to the same, whereby he identifies his field of work as one field among others and functionally interrelated with them. Since the contemporary philosopher certainly is not in the position of one who stands just in front of the threshold of Creation, what this act means concretely is that all the achievements of the human race, all the methods of work, all the products and results that have already been developed by those methods in all other fields are *legitimately* opened for his use. The whole world of human achievement, the world of goods, becomes a community store to which the empirical philosopher has rightful access and from which he may rightfully take what he needs and as he needs it. (And to which, it may immediately be added, he is under obligation to give something in return.) As a matter of fact, even the most non-empirical philosophers have not hesitated to take what they wanted, no matter how empirical the place where they found it. This fact, which Dewey has very amply documented, is not, to be sure, a reflection on their morals, but it is an indictment of their philosophical position.

III

With the assumption of the empirical attitude, the problems *in* philosophy cease to be unique, parthenogenetic creations. They become formulations in philosophy of common problems arising out of common experience. They all have empirical fathers who can be empirically traced, located and identified. And this precisely becomes the task of empirical philosophy, as Dewey conceives it, with respect to the class of problems in philosophy that have by virtue of their formulation acquired the character of being inherently insoluble. From Dewey's empirical standpoint an insoluble problem is of the nature of an intellectual disease; it is what we may call a "diseased formulation" and the empirical remedy (and the only remedy) consists in tracing the "problem" as it appears in philosophy back to its origins in the primary subject-matter of experience and finding out how, in the course of its intellectual genetic-history, it got that way. How complicated and extensive a process this becomes when carried out in some detail can be seen, for example, in *Experience and Nature* and *The Quest for Certainty*.

The fundamental principle of the remedial process is, however, rather simple. Dewey briefly indicated its nature in *Studies in Logical Theory*, and though brief, it is in some ways the best explanation he has given of his own *modus operandi*. It can be most expeditiously described by referring again to the three concentric circles. They comprise the inclusive area within which philosophic inquiry is going on. Examination of the contents will reveal that at least some of the contents in one area appear in other areas in other forms and on different contextual scales. The method Dewey prescribed and has so ex-

tensively and effectively used is that "of working back and
forth between the larger and the narrower fields, transforming
every increment upon one side into a method of work upon the
other, and thereby testing it."[2] Uppermost in Dewey's mind,
at the time of writing, was the function this "double movement"
performs in testing every increment gained. But it also functions to uncover new clews and leads both for solutions and
problems and thus is accumulative as well as corrective. Furthermore, this accumulative and corrective process is the natural
matrix out of which develop new varieties of empirical method.
For empirical method does not consist of a single, linear rule.
It is multi-dimensional and many-potentialed, acquiring different specific forms through use in different specific situations,
and displaying new powers with every new way in which it is
used. When empirical method is deliberately adopted for philosophic use, it has also to be adapted. Since Dewey's "double
movement" is a method of working within the field of philosophy which exhibits the two fundamental features of empirical method as that operates in scientific inquiry it may fairly be
considered as being a natural adaptation of that method.

The concentric circles give, of course, a cross-sectional view,
or the *area* of philosophic inquiry (as Dewey conceived it in
1903). But the actual field of philosophic inquiry has depth
and temporal length as well. It is the socio-cultural world in
its full-dimensional, historical character. The method of working back and forth between the narrower and larger fields
means, therefore, working back and forth between the technical study of the intellectualized problems in philosophy and
the common world of experience, the socio-cultural conditions
and activities, including the scientific, which generate· or *are*
those problems.

IV

In *Studies in Logical Theory*, the distinction between what
we may call "problems in general" and "general problems" is
clearly recognized and made. All "problems in general" or
"problems *überhaupt*" are diseased formulations of general
problems. Thus the problem of "knowledge in general" ("Is

[2] Reprinted in *Essays in Experimental Logic*, 103-104.

Knowledge Possible?") is a diseased formulation of the problem of developing a general theory of knowledge or a general logic. From the scientific empirical standpoint Dewey took in those early essays and which he has maintained ever since, it is just as intelligent for a philosopher to ask "Is Knowledge Possible?" as it would be for a scientist to ask "Is Motion Possible?" There are specific cases of motion and scientific inquiry begins by observing (and experimenting with) these specific cases. Although there is no "motion in general" (and hence no "problem in general") the scientist none the less has a general problem, namely, the problem of developing a general theory of motion or, what is the same thing for him, formulating general laws of motion. The general laws, furthermore, are not proved valid, are not tested and established by their ability to evaporate out of scientific existence the specific cases of motion going on and observed but, on the contrary, their validity is established by their ability to explain or account for the specific cases.

Similarly with the general problem of knowledge which is the concern of the philosopher in his restricted capacity as logician. Any general theory of knowledge, any general formulation he reaches, must be competent to explain or account for the specific cases of knowing going on. However attractive and admirable his general formulation may be in all other respects, if it does not meet this fundamental requirement it is invalid or incompetent. A great deal of rightful enthusiasm has been poured over Newton's general laws of motion. But suppose the characteristic of those laws was that they accounted for "all motion" only by making every actual motion unaccountable. Would we then be as enthusiastic? To ask the question is to answer it. Why then any enthusiasm over general philosophic formulations which display their competence to account for a total field of inquiry by the method of rendering inexplicable and unaccountable everything that actually occurs within that field? Should we not enforce on philosophic generalizations the same demand we enforce on scientific generalizations? For the philosopher who, like Dewey, has taken the empirical attitude only an unequivocal affirmative answer is possible. For by taking the attitude, by identifying his field of work as one among others, he has given up all special privileges, all claims to exclusive, prerogative treatment and consideration. Hence when he concerns himself with the general problem of knowledge he proceeds with the firm and basic understanding that his solution of that problem, the general formulations he reaches must be such that they will include, not exclude, will account for, not render unaccountable, the actual ways of knowing which occur. The common man and the scientist experience no "metaphysical" problem, they suffer from no "metaphysical" fright, when engaged in the enterprise of knowing. For them, knowing and knowledge do not rend their experience into two inexplicably unjoinable parts. For the common man and scientist, knowledge does not divide off and then hermetically seal the divisions. It does just the opposite: it functions to break through divisions that have for other, non-knowledge causes, occurred. Knowledge, as actually exemplified in experience, does not create breaches but heals them; it does not function to disrupt and disintegrate experience but, on the contrary, operatively functions to deepen and to expand, to re-integrate and integrate experience in adequate and more comprehensive and more fruitful ways. The general formulation of the philosopher must therefore meet these specific conditions. If it does not, there is only one conclusion that can be drawn: the philosopher has, in the course of his work, severed all connection between his field of inquiry and all other fields. He has set himself up as an emperor in a self-created and insulated empire of his own.

The philosophic task, then, is to reach generalizations that meet specific conditions. This is Dewey's position. How is this done? Let us quote:

Generalization of the nature of the reflective process certainly involves elimination of much of the specific material and contents of the thought-situations of daily life and of critical science. Quite compatible with this, however, is the notion that it seizes upon *certain* specific conditions and factors, and aims to bring them to clear consciousness—not to abolish them. While eliminating the particular material of particular practical and scientific pursuits, (1) it may strive to hit upon the common denominator in the various situations which are antecedent or primary to thought and which evoke it; (2) it may attempt to show how typical features in the specific antecedents of thought call out diverse typical modes of thought-reaction; (3) it may attempt to state the nature of the specific consequences in which thought fulfills its career.[3]

There is, then, according to Dewey, no opposition or conflict between philosophic concern with the general or generic and interest in the specific. In fact, the etiology of all diseased formulations, for example of the diseased formulation of the general problem of knowledge as the problem of "knowledge in general" is, as Dewey then diagnosed the case, chiefly if not exclusively to be found in the fact that logicians apparently believed that there is an irreconcilable opposition between the two and hence in constructing their general theories always worked to eliminate the specific entirely. Wherefore their theories were doomed to end up as one or other of the extant varieties of diseased formulations, that is, were doomed to end up by presenting in an insoluble intellectualized form the original problem they started out to solve.

Dewey's theory of knowledge or general logic of reflective thought is here introduced for illustration not discussion. It is a specific example of an essential, indeed basic element in his general doctrine in *Studies in Logical Theory* regarding philosophy. There the concern of philosophy with general problems is not only admitted as a legitimate concern but the competence of philosophy to arrive at solutions of general problems, its competence to reach general theories or formulations is insisted upon as the foundation of philosophy's ultimate effectiveness as Dewey then envisioned it.

As there described, philosophy, from an initiating and restricted interest in the logic of reflection develops into a "general logic of experience." When thus developed it "gets the significance of a method." Its business ceases to be that of defending any vested interest or traditional order in society or any entrenched conception of Reality. Its business becomes that of freely and unprejudicially (or scientifically) examining the various typical modes of experience and discovering their relationships to each other and their respective claims. When fully realized as a method, Dewey envisioned philosophy as doing

---

[3] *Essays in Experimental Logic,* 83-84; *italics* in original.

"for social qualities and aims what the natural sciences after centuries of struggle are doing for activity in the physical realm." Philosophy would answer the "social questions" of which some examples were cited earlier. Philosophy alone would answer these questions because only philosophy, in the course of realizing itself, would have acquired the requisite foundation of general method.

The three stages of philosophy's development are diagrammatically represented by our three concentric circles—to refer to this device for the last time. In view of what has already been said, it is clear that Dewey did not conceive of these stages as separate and distinct, as following upon one another in discrete succession. He conceived of the stages in just the opposite way: as indissolubly and interactively interconnected, as discriminable phases of a temporal or natural-historical development. The solution of problems in philosophy can be reached only by working back and forth between the technical or private domain of philosophy and the final or public domain of sociocultural experience. For philosophy to solve its own intellectualized problems it must move into the common field of problematic situations. And just as truly, if philosophy is ever to become able to handle social situations successfully or constructively, it must begin to handle them—its ability progressing in the "double" process: the periodic return of philosophy into its technical domain being an essential phase of the way philosophy perfects its general methods. In sum, for philosophy to develop either way, within its own technical confines or within the inclusive social world, the "double movement" must be continuously maintained. Undoubtedly there is a great temptation to say that answering "social questions" would be "applied philosophy" but such temptation must be resolutely denied. For such a distinction involves the idea that methods and application can be separated, that methods can somehow be developed in some sequestered location and then "applied" to the situations. Which is fundamentally contradictory to Dewey's doctrine. And at any rate in the sphere of "social questions" almost every one admits the inherent absurdity of the idea that

methods and application can be separated. This idea is popularly known as sentimentalism or utopianism.

Dewey did not of course see philosophy as maturing to its
full powers as a "method" immediately or even soon. But it was
in the direction of attaining this maturity that philosophy's
destiny lay, the ultimate end in view of which the reconstruction of philosophy was to be undertaken.

V

In the period between 1903 and 1920, the publication dates
respectively of *Studies in Logical Theory* and *Reconstruction
in Philosophy*, many things happened in the world. For one
thing, the brood of social sciences was growing larger and even
growing up. And they were obviously increasing their business
by taking away the business of philosophy as Dewey had conceived it ultimately to be. By all evidences of the times, philosophy was, in this respect, to repeat its history: its maturation
as the science of society was to be achieved through the maturation of the social sciences.

The second thing we need notice here as having happened
during this period is the World War. It was largely, though
not exclusively, in connection with the social problems created
by the War—while it was in progress and for some years after
—that Dewey developed his publicist activity, directly participating in current, almost day to day, public affairs. By far the
major part of his publicist writings belong to the years 1917-
1923. *Reconstruction in Philosophy*, one of the more widely
read and known of Dewey's volumes, belongs very definitely
to this period. Since it is the only volume of this period that
covers the whole field of philosophy, we may fairly take it as
representative of one of the major changes in Dewey's conception of philosophy referred to at the outset. If the change were
exclusively restricted to this period, or were to be found only in
this book, it would deserve some notice, but only of a passing
sort. But recurrent echoes of the strain here developed are observable, if not in all Dewey's subsequent writings, at any rate,
in a goodly portion of them.

In *Reconstruction in Philosophy* two different, though not unrelated, conceptions of philosophy and its function are advanced. One is the conception that philosophy "is vision" and "that its chief function is to free men's minds from bias and prejudice and to enlarge their perceptions of the world about them."[4] Although this conception of philosophy is not new with Dewey, it is not unreasonable to suppose that the prominence it acquires, not only in this book, but throughout this period and subsequently, is not unconnected with the rise and development of the social sciences.

The other conception of philosophy is a revised version of philosophy as social method, as an "organ for dealing with . . . the social and moral strifes of [our] day."[5] There is, of course, no contradiction or opposition between these two conceptions, they do lead into and out of each other, but there is at least a difference in emphasis between them, which difference sometimes becomes very important, if not crucial. "To say frankly that philosophy can proffer nothing but hypotheses, and that these hypotheses are of value *only* as they render men's minds more sensitive to life about them"[6] is qualitatively different from saying with equal frankness: "the task of future philosophy is to clarify men's ideas as to the social and moral strifes of their own day. Its aim is to become so far as is humanly possible an organ for dealing with these conflicts."[7]

But it is not the relation between these two conceptions of philosophy that we want to discuss just now. It is the second conception only that is of immediate concern. In this book, there is a fundamental conflict in doctrine with respect to this second conception. It occurs throughout, sometimes becoming acute, sometimes practically disappearing entirely. In terms of the foregoing discussion, this conflict may be said to turn on the fact that Dewey recurrently forgets the fundamental distinction he made in *Studies in Logical Theory* and confuses what we called "problems in general" with "general problems"

[4] *Reconstruction in Philosophy*, 21.
[5] *Ibid.*, 26.
[6] *Ibid.*, 22; *italics* mine.
[7] *Ibid.*, 26.

and because of this mistaken identification repeatedly is led from the argument that the former are intellectual chimeras (which they are) to the conclusion that the latter are of the same character (which they are not).

Thus, for example, in considering various theories of society Dewey

plunge[s] into the heart of the matter, by asserting that these various theories suffer from a common defect. They are all committed to the logic of general notions under which specific situations are to be brought. What we want light upon is this or that group of individuals, this or that concrete human being, this or that special institution or social arrangement. For such a logic of inquiry, the traditionally accepted logic substitutes discussion of the meaning of concepts and their dialectical relationship to one another. The discussion goes on in terms of *the* state, *the* individual; the nature of institutions as such, society in general.[8]

Now from this thoroughly sound criticism of "notions in general"—"society in general," "the state in general," "the individual in general"—Dewey passes to a conclusion which is tantamount to a denial of the need for any general theory of society, of the state, of the individual, etc. "The social philosopher, dwelling in the region of his concepts, 'solves' problems by showing the relationship of ideas, instead of helping men solve problems in the concrete by supplying them hypotheses to be used and tested in projects of reform."[9] And on the next page he is even more specific: "In the question of methods concerned with reconstruction of special situations rather than in any refinements in the general concepts of institution, individuality, state, freedom, law, order, progress, etc., lies the true impact of philosophical reconstruction."[10]

A great deal of course can be made of the terms "refinement" and "impact" but a dialectical exegesis is uncalled for. On an earlier page, Dewey writes as follows:

Knowing, for the experimental sciences, means a certain kind of intelligently conducted doing; it ceases to be contemplative and becomes in a true sense practical. Now this implies that philosophy, unless it is to

[8] *Ibid.*, 188; Dewey's *italics.*
[9] *Ibid.*, 192.
[10] *Ibid.*, 193.

undergo a complete break with the authorized spirit of science, must also alter its nature. It must assume a practical nature; it must become operative and experimental.[11]

Now there can be no doubt that the theory of knowing as contemplative was also "operative" in the very important sense that it operated to influence men's minds and thus to some extent guide their conduct, misguidance being also a form of guidance. In fact, to render this theory innocuous or inoperative was the chief purpose of the book under discussion. In a very real sense, it may truly be said that Dewey has dedicated his life's work to the accomplishment of this myriad-formed, if not hydra-headed task. For the accomplishment of this task requires the reconstruction of all philosophic ideas that were formed under the influence of the conception of knowing as inherently and exclusively contemplative, which means, in effect, reconstructing all of them since none escaped this influence. The implication for philosophy of the operative and experimental character of scientific knowing is not that philosophy must change its nature and itself become operative and experimental in the same direct sense in which laboratory science is experimental: the implication is that philosophy must change its ideas, its conceptions. Above all it must reconstruct its conception of knowing so that the operative and experimental character of knowing is made an *integral* part of its general theory of knowledge. This is not accomplished—unfortunately not, needless to say—when philosophers "insert" the characters of operation and experimentation somewhere in their treatises (take "notice" of them so to speak) and then go on with their business as usual. It is also not accomplished when the element of "contemplation" is shoved back so completely that the process of reconstruction becomes one of substituting the operative for the contemplative. And the trend of Dewey's thought, in the period under consideration, was in the direction of making some sort of a substitution. Wherefore the two conceptions of philosophy which are, in reality, two general conceptions of knowledge.

The title of the book—*Reconstruction in Philosophy*—tells

[11] *Loc. cit.*, 121.

the tale without argument. It is philosophy that Dewey is re-constructing. The impact of this reconstruction is to change the world or some portion of it through changing men's minds or ideas. But whatever the ultimate change philosophy brings about in the world, it is a change that it brings about precisely through changing ideas, through reformulating them, recon-structing them. It is in this way that philosophy "gets the sig-nificance of a method." Thus, on the heels of the passage cited where it is asserted that the true impact of philosophical re-construction does not lie in any refinements in the general con-cepts, Dewey proceeds exactly to the task of reconstructing the general concept of individuality, etc. Speaking generally, and I hope without any confusing results, it may be said that Dewey's most important line of reconstruction, along which lie his greatest contributions, is his painstaking reconstruction of a considerable number of "concepts in general" into "general concepts." When thus reconstructed, the specific and special are not eliminated or abolished but brought out and embraced. Hence the general concepts can also function as general meth-ods guiding and controlling action to a prospering and not im-poverishing issue.

As Dewey very clearly puts it in "The Need for a Recovery of Philosophy":

There are human difficulties of an urgent, deep-seated kind which may be clarified by trained reflection, and whose solution may be forwarded by the careful development of hypotheses. When it is understood that philosophic thinking is caught up in the actual course of events, having the office of guiding them towards a prosperous issue, problems will abundantly present themselves. Philosophy will not solve these problems; philosophy is vision, imagination, reflection—and these functions apart from action, modify nothing and hence resolve nothing. But in a com-plicated and perverse world, action which is not informed with vision, imagination and reflection, is more likely to increase confusion and con-flict than to straighten things out.[12]

For good or bad, whether he likes it or not, the philosopher, in his professional capacity, is stuck in the realm of ideas.[13]

[12] *Creative Intelligence*, 65.
[13] Perhaps it should be explicitly stated that the intellectual and socio-cultural changes mentioned in this section were only the *conditions* that occasioned the

VI

In "The Need for a Recovery of Philosophy" Dewey writes as follows:

It is often said that pragmatism, unless it is content to be a contribution to mere methodology, must develop a theory of Reality. But the chief characteristic trait of the pragmatic notion of reality is precisely that no theory of Reality in general, *überhaupt*, is possible or needed. It finds that "reality" is a *denotative* term, a word used to designate indifferently everything that happens. Lies, dreams, insanities, deceptions, myths, theories are all of them just the events they specifically are. Pragmatism is content to take its stand with science; for science finds all such events to be subject-matter of description and inquiry—just like stars and fossils, mosquitos and malaria, circulation and vision. It also takes its stand with daily life, which finds that such things really have to be reckoned with as they occur interwoven in the texture of events.[14]

Here more explicitly than in our earlier examples, we find Dewey going from the proposition that there is no "Reality in general" (which is true) to the conclusion that no general theory of reality is possible (which is false). The passage cited may rightfully be claimed as itself a nuclear or germinal statement of a general theory of reality. But it is quite unnecessary to argue the point. Just as Dewey in *The Public and Its Problems* thoroughly corrected the idea that a general theory of the state and society is not necessary by developing one, so in *Experience and Nature*, which appeared some eight years after the citation above was written,[15] he explicitly developed a general "theory of nature, of the world, of the universe."

Experience and Nature thus marks another major change in Dewey's conception of philosophy, what its task is, what it may and should undertake to do. The only way of getting rid of bad metaphysics is to develop good metaphysics; the only way

emergence of the conflict in doctrine in *Reconstruction in Philosophy*. (A full list of the *conditions* would include, of course, as supplementary conditions, the philosophical controversies between 1903 and 1920.) The *cause* of the split in doctrine is to be found in a fundamental fault (geologically speaking) which lies deep in the original formulation of instrumentalism in *Studies in Logical Theory*. The limits of this essay make it impossible to go into this matter any further.

[14] *Ibid.*, 55; *italics* in original.

[15] In 1925, to be exact.

of getting rid of "Reality in general" is to develop a "general theory of reality." The development of a general theory of reality is not of course to be undertaken as a mere task of riddance. It is a proper and legitimate and needed enterprise on its own. Up to *Experience and Nature* Dewey was preoccupied with the general problem, or the constellation of general problems concerned with locating knowing within experience; and then he took on the still more general problem of locating experience within nature. The more general problem does not abolish or eliminate the less general: it seizes upon the characteristic traits of the latter and includes them in a wider network of meanings. The determination of the place of man within nature is not achieved by eliminating man from the scheme of things. Nor can the scheme of things, or the nature of Nature be determined—as Dewey has comprehensively pointed out—unless we include man as an integral part within that determination. It is a process, again, of working back and forth, only now on an all-inclusive scale, or within an all-inclusive field.

VII

The changes in Dewey's specific doctrines, his changes within the discriminable departments of philosophy, do not concern us here. We may therefore consider *Experience and Nature* as being representative of the final major change in Dewey's conception of the field of philosophy.

In the closing chapter of this book, Dewey redefines his general conception of philosophy as a "criticism of criticisms." In this definitional formula, the two conceptions we distinguished before—philosophy as "vision, imagination, reflection" and philosophy as "social method"—are merged. They are merged but not fused.

Philosophy as a criticism of criticisms differs from other criticisms both by virtue of its generality and of its objective or orientation. Within each specialized occupation, within the boundaries of each profession, technical criticism, competent and restricted to that field, goes on. Specialization, professionalism, even departmentalization are unavoidable and necessary for the successful maintenance and progress of a condition of human society above that of a primordial horde, and of course for such a complex culture as our own. But these necessary conditions, if allowed to develop their particularisms and segregations unchecked would bring about the destruction of culture. The socio-cultural condition—the existential state of affairs, and not some transcendental vision—creates the need for an integrative medium.

Over-specialization and division of interests, occupations and goods create the need for a generalized medium of intercommunication, of mutual criticism through all-around translation from one separated region of experience into another. Thus philosophy as a critical organ becomes in effect a messenger, a liaison officer, making reciprocally intelligible voices speaking provincial tongues, and thereby enlarging as well as rectifying the meanings with which they are charged.[16]

Although terminologically this differs greatly from the conception of philosophy as a "general logic of experience," it is in its final intent not so very far removed from it. For, clearly, by "liaison officer" Dewey does not mean a Western Union boy. And, equally clearly, by a generalized medium of intercommunication he does not mean a "language" into which all statements of the particular voices can be translated so that by learning this language every one can learn what every one else has said (in so far as their sayings have been translated of course). Dewey's generalized medium is one in which the meanings are enlarged and rectified. Sheer translation does not do this—or if it does then it is bad translation. But to enlarge and rectify is precisely what philosophy is to do—the good of it. Philosophy, as a critical organ, is not critically diaphanous.

From the passage cited one might be tempted to conclude that the process of bringing meanings together from different fields is the whole of philosophic activity. Undoubtedly, the *origination* of the "generalized medium" must be conceived in some such way. However, because philosophy, from its inception, has not been a stranger to the ways of men—something from on high, separate and alone—it has, in the course of its history, been able to acquire a mind of its own. This mind—the com-

---

[16] *Experience and Nature*, 2nd ed., 410.

plex of ideas and meanings we call philosophic—is, I think, the "generalized medium" whereof Dewey speaks. For to function as such a medium, or perhaps better said, to *be* such a medium, has been and is, according to Dewey, the rôle of philosophy in the history of civilization.

But to *be* a medium, and consciously and systematically to function as a *critical* medium of *intercommunication* are not quite the same thing. The difference is all-important. Philosophy has at various times been set up as a separate and peculiar science, *sui generis*—the holder of the keys to the universe. This, for Dewey, philosophy is not and has not ever been. The keys to the universe are not exclusively retained in any one pair of hands. They are everywhere about. What philosophy does hold is a key position within the development of sociocultural experience. It is an intermediate between the technical sciences (natural and social) on the one hand, and on the other, the arts and technologies, including among the latter the technologies of associated living, the institutions of society, political and otherwise. An intermediate is not a go-between. An intermediate is a functional activity between two qualitatively differentiated functional activities. Philosophy, as an intermediate between the sciences and the arts, participates in both their functions, being exclusively identifiable with neither. In some phases of its work, philosophy nears the sciences: what Dewey calls the rectification of meanings: this is philosophy as "method." In other phases, it approaches the arts: the enlargement of meanings: this is philosophy as "vision." Neither can be separated from the other. It is a "double movement." And also, it is a "double movement" that does not leave philosophy unchanged. The enlargement and rectification can be effected in the socio-cultural world only as it occurs *in* as well as *through* philosophy. Just as philosophy is not a stranger to the ways of men, so non-philosophic men are not strangers to philosophy. Because of its intermediary function philosophic formulations and ideas have gone out into and penetrated all other fields. A thoroughgoing reconstruction *in* philosophy thus involves reconstruction of ideas in technically non-philosophic domains. And reconstruction of ideas in the latter often brings about and compels reconstruction in philosophy. In the historic spread, the double movement is continuously going on.

The other distinguishing characteristic of philosophy as criticism is its objective. The ultimate orientation of philosophic criticism is towards value. "Criticism is discriminating judgment, careful appraisal, and judgment is appropriately termed criticism wherever the subject-matter of discrimination concerns goods or values."[17] In fulfilling this objective, philosophy accepts "the best available knowledge of its own time and place" and uses this knowledge for the criticism of "beliefs, institutions, customs, policies."[18] If this criticism is not to be a particularistic series of unrelated objections to thises and thats—piecemeal, disconnected, directionless, uncontrolled and uncontrollable— some general concepts, which in their functional sum constitute a "general method" must be developed. In other words, a general logic of experience is necessary. Philosophy, in *Experience and Nature,* just as in *Studies in Logical Theory,* is to be this general logic. And when fully realized, philosophy will do "for social qualities and aims what the natural sciences after centuries of struggle are doing for activity in the physical realm" —*if* by "what the natural sciences are doing" we understand that functional division within the natural sciences which constitutes its theoretical part. When thus understood the comparison is exact: the theoretical division of the natural sciences is the *general logic* of activity in the physical realm and philosophy is (to become) the *general logic* of activity in the socio-cultural realm.

To understand the matter this way, does not involve destroying Dewey's fundamental doctrine concerning the inseparability of theory and practice, for the general logic of experience can be developed only through and in the course of the actual practices of experience as they concretely manifest themselves in the socio-cultural realm. However, in *Experience and Nature* there is a more explicit recognition on Dewey's part of the functional division between theory and practice as this division effects the content and conduct of philosophy itself.

What a general logic of experience looks like, and what is

[17] *Experience and Nature,* 398.
[18] *Ibid.,* 408.

its interwoven relation with practice, can be seen by glancing over the range of Dewey's work. For he has not just been *arguing* that philosophy should become a general logic of experience. He has been *producing* one. This is what his works functionally sum up to, what, in their total integration, they are.

When we take Dewey's works severally, they very naturally group themselves into special (or specific) logics of the typical (or distinctive) modes of experience. Thus to mention only some of his representative works: *Human Nature and Conduct* is the special logic of the socio-ethical mode of experience; *Art as Experience* is the special logic of the esthetic mode; *A Common Faith*—of the religious; the early logical works, *The Quest for Certainty* and *Logic: The Theory of Inquiry*—comprise the special logic of the scientific mode of experience; *The Public and it Problems, Individualism Old and New, Liberalism and Social Action*—comprise the socio-practical or utilitarian; and here belong all the publicist writings which in their dealings with concrete socio-practical problems are tryings out, experimental testings and elaborations of the special logic of the utilitarian mode; *Democracy and Education* and the great body of work of which this is only a representative, cut across and include in various ways all the other special logics for within the school, as Dewey conceives it, all typical modes of experience and all forms of socio-practical problems are involved; the school is not a factory which has an outfit of standardized machines and dies for stamping out standardized parts and a conveyor-belt along which the standardized parts are assembled into standardized models ready for sale. The school, or the total educational institution is, for him, both the germinal and cellular structure of society: the means by which society not only reproduces itself as a socio-cultural world but also the means by which it grows. And finally, *Experience and Nature*. All modes of experience are naturally interconnected, being socio-cultural differentiations of common experience. None, therefore, of the special logics enumerated is separated and isolated from the rest. Common strands weave through them all. The interweaving of these common strands, the integration of the special logics into a comprehensive logic of experience, is the special task of this book. *Experience and Nature* is the logic of common experience considered in terms of widest and most inclusive generality. The inclusive general logic of experience is the inclusive integration of the continuities that are disclosed through man in Nature and through Nature in man.

VIII

To sum up. Fundamental to Dewey's conception is that philosophy is not outside of and above all other human pursuits, cultivating in secrecy and silence a remote, staked-off preserve of its own; philosophy is and works within the open and public domain of all human activities, one among others, differentiated by its scope and function, but in no way set apart.

The keys to the universe are not in any one pair of hands. They are everywhere about. In the history of philosophy, one bunch of keys after another has been selected and set up as *the* keys to the universe, philosophy being the sole true keeper, when not also the one and only discoverer of the keys. And then the unappeasable problem has always arisen: How on earth to get rid of the other keys. Dewey's basic conception of the philosophic task—a conception which has persisted through all his changes and deviations—is just the opposite. Here are all these bunches of keys. We cannot do without any of them. The history of thought and ever-present experience prove this. Besides, even if we could dispose of any, it would be a distinct loss: we would impoverish life by just so much. However, just as it is futile and morally unwise to try to get rid of any, so is it morally unwise and theoretically unintelligent merely to collect them and string them along on a series of "ands."

The philosophic task—in which the moral and intellectual, the "vision" and the "method," fuse—is to bring them all into functional relationship with each other.[19] This does not mean,

[19] In the conception of philosophy as a "criticism of criticisms" Dewey's two general theories of knowledge (or of philosophy) are merged but not fused. The actual fusion is attained in his concept of intelligence. Unfortunately, the fusion is implicitly achieved in his writings rather than explicitly recognized and formulated. An adequate discussion of this matter would carry us far beyond the boundaries of this essay. We must content ourselves with saying that "intelligence" for Dewey is a quality of human behavior which is completely actualized when the experience of living has become an intelligently cultivated art. It is not un-

of course, taking all the keys, melting them down and then constructing one great big key that will be the whole works—the idea that seems to prevail in most quarters. It means to reconstruct the keys so that instead of each one allegedly opening a different lock, they will naturally function to assist each other in the common enterprise. For Nature, after all, is not a set of separate locks and human beings the keysmiths. Indeed, in a very important and fundamental sense it may be said that the keys *are* the locks for they *are* Nature in so far as she constructs herself through our reconstructions.

The construction of one great big key is, in more philosophic language, the construction of a formal set or system of principles. In this sense Dewey has no system and, as far as I know, has never aimed to have one. But when we take the outline of the field of philosophic activity presented in *Studies in Logical Theory* as being of the nature of a rough sketch of a philosophic project, we can see that all of Dewey's work is the systematic fulfilling, expanding, revising, deepening, realizing of that project. All his works together comprehend a "system" but it is a system in a new sense, created in a new way. It was created by working back and forth between one field of experience and another, interweaving the threads of continuity as the creative process of reconstruction proceeded.

Dewey has not "solved" the comprehensive problem of the relation of mind to matter which is just the old terminology for his own comprehensive problem of the relation of theory to practice. But if ever this problem is "solved" the solution I venture to say will be reached only by the method so fundamentally characteristic of Dewey's life-long philosophic procedure. For his method of working—the "double movement"—seems to be the way Nature herself works. Every increment Nature gains on one side she converts into a method of work upon the other, thus accumulating as well as testing her increasingly complicated gains.

JOSEPH RATNER

NEW YORK CITY

natural therefore that one finds Dewey's best and profoundest exposition of his integral conception of philosophy, or the nature of intelligence, in his *Art as Experience*.

2

John Herman Randall, Jr.

DEWEY'S INTERPRETATION OF THE HISTORY
OF PHILOSOPHY

2

DEWEY'S INTERPRETATION OF THE HISTORY OF PHILOSOPHY

I

JOHN DEWEY has written no volume dealing primarily with the history of philosophic thought. Nor, unless in some now long-forgotten youthful indiscretion, did he ever elect to set before a class the simple record of objective and impartial knowledge of the past. That kind of scholarship that is content to display in nice articulation the thoughts that have thrilled the search of uneasy and inquiring minds, and mount them in some museum piece so plausibly arranged as to convey the illusion of a kind of timeless life forever frozen into immobility—that perfection of a past recovered for eternity which German *Gelehrte* have so often sought in vain, and French *savants* have so often captured, none better than M. Gilson in our generation —these Dewey has brushed aside, for in practice as in theory, history has meant for him more than the mere chance to enjoy such fruits of esthetic contemplation. For him it has not been enough to weigh precisely the compulsions that have made great minds what they forever are, so that from their centers of vision the world must even now appear not otherwise than as it presented itself to them.

Not that Dewey has been blind to the appeal and significance of the comprehensive intellectual visions that make the record of what philosophy has seen so revealing a key to human nature and the rich variety of cultures it has created. These imaginative visions—more often he prefers to call them "shared meanings"—he finds indeed the noblest fruits of thought, the goal of the busy labors of all man's cunning arts and contrivings. "Scientific thought itself is finally but a function of the imagination in enriching life with the significance of things. . . . Signifi-

77

cant history is lived in the imagination of man, and philosophy is a further excursion of the imagination into its own prior achievements."[1] And as every reader knows, Dewey's pages are sprinkled with brief but often eloquent sketches of these visions—like the insight into Spinoza in the *Quest for Certainty*, or the portrait of Bacon in *Reconstruction in Philosophy*, or the many passages in which he pays tribute to what the Greeks saw.

No one has been more insistent than Dewey that the ultimate function of knowing is to contribute to the widest possible diffusion and sharing of such meanings—provided they be seen for what they are, visions of man's imagination and not revelations of eternal truth.[2] And surely no one has been more impressed by the power and appeal of vision in human life—a power so great and so seductive that men have been forever tempted to rest in vision without seeking to understand it or the conditions of its enhancement. Seek visions and distrust them, is the counsel born of reflection on the tragic yet magnificent history of the philosophic mind. For visions are not understood by vision, but by the use of another and more laborious intellectual method; and they can be neither generated nor shared save by the practice of intelligence, of the most critical and scientific ways of thinking.

Hence Dewey has found no time to tell, like Santayana, the story of the human imagination, or to repaint at second hand the marvels it has beheld. Even the men of vision and aspiration he has been more anxious to catch in travail than to contemplate their serene achievement. The insights that constantly occur in his writings into the great philosophies and movements of ideas in the past are concerned far more with the intellectual methods whereby they were arrived at than with praise of their fruits. Where Dewey approaches most closely to the narration of a history—as in the *Reconstruction in Philosophy*—it is in following the thread of the development of method. For him, it is

---

[1] *Philosophy and Civilization*, 5.

[2] "Poetic meanings, moral meanings, a large part of the goods of life are matters of richness and freedom of meanings, rather than truth. . . . For, assuredly, a student prizes historic systems rather for the meanings and shades of meanings they have brought to light than for the store of ultimate truths they have ascertained." *Experience and Nature*, 411.

method rather than vision that is fundamental in the history of philosophy, that reflective and critical method that aims to reorganize and reconstruct beliefs.

Yet Dewey has given no straightforward account of the history of intellectual method comparable to the studies of men like Cassirer or Brunschvicg. Here too he has been more interested in making history than in writing it. He has used his wealth of historical knowledge, not for a display of brilliant erudition, but as material to be brought to bear upon the present-day problems of the logic of inquiry. Just because of his deep concern with the immediate future, he has tried to make the most of the successes and the mistakes of the past. Profoundly convinced of the continuity of human thinking, he has seen prior thought always as an instrument which with the proper reshaping might be used to help us in our present discontents. The past is enormously significant; but to be significant is to be significant for something, and that something is the intellectual problems the envisaged future insistently poses for us today. To praise the past Dewey is content to leave to others; he sees his task, rather than to appraise it, as a weapon for the morrow's fight. Toward the history of philosophy his attitude thus differs little from that of the chemist or the biologist: all alike view the chronicle of man's intellectual achievement as an arsenal, or as a warning, but not as an ancestral mansion to be lovingly explored.

Indeed, if Dewey's whole philosophy be taken as he would have it, as scientific method at last come to self-consciousness, as experimentalism aware of itself, its meaning and its implications, developed as a critical instrument and a constructive tool, it might well seem that concern with past thinking deserves to hold as small a place for him as for any scientist. To dwell on the record of history may be a harmless and satisfying luxury, but it can scarcely be a major or essential preoccupation of the philosophic mind. To master what inquiry has achieved that we may inquire further, would be all that wisdom could demand. Should not a scientific philosophy really in control of the best intellectual methods win us emancipation from the sterile historicism of the romantic and backward-looking 19th century? Scientific thought has no further interest in the scaffolings by which it was constructed: it has plenty of work of its own to do. An experimental philosophy, wedded at last to the methods of science, should resolutely face the future with an open mind and an earnest heart. If it think of the past at all, should it not, like our latest fashion in scientific philosophizing, rejoice that it has finally escaped those centuries of bondage to darkness, and put boldly behind it all temptation to traffic with the meaningless nonsense of their unconfirmable speculations?

Now Dewey himself has dwelt so long and so vigorously on the need of just such liberation from persistent tradition, that it is not irrelevant to ask these questions about the true implications of an experimental philosophy. Many who have found that basic drive congenial have indeed raised them. They have been sadly puzzled to find his works overloaded with references to the outworn ideas of thinkers they would themselves prefer to forget. Why all this beating of dead asses? For years it was possible to reach his most penetrating analysis of the logic of inquiry, in *Essays in Experimental Logic,* only through a thick tangle of Lotze, a logician whom it is safe to say no one has seriously read for a generation. And of even his fundamental *Experience and Nature,* it has been not unfairly pointed out, each page is made up half of a fresh grappling with pressing problems worthy of the best laboratory approach, and half of a wrestling with the vagaries of ancient tradition. Why does Dewey insist on conducting his original inquiries in the musty atmosphere of a historical museum? Why does he not throw open the windows to let the fresh breezes of the present blow these dusty cobwebs away? Why, to go forward a step, must he look backward on the whole course already traversed? For all but the most learned of his readers Dewey has seemed weighed down by an obsession with the past. This burden of historical baggage has inordinately increased the difficulties of his pages. What might have been so clear on the authority of a successful scientific method has been obscured by the painful resolve to win every step of the way by ceaseless polemic with the whole long course of philosophical thought. Dewey may never have written specifically on the history of philosophy; but he has rarely set forth his own position save in detailed and lengthy critical opposition to the views and methods of his numerous predecessors.

There is more than the mere matter of rhetorical effectiveness here at stake. It is to be sure not hard to conceive an easier path of persuasion for those who come, without knowledge of philosophy's past, in search of light and power for today. From Dewey's historical analyses such men have gained little enlightenment: they have scarcely yearned to cast off shackles by which they never felt themselves bound. The present emancipation they do need he might well have granted more directly. And there would not then be so many, especially among teachers, whose sole exposure to the career of philosophy has come from Dewey's critically selective treatments, with results a little too weird and painful to narrate. Even for the less unsophisticated one may venture to doubt the wisdom of Dewey's strategy. It is possible the hard-boiled professionals themselves might have been more easily won over to a philosophy of the experimental method, had not their sentimental pieties been so repeatedly and so insistently violated. There is some point in making even a revolutionary philosophy appear the culmination of the great traditions of the past: even experimentalism might have been dressed up as 20th century certainty. The point is all the clearer when one realizes that even the most significant revolutions are not quite so revolutionary as they at first appear, and that tradition is immemorial chiefly in failing to remember how rapidly it has changed.

This vexed question of Dewey's rhetoric is raised only because it alone can explain how many honest readers can quite misconceive his intentions. Intelligent interpreters have asserted that his only interest in the past is to free us from its clogging and stultifying assumptions. Greek thought we must understand, but only because it is the source of all our errors. And others, like the ancient Caliph, have judged it better to forget that past entirely: what is of value has been taken up in Dewey, what he has omitted deserves to be forgotten. Alas, a teacher's worst enemies are often his professed admirers. Such a reading does little credit to Dewey, and less to the readers. Fortunately the danger of falling into it is not today what it was a decade ago. For just such a view, put forth in the name of physical science, has been expressed almost beyond the possibility of caricature by some of the logical positivists; and even the most blind can see that Dewey's experimentalism is hardly of that stripe.

There are places, especially in the *Quest for Certainty*, where Dewey turns to past thought only to criticize its assumptions. But it would be both an insult to Dewey's intelligence, and a confession of sad ignorance in the asker, to request him to repeat once more what he has so often made clear, that the value and importance of the philosophical tradition is not exhausted by the assumptions it has transmitted that need altering. It would be much more to the point to single out that basic element in Dewey's thought which makes constant concern with the great intellectual traditions of our civilization not only compatible with his experimentalism, but actually an essential and integral component of it.

For despite all his analysis of the procedure of the natural sciences, Dewey's experimentalism is not primarily based on the methods of the laboratory. It is at once the experimentalism of practical common sense, and the coming to self-awareness of the best and most critical techniques and concepts of the social sciences. In the broadest sense, it is the experimentalism of the anthropologist, of the student of human institutions and cultures, impressed by the fundamental rôle of habit in men and societies and by the manner in which those habits are altered and changed. Like any honest social scientist, he finds the presence and the influence of natural science in Western culture today both its distinctive trait and its greatest achievement. But for him that science is primarily a cultural phenomenon: it is an institutionalized habit of thinking and acting, a way whereby that culture conducts many of its tasks and operations. It is essentially a social method of doing and changing things, a complex technique that has proved both extraordinarily successful and extraordinarily disruptive of the older pattern of life. It is a method of inquiry, of criticizing traditional beliefs and instituting newer and better warranted ones. It is the best intellectual method our culture, or any culture, has constructed; and as such it must furnish the basis on which any philosophy must build. But it is not a sheer method in isolation, it is a cultural method whereby a society operates on its inherited and traditional materials.

It is just this combination of a critical anthropology and social psychology with his experimentalism, this permeating sense of scientific method and of all inquiry as working in and through and upon a complex social heritage of accustomed ways of believing and acting, that sets Dewey's development of the philosophic implications of scientific method off so sharply from others of the present day. Most of our fashionable "scientific philosophies" are socially far from sophisticated. Arrived at by reflection primarily upon the state of the physical sciences, they are quite innocent of the knowledge gained by a century of biological and social inquiry. For Dewey the task of a scientific philosophy is not confined to the formulation of a consistent system of the entities disclosed in sense-awareness. Nor is it limited to the analysis of the linguistic expressions that constitute science considered as a body of ordered knowledge. Even today, it seems, in the midst of the most thoroughgoing revolution in physical theory and concepts since the 17th century, it is possible to erect philosophies based on mathematics and mathematical physics which may recognize the interesting fact that science has had and may well continue to enjoy a history, but scarcely find that fact relevant to the understanding of what science is and does. For such theories the history of human thinking is indeed of no serious moment. Philosophy is reflection upon what is—in all probability. It has little to do with what men who were mistaken thought, and why they thought that way. But if, as Dewey has learned from the social sciences, knowledge in general and science in particular are rather the ability of a society to do what it must and can, if they are primarily a matter of the intellectual methods whereby a culture solves its specific versions of the universal human problems, then the history of that culture and its problems, and the historical criticism of its methods of inquiry and application, become of the very essence of any philosophy with a claim to scientific inspiration. If science be an institutionalized method of trial and error, or, as James Harvey Robinson put it, of fumbling and success, then the trials, the errors, and the successes are equally instructive for the refinement and improvement and extension of scientific method, of experimentalism.

For Dewey, science is ultimately a conscious and reflective method of guiding the process of changing beliefs, of using the digested lessons of past experience to clarify and learn from fresh inquiry. Indeed, the natural sciences, as a great cultural enterprise, are the best illustration of an institutionalized technique for actively initiating social change. In them has been worked out the way in which originality may be intentionally, critically, and habitually combined with the cumulative preservation of the past's achievements. The scientist does not lightheartedly enter his laboratory to try anything once; if he is worth his salt, he knows what has been slowly built up in the way of accredited techniques and tests and warranted scientific knowledge; and it is that body of laboriously certified tools and materials which both raises his problems and offers him the methods and tests with which to solve them. The history of science is the history of a never-ending reconstruction of ideas and concepts. And it is as just such an enterprise of reconstruction that Dewey regards the criticism that is philosophy, the criticism that makes the philosopher at his best the statesman of ideas, effecting some new synthesis, and at his humblest the politician of the mind, bringing about through his analysis some working agreement to live and let live.

II

More fundamental than any particular interpretation of the history of philosophy is Dewey's view of the historical function of philosophical thought itself. Philosophy is basically a phenomenon of human culture. Its very nature is the rôle it has played in the history of civilizations.[3] The philosophical tradi-

---

[3] "Take the history of philosophy from whatever angle and in whatever cross-section you please . . . and you find a load of traditions proceeding from an immemorial past. . . . The life of all thought is to effect a junction at some point of the new and the old, of deep-sunk customs and unconscious dispositions, brought to the light of attention by some conflict with newly emerging directions of activity. Philosophies which emerge at distinctive periods define the larger patterns of continuity which are woven in effecting the longer enduring junctions of a stub-

tion of the Western world took form in Hellas, and Greek thinkers laid its foundations. "Even if these foundations are not always built upon, it is impossible to understand departures and innovations apart from some reference to Greek thought."[4] But the problems the Greeks thus formulated and transmitted to the West did not evolve in the consciousness of lonely though brilliant thinkers. Rather was Greece, and especially Athens, the intellectual mirror in which men first saw clearly reflected the essential difficulties and predicaments that arise in the collective relation of man to nature and to his fellow man. "These origins prove that such problems are formulations of complications existing in the material of collective experience, provided that experience is sufficiently free, exposed to change, and subjected to attempts at deliberate control to present in typical form the basic difficulties with which human thought has to reckon."[5] Greek life offered both the typical conflicts of man's social experience, and the intellectual freedom, born of the absence of a priestly power and a poetic rather than a dogmatic formulation of religious beliefs, to reflect on them, rationalize them in general terms, and endeavor to deal with them intelligently. Aware of their society as in rapid flux, and imbued with the sense of the power of human art to manipulate its materials, the Greek thinkers worked out programs of moral and political conduct in a natural setting they could hope to fathom and understand.

The Greeks built an intelligible world: they invented the ideas, concepts and distinctions in terms of which they could create an ordered intellectual life. Since their achievement there have been successive attempts to use Greek thought to interpret a novel and alien experience, to deal with new social problems and new schemes of value. The Oriental peoples employed it to express a religious theocracy, the Christians, to rationalize the

---

born past and an insistent future . . . Thus philosophy marks a change of culture. In forming patterns, to be conformed to in future thought and action, it is additive and transforming in its rôle in the history of civilization." *Philosophy and Civilization*, 6-8.

[4] *Encyclopedia of the Social Sciences*, article "Philosophy," Vol. 12, 119.

[5] *Encyclopedia of the Social Sciences*, Vol. 12, 119.

Hebrew-Oriental religious tradition, the schoolmen, to organize medieval society and culture, the moderns, to understand and make rationally consistent a scientific method that has persisted in remaining unintelligible, and to adjust somehow their inherited wisdom to the secular and industrial values of the modern world. Each episode involved a reconstruction of Greek thought, and each a striking off of original ideas. The consequence has been a piling up of confusion, yet at the same time of an extraordinarily rich and fertile mass of intellectual resources. Always it has been the conflicts between old ideas and new ways of acting that have led men to the searching thought that is philosophy, the impingement of novel experience upon traditional beliefs and values that has impelled them to construct their systems and programs, the emergence of new ideas irrelevant to or logically incompatible with the old, which yet had somehow to be adjusted to them, and worked into the accustomed pattern of living and thinking. Philosophic problems arise whenever the strife of ideas and experience forces men back to fundamental assumptions in any field; they are to be understood only as expressions of the basic conflicts within a culture that drive men to thoroughgoing criticism. Philosophy is the expression in thought of the process of cultural change itself: it is the intellectual phase of the process by which conflicts within a civilization are resolved and composed. A civilization that has grown stable and static may have inherited a philosophy, but it produces no philosophic thought.[6]

It is clear how such a view of the historic function of philosophy in human culture makes questions of value integral to its very essence. The changes in philosophic problems and thought are all inherently bound up with new emphases and new

---

[6] "The conception of philosophy reached from a cultural point of view may be summed up by a definition of philosophy as a critique of basic and widely shared belief. For belief, as distinct from special scientific knowledge, always involves valuation, preferential attachment to special types of objects and courses of action. . . . Thus philosophies are generated and are particularly active in periods of marked social change. . . . The chief rôle of philosophy is to bring to consciousness, in an intellectualized form, or in the form of problems, the most important shocks and inherent troubles of complex and changing societies, since these have to do with conflicts of value." *Encyclopedia of the Social Sciences*, Vol. 12, 124.

redistributions in the significance of values. For each philosophy, points out Dewey,

is in effect, if not in avowed intent, an interpretation of man and nature on the basis of some program of comprehensive aims and policies. . . . Each system . . . is, implicitly, a recommendation of certain types of value as normative in the direction of human conduct. . . . It is a generic definition of philosophy to say that it is concerned with problems of being and occurrence from the standpoint of value, rather than from that of mere existence.[7]

In the light of this interpretation, it is not hard to see why "reconstruction" is so dear a word for Dewey. The life of thought, in its humblest as in its most exalted reaches, is a reconstruction of the material it finds at hand. Now reconstruction involves first criticism, the careful appraisal, the exact determination of powers and potentialities, with their limits and their promise, the verification and testing of the values which tradition transmits and emotion suggests. But it also demands a freedom of speculation, a search for new hypotheses and more fertile principles. In its long history philosophy has again and again pruned away accepted beliefs, confined them within new and narrower limits, determined their function more effectively and precisely. But it has also brought fresh and original ideas to birth. The mere piling up of observations unfertilized and unguided by theory is to be found in neither the history nor the procedure of scientific inquiry.

The origin of modern science is to be understood as much by the substitution of new comprehensive guiding ideas for those which had previously obtained as by improvement of the means and appliances of observation. By the necessity of the case, comprehensive directive hypotheses belong in their original formulation to philosophy rather than to science.[8]

This is true not only of scientific notions like the mathematical interpretation of nature, the idea of evolution, of energy, or of the atom; it is still clearer in political and social theory, which

[7] *Encyclopedia of the Social Sciences,* Vol. 12, 122.
[8] *Encyclopedia of the Social Sciences,* Vol. 12, 125.

have derived all their concepts from philosophies that started as battle-cries in some human struggle.

As long as we worship science and are afraid of philosophy we shall have no great science; we shall have a lagging and halting continuation of what is thought and said elsewhere. This is a plea for the casting off of that intellectual timidity which hampers the wings of imagination, a plea for speculative audacity, for more faith in ideas, sloughing off a cowardly reliance upon those partial ideas to which we are wont to give the name of facts.[9]

Dewey's view of philosophy as the intellectual instrument whereby a culture reconstructs itself, in whole or in part, is itself of course a reconstruction of tradition. Like everything touching the social sciences, it owes much to the Hegelian vision of history, and to the long line of idealists who built upon it in their analysis of human culture. It owes much also to the left-wing Hegelians like Marx who bent Hegel's idealism of social experience to the active service of changing the world. But the obvious points of contact should not be taken, as they have sometimes been, to obscure the essential differences. If Dewey escapes the naïve provincialism of the philosophies of physics, that past thinkers have merely wasted their time in a fruitless search for mistaken truths about reality, he differs also from the idealists who have passively appreciated philosophy as the expression of the collective spirit and imagination. For him thought is still thinking and human, not an unrolling of the divine plan. It is active, efficient, and constructive, not in that wholesale fashion that makes it irrelevant to any human problem, but in the specific and piecemeal way that suits the needs of intelligent organisms. It is neither the mere passive reflex of material interests and conditions, nor the slave of an immutable absolute dialectic. Philosophy is the human instrument of groups of men acting as wisely as they may on specific programs and problems. And its imaginative vision has been successful only when disciplined by responsibility to the exacting tests of scientific method. For all their power and insight, the idealists failed to appreciate the liberation that comes from conformity to the regulative principles of scientific inquiry.

[9] *Philosophy and Civilization,* 12.

But if the ultimate context within which philosophy operates is cultural change, and if that social function defines its nature, Dewey is far from therefore taking its value as merely instrumental. Science too is science because of its proper function, because it enlarges our power to act and do what we have intelligently chosen; but that need not prevent the greatest good it brings being the immediate enjoyment of the power of sheer knowing. Just so the great philosophies, born as the programs for some particular task of adjustment, have yet raised themselves some little way above the conflict to a more comprehensive view of life; and those eternal visions glimpsed by men struggling in the circumstances of time may well be now their chief claim to our attention. Philosophy is an art, one of the noblest; and like every art it is at once the instrument for performing a specific function, and an immediate good to be possessed and enjoyed. With Santayana, Dewey agrees that the history of philosophy contains poetry as well as politics. But he urges us to beware lest we confuse the two.

Nor does Dewey follow the Hegelians and Marxians in taking the historical function of philosophy as unilinear and monistic. Rather he finds it inexhaustibly pluralistic in the problems from which it takes its start. There is no one type of conflict that is fundamental and controlling. Dewey is no Marxian; important as is the strife of economic groups, especially in modern times, philosophic thought has played a rôle far richer than that of a mere class ideology. The importance of conflict Dewey learned from Hegel as well as from the facts of history. But the conflicts that have given rise to philosophy he sees not merely as economic, but as in the broadest sense psychological and cultural—for him the two must ultimately coincide. The inertia of habitual ways of acting and believing is forever opposed to the power of new ideas. The specific historical function of philosophy is ultimately to get men to act and believe together in new ways: it is political and educational. That is why he finds the intellectual method of reorganizing and reconstructing habits of belief and action, the method of political education or "coöperative intelligence," of such basic importance.

Yet in modern times there has emerged one central conflict

as the focus for understanding all Western philosophies. It is the ever repeated struggle between the active force of scientific knowledge and technical power and the deflecting force of the lag and inertia of institutionalized habits and beliefs, generating the insistent problem of political education if the potentialities of the new knowledge are to be released.

The conflict is between institutions and habits originating in the pre-scientific and pre-technological age and the new forces generated by science and technology. The application of science, to a considerable degree even its own growth, has been conditioned by the system to which the name of capitalism is given, a rough designation of a complex of political and legal arrangements centering about a particular mode of economic relations. . . . Institutional relationships fixed in the pre-scientific age stand in the way of accomplishing this great transformation. Lag in mental and moral patterns provides the bulwark of the older institutions. . . . Change in patterns of belief, desire and purpose has lagged behind the modification of the external conditions under which men associate. Industrial habits have changed most rapidly; there has followed at considerable distance, change in political relations; alterations in legal relations and methods have lagged even more, while changes in the institutions that deal most directly with patterns of thought and belief have taken place to the least extent. This fact defines the primary, though not by any means the ultimate, responsibility of a liberalism that intends to be a vital force. Its work is first of all education, in the broadest sense of that term. . . . I mean that its task is to aid in producing the habits of mind and character, the intellectual and moral patterns, that are somewhere near even with the actual movements of events. . . . The educational task cannot be accomplished merely by working upon men's minds, without action that effects actual change in institutions. . . . But resolute thought is the first step in that change of action that will itself carry further the needed change in patterns of mind and character.[10]

This is not the place to question or to defend the adequacy of Dewey's program for our present conflicts. If he be right, if it be true that history itself generates change in the method of directing social change, then surely the most insistent problem today is precisely this one of political education. And the achievement of the political intelligence to persuade men to use the intelligence we do as a society possess must be the conscious

___

[10] *Liberalism and Social Action*, 75-76, 58-62.

focus of our philosophies. Instead of many fine generalities about the "method of coöperative intelligence," Dewey might well direct attention to this crucial problem of extending our political skill. For political skill can itself be taken as a technological problem to which inquiry can hope to bring an answer. It is obviously dependent on our acquiring the knowledge how to get men to apply the techniques already available for dealing with our social problems, how to enlist the coöperative support of men in doing what we now know how to do. Thus by rights Dewey's philosophy should culminate in the earnest consideration of the social techniques for reorganizing beliefs and behavior—techniques very different from those dealing with natural materials. It should issue in a social engineering, in an applied science of political education—and not merely in the hope that someday we may develop one.

But whatever our needs and resources in this crucial field, it is the cultural conflict that generates this problem of political education, the strife between new knowledge and power and the lag of institutionalized habit, that gives Dewey the key to his psychological interpretation of history in general and the history of philosophy in particular. In that history philosophy has functioned as an instrument of reconstruction, and the philosopher has ever played the rôle of the adjuster and compromiser, the mediator between old and new, the peace-maker who consciously strives to blend both in a novel pattern which, added as a further deposit, becomes the starting-point of further change.

It may be that Dewey has developed his conception of the essentially critical and reconstructive function of philosophy out of his study of the record of the past. It may be that, himself a critic, he has found his own image in all who have come before. Doubtless both factors were present. But whatever the source of his views, it remains true that he approaches his heritage always as a critic and reconstructor of tradition. And in his constant historical analysis of the materials that have come down to him, it is as a critic of the past that he is to be understood. He is forever bringing men's past experience with ideas to the test of present experience.

It is difficult to avoid reading the past in terms of the contemporary

scene. Indeed, fundamentally it is impossible to avoid this course. . . .
It is highly important that we are compelled to follow this path. For
the past as past is gone, save for esthetic enjoyment and refreshment,
while the present is with us. Knowledge of the past is significant only
as it deepens and extends our understanding of the present.[11]

In the twelfth chapter of his *Logic* Dewey has a brilliant
analysis of the historian's method, which makes plain why historical judgments must be centered on the problems of the present. It is his most penetrating statement of the theory that lies
behind his own practice.

As culture changes, the conceptions that are dominant in a culture
change. . . . History is then rewritten. Material that had formerly been
passed by, offers itself as data, because the new conceptions propose
new problems for solution, requiring new factual material for statement and test. . . . All historical construction is necessarily selective. . . .
If the fact of selection is acknowledged to be primary and basic, we are
committed to the conclusion that all history is necessarily written from
the standpoint of the present, and is, in an inescapable sense, the history
not only of the present but of that which is contemporaneously judged
to be important in the present. . . . Intelligent understanding of past history is to some extent a lever for moving the present into a certain kind
of future. . . . Men have their own problems to solve, their own adaptations to make. They face the future, but for the sake of the present,
not of the future. In using what has come to them as an inheritance
from the past they are compelled to modify it to meet their own needs,
and this process creates a new present in which the process continues.
History cannot escape its own process.[12]

But the details of this functional conception of historical
understanding, suggestive as they are, are not so important as
the insistence that historical knowledge *has* a function. It presents us with material to be criticized and used. This fact has
far-reaching implications for Dewey's treatment of the history
of philosophy. That treatment is carried through consistently
with an eye to what is significant and important for the problems
he judges to be significant today. This explains why he singles
out for attention what he does, and neglects other things, why

[11] *Liberalism and Social Action*, 74.
[12] *Logic: The Theory of Inquiry*, 233, 235, 239.

certain figures are emphasized, certain problems stressed, why method is taken as more controlling than vision. It explains why what he does select he treats as material to be critically reconstructed, rather than as achievement to be enjoyed. The fact that, while the Greeks figure so prominently in his pages, and the empiricists of the liberal tradition, they appear only to see certain of their assumptions drastically attacked, is no longer a paradox. The Greeks and the empiricists would not appear at all were their thought not so important a part of our own instrumentalities. And it helps to explain why, for all his insight and suggestiveness, Dewey seems so often to do less than justice to the great achievements of the past. He is far from denying those achievements; but his concern is with power and not justice, for he fears lest in their complacent celebration we today should rest in their triumphs, instead of building further on the foundations they have laid.

III

In certain quarters Dewey still figures as the iconoclast seeking to destroy utterly the idolatrous worship of the past. Nothing could be further from the truth; and it is difficult to see how any perceptive reader could fail to discern in him the greatest traditionalist among the leading philosophical minds of today. For the true traditionalist does not merely repeat the familiar shibboleths; he understands how to use tradition in facing our present problems. In his discriminating employment of the historical resources of philosophy, Dewey has no rival.

There are two quite different ways of using a method that is essentially critical, two ways well illustrated by two students whom Dewey has taught. One, a brilliant Chinese, despite the fact that Chinese thought exhibits much of the temper of Dewey himself, took Dewey's experimentalism to mean that the slate must be wiped clean for a fresh start. The Chinese past was utterly mistaken, and must be forgotten: men must build anew from scratch, and by assiduous cultivation of the scientific method, develop for China a philosophy embodying all those values which Dewey has found as the permanent deposit of the

Christian and individualistic West. The other was a Hindu, confronted by a culture far different from that in which Dewey has operated, and therefore tempted to sweep it too away. But he took the method of Dewey to indicate rather that one should manipulate reflectively the material at one's disposal; and so he tried to arrive at what the peculiar Hindu values might mean when critically examined in the light of the demands of today. He emerged, not with the scheme of beliefs which Dewey has rebuilt for the West, but with a translation of Hindu spirituality into terms that could stand up in the presence of scientific criticism. To him Dewey offered a method for dealing with his own inherited materials. There is little doubt but that he understood Dewey better than the Chinese, and had a firmer grasp on the spirit of his experimentalism. For he knew that Dewey meant not destruction but reconstruction; he knew that criticism demands a tradition as the material on which to work.

So, however penetrating his criticisms of traditions in the plural and in detail, it is fundamental for Dewey that tradition remains the subject-matter within which the critical method that is philosophy must operate. Material and critical instrument—both are alike essential to any valid and fruitful experimental art. Nowhere has Dewey made this more explicit than in an essay in which he was most anxious to emphasize the need of working also with the present.

A philosopher who would relate his thinking to present civilization, in its predominantly technological and industrial character, cannot ignore any of these movements [18th century rationalism, German idealism, the religious and philosophic traditions of Europe] any more than he can dispense with consideration of the underlying classic tradition formed in Greece and the Middle Ages. If he ignores traditions, his thoughts become thin and empty. But they are something to be employed, not just treated with respect or dressed out in a new vocabulary. Moreover, industrial civilization itself has now sufficiently developed to form its own tradition. . . . If philosophy declines to observe and interpret the new and characteristic scene, it may achieve scholarship; it may erect a well equipped gymnasium wherein to engage in dialectical exercises; it may clothe itself in fine literary art. But it will not afford illumination or direction to our confused civilization. These can proceed only from the spirit that is interested in present realities and that faces them frankly and sympathetically.[13]

The great traditions and "present realities"—they are equally indispensable materials for philosophic reflection, in our present or in any past present; and the philosophic task, ever old and ever new, is to bring them together significantly and fruitfully. From this follow several of the most characteristic traits of Dewey's treatment of the intellectual record. In the first place, there is the thoroughgoing historical relativism with which he views the figures and movements of the past—an objective relativism, to be sure, for the ideas of previous thinkers must be understood as specifically and objectively relative to the particular conditions and conflicts to which they were the answer. Before we can assay the worth of an idea today, we must first find its meaning in terms of the issues faced by the man who formulated it. Traditional concepts are not to be judged by the measure in which they fall short of an illusory eternal truth; the ultimate test, by their availability for our problems, can come only after we have understood their adequacy for the past problems they were devised to meet.

This is well illustrated in Dewey's most recent examination of the Aristotelian logic. This intellectual instrument he is peculiarly tempted to judge by our needs rather than by those of the Greeks. "For Aristotelian logic enters so vitally into present theories that consideration of it, instead of being historical in import, is a consideration of the contemporary logical scene."[14] Yet he is careful to make clear:

It would be completely erroneous to regard the foregoing as a criticism of the Aristotelian logic in its original formulation in connection with Greek culture. As a *historic* document it deserves the admiration it has received. As a comprehensive, penetrating and thoroughgoing intellectual transcript of discourse in isolation from the operations in which discourse takes effect it is above need for praise. . . . Generically, the need is for logic to do for present science and culture what Aristotle did for the science and culture of his time.[14]

[13] *Whither Mankind?*, ed. Charles Beard, ch. 13, "Philosophy."
[14] *Logic: The Theory of Inquiry*, 81, 93-95.

Or take his acute statement of Spinoza's essential problem.

An unqualified naturalism in the sense in which he understood the new science was combined by a miracle of logic with an equally complete acceptance of the idea, derived from the religious tradition, that ultimate reality is the measure of perfection and the norm for human activity. . . . A scientific comprehension was to give, in full reality, by rational means, that assurance and regulation of life that non-rational religions had pretended to give. . . . There have been few attempts in modern philosophy as bold and as direct as is this one to effect a complete integration of scientific method with a good which is fixed and final, because based on the rock of absolute cognitive certainty.[15]

Like so many of Dewey's most suggestive historical insights, these analyses occur in the midst of appraisals of our resources for meeting present problems. There is hardly need to single out professedly historical studies, like his illuminating paper on "The Motivation of Hobbes's Political Philosophy,"[16] in which by viewing Hobbes in terms of his own controversies he brings him into the line of "the protagonists of a science of human nature operating through an art of social control in behalf of a common good;" or his "Substance, Power and Quality in Locke,"[17] in which he is extraordinarily successful in brushing aside conventional views and penetrating to Locke's own difficulties with the certainty of knowledge; or his analysis of Newton in the *Quest for Certainty*. Mention might be made of a somewhat different type of historical analysis that recurs in Dewey's pages, the attempts to characterize the complex cultural features that have generated and sustained certain great movements of ideas. This type of thing is extraordinarily difficult to carry through in detail, as the Marxians and other German historians have discovered to their peril; and at best the keenest insight can hope to attain only shrewd guesses which would take a lifetime of research to verify and refine. Dewey would be the first to admit that his own suggestions are far too simple; yet ever since his essay on "The Significance of the Problem of Knowledge," published in 1897,[18] he has been re-

[15] *The Quest for Certainty*, 53-55.
[16] In *Columbia Studies in the History of Ideas*, Vol. I.
[17] *Philosophical Review*, Vol. XXXV, 1926.
[18] Reprinted in *The Influence of Darwin on Philosophy*.

markably fertile in throwing out such leads. The two central works, *Experience and Nature* and *The Quest for Certainty*, contain enough suggestions of this sort for further investigation to keep a whole historical school going for a generation.

Secondly, out of this objective historical relativism there develops the conception of philosophic thought as cumulative and additive, like the body of science with which it is so closely allied. Especially is this true of intellectual method, which grows in flexibility and power as its problems vary and as new technical devices and skills are built up. Each time an instrument is applied to fresh circumstances, it is itself enhanced and enriched. Greek thought remains the core of the classic tradition; yet the very diversity of the movements and cultural factors on which it has been employed, especially during the modern period, has subjected it to one illuminating criticism after another. Since for Dewey the process of criticism is emphatically the addition of further knowledge and not subtraction, since it reveals that larger context within which ideas are able to function validly and dualisms are disclosed as functional distinctions, these successive critical episodes have added precision of meaning and a delimitation of range of applicability, as well as new hypotheses and suggestions to be criticized in turn. The fortunes of Greek thought under the impact of 18th century empiricism, of the Kantian and post-Kantian movements, and of the new techniques and concepts of 19th century natural and social science, are a cardinal illustration of the cumulative character of a vital intellectual tradition. Another is the building of the liberal tradition in social affairs, the gradual bringing to bear of scientific thought upon men's social relations. And still a third is exhibited in the growth, expansion, and ultimate adjustment of the conceptions of human liberty, as set forth in "Philosophies of Freedom."[19]

In the third place, this objective relativism and cumulative character of the philosophical traditions make possible an intellectual tolerance and comprehensiveness that can find a place for every philosophy and every way of life. No single one can claim exclusive domination; each can be welcomed with under-

---

[19] Reprinted in *Philosophy and Civilization*.

standing appraisal when once its particular and appropriate function has been historically understood. As vision, as the imaginative expression of a definite culture, each has its own unique worth. As method, as a means for composing our own conflicts, each has a *prima facie* claim to be considered—though each must pass the stern test of its fruits. None is immune to philosophic criticism: each, stripped of its assumed unlimited validity, must abide within the bounds its historic operations have revealed. But each great belief of the past has some core of value from which we can learn and which we can use. Breadth and not narrowness of vision, generous reception and not intolerant single-mindedness, mark the spirit of Dewey's recurrent appeals to the past. If we are to assimilate its varied insights, we face a never-ending problem of harmonization and adjustment. And if all are to live in peace, none must be so stiff-necked as to refuse submission to the necessary reconstruction.

At only two points does Dewey's tolerant welcome stop short. The cardinal philosophic sin has been to shrink from practical action to take refuge in an unshakable higher realm of fixed and antecedent Reality. Afraid to seek a shifting and relative security by the efforts of intelligence, men have found consolation in the exaltation of pure intellect and the eternal intelligible perfection it has beheld. This cowardly choice, to accept a world understood instead of trying to change it, Dewey connects, by a somewhat dubious logic, with the quest for an absolute and immutable certainty in the things of the mind. Whatever has appeared in past thought of such a craven yearning for the eternal and unchanging must be dissolved forever in the relativities of time. For complete fixity or absolute certainty there can be no place.

And the great vice of practice has been an equally illiberal and inhumane choice. Men have cultivated the so-called higher values, and disdained the homely goods of common experience. From the poverty-stricken Oriental lands they have inherited despair of ever making widespread the natural and social goods of living. Leaving the latter to the avarice of the worldly, they have aspired to a Good Life located in a far different "spiritual" realm. With righteousness and purity of heart, the great moral faiths of renunciation, they have consoled the penniless beggar, the lame, the halt and the blind—even such can attain the Highest. Such counsels of despair Dewey not unwisely finds irrelevant today. But with them he also dismisses all selection, all concentration on certain values to the inevitable exclusion of the rest. When confronted by the apparent necessity of choice, intelligence must insist that both courses are valuable, and impel an active and aggressive manipulation of conditions until both are made compatible. To reject any values completely is to accept defeat. In his ethical and educational theory Dewey has stood for the Romantic ideal. The richest possible variety of goods must be included: but this very choice of inclusion has excluded the historic values of selection and single-minded devotion. There is no place for any ascetic or Puritan ideal.

IV

What has been here set forth is an attempt to catch the fundamental drive of Dewey's position on how philosophy's past is to be understood and used. Yet men have not always read him thus. These persistent variations raise doubts as to whether he has always consistently practiced his own essential teaching. We may well conclude by formulating these doubts for his adjudication.

First, the equal necessity of tradition, present experience, and reconstructive criticism is intellectually clear. But it is also beyond dispute that the very terms he uses again and again suggest a loading on the side of deep emotional feeling for liberation from the past. In Dewey's lifetime America has emancipated itself from restricting provincialism and narrow and fossilized religious and moral codes. His leadership in that emancipation has been effective and mighty: but it has determined his task and defined his own historic problems. This is both understandable and inevitable. But the warm sympathies so generously enlisted in the struggles of what is now his and not our generation have left their train of misconceptions. The question they raise is, are we to trust his obvious feelings, or his considered words? Are we to approach the past as revolutionaries who would fain forget as much of it as we can, and make a wholly fresh start? or are we to analyze and use it in the interests of experimental reconstruction?

Secondly, there is the method whereby the value of past ideas is to be judged. Again Dewey's basic position is clear: we must summon all our resources of intellectual analysis to ascertain how those ideas have operated, in their generating conditions, in their subsequent career, in our own adjustments. The test must be wholly functional: ideas are to be evaluated by their consequences in experience. Yet here too Dewey's practice has created misconceptions: to critics he has seemed to commit the genetic fallacy, and to admirers, to justify the discrediting of ideas by an account of their origins. For instance, it has not helped for him to say: "The more adequate [Aristotelian] logic was in its own day, the less fitted is it to form the framework of present logical theory."[20] It is not the fact but the method that raises the question. Is the bare discovery of the genesis of beliefs in some past epoch enough to dispose of them? Or is such a genetic analysis only a preliminary to determining the conditions to be satisfied by a genuinely functional test?

Thirdly, there is the unceasing polemic against any traffic with "certainty" that runs as a thread through all Dewey's historical criticisms. To friend and foe this has often appeared the most characteristic feature of his treatment of the history of philosophy. I have deliberately avoided emphasizing it. For though it be essential in his own mind, I doubt whether the future will judge it a very significant part of his contribution to our knowledge of the past. We have thoroughly learned that ideas are relative to a context, and that neither history nor science reveals any fixed absolutes. Those who have not are not likely to learn it from Dewey. He has played his part, and it would be ungrateful to forget it; but Dewey scarcely gave our age its relativism. The constant harping on its previous absence sounds a little like the advice to remember the schoolmen were Christians, or the moderns dwellers in an era of capitalism.

The question is rather about the sources of this ancient illu-

[20] *Logic: The Theory of Inquiry*, 82.

sion. Does the utmost devotion to changing the world through action exclude as a cardinal sin all attempt to change the self in emotion and idea? To be intelligent, must one renounce all wisdom of renunciation? Are there no vital and strengthening arts of consolation? Is not vision itself a power over the passions? Dewey's reasoned answer is clear, and might be abundantly cited. But there are those passages like the one about ideal friendship and the unreality of space and time.[21] Classic thought beheld the vision of the communion of the saints. But moderns have done better: they have invented the telephone and the radio. Is Dewey seriously advising the bereaved to get a medium and ring up their dead? The illustration, I fear, is symbolic. Would Dewey dismiss out of hand all that imagination has done to make existence endurable, just because the world has not yet through action been made quite wholly new?

And finally, there is the judgment of the classic tradition, of Greek thought, of Aristotle. Here Dewey's procedure is more revealing than his words. *Experience and Nature* is not unique, but typical: again and again on every major philosophic issue he first displays the dualisms, the wrenchings apart, the messy confusions of modern thought, only to turn to the Greeks in admiration for their clarity of perception. It is their ideas he deems fruitful material for further critical development. And in contrast to the whole of modern philosophy, save where it in turn has most powerfully felt Greek influence, Dewey himself seems to be working primarily with the conceptions of Aristotle. In his naturalism, his pluralism, his logical and social empiricism, his realism, his natural teleology, his ideas of potentiality and actuality, contingency and regularity, qualitatively diverse individuality—above all, in his thoroughgoing functionalism, his Aristotelian translation of all the problems of matter and form into a functional context—to say nothing of his basic social and ethical concepts—in countless vital matters he is nearer to the Stagirite than to any other philosopher. Where he has used the instruments of a century of critical effort —the empiricists' analysis, the post-Kantian appeal to a more human experience, the biological and social conceptions of

[21] *Reconstruction in Philosophy*, 119-120.

human nature, the lessons of a rapidly changing culture—it has been to carry the Aristotelian attitude still further in the direction in which Aristotle criticized Platonism. It were not difficult to exhibit Dewey as an Aristotelian more Aristotelian than Aristotle himself.

Yet one would hardly realize this from his words. His use of Aristotelian ideas has been remarkably fruitful. But however effective in developing his own position, most of what he has explicitly said about Aristotle has conveyed little real historical illumination: it has been far more relevant to Saint Thomas than to the Greek. Much of what he points to is there; much is not, and is to be found only in the scholastic tradition. It would scarcely be proper and pertinent, even if true, to maintain here that the total impression he gives of Aristotelian thought is nevertheless false. It would be more to the point to ask, why should Dewey view Aristotle through the eyes of the Neothomists? Why should he not see Aristotle for what he is, the greatest functionalist in the philosophical tradition?— he who of all thinkers today can best claim to be the representative of Aristotelian thought, the truest follower of him who likewise in his time most effectively and suggestively brought the criticism of the best scientific thought to bear on the classic tradition.

JOHN HERMAN RANDALL, JR.

DEPARTMENT OF PHILOSOPHY
COLUMBIA UNIVERSITY

3

Donald A. Piatt

DEWEY'S LOGICAL THEORY

3

DEWEY'S LOGICAL THEORY

I

A FAIR evaluation of Dewey's philosophy has been difficult to obtain for a number of reasons. For one thing, philosophers are a bit disingenuous in pretending to be lovers of wisdom and truth; they are more at home in defense and attack than in a coöperative search for common meanings and values; their major premises have the quality of a religious faith, are felt so deeply and to be of such importance that they *must* be saved. It is exceptional for a philosopher to admit that he has made a mistake, and if he does admit it, the mistake is said to lie in his argument rather than in what he set out to prove. For the same reason it is uncommon for a philosopher to make a determined and sympathetic attempt to understand an opponent's position. Far too many of the criticisms of Dewey's pragmatism have been based on misunderstandings which have been repeatedly pointed out. If pragmatism has suffered more from misunderstanding than most philosophies, I think this is due largely to the dogmatic tone of philosophies in general and to the aggressive, militant, and revolutionary character of pragmatism in particular: the attitude of frontal attack I have found stimulating to my own thought, but not conducive to objective and sympathetic understanding.

A second difficulty which dogs pragmatism has already been intimated in the statement of its revolutionary character: just because Dewey differs from most philosophers more than they differ from one another, because he challenges their common premises, misunderstandings easily arise and are hard to remove. Insiders and outsiders speak a different language or, what is worse, use the same words with different meanings, and there is no recognized common referent for getting in and out of

Dewey's thought. In this predicament "clarifications" of meanings fail to clarify and merely repeat the underlying difficulty; no genuine dispute takes place.

Owing to a growing impatience with this kind of frustration, and to my close association in recent years with philosophers of a dominantly realist stamp, I have come to believe and to argue that a rapprochement between pragmatism and realism is possible when certain misunderstandings on both sides have been cleared away. But when I explain and defend Dewey in their terms my realist friends tell me that I have actually abandoned him and that only personal loyalty prevents me from admitting it. This I am not yet prepared to believe, for I think the alleged abandonment is in the main but a change in emphasis and in wording. There are so many different brands of pragmatism, and subjectivism, relativism, voluntarism and anti-intellectualism loom so large in the ensemble that it is no wonder that Dewey's essential realism and rationalism get lost in the shuffle. Yet if it should turn out that on certain important points I disagree with Dewey, it is intrinsic to the logic of inquiry that philosophic as well as scientific beliefs can be modified without any sacrifice of principle. Indeed it has always seemed to me that the pragmatist is the least bound by prior commitments of all philosophers, so that I should not be worried about personal loyalty.

An adequate account of Dewey's logical theory would disclose the idealistic no less than the realistic import of this theory but, because the realists are for the moment more importunate, because they are likely to miss the realism if it is presented in proximity with idealism, and because the latter presupposes the former, I shall concentrate on the realistic aspects of the theory.

Before turning to Dewey's logical theory I wish to say a word regarding the scope of this essay relative to the other essays of the volume, to remind the reader of the historical setting of the theory, and to note certain general assumptions of Dewey's philosophy.

There is bound to be much overlapping in these essays because Dewey's philosophy is all of one piece: metaphysics, epistemology, logic differ not in their ultimate subject matter but in phases or perspectives of the same subject matter. For Dewey as for Hegel, continuity is pervasive and all-embracing. While, to be sure, Dewey's empiricism stresses the specific and differential conditions under which natural events are experienced, and thus differs from Hegel in noting the plurality, individuality, novelty, and piecemeal characters of events; yet these articulations are not alien to one another but fall within a unitary world. Experience and nature are not separate entities conjoined or added together; experience is rather the forms which nature assumes in interactions of non-organic and organic events including human events. Much of the difficulty in understanding Dewey would be obviated if more attention were paid to his naturalism and less to his empiricism. Instrumental and experimental logic is naturalistic, not a logic of a separate world of thought but a logic of natural events which are functioning on a meaning level. By the same token, naturalistic metaphysics may appropriately be regarded as instrumental and experimental because thinking behavior only actualizes and utilizes to better advantage the instrumental and experimental potentialities of natural events. Because of the polarity of the contextual and the perspectival aspects of Dewey's philosophy, because its logical theory is material as well as formal in having to do with natural events in their thought connections, this examination of the logical theory is of necessity an examination of much more than ordinarily passes for logical theory.

The realistic and naturalistic import of Dewey's philosophy is partly concealed by reason of its historical setting and its primary motivation. Dewey's metaphysics is a development of his logical theory, and much of the *Essays in Experimental Logic* was written before realism took shape, and it was written partly as a reaction against and partly as a development of idealism. As a result the terminology is more subjectivistic than it needs to be or means to be. However, the insistence that thought is an agency for *re*constituting existence and that knowledge resolves conflicting impulses or habits and settles an unsettled tensional state of affairs is primarily a result of Dewey's engrossment in education, morals, and politics. In this sense, Dewey has always been an idealist in the proper sense of that term, if I may take that liberty. Where for idealism the world was created as a necessity for the self-realization of moral will and of thought—as a series of obstacles or contradictions to be overcome—for Dewey, the world *is* in its own right precarious, hazardous, challenging. Consequently pragmatic idealism is grounded on a realistic and naturalistic basis. Judgments of value and of practice, of what ought to be done, are grounded both by inception and by "warranted conclusion" in judgments of fact. Dewey looks at the world primarily from the perspective of the moralist, the educator, and the ordinary man; only secondarily and hence instrumentally from the perspective of the theoretical scientist and the metaphysician. The question of what the world is gets a bit squeezed by the question of what we can make of it, of what it is doing to us and of what we can do to it.

In evaluating experimental logic we can do no better than to apply to it the test which it applies to other theories. Philosophic thought depends upon an act of choice and of selective discrimination for a purpose or a preference. "Honest empirical method will state when and where and why the act of selection took place, and thus enable others to repeat it and test its worth."[1] The pragmatist chooses to look at the world temporally, longitudinally, historically rather than spatially, horizontally, and structurally. But one does not have to view the world exclusively or primarily in this way, and there is nothing in empirical method that requires it. One can, and I think one must, acknowledge that knowing is an experimental process in which there is deliberate interference with antecedent existence. Nature itself is reconstituted in the process. But one must also acknowledge—and the casual reader is likely to miss this in Dewey—that the purpose of knowledge in using experiment in science and largely in practical life is to discover what exists and what antecedently existed apart from the experiment. The realist underestimates the force of the active, experimental, transforming nature of the knowing process; and the pragmatist is in danger of overestimating it. Conversion of eventual functions into antecedent existence Dewey regards as *the* philosophic

[1] *Experience and Nature*, 36.

fallacy,[2] but it seems to me that this depends on what antecedent existence we are talking about. The antecedent existences which set the problem for thoughtful inquiry are experimentally transformed; we do not merely change our "thinking." But equally through experimental inquiry in science we creatively *discover* other antecedent existences than those just mentioned which existed quite apart from our inquiry. On this point there is at times confusion in Dewey's language and perhaps overemphasis on the creative power of intelligence, but Dewey himself supplies the correction. Though he stresses the temporal aspect of existence and the transformation made in it by thought (itself an existential process), though he concentrates on the macroscopic traits of nature as it impinges upon us in our ordinary experience, yet he recognizes that thought is as much *inquiry* into the microscopic and stable conditions of nature, which have been settled in nature before they have been settled for us, as thought is a reconstruction of gross existence.

II. Logical Subject Matter

Dewey's philosophy begins and ends in logical theory as the method of *inquiry*. All of the many fields which this philosophy has explored are in terms of differences of subject matter variations upon the central theme of inquiry. A reciprocal relationship binds the theme and its variations: apart from the actual occurrence of different kinds of natural events with distinctive qualities there would be no specific inquiries, much less inquiry into inquiries; apart from a generalized method of inquiry specific inquiries would lack direction and control. The former relationship however is the more important in the sense that all thought must follow the lead of its subject matter, and all that logic can do is to clarify, generalize, and systematize what specific investigations do when they succeed in performing what they set out to do. Dewey is empiricist and naturalist in recognizing the derivative rôle of thought, the dependence of thought upon a non-logical subject matter. He is a rationalist *par excellence* in recognizing the paramount rôle of intelligence in the conduct of life.

[2] *Experience and Nature*, 35.

It will be asked how an instrumentalist, experimentalist, and immediate empiricist can be a rationalist. The answer is, by being a contextualist—by placing thought as inquiry *within* the natural existential context in which alone it can yield warranted assertions. Within such a context inquiry is no more an instrument, tool, servant than a master. When inquiry turns in upon itself it finds that, to produce warranted conclusions, it *must* proceed according to certain rules or stipulations. The stipulations are not arbitrary or conventional save in verbal expression, for though one can choose whether to think or not, if one thinks, one is obliged to follow the *a priori* forms of thought shown by inquiry to be implicit in all previous rational inquiry and necessary for further inquiry.

I must confess that I fail to find an impassable gulf between this rationalism which makes logical forms postulational and ordinary rationalism. If, to adapt Kantian terminology, the rationalist means by pure reason formal factors that are transcendental but not transcendent of empirical subject matter, then logical forms as postulates are forms of pure reason. Identity of meaning in inference, for example, is, if you please, a postulate or a demand or a responsibility which one agrees to make in rational inquiry, it is even a product of inquiry; but it is shown in the process to be necessary for any rational inference regardless of differences of empirical subject matter. Rationalists, I suppose, would concede that with the progress of knowledge and the development of science old logical forms are abandoned as *useless*, some are found to be erroneously formulated through faulty analysis, and new ones are discovered. But rational thought presupposes logically (not temporally) *a priori* rules. Unless the rationalist means by pure logical forms essences which subsist at large apart from thought, and unless Dewey means by logical forms the sort of postulates which can be made and unmade at will, the two positions are only verbally different in basic principle. Voluntarism is always in danger of running riot in pragmatism. We may rightly insist that there is no thought at large but only in the service of interests and needs, that differences in needs *may* and frequently do call for different methods or forms of thought as means, that logical means have a natural history and are continuous with prior non-logical operations; but we must then acknowledge that what makes the instrument serviceable is its intrinsic and definitive character. Beginning as means of solving non-logical problems and of satisfying non-cognitive needs, logical forms become *a priori* ways of determining whether problems have been solved rationally. I suspect that Dewey accepts what he sets down as the basic pattern of inquiry, as the *sine qua non* of all future rational inquiry.

Let us pursue the question of logical subject matter a bit further. When the pragmatist defines logic as methodology he does so, it seems to me, because logic grew out of inquiry into nature and has its primary use in guiding material inference. Dewey has no trouble in showing that Aristotelian logic developed in this way. Now it is because Dewey is interested in logic *for use,* because he is interested in propositions, terms, and their formal relations only as constituents of judgment (judgment being what the rationalist calls "synthetic judgment") that he makes out his case for axioms and first principles as postulates. With respect to the *ultimate* subject matter of logic this argument seems to me perfectly tenable, but the rationalist affirms *a priori* certainty only for the proximate subject matter, only for what Locke would have called "trifling judgments," or for what the rationalist today calls "analytic judgments." Dewey admits that here rationalism and pragmatism seem to amount to the same thing but affirms that there is a radical theoretical difference between them. I fail to see this difference if I am right that the rationalist need not deny the empirical generation of logical forms or the empirical limitations in applying them to empirical subject matter, but basically affirms their certainty within their abstracted formal medium. I am of course assuming that Dewey does not deny the latter.

III. The Existential Matrix of Inquiry

In this section we shall be concerned with the antecedents and the external aspects of inquiry in the organism-environment relation—with the naturalistic and "epistemological" import of the theory, and with "immediate empiricism." These matters take us into deeper strata of the ultimate subject matter of logic, and are the source of much misunderstanding of Dewey's theory.

It is a persistent misconception that pragmatism glorifies common sense and ordinary conduct at the expense of thought, that it belittles theory in behalf of practice, that it is blinded by a preference for doings and makings and so ignores the higher values of life, that it lightly brushes aside the central philosophical problem of the relation of thought to reality and substitutes logically derivative and hence unsupported questions of a biological and psychological rather than a philosophical nature. The truth is that pragmatists accept as central the question of the relation of thought to reality and endeavor to answer the question in the operational and situational context through which the question gets intelligible meaning and is capable of being answered. Unless our minds are already in some ways in touch with reality, unless one connection in some assignable fashion is broken relative to other connections that remain intact, this question is meaningless. Unless thought is a function of an active thinker and unless his thinking is rooted in other activities that on occasion demand thinking and provide a consummating terminal for thinking, thought is a complete mystery—unthinkable even as a mystery. For in that case either we would not think at all or else we would have instantaneous and complete knowledge. In neither case would the *problem* of the existence of reality or the knowledge of it arise. On the other side, if reality were just reality, if there were not different kinds or groupings of reality, and if these did not present themselves ambiguously and unsatisfactorily in our experience in relation to our differential purposes and interests; there would be nothing in nature or existence or "data" (choose any term that suits your philosophy) to offer any ground for the terms "reality" and "appearance."

Dewey's logical theory is an elaboration of the thesis that the only way to secure continuity is to recognize it when you see it and hence to start with it as an indefeasible fact of ordinary experience. He accordingly begins with the common sense world in which people act, love, hate, suffer, in response to a somewhat settled and somewhat unsettled environment—not because he prefers pre-reflective activities and existences, not because they are more real than reflective activities, but because they are the actual and necessary presuppositions of inquiry. Apart from such a world there would be no inquiry. The assertion of the existential basis of inquiry is an assertion that epistemological subjectivism and solipsism are masquerades, impostors, fabrications of thought which is forgetful of its origin and function. The origin consists in natural events which are organisms in *inter*action with other natural events. On this level of primary behavior unsophisticated as yet by reflection about it, the organism finds the environment satisfying or dissatisfying, responsive or unresponsive, stable or unstable; and it finds that the ordering of these qualitative events can in a measure be changed by its own activities in response to its needs. On this primary level of immediate experience, qualities which philosophers distinguish with dubious propriety as primary, secondary, and tertiary are "had" or enjoyed or suffered as qualities of things—not as private data of consciousness for inference to things.

It has not been asserted in the foregoing that the environment of the organism exhausts nature or that the whole of nature depends upon experience. Rather it is the essence of experience that it is in nature, continuous with it, a part of it.[3] Nay more, the immediately experienced qualitative environment is found to act upon us in ways that we cannot, at least for the time, as well as in ways that we can modify. It is this hard factual and resistant trait of things that leads later to the development of the sciences and to the discovery of different kinds of environment—physical, biological, social, and so on. It is a patent fact of experience that much of the world transcends the parts now perceived, that life is restrictive and selective within a world. Or if you please, we are conscious of a fringe beyond which whatever exists is *now* inaccessible. Much of the world may be never directly accessible. Experience is a form of existence, a part of the natural history of existence. Experience is, as such, a part of a wider field of existence. The pragmatist willingly

[3] *Logic*, 33.

acknowledges this dualism *within* the world which the epistemological dualist mistakes usually for a dualism of mind and nature as independent substances. We return to this matter later.

We have said that the external world is immediately experienced, and yet we are claiming to know that what is experienced as external is real. Is this not a paradox? The answer is that our present statements do not, of course, by themselves prove the existence of the external world. The critic can but be asked to have some experience to which we can point and to see for himself what he finds—to see whether qualities are not had as qualities of things in the world rather than as subjective data for inference to an external world. Moreover, what other recourse is there for inquiry and thought if thought is to lead to any knowledge whatsoever, save in facts that are had and are had as not in need of further thought for the problem at hand? How otherwise are we ever to get beyond thinking? If I treat a man who menaces me with a club as a collection of sense-data, and he bumps me with a club, I don't have to make an inference to tell what has happened to me and to tell that the happening has an external source. The immediate experience of such happenings is not said to be immediate *knowledge*, for knowledge is a function of judgment, and no judgment is necessary about what one immediately has.

To the further objection that while our account of pre-reflective experience is plausible enough on the pre-reflective level, yet analysis shows that "immediate experience" is frequently if not always in error, we reply by carrying our own analysis further. We might ask once more how an error of immediate experience could be made out ultimately apart from reference to another immediate experience. But instead we reply briefly to the argument for the subjectivity of "secondary" and "tertiary" qualities. If these are subjective, so are the "primary" qualities, for all qualities rest on complex causal conditions, some of which involve the nervous organization of sense organs and the brain. But there is no good reason for regarding any of these qualities as subjective. The argument confuses an effect with its organic cause. In perceiving qualities, we do not perceive their causes; and if we did, we might as well perceive the physical causes as the organic ones, for all qualities rest partly on physical causes. It must be noted that the pragmatist does not say that qualitative objects are external in the sense of being independent of organisms; these objects belong to our environment, and our environment is a function of our organic structure as much as of the structure of inanimate things. Moreover, organisms belong to nature as much as inanimate things do.

Another argument is to the effect that we perceive qualities differently when we are grown than when we are infants. To this contention and its variations we reply by admitting the facts and by questioning the interpretation of them. The fact that earlier perceptual or sensory qualities are modified, by reason of modifications in brain paths that have occurred with or without *previous* inferences, is mistaken to mean that we are *now* making an unconscious inference from subjective images to objective independent things. The qualities themselves have changed because of the change in organic conditions that affect them; we don't make an inference from the old qualities or "data" to the new qualities.

It is interesting that Professor Reichenbach agrees with Dewey that perceptual qualities are not subjective data used in inference to things but are rather immediately experienced qualities of things. This is notable because he goes on to claim nevertheless that secondary and tertiary qualities are qualities of "immediate existences" which are in so far forth subjective. His argument takes the line that illusions and dreams prove the point: we can be mistaken in perception whether we are making an inference or not. In so far as we are mistaken, "immediate existence" is subjective; in so far as we are right, "immediate existence" is objective.[4] But this objection seems to me terminological. He admits that a camera would register as bent the stick partly submerged in water, but he argues that nevertheless the stick is straight. Just as the stick is fortunately not affected by all the abuse which has been heaped upon it, it is not affected by the diffraction of light in water which only makes it appear bent. The answer is that this is an existential question of physical operations, not a question of failure of perception to report what

[4] *Experience and Prediction*, 198 and *passim*.

is there in the *given* physical perspective. A camera does not make inferences and we do not make an inference in perceiving the bent stick. Illusion could occur if we took the optical stick as a datum or sign for an inference that the optical stick is altogether like the tactual stick or like the optical stick out of water, or that in perception of either sort we have a safe datum for inference to the physical conditions underlying the apparent-and-real stick. Realists misinterpret Dewey by supposing that in saying that we perceive a natural event he means that we perceive the causes of its occurrence or properties of its behavior in other environments than the perceptual one specified. Dewey expressly states that the existential matrix of inquiry is the inter-action of organism and environment. This is why I suspect that Mr. Reichenbach's objection is lexicographic.

I am not optimistic enough to suppose that the difficulties cited have been cleared up, and I do not say that there are no genuine difficulties, but we must understand the theory before we can criticize it. Realists think that Dewey's claim that perception is not a case of knowledge is undone by his claim that perceptual objects are real. For if they are real, must this not mean that a perceptual judgment conscious or unconscious has been ex-cogitated to the effect that the datum is in fact the external object as the cause of the datum? The answer is that on the primary qualitative level of perception (a secondary cognitive level will be examined in the next section of this essay) what is had is no more an inference than coughing, breathing, or sneezing is an inference. These are all natural occurrences involving the organism *and the environment*. Things had in this way are not affairs of knowledge because there can be no question about their occurrence for thought to raise, no doubt that they exist as they appear, and because things must be had before they can become affairs of knowledge or inquiry. They become affairs of inquiry, of thoughtful discrimination, of careful noting when there is a question of having them again or of what they mean relative to other things had or relative to their conditions and consequences. Thus when a physicist uses physical instruments he may reasonably doubt whether the instruments are adapted to the use to which he puts them, but he does not doubt the existence of the instruments. When he makes observations for purposes of testing a theory he does not think he is observing his own mind. When a scientist observes a fact contrary to what prior knowledge or law led him to expect he does not regard the fact as psychical; science requires that the prior law be reformulated to include the exceptional instance. Of course, these citations are illustrations of inquiry rather than of pure immediate experience; nevertheless they point to the experienced existential basis of inquiry and indicate that we inquire into the meaning of existence and not into the meaning of "psychical data."

I think this whole question of the non-cognitive status and of the reality of the perceptual situation (I say situation because the realist's "data" are post-analytic discriminated components of the perceptual situation and not the situation originally had) can be clarified if we keep in mind the difference between the realist's and the pragmatist's meaning of knowledge. For the realist it seems, if he is consistent, any experience is knowledge— breathing I dare say as much as perception of a colored patch— in so far as what is experienced is in fact independent of the experient and belongs to the "physical" world. For the pragmatist, experience is not a knowing-experience save as there is in the existential situation experienced something dubious or problematic, calling for judgment about and hence inquiry into the meaning (not the existence) of the situation. Inquiry passes into knowledge or rather warranted assertion when inference from features of the situation taken as data or signs is actively followed out to other existential occurrences signified, in such a way that the initial dubious situation becomes reconstituted and settled. Only relative to other natural events is the initial perceived situation cognitive or problematic.

Now it seems to me that it is practically unimportant whether we say with some realists that dreams, "illusions," and *some* qualities in ordinary normal perception are subjective, or say with the pragmatists that all qualities perceived or had are real, and that in the case of some qualities the requisite conditions for their occurrence lie more within the organism than without. What is theoretically important is that the dualistic realist cannot make out a case for subjective "data" without appealing to conditions that are "subjective" in relation to other conditions that are "objective." There is no harm in speaking proleptically of dreams as subjective on the ground that their major conditions are organic, but it is a serious confusion of thought to treat perceptual qualities in general as psychical, for the "problem" of getting to an external world is then insoluble. The actual facts in inquiry are the same for the realist as for the pragmatist. The astronomer makes warranted assertions about stellar events on the basis of observations which he certainly does not regard as subjective. Yet he knows that all perceptual qualities rest partly on organic conditions. Notwithstanding the organic conditioning of the visible star, he regards the visible star as on the same level of reality as the astronomical star which is its physical cause. The visible light is a physical occurrence continuous with its physical cause. The astronomer does not mistake the perceived effect for its cause; on the contrary, since he is not dealing with a representative mental content but a physical event, he is able to trace the process back to its cause. Realist, pragmatist, and astronomer all believe in distant physical events that do not depend on the observer, that are not themselves perceived. All three believe that these events can be known. This is possible, according to the pragmatist and the astronomer, because the percept is itself a natural object and not a content in the mind purporting to represent an independent external object. The pragmatist and the scientist are the true realists because they do not open the door to a subjective mental world, then close it against the objective world, then forget how they got in, and then hunt for cracks in the wall by which they hope to "see" out.

IV. DATA AND MEANINGS

Attention has been directed to the pre-reflective existential situation in order to emphasize the continuity of experience and nature and the continuity of both with inquiry. Nature undergoes inquiry when natural events act upon human organisms in certain ways and when these organisms react in certain ways; by reason of this interaction, within nature, of organisms and their environment, natural events behave differently, take on new properties, become subject to a measure of control, and are forced to reveal hidden structural relations among themselves as a result of the existential operations of the process of inquiry. Why inquiry occurs, what it is about, how it proceeds, what consummates and terminates it are all questions pertaining to natural existence. Central to these questions is the rôle of data, meanings, and the objects of knowledge. We consider the interplay of data and meanings in this section, and the objects of knowledge which eventuate through this interplay in the following section, though in so doing we lose perhaps as much as we gain in clarity of exposition.

Perception has been treated so far as a non-cognitive occurrence, as an immediate experience of qualitative events of the environment. Things are had and used, Dewey repeatedly tells us, before they are known. The purpose of knowing is to be able to have and use them in a better and more secure manner. But realists and others will ask whether this clean-cut distinction between having and using on the one side and knowing on the other is warranted. Is not perception, at least in human beings, always cognitive? Dewey has been misunderstood on this point for he does not deny this allegation (though our previous argument represents him as denying it) but only asks us to consider *in what way* perception is cognitive. Does it follow, he asks, that because perception involves inference it requires that the datum be in the mind? And what is the nature of this inference?

In perception we experience clouds as a sign of rain or a patch of darkish sky as a sign of a cloud. If we take our experience at its face value, we must admit that a good share of the time we perceive things more in terms of what they suggest than in terms of what they directly appear to be and, Dewey would add, of what they are. We look at objects in our hurried and practical life for what we can do with them, for their existential connections with other objects that we want to get or have to get. Inference is from one thing as means to another as end, not from the mind to the world. So Dewey does not deny that perception is cognitive; in fact, he states that it is precisely because things are so prolific in their suggestions and so uncertain as signs that inquiry is necessary to control the suggestions.

The realist will not deny that phenomenally this sort of

thing occurs. The theory is perhaps now clearer to him but he is still not satisfied. He will say that the non-problematic basis in the seen cloud for the suggestion of rain seems non-problematic and immediate only because we have not stopped to ask whether there is really a problem there. The cloud itself is an inference so far as our experience is concerned. Dewey, I think, would reply to this crucial question by saying that there are two points here to be distinguished. First, the perceived cloud is not necessarily an inference, it is ordinarily a fact in the minded-organism-environment in which it occurred, and we take it to be an inference only because we confuse a later judgment with the fact. Secondly, while the perceived cloud is a natural event in the perspective noted, it can of course become an affair of knowledge, we can ask (as the realist has asked) whether what we are looking at is a cloud or indicates a cloud. But in this case inference in principle is the same as before: where before we took the cloud as a sign of rain, we now take what is seen as a sign of a cloud. Inference goes from one aspect of nature to another, actual or possible, not from a mental content to nature. Whenever we ask whether what we see is real we are asking what it indicates as to its connections with other things, things not now given.

We return from this objection to the main topic. The perceptual situation ordinarily is one of qualitative things given as such; it is not a presentation of "sense-data" as an appearance or representation of objects, much less of the external cause of the "sense-data." But ordinarily what is given with its own qualitative integrity and intrinsic meaning—a table, a cloud, or any of the familiar objects of our experience—is attended to more for what it suggests than for what it is. Ordinarily things are instruments for use in securing or avoiding other things not present; they are not objects of knowledge or even just objects had. Things that occur usually occur as appearances or representations, and it is this circumstance that makes plausible the realist's theory that perception is essentially a judgment. However, things are appearances or representations usually of other things that are to follow or that may follow, as rain may follow the gathering clouds. The extrinsic office by which things point to other things Dewey defines as the primary relation of inference. Inference is the "sign-significance" relation.[5] Inference from clouds as a natural sign to rain as what is indicated is, if you please, cognitive; but it is not judgmental or does not have to be. It is a matter of habit and of expectation. We do not have to think to make such inferences, for the expectation is grounded in natural occurrences. Meanings are in things before they are "in minds." If Dewey at times seems to deny that such expectations are cognitive, he means then that they are not the work of thought. Signs are as much immediately experienced as are things.

Much has been made of the existential setting of inquiry. We have just said that expectation is grounded in natural occurrences, but we have also said that this does not mean that the worth of the expectation is so grounded. Valid inference has to be established in inquiry. A bell rings and we go to the door perhaps to find nobody there; then there is a problem for inquiry. Inquiry takes place by the interplay of data and meanings, so that we must now consider in what way data and meanings function.

On the one side, meanings are functions of things in the environment; on the other side they are functions of thought. The success of inquiry turns on this fact: that existential meanings and ideational meanings are quite different and are yet in inquiry, as will presently be noted, closely related to each other. We say that smoke seen means fire, and we say that the idea or thought of smoke means or implies fire. In the first case, one actual event indicates another event as possible or as expected. In the second, one concept means another. To avoid confusion, Dewey sharply distinguishes the former relation as that of "sign-significance" from the latter relation as that of "symbol-meaning." The former relation defines inference; the latter defines implication.[6]

Now signs, or more properly natural signs, and symbols have in common the fact that they are existential events. The word smoke as written, seen, spoken, or heard, is a particular physical

[5] *Logic*, 51, 56.
[6] *Logic*, 51-56.

thing; but, unlike the smoke seen, it functions as a universal in discourse. Granted that reasoning operates with ideas or concepts, it does so only by the manipulation of symbols arranged as terms, propositions, and the like. There is no thought without language behavior. The advantage of language is of course that it provides tools of thought that can be manipulated quite independently of external events: it gives us the mixed blessing of formal logic. Language has however, save for philosophers, the further advantage that it takes us away from actual smoke and fire to symbols as substitutes so as to bring us back with the means of identifying, recognizing, understanding, and controlling smoke and fire. Qualitative events existentially connected become converted into definite objects, that is, into events having characters and not just qualities and sign-values. Language enables us to invest existential events with properties that they owe to their existential involvements in the way of causes, effects, and correlates. Things are no longer simply had and used but are meaningfully had and used; they can be known whenever there is any occasion to induce inquiry. The ways in which things can operate as signs of other things are vastly multiplied. Inference no longer has to be a matter of luck; it becomes grounded in science and previous inquiries, and it is subject always to fresh inquiries. Yes, language is indeed man's greatest invention.

Three different kinds of meaning have been noted, and even these are not exhaustive. In review, they are as follows: (1) Some meanings are intrinsic to natural events as experienced; they are had as immediately and as directly as qualities. Qualities of pre-analytic and also of post-analytic experience are qualities of things. Animal psychology and especially gestalt psychology have established the situational nature and the wholeness of the perceptual environment. Prior to the development of language, animals react to whole objects—not to qualities out of which they construct objects. The Lockean psychology, according to which qualities are primitive data or "simple ideas" and things are "complex ideas," has been discredited. When reflection begins, it operates by abstraction and discrimination rather than by addition and comparison. Equally, the objects of

our world which we take to be there without any question because they are objects of *past* knowledge, so well established
that there is no longer any occasion to think about them, are
cases of intrinsic meanings. We have learned that fire is a dangerous thing; it has the intrinsic meaning of danger. As Dewey
puts it, pre-analytic and post-analytic objects are objects because they make "sense," they have significance in themselves.
Much of logical theory and of logical positivism has been artificial because it has ignored the fact that meanings are given
in things before they are taken in language and thought.

(2) A second kind of meaning has been noted in the "sign-
significance" relation of inference. I would speak of "signification" rather than of "significance," because this kind of meaning, in contrast with the previous kind, is extrinsic or instrumental. Corresponding to the two sub-types of intrinsic meaning, there are two sub-types of extrinsic meanings of things. In
the simpler case, one thing suggests another, leads us to expect
the other, without instigating reflection or inquiry. In the more
complex case, the inference from the one thing to the other is
made explicit through inquiry. We stop to analyze the first thing
to determine what there is about it that will warrant the appearance of the other thing. We want to know whether the cloud
that suggests rain is one that really means (signifies) rain,
whether what appears as a cloud really is (signifies) a cloud,
and what kind of a cloud it is. In this inquiry, we pass from one
object to another object—from the cloud to the rain—by means
of intermediate symbols or ideas. But while these symbol-meanings are important, it must be emphasized that they are intermediate, they are what we think with and not what we think
about. As Dewey says, "What a thing means [signifies] is
another *thing;* it doesn't mean a meaning."[7]

(3) A third class of meanings is this class of symbol-meanings which we acquire and use in language operations in developing implications. Meaning is at bottom a functional relationship
between things as signs and other things as signified, but *a*
meaning is an idea, a gesture, a symbol as a substitute for what
is existentially indicated.[8] Now symbol-meanings point in two

[7] *Essays in Experimental Logic,* 430.
[8] *Ibid.,* 432.

directions: they are meanings of thought in their own medium of language but they refer or may refer indirectly to existential happenings. Hence if we ask what are the meanings of words, the question is ambiguous. Ideas or symbols mean things only in the sense that (to use Dewey's words) they "refer" and have "application" to things, and their application is by way of observation of and experiment with existential happenings. Neither ideas nor statements nor propositions mean things in the sense of implying them and supplying evidence for them. Symbol-meanings mean or imply other symbol-meanings, and in reasoning or ratiocination we elaborate and clarify the implications or meaning of an hypothesis. Any symbol, any word, is a meaningful term of discourse and of that talking with oneself which constitutes thought because any word is a part of a system of words, having no meaning apart from the system. That we engage in reasoning despite its tautological character is due to the fact that we cannot hold all the implications of an idea in our mind, that we can make mistakes in drawing implications, and that some and not other implications are relevant to the inquiry that we are conducting regarding matters of existential fact. But the point to be stressed is that no existential fact can be deduced from symbol-meanings, from any system of such meanings, or from any amount of reasoning with such meanings. The conclusions from reasoning are as hypothetical as the hypothesis from which they start.

It is hoped that this discussion of meaning will clarify the pragmatist's position relative to the realist's. If the realist maintains that ideas as such mean existential objects by being representations of them, and further maintains that by reasoning we can establish the truth or probability of ideas arranged in the form of propositions, the pragmatist dissents. He asserts that meaning and warranted assertions are fundamentally a connection of inference between a thing meaning and a thing meant or, as Dewey now puts it, between a *thing* signifying and a *thing* signified. He admits that reasoning is important but claims that it is distinct from inference and powerless apart from inference. The power of reasoning is the power of language in reconstituting a natural sign into a significant sign, and in reconstituting a thing or situation indicated into a significant indication. We turn now to the rôle of data in order to explain how this power of thought is exerted and how the gap between thought and existence is bridged.

It is customary to speak of data as entities that are given, one school of realists holding that these entities are mental or logical contents as representations, and another school holding that they are external existential events either as identical with the external object of knowledge or as a part of that object. For Dewey, the datum is not what is given but what is *taken*, selected, noted, observed, discriminated for the purpose of inference. What is given is the whole perceptual situation. What is taken as datum depends on the specific purpose of the inquiry, and purposes are manifold. Much of what is given may be irrelevant to the matter in question. In much of our practical life, as previously mentioned, we pay scarcely any attention at all to the objects around us and look only for the things that they indicate. If the doorbell rings, the question may be whether to go to the door and who is the intruder and is he a welcome guest. In science and in more complicated problems, the question is what the datum is in its sign connection with other things. But in no case can there be any question concerning the given as such, can the datum be identical with the given, for we cannot inquire into what we indubitably have.

Now inferences occur with and without judgment or inquiry. Hence it might be said that in either case a natural sign is a datum for a *quaesitum*, for a thing indicated. If a dog follows a scent and picks up a bone, the odor as a sign is a datum if you please. Dewey, however, reserves the term "datum" for those signs which are problematic for thought, which are judged uncertain as to their outcome and signification. Since logical theory is concerned with judgment, this usage is not arbitrary, and no one will question the difference between the two situations. In this restricted sense then, a datum is an existential happening or some phase of the perceptual situation which poses a problem and helps to define it. I hear a rumbling noise and ask: "What is that?" I am asking what the sound signifies. I am asking for the meaning in the sense of signification, in this case for the indicated cause. My attention is focused on the noise, alert, trying to discriminate what kind of noise it is, in order to ascertain the cause that it signifies. Suggestions of possible significations pop into my mind from my store of symbol-meanings. These significations are symbol-meanings. It may be an earthquake, and it may be the detonation of guns from the battleships off shore. It may be any one of a number of things. The point for the moment is that nothing is a datum in isolation, simply as given or as presented; a datum is always representative, involves a disturbed connection with what is not given, requires a careful determination of present fact as much as of other facts not present. The point is also that no event can qualify as a datum save as it is reconstituted in inquiry as a signification of other events by the intervention of symbol-meanings. Data and meanings are correlative.

The enduring truth of idealism is that factuality must be qualified by meanings before we can make judgments about it. The enduring truth of realism is that factuality must have a brute quality and articulate structure of its own before judgments can have relevance and validity. The enduring truth of pragmatism is that, as active organisms, we are in the world and of it, we don't altogether have to acquiesce in facts as they come, we can alter the facts as they affect us by operationally applying our purposes and meanings to them so that they become data for knowledge by becoming data for successful action.

We may pause here to consider an ambiguity in the term "given" which I suspect is the source of what may turn out to be a merely verbal dispute between pragmatism and a recent version of realism. My colleague, Professor Donald C. Williams, has made an ingenious attempt to save direct realism by maintaining the "innocence of the given."[9] A bush may be given or presented to me in perception, he would say, and I may perceive it as a bush or as a man or as something else. On this position, perception is always a cognition of the given, but neither the perception nor what is given to perception guarantees that the perception of the given is true. Only a further cognition

[9] *Journal of Philosophy*, Vol. 30, No. 23 (1933), 617-628.

in terms of further evidence can authenticate the initial perception, and this authentication is inductive and a matter of probability. Now obviously this position differs from Dewey's in two respects: perception is treated simply as a kind of knowing, and yet the objectivity and independence of the given prevent us from knowing it or knowing that we know it at the time it is given. It is no wonder therefore that Professor Williams is incredulous at the pragmatist's thesis that the given, as taken, as datum, is transformed in inquiry. Quite the contrary, if the given object is what is existentially there apart from our experience of it, then by definition it is certainly not modified in inquiry. It is so unmitigatedly innocent that I fail to see why inquiry should ever be concerned with it at all. But I wish to honor and not to damn the realist here, and Mr. Williams seems to me to have put his finger on the essential truth of realism—namely, that what is given to us in perception and recognized for what it is, is connected with (though not identical with) events which are independent of the perceiving subject. The pragmatist's thesis is that, if the given be recognizable real features of the perceptual environment of the organism, and if inquiry can so control the given as to establish reliable features within it as data or signs for inference to what is not given, then we can so modify the perceptual situation given as to reveal what is there apart from the perceiving subject. The independence of the "given," as referred to by Mr. Williams, is not disputed: a bush is a bush, regardless of the way in which we perceive it or think about it.

We return to this matter presently when we consider the status of the object of knowledge or the *cognoscendum*. For the moment we must gather together our statements of the rôle of data and meanings in order to explain the reciprocal relationship between them and the part played by induction and deduction in the mutual determination of data and meanings. Dewey is charged by many critics with overlooking the essential difference between induction and deduction, and with failing to solve *the* problem of induction. Adequate treatment of these matters is impossible here, and it will have to suffice to show that induction and deduction are complementary phases of any real judgment or inquiry, and that this is due to the protean nature of data.

A situation figures as a datum, we have said, when it is taken as a problem for thought. It makes no difference how the problem arises; it is a datum the moment we ask what it signifies. Pragmatists have made unnecessary trouble for themselves by stressing the practical nature of the problem, by focusing attention on habits of action that are impeded or blocked, and hence by seeming to insinuate that inquiry is motivated simply by the need of facilitating action. Let the motive be what it will, the wonderment of a child, the pressing need of escape from a burning building, the pure unadulterated curiosity and love of knowledge of the theoretical scientist; the logic of inquiry is the same: there is a subject matter at hand that is unsettled and dubious as to its signification. Something has to be done to change the situation, to clear it up. What has to be changed, if warranted assertion is desiderated, is not our thinking about it, is not simply the facilitation of our own action or the promotion of our own comfort; else the ontological argument or the will to believe would prove the existence of God. What has to be changed is the objective given situation.

Now to solve the problem is *prima facie* simply a matter of finding out what the datum signifies, a matter of attaching the right predicate to the present fact as subject of a judgment, in science a matter of going by induction from a particular fact to a universal law. But this atomistic way of looking at the world does not square with the facts, either of practical or of scientific inquiry. If what we perceive is a fact established by previous inquiry, if present subject matter is settled, there is no problem for thought; we perceive an object, not a datum. But if there is a problem in what we perceive, what we want to know is no more the predicate than the subject of judgment, no more the thing or law signified than the thing signifying. What we want to know is whether the thing before us is a reliable case or instance of the law that we are seeking. In short, data are not given but have to be found and determined as such. They are post-analytic and not pre-analytic facts of inquiry. The scientist does not attempt to solve his problem until he has made sure of what the problem is, until he has experimentally established the facts that can be depended upon in further research. Nay more, when the particular problem is fully defined that problem is solved.

In defining a problem we transform temporally antecedent subject matter into data. The pragmatist says that in this process the *object* undergoes reconstruction, but this is misleading. The object to be known certainly does not undergo reconstruction: the bush or a star is not made by inquiry. What is changed is *the existential subject matter.* Data as fragmentary and problematic indicate that as yet we don't have an object, and our problem is to find one. A child complains of being sick and we want to know what is the matter with him. To find the cause of his ailment is the object of our inquiry, but this requires a diagnosis of symptoms (data). The inductive phase of the inquiry consists in the observational and experimental operations by which we work over the crude symptoms and refine them so that they indicate meanings—indicate them not only by way of suggesting them but by way of testing them. A flushed face suggests the idea (symbol-meaning) of fever. We test the idea of fever in thought by asking what fever means or implies. For a physician it implies so many meanings that this idea by itself is of no great help, but of course it implies the idea of using a thermometer. This process of experimenting with symbol-meanings in thought is the deductive phase of inquiry, and its purpose is to provide tools and guides for further observation and experiment with facts. The idea of fever does not establish that this is a factual case of fever; it only points to operations by which we can hope to establish that fact. It sends us back for further and more exact data. We not only use the thermometer to get an overt test of the idea of fever, but we look for other symptoms associated with the idea of fever. Whenever we go from facts or data to possible meanings or in the reverse direction we are practicing induction. Whenever we ask an "if-then" proposition, ask what is implied in, or what is the meaning of, a suggested hypothesis, we are practicing deduction. We deduce not a fact but an idea of a fact from an hypothesis.

We may now summarize our discussion of data and meanings. Data exhibit the reciprocal interplay of facts and meanings or of signs and symbols. Data exhibit in this process the interplay of induction and deduction: induction in so far as the problem gets defined, in so far as natural signs are made reliable indications of what they signify; deduction in so far as suggested meanings, ideas, or hypotheses are elaborated and clarified in their implications. Induction is not a process simply of going from a particular to a universal; universals are symbol-meanings and their range of application therefore extends far beyond what can be existentially established in inquiry. Induction seems to be from particulars to universals only because the situation or subject matter which instigates inquiry is fragmentary as it stands, and is more settled and complete when the inquiry is consummated. Deduction seems to be from universals to particulars only because the final reference and application of implied meanings is to particular matters of fact, but only meanings can be deduced from meanings, and all meanings are universals. Since data and meanings modify each other in the course of inquiry, it is all one to say that in the end we have solved our problem or have correctly defined it: a complete diagnosis of symptoms or determination of data defines not only the malady but the cause, not only the natural sign but the thing signified. In other words, judgment is no more affirming a predicate of a subject than determining the proper subject for the predicate. When the subject is known the predicate is known because the purpose of inquiry is to convert ill-defined subject matter into an articulate existential connection between a subject and a predicate. The copula of a real judgment, a "synthetic judgment" is not at all like the conjunctive copula of a mere proposition or statement. It consists in the existential operations of observation, action, experiment by which meanings apply to data and data come to signify objects; together with the operations of discourse by which meanings are made fruitful guides to observation and experiment. The copula converts problematic subject matter into an object of knowledge.

V. The Object of Knowledge

An object and an object of knowledge are basically the same thing, for an object arises as an existential state of affairs gets settled in and by inquiry. We have previously explained that things, like tables, chairs, and the thousands of other things that no one questions, are given and are there in perception with intrinsic meanings because they are the product of previous inquiries. No questions have arisen to bring us to doubt them. They are now had or enjoyed and used—had for what they intrinsically are, used confidently as signs of other things. They are not objects of knowledge now but just objects, unless bare recognition be called knowledge; they are, as the direct realist says, simply presented. But what he forgets to say is that they were established by previous judgment, they were consummations before they were presentations. After a house is built it functions as a house but it stands up because of the materials used and the operations employed.

Anything is an object, or an object of knowledge, or objective, in so far as it is settled, dependable, can be counted on in further inquiry or in further action. Now, objects which have been established as objectives of previous inquiry of course serve as means of further inquiry or of further action. If in the course of this action the object is a questionable means for the purpose at hand, it becomes subject matter for judgment, it loses its objective character as a sign, it becomes functionally subjective because uncertain. The uncertainty is not simply one of thought nor one of action; the uncertainty of our response is due to the uncertainty of the stimulus. Subjectivity is no more a function of ideas than of existential subject matter.

When the situation becomes subject matter for inquiry, we employ ideas or symbol-meanings. These are subjective in two ways: they register the uncertainty of the subject matter, and they are tools for removing that uncertainty. Ideas are plans of action for determining data and for determining things not yet present but signified by the data. In an oft-quoted illustration of Dewey's, if we come home and find things in disarray, we start inquiry into the signification of the situation. The idea of being robbed registers an uncertain but also a possible meaning. It implies the idea of valuable articles missing. That idea in turn leads to action and observation for the purpose of transforming the subject matter into definite data. If we find our valuables intact or missing, in either case something factual and objective has been established. As fulfilling the reference of the idea, a datum becomes an object known. We don't know yet, to be sure, that we have been robbed, we don't yet know *the* object of knowledge, the *cognoscendum* that we are after. But with each step of observation and experiment in which we determine facts or data, e.g., that my watch is where I left it, that no window or door has been tampered with, we secure objects known or data whose signification is settled. We eliminate or narrow suggested meanings and we get a more definite problem. Meanings get established objective reference, and subject matter breaks up into definite objects.

We have now distinguished two ways in which things figure as objects, or objects of knowledge: 1) as a result of previous inquiry, objects are so settled that we treat them simply as objects; 2) as a result of present inquiry, we transform ill-defined subject matter into definite data, and in so far as there is still a problem we continue to call these objects data, evidence, or signs. Their final significance for our inquiry is not yet known, for they have not yielded the *cognoscendum* as the objective of our inquiry.

What then is the precise status of the *cognoscendum?* In our illustration, from the standpoint of ongoing inquiry, it is what the partly defined and partly ill-defined subject matter and our ideas point to as the objective. It is whatever is the cause of the condition in which we find our house. From the standpoint of closed or consummated inquiry, it is the settled objective that we were looking for. If we find burglars leaving the place, possessing a passkey and articles that belong to us, the object of our inquiry is established as a warranted conclusion. The *cognoscendum* is known because it is evidence which settles and clears up the problematic subject matter. The *cognoscendum* is evidence also which confirms the objective reference of the idea or symbol-meaning, *burglars.*

It may be granted that in practical life the *cognoscendum* is or may be identical with evidence that we can experience. But the realist will insist that in theoretical or scientific knowledge the *cognoscendum* is not the evidence. Our previous discussion was pointed for this objection. In practical knowledge we are concerned with ends to be reached, with things to be done, with objects that can be known because they can be had. But in science, the realist will argue, objects of knowledge are transcendent: judgment is aimed at an external object and not at the evidence. It is true if it corresponds with the object; the object is not modified in the knowing of it.

The reply is that to suppose Dewey believes otherwise is to misunderstand him. In practical knowledge we are interested in things that we can change and settle, but in science we are interested in changes that have already occurred, in what has already been settled apart from us. Scientific judgments certainly refer to, and aim to know, what lies beyond our qualitative objects. Atoms are not convenient fictions, not thought constructions. Dewey indeed speaks of scientific objects as instruments, but this is to say that they are means in nature that have been settled in inquiry so that they can be used. They are data or facts that have been established. Gross perceptual subject matter has been experimentally modified so that we can discover what goes on in nature when we are not experimenting.

The atoms as objects of knowledge are of course not the same things as the evidence which makes them objects of warranted assertion. But what warrants the assertion, what makes the atoms known as far as they are known, is the experimental evidence. Scientific objects are operationally arrived at, and present-day physicists are well aware that new evidence or different operations may call for a reconstruction of these objects. The reconstruction is not a creation of thought; it is guided by thought tools but it is conducted by physical instruments that are subjected to physical materials having their own indefeasible properties. These properties, however, display themselves as objects of knowledge or as reliable data, only as they are put to work in interaction with other things. We know the properties of oxygen by noting how it behaves and what it does to other things. We don't know any things-in-themselves; we only know what things are under these or those specified conditions.

What we have said should dispel the misconception that analysis, for Dewey, is distortion. Analysis need not distort so long as it knows what it is about. Analysis proceeds *within* the world and not within the mind of a thinker outside the world. Analysis of the physical world is always provisional, is always guided by some purpose and conducted by experiment. Physical elements that are ultimate for one analysis may not be ultimate for a later one. Objects of knowledge are ends of inquiry and means to further inquiry.

DONALD A. PIATT

DEPARTMENT OF PHILOSOPHY
UNIVERSITY OF CALIFORNIA AT LOS ANGELES

4

Bertrand Russell

DEWEY'S NEW *LOGIC*

DEWEY'S NEW *LOGIC*

DR. DEWEY is the foremost representative of a philosophy which, whether one accepts or rejects it, must undoubtedly be judged to have great importance as a social phenomenon. Unlike most academic professors, Dr. Dewey is interested in this aspect of a philosophy. He accounts for much in Greek theory, and more particularly in Aristotelian logic, by the social system of that age. The persistence, among the learned, of elements derived from the Hellenic tradition is one of the reasons for the divorce between university philosophy and practical affairs which is characteristic of our time. Dr. Dewey has an outlook which, where it is distinctive, is in harmony with the age of industrialism and collective enterprise. It is natural that his strongest appeal should be to Americans, and also that he should be almost equally appreciated by the progressive elements in countries like China and Mexico, which are endeavoring to pass with great rapidity from medievalism to all that is most modern. His fame, though not his doctrine, is analogous to that enjoyed by Jeremy Bentham in his own day—except that Bentham was more respected abroad than by his compatriots.

In what follows, I shall not be concerned with these general matters, but only with one book: *Logic: The Theory of Inquiry*. This book is very rich and varied in its contents; it contains highly interesting criticisms of past philosophers, very able analyses of the prejudices inspiring traditional formal logic, and an intimate awareness of the realities of scientific investigation. All this makes the book far more concrete than most books called "Logic." Since, however, a review should be shorter than the work reviewed, I shall ignore everything that occurs by way of illustration or history, and consider only those positive doctrines which seem to me most characteristic.

In every writer on philosophy there is a concealed meta-physic, usually unconscious; even if his subject is metaphysics, he is almost certain to have an uncritically believed system which underlies his explicit arguments. Reading Dr. Dewey makes me aware of my own unconscious metaphysic as well as of his. Where they differ, I find it hard to imagine any arguments on either side which do not beg the question; on fundamental issues perhaps this is unavoidable.

One of the chief sources of difference between philosophers is a temperamental bias toward synthesis or analysis. Traditionally, British philosophy was analytic, Continental philosophy synthetic. On this point, I find myself in the British tradition, while Dr. Dewey belongs with the Germans, and more particularly with Hegel. Instrumentalism, his most characteristic and important doctrine, is, I think, compatible with an analytic bias, but in him it takes a form associated with what General Smuts calls "holism." I propose to consider first the "holistic" aspect of Dr. Dewey's logic, and then the instrumentalist doctrine as he sets it forth.

Dr. Dewey himself has told of his debt to Hegel in the article which he contributed to *Contemporary American Philosophy* (1930). Hegel's thought, he says,

Supplied a demand for unification that was doubtless an intense emotional craving, and yet was a hunger that only an intellectualized subject-matter could satisfy. . . . The sense of divisions and separations that were, I suppose, borne in upon me as a consequence of a heritage of New England culture, divisions by way of isolation of self from the world, of soul from body, of nature from God, brought a painful oppression— or rather, they were an inward laceration. . . . Hegel's synthesis of subject and object, matter and spirit, the divine and the human, was, however, no mere intellectual formula; it operated as an immense release, a liberation. Hegel's treatment of human culture, of institutions and the arts, involved the same dissolution of hard-and-fast dividing walls, and had a special attraction for me. (19)

He adds, a page or two later: "I should never think of ignoring, much less denying, what an astute critic occasionally refers to as a novel discovery—that acquaintance with Hegel has left a permanent deposit in my thinking." (21)

Data, in the sense in which many empiricists believe in them, are rejected by Dr. Dewey as the starting point of knowledge. There is a process of "inquiry" (to be considered presently), in the course of which both subject and object change. The process is, in some degree, continuous throughout life, and even throughout the history of a cultural community. Nevertheless, in regard to any one problem, there is a beginning, and this beginning is called a "situation." A situation, we are told, is a "qualified existential whole which is unique."[1] Again: "Every situation, when it is analyzed, is extensive, containing within itself diverse distinctions and relations which, in spite of their diversity, form a unified qualitative whole." "Singular objects exist and singular events occur within a field or situation." We point *out* rather than point *at*. There is no such thing as passive receptivity; what is *called* the given is selected, and is taken rather than given.

There are a few further statements about what the world is apart from the effects which inquiry has upon it. For instance: "There is, of course, a natural world that exists independently of the organism, but this world is *environment* only as it enters directly and indirectly into life-functions." (The words "of course," here may be taken as indicating an underlying metaphysic.) Again: "existence in general must be such as to be *capable* of taking on logical forms." We are told very little about the nature of things before they are inquired into; we know, however, that, like dishonest politicians, things behave differently when observed from the way in which they behave when no one is paying attention to them.

The question arises: How large is a "situation"? In connection with historical knowledge, Dr. Dewey speaks of the "temporal continuity of past-present-future." It is obvious that, in an inquiry into the tides, the sun and moon must be included in the "situation." Although this question is nowhere explicitly discussed, I do not see how, on Dr. Dewey's principles, a "situation" can embrace less than the whole universe; this is an inevitable consequence of the insistence upon continuity. It would

[1] This and all further quotations in this essay are from Dewey's *Logic: The Theory of Inquiry,* unless stated otherwise.

seem to follow that all inquiry, strictly interpreted, is an attempt to analyze the universe. We shall thus be led to Bradley's view that every judgment qualifies Reality as a whole. Dr. Dewey eschews these speculations because his purpose is practical. But if they are to be invalid, it will be necessary (so at least it seems to me) to give more place to logically separable particulars than he seems willing to concede.

The relation of perception to empirical knowledge is not, so far as I have been able to discover, made very clear in this book, what is said on the subject being chiefly negative. We are told that sense-data are not objects of knowledge, and have no objective existential reference. (The word "existential" occurs frequently in the book, but its meaning is assumed to be known. Here, again, we find evidence of the underlying metaphysic.) When it is said that sense-data have no objective existential reference, what is meant, no doubt, is that sensation is not a relational occurrence in which a subject cognizes something. To this I should entirely assent. Again we are told that there are three common errors to be avoided: (1) that the common-sense world is perceptual; (2) that perception is a mode of cognition; (3) that what is perceived is cognitive in status. Here, again, I agree. But since, clearly, perception is in some way related to empirical knowledge, a problem remains as to what this relation is.

The question of the relation of perception to knowledge is important in connection with "holism." For it seems clear that we perceive some things and not others, that percepts are links in causal chains which are to some extent separable from other causal chains, and that some degree of mutual independence in causal chains is essential to all empirical knowledge. Let us examine this question in connection with perception.

Dr. Dewey denies "immediate" knowledge and its supposed indispensability for mediated knowledge. But he admits something which he calls "apprehension," which has, for him, functions very similar to those usually assigned to "immediate knowledge." On this subject he says:

A certain ambiguity in words has played a very considerable rôle in fostering the doctrine of immediate knowledge. Knowledge in its strictest and most honorific sense is identical with warranted assertion. But "knowledge" also means understanding, and an object, or an act (and its object) that may be—and has been—called *apprehension*. . . . Just as, after considerable experience, we understand meanings directly, as when we hear conversation on a familiar subject or read a book, so because of experience we come to recognize objects on sight. I see or note directly that *this* is a typewriter, *that* is a book, the other thing is a radiator, etc. This kind of direct "knowledge" I shall call *apprehension;* it is seizing or grasping, intellectually, without questioning. But it is a product, mediated through certain organic mechanisms of retention and habit, and it presupposes prior experiences and mediated conclusions drawn from them (143).

I still have no criticism to make, except that the "organic mechanisms of retention and habit" and the "prior experiences and mediated conclusions" deserve more attention than they receive in this volume. Consider the habit of saying "book" on certain occasions. We may use this word, as a parrot might, merely because we hear some one else use it. We may use it because we "think of" a book—whatever may be the correct analysis of this phrase. Or we may use it because we see a book. We cannot do this last unless we have frequently heard the word "book" at a time when we saw a book. (I am assuming that the word had for us originally an ostensive definition, not a definition derived from the dictionary.) Thus the use of the word "book" presupposes frequent simultaneity of books and instances of the word "book" as perceived objects, and the causal law according to which such frequent simultaneity generates a habit. When the habit in question has been formed, it is not the whole environment that causes us to use the word "book," but only one feature of it; and the effect is only one feature of what is happening in us at the time. Without such separable causal chains the use of language is inexplicable.

Let us pursue a little further this question of "apprehension." The common-sense belief "there is a book," or (what comes to much the same thing) the impulse to use the word "book" demonstratively, arises as the result of a stimulus of a certain kind. The immediate stimulus is in the brain; before that, there is a stimulus in the optic nerve; before that, at the eye; and, when the common-sense belief is justified, there are light-waves travelling from the book to the eye. We have thus, when the common-sense belief is justified, a rather elaborate causal chain: book, light-waves, eye, optic nerve, brain, utterance of the word "book." If any intermediate link in this causal chain can be produced without the usual predecessors, all the subsequent links will be produced just as they would be if the causation had been of the normal sort. Now unusual causes are possible at each stage: physical, by means of mirrors; optical, by defects in the eye; nervous, by suitable stimulation of the optic nerve; cerebral, by the kind of disturbance that produces a hallucination. Consequently, while it is true that the common-sense judgment expressed in the utterance of the word "book" is not perceptual, it is also true that the common-sense judgment may be erroneous, and the only warranted assertion is: "A bookish percept is occurring." It is such considerations that lead me to stress percepts as opposed to common-sense judgments.

Consider, from a purely physical point of view, what is involved in our seeing various objects simultaneously. If the common-sense point of view is to be in any degree justifiable in ordinary circumstances, we must suppose that each visible object is the starting-point of a causal chain which remains, at least in some respects, independent of all the other simultaneous causal chains that lead to our seeing the other objects. We must therefore suppose that natural processes have the character attributed to them by the analyst, rather than the holistic character which the enemies of analysis take for granted. I do not contend that the holistic world is logically impossible, but I do contend that it could not give rise to science or to any empirical knowledge.

The same conclusion may be reached through consideration of language. Words are discrete and separable occurrences; if the world had as much unity as some philosophers contend, it would be impossible to use words to describe it. Perhaps it is impossible; but in that case there can be no excuse for writing books on philosophy.

Dr. Dewey would reply that it is not the purpose of such books to *describe* the world, but to *change* it. This brings us to what is perhaps the most important aspect of his philosophy.

I come now to what is most distinctive in Dr. Dewey's logic, namely the emphasis upon inquiry as opposed to truth or knowledge. Inquiry is not for him, as for most philosophers, a search for truth; it is an independent activity, defined as follows: "Inquiry is the controlled or directed transformation of an indeterminate situation into one that is so determinate in its constituent distinctions and relations as to convert the elements of the original situation into a unified whole" (104). I cannot but think that this definition does not adequately express Dr. Dewey's meaning, since it would apply, for instance, to the operations of a drill sergeant in transforming a collection of raw recruits into a regiment, or of a bricklayer transforming a heap of bricks into a house, and yet it would be impossible to say that the drill sergeant is "inquiring" into the recruits, or the bricklayer into the bricks. It is admitted that inquiry alters the object as well as the subject: "Inquiry is concerned with objective transformations of objective subject-matter." Propositions are merely tools in effecting these transformations; they are differentiated as means, not as "true" or "false" (287).

Before examining this doctrine, it may be worth while to repeat, what I have pointed out elsewhere,[2] its close similarity to that of another ex-Hegelian, Karl Marx, as stated in his *Theses on Feuerbach* (1845), and afterwards embodied in the theory of dialectical materialism (which Engels never understood).

The chief defect of all previous materialism [says Marx] is that the object, the reality, sensibility, is only apprehended under the form of the object or of contemplation, but not as human sensible activity or practice, not subjectively. Hence it came about that the active side was developed by idealism in opposition to materialism. The question whether objective truth belongs to human thinking is not a question of theory, but a practical question. The truth, *i.e.*, the reality and power, of thought must be demonstrated in practice. Philosophers have only *interpreted* the world in various ways, but the real task is to *alter* it.

Allowing for a certain difference of phraseology, this doctrine is essentially indistinguishable from instrumentalism.

One of the chief difficulties in this point of view—so, at least,

[2] *Freedom Versus Organization* (New York, 1934), 221.

it seems to me—consists in distinguishing inquiry from other kinds of practical activity such as drilling recruits or building houses. Inquiry, it is evident, is some kind of interaction between two things, one of which is called the object and the other the subject. There seems to be an assumption that this process is more or less in the nature of an oscillation of which the amplitude gradually grows less, leaving it possible to guess at an ultimate position of equilibrium, in which, when reached, the subject would be said to "know" the object, or to have arrived at "truth" concerning it. "Truth" is not an important concept in Dr. Dewey's logic. I looked up "truth" in the index, and found only the following: "Defined, 345*n*. See Assertibility, Warranted." The note, in its entirety, is as follows:

> The best definition of *truth* from the logical standpoint which is known to me is that of Peirce: "The opinion which is fated to be ultimately agreed to by all who investigate is what we mean by the truth, and the object represented by this opinion is the real." *Op. cit.*, Vol. V, p. 268 [*Collected Papers of Charles Sanders Peirce*]. A more complete (and more suggestive) statement is the following: "Truth is that concordance of an abstract statement with the ideal limit towards which endless investigation would tend to bring scientific belief, which concordance the abstract statement may possess by virtue of the confession of its inaccuracy and one-sidedness, and this confession is an essential ingredient of truth" (*Ibid.*, 394-5).[3]

Although these two definitions of "truth" are Peirce's, not Dr. Dewey's, the fact that Dr. Dewey accepts them makes it necessary to discuss them as if they were his own. The discussion is required in spite of the unimportance of "truth" to Dr. Dewey, for those of us who make it fundamental are concerned to examine the consequences of giving it such a humble and derivative position.

The acceptance of such a definition as Peirce's makes it natural to mention "truth" only once, and that in a footnote; for if "truth" is to be so defined, it is obviously of no philosophical importance. The two definitions are not in complete agreement. According to the first, when we say that a proposition is "true" we are making a sociological prophecy. If the definition is in-

[3] *Logic,* 345n.

terpreted strictly, every proposition which is investigated by no one is "true," but I think Peirce means to include only such propositions as some one investigates. The word "fated" seems merely rhetorical, and I shall assume that it is not intended seriously. But the word "ultimately" is much more difficult. As the second definition makes plain, the word is intended in a mathematical rather than a chronological sense. If it were intended chronologically it would make "truth" depend upon the opinions of the last man left alive as the earth becomes too cold to support life. As he will presumably be entirely occupied in keeping warm and getting nourishment, it is doubtful whether his opinions will be any wiser than ours. But obviously this is not what Peirce has in mind. He imagines a series of opinions, analogous to a series of numbers such as $\frac{1}{2}$, $\frac{3}{4}$, $\frac{7}{8}$ ... tending to a limit, and each differing less from its predecessor than any earlier member of the series does. This is quite clear in the second definition, where Peirce speaks of "the ideal limit towards which endless investigation would tend to bring scientific belief."

I find this definition exceedingly puzzling. To begin with a minor point: what is meant by "the confession of its inaccuracy?" This seems to imply a standard of accuracy other than that indicated in the definition. Or is "accuracy" a notion wholly divorced from "truth?" If Peirce is to be interpreted strictly, he must mean that a statement is "true" because it says it is inaccurate. This would enthrone Epimenides as the only sage. I think that Peirce, when he says "inaccurate," means "unprecise." The statement that Mr. A is about 6 feet tall may be perfectly accurate, but it is not precise. I think it is such statements that Peirce has in mind.

The main question is: why does Peirce think that there is an "ideal limit towards which endless investigation would tend to bring scientific belief?" Is this an empirical generalization from the history of research? Or is it an optimistic belief in the perfectibility of man? Does it contain any element of prophecy, or is it a merely hypothetical statement of what would happen if men of science grew continually cleverer? Whatever interpretation we adopt, we seem committed to some very rash assertion. I do not see how we can guess either what will be believed, or what would be believed by men much cleverer than we are. Whether the theory of relativity will be believed twenty years hence depends mainly upon whether Germany wins the next war. Whether it would be believed by people cleverer than we are we cannot tell without being cleverer than we are. Moreover the definition is inapplicable to all the things that are most certain. During breakfast, I may have a well-grounded conviction that I am eating eggs and bacon. I doubt whether scientists 2000 years hence will investigate whether this was the case, and if they did their opinions would be worth less than mine.

"Truth," therefore, as Peirce defines the term, is a vague concept involving much disputable sociology. Let us see what Dr. Dewey has to say about "assertibility warranted," to which he refers us. We must remember that Dr. Dewey's *Logic* has as its sub-title "The Theory of Inquiry." "Inquiry" might, from other points of view, be defined as "the attempt to discover truth," but for Dr. Dewey inquiry is what is primitive, and truth, or rather "warranted assertibility," is derivative. He says (7):

"If inquiry begins in doubt, it terminates in the institution of conditions which remove need for doubt. The latter state of affairs may be designated by the words *belief* and *knowledge*. For reasons that I shall state later I prefer the words 'warranted assertibility'."

Again Dr. Dewey says:

Were it not that knowledge is related to inquiry as a product to the operations by which it is produced, no distinctions requiring special differentiating designations would exist. Material would merely be a matter of knowledge or of ignorance and error; that would be all that could be said. The content of any given proposition would have the values "true" and "false" as final and exclusive attributes. But if knowledge is related to inquiry as its warrantably assertible product, and if inquiry is progressive and temporal, then the material inquired into reveals distinctive properties which need to be designated by distinctive names. As *undergoing* inquiry, the material has a different logical import from that which it has as the *outcome* of inquiry (118-119).

Again: "An inferential function is involved in all warranted assertion. The position here defended runs counter to the belief that there is such a thing as immediate knowledge, and that such knowledge is an indispensable precondition of all mediated knowledge" (139).

Let us try to re-state Dr. Dewey's theory in other language. I will begin with what would certainly be a misinterpretation, though one for which his words would seem to afford some justification. The position *seems* to be that there is a certain activity called "inquiry," as recognizable as the activities of eating or drinking; like all activity, it is stimulated by discomfort, and the particular discomfort concerned is called "doubt," just as hunger is the discomfort that stimulates eating, and thirst is the discomfort that stimulates drinking. And as hunger may lead you to kill an animal, skin it, and cook it, so that though you have been concerned with the same animal throughout, it is very different when it becomes food from what it was to begin with, so inquiry manipulates and alters its subject-matter until it becomes logically assimilable and intellectually appetizing. Then doubt is allayed, at least for the time. But the subject-matter of inquiry, like the wild boar of Valhalla, is perpetually re-born, and the operation of logical cooking has to be more and more delicately performed as the intellectual palate grows more refined. There is therefore no end to the process of inquiry, and no dish that can be called "absolute truth."

I do not think that Dr. Dewey would accept what has just been said as an adequate account of his theory. He would, I am convinced, maintain that inquiry serves a purpose over and above the allaying of doubt. And he would object that the revival of an inquiry after doubt has been temporarily quieted is not merely a question of refinement of the intellectual palate, but has some more objective basis. He says (to repeat a quotation already given): "If inquiry begins in doubt, it terminates in the institution of conditions which remove *need* for doubt" (my italics). I do not know what he means by "need for doubt," but I think he means something more than "cause of doubt." If I doubt whether I am a fine fellow, I can cure the doubt by a suitable dose of alcohol, but this would not be viewed by him as "the institution of conditions which remove the *need* for doubt." Nor would he reckon suicide a suitable method, although it would be eminently effective in removing doubt. We must therefore ask ourselves what he can mean by "need for doubt."

For those who make "truth" fundamental, the difficulty in question does not arise. There is need for doubt so long as there is an appreciable likelihood of a mistake. If you add up your accounts twice over, and get different results, there is "need for doubt;" but that is because you are persuaded that there is an objectively right result. If there is not, if all that is concerned is the psychological fact of inquiry as an activity stimulated by doubt, we cannot lay down rules as to what *ought* to remove the need for doubt: we can only observe what does in fact remove doubt. Inquiry can no longer be regulated by canons. To say that one man is a better inquirer than another can only mean that he allays more doubts, even if he does so by a brass band and ingenious spot-lighting. All this is not what Dr. Dewey means; but if it is not to follow from what he says, inquiry will have to have some goal other than the removal of doubt.

I ask again, therefore: what can he mean by "the need for doubt?"

The word "pragmatism" is not mentioned in the index to Dr. Dewey's *Logic,* but the preface contains the following passage:

The word "Pragmatism" does not, I think, occur in the text. Perhaps the word lends itself to misconception. At all events, so much misunderstanding and relatively futile controversy have gathered about the word that it seemed advisable to avoid its use. But in the proper interpretation of "pragmatic," namely the function of consequences as necessary tests of the validity of propositions, *provided* these consequences are operationally instituted and are such as to resolve the specific problem evoking the operations, the text that follows is thoroughly pragmatic (iii-iv).

Perhaps, in view of this passage, we may say that there is "need for doubt" so long as the opinion at which we have arrived does not enable us to secure desired results, although we feel that a different opinion would do so. When our car breaks down, we try various hypotheses as to what is wrong, and there is "need for doubt" until it goes again. This suggests a way out of our difficulty, which I will try to state in quite general terms.

Beliefs, we are now supposing, may be tested by their consequences, and may be considered to possess "warranted assertibility" when their consequences are of certain kinds. The consequences to be considered relevant may be logical consequences only, or may be widened to embrace all kinds of effects; and between these two extremes any number of intermediate positions are possible. In the case of the car that won't go, you think it may be this, or it may be that, or it may be the other; if it is *this* and I do so-and-so, the car will go; I do so-and-so and the car does not go; therefore it was not *this*. But when I apply the same experimental procedure to the hypothesis that it was *that*, the car does go; therefore the belief that it was *that* has "warranted assertibility." So far, we have only the ordinary procedure of induction: "If p, then q; now q is true; therefore p is true." *E.g.*, "If pigs have wings, then some winged animals are good to eat; now some winged animals are good to eat; therefore pigs have wings." This form of inference is called "scientific method."

Pragmatism, however, involves something more than induction. In induction, we have two premises, namely "if p, then q," and "q." Each of these has to be true in the ordinary sense if they are to confer inductive probability upon "p." In order to enable pragmatism to dispense with "truth" in its ordinary sense, we need some further steps. It will be remembered that Dr. Dewey distinguishes "knowledge" from what he calls "apprehension," which contains such statements as "this is a typewriter." In dealing with the car, we shall, in Dr. Dewey's terminology, "apprehend" that it is going or that it is not going; this sort of thing, which I should take as the quintessential form of knowledge, is no longer to count as such. "If p, then q" may be a mere bodily habit: I think "perhaps there is no petrol" and I pour some in, without further thought. I hope to apprehend q, *viz.*, "the car goes," but I do not. So I try something else. My behaviour is just like that of an animal trying to get out of a cage, and may have just as little intellectual content.

We may, eliminating the intellectual element as far as possible, schematize our behaviour as follows: we desire a certain change C (in our illustration, the change from rest to motion on the part of the car); in our past experience, various acts A_1, A_2, A_3 . . . have been followed by this change; consequently there exists an impulse to perform some one of these acts, and, if it fails to be followed by C, some other of them, until at last, with luck, C takes place. Suppose the act A_n is followed by C; then A_n is appropriate to the situation. So far, everything that I have been describing could be done by an animal and is done by animals that are actuated by strong desires which they cannot immediately gratify. But when we come to human beings, with their linguistic proclivities, the matter becomes somewhat different. The acts A_1, A_2, A_3 . . . may all be sentences: "Perhaps it is this," "Perhaps it is that," "Perhaps it is the other." . . . Each of these sentences causes certain further acts, which, in turn, set up a chain of effects. One of the sentences causes a chain of effects which includes the desired change C. If this sentence is A_n, we say that A_n is "true" or has "warranted assertibility."

This suggestion needs a good deal of clarification before it becomes a possible hypothesis. As it stands, it is as follows: A hypothesis is called "true" when it leads the person entertaining it to acts which have effects that he desires. This obviously is too wide. Acts have many consequences, of which some may be pleasant and others unpleasant. In the case of the car, it may, when it finally moves, move so suddenly that it causes you serious bodily injury; this does not show that you were mistaken as to what was the matter with it. Or take another illustration: In a school, a prize is offered for the child that shows most general intelligence; on class-work, four are selected, and the final test is by a *viva voce;* the *viva* consists of one question, "who is the greatest man now living?" One child says Roosevelt, one says Stalin, one says Hitler, and one says Mussolini. One of them gets the prize, and has therefore, by definition, answered truly. If you know which gets the prize, you know in what country the test was made. It follows that truth is geographical. But this consequence, for some reason, pragmatists would be unwilling to admit.

The first limitation is that we must not take account of *all* the consequences of a hypothesis, but only of those that are relevant to a certain specified desire. You desire the car to move, but not to move into the ditch. If you are only thinking of getting it to move, the truth of your hypothesis is only to be judged by whether it moves, not by whether it moves along the road or into the ditch.

There is another more difficult limitation. The consequences of which account is to be taken must be only such as are considered "scientific." The pleasant consequences to the successful school-child depend upon the psychology of the teacher, which is considered logically irrelevant. I am not clear what this means, except that the same experiment in a different environment would give different results. It is difficult to imagine any experiment of which the result *cannot* be affected by the environment, but this is a matter of difference of degree. If all *usual* environments give the same result, the environment is irrelevant except on rare occasions.

We may say, therefore: An hypothesis H is to be called "true" if, in all normal environments, there is a kind of event C such that a man who desires C and entertains the hypothesis H will secure C, while a man who desires C but does not entertain this hypothesis will not secure C.

Thus before we can know H we must have observed large numbers of instances, in many different environments, in which people entertained H, desired C, and secured C. After we have made all these observations, we "know" H. We did not "know" that H was entertained, that C was desired, or that C was secured, in any of the many instances; for to "know" these things, we should have had to apply the pragmatic tests to them. To "know" that A entertains the hypothesis H, we shall have to find many instances of people who suppose that he does and consequently achieve their desires; similarily to "know" that A desires C or achieves C. All these things, in Dr. Dewey's phrase, will have to be "apprehended," not "known." We cannot possibly "apprehend" the whole multiplicity of instances at once; therefore the generalization must be not a belief, but a bodily habit, which is the pre-intellectual ancestor of belief in a general proposition.

Even so, there are still difficulties. Dr. Dewey and I were once in the town of Changsha during an eclipse of the moon; following immemorial custom, blind men were beating gongs to frighten the heavenly dog, whose attempt to swallow the moon is the cause of eclipses. Throughout thousands of years, this practice of beating gongs has never failed to be successful: every eclipse has come to an end after a sufficient prolongation of the din. This illustration shows that our generalization must not use merely the method of agreement, but also the method of difference. As all this is to be done by the body before knowledge begins, we must suppose the body better versed in Mill's Canons of Induction than any mind except that of a logician. I find this a somewhat difficult hypothesis.

Leaving these questions of detailed definition, let us consider the general problem of the relation of knowledge to the biological aspects of life. It is of course obvious that knowledge, broadly speaking, is one of the means to biological success; it is tempting to say, generally, that knowledge leads to success and error leads to failure; going a step further, the pragmatist may say that "knowledge" means "belief leading to success" and "error" means "belief leading to failure." To this view, however, there are many objections, both logical and sociological.

First, we must define "success" and "failure." If we wish to remain in the sphere of biology, we must define "success" as "leaving many descendants." In that sense, as every one knows, the most civilized are the least successful, and therefore, by definition, the most ignorant. Again: the man who, wishing to commit suicide, takes salt under the impression that it is arsenic, may afterwards beget ten children; in that case, the belief which saved his life was "true" in the biological sense. This consequence is absurd, and shows that the biological definition is inadequate.

Instead of the objective biological test of success, we must adopt a subjective test: "success" means "achieving desired ends." But this change in the definition of "success" weakens the position. When you see a man eating salt, you cannot tell whether he is acting on knowledge or error until you have ascertained whether he wishes to commit suicide. To ascertain this, you must discover whether the belief that he wishes to commit suicide will lead to your own success. This involves an endless regress.

Again: if A and B have conflicting desires, A's success may involve B's failure, so that truth for A may be falsehood for B. Suppose, for example, that A desires B's death but does not wish to be morally responsible for it; and suppose B has no wish to commit suicide. If B eats arsenic thinking it is salt, and A sees him doing so, also thinking it is salt, A achieves his desire and B does not; therefore A's belief that the arsenic was salt is "true" while B's identical belief is "false."

The pragmatist may say, in reply, that the success which is a test of truth is social, not individual: a belief is "true" when the success of the human race is helped by the existence of the belief. This, however, is hopelessly vague. What is "the success of the human race?" It is a concept for the politician, not for the logician. Moreover, mankind may profit by the errors of the wicked. We must say, therefore: "A belief is 'true' if the consequences of its being believed by all whose acts are affected by it are better, for mankind as a whole, than the consequences of its being disbelieved." Or, what comes to much the same thing: "A belief is 'true' if an ideally virtuous man will act on it." Any such view presupposes that we can know ethics before we know anything, and is therefore logically absurd.

Some beliefs which we should all hold to be false have greatly helped success, for example, the Mohammedan belief that the faithful who die in battle go straight to Paradise. When we reject this belief, do we mean merely that it proved an obstacle to science, and therefore to war-technique, and so led ultimately to the subjugation of the Mohammedans by the Christians? Surely not. The question whether you will go to Paradise when you die is as definite as the question whether you will go to New York tomorrow. You would not decide this latter question by investigating whether those who believe they will go to New York tomorrow are on the whole more successful than those who do not. The test of success is only brought in where the usual tests fail. But *if* the Mohammedan belief was true, those who entertained it have long since had empirical evidence of its truth. *Such* evidence is convincing, but the argument from success is not.

The pragmatist's position, if I am not mistaken, is a product of a limited scepticism supplemented by a surprising dogmatism. Our beliefs are obviously not always right, and often call for emendation rather than total rejection. Many questions of the highest emotional interest cannot be answered by means of any of the old conceptions of "truth," while many of the questions that can be answered, such as "is this red?" are so uninteresting that the pragmatist ignores them. But in spite of his scepticism, he is confident that he can know whether the consequences of entertaining a belief are such as to satisfy desire. This knowledge is surely far more difficult to secure than the knowledge that the pragmatist begins by questioning, and will have to be obtained, if at all, not by the pragmatist's method, which would lead to an endless regress, but by that very method of observation which, in simpler cases, he has rejected as inadequate.

There are certain general problems connected with such a theory as Dr. Dewey's, which perhaps deserve consideration although he does not discuss them. Inquiry, in his system, operates upon a raw material, which it gradually transforms; it is only the final product that can be known. The raw material remains an Unknowable. That being the case, it is not quite clear why it is supposed to exist. A process, not unlike the Hegelian dialectic apart from the triadic form, starts from Pure Being and ends with—what? Presumably a world in which everything can be successfully manipulated owing to the progress of scientific technique. Just as, in Hegel, the earlier categories are not quite real, so, in Dr. Dewey's system, nothing can be fully known except the ultimate result of "inquiry."

I find this view difficult, not only theoretically, but in view of the actual history of scientific knowledge. The first science to be developed was astronomy, yet it can hardly be supposed that the sun and the planets are much altered by the observations of the astronomers. Telescopes, it is true, alter the sense-data by means of which we know about the heavenly bodies, but sense-data, according to Dr. Dewey, are not the subject-matter of knowledge.

"Knowledge" as traditionally conceived is, no doubt, something of a false abstraction. Human beings find themselves in an environment to which they react in various ways; some of these reactions may be regarded as showing "knowledge" and others as showing "error." In the older philosophies, knowledge was conceived too passively, as though it consisted merely in receiving an imprint from the object. I think, however, that, with modern terminology, something not wholly unlike this passive conception of knowledge may still be justified. The circumstances in which we most naturally speak of "knowledge" are those in which there is a delayed reaction. For instance, I know Mr. A's address, but this only leads to action on certain occasions. The reason for isolating knowledge is that what we know not only gives a possibility of successful action, but is in the meantime a part of our constitution. When we consider this aspect of it, we are led to regard it as something not essentially concerned with action, and, owing its capacity for promoting success, as a relation to the object, which can be studied and defined without bringing in the relation to action.

Perhaps the objections which I feel to the instrumentalist logic are merely emotional, and have no logical justification, although I am totally unable to believe that this is the case. Knowledge, if Dr. Dewey is right, cannot be any part of the ends of life; it is merely a means to other satisfactions. This view, to those who have been much engaged in the pursuit of knowledge, is distasteful. Dr. Dewey himself confesses to having felt this, and resisted it as a temptation. The emphasis upon the practical in his later writings, he says, "was a reaction against what was more natural, and it served as a protest and a protection against something in myself which, in the pressure of the weight of actual experience, I knew to be a weakness." Even those who doubt whether such asceticism is necessary either practically or theoretically, cannot but feel the highest respect for the moral force required to practice it consistently throughout a long span of years.

For my part, I believe that too great emphasis upon the practical robs practice itself of its *raison d'être*. We act, in so far as we are not blindly driven by instinct, in order to achieve ends which are not merely further actions, but have in them some element, however precarious and however transient, of rest and peace—not the rest and peace of mere quiescence, but the kind that, in the most intense form, becomes ecstasy. When what passes for knowledge is considered to be no more than a momentary halting-place in a process of inquiry which has no goal outside itself, inquiry can no longer provide intellectual joys, but becomes merely a means to better dinners and more rapid locomotion. Activity can supply only one half of wisdom; the other half depends upon a receptive passivity. Ultimately, the controversy between those who base logic upon "truth" and those who base it upon "inquiry" arises from a difference of values, and cannot be argued without, at some point, begging the question. I cannot hope, therefore, that anything in the above pages has validity except for those whose bias resembles my own, while those whose bias resembles Dr. Dewey's will find in his book just such an exposition as the subject seems to them to require.

BERTRAND RUSSELL

DEPARTMENT OF PHILOSOPHY
THE UNIVERSITY OF CALIFORNIA AT LOS ANGELES

5

Hans Reichenbach

DEWEY'S THEORY OF SCIENCE

5
DEWEY'S THEORY OF SCIENCE

PHILOSOPHIC systems, though of abundant varieties as to their specific content and form, may be classified into two great groups if we consider the motive forces behind them. In the first group we find the systems of negative attitude towards our world, interpreting knowledge and feeling as messengers from, or as bridges towards, another world; the world we live in seems to philosophers of this group deeply unsatisfactory, insignificant, delusive, and seems bearable only because we know about another world of transcendent beings and values which sheds its lustre and splendor into our imperfect and transient existence. In the second group we meet the systems of affirmative attitude towards our world; life for them bears its value in itself and does not derive it from supernatural entities; knowledge for them is directed towards this world, and all transcendent interpretations appear to these philosophers as turning away from the sound basis of our existence, as flight from this world. It is well known how the different philosophical systems divide into these two groups of "other-world philosophies" and "this-world philosophies," into transcendence and immanence systems. Plato in his allegory of the men in the cave who see the shadows of passers-by on the wall and take them for real beings, has created a poetic image for philosophies of the first group, at the same time giving in his doctrine of ideas a far-famed intellectual formulation of transcendentalism; besides his system, religious and rationalistic philosophies of all kinds have expressed in various forms the idea of a supernatural world "behind" the world we live in. The second group is characterized by such names as materialism, empiricism, sensationalism. It is as old and as young as the first, and the history of philosophy from the time of the Greeks up to our days represents a constant struggle between these two fundamental conceptions.

It is the outspoken character of John Dewey's philosophy that it belongs to the second group, that it is a "this-world philosophy." If the present writer ventures in the following pages a criticism of Dewey's philosophy of science, he feels encouraged to do this because he considers himself a member of the same group, criticism promising positive results only in case both author and critic stand on the same basis. He may be allowed to add that his criticism is based on admiration, that he suggests some alterations only because he agrees so much with the author as to his main tendencies, and that he knows quite well how much any success of his own work and that of his friends is due to the enormous contribution to philosophic education achieved by scientific personalities of the type of John Dewey. In an imposing series of books carried by an eloquence convincing both in its dark and its brilliant parts, Dewey has spread the impulse towards a life affirming philosophy over all the world; if some part of his echo comes back in a critical form, he will not, I think, refuse it as a present on his eightieth birthday.

I

Empiricist philosophies have been maintained in all phases of the history of ideas; however they have appeared in different forms according to the specific characters of the historic trends. Within the last hundred years, the sensationalism of British empiricists and the materialism of French and German philosophers have been replaced by two modern empiricist movements: by American pragmatism and European positivism.

Empiricism as an epistemological principle needs a complement on the logical side. It is a common feature of both pragmatism and positivism that they find this logical complement in nominalism, thus combining in their systems the empiricist trend with a line of development originating in logic. Out of this combination grew a specific version of empiricism in which the stress is laid, not so much, as in materialism, on an incorporation of the human mind into the physical world, as on a logical analysis of this physical world in terms of the world as it is originally given. The primitive world of concrete things, full of colours and sounds and feelings and emotions, stands at the basis of this construction; to this basis are reduced all the complex objects of scientific thought, the method of reduction being the nominalistic reduction of abstracta to concreta.

It is well known how this principle works. Nominalism has shown that abstract terms such as "the race of negroes" are reducible into statements about individual negroes, that the abstractum is to be conceived as a kind of shorthand for groups of complicated statements about concreta, not however as concerning an independent self-existent entity. Applying this principle to scientific concepts such as "atom," "electricity," "cause," "social movements," etc., pragmatists and positivists repeatedly assure us that all that is meant by those abstract concepts can be exhaustively formulated in terms of the immediate world around us. C. S. Peirce in his famous pragmatic maxim states that all effects of practical bearing resulting from a scientific conception together define the whole meaning of this conception; William James speaks of these practical bearings as the "cash value" of an abstract idea; John Dewey calls the scientific object an "instrumentality of multiplied controls and uses of the real things of everyday experience;"[1] E. Mach calls the physical thing a "complex of elements"[2] each of which is directly given to us in immediate experience; all of these state in various forms the nominalistic program of the reduction of abstracta applied to the relation between the world of science and the world of every day life. It is this principle of reduction which marks the decisive turn empiricism has made with the appearance of pragmatism and positivism.

Apart from this common feature, however, there is a remarkable difference between pragmatism and positivism. The latter considers the world of every day life as something complex, as not primitive, and tries to reduce it to further "elements," to "sense data" such as "hot," "blue," "sweet," "loud," etc. The thing of every day life, the table, the flower, then, are considered as being already complexes of those elements; and the

---

[1] *Quest for Certainty*, 106.
[2] *Analyse der Empfindungen* (9th ed., Jena, 1922), 13.

immediate world of the positivist is therefore a world of nothing but sense data. The pragmatist, however, does not follow this further reduction. It is one of the great merits of Dewey, it seems to me, to have insisted upon the idea that sense data are abstractions as much as are objects of physical science, that in immediate experience no "blue" or "hot" are given, but a blue flower and a hot oven; that the immediate reality is composed of *things*, not of *qualities*. The basis of all knowledge is the world of concrete things around us. This conception distinguishes the pragmatist from the positivist whose basis psychologically speaking is an artificial construction.

Dewey adds an important remark. Concrete things around us are not only provided with what is called since Locke "secondary qualities," *i.e.*, with those qualities such as "blue" and "hot," produced, physiologically speaking, in the sense organ. They possess also emotional qualities such as "beautiful" and "ugly," "lovable" and "contemptible," "adorable" and "awful."[3] Using a well-chosen term of Santayana, Dewey calls them "tertiary qualities," indicating by this term that these qualities are originally given to us not as emotional states of our own, but as qualities of things. There seems to me no doubt that this conception is correct. The thunder we hear is, in the same sense, loud and frightful; it is only a result of later reflection that "fright" is something not to be located in the thunder but in ourselves. Language has preserved this original interpretation of emotional qualities as qualities of things in expressing them by adjectives used in the same way as and along with adjectives denoting physical qualities.

We reach here a point where a directive tendency of Dewey's philosophy becomes manifest. In restoring the world of everyday life as the basis of knowledge, Dewey does not only want to establish knowledge in a better and more solid form. What he intends, and perhaps to a greater extent, is establishing the sphere of values, of human desires and aims, on the same basis and in an analogous form as the system of knowledge. If concrete things as immediately experienced are the truly "real" world, if the scientific thing is nothing but an auxiliary logical

[3] *Experience and Nature*, 21.

construction for better handling of the "real" things, then ethical and esthetical valuations are "real" properties of things as
well as are the purely cognitive properties, and it is erroneous
to separate valuations as subjective from cognitive properties
as objective. In persuasive language and in ever renewed form
Dewey insists upon this outcome of his theory, the establishment
of which seems to be the motive force in the work of this eminently practical mind, "practical" to be taken in both its implications as "moral" and "directed towards action." Dewey attacks as "intellectualism"[4] a conception for which the scientific
thing is the real thing; he asks us to consider the problem of
knowledge free from the prejudice of "intellectual habits," with
a "cultivated naïveté" which is accessible to us even though
"primitive naïveté" is for ever lost to anybody who has gone
through the school of philosophic thought.[5] Values have been
discarded from the real world by a preference of thought over
experience, by a predominance of cognitive over emotional
powers; if we free ourselves from this bias we are able to construct objective ethics and esthetics in the same way as we have
founded an objective natural science.

To this Dewey adds an epistemological remark. He believes
that the introduction of transcendent beings, of Platonic "ideas,"
of Kant's "things in themselves," as real beings "behind" the
world of experience, is psychologically explicable as an outcome
of the "intellectualism" described. The scientific world, empty
of values and ends and of everything that makes life worth
while, had become unsatisfactory to the human mind and could
not answer his "quest for certainty" as to moral aspirations. In
compensation for that, value and aim were shifted into an
imaginary sphere of "real beings" and essences, and thus originated transcendence philosophies of all kinds. We come back
here to the division of philosophies given in the beginning of
this paper, which found Dewey on the side of immanence philosophy. Let us leave further explanation to his own words:
"The ulterior issue is the possibility that actual experience in its
concrete content and movement may furnish those ideals, mean-

_____

[4] *Ibid.*, 21.
[5] *Ibid.*, 37.

ings and values whose lack and uncertainty in experience as actually lived by most persons has supplied the motive force for recourse to some reality beyond experience." This subterfuge, continues Dewey, is not necessary: "a philosophy of experience may be empirical without either being false to actual experience or being compelled to explain away the values dearest to the heart of man."[6]

II

We turn now to a criticism of Dewey's theory of science and reality. In anticipating our result let us say: we do not think that Dewey's nonrealistic interpretation of scientific concepts is tenable.

Let us first explain Dewey's viewpoint in his own words. The passage quoted above reads more completely:

Water as an object of science, as H_2O with all the other scientific propositions which can be made about it, is not a rival for position in real being with the water we see and use. It is, because of experimental operations, an added instrumentality of multiplied controls and uses of the real things of everyday experience.[7]

And in a later passage, he writes: "the physical object, as scientifically defined, is not a duplicated real object, but is a statement . . . of the relations between sets of changes the qualitative object sustains with changes in other things."[8]

There is a serious objection against this dissolution of scientific objects into relations of "qualitative" objects. It is based on the fact that inferential processes of the type leading to scientific objects are not restricted to science, but occur as well within the sphere of objects of everyday life, sometimes denying reality to these objects, sometimes replacing them by other objects of the same qualitative kind. The objects we dream, for instance, are judged as being not real by inferences never trespassing everyday's experience; other objects like the bent stick in water or the Fata Morgana in the desert are judged as being different from what there is in their place, objectively speaking. The real object in the latter case is not an "abstract"

[6] Quest for Certainty, 107.
[7] Ibid., 106.
[8] Ibid., 131.

excluded forever from human experience like H_2O, but it is itself a "qualitative" object in Dewey's sense; saying that the stick is really straight means replacing the seen stick by another stick seeable in principle although not seen under present conditions; saying that there is no water but dry hot sand means replacing the object seen in the Fata Morgana by another object well known in everyday experience though not simultaneously seen in the place of the pseudo-object. Thus there are cases in which primitive experience compels us to abandon the perceived objects and to replace them by inferred objects the reality of which is better founded than that of the perceived objects. Why then not admit the possibility of similar corrections by the methods of science? These methods do not differ in principle from the correcting methods applied in the examples quoted, although they are of course much more efficient.

But "dream, insanity and fantasy are natural products, as 'real' as anything else in the world,"[9] writes Dewey. In saying so, however, Dewey uses the word "real" in a sense different from that of everyday life. I have to appeal here to a judgment of "cultivated naïveté" which Dewey has so convincingly demanded for correct reasoning in basic questions of existential import. The distinction between "appearance" and "reality" is a basic need for constructing a consistent picture of the everyday world, in particular for the world of actions. The pragmatists have greatly emphasized the fact that thought is directed by the necessity of action: well then, our program of daily activities would be rushed into a tremendous disorder if we should for one moment forget the distinction between real and apparent objects.

I interpret Dewey's statement that dreams and fantasies are real on the assumption that his word "real" is to mean "real or apparent," the latter word "real" here having the ordinary meaning. There are reasons indeed for forming the logical sum (or disjunct) of the two concepts, since they have many features in common. The kind of presentativeness is the same both in dream and waking, or in fantasy and correct observation; besides, apparent objects may be used as bases of inferences which,

9 *Ibid.*, 243.

though not resulting in a confirmation of these objects, establish the presence of some determinate other objects. Thus we may infer from the observation of a Fata Morgana the presence of layers of hot air, from certain dreams past events in the life of a person such as is frequently done in psychoanalysis. But we should not use the term "real" in two senses; moreover, we should not appeal for naïveté in judging about real things when we are using the term "real" in the non-naïve sense of the disjunct. I have proposed the term "immediate existence" for the disjunct; immediate existence then divides into the subjective existence of the things of dream and fantasies, and the objective existence of observable "real" things, this word "real" taken in the usage of everyday life as denoting things that stand the test of continued inquiry. We have to add that there are many things which never can have immediate existence but have objective existence or reality; such are the scientific things like H_2O, or electricity, which are not directly observable. I have proposed for these things the term "illata," i.e., inferred things. The division of immediate things into subjective and objective things is not always performed directly by the observation, but is in general achieved by inferential methods starting from the basis of immediate existence; thus an immediate thing may lead to the inference that it is only subjective and that an objective thing of different character holds its place in the real world, or even that there is no objective thing at all in its place as in the case of dream.

We interpreted Dewey's statement about the reality of dreams and fantasies by translating his term "real" into our term "immediate existence;" this is however not the only interpretation possible. Another interpretation is obtained by the idea that dreams and fantasies prove the existence of real things, "real" now in our sense of objective existence, in so far as they prove that there are processes of a determinate kind in our sense organs, processes of the same kind as would happen if we were to observe real things similar to the seen subjective things. The statement, in this interpretation, is of course also true. But the real *processes* in the sense organ to which the statement then refers have no similarity to the immediate and subjective things seen, they are not observed but inferred by scientific methods, and they are not accessible to direct view. They are real in our sense, but not immediately existent.

There is a third way of interpreting the "reality" of phenomena such as the bent stick in water; this way (which however does not apply to the case of dream) makes use of geometric conventionalism. Analysis of the philosophical problem of geometry has shown that we cannot speak of a geometric form without giving beforehand certain "coördinative definitions." These being arbitrary it might be possible to introduce a geometry such that the stick is bent at the point it enters into the water; the stick as a whole then would not be straight, objectively speaking. But this is nothing but a change in the definition of the physical term "straight" which then for instance would not mean "line as determined by a pulled string." This escape into conventionalism would therefore be only a change of physical terms and would not make superfluous the distinction between objective things and subjective things. We can eliminate the problem of coördinative definitions by saying: we see the stick in a form which is different from the usual form of a pulled string, although a pulled string in its place would show the same form. Or in other words: we see the stick in a form the implications of which, determined in the usual way, contradict the actual implications. As the meaning of a term should include the meaning of its implications, we should therefore not say: the stick *is* bent, but the stick *appears* bent.

The distinction between subjective and objective things presupposes of course that strict meanings of the physical terms have been defined. If we understand by water any physical thing that looks like water, the water of the Fata Morgana would be an objective thing; but the term "water" in this case would not have the usual meaning, as it would include layers of dry air. The conventionalistic interpretation is of the same kind; it is nothing but a change in the meaning of words. But juggling with physical terms cannot solve the problem of illusions of the senses. I do not think therefore that interpretations of the conventionalist kind are seriously maintainable in dealing with these problems; nor do I believe that the pragmatists are inclined to conceptions of this type.

It is astonishing that quarrels about appearance and reality play such a great rôle in philosophic discussions. The diversity of opinions here is by no means paralleled by a diversity in the field of action. In everyday life everybody knows fairly well what to do if distinctions of the considered kind become relevant; it is only when they come to questions of terminology that philosophers never "come to terms." Both the pragmatist and the realist know very well that when they dream of a bank account of a million dollars they had better not draw checks on this amount after awaking; but they will not agree as to the way in which this knowledge is to be formulated. I suggest therefore the use of a terminology which follows as much as possible the naïve realism of everyday life.[10] I know quite well that there is more than one admissible terminology; but if different terminologies are correct, they will all be translatable into each other, and none of them will be able to erase the difference which conversational language expresses by the distinction between appearance and reality.

It seems that Dewey wants to avoid this "duplication" of things because he is afraid that it might lead to the conception of transcendent things such as Kant's "things-in-themselves." I do not think, however, that there is any danger of that kind if the terminology is scientifically elaborated. Phenomena of the kind leading to the distinction between appearance and reality are not the cause of transcendent philosophies. The fisherman who dips his oar into the water and sees it bent does not turn transcendentalist if he says that this is only appearance, and that in reality his oar is not bent. Why then should the physicist be a transcendentalist if he says that the same oar, strictly speaking, is not a continuous mass but built up of fine grains with interstices between them so small that even the microscope cannot show them? The inferences leading him to

[10] The terminology which I propose and which I indicated above is explained in my book *Experience and Prediction* (Chicago University Press, 1938), §24. I have to refer to this book in general for further exposition of the viewpoints expressed in this paper.

this contention are of the same type as those convincing the fisherman of the straightness of his oar. The discrepancy of the seen bent oar and the inferred straight one is repeated, on a higher level, in the discrepancy between the seen continuous nature of its wood and the inferred atomistic pattern; in both cases the objective thing is different from the seen subjective thing. What we see is only a substitute thing, not the real thing in all its details. If the deviation is great as in the case of the bent oar, conversational language does not hesitate to admit the substitute character of what we see. If the deviation is small as in the case of the continuous substance and the atomistic one, we may neglect it for many purposes and consider the seen subjective thing as identical with the objective thing; for strict considerations only we have to admit that even in this case the subjective thing is only a substitute, though of a good approximation.

We may add here some remarks concerning the reason which necessitates, physically speaking, the distinction between subjective and objective things. The human sense organs may be considered as registering instruments in which certain external causes like light rays or sound waves produce specific effects, which are however gauged in such a way that not the effect but the external cause is indicated. Instruments of this kind are frequently used for technical purposes; thus the speedometer of a car is gauged in the speed of the car, whereas the effect produced in the instrument is the angular deviation of a needle. Correspondingly our eyes are "gauged" in such a way that they indicate external things, not the processes occurring in the eye. We may say that they are gauged in "stimulus language;" we see the things which emit the light rays, not these light rays, nor the chemical processes released by the light rays in the retina. This method of gauging however involves the disadvantage that the indications presented are correct only under normal conditions, *i.e.*, the gauging can be made only for a certain set of external stimuli, and the instrument will furnish false indications in case it is affected by stimuli of another kind which produce the same reactions in the instrument. If we mount for instance a speedometer into a car whose wheels do not fit the speedometer gear, the speedometer will furnish false indications about the speed of that car. We may even take the speedometer out of the car and produce a deviation of the needle by means of a magnet brought near to it; this new kind of "stimulus" then will be registered by our speedometer like the normal one, *i.e.*, in terms of miles per hour. It might even happen that the speedometer indicates a speed without any external cause; an internal cause like a broken spring in the mechanism of the instrument may produce this effect.

The analogy with the human eye is evident; the eye is gauged only for stimuli in normal conditions and will falsely indicate in case it is affected by stimuli of another kind. The case of illusions like the bent stick or the Fata Morgana corresponds to the case of a speedometer mounted in combination with an inappropriate gear, or of a speedometer influenced by a magnet; the case of dream corresponds to a speedometer the speed indication of which is due to internal processes only. It is however obvious that the indications of such a speedometer are, although false, not useless; they may be used as a basis of inferences to the real external causes if we have sufficient knowledge about the external conditions in which the speedometer is working. Thus the miles per hour of the instrument may be used to measure the strength of a magnet which turns its needle. Using the language which we apply in the analogous case of the eye we may say that the speedometer registers here the subjective thing "speed of fifty miles" but that we infer from this the objective thing "magnetic force of a certain amount."

This makes clear why we sometimes have to call the things perceived by our sense organs subjective, although they may be used for inferences to objective things of a different kind. The possibility of such inferences may be further illustrated by our example. Although in the case described the speed of fifty miles is only a subjective thing, it is an objective fact that the speedometer points at fifty miles; this is the objective fact from which inferences concerning the power of the magnet start. In the same way, if a person sees a subjective thing, it is an objective fact that the person sees this subjective thing; this objective fact enables us to make inferences concerning objective things which we assume in the place of the subjective thing.

Pragmatists may defend their "reality" of illusions by pointing out that these are sometimes due to objective physical conditions. The phenomenon of the bent stick for instance is due to the refraction of light rays which produces the same perspective as a bent stick would have outside the water. The eye, they might say, makes no mistake here. However I could not agree to this interpretation. It is the mistake of the eye that it continues to furnish its indications in a stimulus language which is appropriate only for normal conditions, no longer for the physical conditions present in the case of the illusion. The eye, so to speak, is "cheated" by the refracted light rays as is the speedometer by the magnet which turns its needle. We may add here the remark that the human eye is much superior to technical instruments in so far as it in many cases corrects the indication in correspondence with the changed stimulus. If for instance a person walks away from us in a room, the angular perspective of the light rays sent from his body into our eyes changes considerably; however our eye sees the man always in the same size. The diminution of the angle of the perspective may here be rather great, and is certainly above the threshold of perception; our eye however changes its gauging relative to the distance of the object. Inversely there are cases in which the same angular perspective may be interpreted as indicating different objective sizes, such as occur for peripheral optical objects the size of which varies with the distance in which the object is located. The "mistake" of the eye in the case of the bent stick in water consists in its inability to correct the seen object in correspondence to the abnormal physical conditions in which the object is presented.

Pragmatists denying any "mistake" of the eye have referred to the fact that a photographic camera would furnish the same picture of the stick as does the human eye. But why should we not say that sometimes a photographic camera makes mistakes either—even more than the eye—because it never "corrects" its report in the case of abnormal conditions of the observations? The photographic picture can be interpreted in two ways. First we may conceive it as a report about the stick; then it is false in the same sense as is the report of the speedometer or the report of the human eye. Only in a second interpretation the report made by the camera would be correct; the photographic picture then has to be conceived as a report about the projection of the stick on the film. This projection is indeed bent, although, as we know from the laws of physics, this is du ιo the bending of the projecting light rays and not to a bending of the stick. If we should try to apply this interpretation to the case of the human eye we should have to say: there is a bent projection of the stick on the retina. This is of course true, but it is not what we *see*. The eye reports in stimulus language, not in a language about the process within the eye. This is the reason that the human eye sometimes makes mistakes.

To avoid a term like "mistake" we prefer to speak of "subjective things." The distinction between objective and subjective things therefore is nothing but the expression of the fact that our senses speak stimulus language; it does not involve any "metaphysics." It is not this distinction, only misinterpretations of it which may lead to metaphysical conceptions opposed to empiricism. There have been mainly two such misinterpretations presented in the history of philosophy. The first considers the subjective things as carrying with themselves a specific reality; these things then are conceived of as existing in the "mind," as "psychical entities," and with this a dualism of two kinds of reality, of mind and matter, is established. It seems to us that the pragmatist terminology which calls subjective things real is much more susceptible to this misinterpretation than our terminology for which subjective things are unreal. The second misinterpretation is transcendentalism. It considers legitimate a recapitulation of the distinction between subjective and objective things on a higher level, leading to "things in themselves" which are supposed "behind" the objective things in the same sense as the objective things are assumed "behind" the subjective things. However I do not see any argument against our terminology in the very fact that the analogy as indicated has indeed been used by transcendentalists, for it is by no means justified. Our realistic terminology should not be made responsible for such a misinterpretation. Our objective things are not of the type of "noumena" because we do not consider the *unobservable* things as *unknowable*. On the contrary, science gives us methods of studying them, and just because we know them we conclude that what we see is different from them. The psychological motives for transcendentalism which both pragmatists and empirical realists reject derive from other sources. I think Dewey is quite right in pointing out that one of these sources is the quest for certainty in *ethical* decisions; another source is the desire to show human knowledge as a very imperfect instrument and to make men amenable to the doctrines of religion.

The possibility of misinterpretations should not retain us from using concepts indispensable for an analysis of the process of human knowledge. Carried through within a correct terminology the distinction of subjective and objective things will lead neither into the metaphysics of dualism nor into that of transcendentalism, but into a philosophy of knowledge which considers science, and the pre-scientific inferential methods of daily life, as the only approach to reality.

III

Discussions about terminology have a more than terminological import if they turn into an analysis of material conceptions behind the verbal form. After having shown that it is erroneous to assume a metaphysical dualism or transcendentalism as the necessary background of a realistic terminology, let us now inquire along the same line into the conceptions which stand in the background of the pragmatist terminology. There are, we think, two main ideas at work behind the pragmatist conception of reality; one is of a logical nature, the other of the nature of an ethical program. Leaving the discussion of the second idea to the following section, we turn now to an inquiry into the structure of the first idea.

This logical idea which seems to us involved in the pragmatist denial of independent reality to scientific objects is a nominalistic theory of meaning. We indicated this idea already in I when we referred to quotations of Peirce, James, Dewey, Mach; we have now to enter into a more profound analysis of this conception.

It is well known, and has for good reason recently been emphasized by Carnap, that questions concerning the existence of things assume a form more easily to be answered if they are turned into questions concerning the meaning of propositions. Instead of speaking of existing objects, we then shall speak of true propositions; the distinction between objective and subjective things will be translated into a distinction between objectively true and subjectively true propositions; and the question concerning the reducible or independent reality of scientific things will assume the form of a discussion of the equivalence or nonequivalence of propositions. Problems of this form are more easily to be solved because they are less subject to the psychological constraint of traditional associative representations.

If we apply this transformation to Dewey's theory of scientific things, this conception turns into the theory that every scientific statement is equivalent to statements about observable concrete objects. The latter statements concern those observations from which, as we usually say, the scientific statement is inferred; this inference, so goes the pragmatist interpretation, is not synthetical, but analytical, i.e., it is nothing but a logical equivalence. If for instance the existence of electricity is inferred from observations about sparks, the moving of needles, burning of bulbs, etc., every statement about electric processes is nothing but a shorthand expression for statements about sparks, moving needles, burning bulbs, etc. This conception, which forms one of the basic principles of pragmatism and positivism, which has been applied with much success in modern physics under the name of operationalism, and which forms a special application of the well-known principle of nominalism, has been discussed in recent times by the name of the *verifiability theory of meaning*. A proposition has meaning only in so far as it is verifiable, and an abstract statement has therefore only so much meaning as has the group of concrete statements to which it refers—this is the logical background of Dewey's theory of instrumentalism of scientific concepts.

We cannot enter here into an analysis of this theory, but must confine ourselves to a short report on the discussion this theory has been submitted to in the last years. There can be no doubt that this theory of meaning represents a very important point reached in modern logic, and that it played an important rôle in the development of modern scientific philosophy. Because of the establishment of this theory of meaning the work of pragmatists and positivists will occupy, without any doubt, a leading position in the history of modern philosophy; we are glad to be able to express this acknowledgement in the present collection of papers to one of those who contributed so much to the foundation and propagation of this theory at a time when it was not yet so widely acknowledged.

However, we have to add here the remark that recent discussion has shown this theory to be not the last word in the problem of meaning. It is, so to speak, only the first approximation in the approach to an empiricist theory of meaning; the second approximation is much more complicated and leads, as regards certain consequences, to different results. The verifiability theory of meaning as explained starts from the assumption that propositions are either true or false; *i.e.,* in logical terms, from the assumption that propositions are *two-valued.* But a more precise consideration shows that this is a simplification approximately valid in many cases but which cannot be carried through universally; scientific propositions, and also propositions of everyday life, are correctly speaking *more or less true* and should be incorporated therefore into a *multivalued* logic the scale of which varies continually from zero to one. In the concept of probability, logic and mathematics have created a concept the rules of which furnish the appropriate form of such a generalized logic. This latter has been systematically developed within the frame of mathematical logic, or logistics.

After these results, the problem of meaning was to be discussed anew, this time in terms of probability logic. It turned out that in the frame of this generalized logic the equivalence theory of meaning as explained was no longer tenable. To state it more correctly: the nominalistic principle of the equivalence of meaning is not wholly superseded, but its application is restricted; it does hold for propositions which possess the same degree of probability relative to all possible observations, and so it holds for the usual relation of abstracta to concreta, but it does not hold for the relation of inductively inferred propositions to observational propositions[11] and therefore not for the relation of "illata" to concreta. The inference leading from observed facts to hypotheses is not an equivalence, but a probability inference which adds something new to the premises; the addition finds its expression in an unlimited and even never determinable class of predictions of new facts which the hypothesis involves.[12] This "overreaching" character of probability inference excludes the application of the nominalistic reduction to the relation of scientific concepts and experiential observations. If we understand by "semantic language" a language of a higher level dealing with propositions, and by "object language" the usual language dealing with things, we may say: the nonequivalence between scientific propositions and observational propositions expresses in semantic language what the realistic interpretation of scientific concepts as independent entities expresses in object language.

Now it is very interesting to note that this very idea of probability replacing truth is one of the fundamental ideas of Dewey. He attacks the "quest for certainty" not only on the ethical side, but also on the theoretical side; he knows that "inquiry into existence can only arrive at conclusions having a coefficient of some order of probability,"[13] and, transferring this result about empirical knowledge in general to the problem of human action, he emphasizes that knowledge applicable to practical purposes is never absolutely true, that "judgment and belief regarding actions to be performed can never attain more than a precarious probability."[14] Dewey's emphasis upon the fact that empirical knowledge is written in terms of probability and not of truth is one of the great merits of this thoroughly empiricist

[11] The proof of this idea is given *in extenso* in chapter II of my book *Experience and Prediction*. Although the inquiry of that chapter is attached to the positivistic conception of "impressions" as the observational basis of inferences, it applies as well to the pragmatist conception which considers statements about concrete physical objects as the basis, but which conceives all scientific statements as derived from this basis by equivalence transformations.

[12] We may add here that even if we include statements about an infinity of predicted new observable facts in the class of observational propositions, the equivalence with the hypothesis cannot be maintained; cf. *Experience and Prediction*, §17.

[13] *Logic*, 390.

[14] *Quest for Certainty*, 6.

philosopher, placing him into one line with C. S. Peirce in the struggle for a theory of science free from the preoccupations of traditional rationalism and absolutism. We should be glad if he could be convinced that a probabilistic empiricism opens new ways for a realistic interpretation of scientific concepts not imperiled by any transgression into a domain of unknowable "things in themselves."

IV

We turn now to some consequences our analysis involves for Dewey's theory of secondary and tertiary qualities. We presented in Part I Dewey's idea that, if the immediate things of everyday life are the only real things, the reality of secondary and tertiary qualities is demonstrated; Dewey considers this proof as one of the fundamental issues of his epistemology. We have to inquire whether this result is tenable in the sense in which Dewey interprets it.

We explained above that we agreed with Dewey in his conception that secondary and tertiary qualities are qualities of immediate things, using our term introduced in Part II. But it can easily be shown that they are, if we continue using our terminology, subjective qualities, *i.e.*, qualities which do not belong to objective things. They are qualities of things only for those persons whose bodies possess sense organs of a specific kind, not for other persons. The things of the colour-blind man have no colours, but show only shades of grey in all variations. If, therefore, we understand by objective qualities those qualities of things which are the same for all men we have to cross out colours from the objective qualities. The same holds for emotional qualities; a black cat may appear frightful to one man, whereas another sees it as a graceful and tender animal. This is why we call these qualities subjective.

The term subjective seems to us appropriate because it expresses the fact that the nature of the subject, of the observer, produces these qualities. The world as we see it is a resultant of properties of the objective world and of properties of the observer. It is the aim of science to eliminate the latter influence as far as possible. Once more we have to say that the methods science uses for this purpose are not different, in principle, from methods applied for the same purpose in everyday life. When we look through blue spectacles the world turns blue; but we know that this is due to our spectacles only. In the same sense the scientist shows that colours in general are products of human sense organs. He shows at the same time that even the eye of the normal man has only a very limited range of sensitivity, that we are all colour-blind, even *blind*, relative to electric waves outside a small range of wave lengths. Reference to this fact has often been made in philosophic discussions: if our eyes were sensitive to ultraviolet or infra-red rays, the world would be richer in colours and look different from what it looks now; if they were sensitive to cosmic rays, the sky at night would be bright with a maximum zone of brightness near the galaxy, etc. I think the physicist is quite reasonable when he refuses a terminology in which such changes would be called changes in the objective or real world.

Now if the pragmatist intends with his characterization of secondary and tertiary qualities as real nothing but a change of terminology, if he understands by "real" what we call "immediate," there would be at least no material difference in these conceptions. But it seems to us that there is more than a terminological difference involved in the pragmatist's conception. We come here to a problem which, we suppose, reveals the motive force of the pragmatic conception of reality. If the pragmatist considers secondary and tertiary qualities as real he does so because he wants to establish esthetics and ethics as aspects of reality comparable to physics; because he wants to show that esthetic and moral judgments are statements of facts in a sense analogous to statements of physical facts. It is the desire to establish objective esthetics and ethics, as opposed to subjective conceptions of esthetics and ethics, which stands behind the pragmatist's theory of reality.

We cannot subscribe to this interpretation. If the term "objective esthetics and ethics" is to have any meaning utilizable for a theory of action it must mean that esthetical and ethical properties can be demonstrated to every man as properties of things, *i.e.*, that they are *intersubjective* properties. But we know that this is not possible. Any attempt to convince a colour-blind man of a visible difference in two things the normal man sees as red and green would be nonsensical. However by means of physical devices we can convince him that these two things emit light rays of different wave lengths. This is why we distinguish between objective and subjective qualities, and call the secondary qualities subjective. The same is easily demonstrated for tertiary qualities.

We called the secondary and tertiary qualities resultants of qualities of the things and of the observer. It is true that also many other qualities which we consider as being qualities of one thing are correctly speaking relations of this thing to other things, and that therefore secondary and tertiary qualities are special cases of what may be called "interactional" qualities of things. If the chemist calls lemon acid *sour*, this term is to mean that *if* other liquids such as alkalis are brought into contact with lemon acid a certain reaction occurs. Similarly if we call a lemon *sour* in conversational language, this is to mean a reaction which would occur if the lemon contacts our tongue. The difference between the two cases, however, consists in the fact that in the second case the "test-body" is just the observer; this is why in this case we speak of subjective qualities, and exclude them from a description of the world if this description is to be independent of the observer.

On the other hand this analysis shows that secondary and tertiary qualities may be characterized as objective if we include the observer into the description. We can for instance convince a colour-blind man that a normal man sees a difference between two things he himself sees as equally coloured. This is the reason that an objective psychology is possible; though psychology deals with subjective things it is objective because it states that persons of a certain type under certain conditions observe these subjective things. With this interpretation as objective however the secondary and tertiary qualities are no longer *qualities* of things, but *relations* between thing and observer, varying therefore with the nature of the observer.

Now our immediate world does not show these qualities as relations but as qualities of things; their relational character is a discovery due to inferential operations. As long as we stay in the immediate world of experience we therefore have to call secondary and tertiary qualities subjective; considering them

as objective relations is replacing immediately verifiable statements about the world of things around us by inferred statements about a more comprehensive world including the observer as an object. The lack of intersubjectivity which characterizes those qualities in the first conception finds its analogue
in the second conception by the very fact that the objective relations which take the place of those qualities vary with the nature
of the observer. This analysis points out where the terminology
of the pragmatist may become misleading: if he calls the *qualities* real, this word "real" does not involve the meaning of
"intersubjective;" if he calls the *relations* real, the very fact
that he has to speak here of relations makes them functions of
the observer.

   We see that in both interpretations the pragmatist's "reality"
of secondary and tertiary qualities cannot furnish the very feature which would justify a characterization of esthetics and
ethics as objective: it cannot furnish a *compulsory* character of
esthetic and ethical judgments. We are afraid that the pragmatist conception may lead for this reason to dangerous misunderstandings of value-judgments in so far as it may suggest
a theory of ethics which considers moral judgments as *binding*
as physical judgments. There are ethical systems which for
instance consider the idea that private property is sacrosanct as
a demonstrable truth, in the same sense as it is demonstrable
that private property is destructible by fire. It is the danger
of pragmatism that its theory of reality is made to order for
ethical philosophies of this type, although the pragmatists themselves may not intend these implications. It seems to us a basic
insight of modern ethics that moral judgments vary with the
structure of the individual, and that, as this structure is highly
determined by the social environment, moral judgments vary
with the social structure of society. This conception is acceptable
only for an epistemology which does not consider tertiary qualities as qualities of objective things but of subjective things, and
therefore as qualities depending on the nature of man. Compared with secondary qualities, tertiary qualities are subjective
to an even higher degree: secondary qualities are at least biological constants, *i.e.*, determined by the biological structure
of the human body and therefore not susceptible to change;

whereas tertiary qualities depend on the social milieu of the observer and are amenable to change by education and new social adjustment.

Our refusal to consider tertiary qualities as "real" does not mean that science is without any import for ethical considerations. There are two different functions which science has to perform in respect to ethics. First it will collect material in the form of statements about ethical conceptions of different persons, classes, nations, of the present and of ancient times; *i.e.*, science will show us ethical concepts as functions of human beings in their environment, not of things independent of man. Second it will construe the implications between intended aims, and means of their realization; considerations of this kind may sometimes lead to the result that two aims involve each other, or that they are incompatible. Statements of both these kinds can be made without any claim of reality for tertiary qualities because the logical form of these statements is a relation between ethical values and men as their bearers. This *regulative* function is all that science can perform in the field of ethics—there is no way of establishing a *normative* ethics by means of scientific method.

Throughout the history of philosophy we observe ever renewed attempts at establishing the human system of moral values in a form similar to the system of physical truths. The Platonic doctrine of Ideas is the first great realization of this everlasting dream of mankind; from that time there runs a continuous line of similar attempts through various forms of theology up to Kant's three *Critiques* the titles of which express in their deliberate parallelism the very program of a philosophy which considers physical science, esthetics and ethics as three congenerous approaches to reality. It seems to us that this line, perhaps transferred through influences of Hegel, has found a continuation in the pragmatist conception of reality. We should think, however, that it is time now to develop a theory of values as volitional decisions which needs no artificial spine of a quasi-cognitive theory of values, which admits frankly that volitional decisions are not justifiable in the sense of discoveries of qualities in the objective world, but for which, on the other hand, the obligation involved in ethical impulses and decisions is not diminished by the fact that these decisions are products of nothing but our nature as biological and social beings. We hope that a sound empiricism, not afraid of differences between appearance and reality, may lead the way towards such an ethics of human volition purified from all claims of a pseudo-objectivity.

V

We turn now to a consideration of Dewey's analysis of scientific method. It is in this field that the truly empiricist character of Dewey's philosophy becomes most visible, revealing its author as a pioneer of ideas which have become the common property of the present generation of empiricist philosophers.

It is the basic idea of Dewey that the method of modern science becomes understandable only if we drop the conception of science as a system of absolute truths. If the scientific work of Antiquity and of the Middle Ages seems so inefficient in comparison with the science of Modern Times, the reason is to be found in the fact that the science of the ancients was a search for necessities and essences, a "quest for certainty." As reason alone, and not experience, seems able to promise absolute certainty, ancient science turned to a striking overestimation of rational and speculative methods as compared with experimental procedure. In an interesting analysis Dewey points out that the fault of ancient science consisted not so much in insufficient observation of natural phenomena—on the contrary, "the Greeks were keenly sensitive to natural objects and were keen observers"[15]—as in a lack of insight into the necessity of checking scientific theories by an inquiry involving active intervention in the conditions of natural processes, *i.e.*, by experimental methods. Once a scientific hypothesis had been suggested by observation of natural phenomena, its further implications were never tested by appropriate experiments but accepted through confidence in the "inherent 'rationality' of the conclusion."[16] Only a natural science the results of which were never checked by experiments could be conceived of as a system of eternal truths.

The very fact that modern science introduced experimental methods of testing hypotheses led to the discovery that scientific

[15] *Quest for Certainty*, 88.
[16] *Logic*, 430.

theories can never be considered as absolutely true, that they must be submitted to continuous improvements by further inquiries. The modern scientist is glad if he finds an assumption which at least holds for a determinable group of phenomena within the limits of a sufficient approximation; he will maintain this hypothesis as long as it is good, but he is always prepared to improve or even to reject it in the face of new experimental data. For the modern mind knowledge is therefore not a system of truths—it means nothing but "warranted assertibility."[17] Dewey refers to Leonardo's remark that "true knowledge begins with opinion"[18] and defends the rôle of guessing in scientific research; "opinion as a venture, as an 'it seems to me probable,' is an occasion of new observations, an instigator of research, an indispensable organ in deliberate discovery."[19] Guessing as method is justified because its results are submitted to experimental tests and therefore amenable to improvement; but what we obtain by such a procedure is never certainty, it is at best only "warranted assertibility."

In an instructive analysis of some simple examples, such as the explanation of dew[20] and the investigation of the malaria disease,[21] Dewey illustrates this deep insight into the logical structure of modern scientific method. He uses the comprehensive term "inductive methods" for the various procedures which lead from observational data to hypothetical assumptions; by deductive methods inversely new observational predictions are inferred from the hypotheses the experimental test of which confirms or disproves the hypothetical assumption. Scientific inquiry is thus hypothetical-deductive. In opposition to other representatives of this conception Dewey makes it, however, very clear that this procedure cannot be interpreted in the frame of a logic for which knowledge is either true or false. Experimental tests of the implications of a hypothesis cannot strictly verify—we may add here: nor strictly falsify—the original assumption; all the tests can perform is increasing or lessening

[17] *Ibid.*, 7.
[18] *Experience and Nature*, 155.
[19] *Ibid.*, 155.
[20] *Logic*, 429.
[21] *Ibid.*, 433.

the probability of the hypothesis. On the other hand, the very facts from which the hypothesis was in the first place inductively inferred must be such that they already confer a probability, though a smaller one, to the assumption; this material upon which the hypothesis is based must be already "a factor in warranting its validity."[22] There is no difference of principle, only a difference of degree, between the logical situation before and after the test; all observational material is to have "conjunct inferential and testing force."[23] The relation from observational data to "warranted assertibility" is therefore understandable only within the frame of an inductive logic which ascribes degrees of truth, or, better, degrees of probability, to scientific generalizations and hypotheses.

In the exposition of these ideas of Dewey's about scientific method the present writer, in part, has used a terminology which he himself has developed for similar purposes; he hopes, however, that his interpretation of Dewey's ideas is correct. He would be glad to be entitled to assume a close correspondence of his own views of the problem with those of one of the leaders of pragmatism. Just because of this agreement in basic conceptions he may be allowed to add now some critical remarks concerning further parts of Dewey's theory of induction.

VI

Dewey distinguishes, as usual, induction by simple enumeration from the more general methods of induction. He then endeavors to show that the first plays only a subordinate rôle, that the important form of scientific induction is represented by inferences different from induction by simple enumeration and not reducible to it. He even wants to show that in induction by simple enumeration there is another principle involved, the principle of finding "the representative," and that mere enumeration does not add any cogent force to the inference.

We start with the latter objection. Dewey writes:

The problem of inductive inquiry, and the precautions that have to be observed in conducting it, all have to do with ascertaining that the

[22] *Ibid.*, 428.
[23] *Ibid.*, 429.

given case *is* representative, or is a sample or specimen . . . the validity of the inferred conclusion does not depend upon their number. . . . The moment any *one* case is determined to be such that it is an exemplary representative, the problem in hand is solved.[24]

Dewey does not explain to us what he understands by, or how he determines, a specimen. I think if he should do so he would come to define a specimen as that form of the case which we would encounter in future repetitions of the same observation. The question under discussion, then, is the question whether repeated occurrence of past observations is a sufficient reason to assume that the conditions of a specimen are fulfilled. There seems to me no doubt that in many cases, we indeed make this assumption; for these cases then, the principle of the representative leads back to induction by simple enumeration; *i.e.*, to an inference from "some" to "all." If we observe, for instance, that a stifling hot day is followed by a thunderstorm at night we consider this case as a specimen and infer that the same atmospheric change will always, or mostly always, follow a day of that kind. But why do we assume that? Because this sequence has frequently been observed. The interpretation of induction by reference to the sample case instead of enumeration seems to us nothing but a change of the linguistic expression, the sample case being definable only in terms of enumeration. Dewey's analysis includes the correct idea that counting cases and making predictions of their repetition involves a classification, and that therefore "making correct predictions about repeated occurrence" can be translated into "making the correct classification;" but then the correct classification is the one which leads to repeated occurrence.

We think that what is behind this analysis by Dewey is not so much an attack upon the logical structure of induction by simple enumeration as the idea that many cases which usually are considered to be cases of this form of induction are correctly speaking more complex cases. If, for instance, we assume that stifling hot days are mostly followed by a thunderstorm we base this assumption not only on observation of past experiences of this kind, but also on an analysis of the electrical mechanism of a

[24] *Ibid.*, 436-437.

thunderstorm which shows that the forming of a high electrical tension between clouds and its subsequent discharge is favored by heat and moisture, etc. In other words: the number of observed cases is relevant, but it is not the only reason for inductive inference. This leads us to the second of Dewey's contentions which concerns the idea that there are further principles involved in scientific inductions beyond simple enumeration.

This critique forwarded by Dewey seems to us good in so far as it attacks some primitive theories of induction which do not take into account the complex structure of scientific inference and maintain that inductive inference *directly represents* nothing but enumerations. However this critique seems to us incorrect if it is to contend that the additional principles involved in inductive inference are not *indirectly reducible* to enumeration. Returning to our example we may say: an analysis of the influences occurring in the theory of the electrical mechanism of a thunderstorm may show that these inferences turn out to be once more inductions by simple enumeration. A case which we call one inductive inference may therefore disintegrate into a network of inductive inferences; the first, considered directly, may represent more than a simple enumeration, but the elements to which it is indirectly reduced are inductions by enumeration.

We suppose that this was the conception of Hume and of others who have developed the idea that all inductive inference reduces to enumeration. I do not think, however, that they had a good proof of this assumption. I shall explain now why I think that today we can give a proof of it.

Let us introduce the term "macroscopic inferences," for the inferences as they are directly applied, connecting comprehensive scientific concepts such as "thunderstorm," "the theory of electricity," "weather," etc. We shall then call "microscopic inferences" the elements to which macroscopic inferences are reducible. Our thesis then is that it is possible to reduce all macroscopic inferences to microscopic inferences which are inductions by simple enumeration.

The demonstration of this thesis is based upon the fact that, apart from purely deductive methods, the application of the calculus of probability to physical objects can be shown to involve only one axiom: this is the axiom of induction by simple enumeration. This fact has been established in the axiomatic of the mathematical theory of probability.[25] Thus to give our proof we have to assume only that all macroscopic scientific inference conforms to, and is interpretable in terms of, the calculus of probability. This is, I think, scarcely deniable, as the scientists would never tolerate inferences which are not justifiable by the rules of probability. Our theory explains why macroscopic inference seems so often of a form different from induction by enumeration. If we maintain that in spite of such difference all inferences reduce to inductions by simple enumeration this may be illustrated by an example from mathematics: it is known that higher arithmetical operations such as taking the square root, etc., are reducible to additions of the form $1 + 1$, although the direct structure of these higher operations is very different from a simple addition. In the same sense, all inductive inferences are reducible to inductions by simple enumeration.

VII

We turn now to the question of the justification of the principle of induction. I was glad to see from his latest book that Dewey considers this a serious problem and does not share the opinion of many a modern writer who tries to get rid of this problem by calling it a pseudo-problem. In his analysis of the problem, Dewey[26] refers to some ideas of C. S. Peirce; so we have to discuss jointly the conceptions of both Dewey and Peirce.

There is no doubt that the contributions of Peirce mark the first forward step towards a solution of this problem since it had been pointed out so seriously by David Hume. There are two main ideas which Peirce has introduced into the discussion of this problem. The first is that a justification cannot concern one single inductive inference in isolation, but that we have to consider induction as a continuous procedure of assumptions and later corrections. With this conception in view Peirce writes: "The justification of it is that, although the conclusion at any stage of the investigation may be more or less erroneous, yet the further application of the same method must correct the

---

[25] For the demonstration of this I refer to my book, *Wahrscheinlichkeitslehre* (Leiden, 1935), and to chapter V of *Experience and Prediction*.

[26] *Logic*, 469-470.

HANS REICHENBACH

error."[27] Dewey, who quotes this passage of Peirce, adheres to it in saying that the problem of induction is soluble only "on the ground of the continuity of inquiry." The second main idea presented by Peirce is attached by him to wha⁺ he calls "abduction." Without entering upon an analysis of what Peirce means by this term we may interpret it as "induction in a wider sense" and thus apply his idea to the problem of induction in general; the idea then reads: the justification of induction is "that if we are ever to understand things at all, it must be that way."[28]

Reading Peirce's collected papers has always been for me a high intellectual enjoyment combined with the suspicion of a personal tragedy behind all these scattered utterances of a brilliant mind. There is an enormous collection of important material and deep insights presented in these papers, however, interspersed with dark and sketchy passages of unclarified meanings, sometimes apparently derived from a Hegelian past not completely stripped off. It seems Peirce never found the time to elaborate his ideas, and to carry through promising beginnings into a definitive form. I do not know whether he was withheld from it by the constraint of an unsatisfactory economic situation which forced him to publish his ideas as they came, in scattered articles, with permanent repetitions, or whether there are other psychological conditions behind this dispersion of exceptional intellectual talents. What remains for us of Peirce's work is not solutions but directions, not an elaborate philosophy but a philosophic program. Let us be glad that we have at least this—there are not many philosophers who leave a program to posterity. But we cannot refer to Peirce if we want elaborate solutions.

These general remarks apply as well to his contributions to the problem of induction. The two ideas we quoted form a pro-

---

[27] Peirce, *Collected Papers*, V, 90.

[28] *Ibid.*, p. 90; similar remarks in II, pp. 497, 502. It is difficult to give a clear interpretation of what Peirce means by "abduction." Sometimes it has the meaning of what I call "macroscopic inductive inference;" sometimes it refers to the psychological process of finding new hypotheses. It then would belong to what I call the "context of discovery" (cf. my book, *Experience and Prediction*, pp. 7, 382). In this frame, however, a question of justification cannot be raised; or in other words: the justification of actually used psychological methods consists in repeatedly observed success of these methods. This being itself an inductive inference the problem of abduction is turned back to the justification of induction.

gram, not a solution. They can be worked into a solution; based on a combination of the same ideas I have myself developed a solution of the problem although at a time when I did not know these ideas of Peirce. I am particularly glad to have taken paths which at a so much earlier time a philosopher of the rank of Peirce had indicated, and I may be allowed to consider it as a proof of sound method that philosophic movements of so different an origin as American pragmatism and German philosophy of science converge in the solution of this basic problem of all empiricist philosophy.

If I cannot call Peirce's ideas a satisfactory solution of the problem of induction, it is because he does not give a sufficient foundation for these ideas. To say, first, that continued application of inductive inference must lead to success is correct only on the basis of some presuppositions; the validity of these presuppositions for natural objects cannot be taken for granted. Those presuppositions to which Peirce refers include even the whole calculus of probability as he derives this thesis from the theorem of Bernoulli. This is clear from an exposition of the same idea he gives in another paper.[29] He does not see that, although induction is *confirmed* by mathematical considerations lying *within* the calculus of probability, its *justification* must be given by considerations *outside* the calculus; as the very calculus, in its application to physical objects, presupposes the principle of induction, any other reasoning would be circular. Second, Peirce's idea that induction is justified because if success is possible at all it must be with the help of inductive methods, though it presents a thoroughly sound program, must be *proved* before it can be considered as a solution. I have not found such a proof in Peirce's papers. The proof of this second thesis, which I consider to be the right one, is based on the idea that all kinds of induction are reducible to induction by simple enumeration, an idea contrary to Peirce's conceptions but without which a proof of the thesis in question scarcely could be constructed. This proof therefore presupposes an axiomatic of the theory of probability which shows that this theory can be deduced from the frequency interpretation, without any further presuppositions. Such

---

[29] Peirce, *Collected Papers*, II, 428.

further presuppositions would be assumptions of an "irregularity" of probability series as they are for instance presupposed in the theorem of Bernoulli. The axiomatic constructed by me needs no such presuppositions because all assumptions of this kind, occurring in physical problems, can be tested as to their validity by continued application of the inductive principle. Only after the construction of a theory of induction and probability as sketched in these remarks may we proceed to a foundation of the second idea of Peirce. Combining it with the first idea which, however, we base on nothing but certain properties of the definition of a limit of the frequency, we come to show that we are entitled to say: if success is possible at all it can be obtained by continued application of the principle of induction.

Returning to Dewey's theory of inquiry, I am glad to be able to remark that some ideas developed by myself coincide so well with the general draft of his empiricist program. The problem of induction is no longer a barrier to an empiricist solution of the theory of inquiry; within the frame of a philosophy which definitely abandons the "quest for certainty" and contents itself with "warranted assertibility"—I speak in the same sense of "posits" or "wagers"—the inductive principle can be shown to be our best guide towards predictions of future experiences.

VIII

What is to be the future prospect for an empiricist theory of inquiry? This question may seem pertinent if one of the builders of its present stage is being presented with a survey of the reactions his work has found in the scientific world.

In the foreground of present discussion we still see the analysis of scientific method in terms of probability. Here a good deal of work has already been done. The concept of probability has been analyzed from the mathematical and the logical side. More and more older conceptions of probability as an expression of rational belief are recognized as remnants of philosophic rationalism and are being discarded; in their place the frequency interpretation of probability which has been applied with so much success in all sciences is carried through. The last hidden corners into which a rationalistic interpretation of probability has retired, though under new names, contain problems such as the probability of historical events, and of scientific theories. There seems to me no doubt that the frequency interpretation is able to give an account of the usage of the term "probable" in all these cases. Some attacks directed against this conception have not been able to present any serious objection. Thus it is no objection that in many cases the statistical material we actually possess is not sufficient to permit numerical determinations; all that a logician can be asked for is to indicate, in principle, the way that such statistics can be worked out. I am glad to see that Dewey adheres to the frequency interpretations for both historical facts and scientific theories;[30] some qualifications he adds, referring to insufficiency of actual statistical material, do not seem to modify this general view relevantly. If for instance actual material permits only a statement of the form that the probability *for* an assumption is greater than that *against* it, this determination in the form of an inequality may be improved by further material into a numerical determination of a probability, at least within some serviceable limits. Besides questions of the availability of statistical material there is included in these discussions another problem which may be called the problem of the application of the frequency interpretation to the single case; this problem is solved, I think, by the idea that speaking about the probability of a single case is an elliptic mode of speech translatable into statements about frequencies.[31]

However, there remains still much work to be done. Analysis of scientific method will always remain unsatisfactory as long as it is not accomplished in close connection with actual scientific procedure in all its technicality. In as much as modern physics in particular is intrinsically mathematical, philosophic analysis of modern science cannot be achieved without a profound study of mathematical methods. This is why in our time a qualified philosopher has to be a good mathematician—a maxim which our students of philosophy should note. This applies not only to the analysis of probability; modern logic will remain unintelligible to anyone who did not study the calculus of classes and the methods of modern axiomatics; philosophy of space and

---

[30] *Logic*, 472, 478.
[31] For further explanation of this conception cf. *Experience and Prediction*, 309-312.

time involves a study of differential geometry and the calculus of tensors; philosophy of quantum mechanics demands a profound knowledge of an abstract calculus constructed by mathematical physicists in the pursuit of their inquiry. It is in particular the analysis of this last creation of mathematical physics which promises new insights into the nature of knowledge; problems of the definition of the physical object in its relation to the observer, of the replacement of causal laws by probability laws, of the applicability of macroscopic concepts of space and time to the world of electrons and positrons, including even the applicability of classical logic, are still to be solved. Many a leading physicist has turned a philosopher in his efforts to develop new methods in this field; it is time that philosophers who have turned physicists and mathematicians come to their aid.

The early period of empiricism in which an all-round philosopher could dominate at the same time the fields of scientific method, of history of philosophy, of education and social philosophy, has passed. We enter into the second phase in which highly technical investigations form the indispensable instrument of research, splitting the philosophical campus into specialists of its various branches. We should not regret this unavoidable specialization which repeats on philosophic grounds a phenomenon well known from all the other fields of scientific inquiry. Let us hope that in each of these branches of future philosophy we shall be presented with scientific personalities of the seriousness, the effectiveness, and the caliber of John Dewey.

Hans Reichenbach

Department of Philosophy
University of California at Los Angeles

6

Arthur E. Murphy

DEWEY'S EPISTEMOLOGY AND METAPHYSICS

DEWEY'S EPISTEMOLOGY AND METAPHYSICS

IN HARMONY with Spinoza's observation that Peter's idea of Paul is likely to give us a better notion of Peter than of Paul, it will doubtless be observed that the essays in this volume reflect the preconceptions and interpretative limitations of their authors at least as much as the actual content and implications of Mr. Dewey's philosophy. The danger in such cases is that what is presented as a critical analysis will in fact amount to little more than a translation of what, from the standpoint of an opposing philosophy of questionable validity, Mr. Dewey really must have meant and ought to have said. This risk is not altogether avoidable, for one can only criticize what he takes to be confused and inadequate by reference to clarity and adequacy as he sees them. It can, however, be minimized if the critic states at the outset the standpoint from which his analysis is to be made and the interest that directs it. The reader should then be in a position to consider the interpretation offered explicitly as an hypothesis, to be tested by its success in clarifying a theory which he has, on his own account, been trying to understand.

In the account here presented of Mr. Dewey's theory of knowledge and of nature, primary importance is attached to his insistence on the interpretation and criticism of statements made in terms of their use and testable validity in the contexts in which, prior to either epistemological or metaphysical analysis, they have a discoverable use and meaning. I shall term this reference of ideas to and their testing in specific situations 'contextual analysis.' The name does not particularly matter, but the procedure it calls attention to does, and the name suggested will serve, I think, as well as any other. It appears to me that a contextual analysis and testing of the ideas used in philosophical discussion is the indispensable basis for any adequate theory of either knowledge or nature and that Mr. Dewey in insisting on this fact and sometimes in carrying out the analysis or criticism required, has contributed very substantially to the progress of inquiry in these fields. I propose, therefore, in the first place, to indicate what this method is and what, by its consistent use, we could reasonably expect to find out about knowledge and its place and function in the natural world.

It will be apparent, however, on further investigation, that the results he has actually reached are in many respects not consistent with the theory thus suggested. The non-philosophical inquirer who studies Dewey's theory of 'inquiry' in the *Logic* or of 'experience' in *Experience and Nature* will not find what, on the basis of the prospectus offered, he may well feel he had a right to expect. Instead he will discover that the context in terms of which Mr. Dewey interprets knowledge is one not appropriate to the actual procedures and claims of scientific or practical inquiry, and that his theory of nature is compromised and confused by this fact. It becomes necessary, therefore, to discriminate between those elements in the total theory which can be justified by the method recommended and those which tend to impede its satisfactory use. I believe that this discrimination can be made, that the complications and inconsistencies can then be accounted for by reference to the conditions under which Mr. Dewey's theory developed and the controversies in which it was involved, and that, finally, it can be shown that their elimination leaves the method originally outlined more clearly and reliably usable than it has so far been.

The interpretation thus presented is not offered as an account of what Mr. Dewey really meant, or as a rival theory which might increase its prestige by disposing argumentatively of so formidable a contender for epistemological or metaphysical supremacy. I have not been able to understand Mr. Dewey's philosophy as having any single clear or unequivocal meaning, and I do not suggest that the elements I have selected for favorable attention are any more 'really' or 'ultimately' what the author had in mind than much else that seems inconsistent with them. And it is certainly not my purpose to 'refute' Mr. Dewey. On the contrary, I have learned so much from him that any criticism made will be based, in large part at least, on what, from his own writings, I have come to believe that philosophy ought to be and can be if philosophers take pains to know what they are talking about and to test their theories by reference to situations in which they have a testable meaning. It is in the interest of that sort of philosophy that I have here tried to discriminate those factors in Mr. Dewey's own theories which are permanently useful from those which, as it seems to me, have tended to impede its development.

I

I shall first discuss Mr. Dewey's theory of knowledge since, as will be shown later, it is only in terms of it that the more puzzling features of his empirical metaphysics are to be understood. And here some examination of the use of the term 'epistemology' is at once required. In a common philosophical usage 'epistemology' simply means 'theory of knowledge' or 'philosophical analysis of the nature of knowing and the meaning and criteria of truth.' In this sense, Mr. Dewey not only has an 'epistemology' but gives it a quite fundamental place in his philosophy. He himself, however, has habitually reserved the word 'epistemology' as the designation for a particular sort of theory of knowledge of which he disapproves. This has led to some confusion, and has in particular left him open to the specious objection that he has not been able to avoid 'epistemology,' since he, too, has a theory about knowledge.

The difficulty is easily resolved. There are, on Dewey's view, two main sorts of philosophical accounts of knowledge, the epistemological and the contextual. And he has said quite plainly what the essential difference between these is. For him, as he explains in the first chapter of the *Logic*, 'knowledge' has no meaning independent of inquiry so that "that which satisfactorily terminates inquiry, is by definition, knowledge," while for theories of the type to which he objects "knowledge is supposed to have a meaning of its own apart from connection with and reference to inquiry. The theory of inquiry is then necessarily subordinated to this meaning as a fixed, external end. The opposition between the two views is basic."[1]

This distinction seems to me quite fundamental. Any stu-

[1] *Logic*, 8.

dent of the theory of knowledge is acquainted with the interminable and inconclusive controversies which arise when the disputants start with incompatible, but presumably quite evident, notions of what knowing must really be and then proceed to test the validity of all knowledge-claims by reference to or derivation from what is thus really known. If the datum in knowledge must always be other than the 'real' object which is the true objective of knowing, since all knowing involves transcendence, then of course all knowing is indirect and we are 'epistemological dualists.' If, on the other hand, it is quite evident to us that real knowing must be a grasp of being itself as this is directly 'present to the mind,' then epistemological monism, according to which the real object is itself the given, is the doctrine to be accepted. Such theories are admirably suited to dialectical elaboration and defense against opponents, since the partisan of either view has only to assume the validity of his own definition of knowing in his criticism of his opponent in order to show that the theory criticized either denies the possibility of 'knowledge,' so defined, and thus reduces to scepticism or else, when its 'real' meaning is seen, reduces to his own theory and thus reluctantly and against its will testifies to the essential truth. Since this procedure is open to each of the contestants, if he is sufficiently tenacious in his insistence on his original stipulation, the controversy is in principle endless. Its defect is that it has, as experience has shown, very little connection with what reliable knowing shows itself to be outside the limits and stipulations of the debate, and in terms of the methods by means of which, in the sciences and in practical life, grounded knowledge is distinguished from unsubstantial and unsubstantiated opinion. Hence if we are to get any light on the nature of knowing as it operates in these cases, and to provide the sort of philosophical clarification that is urgently needed of some of the notions that are involved in it, we shall have to turn our attention away from the debate and find out in the first place what such knowing is, what the claims made for it mean in use, and how they are tested in the context of their primary and reliable application. And since it is by inquiry and investigation that most reliable knowledge is acquired, it is to inquiry that we must go to find out what it is.

'Epistemology,' in Dewey's usage, is a designation for theories of knowledge that neglect this essential reference.

Theories of knowledge that constitute what are now called epistemologies have arisen because knowledge and obtaining knowledge have not been conceived in terms of the operations by which, in the continuum of experiential inquiry, stable beliefs are progressively obtained and utilized. Because they are not constructed upon the ground of operations and conceived in terms of their actual procedures and consequences, they are necessarily formed in terms of preconceptions derived from various sources, mainly cosmological in ancient and mainly psychological (directly or indirectly) in modern theory.[2]

The alternative proposed is simply, in the first instance, a reference back to the specific situations in which a difference between true and false beliefs can reliably be made out, and a careful account of what, in these situations, the meaning and validity of various truth claims is found to be. We shall only then be in a position to indulge in philosophical criticism or synthesis.

I shall follow Dewey, in this paper, in describing theories of the first type as 'epistemological' and shall designate as 'contextual' those that belong in the second group. I do not want to suggest, as Dewey seems at times to do, that all accounts of knowledge prior to his own have been primarily of the epistemological type. There is much careful observation and substantial wisdom in Locke's theory of knowledge, in Spinoza's, and in those of Aristotle and Aquinas, and much that the most up to date devotee of 'contextualism' might with much profit learn from them. There is, however, a persistent tendency in theories of knowledge to lose touch with the situations in which knowledge-getting occurs and to substitute a dialectical elaboration of the 'real' nature of knowledge for a contextual examination of the specific manner of functioning and meaning in use of the processes and claims of inquiry. In the period during which Mr. Dewey's own philosophy was developed this tendency reached an unhappy maximum in idealistic theories of 'thought' and its relation to 'reality' and in the great debate among the realists about the real or true object of knowledge

[2] *Ibid.*, 534-5.

and the essential nature of the mind's relation to it. To have insisted on the essential sterility of these theories and the need for philosophy to get into touch once more with the facts of knowledge-getting and testing was a needed contribution to the subject and one that Mr. Dewey has made in quite decisive fashion.

Stated summarily, the standpoint for a philosophical analysis of knowledge by reference to the contexts in which various knowledge-claims have meaning and testable validity in use is substantially this: (1) The philosopher has no special access to the nature of knowledge or of reality, or to the circumstances of their relation to each other. The knowledge-claims that it is his business to examine, understand, and unify so far as possible into a comprehensible whole, occur in the first instance in non-philosophical activities and are to be understood by reference to their rôle in such activities. (2) These activities are various and are concerned not with reality as such or as a whole, but with those aspects or features of the world which are relevant to the particular requirements of the activity in question. (3) A reference to the circumstances under which, in the course of such activities, truth-claims are made and tested, is essential for an understanding of their meaning. To suppose that the statements in which the results of inquiry are summed up can retain their meaning when they are used for other purposes and in other contexts than those of their primary application is quite unwarranted, and leads to confusing results, as when, for instance, the validity of common sense statements is philosophically 'criticized' as though they were claims to a sort of knowledge with which, in their ordinary and reliable use, they are not at all concerned, or scientific knowledge is treated as a highly inadequate attempt to characterize reality as a whole and is thus, in its own nature, essentially defective. (4) It is, none the less, philosophically legitimate and important to discover how far what can be found out by any one method of inquiry is relevant to what, on other grounds, we have reason to believe, and especially to our beliefs about what, in the sort of world we live in, is humanly possible and desirable. If 'metaphysics' were simply an inclusive and necessarily provisional estimate of the place and prospects of human experience and aspirations within the natural world, then an empirical metaphysics would be a meaningful and useful investigation.

In some aspects of his philosophy, celebrated elsewhere in this volume, Mr. Dewey has given us this sort of theory. In the theory of knowledge, however, his position is much less clear. To see its significance we had best turn directly to his latest and most comprehensive account of the nature of knowledge, in the *Logic*.

Knowledge, as already noted, is to be understood as the appropriate outcome of inquiry. What, then, is inquiry? The answer to this question does not take us, as it should, to such specific sorts of inquiry as serve in practice as our means of finding out about the 'antecedent' environment or the consequences of human behavior in it. It refers us instead to a theory about the rôle of ideas as instruments to be used in so altering a present indeterminate situation that an enjoyed future experience, itself non-cognitive but worth while on its own account, will reliably ensue, through the use of procedures which have proved their instrumental value in this capacity. The ultimate objective of knowing is held in all cases to be such an existential transformation of the subject-matter of knowledge, and the only object to which ideas ultimately refer is the experienced outcome of this transformation, as this is later to be 'had' or immediately experienced. This does not seem, *prima facie*, to correspond to the intent of knowing or the manner of its use and validation in many sorts of inquiry, and a closer examination will tend to confirm the suspicion that the discrepancy is a radical one. I propose to examine this discrepancy as it first enters into and complicates Dewey's theory of 'inquiry,' and to show how the confusions it engenders are explained by the antecedent epistemological entanglements in which his notion of the relation of ideas to experience and of cognitive inquiry to practice is involved.

"Inquiry," Mr. Dewey tell us, "is the controlled or directed transformation of an indeterminate situation into one that is so determinate in its constituent distinctions and relations as to convert the elements of the original situation into a unified whole."[3] The appropriate outcome of inquiry is a judgment "warrantably assertible" as following validly from the correct use of appropriate methods, but the objective of this judgment is simply the reconstitution of the situation in which thinking arose as response to the indeterminate or doubtful, in such wise that a final state of determinate resolution and unification is achieved.[4] Propositions about matters of fact or possible courses of action are used in the process of reaching the final judgment and resolution. But these

are neither self-determined nor self-sufficient. They are determined with reference to an intended future issue and hence are instrumental and intermediate. They are not valid in and of themselves, for their validity depends upon the consequences which ensue from acting upon them—as far as these consequences actually ensue from the operations the propositions dictate and are not accidental accretions.[5]

All thought contains a practical factor, "an activity of doing and making which reshapes antecedent existential material which sets the problem of inquiry,"[6] and since the ultimate reference of the ideas involved in this reshaping is to the reconstruction to be achieved, "The ultimate ground of every valid proposition and warranted judgment consists in some existential reconstruction ultimately effected."[7]

Mr. Dewey's development of this theory is accompanied by many illustrations of the way in which inquiry and investigation do alter antecedent situations by bringing to light facts and suggesting hypotheses relevant to the problem being investigated and are thus instrumental to finding out whatever it was that the investigator was previously in doubt about. Equally important in his exposition is the manner in which knowledge once attained is instrumental to further and non-cognitive interests, not least among them the interest in enjoying the outcome of knowing in a cleared-up situation as something worth having on its own account. Of the antecedents in preliminary analysis, hypothesis and the like, and of the consequences of

[3] *Logic,* 104-5.
[4] *Ibid.,* 134.
[5] *Ibid.,* 164.
[6] *Ibid.,* 160.
[7] *Ibid.,* 489.

knowing for many other humanly desirable ends Mr. Dewey has a great deal that is enlightening to say. But at the center of the theory there remains an ambiguity that is likely to puzzle even those most anxious to profit by its teachings. One's natural tendency is to suppose that what the ideas used and the analyses performed in the course of inquiry are instrumental to is finding out whatever it is that the particular inquirer was investigating, which might be immediate experience, or unperceived antecedent existence, or the structure of some purely hypothetical logical system, or anything else, existent or non-existent, which can in any way be investigated. And similarly we are inclined to suppose that the worth of knowledge for improving man's estate, or ushering in immediate experiences non-cognitively enjoyed, though enjoyed as the fruit of previous cognition, is essentially distinct from its worth as knowledge, as true belief about its own intended object in the sense that what it asserts to be so is so and is based on adequate evidence or arrived at by a method which leads reliably to true conclusions. Something of this sort seems to be presupposed in inquiry as ordinarily pursued. If we look for its equivalent, however, in Mr. Dewey's description of inquiry, we shall be at a loss to find it.

The most puzzling feature of this instrumental theory of knowledge is that, in the picture of inquiry it offers, knowing, in the sense in which it was understood in the preceding paragraph, seems not to occur at all. There are steps that would ordinarily be thought of as leading up to it—the 'jam tomorrow' stage in which experienced events are not simply known on their own account but are used as signs, or instruments, or evidence for something else that is *to be known*. And there are steps leading away from it, the 'jam yesterday' stage, at which the use of what is *already* known as a means for the attainment of some further satisfaction is stressed. But what, on the ordinary view, ought to occupy the central place between these two processes and to lend its significance to both, is just not there. It was Mr. Lovejoy, I believe, who observed that "I am about to have known" is the appropriate pragmatic equivalent for "I know." The comment, as applied to Mr. Dewey's theory, is enlightening.

It must not, of course, be supposed that this result is due to any inadvertence on Mr. Dewey's part. It means simply that if he is right, what I referred to as the 'ordinary' view of knowing is in need of further analysis, and that when this is supplied the apparent reference to antecedent existence, to a cognitive validity of truth-claims essentially distinct from their efficacy in reconstructing experience, is replaced by a reference of ideas to future experience and to the means for so altering a present situation that a desired and anticipated future will reliably ensue. I am not at present concerned to deny that this is what knowledge 'really' is, or that the ultimate objective of knowing may be what he takes it to be. Any decision on these points depends so largely on antecedent epistemological commitments that it is not, on the whole, a matter for fruitful discussion. It is important, however, to observe that this is not what knowing is 'known as' when we take it for what it shows itself to be in physical, historical or sociological research and that the attempt to understand these activities in terms of the theory that Mr. Dewey has offered is more fruitful of epistemological controversy, in the disparaging sense in which he uses that term, than of philosophical enlightenment.

The particular issues that will serve best to illustrate the contrast between the theory of knowledge which a contextual analysis would appear to require and that to which Mr. Dewey, as a result of previous epistemological commitments, has been led, are those which concern the true or ultimate object of cognition and the relation of cognition to other and non-cognitive modes or access to reality. It will appear, I believe, that his discussion of these issues is not intelligible until we refer it back to the idealistic and realistic philosophies in relation and opposition to which it was developed, and that while it can be controversially justified as an alternative to them, its fruits in contextual application are of questionable value.

In *The Quest for Certainty*, Mr. Dewey has insisted at length that the assumption that "the true and valid object of knowledge is that which has being prior to and independent of the operations of knowing" is unwarranted and that on the contrary, "the true object of knowledge resides in the consequences of directed action."[8] This is held to be particularly

---
[8] *The Quest for Certainty*, 196.

true and important in the case of the sciences, where it must be seen that "scientific conceptions are not a revelation of prior and independent reality,"[9] but that, on the contrary, "scientific men accepted the *consequences* of their experimental operations as constituting the known object,"[10] and cared nothing for an antecedent archetypal reality.

What precisely do these statements mean? In the procedure of inquiry, whether into the structure of the atom, the cause of infantile paralysis, or, if anyone is interested to investigate, the batting averages of all members of the New York Yankees baseball team in 1921, the true object of knowledge is surely just whatever it is that the inquirer wants to find out about. That antecedent being, as it existed prior to the operations of inquiry, can in this sense be a true and legitimate object of knowledge and even an archetype in so far as knowledge of it must conform to what it was, if it is to be the truth about it, seems not really doubtful. It is of course true that antecedent existence is not *the* true and valid object of knowledge, the only or exclusive one. On this point we should be inclined to say, if we came at the matter directly, that the question as to *the* true object of knowledge is a puerile one, since anything whatever can be *an* object of knowledge if there is any humanly possible way of finding out about it and if anyone is interested in finding out, and that the attempt to set up any such object as preeminently the true or genuine article is inspired by such extraneous moral or epistemological considerations as, e.g., that it is something important or desirable to know about or that it is what we must *really* be knowing if somebody's theory of knowledge is the true one. The objects of science are any objects about which the sciences can give us reliable information; and that some scientific conceptions *are* revelations of a prior and independent reality in that, by the use of them, true and warranted statements can be made about events and objects that existed before cognitive situations ever occurred and independent of such situations, is, I should think, as sure as anything can be in this uncertain world.

The inquirer interested in understanding what scientists are

[9] *Ibid.*, 165.
[10] *Ibid.*, 185.

talking about, how their various theories and conceptions are instrumental to finding out, in an approximate but on the whole reliable way what is going on, has gone on and is likely to go on in the world, and what sort of evidence is available for testing statements made on these matters, will get no light from a discussion of the "true" object of knowledge. And when he discovers that Mr. Dewey, in order to emphasize the experimental and operational nature of scientific concepts, is forced to assert that these conceptions do not 'ultimately' refer to past events, or indeed to anything but the empirically observable consequences of acting upon them, he is likely to be more confused than enlightened.

Why should Mr. Dewey have introduced such claims into his theory of knowledge? The answer is to be found not in the nature of scientific procedure but in that of Mr. Dewey's antecedent quarrel with a "spectator theory of knowledge." He defined the issue quite clearly in his *Essays in Experimental Logic.*

The new realism finds that it [thinking] is instrumental simply to knowledge of objects. From this it infers (with perfect correctness and inevitableness) that thinking (including all the operations of discovery and testing as they might be set forth in an inductive logic) is a mere psychological preliminary, utterly irrelevant to any conclusions regarding the nature of objects known. The thesis of the essays is that thinking is instrumental to a control of the environment, a control effected through acts which would not be undertaken without the prior resolution of a complex situation into assured elements and an accompanying projection of possibilities—without, that is to say, thinking.[11]

Whether or not this characterization of the new realist's position is adequate is not here important. The essential fact is that when thinking is held to be instrumental to a knowledge of 'reality' this 'reality' is thought of by Dewey as something that is supposed to be known antecedently to and independently of the processes by means of which scientific investigation takes place. The 'spectator' theory of knowledge thus stands in his mind for the view that we can know things by passively contemplating them or accepting preconceived ideas about them as adequate bases for conclusions as to their essential natures. It follows of course that scientific method, with its experimental

[11] *Essays in Experimental Logic,* 30.

manipulation of given data and constant modification of antecedently accepted ideas, is out of harmony with any such theory of knowledge. If this be knowledge of antecedent being, then neither scientific method nor experimental logic gives such knowledge.

It is clear, I think, that if we want to understand Mr. Dewey's puzzling denial of what seems, on the face of it, the obvious import of some reliably tested knowledge-claims, we must think of him as referring to theories of this sort. His statements are simply not comprehensible apart from such reference. That is why, after burying the spectator theory of knowledge in one volume after another, he has been obliged to dig it up again in subsequent works to justify by contrast his own insistence that *the* true object of knowledge is not only got at by experimental methods but simply *is* the observable outcome of such experimental procedures. But while this is intelligible, in terms of the controversy in question, it is not at all helpful as a characterization of the actual aims of experimental science, where it is not simply what will happen when an experiment is performed that is in question, but also what evidence this supplies about the nature and behavior of other objects which may themselves be beyond the range of observation but can be known about by means of experimental evidence. Mr. Dewey evidently does not mean to deny that in some sense we have such knowledge, but he does insist on stating the nature and aims of knowing in such fashion as to make any clear analysis of it impossible. And this is done because a straightforward statement suggests to him, though it does not by any means imply, an epistemological theory which he is extremely anxious to avoid. The epistemological controversy has thus impeded and confused the contextual analysis that was wanted.

A related matter on which Mr. Dewey finds it very important to insist is the falsity of the assumption "that knowledge has a uniquely privileged position as a mode of access to reality in comparison with other modes of experience."[12] Actually, things can be 'had' in immediate experience, as well as known, and in such 'having' "we experience things as they really are apart from knowing" while knowing is that *special* mode of

---

[12] *The Quest for Certainty*, 106.

experiencing things "which facilitates control of objects for purposes of non-cognitive experiences."[18] Cognition thus is not, as philosophers have in the past assumed, "the measure of the reality found in other modes of experience," and an insistence on this fact is held to be of great significance.

The difficulty one finds in understanding these passages, and many others like them in Dewey, is that knowledge or cognition appears to be used in them in two different but not adequately distinguished senses. Referred to ordinary operations of investigation, knowledge consists of true statements or beliefs arrived at by a reliable method. The cognitive interest is that in the acquisition and adequate testing of such beliefs; and nothing can be directly relevant to the cognitive goodness of a belief or the satisfaction of the interest in knowing except that which tends to confirm or confute the belief in question by serving as evidence of the nature of its object.

It is only because some connection with this meaning for knowledge and the tests of its validity is carried over into Mr. Dewey's discussion that it retains its appearance of pertinence to inquiry in the sciences and practical affairs. But at the same time this is not what Mr. Dewey himself, in his specific epistemological analyses, takes knowing to be. Instead, as we have already seen, he regards it as a use of ideas as signs of possible future experiences and means for effecting the transition to such experiences in a satisfactory manner. These future experiences, in so far as they terminate inquiry, will not be cases of 'knowing,' i.e., of the use of given experiences as signs of something else. Hence what justifies cognition is not anything in the same sense 'known' at all, but the occurrence of a non-cognitive satisfaction, and the goodness of cognition in its own primary aim or intent, is determined by its use in bringing about such experiences.

Each of these accounts is intelligible enough in itself, but when we try to apply to non-philosophical inquiry the results reached on the epistemological level, confusions arise which have always surrounded the 'instrumental' theory of knowledge. Are we actually to suppose that the validity of ordinary truth-claims as true is to be determined by something else than

[18] *Ibid.*, 98.

what we can find out as to the nature of their objects, or that we are to regard as evidence of their truth the fact they are instrumental to non-cognitive satisfactions? And does the claim that we have non-cognitive access to 'reality' mean that we have any way of finding out what really exists or is the case, that is not, just in so far as it *is* a way of finding out, a way of knowing or of cognition? Of course we are related to our environment in many other ways than framing and testing beliefs about it. We 'grasp reality' in seeing and handling perceptual objects, in enjoying good health and in doing all manner of things that are not knowing, and may be more satisfactory than knowing. But if the question arises as to what, in any of these ways of experiencing or behaving we *find out* about 'reality,' the only possible answer is a 'cognitive' one, namely, in the first place a statement of what these experiences are, what, other than themselves they are evidence for and how they are relevant to the rest of what, in our various relations with it, we find the world to be. If "practice" reveals the nature of 'reality' in any significant sense, it is surely because we find out something through our practical relations with things that we should not otherwise have known. And similarly, if, as Dewey maintains, we experience things as they really are apart from knowing, this is itself something that can be known, where 'knowing' is not a reference to some future experience later to be noncognitively enjoyed as a result of present intellectual operations, but a true belief, tested by inspection of the very experiences in question, as to what these experiences are. Mr. Dewey himself makes many statements about immediate experience that he evidently regards as verifiably true in this sense.

In all this, however, we are putting 'cognition' in a context other than that to which his own analysis refers. If cognizing is only what, for epistemological purposes, he takes it to be, then there *are* ways of finding out about objects, e.g., observing our own immediate experiences and making a true report of them, which are not 'cognitive,' since they are not ways of using the experiences in question as signs of future experiences. We then have 'access to reality' which is not 'cognitive' but nevertheless is a source of information about its intended object. And we have a goodness of ideas in the instrumental sense which bears no clear relation to their goodness as evidence for or information about the objects of which they purport to supply knowledge, but which nevertheless is somehow intended as an equivalent for truth in the more usual sense.

The controversy about pragmatism or instrumentalism has always been a particularly unrewarding one, in which neither party seemed at all able to understand what the other was saying, and any criticism offered from a non-pragmatic standpoint was rejected by the pragmatists as a misrepresentation. It is not my purpose to revive that controversy. What I want to point out is that its inconclusiveness and the misunderstandings on both sides were due to the fact that what Mr. Dewey says about cognition is true of it as he defines it, and false of it as more ordinarily understood, and that the attempt to interpret what he has to say in terms of the ordinary use of the term 'truth' leads only to ambiguity. The truth-relation on his view is that of an idea to a future experience, when the idea is intended to suggest a way of behaving that will lead the thinker, if he acts upon it, to enjoy that future experience, and the goodness of an idea in that connection *is* its capacity to serve reliably for the purpose intended. The question of its truth in any other sense does not arise, and it is the essence of this extremely ingenious theory to see to it that it shall not arise. Once admitted into Mr. Dewey's epistemological universe of discourse, the critic will find himself quite unable to make the objection he had intended. It will be quite impossible to 'know' immediate experience as it is in its own qualitative being, since to know anything is not to attend to it on its own account, but to use it as a sign of something else. Yet immediate experience will provide 'access to reality,' indeed, our only first-hand approach to it. Hence the claims of non-cognitive experience to epistemological primacy. And when ideas are used cognitively their intent as cognitive, as instruments for the resolution of an indeterminate situation, will be to eventuate and find their justification in something not in the same sense known at all. The subtlety with which this theory has been developed is of the highest order.

The crucial question is, however, for what was it devised, and for what is it useful? As an analysis of the interest and criteria of knowing in non-philosophical research it is not really helpful, for the terms in which it is stated and the assumptions on which it is based are not comprehensible except in relation to epistemological controversies on a quite different level, and when applied directly to the ordinary business of truth-seeking, result in endless misunderstanding. But if one recalls the idealism out of which Dewey's theory developed, the situation is altered. The limitation that Mr. Dewey puts on 'cognition' and his insistence that it is to be justified by its furtherance of interests and satisfactions not in the same sense cognitive are the direct result of his rejection of his idealistic antecedents, and find their explanation in their relation to it.

In objective idealism 'thought' had long since been divorced from the ordinary business of acquiring information. For reasons with which every student of epistemology will be familiar, thought had come to be regarded as a kind of construction, having its point of departure in immediate experience but transcending such experience in its search for an object that would fully satisfy thought's own demand for completeness and consistency. The cognitive interest was just this interest in systematic completeness and coherence, and proofs were not lacking that 'Reality' must correspond to our ideas, satisfy the demands of thought, and the like.

The pragmatic revolt against this idealism was a thoroughly salutary one. Thinking, we were told, was to have its test not simply in meeting its own demands for consistency, but in meeting the demands of the situations in which it arose. This reference to 'actual situations,' which the *Studies in Logical Theory* brought to the center of philosophical discussion, was intended to correct the arbitrariness and isolation of a 'thought' 'absolute and self-inclosed' and to place the tests of thinking in its capacity to serve other ends than its own. That 'cognition,' in the sense *in which the idealists had understood it,* is 'mediate' essentially and finds its justification in its relation to specific situations, is surely true. But that what justifies cognition is its relation to the objects, or facts, or events or whatever else, by its means, we can find out about was not, for Dewey, a live alternative. He was still too much of an idealist to refer directly from thought to its object. The reference was instead to immediate experience, to 'practice' and, in general, to the satisfaction of other interests than knowing. The result was that, in denying the right of 'thought' to lay down its own laws as to what 'reality' must be and insisting on its essential responsibility to something beyond mere thinking, he was impelled to maintain the essential dependence of 'cognition' for its validity on its capacity to satisfy 'non-cognitive' demands. Such is the primary basis of 'instrumentalism.'

A position arrived at as a modification of idealism proved further useful in eliminating all reference to 'antecedent,' 'transempirical,' and otherwise undesirable objects on which the realists were by this time insisting. In the reflective situation as Dewey defines it no such reference occurs, for the only object an idea can be about is that empirically attainable future to which it serves as a guide. As a means of avoiding questions which, given this definition of knowledge, it would be difficult to answer, it is a model of its kind. But that kind is precisely the kind called by Mr. Dewey 'epistemology,' the kind that stipulates on grounds (mainly psychological in modern philosophy) what knowing is to be, and acknowledges only those operations which can be fitted into its pattern: the preliminary operation in which data are manipulated for use as evidence and the consequent operation in which the results of knowledge are used for the benefit of man's estate, but not the central and primary operation which is the finding out, on the basis of evidence, of those reliably ascertainable conclusions which can be used in a subsequent practical reconstruction because, on their own account, they constitute knowledge of the 'situation' to which they refer.

We have now to assess the consequences of this view for an understanding of 'knowledge,' and an adequate theory of its nature. These will have to be judged on two levels. So far as the epistemological controversy is concerned, the theory is a formidable one. Once inside the 'reflective situation' as Dewey describes it, there is no escape from his conclusions, and there are persuasive considerations that recommend such an analysis as opposed to those of its rivals. It is 'empirical,' 'practical,' even 'operational' and these are all terms of praise in the market-place of current discussion. The view can be 'refuted,' of course, as it has been many times, but the refutations proceed from assumptions about knowledge which have their own difficulties and whose results are in many respects out of harmony with facts to which Mr. Dewey and his followers can legitimately refer for support.

When the test is made, however, by reference to the measure in which the theory enables us to understand better and test more justly the knowledge-claims that are made in the course of non-epistemological inquiries, the result is a less favorable one. This does not mean that Mr. Dewey has not made valuable contributions to the subject. No one, certainly, has been at more pains to draw from the procedures of experimental science material illustrative of the thesis he is defending, or to insist that the test of any such theory must be found in its application to the actual subject. This interest in application, and in experimental procedures gives Mr. Dewey's *Logic* a solid content which more orthodox treatises on the subject rarely possess. He has shown us the environment, physical, biological, and social, in which such inquiry has to operate, and thus provided useful and philosophically relevant information about it. There are very few epistemological theories in the current crop of which as much can be said.

The difficulties that persist in any consistent attempt to apply his theory in contextual analysis or criticism of knowledge, however, are two. The first is an inescapable vagueness, a tendency to see all around the specific object, but never to focus clearly on the object itself. The suggestion that this is the effect of Mr. Dewey's manner of expressing himself is quite misguided. On the contrary, he has said just what, in terms of his epistemology, he *ought* to say, with great skill. The point rather is that his theory focuses attention exclusively on the antecedents and consequences of knowing. Hence when we try to fix our gaze on the object, logical, scientific, or qualitative, as itself an object of knowledge, what at a distance seemed substantial enough becomes diffused and spreads out over its immediate neighborhood. And when we insist on locating it more exactly, we are met by statements not about *it* at all, or our means of finding out about it, but rather about the inaccessibility of an 'antecedent' or archetypal reality, the futility of 'self-enclosed' thought, and the value of thinking as a means of enriching the life of men. It then becomes apparent that the theory is afflicted with epistemological strabismus, that one eye has been fixed all the time on the defects of opposing theories, and that the specific nature of cognitive inquiry has, in consequence, been blurred.

The second difficulty in application arises not in understanding the various knowledge-claims made but in estimating their validity. Since all thinking is 'practical,' according to Dewey, and all is justified by the reconstitution of experience it is instrumental in achieving, we should expect to judge of the 'worth' of thinking by its results. But here it is important to distinguish between the goodness of knowing for its own primary objective *as knowing* and its goodness as a means to other ends. It is, again, of the essence of Dewey's theory that it prevents us from making this distinction in any clear way. Intellectual inquiry is practical in that it involves making choices, manipulating materials, testing hypotheses, and so far as the inquiry is successful, changing the situation in which the investigator is doubtful into one in which his mind is at rest on the point at issue. Hence "the conduct of scientific inquiry, whether physical or mathematical, is a mode of *practice;* the working scientist is a practitioner above all else, and is constantly engaged in making practical judgments: decisions as to what to do and what means to employ in doing it."[14]

Yet it is quite evident that the outcome of all this 'practice' may be a well grounded theory which is not 'practical' in the sense that it has the least use in or relevance for any further ends, and, in particular, for those that are socially significant or regarded by wise and good men as of primary importance. Whether all knowledge that a man with a social conscience ought to permit himself to pursue must be in this *further* sense 'practical' is a genuine moral question, but it is not the same at all as the question whether the 'practice' involved in his in-

[14] *Logic,* 161.

quiry itself has justified, i.e., verified or given grounds for believing in the truth of, the hypothesis with which he was working. There is, then, a practice intrinsic to knowledge-getting, and a 'practice' to which it may or may not be relevant, and which is of much moment for its moral or social worth but need be of none at all—unless the hypothesis happened to be about social uses and worth—in testing its truth.

This distinction is, in our own time, of some importance. For earnest men in a hurry are likely to be impatient of inquiries whose relevance to their own socially reconstructive aims is not apparent. If they are encouraged to confuse the practical value of such inquiries for the ends which they take to be of primary importance, with their cognitive validity, they will inevitably judge them unfairly and make utility for the furtherance of their preferred interests the final measure of what is actually true about the world.

That Mr. Dewey himself intends to subordinate scientific method to more immediate social interests is not even plausible enough as a suggestion to make its denial important. No one in this generation has done more than he to celebrate the value of scientific thinking or to discredit attempts to subordinate the pursuit of truth by its means to ulterior interests. But that is precisely because he believes that scientific method is 'practical' in the social and moral sense as well. When he comes to deal with intellectual inquiries of whose relevance to the interests he regards as important he is less convinced, his position is a more dubious one. In a recent contribution to the *International Encyclopedia of Unified Science*, he has drawn a sharp line between those types of inquiry that manifest a scientific attitude and are therefore, in his view, to be approved, and those that do not. And one of the bases for distinguishing a scientific from an unscientific attitude is stated as follows:

Above all, it [the scientific attitude] is the attitude which is rooted in the problems that are set and questions that are raised by the conditions of actuality. The unscientific attitude is that which shuns such problems, which runs away from them, or covers them up instead of facing them. And experience shows that this evasion is the counterpart of concern with artificial problems and alleged ready-made solutions. For all problems are artificial which do not grow, even if indirectly, out of the conditions under which life, including associated living, is carried on.[15]

Now, even artificial problems have presumably grown somehow, since some people are concerned with them, and if the conditions of living are not accountable for them, this must be because 'living' is here used in a eulogistic sense, to refer to such conditions as Mr. Dewey thinks are important. Either all problems whatever arise in conditions of life and actuality since they do actually arise in the life history of human beings, or else 'life' and 'actuality' stand for the conditions in which *important* problems arise, or those we *ought* to take account of. And when we recall that it was the cognitive goodness of scientific method that was in question here, as opposed e.g. to that of the sort of metaphysics and compensatory religious belief of which Mr. Dewey disapproves, we can see how fatally easy it is to make relevance to conditions felt to be important a primary criterion of the goodness of knowledge as knowledge.

With Mr. Dewey's valuations on this subject I have no quarrel. But with his tendency to make such valuation the test of what is valid as knowledge, I have. The essential fact is that where the distinction between the value of an idea as a means for discovering the truth has been confused with its value as a means for subserving interests felt on other grounds to be important, there is simply no basis left for an independent estimate of truth as such. Mr. Dewey's theory, however liberal its intentions, does involve this confusion and does therefore in practice leave all claims to knowledge at the mercy of ulterior preconceptions about what is 'actual,' 'living,' or 'socially significant.' The theory would be sounder and more useful with this epistemological confusion eliminated.

II

The term 'metaphysics,' like 'epistemology,' has often in recent years been used in a derogatory sense. But on this point Dewey does not as a rule adopt the current fashion. In *Experi-*

[15] *International Encyclopedia of Unified Science,* Vol. I, No. I, 31.

ence and Nature, he takes metaphysics as "a statement of the generic traits manifested by existences of all kinds without regard to their differentiation into physical and mental,"[16] and maintains that an adequate metaphysic can supply a ground-map of the province of criticism. To note, for example, that contingency is a pervasive trait of natural events, and to bring this fact into connection with concrete situations of life, is to provide a metaphysical basis for value judgments. And, in general,

the more sure one is that the world which encompasses human life is of such and such a character (no matter what his definition), the more one is committed to try to direct the conduct of life, that of others as well as of himself, upon the basis of the character assigned to the world.[17]

The understanding of man with his wants and hopes and limited capacities as a factor in the natural world out of which the human organism has developed and with which, in even its loftiest flights, the human spirit remains essentially continuous, is then the primary task for this metaphysics, and one which, as Mr. Dewey rightly observed, would provide a sound basis for that criticism of values and meanings with which philosophy in his view is primarily concerned.

In one sense this is a very modest project. "This is the extent and method of my metaphysics: the large and constant features of human sufferings, enjoyments, trials, failures and successes together with the institutions of art, science, technology, politics and religion which mark them, communicate genuine features of the world within which man lives."[18] No more 'transcendent' reality than the world of natural events is referred to, and the situation of human experience within nature provides the limited but reliable basis on which this 'empirical naturalism' is to be built.

In another sense, however, the task that Mr. Dewey has set himself is more arduous than that of traditional metaphysics. For he proposes to use an empirical method throughout, and this has by no means usually been the procedure in these matters.

[16] *Experience and Nature,* 412.
[17] *Ibid.,* 413-4.
[18] *Journal of Philosophy,* Vol. XXIV, 59.

In concrete experience

things present themselves in characteristic contexts, with different savors, colors, weights, tempos and directions. Experience as method warns us to give impartial attention to all of these diversifications. Non-empirical method sets out with the assumption that some one of these groupings of things is privileged, that it is supreme of its own right, that it furnishes a standard by which to measure the significance and real quality of everything else.[19]

This seems to me a remarkably sound and important point. The word 'empirical' is perhaps not happy in this connection, but there is no need to argue over terminology. The fact, which badly needed emphasis, and which in the passage quoted admirably receives it, is that we do come at things in a variety of contexts and that while each of these reveals the 'real' nature of things as thus discovered, there is no good reason to believe that any one among them provides a unique approach to 'reality' as such, or a preferentially ultimate basis for metaphysics. The attempt to discover a reality thus ultimate and inclusive, to which all that in any fashion we find out about the world must be referred if we are to understand its kind and degree of 'reality,' whether this be 'matter' or 'mind,' God or Nature, the Absolute or the inevitable dialectical development of history, has not proved, on the whole, an enlightening one. The 'reality' discovered is always at best an aspect of the world for which it is supposed to provide the final explanation, and to attempt to unify all experience by reference to or derivation from this metaphysical ultimate will finally confuse our notion of the world and leave us vainly trying to connect this 'reality' with what, on other and more substantial grounds we know to be the case. It is no wonder that 'metaphysics,' thus understood, has fallen into disrepute. Mr. Dewey's attempt to provide a basis for philosophical criticism by reference to the pervasive features of existence which are found alike in human experience and striving and in the world of events with which that striving is inevitably bound up, and to do this without recourse to metaphysical simplification of the sort he condemns as 'non-empirical,' is an uncommonly hopeful and promising one.

[19] *Experience and Nature,* 15.

The title of his principal work on metaphysics, *Experience and Nature*, indicates the point of departure for his theory. Its center is the human situation, as this is disclosed in the whole course of our experience of or commerce with the world. The essential fact is that "this human situation falls wholly within nature. It reflects the traits of nature, it gives indisputable evidence that in nature itself qualities and relations, individualities and uniformities, finalities and efficacies, contingencies and necessities are inextricably bound together."[20] Experience is continuous with the rest of nature in that it is both a consequence of purely natural (physical, biological and social) interactions and also a fair sample of what natural events really are. The pervasive traits of human experience are traits of nature itself and can be used in metaphysics as a guide to its character. "Man fears because he exists in a fearful, an awful world. The *world* is precarious and perilous."[21] And so, as Dewey has so frequently insisted, the indeterminate situation which elicits thought and requires reflection for its adequate resolution is as objective as any other natural situation. A change in it is brought about in a satisfactory and reliable way only when we have altered factors in the environment, not merely our feelings or beliefs about it. Thought in its dealing with the doubtful or precarious is itself a development within the natural world, and the changes it initiates are as 'real' as a thunderstorm or an earthquake and as genuinely, though not as a rule as catastrophically, effective in altering the world of nature.

In academic discussion, this view has sometimes been described as 'objective relativism,' in order to stress the fact that the experienced world is *at once* in some of its major features dependent on and conditioned by the special relations in which sentient (and more particularly human) organisms stand to their environment *and also* a direct presentation of that environment itself, or the order of natural events, as it is under such conditions. Nature is not something essentially beyond the range of perceptual inspection, having its exclusive being in characters independent of all relation to human responses to it. Far more in the natural world than we can ever experience

[20] *Ibid.*, 421.
[21] *Ibid.*, 42.

there certainly is and must be. But unless what we experience *also* belongs to and is, under the special but entirely natural conditions of organic interaction, a sample of the nature to which we claim to refer, then our relation to this ulterior nature becomes problematic, and the conditions of interaction which are in fact our means of getting in touch with it are treated as barriers to knowledge of what it is. It is evident, I think, that if metaphysics is to unify our knowledge by stressing the connections between what we experience the world as being and what, more indirectly, we find out about its nature and behavior under conditions in which we cannot ourselves observe it, some such principle is essential. The alternative appears to be, as in fact it has proved to be, an essentially unplausible attempt to predicate of the natural world, as it exists independently of any sentient organism's response to it, the characters which it takes on, so far as we know, only under these special conditions, or, failing this, to insist that the world as experienced and in its empirically discoverable connections is not the 'real' world at all, but only an inadequate subjective counterpart of it. From that point on, the relation between experience and nature will be whatever the metaphysician chooses to take it to be; for his only real ground for supposing that there is a connection will be some remnant of those empirically discoverable interactions which his theory actually has rendered dubious but which for epistemological reasons or as a result of 'animal faith' he insists on retaining. In asking philosophers to turn their attention rather to that relation between experience and nature which consists in the fact that what we experience is the outcome of natural and scientifically describable processes and that it is itself an instance and, within its contextual limits, a fair sample, of what nature is and thus a sound basis for a further exploration of it, Dewey has served his subject well and has brought the whole discussion back to a point from which a comprehensive estimate of man's place in nature might profitably proceed.

The 'naturalism' of such a theory is founded partly on fact, in so far as it stresses the dependence of the 'higher' or more spiritual aspects of human behavior on the physical, biological and social environment in which they are manifested, and partly on a decision that the whole of experience is to be interpreted as falling within the situation which this environment determines. No conclusive proof for such a comprehensive naturalism is possible, since demonstrations of the traditional type that 'nature,' whether identified with matter, or space-time, or the evolutionary process, is all that can be real, have been ruled out by the method of this empirical metaphysics. It does, however, provide a standpoint for the organization of experience as a whole in which everything on other grounds reliably verifiable finds a credible place, and in which 'value' and 'meanings' are freed from dubious speculative and supernatural entanglements without being robbed of any of their human validity in the process. As such many reasonable men will prefer it to any speculative alternative and will find it justified to the extent in which it gives order, proportion, and a basic and essential sanity to their total view of things. While it cannot be said that Mr. Dewey has worked out a fully satisfactory theory along these lines, he has made very notable contributions to it.

There is, nevertheless, a skeleton in the closet of this admirably planned metaphysics, which has seriously compromised its good repute and thus given aid and comfort to its speculative rivals. It consists in an unhappy discrepancy between experience as it ought to be if its place in the natural world is to be made intelligible, and experience as it must be if Dewey's epistemology is correct. In the former capacity, "experience" is the essential link between man and a world which long antedates his appearance in it. In the latter, "experience" is the terminus of all knowing, in the sense that all our cognitive claims refer ultimately to what experience will show itself to be in a 'resolved' situation and to nothing else. If this latter account is true, all statements about a natural environment outside of these immediate experiences become on analysis simply means of facilitating cognitive transitions to such enjoyed immediacies and the world which should have provided the background for our experience, and the measure of its metaphysical significance, "collapses into immediacy," and Mr. Dewey's naturalism reduces, as Mr. Santayana has said, to a "philosophy of the foreground."[22]

<hr />

[22] See Santayana's review of *Experience and Nature* in the *Journal of Philosophy*, Vol. XXII, 680 ff., and Dewey's reply in Vol. XXIV, 57 ff.

The difficulty does not arise from Mr. Dewey's laudable attempt to treat experience as continuous with the rest of nature. It is the result of a misinterpretation of the way in which experience functions in knowing, and its consequence is that the reference to 'experience' cuts us off from, instead of connecting us with, the circumambient environment, in which experience must be placed if it is to retain its status as a natural event.

The precise nature of this difficulty can be specified by reference to the relation described in *Experience and Nature,* of scientific objects to qualitied events as these are immediately experienced. The latter are held to be 'ends' both for knowledge and in nature, the former are relational and 'instrumental,' the conceptual means we use for establishing connections between qualitied events. These qualitied events are taken as the type of what a natural event, in its concrete individuality, is, and it follows from this that the objects with which the physical sciences deal, representing the statistical outcome of complex processes of measurement and comparison, are not "individual existential objects" in this primary sense at all. "The procedure of physics itself, not any metaphysical or epistemological theory, discloses that physical objects cannot be individual, existential objects. In consequence, it is absurd to put them in opposition to the qualitatively individual objects of concrete experience."[23] The difference between the "world of physics" and the "world of sense" is to be explained as that between objects of thought, when thought is essentially instrumental to the satisfactory reconstruction of experienced and "qualitied" situations, and objects of immediate enjoyment—the ends or termini of thinking, in their directly apprehended being.

Thus "the proper objects of science are nature in its instrumental characters"[24] and hence science "is not a final thing. The final thing is appreciation and use of things of direct experience."[25]

This seems to me to violate the primary principle of Dewey's 'empirical method' as previously laid down. The objects about which the physical sciences provide abstract and schematic but

[23] *The Quest for Certainty,* 241.
[24] *Experience and Nature,* 137.
[25] *The Quest for Certainty,* 221-2.

nonetheless reliable information are not in their own nature 'instrumental' at all. Our knowledge of them is instrumental in so far as we can use it to make life in other respects more satisfactory and in this instrumental use science is, of course, not a final thing. But to suppose that the whole meaning of what science tells us about the physical environment is reducible to this instrumental function is to treat one context in which things come to us as ultimate for metaphysics, and this is an irreparable mistake.

For we actually need scientific information *not* merely in this instrumental capacity, but as information about the causes and conditions of human experience, if our naturalism is not to lapse into a hopelessly anthropocentric view of things. Of course the things we directly experience are more 'concrete' than the objects of science, since they are the only things we can get at in terms of sensuous content and emotional associations and practical uses. They owe this special status, however, precisely to the fact that we stand in special relations to them. Whatever the 'individuality' of an object beyond the range of direct experience may be it will always *for us* remain abstract and relational, since all we can know about it is what can be inferred from its relations to other things. To take 'concreteness' in this sense as the measure of individual reality, and abstractness as evidence of a merely 'relational' or instrumental character *in nature* is to make the special conditions under which a sentient organism gets into connection with things the measure of their reality. It is the basis for every sort of panpsychism and animism, but hardly for an empirical naturalism.

Since Mr. Dewey has no leanings toward animism or other such attempts to reduce the world to the human scale, it is in a different direction that we must look if this unhappy situation is to be explained. We have not far to look. If conceptual knowing as it functions in physics is a way of finding out by such means as we can what the physical environment is, then experience is not its exclusive object. Objects that cannot be come at directly must of course be known about through such report as other things give of their nature. Experience in such investigation is not the terminus of knowing but a means to knowing about something else. And it is what is thus indirectly known that gives 'experience' the meaning that Dewey wants to place on it as a natural event. It would be quite illegitimate to suppose that the reference to such objects renders what we experience 'unreal,' or 'bifurcates' nature. Neither scientific investigation nor empirical observation and enjoyment can be the measure of any other reality than that of its own appropriate object. But it is essential to acknowledge that we know both what the world is like under the conditions of observation and enjoyment and also what, in a much more general and approximate way, the unexperienced environment is by which experience is conditioned. If we could not know this there would be no sense in calling this environment 'nature' and regarding experience as our means of finding out about it. On any contextual analysis of knowing this is a feasible and straightforward interpretation.

If, however, the meaning of conceptual inquiry is defined simply as its capacity to refer to and satisfactorily initiate future experiences, experience loses this 'vehicular' significance altogether and the limits of what we can enjoy or immediately 'have' become the limits of the world to which we can significantly refer. And since these limits are relatively narrow ones, we are left with a reality far too limited for what, outside metaphysics and epistemology, we find the world to be. Mr. Dewey himself warned us of where such a non-contextual metaphysics would lead and the result is an impressive verification of his warning.

The attempt to establish this has necessitated a somewhat ungrateful emphasis on the defects of a theory which, as compared with its rivals, has very much to recommend it and which stands today as the most significant contribution America has made to philosophic enlightenment. It would have been possible, of course, to stress this aspect of the matter more, and to write an essay, as many have been and will be written, in praise of this philosophy. But this outcome, though more laudatory, would have been less appropriate, I think, to the actual merits of its subject. For Mr. Dewey did not compose a philosophy to be appreciated, along with other speculative and literary monuments, as an impressive specimen of man's answer to the riddle of existence. He developed rather a method for clarifying ideas and testing theories in such fashion that men, less interested in even ultimate riddles than in knowing what their statements mean and what, in relation to their own more inclusive purposes, their various activities are worth, could see more clearly and judge more sanely in these matters. In this he has placed us all greatly in his debt. This is a continuing work, and one in which there is still very much to do. We need to know how best to do it, and to decide, more definitely than was possible when Dewey's own work began, what elements in the theory presented are reliable for the purpose in hand. It is because I believe this work is profoundly worth continuing that I have tried here to suggest the line along which work can now most profitably proceed.

The conclusion "warrantably assertible" as the outcome of the preceding analysis is, I believe, the following: Mr. Dewey's epistemology is not, either in its method or results, in harmony with the philosophical procedures he has recommended or the empirical metaphysics he proposes to develop. The procedure would be more directly applicable in non-epistemological contexts and far less open to misconstruction, the metaphysics freed from a serious and quite gratuitous difficulty, if this epistemology were abandoned. In so far as Mr. Dewey's philosophy is one of the rival 'positions,' developed in the last generation as competing accounts of the 'true' object of knowledge and the 'final' meaning of truth, this conclusion amounts to the claim that that position is in a fundamental respect untenable. In so far, however, as this philosophy has been, more than any other of the period, a project for the use of philosophic analysis and criticism for the clarification of basic ideas and the coördination of the various aspects of the world as experienced and known, the conclusion offered amounts to a suggestion for its wider and more consistent application. It is the enduring worth of Mr. Dewey's philosophy in this latter aspect that lends whatever significance it may have to this discussion.

ARTHUR E. MURPHY

DEPARTMENT OF PHILOSOPHY
UNIVERSITY OF ILLINOIS

7

Dominique Parodi

KNOWLEDGE AND ACTION IN DEWEY'S PHILOSOPHY

7
KNOWLEDGE AND ACTION IN DEWEY'S PHILOSOPHY[1]

THE work of John Dewey inspires respect and admiration not only on account of its extent and its richness, but on account of its sincerity, its integrity and the vigorous resoluteness with which even a leading idea is analysed and considered under all its aspects, is examined thoroughly and applied to every field of philosophy. Less brilliant perhaps than that of James, it has more coherence and unity; it advances further the attempt to attain consistency and to test its specific principles. In it, undoubtedly, we find the most complete expression of that great movement of ideas which pragmatism has been and which, although it seems it has already completed its development, has nevertheless left so many traces even in those recent modes of thought where one does not dream of noticing them any more: pragmatism, which constitutes one of America's most original contributions to universal philosophy.

Although, aside from his pedagogical writings, few of his works have been translated, John Dewey's philosophy is well known in France and greatly appreciated. He himself has given us straightforward summaries of it, both in the article entitled "Développement du pragmatisme américain,"[2] which he wrote for the special number devoted to American thought of the *Revue de Métaphysique et de Morale* (in 1922), and in the paper which he read before the *Société française de Philosophie* on November 7th, 1930, under the title "Trois facteurs indépendents en matière de morale." One may find penetrating accounts of the whole of his philosophy in the two great works, *Les philosophes pluralistes d'Angleterre et d'Amérique* (1920),

[1] Translated from the French by Walter Gieseke.
[2] Published in English under the title *Philosophy and Civilization*.

by M. Jean Wahl, and *Le Pragmatisme américain et anglais* (1923), by M. Emmanuel Leroux, and furthermore in such a study as that which M. Duprat has devoted to the most impórtant works among Dewey's later books, in the *Revue de Métaphysique et de Morale* (Nos. October 1930 and January 1931), entitled "Rapports de la Connaissance et de l'Action d'après John Dewey."

In the present study we would like to attempt—by referring especially to three main works, the *Essays in Experimental Logic* (1916), *Reconstruction in Philosophy* (1920), and *Human Nature and Conduct* (1922)—to set forth what seems to us the central doctrine of his entire philosophy, both in its speculative and in its moral aspect, and to state clearly the difficulties which it seems to us to present.

I

One may, we believe, consider Dewey's philosophy as the most successful attempt to remould the traditional Anglo-Saxon empiricism, by freeing it from the intellectualistic and especially the static prejudices which in his eyes vitiated it, almost to the same degree as the contrary doctrines, a-priorism, rationalism, idealism. He wanted to see in intelligence, though asserting its primacy in human endeavour, only the instrument of action, the sole effective means of universal reconstruction in a civilization which he, in spite of all denials of today, considers as essentially human, natural and democratic and which must—at its own risk—pursue its indefinitely progressive destiny through the unknown and the adventurous. Whereas in James remain some obscure elements, linked with his conception of the will to believe, Dewey has essayed with a radical and forceful candor to recover all the advantages of a practical idealism in a broadened positivism which is exclusively concerned with experience. His central purpose then seems to be to re-integrate human knowledge and activity into the general framework of universal evolution, without, at the same time, taking from man what distinguishes and exalts him among living creatures.

The great error of philosophy since classical antiquity has been, according to John Dewey, to put the static and the changeless above the moving and the changing; to conceive knowledge as an ensemble of absolute truths and certainties, morality as obedience to principles or to ends also absolute; and to strive to construct reality in all its aspects out of fixed and ready-made elements. Hegel in philosophy, Darwin and the evolutionists in the natural sciences have finally made the opposite idea triumph. Henceforth reality is conceived as an unending process of ever new events, all of them in continuity with each other; and knowing is only a peculiar type of such events among others, events that have their specific conditioning in those that precede them and which in turn react upon those that follow: "Thinking is . . . a specific event in the movement of experienced things, having its own specific occasion or demand and its own specific place."[3] "Knowing is something that happens to things in the natural course of their career . . ." Thus from the beginning the existing conflict between idealism and realism finds itself resolved: it is a strange illusion to want to take consciousness as a point of departure and then to ask oneself whether anything exists outside of it: whereas actually consciousness cannot be conceived without it being the consciousness of something; it presupposes countless data anterior to it, just as it is an activity which has consequences in the future. Every conception of knowledge, idealism included, implies an existing world, outside of it; every change, of form or color for example, cannot be defined except "in respect to a temporal continuum of things anteceding and succeeding." Psychology therefore is not a science of states of consciousness, but of ways of acting, of continuous readjustments of our habits and our impulses to circumstances always new. Knowing is nothing but a series of organizing acts.

Indeed, when our activity is carried on with ease and without encountering an obstacle, when, thanks to habit and to previous acquisitions, it finds itself in harmony with the environment in which it manifests itself, there is properly speaking neither consciousness nor knowledge; "there are just things."[4] "When we already have what we want, namely existence,

[3] *Essays in Experimental Logic*, 127.
[4] *Ibid.*, 229.

reality, why should we take up the wholly supernumerary task of forming more or less imperfect ideas of those facts?"[5] But let a difficulty arise, let a situation occur the different factors of which are more or less incompatible with each other, then the situation itself tends to remould and to reorganize its elements, and thinking intervenes. "The thought-situation is only a constant movement toward a defined equilibrium."[6] It is thus an ensemble of means to give or to restore to experience its unity, its coherence, and thereby its efficacy. Its rôle is instrumental and functional; it brings about "the transition from a relatively conflicting experience to a relatively integrated one."[7] It is valid in so far as it succeeds; that is, of course, as it succeeds in the function of thought, giving to the thinking activity its coherence and practical bearing.

Such a conception involves a corollary the paradoxical nature of which does not halt Dewey. Sensations and perceptions are not in themselves knowledge, no more than a shower or an attack of fever, but mere natural phenomena, arising in certain physical conditions (external stimulation, transmission by the nerves, etc.). The average man, in his common sense, does not consider the noises he hears, the colors he sees, "as mental existences . . . neither . . . as things known: that they are just things is good enough for him."[8] Perceptions taken as a kind of knowledge: that would be the door open to idealism. "But,— crede experto—let them (the realists) try the experiment of conceiving perceptions as pure natural events, not as cases of awareness or apprehension, and they will be surprised to see how little they miss—save the burden of carrying traditional problems."[9]

But if the perceptions can be regarded as existing facts, with certain qualities and in certain spatial and temporal relationships, there is knowledge only when another relationship is added: that of a present thing to an absent thing which it signifies or which it announces: "When there is knowledge, another

[5] *Ibid.*, 232.
[6] *Ibid.*, 123.
[7] *Ibid.*, 170.
[8] *Ibid.*, 297.
[9] *Ibid.*, 262.

relation is added, that of one thing meaning or signifying another."[10] All knowledge has thus a symbolic character, it prepares for or constitutes an inference. Perceptual events become cases of knowledge when habit—a natural function, and not a psychical or epistemological one—associates them with others as their signs. The body of the propositions of the natural sciences rests thus upon perceptions, but only by considering them as indications or signs of each other; and this is what finally obscures their real nature, "that of being simply natural events."

Knowledge, according to such a conception, is then essentially a signification, a "meaning," and the word will have different shades of meaning according to whether objects, ideas or truths are concerned.[11] If an object is concerned, the "meaning" will be the totality of the practical responses which it elicits from us: an armchair is the totality of usages and habits that it suggests to us. If an idea is concerned, the "meaning" designates a plan of action, a series of changes to bring about in the existing things. If truth is concerned, it expresses its value, its import. Ideas and truths then are "working hypotheses." They do not depend, as William James seemed to admit, upon any consequences, favorable or unfavorable, which, taken as ready-made structures of thought, they might have: but they serve to clarify their very meaning as a programme of behavior (as a *modus operandi*); they help to criticize, to revise and to determine the very sense of their formula. As if someone drank a liquid to verify whether or not it were poison and would, by the effect, both find out the correctness of his hypothesis and die. Truth is not verified by just any kind of satisfaction, but only by that satisfaction which is born of the fact that a working hypothesis or an experimental method applies to the facts which it concerns and affords a better ordering of them. No misconception concerning the instrumental logic of pragmatism has been more persistent than the belief that one would want to make of thought merely a means for a practical end,—"practical" being taken in the sense of certain material utilities, like drinking and eating. But what Dewey affirms on the contrary is that the principle of pragmatism lies in that rule of logic which refers each

[10] *Ibid.*, 246.
[11] *Ibid.*, 302 ff.

thought, every reflective consideration "to *consequences* for final meaning and test."[12]

Thus understood, knowledge is wholly oriented towards future consequences; it draws its validity only from "its relationship with its own product;" it goes essentially from the known to the unknown. The implied agreement with the facts is in no way conformity with the given, present or past, but a better organization of activity in process moving in the direction of the future; it is a method, a plan of action; a certain conception of what is given in its hypothetical relations to what is not yet given, so as to bring it about or to avoid it. Contrary to what it was in classical empiricism as well as in classical rationalism, it becomes a dynamic and not a static process. Logic is experimental; it tends to push back the frontiers of science, "not to mark by signs those that are already attained." "Inventio" is more important in it than "judicium," discovery more than proof. The paradox of the relations of theory to practice is that of all the modes of practice, theory is the most practical of all.[13]

II

If all knowing is thus an act, judged by its consequences and practical by nature, what then will one call the more specifically practical judgments, when one contrasts them with others that are not so either in the same degree or else in the same sense? It is the moral aspect of the doctrine that we must now try to define more precisely.

In a strict sense all judgments are indeed practical in as much as they originate from an incomplete or an uncertain situation which is to be completed or organized. But there are some judgments that have—among other less essential differences—both of the following characteristics: (1) the situation is conceived as being capable of completion in several different ways, and (2) the proposition itself is a factor necessary to complete or to organize it. If I say: "the house is burning," the judgment consists in ordering my impressions or my ideas by verifying the truth of a fact and does not consist in acting upon the external

[12] *Ibid.*, 330.
[13] *Ibid.*, 441.

events. But if I say: "let it burn," or: "direct the stream from the fire-engine upon it," I am dealing with practical judgments, for firstly, they express two possible ways of reacting to the event, and, secondly, they express two ways of reacting on my part, each of which presupposes the judgment itself as a condition. Judgments of this sort may also be called judgments of value or of evaluation. But here a distinction must be made. We must distinguish, on the one hand, between the experience of a good or of an evil, which consists, under the influence of instinct or habit and apart from reflective judgment, in hanging on to a thing or in separating oneself from it, in acting in such a way as to perpetuate its presence or to avoid it; such experience is only a way of behaving toward a thing; a sort of organic reaction. In the second place, experience of a good or evil may consist in an intellectual act of weighing, of evaluating. It is the difference between eating something and investigating the food properties of the thing eaten. The practical judgment, the evaluation, takes place only in the case where the individual undergoes some perplexity, where he reflects that—although it does not well please him—the food is wholesome, that he needs to rebuild his strength, etc. This means to foresee and to calculate the consequences, or to compare the various possible actions.

To evaluate, then, supposes a relationship of means to an end; but the value is not given in advance [to the evaluating act], it will not be determined except by the judgment itself. As long as I deliberate, the value remains undetermined. The lobster will give me, if I eat some, delight now but indigestion later; shall I take my act as means to present enjoyment or as a (negative) condition of my future health? "When its status in these respects is determined, its value is determined; judgment ceases, action goes on."[14] The position of a value then shows itself only if the continuation or the completion of a process is questioned: a value exists only where desires oppose each other and where the need arises to deliberate in order to choose between them. Spontaneous action under the influence of need or desire is here left by Dewey to the pure and simple world of natural events, as a moment ago was the merely sensory and

[14] *Ibid.*, 361.

perceptive activity. But there is nothing in this entire process that resembles the imitation of a model or ideal ready-made and given in advance: "the standard of valuation is formed in the process of practical judgment or valuation."[15] This "standard" changes continually with the circumstances. The specific object of a judgment of valuation is to release new factors which, being new, cannot be measured on the basis of the past alone. To determine the standard means to appeal to the present situation as involving an original re-organization, namely, the unification which it lacked. The very incompleteness of each situation is specific; even a moral rule acts only as a guiding idea, a working hypothesis.

The same conceptions, the same distrust of the abstract, of the theoretical and of all finality may be found, in a slightly different terminology, in the work entitled *Human Nature and Conduct*. In it John Dewey represents living as an ensemble of dispositions to act, as a complex of habits; so much so, that one can affirm without being paradoxical that, in the living person, it is the acquired which is primitive. It is a fact of primary importance that each human being begins his life with complete dependence upon others. Morality, therefore, must unreservedly appear as wholly social. The act must come before thought, and habit before the capacity to appeal to thought. But habit is not routine or automatism: it is re-adjustment, adaptation of antecedent dispositions to new circumstances. Let this re-adjustment become difficult and painful, then an appeal will be made, on the one hand, to individual impulses or tendencies which until then are more or less hidden and disciplined, and, on the other hand, to reflection or thought; which means that the acts to be carried out will be conceived in advance and pursued in their possible development. From then on the act will involve motives, a relationship of means to ends.—But there is no essential difference between the end and the means: it is the same series of possible acts, imagined either as remote or in their nearest elements; or else the end is a series of these acts taken collectively, the means being the term designating the same series distributively.[16]

[15] *Ibid.*, 374.
[16] *Human Nature and Conduct*, 34, 36.

Let us go further: the object of this anticipation of the consequences is not to predict the future: it is to give to present activities their signification and to organize them, to put an end to the conflict that has stirred up the activity. This termination marks the final point of deliberation, though not of action; it is the "turning point in the course of activity." To have an end or an aim[17] is a characteristic feature of *present* activity: it is the means by which activity becomes unified and adjusted, when otherwise it would be blind and disorderly; or whereby it acquires a meaning when it would otherwise be wholly mechanical. A foreseeable end is only a means in the present action; the present action is not a means towards a remote end. Are not our ends, therefore, of necessity beginnings in their turn? The port is just as truly, for a sailor, the beginning of a new kind of activity, as it is the end of his present activity; it is only during the course of the voyage itself that it has been an end. Life is continuity. Peace in the action itself, and not after it, is the contribution of the ideal to conduct. To see the goal only in the future means to deprive oneself of the surest means of attaining it, namely, being aware of the full use of our present resources in the given situation.[18] Rules, precepts, principles are only instruments and working methods. "Instruction in what to do next can never come from an infinite goal, which for us is bound to be empty. It can be derived only from study of the deficiencies, irregularities and possibilities of the actual situation."[19]

Then the moral problem can only be a problem of continuous fundamental re-adaptation.[20] It does not assume the unity of a principle or of an end, but tends only to achieve always a somewhat greater unity of the present and the real. Morality then does not involve any transcendental element, it is a wholly human and social matter; not in the sense that it *must* be so, but in the sense that it *is* in fact. It implies an interaction of the person and his environment, no more and no less than walking is an interraction of the legs and of the natural surroundings. It

[17] *Ibid.*, 226.
[18] *Ibid.*, 267.
[19] *Ibid.*, 289.
[20] *Ibid.*, 240.

presupposes, finally, freedom; but not some indefinite, vague power which is transcendental and hardly intelligible; but rather as effective power to modify the milieu in which we live; thus freedom is not a psychological or metaphysical problem, but one which is again practical. "A world that is at points and times indeterminate enough to call out deliberation and to give play to choice to shape its future is a world in which will is free."[21] A certain indetermination in the things themselves and in our knowledge is thus a condition favorable for man's activity; love of certainty and of the absolute would at bottom be only a demand for an advance guarantee of the action and to keep us from engaging in it. Truth is not acquired except by risk and adventure. "Fixed ends upon one side and fixed 'principles,'—that is authoritative rules,—on the other, are props for a feeling of safety, the refuge of the timid, and the means by which the bold prey upon the timid."[22]

III

The work of John Dewey is notable in scope and touches all the great problems that confront contemporary thought; its educational and its social aspects, both of such importance, are particularly well known. But nevertheless—if we are not mistaken—it is the theory of knowledge and action, the principle of which we have tried to point out, which constitutes its inmost logic and grounds its unity. It appears quite modern in most of its features and approaches in a good many points those contemporary doctrines which, in inspiration and general intent, would seem most remote from it. In reaction to Hegelian idealism, which fifty years ago was held in great esteem in the Anglo-Saxon world, it is a powerful realism. In his thesis that perception is not really knowledge and must be taken as in itself objective, Dewey is not very far away from the Bergsonian conception, which in this respect he appreciates greatly, while at the same time protesting against the value given by the French philosopher to intuition.[23] In the restricted sense in

[21] *Ibid.*, 310.
[22] *Ibid.*, 237.
[23] Cf. in *Philosophy and Civilization* the study entitled "Perception and Organic Action."

which he uses the word "knowledge" and in the narrow limits within which he confines it, so that on all sides the world of existence and experience overflows it, he is not really very far from certain attitudes of the recent "phenomenological" or "existential" philosophies.

Yet, on the other hand, his doctrine opposes all prevailing conceptions of today by the positive and intellectualistic character which it courageously proclaims, and which makes it, as has been said, the heiress of the thought of the eighteenth century and of the philosophy of the enlightenment; this is particularly true in epistemology and social thought. It is in scientific knowledge alone that Dewey sees the privilege of humanity; upon it alone he makes its progress depend. He scorns metaphysics altogether and is inclined to see in several of its classical problems only illusions and verbal difficulties. Though continuing it, he also renews and deepens the great tradition of empiricism and positivism.

Nevertheless, however honest and clear the position which he thus takes may be, is it tenable? Have the problems of being and of knowing and of their relationships really been made to disappear?

First of all it must be said that science, as Dewey defines it, is almost exclusively physical and natural science; it is hardly mathematical science. He conceives nature not as a totality of intelligible and necessary relationships, but as a succession of more or less continuous and coherent phenomena; without excluding an element of contingency from it; thus he leaves it open for human initiative and invention. But he hardly tries to specify or to give an account of the rôle of contingency on the one hand, and of regularity and necessity on the other. The idea of explication and intelligibility is not in the foreground in this philosophy; it is to some extent sacrificed to that of scientific probability and practical efficiency. We find ourselves, indeed, in the presence of a positivistic theory.

It is Dewey's original contribution to have attempted to integrate everything into the precise framework of natural phenomena thus understood, and to intend to make every distinction of the subjective and the objective, of the psychical and the physical disappear for the sake of a totalitarianism of experience. He takes perceptions to be natural events which follow the physical and physiological modifications of which the scene of action is the organism and which are a part of the same unfolding of phenomena; which then determine a better coördination and adaptation of our ideas and which culminate finally in oriented and efficacious actions. He likewise describes deliberation and decision as a series of acts which, without any gap of continuity, interpose themselves between the momentarily conflicting habits or impulses and the fitting practical adjustments. But is the continuity of this process—in which one seems to end by putting physical phenomena and conscious phenomena on the same level—truly intelligible? For it is from the outside that we experience both the vibrations which constitute for the physicist say, the color red, and the modifications of the nerves which transmit them (*i.e.*, the impressions) to the brain; and we would, if we could follow its course farther, undoubtedly find in the brain itself a new series of phenomena of a mechanical or chemical nature, which on their part determine centrifugal nerve currents and bring finally our muscles and our limbs into play; but nowhere, certainly, should we meet, from this point of view, the color red as something felt, as the sensation or the perception properly so called. It seems indeed that, in order to apprehend something like that, it is necessary to change one's point of view and to place oneself into the very center of the consciousness of the subject who perceives.

In any case, the paradox remains just as perplexing when one attempts to take this new attitude. We are told that sensations and perceptions, which are, until that moment, simple natural facts, become acts of knowledge when they serve as signs and announce or suggest other facts which are not yet present in the experience of the senses: but, if they were in the beginning only natural facts (which means, undoubtedly, that they were not yet data of consciousness), how could they enter as terms into these conscious relationships or thoughts which constitute our inferences and which permit us to foresee and to estimate consequences? Would they not suddenly have to change their nature in the most mysterious manner? It seems indeed that, if one places himself on the standpoint of exterior observation, it is necessary to stick to it to the end and to come finally to "behaviorism" proper, trying to get along entirely without the benefit of consciousness, whether it be that one means to deny its existence, or whether it be that one sees in it only a perfectly useless and completely unintelligible epiphenomenon.

A similar obscurity presents itself when action or voluntary decision is concerned. Undoubtedly, every conception of an end, every judgment of value, can be considered as a coördination of our habits, of our desires, or of our motives, a coördination which is an act and is performed only in the present; and no doubt, each goal achieved is the beginning of a new activity. But the analysis, however exact and valuable it may be, is still made from the outside, from the standpoint of the psychologist or the logician. However, for the subject itself which deliberates and which finally "wills," the end—in the present, undoubtedly—is imagined as belonging to the future. It constitutes indeed a guiding idea, which until its final realization, remains present in consciousness and is conceived as identical with itself in order to guide and to organize our movements and our acts as means for its realization. Thus, during all the time of the construction of the house the workers refer to the architect's plan previously established and precisely fixed. To be sure, an activity satisfactorily concluded is the point of departure for a new activity directed toward another end; but, in the consciousness of him who thinks and acts, it constitutes properly a completion, an end; it constitutes, together with its means, an activity which is, quite apart from those which are going to follow, unified and intelligible. Nature undoubtedly is universal and continuous becoming: but the mind that reflects sees in it points of arrest and gives it, by means of abstraction, an ideal stability; it considers as stable even that which in its manifestation or its external unfolding is always in flux. Viewed from without, all is undoubtedly history and change, an uninterrupted succession of movements: but to think means to fix, to abstract and to define, to give consistency, permanence, and intelligible unity to our ideas and our purposes. Permanence and change are perhaps dialectical moments that have meaning only in and through their very opposition, but both are equally necessary for the conceiving and regulating of experience. To understand, to explain, to demonstrate, to prove are undoubtedly intellectual acts; from the start these acts are—and Mr. Dewey has seen it and maintained it with a beautiful clearness—disinterested and foreign to all seeking of material advantages; and moreover, we would add, they are acts conceived as above time, as freed from the future, and viewed—to the extent to which they are true—*sub specie aeternitatis.*

Either one describes the universe—the spiritual as well as the physical—in terms of material existence and of objectivity, and then one has to go as far as to "epiphenomenalism" and consent never to meet anything that might resemble what we call consciousness, idea, finality, will. Or else one agrees to place oneself at a given moment into the very center of consciousness and to start from the *cogito;* in this latter case one will meet above the Heraclitean becoming the Platonic world of essences, and at the same time the inevitable problems of idealism and realism, of the subjective and the objective, of being and thought. Such is the alternative which, even after the admirable attempt made by Mr. Dewey, seems to us still to confront human reflection.

DOMINIQUE PARODI

PARIS, FRANCE

8

George Santayana

DEWEY'S NATURALISTIC METAPHYSICS

8

DEWEY'S NATURALISTIC METAPHYSICS[1]

HERE[2] is a remarkable rereading of things with a new and difficult kind of sincerity. For my part, I am entirely persuaded of the genuineness and depth of Dewey's views, within the limits of his method and taken as he means them. He is, fortunately, not without an active band of followers who will be able to interpret and elaborate them in his own spirit. I am hardly in their case, and all I can hope to accomplish is to fix the place and character of this doctrine in relation to the points of view which I instinctively take or which seem to me, on reflection, to be most comprehensive. And I will append such conclusions as I may provisionally reach on this subject to a phrase by which Dewey himself characterizes his system: *Naturalistic Metaphysics*. In what sense is this system naturalistic? In what sense is it metaphysical? How comes it that these two characters (which to me seem contradictory) can be united in this philosophy?

Naturalism is a primary system, or rather it is not a special system at all, but the spontaneous and inevitable body of beliefs involved in animal life, beliefs of which the various philosophical systems are either extensions (a supernatural environment, itself natural in its own way, being added to nature) or interpretations (as in Aristotle and Spinoza) or denials (as in idealism). Children are interested in their bodies, with which they identify themselves; they are interested in animals, ade-

[1] EDITOR'S NOTE: This essay is, essentially, Mr. Santayana's review of Dewey's *Experience and Nature*, a review which first appeared in *The Journal of Philosophy* (December 3, 1925). Mr. Santayana believes that Dewey's Carus Lectures of 1922 still contain the essence of Dewey's philosophy. In view of this fact the editor is happy to have Mr. Santayana's permission to reprint the review here with a few minor changes made by Mr. Santayana himself for the present purpose.

[2] In Dewey's *Experience and Nature* (1925).

245

quate playmates for them, to be bullied with a pleasing risk and a touch of wonder. They are interested later in mechanical contrivances and in physical feats and adventures. This boyish universe is indefinitely extensible on its own plane; it may have heaven around it and fairyland in its interstices; it covers the whole field of possible material action to its uttermost reaches. It is the world of naturalism. On this material framework it is easy to hang all the immaterial objects, such as words, feelings, and ideas, which may be eventually distinguished in human experience. We are not compelled in naturalism, or even in materialism, to ignore immaterial things; the point is that any immaterial things which are recognized shall be regarded as names, aspects, functions, or concomitant products of those physical things among which action goes on. A naturalist may distinguish his own person or self, provided he identifies himself with his body and does not assign to his soul any fortunes, powers, or actions save those of which his body is the seat and organ. He may recognize other spirits, human, animal, or divine, provided they are all proper to natural organisms figuring in the world of action, and are the natural moral transcript, like his own feelings, of physical life in that region. Naturalism may, accordingly, find room for every sort of psychology, poetry, logic, and theology, if only they are content with their natural places. Naturalism will break down, however, so soon as words, ideas, or spirits are taken to be substantial on their own account, and powers at work prior to the existence of their organs, or independent of them. Now it is precisely such disembodied powers and immaterial functions prior to matter that are called metaphysical. Transcendentalism is not metaphysical if it remains a mere method, because then it might express the natural fact that any animal mind is its own center and must awake in order to know anything: it becomes metaphysical when this mind is said to be absolute, single, and without material conditions. To admit anything metaphysical in this sense is evidently to abandon naturalism.

It would be hard to find a philosopher in whom naturalism, so conceived, was more inveterate than in Dewey. He is very severe against the imagination, and even the intellect, for having created figments which usurp the place and authority of the mundane sphere in which daily action goes on. The typical philosopher's fallacy, in his eyes, has been the habit of hypostatizing the conclusions to which reflection may lead, and deputing them to be prior realities—the fallacy of dogmatism. These conclusions are in reality nothing but suggestions or, as Dewey calls them, "meanings" surrounding the passing experience in which, at some juncture, a person is immersed. They may be excellent in an instrumental capacity, if by their help instinctive action can be enlarged or adjusted more accurately to absent facts; but it would be sheer idolatry to regard them as realities or powers deeper than obvious objects, producing these objects and afterwards somehow revealing themselves, just as they are, to the thoughts of metaphysicians. Here is a rude blow dealt at dogma of every sort: God, matter, Platonic ideas, active spirits, and creative logics all seem to totter on their thrones; and if the blow could be effective, the endless battle of metaphysics would have to end for lack of combatants.

Meantime there is another motive that drives Dewey to naturalism: he is the devoted spokesman of the spirit of enterprise, of experiment, of modern industry. To him, rather than to William James, might be applied the saying of the French pragmatist, Georges Sorel, that his philosophy is calculated to justify all the assumptions of American society. William James was a psychologist of the individual, preoccupied with the varieties of the human imagination and with the possible destinies of the spirit in other worlds. He was too spontaneous and rare a person to be a good mirror of any broad general movement; his Americanism, like that of Emerson, was his own and within him, and perhaps more representative of America in the past than in the future. In Dewey, on the contrary, as in current science and ethics, there is a pervasive quasi-Hegelian tendency to dissolve the individual into his social functions, as well as everything substantial or actual into something relative or transitional. For him events, situations, and histories hold all facts and all persons in solution. The master-burden of his philosophy, which lends it its national character, is a profound sympathy with the enterprise of life in all lay directions, in its technical and moral complexity, and especially in its American form, where individual initiative, although still demanded and prized, is quickly subjected to overwhelming democratic control. This, if I am not mistaken, is the heart of Dewey's pragmatism, it is the pragmatism of the people, dumb and instinctive in them, and struggling in him to a labored but radical expression. His pragmatism is not inspired by any wish to supply a new argument to support some old speculative dogma. Nor is he interested, like Nietzsche and Vaihinger, in a heroic pessimism, desperately living as if postulates were true which it knows to be false. He is not interested in speculation at all, balks at it, and would avoid it if he could; his inspiration is sheer fidelity to the task in hand and sympathy with the movement afoot: a deliberate and happy participation in the attitude of the American people, with its omnivorous human interests and its simplicity of purpose.

Now the philosophy by which Americans live, in contrast to the philosophies which they profess, is naturalistic. In profession they may be Fundamentalists, Catholics, or idealists, because American opinion is largely pre-American; but in their hearts and lives they are all pragmatists, and they prove it even by the spirit in which they maintain those other traditional allegiances, not out of rapt speculative sympathy, but because such allegiance seems an insurance against moral dissolution, guaranteeing social cohesion and practical success. Their real philosophy is the philosophy of enterprise. Now enterprise moves in the infinitely extensible boyish world of feats and discoveries—in the world of naturalism. The practical arts, as Dewey says, presuppose a mechanical unity and constancy established in the universe. Otherwise discoveries made today would not count to-morrow, inventions could not be patented, the best-laid plans might go astray, all work might be wasted, and the methods of experts could not be adjusted more and more accurately to their tasks. This postulated mechanical system must evidently include the hands and brain of the worker, which are intertwined inextricably with the work done. It must also include his mind, if his mind is to be of any practical account and to make any difference in his work. Hence the implicit American philosophy, which it is

Dewey's privilege to make explicit, involves behaviorism. This doctrine is new and amazing if taken to deny the existence of thought; but on its positive side, in so far as it puts all efficient processes on one level, it has been an implication of naturalism from time immemorial. For a naturalist nothing can be substantial or efficacious in thought except its organs and instruments, such as brains, training, words, and books. Actual thought, being invisible and imponderable, eludes this sort of chase. It has always been rather ignored by materialists; but it remained for American optimists to turn their scorn of useless thought into a glad denial of its existence. This negative implication of behaviorism follows also from the commonsense view that mind and body act upon each other alternately; for when his view is carried out with empirical rigor, it corrects the speculative confusion which first suggested it. What it called mind turns out never to have been anything but a habit in matter, a way people have of acting, speaking, and writing. The actuality of spirit, mystically momentary, does not fall within the purview of this empirical inventory any more than the realm of truth, invisibly eternal. Men of affairs, who can easily tell a clever man from a fool, are behaviorists by instinct; but they may scout their own conviction when it is proposed to them by philosophers in paradoxical language. The business intellect, by the time it comes to theorizing, is a little tired. It will either trust a first impression, and bluff it out, or else it will allow comfortable traditional assurances in these hazy regions to relieve it of responsibility.

Is Dewey a behaviorist? On the positive side of the theory, he certainly is; and it is only when we interpret what he says about ideas, meanings, knowledge, or truth behavioristically, that the sense and the force of it begin to appear. Often, indeed, he seems to jump the barrier, and to become a behaviorist in the negative sense also, denying the existence of thought: because it would be to deny its existence if we reduced it to its material manifestations. At least at one point, however, the existence of thought in its actuality and spiritual concentration is admitted plainly. Not, indeed, on the ground which to most philosophers would seem obvious and final, namely, that people sometimes do actually feel and think. This consideration might seem to

Dewey irrelevant, because actual feeling and thinking are accounted for initially, on his view, by the absolute existence of the specious or conventional world: they do not need to be introduced again among its details. An impersonal transcendental spectator, though never mentioned, is always assumed; and the spectacle of nature unrolled before him may be, and strictly speaking must be, wholly observable and material. There can not be any actual mind in experience except the experience itself. The consideration which nevertheless leads Dewey to graft something consciously actual and spiritual upon the natural world is of quite another sort. Essentially, I suspect, it flows from his choice of "events" to be his metaphysical elements (of which more presently); incidentally it is attached to the sympathetic study which he has made of Aristotle. Events, he thinks, have natural "endings," "culminations," or "consummations." They are not arbitrary sections made in the flux of nature, as if by geometrical planes passed across the current of a river. They are natural waves, pulsations of being, each of which, without any interruption in its material inheritance and fertility, forms a unit of a higher order. These units (if I may express the matter in my own language) fall sometimes into the realm of truth, when they are simply observable patterns or rhythms, and sometimes into the realm of spirit, as in animal perception or intent, when the complex tensions of bodily or social life generate a single sound, an actual pang, or a vivid idea. Mind at such moments possesses a hypostatic spiritual existence, over and above the whole behaviorist or pragmatic ground-work of mind: it has become conscious, or as Aristotle would say, has reached its second entelechy and become intellect in act. This hypostatic spiritual existence Dewey seems to recognize at least in esthetic contemplation; but evidently every actual feeling or idea, however engrossed in action or however abstractly intellectual, is in the same case.

Such an admission, if taken to heart, would have leavened this whole philosophy; but Dewey makes it grudgingly, and hastens to cover it up. For instance, when he comes upon the phrase "Knowledge of acquaintance," he says that acquaintance implies recognition and recognition familiarity; on the ground,

I suppose, that people are called "acquaintances" when they bow to one another: and we are left with an uncomfortable suspicion that it is impossible to inspect anything for the first time. In another place we are told that consummations are themselves fruitful and ends are also means. Yes, but in what sense? Of course, no earthly flame is so pure as to leave no ashes, and the highest wave sinks presently into the trough of the sea; but this is true only of the substance engaged, which, having reached a culmination here, continues in its course; and the habit which it then acquired may, within limits, repeat the happy achievement, and propagate the light. One torch by material contact may kindle another torch; and if the torches are similar and the wind steady, the flames, too, may be similar and even continuous; but if anyone says that the visible splendor of one moment helps to produce that of another, he does not seem ever to have seen the light. It will therefore be safer to proceed as if the realm of actual spirit had not been broached at this point, and as if the culminations recognized were only runs or nodes discoverable in nature, as in the cycle of reproduction or in sentences in discourse. The behaviorist landscape will then not be split by any spiritual lightning, and naturalism will seem to be established in its most unqualified form. Yet in this case how comes it that Dewey has a metaphysics of his own, that cosmology is absent from his system, and that every natural fact becomes in his hands so strangely unseizable and perplexing?

This question, which is the crux of the whole system, may be answered, I think, in a single phrase: *The dominance of the foreground.* In nature there is no foreground or background, no here, no now, no moral cathedra, no centre so really central as to reduce all other things to mere margins and mere perspectives. A foreground is by definition relative to some chosen point of view, to the station assumed in the midst of nature by some creature tethered by fortune to a particular time and place. If such a foreground becomes dominant in a philosophy naturalism is abandoned. Some local perspective or some casual interest is set up in the place of universal nature or behind it, or before it, so that all the rest of nature is reputed to be intrinsically remote or dubious or merely ideal. This dominance of the foreground has always been the source of metaphysics; and the metaphysics has varied according as the foreground has been occupied by language or fancy or logic or sceptical self-consciousness or religious rapture or moral ambition. Now the dominance of the foreground is in all Dewey's traditions: it is the soul of transcendentalism and also of empiricism; it is the soul of moralism and of that kind of religion which summons the universe to vindicate human notions of justice or to subserve the interests of mankind or of some special nation or civilization. In America the dominance of the foreground is further emphasized by the prevalent absorption in business life and in home affections, and by a general feeling that anything ancient, foreign, or theoretical can not be of much consequence.[3] Pragmatism may be regarded as a synthesis of all these ways of making the foreground dominant: the most close-reefed of philosophical craft, most tightly hugging appearance, use, and relevance to practice today and here, least drawn by the lure of speculative distances. Nor would Dewey, I am sure, or any other pragmatist, ever be a naturalist instinctively or on the wings of speculative insight, like the old Ionians or the Stoics or Spinoza, or like those many mystics, Indian, Jewish, or Mohammedan, who, heartily despising the foreground, have fallen in love with the greatness of nature and have sunk speechless before the infinite. The pragmatist becomes, or seems to become, a naturalist only by accident, when as in the present age and in America the dominant foreground is monopolized by material activity; because material activity, as we have seen, involves naturalistic assumptions, and has been the teacher and the proof of naturalism since the beginning of time. But elsewhere and at other periods experience is free to offer different perspectives into which the faithful pragmatist will be drawn with equal zeal; and then pragmatic metaphysics would cease to be naturalistic and become, perhaps, theological. Naturalism in Dewey is accordingly an

---

[3] I can imagine the spontaneous pragmatism of some President of a State University if obliged to defend the study of Sanskrit before a committee of Senators. "You have been told," he would say, "that Sanskrit is a dead language. Not at all: Sanskrit is Professor Smith's Department, and growing. The cost is trifling, and several of our sister universities are making it a fresh requirement for the Ph.D. in classics. That, Gentlemen, is what Sanskrit *is*."

assumption imposed by the character of the prevalent arts; and as he is aware that he is a naturalist only to that extent and on that ground, his naturalism is half-hearted and short-winded. It is the specious kind of naturalism possible also to such idealists as Emerson, Schelling, or any Hegelian of the Left, who may scrupulously limit their survey, in its range of objects, to nature and to recorded history, and yet in their attitude may remain romantic, transcendental, piously receiving as absolute the inspiration dominating moral life in their day and country. The idealists, being self-conscious, regarded this natural scene as a landscape painted by spirit; Dewey, to whom self-consciousness is anathema, regards it as a landscape that paints itself; but it is still something phenomenal, all above board. Immediacy, which was an epistemological category, has become a physical one: natural events are conceived to be compounded of such qualities as appear to human observers, as if the character and emergence of these qualities had nothing to do with the existence, position, and organs of those observers. Nature is accordingly simply experience deployed, thoroughly specious and pictorial in texture. Its parts are not (what they are in practice and for living animal faith) substances presenting accidental appearances. They are appearances integrally woven into a panorama entirely relative to human discourse. Naturalism could not be more romantic: nature here is not a world but a story.

We have seen that the foreground, by its dominance, determines whether the empirical philosopher shall be provisionally a naturalist or shall try being something else. What now, looked at more narrowly, is the character of this foreground? Its name is Experience; but lest we should misunderstand this ambiguous word, it is necessary to keep in mind that in this system experience is impersonal. It is not, as a literary psychologist might suppose, a man's feelings and ideas forming a life-long soliloquy, his impressions of travel in this world. Nor is it, as a biologist might expect, such contact of sensitive animals with their environment as adapts them to it and teaches them to remember it. No: experience is here taken in a transcendental, or rather in a moral, sense, as something romantically absolute and practically coercive. There exists a social medium, the notorious scene of all happenings and discoveries, the sum of those current adventures in which anybody might participate. Experience is deputed to include everything to which experience might testify: it is the locus of public facts. It is therefore identical with nature, to the extent and in the aspects in which nature is disclosed to man. Death, for instance, should be set down as a fact of experience. This would not be possible if experience were something personal, unless indeed death was only a transition to another life. For so long as a man's sensations and thoughts continue, he is not dead, and when dead he has no more thoughts or sensations. But is such actual death, we may ask, the death that Dewey can have in mind? The only death open to experience is the death of others (here is a neat proof of immortality for those who like it); and death, for the pragmatist, simply *is* burial. To suppose that a train of thoughts and feelings going on in a man invisibly might at last come to an end, would be to place the fact of death in a sphere which Dewey does not recognize, namely, in the realm of truth; for it would simply be true that the man's thoughts had ceased, although neither he nor anybody else could find that fact in experience. For other people it would remain a fact assumed and credited, for him it would be a destiny that overtook him. Yet Experience, as Dewey understands it, must include such undiscoverable objects of common belief, and such a real, though unobserved, order of events. The dominant foreground which he calls Experience is accordingly filled and bounded not so much by experience as by convention. It is the social world.

How conventional this foreground is will appear even more clearly if we note the elements which are said to compose it. These are events, histories, situations, affairs. The words "affairs" and "situations," in their intentional vagueness, express very well the ethical nerve of this philosophy; for it is essentially a moral attitude or a lay religion. Life is a practical predicament; both necessity and duty compel us to do something about it, and also to think something about it, so as to know what to do. This is the categorical imperative of existence; and according to the Protestant tradition (diametrically opposed to the Indian) the spirit, in heeding its intrinsic vocation, is not alienated from earthly affairs, but on the contrary pledges itself anew to prosecute them with fidelity. Conscience and nature here exercise their suasion concurrently, since conscience merely repeats the summons to enter a field of responsibility—nature—formed by the deposit of its past labors. The most homely business, like the widest policies, may be thus transfused with a direct metaphysical inspiration; and although Dewey avoids all inflated eloquence on this theme, it is clear that his philosophy of Experience is a transcendental moralism.

That the foreground of human life is necessarily moral and practical (it is so even for artists) and that a philosophy which limits itself to clarifying moral perspectives may be a very great philosophy, has been known to the judicious since the days of Socrates. Why could not Dewey have worked out his shrewd moral and intellectual economy within the frame of naturalism, which he knows is postulated by practice, and so have brought clearness and space into the picture, without interposing any metaphysics? Because it is an axiom with him that nothing but the immediate is real. This axiom, far from being self-evident, is not even clear: for everything is "real" in some sense, and there is much doubt as to what sort of being is immediate. At first the axiom produced psychological idealism, because the proudly discoursing minds of philosophers took for granted that the immediate for each man could be only his own thoughts. Later it has been urged (and, I think, truly) that the immediate is rather any object—whether sensible or intelligible makes no difference—found lying in its own specious medium; so that immediatism is not so much subjective as closely attentive and mystically objective. Be it noted, however, that this admitted objectivity of real things remains internal to the immediate sphere: they must never be supposed to possess an alleged substantial existence beyond experience. This experience is no longer subjective, but it is still transcendental, absolute, and groundless; indeed it has ceased to seem subjective only because it seems unconditioned; and in order to get to the bottom and to the substance of anything, we must still ask with Emerson, What is this *to me*, or with William James, What is this *experienced as*. As Dewey puts it, these facts of experience simply *are* or *are had,* and there is nothing more to say about them. Such evidence flooding immediate experience I just now called mystical, using the epithet advisedly; because in this direct possession of being there is no division of subject and object, but rapt identification of some term, intuition of some essence. Such is sheer pleasure or pain, when no source or object is assigned to it; such is esthetic contemplation; such is pure thinking, the flash of intellectual light. This mystical paradise is indefinitely extensible, like life, and far be it from me to speak evil of it; it is there only that the innocent spirit is at home.

But how should pragmatism, which is nothing if not prehensile, take root in this Eden? I am afraid pragmatism is the serpent; for there is a forbidden tree in the midst, the tree of Belief in the Eventual, the fruit of which is Care; and it is evident that our first parents must have partaken of it copiously; perhaps they fed on nothing else. Now when immediate experience is crossed by Care it suffers the most terrible illusion, for it supposes that the eventual about which it is troubled is controllable by the immediate, as by wishes, omens, or high thoughts; in other words, that the essences given in the immediate exist, generate their own presence, and may persist and rearrange themselves and so generate the future. But this is sheer superstition and trust in magic; the philosophy not of experience but of inexperience. The immediate, whether a paradise or a hell, is always specious; it is peopled by specters which, if taken for existing and working things, are illusions; and although they are real enough, in that they have definite character and actual presence, as a dream or a pain has, their reality ends there; they are unsubstantial, volatile, leaving no ashes, and their existence, even when they appear, is imputed to them by a hidden agency, the demon of Care, and lies wholly in being perceived. Thus immediate experience of things, far from being fundamental in nature, is only the dream which accompanies our action as the other dreams accompany our sleep; and every naturalist knows that this waking dream is dependent for its existence, quality, intensity, and duration on obscure processes in the living body, in its interplay with its environ-

ment; processes which go back, through seeds, to the first beginnings of life on earth. Immediate experience is a consummation; and this not in esthetic contemplation alone, but just as
much in birth-pangs or the excitement of battle. All its episodes,
intermittent and wildly modulated, like the sound of wind in
a forest, are bound together and rendered relevant to one another only by their material causes and instruments. So tenuous
is immediate experience that the behaviorist can ignore it altogether, without inconvenience, substituting everywhere objects of conventional belief in their infinite material plane. The
immediate is, indeed, recognized and prized only by mystics,
and Dewey himself is assured of possessing it only by virtue of
his social and ethical mysticism, by which the whole complex
theater of contemporary action seems to him to be given immediately: whereas to others of us (who are perhaps mystical
at other points) this world of practice seems foreign, absent
from our better moments, approachable even at the time of
action only by animal faith and blind presumption, and com-
pacted, when we consider its normal texture, out of human conventions, many of them variable and foolish. A pragmatist who
was not an ethical or social mystic, might explore that world
scientifically, as a physician, politician, or engineer, and remain
throughout a pure behaviorist or materialist, without noticing
immediate experience at all, or once distinguishing what was
given from what was assumed or asserted. But to the mystic, if
he is interested in that world, it all comes forward into the immediate; it becomes indubitable, but at the same time vague;
actual experience sucks in the world in which conventional experience, if left to dogmatize, would have supposed it was going
on; and a luminous cloud of immediacy envelops everything
and arrests the eye, in every direction, on a painted perspective;
for if any object becomes immediate, whatever it may be, it becomes visionary. That same spiritual actuality which Dewey,
in passing, scarcely recognized at the top of animal life, he now
comes upon from within, and without observing its natural
locus, lays at the basis of the universe. The universe, in his system, thereby appears inverted, the accidental order of discovery

being everywhere substituted for the natural order of genesis; and this with grave consequences, since it is not so easy for the universe as for an individual to stand on its head.[4]

Consider, for instance, the empirical status of the past. The only past that ever *is* or *is had* is a specious past, the fading survival of it in the present. Now the form which things wear in the foreground, according to this philosophy, is their *real* form; and the meaning which such immediate facts may assume hangs on their use in executing some living purpose. What follows in regard to past time? That the survival or memory of it comprises all its reality, and that all the meaning of it lies in its possible relevance to actual interests. A memory may serve as a model or condition in shaping some further enterprise, or may be identified with a habit acquired by training, as when we have learned a foreign language and are ready to speak it. Past experience is accordingly real only by virtue of its vital inclusion in some present undertaking, and yesterday is *really* but a term perhaps useful in the preparation of tomorrow. The past, too, must work if it would live, and we may speak without irony of "the futurity of yesterday" in so far as yesterday has any pragmatic reality.

This result is consistent with the general principle of empirical criticism by which we are forbidden to regard God, truth, or the material cosmos as anything but home vistas. When this principle is applied to such overwhelming outer realities, it lightens

---

[4] A curious reversal of the terms "natural" and "ideal" comes about as we assume that the immediate is substantial or that it is visionary. Suppose I say that "everything ideal emanates from something natural." Dewey agrees, understanding that everything remote emanates from something immediate. But what I meant was that everything immediate—sensation, for instance, or love—emanates from something biological. Not, however, (and this is another verbal snare) from the concepts of biological science, essences immediately present to the thoughts of biologists, but from the largely unknown or humanly unknowable process of animal life. I suppose we should not call some of our ideas scientific if they did not trace the movement of nature more accurately and reliably than do our random sensations or dramatic myths; they are therefore presumably truer in regard to those distributive aspects of nature which they select. But science is a part of human discourse, and necessarily poetical, like language. If literal truth were necessary (which is not the case in practice in respect to nature) it would be found only, perhaps, in literature—in the reproduction of discourse by discourse.

the burden of those who hate external compulsions or supports; they can henceforth believe they are living in a moral universe that changes as they change, with no sky lowering over them save a portable canopy which they carry with them on their travels. But now this pleasant principle threatens the march of experience itself: for if my ancestors have no past existence save by working in me now, what becomes of my present being, if ever I cease to work in my descendants? Does experience today draw its whole existence from their future memories? Evidently this can not be the doctrine proposed; and yet if it be once admitted that all the events in time are equally real and equally central, then at every point there is a by-gone past, intrinsically perfectly substantial and self-existent; a past which such memories or continuations as may be integral to life at this later moment need continue only very partially, or need recover only schematically, if at all. In that case, if I ever find it convenient to forget my ancestors, or if my descendants find it advantageous to forget me, this fact might somewhat dash their vanity or mine if we should hear of it, but can not touch our substantial existence or the truth of our lives. Grant this, and at once the whole universe is on its feet again; and all that strange pragmatic reduction of yesterday to tomorrow, of Sanskrit to the study of Sanskrit, of truth to the value of discovering some truth, and of matter to some human notion of matter, turns out to have been a needless equivocation, by which the perspectives of life, avowedly relative, have been treated as absolute, and the dominance of the foreground has been turned from a biological accident into a metaphysical principle. And this quite wantonly: because practice, far from suggesting such a reduction, precludes it, and requires every honest workman to admit the democratic equality of the past and the future with the present, and to regard the inner processes of matter with respect and not with transcendental arrogance. The living convictions of the pragmatist himself are those involved in action, and therefore naturalistic in the dogmatic sense; action involves belief, belief judgment, and judgment dogma; so that the transcendental metaphysics and the practical naturalism of the pragmatist are in sharp contradiction, both in logic and in spirit. The one expresses his speculative egotism, the other his animal faith.

Of course, it is not Dewey nor the pragmatic school that is to blame for this equivocation; it is a general heirloom, and has infected all that criticism of scholastic dogma on which modern philosophy is founded. By expressing this critical principle more thoroughly, the pragmatists have hoped to clear the air, and perhaps ultimately may help to do so. Although I am myself a dogmatic naturalist, I think that the station assumed by Dewey, like the transcendental station generally, is always legitimate. Just as the spirit has a right to soliloquize, and to regard existence as a strange dream, so any society or nation or living interest has a right to treat the world as its field of action, and to recast the human mind, as far as possible, so as to adapt it exclusively to that public function. That is what all great religions have tried to do, and what Sparta and Carthage would have done if they had produced philosophers. Why should not America attempt it? Reason is free to change its logic, as language to change its grammar; and the critic of the life of reason may then distinguish, as far as his penetration goes, how much in any such logic or grammar is expressive of material circumstances, how much is exuberant rhetoric, how much local, and how much human. Of course, at every step such criticism rests on naturalistic dogmas; we could not understand any phase of human imagination, or even discover it, unless we found it growing in the common world of geography and commerce. In this world fiction arises, and to this world it refers. In so far as criticism can trace back the most fantastic ideas—mythology, for instance—to their natural origin, it should enlighten our sympathies, since we should all have lived in the society of those images, if we had had the same surroundings and passions; and if in their turn the ideas prevalent in our own day can be traced back to the material conditions that bred them, our judgment should be enlightened also. Controversy, when naturalism is granted, can yield to interpretation, reconciling the critical mind to convention, justifying moral diversity, and carrying the sap of life to every top-most intellectual flower. All positive transcendental insights, whether empirical, national, or moral, can thus be honored (and disinfected) by the baldest naturalism, remaining itself international, Bohemian, and animal. The luminous fog of immediacy has a place in nature; it is a meteorological and optical effect, and often a blessing. But why should immediacy be thought to be absolute or a criterion of reality? The great error of dogmatists, in hypostatizing their conclusions into alleged preëxistent facts, did not lie in believing that facts of some kind preëxisted; the error lay only in framing an inadequate view of those facts and regarding it as adequate. God and matter are not any or all the definitions which philosophers may give of them: they are the realities confronted in action, the mysterious but momentous background, which philosophers and other men mean to describe by their definitions or myths or sensible images. To hypostatize these human symbols, and identify them with matter or with God, is idolatry: but the remedy for idolatry is not iconoclasm, because the senses, too, or the heart, or the pragmatic intellect, can breed only symbols. The remedy is rather to employ the symbols pragmatically, with detachment and humor, trusting in the steady dispensations of the substance beyond.

GEORGE SANTAYANA

ROME, ITALY

9

Gordon W. Allport

DEWEY'S INDIVIDUAL AND SOCIAL
PSYCHOLOGY

DEWEY'S INDIVIDUAL AND SOCIAL PSYCHOLOGY

JOHN DEWEY's productive years span almost exactly the lifetime of modern scientific psychology. Born in 1859, his formative period coincided with the formative period of the New Psychology. In 1882, just three years after the founding of the first psychological laboratory, he began to write on topics of mental science—at first with a broad philosophical touch, but soon also with a concreteness better fitted to the aspirations of a young science. His distinguished work continues into the present, and taken as a whole constitutes a remarkable story of intellectual leadership over a period of more than fifty years.

Although we are interested here only in Dewey's psychological work, it is impossible to trace its development entirely apart from the course of his philosophical thought. He himself assigns his pyschology to a subordinate position. Primarily he is concerned with the *norms* of experience and conduct; with their psychological machinery he has less to do. Yet, at the same time, so close is the dependence of his philosophy upon the actual conduct of living men that he finds himself frequently forced to deal with psychological principles. Thus psychology constitutes a necessary and prominent support to his philosophical thought. It is in this light that we must describe and evaluate it.

I. EARLIEST PSYCHOLOGICAL WORK

Dewey's first psychological work consisted of a group of papers wherein he attempted to gain for himself a surer understanding of the concept of *experience*. In the *Andover Review* he expounded at the age of twenty-five the New Psychology with reference to the implications of laboratory researches for a philosophy of experience. Dewey observed that the new science was willing to throw itself upon experience, making "no attempts to dictate to this experience, and tell it what it *must* be in order to square with a scholastic logic."[1]

Yet experience, he felt, is not a matter of mere sensational impressions. The sensationalistic views of the so-called empirical psychologists he rejected as a species of peculiarly degrading anthropomorphism, an anthropomorphism which sets up "the poorest elements of its own feeling, a sensation, and reverences that as its own and the universe's cause."[2] We shall never account for experience, Dewey insisted, by referring it to something else. Sensation is not prior to consciousness or knowledge; it is but a consequent that depends upon experience. In the fullness of experience, which is our starting point, we find a fusion of subject and object.[3] Psychology does not deal with mere subjective states minus the object world, because both subject and object are contained within the experiential whole; they cannot be characterized separately. It is the work of psychology to determine the relations of subject and object as they arise *within* consciousness.

One sees here the powerful influence of Hegel. Dewey named the position he was defending "absolute idealism," and his critic Hodgson added a bit crisply that if such transcendentalism is to be admitted as psychology, then Dewey should in simple fairness label it "psychology: human *and divine.*"[4]

As one might expect, *Psychology*, Dewey's textbook of 1886, was caught in the same turmoil of ebbing transcendentalism and upsurging positivism. The text supports the older rationalistic, soul psychology, on the one hand, and the newer sensory and reaction psychology, on the other. Introspection is the preferred method. Sensation is important, though not all-important. The researches of Helmholtz, Hering, Volkmann, Stumpf, and Wundt are faithfully recorded. Habit—lightly touched—is a matter of successive associations that tend with repetition to become somehow simultaneous. Reaction-forms

---

[1] "The New Psychology," *Andover Review*, 1884, 2, 268.
[2] "Psychology as Philosophic Method," *Mind*, 1886, 11, 169.
[3] "The Psychological Standpoint," *Mind*, 1886, 11, 1-19.
[4] S. H. Hodgson, "Illusory Psychology," *Mind*, 1886, 11, 488.

are described, and there are other adumbrations of the functional psychology to come. It is because of these features that Brett characterizes the text as "the first gray dawn of that tomorrow for which the psychology of the American colleges was waiting."[5]

At the same time the text still invokes the Soul to assist in the psychologizing. The unity of mental life must be accounted for, and Dewey saw no way to obtain unity excepting through the activity of the self, defined, a bit circularly, as "the activity of synthesis upon sense."[6] Attention, for example, is "the activity of self in combining units." Apperception "organizes the world of knowledge by bringing the self to bear upon it." Eight years later Dewey would regard the unifying self as a useless redundancy, accounting in other terms for such unity as mind achieves; but in 1886 he was still far from this position.

II. FUNCTIONALISM

It was James's *Principles* that helped lift Dewey from the fence where his early writings had precariously perched him. So assured was James in his endorsement of the positive premises of the new psychology that his younger colleague felt encouraged to abandon transcendental psychology for good and all in favor of a more earthy functionalism.[7]

But Dewey was no blind follower. He quickly perceived inconsistencies in James that needed to be remedied, as well as insights that merited expansion. Immediately following the publication of the *Principles* came Dewey's heaviest concentration on the special problems of psychology.

In 1894 he reported a minor observational study on the language of a young child, stressing characteristically the importance of its predicative character. Even though nouns prevail in the child's vocabulary, their predicative significance in the

[5] G. S. Brett, *A History of Psychology*, 1921, Vol. 3, 261.

[6] "On Some Current Conceptions of the Term 'Self,' " *Mind*, 1890, 15, 58-74.

[7] Another influence doubtless was Dewey's growing interest in education. His *Applied Psychology* (1889) demonstrated to him the urgent need for a less formalistic psychology of will. Habit, interest, and adjustment were the concepts he needed, and these he could not evolve so long as he treated will in the manner of Hegel or Herbart.

child's striving for better contact with his environment must not be overlooked.[8]

At the same time the James-Lange theory of emotions engaged his attention. He perceived a contradiction between Darwin's theory of emotion as *expression* and James's theory of its *peripheral* origin during acts of adjustment. The opposition he resolved by demonstrating that expression itself is a mode of adaptation. Emotion follows an interference with a smoothly coördinated tendency to action. It occurs only when there is a temporary struggle among habits and partial inhibition. Its origin is indeed peripheral, as James says, but its significance for survival and its relation to the situation of the total organism at the moment are compatible with Darwin's views. A significant concept introduced in these papers on emotion is that of *interest*. Interest, Dewey maintains, is the antithesis of emotional seizure, existing only when an adjustment is well coördinated, when conflict—and hence emotion—are virtually absent.[9]

So whole-hearted is his conversion to the functional position that Dewey accuses James of faint-heartedness. In particular it is the self, with which Dewey had such deep concern in 1886, that he is now bent on ruling out of court. With James's *Fiat* he will have nothing to do; not even the mildest endorsement of indeterminism is allowable. The individual and his actions are one, says Dewey. There are concrete attitudes, habits, desires, ideas and ignorance; but there is no ego behind these states. There is no call to recede into the ego to explain will, any more than to explain consciousness. If James can dispense with the Pure Ego in thought, he should dispense likewise with the Pure Mover in conduct. "If the stream of thought can run itself in one case, the stream of conduct may administer itself in the other."[10]

In a similar vein Dewey criticizes Baldwin's theory of ef-

---

[8] *Psychol. Rev.*, 1894, 1, 63-66.

[9] *Psychol. Rev.*, 1894, 1, 553-569; *ibid.*, 1895, 2, 13-32. McDougall has questioned Dewey's claim that emotion comes merely from the clash of habits. For McDougall, of course, emotion accompanies the operation of primary instincts, whether or not a state of frustration exists. It is therefore fully present in interests. *Amer. J. Sociol.*, 1924, 29, 657-676.

[10] "The Ego as Cause," *Philos. Rev.*, 1894, 3, Ftn. 340 f.

fort.[11] Effort is not, as Baldwin says, "consciousness of opposition between what we call self and muscular resistance." There is for Dewey no longer any self separate from musculature. Effort now is viewed merely as "the critical point of progress in action arising whenever old habits are in process of reconstruction or of adaptation to new conditions." Nor is attention any longer one of the capacities of selfhood; it does not cause the sense of effort. It *is* the sense of effort.

By 1894, then, we see that Dewey has repudiated completely both the substance and the shadow of soul psychology. He will have nothing more to do with an active self, as knower or as effective agent in will; nor does he see any need for the passive self, preserved by Calkins, as the unique ground for all experience. Dewey insists upon the seamless character of experience. To be aware of oneself is merely a part of the total circuit of awareness. It is an event belonging to a larger whole. No need to postulate a substantive person as carrier and locus of a circuit.[12]

We come now to the most important psychological paper of the nineties and probably, so far as psychology is concerned, Dewey's most influential essay, "The Reflex Arc Concept in Psychology."[13] Having abandoned the remote unifying agency from his conception of mental life, he is looking around for a new guarantee of consecutiveness and coherence in behavior. He finds at hand the concept of the reflex arc, recently borrowed by psychology from physiology. But on examination he rejects it, for it makes activity "a patchwork of disjointed parts, a mechanical conjunction of unallied processes."[14]

A burn does not merely induce us to jerk our finger from the flame. It brings not only a withdrawal reflex but at the same

---

[11] "The Psychology of Effort," *Philos. Rev.*, 1897, 6, 43-56.
[12] At about this time Dewey rejects also the sharp distinction then prevailing between functional and structural psychology. The problem of Psychology, he says, is the total course of experience in the individual mind. The distinction between structuralism and functionalism seemed to him about as reasonable "as a division of botanists into rootists and flowerists." ("Psychology as Philosophic Method," Berkeley, Univ. Chronicle, 1899.) Yet in spite of this stricture Dewey's own stress was so consistently upon the stream of consciousness and so seldom upon its states that he must be classified with the functionalists.
[13] *Psychol. Rev.*, 1896, 3, 357-370.
[14] *Ibid.*, 358.

time affects the ocular perception of the inviting flame in such a way that its stimulating character is forever changed. Or, we turn our head to catch a whisper. Is the act thus completed? No, our response is as closely related to the sound that is now becoming effective as it was to the unintelligible sound that served as the first stimulus. The stimuli of both the beginning and the end situation belong to the same act. Every reaction is a circuit, leading to a redistribution of stress and tension. Adjustment is not a matter of response to a stimulus but of re-established rapport within one's environment.

III. Habits

Dissatisfied with the reflex-arc, Dewey felt his way toward a unit that might better express the circuit character of all behavior. Twenty-six years after his attack upon the reflex-arc he finally proposed *habit* as the unit most suitable for psychology to employ.

Habit was not a new concept in Dewey's thinking. On the contrary, it had always been a favorite with him. But in his early years he seemed content with the traditional definition in terms of the fusion of successive associations into one simultaneous pattern. Then came the brilliant and melodramatic chapter by James that set a fashion hard to break. Though James, no less than Dewey, was a believer in an open universe and in man's capacity to modify his behavior step by step, James was never troubled by the excessive rigidity he ascribed to habit. But Dewey, always more consistent than James, saw the consequences of this view and never subscribed to the ball-and-chain conception.

He sought rather in his doctrine of habit to represent both the lag that is characteristic of human behavior and of social custom, and at the same time the adaptability and range of equivalence found in conduct. Habit, he also felt, should be credited with a dynamic or motivational character. When between 1917 and 1922 he decided to dispense with instincts, the need for a dynamic unit, one that should be "assertive, insistent, self-penetrating" became all the more urgent.[15]

[15] The dates represent the publication of "The Need for a Social Psychology," *Psychol. Rev.*, 24, 266-277, and *Human Nature and Conduct*, respectively.

In the following passage Dewey characterizes habit as he now conceived it, setting it against the traditional view established by James and the elder associationists:

While it is admitted that the word habit has been used in a somewhat broader sense than is usual, we must protest against the tendency in psychological literature to limit its meaning to repetition. This usage is much less in accord with popular usage than is the wider way in which we have used the word. It assumes from the start the identity of habit with routine. Tendency to repeat acts is an incident of many habits but not of all. A man with the habit of giving way to anger may show his habit by a murderous attack upon someone who has offended. His act is nonetheless due to habit because it occurs only once in his life. The essence of habit is an acquired predisposition to *ways* or modes of response, not to particular acts except as, under special conditions, these express a way of behaving. Habit means special sensitiveness or accessibility to certain classes of stimuli, standing predilections and aversions, rather than bare recurrence of specific acts. It means will.[16]

Habits, though elements of behavior, are not independent of one another; the exercise and development of one affects all. Were it not so, our acts would be "simply a bundle, an untied bundle at that."[17] Character could not exist. It is the consecutiveness and consistency among habits, achieved through a gradual process of selection, that constitute character. But be it noted that the selection occurs only through modifying surrounding conditions, not by fiat or will. Selection, or choice, becomes effective when the organism learns to coöperate with environmental conditions in a deliberative manner; deliberation being nothing more than "an experiment in making various combinations of selected elements of habits and impulses, to see what the resultant action would be like if it were entered upon. Deliberation and will are a matter of trial acts executed incipiently in imagination not in overt fact."[18]

Here Dewey's conception of habit leads into his philosophy of morality. Indeed it is in the interests of ethics that the doctrine of habits was evolved. It has a decidedly deductive cast. It is not advanced with experimental evidence, nor is it com-

[16] *Human Nature and Conduct,* 41 f.
[17] *Ibid.,* 38.
[18] *Ibid.,* 190.

pared in any detail to similar units, especially *attitudes*, proposed by other psychologists.[19]

Dewey's conception of habit is not altogether successful; it is neither explicitly defined nor consistently employed. To give one example of inconsistency: after stating that repetition of acts is not the essential fact of habit Dewey later declares that "with habit alone there is a machine-like repetition, a duplicating recurrence of old acts."[20] To add to the confusion we are told that habit covers "the very make-up of desire, intent, choice, disposition which gives an act its voluntary quality."[21] Because he ascribes so many contradictory attributes (variability and stability, lag and progress, compulsiveness and choice) to the habit mechanism, psychologists have failed to adopt Dewey's account of it in detail. But the conception has had its influence none the less.

IV. MOTIVE

To understand sympathetically Dewey's psychology of motivation it is necessary to grant his primary assumption that the first need of the organism is to live and to grow. What man wants is not so much the satisfaction of separate autochthonous drives as a way of controlling the environment in relation to the diversified and almost limitless array of goals involved in the life process. Even though our first wants are determined by what our body calls for, we soon come to want the instruments of satisfaction of these wants for their own sakes. Means and ends seldom are as sharply distinguished as instinct psychologists would have us believe. Even in primitive agricul-

[19] Here we have an example of the isolationism that afflicts Dewey's psychology. Granted that relatively little work had been done in 1922 upon the perplexing problem of units of personality, still there were many contacts that he could have made with profit.

Present-day readers of Dewey will do well to check his doctrine of habit against other comparable concepts. See W. McDougall, "Tendencies as Indispensable Postulates of all Psychology," Paris: *Proc. XI Internat. Congress of Psychology*, 1937; likewise G. W. Allport, "Attitudes," *Handbook of Social Psychology*, Worcester: Clark University Press, 1935, Ch. 17; also *Personality: A Psychological Interpretation*, New York: Holt, 1935, Chs. 9-12.

[20] Cf. *Human Nature and Conduct*, 42 and 180.
[21] Dewey and Tufts, *Ethics*, revised edition (1932), 181.

tural societies man does not define his end to be the satisfaction of hunger as such.

Agriculture is so complicated and loaded with all kinds of technical activities, associations, deliberations and social divisions of labor, that conscious attention and interest are in the process and its content. Even in the crudest agriculture, means are developed to the point where they demand attention on their own account.[22]

This quotation, written twenty years before the publication of *Human Nature and Conduct,* contains the essence of Dewey's later doctrine of motivation. Man, so Dewey is convinced, quickly loses sight of his simple original impulses. Motives are vastly more numerous than instincts—"as numerous as are original impulsive activities multiplied by the diversified consequences they produce as they operate under diverse conditions."[23]

He has no use for sex, hunger, anger, or fear, treated as if they were "lump forces, like the combustion or gravity of old-fashioned physical science."[24]

Even in the cases of hunger and sex, where the channels of action are fairly demarcated by antecedent conditions (or 'nature'), the actual content and feel of hunger and sex, are indefinitely varied according to their social contexts. Only when a man is starving, is hunger an unqualified natural impulse.[25]

The treatment of sex by psycho-analysts is most instructive, for it flagrantly exhibits both the consequences of artificial simplification and the transformation of social results into psychic causes.[26]

Nor is Dewey well disposed toward the simple and sovereign motivational forces advanced by the simplicist social scientists.

We have no generalized will to power, but only the inherent pressure of every activity for an adequate manifestation.[27]

Egoism holds no appeal:

[22] "Interpretation of Savage Mind," *Psychol. Rev.,* 1902, 9, 217-230.
[23] *Human Nature and Conduct,* 122.
[24] *Ibid.,* 150.
[25] *Ibid.,* 153.
[26] *Loc. cit.*
[27] *Ibid.,* 141.

The fallacy consists in transforming the (truistic) fact of acting *as* a self into the fiction of acting always *for* self.[28]

Hedonism is equally deceptive. The utilitarians are as far off as any other instinct-mythologists.

Of all things [future pleasures and pains] lend themselves least readily to anything approaching a mathematical calculus.[29]

The present not the future is ours. And in the present we find that our motives are nothing more than impulses viewed as constituents of habit. Impulses never exist by themselves. The primary fact in conduct is the habit. It is our habits that enable us to live—or someone else's habits, as in infancy where the first determiners are parental habits. By the time the young child's impulses rebel at parental regulation, he has his own habits of self-regulation.

Only when impulses are acute and not taken care of in the ordinary habitual channels do they become actually decisive and prepotent in conduct, pivots upon which the reorganization of activities turns, giving new directions to old habits and reshaping them.

Impulses like stimuli are only mediative. Having once provoked a response, their own nature is altered. This back reference of experience into impulse is simply an extension of Dewey's doctrine of the evolving stimulus-response circuits with which he sought (in 1896) to replace the concept of the reflex-arc. Motives like all other units of behavior are constantly changing.[30]

The critique of Dewey's motivational psychology takes various forms. McDougall is a sharp critic of its lack of incisive-

[28] *Ibid.*, 136.
[29] *Ibid.*, 203.
[30] The consequences for ethics of this doctrine of evolving circuits is important. It follows that "good" conduct can never twice be the same. Only if impulse and habit were rigid to the point of immobility could exactly the same good ever recur. Since impulse and habit are in reality ever-changing, we must conclude that "ends are, in fact, literally endless, forever coming into existence as new activities occasion new consequences." *Human Nature and Conduct*, 211. The good is a matter of rectifying *present* trouble through the coöperation of habit, impulse, and thought. Trouble is eternally fresh trouble, and "good" solutions are forever new.

ness.[31] He objects that one cannot discover just how much dynamic force Dewey intends to ascribe to habit. Some habits Dewey clearly regards as mechanical, automatic, and as auxiliary to other forms of motivation. Other habits are "energetic and dominating ways of acting," " assertive, insistent, self-perpetuating." They are "propulsive" and moving always toward some end. Criteria are lacking for distinguishing between a habit that is motivational and one that is passively instrumental.

Further, some psychologists, McDougall among them, are dissatisfied with the secondary rôle assigned to impulse and instinct. According to Dewey impulse arises only when habits prove inadequate to the perpetual task of coming to terms with the environment. Habits blocked engender impulse; but impulse is serviceable only for the restructuration of habits. And impulses are never twice the same. Such constant evolving and interweaving, stressing now habit and now impulse, is fatally opposed to all attempts at psychological classification. The traditional thing to do is to erect a systematic psychology of motivation upon the hypothesis of one simple and sovereign motivational force, or upon an assumption of a plurality of separate instincts, drives, desires, or wishes; it is even possible to handle compounds, fusions and hierarchies of motivational forces, together with their conditioning and modification so long as these motivational forces are named and defined. But when Dewey, or anyone else, proposes to take away the anchorage of fixed categories and fixed mechanisms, the possibility of conceptual manipulation disappears and the science of human nature seems built not upon solid rock but upon shifting sand.

Yet Dewey's path may be that of wisdom. The desire to classify and to standardize motivational forces is perhaps an instance of wholly misguided taxonomic enterprise. Psychology may have to resign itself to the admission that motivation *is* unique, that no two habit systems, no two sets of impulses, no two ends-in-view are identical in different people. Regrettable as it may seem from the point of view of nomothetic science, there may be no escape from this conclusion. Dewey's picture

[31] *Amer. J. Sociol.*, 1924, 29, 657-676.

of motivation may lack the incisiveness of McDougall's, Freud's, Kempf's, or Murray's, yet he may perceive more clearly than they the infinite variety of ways in which man can accomplish his primary task of adapting and growing within the surrounding world.

Although the picture of evolving motives, changing step by step as proximate goals are reached, successfully challenges the easy classifications of dynamic psychology, it leads at the same time to an exaggeration of change within any given individual. Dewey's stress on evolving goals and evolving mechanisms takes his attention away from the stability of organization in the individual personality. It is all to the good to conclude that motives are not uniform within the species, that they grow with experience, and that they exist independently of their origins, involving peculiar blends of habit, impulse, and thought; but it is not helpful to be left without any way of conceiving the patterning of motives within personality over a range of years. He seems not to have asked himself how long-lived an interest may be, or how enduring a habit. Nor has he considered the variable range that thoughts and impulses may have and still retain the same essential significance for the individual. He deals, in short, more adequately with the progressive shifts in personality than with its stability of structure.

V. Thought

The problems of thought, or, as he now prefers to say, the problems of inquiry,[32] have always been for Dewey a matter of major concern. We have already called attention to his doctrine that "thought is born as the twin of impulse in every moment of impeded habit." Its function is to increase the meaning of the present experience and lead to novel solutions beyond what is possible through merely impulsive or routine (habitual) action. Yet thought is more ephemeral than either impulse or habit: "unless it is nurtured, it speadily dies, and habit and instinct continue their civil warfare."[33] Left to itself without training, thought accomplishes nothing. Without training it is unable to

[32] Cf. *Logic*, 21.
[33] *Human Nature and Conduct*, 171.

resist the idols and inadequate beliefs that beset every state of perplexity. Rapid, comforting solutions, the product of untrained thought—sentimental, romantic, self-justifying fantasies—serve only to blunt the misery of the moment. Emotional disturbance, even though it is the original incentive to thought, is at the same time the chief cause of unwarranted belief and conviction. "Nothing is so easy to fool as impulse and no one is deceived so readily as a person under strong emotion."[34]

Dewey's treatment of thought is thoroughgoing in its functionalism. Thought is always *mind in use*. It is not a matter of images, *Bewusstheiten*, or postures of consciousness. It is rather active search for coherent meaning serviceable to practical activity. Thought is an instrument virtually equated with intelligence. Both are the means by which we foresee the future, giving our next action order and direction.[35]

Although Dewey assigns intellect an instrumental rôle, auxiliary to impulse and habit, he gives it more significance than do the true anti-rationalists.

Impulse is primary and intelligence is secondary and in some sense derivative. There should be no blinking of this fact. But recognition of it as a fact exalts intelligence. For thought is not the slave of impulse to do its bidding. . . . What intelligence has to do in the service of impulse is to act not as its obedient servant but as its clarifier and liberator. . . . Intelligence converts desire into plans. . . .[36]

What he says of intelligence and thought is equally true for judgment, deliberation, reflection, and reason. They all have one and the same function: to restore that balance which because of

---

[34] *Ibid.*, 255.

[35] Here we must comment on Dewey's lack of interest in *capacity* psychology. Intelligence testing concerns him not at all. *Anyone* is capable of thinking and so improving his adaptations and mastery within his environment. A pupil labelled as hopeless, he points out, may react in a quick and lively fashion when the thing in hand seems to him worth while. He has likewise written, "Barring physical defect or disease, slowness and dullness in all directions are comparatively rare." (*How We Think*, 35.) There is no homogeneous faculty of thought nor any uniform power of intelligence that would, because of differential possession, make education for some pupils unnecessary and for others worthless. In short, individual differences in capacity are of far less consequence than is the fact that everyone can be taught to think more effectively than he does.

[36] *Human Nature and Conduct*, 254 f.

changing internal and external conditions is constantly interfered with in spite of all habit can do. Such a totally functional
view leaves no room for fine distinctions between the various
higher mental processes. They are all functionally equivalent.
Dewey disdains the subleties of *Denkpsychologie*. Even in *How
We Think* (1910) there is no mention of the flood of introspective studies coming from the German and American laboratories
of that time. He early lost interest in structural psychology.
Apperception, the texture of ideas, the fusion of percepts, the
feeling of relation, vanished from his writings. He cares only
about the use of the states and processes of consciousness in the
service of education for straight thinking. For this reason
Dewey's writings on thought are not a systematic contribution
to the psychology of the higher mental processes. His nearest
approach to an orderly analysis is the widely quoted five-fold
steps in reflective thinking: (i) a felt difficulty; (ii) its location
and definition; (iii) suggestion of possible solution; (iv) development by reasoning of the bearings of the suggestion; (v)
further observation and experiment leading to its acceptance or
rejection, that is, the conclusion of belief or disbelief.[37]

The *Logic* (1938) adds little to the psychological analysis of
thought, even though it regards psychology as "more directly
concerned with the focal center of initiation and execution of inquiry than are other sciences."[38] But just what psychology has
to contribute is not explained. We do, however, find in the *Logic*
two developments that have important bearings on psychological theory and practice. One is the author's complete repudiation of the dualistic position.

Although in the *Logic* Dewey does not free himself from subjective terminology, he is quite certain that terms like thought,
judgment, idea, suggestion and reason can be interpreted in
objective ways. He writes, "I am not aware of any so-called
merely 'mental' activity or result that cannot be described in
the objective terms of organic activity modified and directed by
symbols-meaning, or language, in its broad sense."[39] The sub-

[37] *How We Think*, 72.
[38] *Logic*, 36.
[39] *Ibid.*, 57.

ject or self vanishes, and in its place Dewey establishes the "biological-cultural human being." The felt needs and perplexities of this biological-cultural being are not to be viewed as subjective; they arise because "the situation is inherently doubtful." It is not a hunger drive, for example, that leads to searching behavior but rather a whole problematic situation in which the organic imbalance of hunger plays an interdependent part with all other phases of the situation: "The habit of disposing of the doubtful as if it belonged only to *us* rather than to the existential situation in which we are caught and implicated is an inheritance from subjectivistic psychology."[40]

It is true that possible solutions present themselves as *ideas*, "but an idea is merely an organic anticipation of what will happen when certain operations are executed under and with respect to observed conditions."[41] The organism is caught in an indeterminate situation requiring some transformation for the organism's own welfare. Then follows a progression of finer discriminations and better objective relationships, until a balanced condition ensues. The resolution of indeterminate situations suggests Köhler's principle of requiredness, and the reduction of the problem to what is objectively accessible—the methodological procedure—recalls contemporary operational behaviorism.

The second concept in the *Logic* of special significance for psychology is that of the "situation." Suggestive as it is of the "field" of Gestalt theorists, "situation" has considerably broader reference. It is more than a mere perceptual field. Psychologists err in treating perception in an isolated way, apart from many other effective parts of the situation. "In actual experience, there is never any such isolated singular object or event; *an* object or event is always a special part, phase, or aspect, of an environing experienced world—a situation."[42] And Dewey goes so far as to deny the capacity of psychology to study the nature of a problematic situation in its entirety.

One of the failures of perception psychology is its neglect of

[40] *Ibid.*, 106.
[41] *Ibid.*, 109.
[42] *Ibid.*, 67.

the economic and political conditions that are important factors in many, if not most, of the indeterminate conditions that we are striving to resolve. Perceptually we are usually unaware of such important influences as these. The cultural and social sciences recognize them, and psychology would do well to allow more generously than it does for the unconscious influence upon conduct of our status, our memberships, and the times in which we live.

With its operational and Gestalt flavor, and with its acceptance of situational and cultural determinism, the *Logic* brings Dewey's general philosophy of human behavior to mature expression, but adds little to the narrower psychology of thought.

VI. Educational Psychology

The secret of Dewey's great devotion to education lies in his conviction that no man ever realized his potentialities merely by being left alone. If democracy is, as he believes, the most advanced way of community living, it must be continually born anew in every generation, for man's original nature by no means leads to the spontaneous exercise of the powers of inquiry and self-reorganization that is demanded by democratic life. A set of cheap and easy absolutes may satisfy adherents of a totalitarian state but not of democracy. The authentic democrat takes fright at the appearance of rigid formulations set for the guidance of his conduct. He is satisfied only with an educational policy that keeps the mind limber, and enables it to participate in its own destiny. Especially objectionable are those psychological theories that set fixed limits to the capacity of human beings for self-improvement. A rigid doctrine of instinct, for example, may be used to discourage educational progress and so lead to the defeat of the democratic ideal of participation by all. Even the conception of the constant I.Q. savors of conservative aristocracy.

Among psychological theories that lead to educational stagnation Dewey attacks imitation. There is, of course, no instinct of imitation, and if imitativeness is encouraged in the child by routine drill, it inhibits his power to re-make old habits. Drill at best generates skill in a *particular* performance. In itself it does not lead to new perceptions of bearings and connections. The environment constantly changes, and since this is so any stereotyped way of acting may become disastrous at some critical moment. A vaunted, highly-trained skill may then turn out to be merely a gross ineptitude. Learning must bring with it capacity for constant adaptation. Every skill should be transferable, every hypothesis tentative, every channel of thought versatile in its combination and intercommunication with other channels; for education is that "reconstruction or reorganization of experience which adds to the meaning of experience, and which increases ability to direct the course of subsequent experience."[43]

A properly formulated psychology will inevitably work hand in hand with the instrumental ideal of education. True psychology is itself "a conception of democracy," for it believes in the efficacy of training, of communication, participation and action, as ways of changing human conduct. It does not deal with absolutes. Rather, it proceeds step by step, asking what the organism is going to do next. And it marches hand in hand with the ethics of instrumentalism asking what it is *better* to do next.

Psychology provides the teacher with tools for discrimination and analysis. She cannot deal with a total, unanalyzed personality. She needs instruments of discernment to confront a personality in the forming. Specifically, psychology must tell the teacher what stimuli shall be presented to the sense-organs to obtain a desired result; what stable complexes of associations may be created; what coördinations and adaptations can be evoked and what their effect will be. Hence the application of psychology to education is the only way of achieving particular ends within the broadly conceived ethical goal of democracy and self-realization.

The close linkage between psychology and education is a long-standing conviction with Dewey. As early as 1889 he entitled his Introduction to the Principles and Practice of Education *Applied Psychology.*[44] And in 1895 in *The Psychology of Number* he again insisted that only a knowledge of psychology

[43] *Democracy and Education* (1916), 89.
[44] J. A. McLellan was co-author of both *Applied Psychology* and *The Psychology of Number.*

will supply education with the conditions which will enable psychical functions to mature and to pass into higher stages of integration.

The true purity of psychology as a science exists only in its application, never apart from it. If psychology is not actively concerned with education, or health, or adaptive thought, or social relations, then it has no reason for being. To be a science lockstitched with life is the highest tribute Dewey can pay psychology. He has only scorn for the snobbish notion that applied knowledge is somehow less worthy or less desirable than pure knowledge.

Yet Dewey does not fall into the trap of psychologism. He does not regard psychology as all-powerful and all-inclusive. It cannot, for instance, supply us with our *ideals* for education, nor can it test the *correctness* of thought nor the *value* of conduct. But it can give us a definite base line from which to measure ethical claims by telling whether ideals are attainable, and how to go about attaining them.

All these considerations lead Dewey to foster the closest and friendliest relations between education and psychology. He sees psychology as an infant science, perhaps offering little as yet to the cause of sound pedagogy. But great is his faith that ultimately the psychology of functional and organic development will expand, dealing more adequately than now with progressive adaptations within complex situations. Such a psychology will implement and advance immeasurably the aims of education and therewith the aims of democracy itself.

VII. Social and Political Psychology

As early as 1899 Dewey made the striking observation that the system of postulates and theories that one adopts in psychology is likely to be politically conditioned.[45] In particular the estimate people place upon the significance of individuality varies according to the political frame within which psychology is written. An aristocracy sees the individual as unimportant unless the individual is of the higher classes. Apologists for the *status quo*

---

[45] "Psychology as Philosophic Method," Berkeley: University Press, 1899. Reprinted as "Consciousness and Experience" in *The Influence of Darwin on Philosophy and Other Essays* (1910), 242-270.

draw support from psychological doctrines that declare human nature to be virtually unalterable.[46] In present times Dewey could find additional proof for his contention in the psychological dicta of the National Socialist and Communist ideologies. His recognition of the ideological factor, it should be noted, antedates the work of Mannheim and other *Wissenssoziologen*.

So important to Dewey are the political consequences of psychological theory that he takes considerable pains to discredit social psychologies that seem to him undemocratic in their orientation. He does not combat these theories by marshalling contradictory evidence but repudiates them frankly upon the basis of their ideological affiliations. What Dewey wants is a psychology compatible with democracy and he rejects any mental science having contrary implications. His opposition to the theory of fixed instincts, to the French school of Imitation, to Durkheim's school of the collective mind, can be understood on this ground, likewise his suspiciousness of capacity psychology and his discrediting of the intelligence quotient.

Other concepts are equally uncongenial to him. He has little use for Wundtian folk-psychology, since it employs the rubrics of introspective psychology. In fact, introspective categories, he holds, are the chief cause for the backwardness of social psychology.[47] Interestingly enough, he rejects the dualism of introspective psychology partly for its political implications.

Those who wish a monopoly of social power find desirable the separation of habit and thought, action and soul, so characteristic of history. For the dualism enables them to do the thinking and planning, while others remain the docile, even if awkward, instruments of execution. Until this scheme is changed, democracy is bound to be perverted in realization.[48]

Dewey compels even a metaphysical postulate to give way unless it is democratically oriented.

[46] "The ultimate refuge of the standpatter in every field, education, religion, politics, industrial and domestic life, has been the notion of an alleged fixed structure of mind. As long as mind is conceived as an antecedent and ready-made thing, institutions and customs may be regarded as its offspring." *Psychol. Rev.* (1917), 24, 273.
[47] "The Need for Social Psychology," *Psychol. Rev.* (1917), 24, 271.
[48] *Human Nature and Conduct*, 72.

To complete his list of rejections, Dewey discounts all social psychology that neglects the outside forces that play upon the organism. For unless we believe in the potency of the environmental situation, it does no good to press for social reform. Even in 1917, when he favored the hypothesis of instincts, he insisted that instincts become real events only when they are related to the situation. Besides instinct or impulse the rubrics of social psychology must include many others—habit, discrimination, thought, coördination, adaptation, and custom. Custom is particularly significant, for it supplies the inescapable framework of conception within which individual thinking is compelled to move.[49]

Custom is the first teacher of habits, and it is the primary duty of social psychology to illuminate the ways in which customs shape habits, and with them desires, beliefs, and purposes. Social psychology rests, of course, directly upon the biological or functional psychology that the previous pages have described. Both begin with the living organism engaged in some act, some coördination. When this coördination is interrupted, when an inadequate habit is broken up, we have the possibility of new coördination, novel conduct, effected through impulse, discrimination, attention, association and thought. This brief formula sets the problems for individual psychology, but whenever custom plays a part in the new coördination, or when other individuals are involved, social psychology is called for.

Some of the special problems of social psychology arise when new coördinations are frustrated and the reconstruction of habits prevented. In such a case emotion rises like a tide. Perhaps this emotion will be diverted into side channels of substitute habits

[49] It should be noted that in his most recent book, the Logic, Dewey widens his concept of framework to include not only custom, but also physical conditions such as soil, sea, mountains, climate, tools, and machines. Conduct is only in part determined by subjective wants, beliefs, and skill, and only in part by the social frame of custom. Both in turn are conditioned by physical phenomena and their laws. By stressing here physical and ecological factors, Dewey diminishes proportionately the place he would give to psychology in accounting for social life. Indeed, he says explicitly that his broadened account of the nature of the surrounding situation is "fatal to the view that social sciences are exclusively, or even dominantly, psychological." Logic, 492.

and disperse itself aimlessly. But perhaps it will rise higher and be met by corresponding emotions in other people. There may result a wave of enthusiasm for some reform, or a violent reaction against some threatening novelty. In any case the conditions of the so-called mob mind are fulfilled. The crowd and mob come into existence because of a disintegration of habits which releases impulses that can be manipulated by skilled demagogues and by propaganda.

Far more stable than the crowd or the mob are the group, the club, the political party. It is this level of human association that interests Dewey particularly, for it is here that the public exists and democratic activity is achieved.

The *Public and Its Problems* sets forth the broad framework of a system of political psychology, much as does Hobbes' *Leviathan*, Rousseau's *Social Contract*, or McDougall's *Group Mind*. But Dewey's views agree with none of his predecessors. He rejects all time-honored conceptions of the common will, the Sovereign People, the group mind, and the Great Society. Political groupings, he insists, have no super-personal character. Nor are they based upon social instincts. Wants, choices and purposes are diverse acts of single human beings, not springing from any native social propensity.

A public, instead of being a mystical entity or the expression of social instinct, is nothing but the by-product of social activity between individuals. So long as A and B have direct private transactions no public is involved. But let the consequences of their transactions extend beyond their own lives, affecting the lives and welfare of others, and a public, based on common interest, springs into being. In itself such a public is unorganized and formless, comprised merely of common segments of certain individuals' interests. One public is created by the existence of motor cars, another by the existence of schools, another by the practice of taxation. As soon as officials are elected, or in some other way recognized, the formless public becomes organized. The officials themselves, of course, are single beings, but they exercise special powers designed to protect the common interests of the members. A comprehensive public articulated and operating through officers who are expected to subordinate their private interests for the good of all, is a State.[50]

Unfortunately the same forces which have brought about our form of democratic state have brought about conditions which impede the effective practice of democracy. Technology alone has created *many* publics, with conflicting interests. Each of us is a member of many unrelated, and sometimes even antagonistic groups. For us to elect an official who represents *all* of our diversified interests is impossible. We do not even *understand* the vast industrial and economic enterprises with which we are related in we know not how many ways, and for that reason do not know even in what direction our interests lie. Our so-called popular elections often express nothing more than the will of a certain group of financial forces, propagandists, or selfish leaders. There results an "eclipse of the public." Democracy becomes ineffective.

These observations of the plight of an "inchoate and unorganized" democratic public lead Dewey to plead for the invention of new ways of securing full expression of the wants and interests of whole personalities. Free discussion concerning public policy will help; information on matters now reserved for the expert alone will also help. We need education to free us from stereotyped emotional habits centering around signs and symbols, to give us greater latitude of communication. Freedom of communication is especially needed.

Dewey's picture of the ineffective functioning of democracy is realistic and sorrowful. Probably few will question its correctness, and all believers in democracy will subscribe to his proposed educational remedies. He is never more convincing than in his repeated demonstration that the improvement of the methods and conditions of debate, discussion and deliberation are necessary for the support of democracy. Each public must become a participant public, every member helping to shape its destiny. Becoming active within the publics to which we belong, we find our own well-being.

It is here, however, that one serious difficulty arises. Does Dewey himself see the inherent contradiction that exists be-

[50] *The Public and Its Problems,* 67.

tween his advocacy of the community of *whole* individuals as the ideal unit of public organization, and his hope to harmonize the *segmental* types of public based upon common but highly specialized interests? The latter type of public, as he admits, is an abstraction derived from the separation of one partial segment of life from the remainder of that life. A single individual may belong to many, many publics. His interests as an individual are not truly fulfilled by his being partially included in multiple groups. If a given citizen is, say, a veteran, a "dry," a believer in free trade, a broker, a motorist, a home owner, an urbanite, a pacifist, how shall he vote to gain total inclusion for his pattern of interests? Or what groups shall he join that will bring unity into his life? As complications develop under modern conditions, total inclusion of the personality in specialized publics becomes increasingly difficult to achieve.[51] In a simple, primitive community such inclusion may conceivably be accomplished, but not under the complex conditions of modern society.

The question is then how to reconcile personality as an ethical end with the inevitable increase in the number of special publics that include mere segments of the personality and never the whole. In advocating the face-to-face community Dewey is on solid enough ground; but such a totally inclusive community cannot be achieved by the multiplication of partial publics separated in space. More and more vigorous participation in the segmental activities of a democratic state will not achieve unity for the individual. The problem is a serious one and it remains, in spite of Dewey's efforts, unsolved.

VIII. CONCLUSION

What is the nature of John Dewey's influence on modern psychology? That an answer is not to be sought in conventional directions is clear from our present survey. He is not a laboratory psychologist; there is no record of his conducting a controlled experiment, nor devising nor administering a psychological test. In his bibliography we had only one minor and now forgotten observational study (on infant language). He has not

---

[51] This dilemma as found in Dewey's political philosophy has been discussed at length by F. H. Allport, *Institutional Behavior*, 1933, Chap. 5.

dealt clinically with single cases. He has created no systematic classifications to guide psychologists in their researches, nor has he founded a well-defined school of psychology. Though he spends much time in evaluating psychology, he makes no use of the accumulated researches in its archives. He is thus not an historian nor a bibliographer. He does virtually none of the things that present-day psychologists are supposed to do.

Yet he writes extensively on the very subjects that psychologists are interested in, and he has fashioned his views into a coherent scheme. Is he than a systematist? Many psychologists would say no, for the system Dewey offers is of such nature that it lacks fixed points of reference. It is elusive and difficult to grasp. The reciprocal interpenetration of impulse, habit and thought, the continuous relating of these functions with the properties of the environment, which in turn is regarded as continuously evolving in terms of the properties of *both* the organism and the environment *as* related—such a flux of processes and events makes it difficult for the psychologist to gain a familiar hold. He finds it much easier to redact his observations into the fixed categories of behaviorism, Freudianism, hormic psychology or even the elder categories of structuralism and simple Jamesian functionalism. Evolving circuits may indeed be, as Dewey insists, the course of mental life, but spiraling processes make orderly analysis in terms of separate variables impossible. Unless situations remain fixed and can be relied upon to recur, how can the pychologist plot those definite functions that are said to constitute scientific law, or having plotted them how can he apply them to ever novel situations?

But Dewey is unmoved by such criticism. To those who wish to work only with fixed categories and isolable variables he replies:

When we assume that our clefts and bunches represent fixed separations and collections *in rerum natura*, we obstruct rather than aid our transactions with things. We are guilty of a presumption which nature promptly punishes. We are rendered incompetent to deal effectively with the delicacies and novelties of nature and life.[52]

[52] *Human Nature and Conduct*, 131.

It is this warning, repeated with all manner of variations in his writings, that constitutes one secret of Dewey's influence. He has taught his readers to be wary of "clefts and bunches." His insistence upon the complete process of coördination leads them to be suspicious of the fragments produced by neat analysis. When the laboratory wheels turn and the knives cut, and some exuberant investigator holds up an excised segment of behavior for acclaim, Deweyites are not edified. They know that true statements cannot be made about fragments snatched from their natural context. They have little use for a psychology that isolates separate functions within the total course of experience, and prefer a thoroughgoing organismic psychology, preferably one that has a strong social emphasis.

It is another mark of Dewey's influence that he has made psychological propositions indispensable to philosophy. Morals, for him, deal with aims as they are tied to wants, habits, and choice; and wants, habits and choice are whatever psychology says they are. Logic is the science of inquiry, but the act of inquiry can proceed only according to psychological canons. Art is experience, but experience must be revealed by a study of typical attitudes and habits which psychology identifies. Politics too depends upon psychological discoveries concerning the nature of communication, discussion, and persuasion. At every step education likewise must employ psychological rubrics and rules. The whole pragmatic philosophy of proximate goals, next steps, "ends that are literally endless" must tie in at every point with a psychology that treats the successive stages of organic conduct. Dewey's own interests are primarily normative, but he constantly exposes his norms to the actualities of human conduct. It is because he does so that one feels that psychology has a part to play in human progress. Human betterment becomes plausible and practicable, and psychology receives recognition and boundless encouragement.

Finally, deep and far-reaching significance lies in Dewey's perception of the inherent relation between psychology and democracy. Psychology is in essence the science of democratic living:

The cause of modern civilization stands and falls with the ability of the individual to serve as its agent and bearer. And psychology is naught but the account of the way in which individual life is thus progressively maintained and reorganized. Psychology is the attempt to state in detail the machinery of the individual considered as the instrument and organ through which social action operates.[53]

Psychology studies progressive mental adaptation; democracy is the means of achieving that adaptation. The two must go hand in hand. Both have to do with human experiments in living. While psychology provides the knowledge with which to make democracy effective, democracy provides the congenial, progressive, beneficial frame in which psychology can be productive.

In 1939 Dewey's perception is seen for its true brilliance. It is true beyond shadow of doubt that within no other frame than democracy does psychological inquiry proceed with even a relative freedom, and equally true that the perils and weakness of democracy are to a large extent psychological in origin and must be psychological in cure. The times have caught up with Dewey. We realize at last what he has long contended, that without democracy psychology cannot succeed, and without psychology democracy will surely fail.

GORDON W. ALLPORT

DEPARTMENT OF PSYCHOLOGY
HARVARD UNIVERSITY

[53] "The Significance of the Problem of Knowledge," in *The Influence of Darwin on Philosophy and Other Essays* (1910), 302.

10

Henry W. Stuart

DEWEY'S ETHICAL THEORY

DEWEY'S ETHICAL THEORY

I

ONE of the later chapters of *The Quest for Certainty* is entitled "The Supremacy of Method." The phrase is arresting, for, usually at least, we think of a method as in the nature of the case something instrumental and subordinate. A method is a procedure of some kind, an ordered sequence of operations, physical or mental, which is intended to effect a result. If the intended result does not come to pass our supposed method is no method at all. Methods are justified only by their success; results derive none of their worth from the method by which they have been brought to pass. Thus supremacy seems an attribute or status to which no method can properly lay claim. By definition, those patterns of behavior which we call methods are set apart from "consummatory" patterns—which, for their brief moment of concrete realization in experience at least, are their own excuse for being and ask no ulterior justification. In this way, these latter may be said to enjoy a kind of "supremacy" over those step-by-step procedures of the experiencing individual which bring about their concrete realization and look to this for justification.

The supremacy which Professor Dewey ascribes to method is however of another kind. When we declare that no method can be supreme we mean that, for an individual conforming his procedure to such a pattern, what is legislative is obviously the result which he desires and intends. Our standpoint in making such a statement is that of the individual whose employment of the method we are observing and in whose place we have put ourselves. On the other hand, Professor Dewey's standpoint in the chapter in question is that of a logician or epistemologist who views employment of method with his own special problems in

294   HENRY W. STUART

mind, seeking an explanation of the actual agent's conceptions and categories. The agent, let us say (following Professor Dewey), becomes suddenly aware of an environment over-against him and of a character of doubtfulness, uncertainty, peril-ousness, threatfulness suffusing or clouding it more or less darkly. This character is objective in a perfectly realistic sense, as objective as any particular quality or detail which the environment presents. It is accordingly an environment in itself inherently precarious that must be faced with such fortitude and detachment as the agent can muster and then grasped as a whole as problematic. Determinations of "here" and "now" and "there" and "then" must be made—distinctions of "this" and "that," of "thing" and "quality," of "I" and "we" and "it," of "mind" and "body" and "outer world." These determinations and concepts emerge in, and as aids towards, the analysis and articulation of the situation at first taken as a whole in its problematic character. The whole array makes up an inventory of "the intellectual phase of mental action."[1] The intellectual, the emotional and the volitional phases together constitute the indivisible unity of mental action. By way of definition of the mental, Professor Dewey states that it is in the degree that responses (of the "organism") take place to the doubtful *as* the doubtful "that they acquire mental quality."[2] Further, if the responses of the "organism" are "such as to have a directed tendency to change the precarious *and problematic*[3] into the secure and resolved, they are *intellectual* as well as mental."[4]

It lies in the province of other contributors to the present volume to set forth and discuss these views at length. My own concern with them is only to point out that they issue in Professor Dewey's conception of the *supremacy of method* and illustrate the sense in which he holds it. ". . . inquiry," he writes,

[1] *The Quest for Certainty*, 226.
[2] *Ibid.*, 225.
[3] *Italics* mine. Apparently apprehension of a situation as problematic is, or at least may be, pre-intellectual. If so, the intellectual phase must be introduced or brought about by the factor of "direction" to which reference seems to be made. I find the conception of objective doubtfulness or precariousness difficult but that of objective "problematicality" still more so.
[4] *Ibid.*, 225.

is a set of operations in which problematic situations are disposed of and settled. Theories which have been criticized [above] all rest upon a different supposition; namely, that the properties of the states and acts of mind involved in knowing are capable of isolated determination—of description apart from overt acts that resolve indeterminate and ambiguous situations. The fundamental advantage of forming our account of the organs and processes of knowing on the pattern of what occurs in experimental inquiry is that nothing is introduced save what is objective and is accessible to examination and report.[5]

Thus experimental inquiry, or method, is the locus within which, or the supreme principle by which, conceptions of philosophy that are really significant can be understood. It is in this sense, according to Professor Dewey, that method—that is to say, the method of experimental inquiry—is supreme.

All this, of course, is an integral part of the general argument of *The Quest for Certainty*. We have now to note that such a use of the expression "the supremacy of method" is in no way inconsistent with the view that method, considered as a procedure of the actual knower, engaged not in epistemological inquiry but in the direct solution of a first-hand problem in his experience, is not and cannot be "supreme." This, in fact, I take to be the view of Professor Dewey; at all events it seems to me to be implicit in the naturalism which is the dominant theme of his later major writings. For, according to Professor Dewey, the situation presenting itself to the knower is first of all and characteristically doubtful, and doubtfulness means essentially the imminence of more or less of peril. The situation is precarious. "That which is precarious" might, in fact, serve as the very definition of a situation, for to say what we mean by the term "precarious" is impossible without exhibiting, in its full tensional articulation of component elements, the generalized form of precisely what is realistically present to the knower as his environment in a particular case of problem-solving. The situation before him, perhaps we had better say, is not so much "precarious" as *a particular "precariousness."* Precariousness, which is of the essence, or at least a property, of a situation, is, for Professor Dewey, necessarily as objective as

⁵ *Ibid.,* 229.

the other component elements which become apparent on a more analytic view. It is the knower's first awakener or cue to action in his rôle; the articulation of the situation, to which more particular attention must at once be given, tends to obscure the initial and pervasive aspect. Thus precariousness apprehended is the occasion for the knower's resort to method—if control of the emotions, patience, and perhaps the "delight in the problematic" which is the mark of a disciplined mind make this possible.[6] But until it is called thus into play, method is in abeyance. Only then can method set about its work. Its work done, method subsides again into inaction. "Were existing conditions wholly good, the notion of possibilities to be realized would never emerge,"[7] and without emergence of this notion, method would be superfluous and as good as non-existent. In Kant's words, a method in this type of situation is a "formula of skill, to be used as needed,"[8] and, as such, cannot be supreme.

I have said "in this type of situation." Is there then, after all, another type of situation in our experience, differing from the perhaps more frequent and obvious one in which method must be merely instrumental and subordinate? If so, what different relation to method is characteristic of this type of situation? Are there situations in our experience which, instead of "releasing" method for action, are themselves brought into existence and urgency by it and must therefore acknowledge it as in so far "supreme?" Is it really and universally true that were existing conditions wholly good, "the notion of possibilities to be realized would never emerge?" Is the "fear of violent death," which was Hobbes' equivalent for the apprehension of objective "precariousness," the sole and ultimate source of all reflection and all knowledge? And if not, are there then, besides those situations of the more frequent sort that frighten method out of dormancy and compel mankind on pain of death or misery to move forward, other situations also, coming into view and

[6] *Ibid.*, 228.
[7] *A Common Faith*, 45.
[8] In a passage, to which I shall refer again, from the Prize Essay of 1762 (Prussian Acad. Ed. of Kant's Collected Works, Vol. II, 299). I owe the reference to Professor Paul A. Schilpp's *Kant's Pre-Critical Ethics* (1938), 26.

urgency through an alert initiative and incitement of method itself?

I trust that, as we proceed, these questions will lose their possible appearance of gratuitous artificiality. For I believe that from an ethical point of view it matters little, perhaps not at all, whether precariousness is regarded as a comment of ours upon situations or as an entity or character objectively present, like heat or gravitation, in them. Whether predominantly emotional or cognitive, the awareness or "acknowledgment" of precariousness is not ground in which the ethical interest can take its rise and grow. A precarious situation is one in which what we already prize and are determined to prize is endangered. In an ethical situation nothing is for us in danger but our success in achieving what shall be better worth our prizing. To identify these two dangers is to empty individual experience and human history of all distinctive meaning.

II

In the *Ethics* of 1908[9] Professor Dewey introduces the theoretical part of the work with an analysis of the "moral situation."[10] There are, we read,

two differing types of conduct; two differing ways in which activity is induced and guided by ideas of valuable results. In one case the end presents itself directly as desirable, and the question is only as to the steps or means of achieving this end. . . . Such is the condition of things *wherever one end is taken for granted by itself without any consideration of its relationship to other ends.* It is then a technical rather than a moral affair . . . a question of taste and of skill. . . . There are many different roads to most results, and the selection of this path rather than that, on the assumption that either path actually leads to the end, is an intellectual, aesthetic, or executive, rather than an ethical matter. . . . The moral issue does not arise. . . .

However there are cases in which our choice has to be, not of a particular path or means to a given end which latter there has

[9] By John Dewey and James H. Tufts. The preface designates the respective shares of the work for which the authors are primarily responsible.

[10] In the "revised edition" of 1932 a shortened and simplified statement is given under the caption "Reflective Morality and Ethical Theory" (171). In both versions the terms "moral" and "ethical" appear to be used interchangeably, as do also the terms "right" and "good."

been no occasion to question, but of some one end from among a number or of an end which shall supplant all. In such a case,

> Let the value of one proposed end be felt to be really incompatible with that of another, let it be felt to be so opposed as to appeal to a different kind of interest and choice, in other words, to different kinds of disposition and agency, and we have a moral situation. . . . We have [now] alternative ends so heterogeneous that choice has to be made; an end has to be developed out of conflict. The problem now becomes, what [end] *is* really valuable, [and this decision inevitably involves the theoretical question], what is the *nature* of the valuable, of the desirable? . . .

This, however, is only an objective rendering of the ultimate ethical question, which, adequately stated, runs in terms of personality or character. The *"nature"* of the valuable is that it makes the "supreme appeal." But what makes the "supreme appeal" to any man depends upon "what sort of an agent, of a person," that man is. And therefore,

> This is the question finally at stake in any genuinely moral situation: What shall the agent *be*? What sort of character shall he assume? . . . What kind of a character shall control further desires and deliberations? When ends are genuinely incompatible, no common denominator can be found except by deciding what sort of character is most highly prized and shall be given supremacy.[11]

The ends in an ethical situation are, then, variously described in the above as incompatible, discrepant, heterogeneous, opposed. They get in each other's way; they cannot readily be measured

---

[11] Pp. 206-210. The statement of the revised edition is, in substance, as follows: "Moral theory begins, in germ, when anyone asks, 'Why should I act thus and not otherwise?' . . . 'What right has anyone to frown upon this way of acting and impose that other way?' . . . Moral theory cannot emerge when there is positive belief as to what is right and what is wrong, for then there is no occasion for reflection. It emerges when men are confronted with situations in which different desires promise opposed goods and in which incompatible courses of action seem to be morally justified. . . . When an individual is tempted to do something which he is convinced is wrong [the occasion is not one] of moral theory. We have such an occasion when one is 'torn between two duties' . . . between incompatible values . . . each of which is an undoubted good in its place but which now get in each other's way. [One] is forced to reflect in order to come to a decision. Moral theory is a generalized extension of the kind of thinking in which he now engages." (173-175.)

and chosen, one as against the others, because no common denominator can be found in terms of which to express their relative worth. In an ethical situation, that is to say, the rival ends toward which the individual finds himself attracted are found to be incommensurable—this perhaps is the best description —whereas in the typical situation of end and means the end is unquestioned and the possible ways of accomplishing it are commensurable in terms of the time they require, their cost in physical effort or in money, their incidental advantages or drawbacks and the like. It cannot, of course, be held that the measurement of commensurable means is necessarily an easier or simpler matter than the consideration of incommensurable ends. Measurement of the means may be quite difficult in particular cases; but the difficulty lies in factual uncertainties as to cause and effect attaching to the various means, not in the absence of significant and decisive standards of measure. Toward whatever is for us once definitely in the category of means we are ordinarily, in the end, quite ruthless. In general, and barring occasional qualms of affectionate regret in discarding an ancient typewriter or an old coat, we value means, when the question can no longer be put off, for what they can do for us. Their failure of performance is evident in retardation, interruption, break-down of activities of ours which they have been serving. There are as many ways of estimating their worth, as many common denominators for comparing them with possible substitutes, as there are ways in which they can show themselves doubtful, "precarious," or threatening.

If then there is in our experience a type of situation requiring in some distinctive sense to be set apart as ethical, I hold that the reason lies only in the incommensurability of the ends whose rivalry initially constitutes it. If incommensurability is only an illusion of impatience which may speedily dissolve, then there is no ethics. If there is a field of ethics that is to be more than a grudgingly tolerated annex to biology, then this is because we find ourselves sometimes confronted with choices which no available rule of conduct or conceptual standard is found competent to make for us. That there are such situations in the experience of individual persons and in the history of any free society cannot, I think, be questioned. It is true that many questions apparently about ends are, as Professor Dewey has said, "in reality questions about means."[12] Which of two professions to enter may be only a question of how more safely to assure oneself within a reasonable time of a certain annual income. Whether public funds shall be spent for a park or a common school or study of the rate of expansion of the Cosmos may be promptly decided by the social ideal which the individual called upon to vote may happen to entertain. If so we have no present ethical problem. On the other hand a problem of vocation may well be baffling, and in a way that makes it ethical, because one finds the criterion of promised income somehow irrelevant. Likewise it may be that the citizen's conception of social order and well-being proves unexpectedly deficient at just the points which are critical for his decision. Indeed, in a democratic state the good citizen does well, in anticipation of such emergencies, not to hold to even a satisfying conception too firmly and complacently.

III

So far, I think, there can be no question. In the ethical situation, incommensurable ends; in the adaptive or "precarious" situation, commensurable means measured without scruple in terms of their fitness to effect an end—which, whether definite or indefinite, is at all events unquestioned. But we have now to see that this is only the beginning of an adequate analysis of the ethical situation. I hold that so far in making this distinction between ethical and other situations we are merely noting a *prima facie* descriptive difference. It is not enough merely to mark this difference by the verbal tag of incommensurability. We must try to see how much or how little our verbal tag may mean, to determine in what way or in what sense it is that this relation of incommensurability pertains to ends of ours. Is it something absolute, a relation grounded in the intrinsic natures of the several ends? Or is it an "external" relation somehow supervening upon the ends or entangled by chance amongst them and setting them in a mutually repellent opposition? Certainly further analysis of the ethical situation

[12] *Ethics* (first ed.), 209.

cannot be avoided unless we are content merely to identify it by its difference from the adaptive type.

The side and the diagonal of a square (and sometimes other rectangles) cannot both be measured without fractional remainder by any single unit marked off on a straight-edge. Some unit obviously can be taken for each line in turn which will measure it exactly, but no unit which does so for the one will do so for the other. But is ethical incommensurability more than distantly analogous to what we seem to have in cases such as this? Just what mathematical incommensurability may mean or issue from or be constituted by is, I think, hardly necessary to consider for the present purpose. If we found a relevant answer in mathematical terms, the question would still remain whether the same type of explanation were applicable in other fields. We should still be required in the end to determine independently the meaning of ethical incommensurability in terms appropriate to the ethical situation. We may as well do this first as last.

Whether or not, in any other field of being or of experience, incommensurability is due to the inherent natures of the entities in question or to the structure of the complexes of which they are members, this can hardly, I think, be seriously thought to be the case in ethics. For ethical ends, if incommensurable, are, in the nature of the case, *not* then and there members in any complex of which we can conceive or guess the structure; and their intimacy of relation to the troubled individual's basic drives and interests seems to preclude the other possibility. Thus, we declare the welfare of one's country, whether in peace or war, to be clearly incommensurable with considerations of private pecuniary gain or physical security, of personal ambition and advancement to power, of personal vengeance for one's country's indifference or distrust. For us, that is to say, the opposition of loyalty and self-interest or loyalty and resentment presents an ethical problem. Perhaps. But history and the current experience of all of us suggest caution in concluding that in this matter all men are as we are. It is abundantly evident that men today as in antiquity are most unequally sensible of the inherent difficulty supposedly present in such problems. For many persons, and in situations presenting the general issue in particular ways, conceptions of good appear to be at hand which make such decisions, on the contrary, quite easy. An inherent characteristic of incommensurability seems at the critical moment not to be apparent. It is a sound principle of common sense and logic that if any alleged object or quality fails in fact to put in an appearance when, so far as one can judge beforehand, the requisite conditions for its appearance have been set up, its objective existence is, to say the least, fairly open to suspicion. This must be as true for an alleged objective fact or relation of incommensurability between purposes as for fairies in Ireland or canals on Mars or malaria-parasites looked for in the blood of a supposed victim of that disease. Objective or realistic or (shall I say?) "naturalistic" incommensurability subsistent between such rival ends as loyalty and treason too often fails to impress itself effectively—too often, from the present point of view, not so much for the good of mankind as for the credibility of the objective hypothesis. It is difficult indeed to conceive how ends of desire and effort, never appealing to single and securely insulated interests but representing instead diverse perspectives and proportionings of all our interests together, can ever really be, for the individual, so radically alien, each to the others. Each of these perspectives has its appeal and its moving power. In the nature of the case there are at all times in the course of an ethical inquiry identical elements and continuous lines of affiliation joining closely or distantly the developing rival possibilities of action. By availing himself of such dimensions of commensurability the individual may all too easily escape, if he will, the intellectual difficulties of his problem and the inconveniences and sacrifices to which prosecution of his inquiry may subject him in the end.

He may do this, and on the other hand he may not. I am suggesting that whether the alternatives before him in any given juncture of his inquiry are to be dealt with as commensurable or as incommensurable must depend, in principle, upon the individual's own decision. Shall he accept and apply *some* available common-measure, which in all cases he can do, or shall he refuse to do so? If the latter is his choice, he sets before himself thereby an ethical problem, in which incommensurable

alternatives confront him. For incommensurability is the form
of the ethical problem. No doubt most of our choices are not,
and ought not to be, of the ethical type; although *when* to dis-
card available common-measures in problems of conduct is, I
think, a question admitting of no general answer. It is like
asking just when to stop relying on some long established judgment of historical fact, or conception of the nature of gravitation,
or recognized surgical procedure.

We cannot say, in general terms. It is more hopeful to
consider how to proceed, once one has resolved to give oneself
to such a problem. What it is to be logical can be known and
profitably reduced to formulas. *When* to be logical in our
attitude toward a situation; whether, in a problem of human
relationship, to be logical after the distinctively ethical fashion
or after the adaptive—these are quite other matters. The perplexities and hesitations that trouble the conscientious person
who must face these most crucial and difficult questions of time
and circumstance are, so far as I can see, inescapable incidents of
our mortal lot. We can only use our best judgment, invoke our
sense of humor, appeal to our common sense and tact—phrases
which, if they mean anything, are only disarmingly prosaic and
modest equivalents for "the good will." But the good will,
which is the source and life of the ethical interest and of ethical
theory, is neither a descriptive standard nor a solvent formula.
Between moralistic fanaticism, for which ethical problems do not
exist, and hypocrisy, which keeps its eye to the main chance
while protesting overmuch its anxious concern with them, there
is no sharp line. Nevertheless, with belief in itself, which no
amount of adverse suggestion is in principle competent to
destroy, the good will must declare, as boldly and justly as it
can, whether the case in hand shall be one of commensurable
means or of incommensurable ends.[13] Thus incommensurability

[13] "In fact, it is absolutely impossible to make out by experience with complete
certainty a single case in which the maxim of an action, however right in itself,
rested simply on moral grounds and on the conception of duty . . .; . . . [we cannot "with the sharpest self-examination" be sure] that it was not really some
secret impulse of self-love, under the false appearance of duty, that was the actual
determining cause of the will" (Kant's *Metaphysic of Morals* [*Grundlegung*
of 1785], Abbott's trans., 23-24). Kant has here in mind the *outcome* of ethical

is quite other than the "natural" opposition or incompatibility of ends. All ends are in a perfectly obvious way opposed, heterogeneous and incompatible. One cannot do two things at once: even the convenient compromise of doing first one and then the other makes each, perhaps in some small degree, perhaps with all the difference in the world, a different act. Beyond acknowledging it as a character of physical reality like the impenetrability of matter or inertia, ethical theory has no concern with the "natural" incompatibility of every end with every other end. The sole concern of ethics is with oppositions which the ethical interest itself sets up.

IV

In ethics, accordingly, we have the field of a method which may be regarded as in a sense "supreme." Unlike the adaptive method which, on the spur of compulsive occasion, comes into action for the abatement of an intrusive objective "precariousness," ethical method has its inception in a self-assertive attitude of quest originative of situations which will have to be constructively resolved. In the adaptive situation, a drive, encountering hindrance or worse by its own inertia, attains, by adaptation, not indeed, says Professor Dewey, to "restoration of the previous state of the organism" but to reinstatement of "the form of the previous relation of interaction with the environment." The organism's need for whatever it seeks

remains a constant factor but it changes its quality. . . . The conservative tendency is strong; there is a tendency to get *back*. But at least with the more complex organisms, the activity of search involves modification of the old environment, if only by a change in the connection of the organism with it.[14]

In the ethical situation, on the other hand, it is quest, not "animal drive" that motivates the process of reflection throughout

reflection in the concrete case. Not less exposed to doubt is the will to reflect, upon which actual reflection waits in the particular case. Apparently, according to Kant, the only empirical evidence for the good will is the "indefinite progress of one's maxims" and "their steady disposition to advance." (*Critique of Practical Reason, ibid.,* 121.) Presumably the defender of the good will is to accept, for the sake of the argument, the attacker's explicit or implicit measure of "progress" and "advancement."

[14] *Logic,* 27-28.

its course. And quest, while it may indeed incidentally encounter "perilous" situations created by its own activities or by environmental changes otherwise caused, does not owe its arousal to such occasions. Its "supremacy" lies in its creation of its own problems by determining that alternatives presented in the course of experience shall be dealt with as incommensurables. As Professor Dewey has said, indeed: "Conscientiousness . . . will always be on the lookout for the better. The good man not only measures his acts by a standard but he is concerned to revise his standard. . . . The highest form of conscientiousness is interest in constant progress."[15] But it is the essential characteristic of this "concern," this "interest," that it can and does "emerge" when "existing conditions" are by every present measure "wholly good."[16]

The point calls for insistence. Conditions which are "wholly good" are in principle, precisely and logically, the appropriate occasions for the emergence. If conditions when encountered are found *not* "wholly good," it is because some present end of the individual finds itself adversely affected by them. In such a situation we have, according to the scheme of Professor Dewey's naturalism, the drive or inertia of the "organism's" disturbed or interrupted activity seeking to push forward. Pushing forward, it spreads out in continuously ramifying trains of attentive and manipulative behavior by which the environment is explored and reconstructed. I hold that in such a situation the aggressive and deploying drive is itself the standard. "The good man," says Professor Dewey, "not only measures his acts by a standard but he is concerned to revise his standard"—suggesting that the latter "concern" is only a continuous extension and fulfillment of the "goodness" already manifest in the measurement referred to. This must of course be the position of naturalism. On the contrary, however, I hold the two procedures in question to be discontinuous and opposed in character. The latter only is ethical; the former is at best ethically neutral, finding room within its scope for a great variety of phenomena—the pathetic fanaticism of a Javert or the ferocious fanaticism of the Indian

[15] *Ethics* (1908), 422.
[16] Above, p. 296, top paragraph.

Thug, the right of a "consciously" superior race or class to enslave or exploit their inferiors, the assumption of cultivated individuals to dogmatize for the uplift of the generality, the assurance of a political party of its own exclusive fitness to rule, *as well as* the more edifying moral fortitude of a conscientious man resisting temptation. The good man's measurement of his acts by a standard is ethically good only when the standard is ethically good; and a standard claims ethical goodness not as a projection of the "organism's" interrupted drive but as emergent from ethical reflection upon incommensurables, acknowledging no authority of a higher standard.[17]

I do not, of course, mean to say that whenever, by any chance, "existing conditions are wholly good" there promptly ought to be or inevitably must be discontent. Not every good custom must infallibly corrupt the world. It is only necessary for persons of good will to recognize and, on occasion, act upon the principle, that *although* they find a custom good it *still* may *possibly* corrupt the world—may possibly be doing so even while they cherish it. We must be quite clear upon the point that in principle, it is only against a background of activity wholly satisfactory in an environment of "conditions wholly good" that any intrusive incentive can stand out in its full character as an ethical incommensurable. For when "existing conditions" are "wholly good" there is, by hypothesis, at least a momentarily ruling end. The environment suggests to us, in their convenient and obvious

[17] Twenty-three years before the publication of the *Grundlegung*, Kant wrote as follows: ". . . an immediate supreme rule of all obligation would have to be absolutely indemonstrable. For from no inspection of any concept or thing is it possible to know or to conclude what one ought to do, unless what is presupposed is an end and the action is a means. But this assumption is impossible, for then there would be no formula of obligation, but only one of skill to be used as needed." (Prize essay of 1762.) As Professor Schilpp says, in commenting on this passage, "The supreme rule of obligation, supposing that there is one, must be directly embraced, self-evident in its own right, and its obligatory character must be a wholly indemonstrable finality." Supposing that there is no substantive supreme rule of obligation, but that obligation attaches directly to concrete ends of action as they emerge out of ethical reflection in particular cases, Kant's logic then gives us the result that "A moral choice . . . is not a choice for the sake of something else but for its own sake." See footnote 8, p. 296 above.

order only subordinate activities happily conducive thereto. Our knowledge of the environment in these idyllic circumstances is indeed a 'joyous science.' And now, if "conditions" presently become wholly or perhaps only slightly 'bad,' the ruling activity may still persist. Half the time in our experience, three quarters of the time, nine tenths of the time perhaps, the demand will and must be that "conditions" which have become 'bad' be made 'better'—and better, observe, by the criterion or standard which the drive and inertia of the ruling activity itself automatically sets. And I insist that a man who holds to such a standard and "measures his acts" by it, though certainly not thereby infallibly or by normal presumption a bad man, can equally certainly not for that reason alone set up a special claim to ethical goodness.

I hold that he can do this (or that we can do so for him) only when "conditions wholly good" have first been disturbed by the intrusion of an incentive which the ruling activity, if it had its way, would straightway overbear and crush. But the ruling activity is not permitted to overbear it. The new incentive has aspects which strangely, surprisingly, hauntingly, appealingly engage his interest and allegiance. These aspects root the incentive firmly in its place and win it acceptance and tenure not as a competing drive but in a position of incommensurable opposition to the ruling drive. The situation is now ethical. And the difficulty—the tragedy, it may be—of the situation is that "conditions" are still "wholly good" or as good as they ever were, so far as judgment in terms of hitherto and still acknowledged standards is concerned. The question now troubling one is whether *these standards* are as good as conceivably they might be made, if in some way or to some extent not indicated or as yet even guessable the intrusive and disturbing motivation were accepted. In ethics there can be no easy and coolly rational way: we cannot identify being ethical with even a serene and dogmatic liberalism. In a problematic situation which he has himself in the last analysis elected to become entangled in, the individual must eventually act in a manner radically experimental. Toward ethical action, experimental inquiry into matters of

objective fact, however necessary in particular cases, can never
be decisive or more than incidentally contributory.[18]

[18] Professor Charner M. Perry, in an interesting article entitled "The Arbitrary
as a Basis for Rational Morality" (*International Journal of Ethics*, XLIII, 127-
144), advances a view of ethical decision similar to the above. He writes (140):
". . . man is always on the brink of the bottomless pit of reflection. Usually he
is saved by the pressure of events; but as he becomes more reflective, it is only by
an arbitrary act of will that he pulls himself back. In ordinary decisions such
an act of the will is an affirmation and expression of the existing self. At times,
however, when the self is at a crucial point, when the future nature of the person
depends upon the choice to be made, then the choice results from an arbitrary act
of the will. Such a choice is rational in the sense that it follows a survey of the
possibilities, and that it results from recognition of the fact that a choice must be
made. It is not irrational in the sense of being contrary to reason. But it is non-
rational in that the direction taken by choice is not determined by the evidence
or principles that can be applied." Professor Perry apparently means by "reflection" a valuation or appraisal of "the evidence or principles that can be applied"
in accordance with a theory of value which is abstract or axiomatic or *a priori*
and excludes all consideration of empirically actual beliefs, purposes, or interests
which at the time are not questioned. So understood, reflection seems to be indeed
well described as a "bottomless pit." But after all this may perhaps not be
Professor Perry's real view. For we are told that a choice, even though it "result" from "an arbitrary act of the will," deserves nevertheless to be called "rational" if it "follows a survey of the possibilities." From this asserted character
of rationality, I should suppose the "following upon a survey," which confers it,
to be, in Professor Perry's view, not a mere temporal coming-after but, in some
manner, an emergence out of, and a generation by, the taking of the "survey."
But if so, this taking of the "survey" would seem to be precisely what properly
ought to be meant by the term "reflection," provided the survey is understood to
be not a mere descriptive canvass of alternative trains of consequences taken at
their conventional moral valuations, but a methodical weighing of them in the
light of the trustworthiness or "authority" of the respective incentives which propose them for acceptance (see below, pp. 319-320, esp. 320).

Professor Donald C. Williams has a like perception of the transcendence of
past experience characteristic of a genuinely ethical decision ("Ethics as Pure
Postulate," *Philosophical Review*, vol. XLII, (1933), 399-411). Decision in his
view is postulational and apparently quite cut off from any organic relation to
reflection—which indeed, in Professor Williams' conception of choice, seems to
have no part to play. What he seems not to realize is the entire consistency of
dependence upon reflective process with radical novelty and independence of the
past in an ethical decision. The analogy of decisions and resolves with postulates of
science and mathematics appears to be entirely superficial if not misleading, although undoubtedly very much in the current vogue. I should say that ethical
decisions, in their aspect here in question, probably have far more significance for
the explanation of postulates than postulates have for them.

One is reminded by these articles of Kant's term *Willkür* in the *Critique of
Practical Reason* (translated "elective will" by Abbott in *Kant's Theory of
Ethics*, 157).

For the two types of situation we are here considering differ fundamentally, from a logical point of view, as regards the method of their resolution. In the first type, in which the interrupted drive of the "organism" persists and is permitted to set the standard, the interruption may, indeed, be due to some physical change in the environment, caused by the activities of the organism itself or otherwise. This is the adaptive, the ostensibly "scientific" sort of case, to which the thoughts of naturalism ever return and on which they seem to dwell with a kind of awe. But in the real world of human affairs and values, in which after all we live and with which a genuinely matter-of-fact ethical theory must be concerned, the intrusion may well be of another kind. Monotonous labor may suddenly become strangely irksome as one catches, through some chance suggestion, a vision of a more spacious and a freer life. In one's own behalf or in behalf of another, one may flare up in resentment against a master or employer or impersonal institution. Or again, one's sympathy may be appealed to for a change of one's own opinion or behavior or the surrender of some advantage or prerogative of one's class. Condemnation may be encountered coming from some authoritative source—not necessarily priest or policeman; perhaps tradition, "public opinion" or the code of one's class, a friend's disapproval, the example of a saint or hero, the word of a wise man, a long-settled rule of one's own conscience. Nevertheless, in the first type of situation, which we are now considering, the interrupted drive is assumed to persist. And persisting, it may overbear the intrusion or, if it must, it may seek an "adjustment"—in which however, as Professor Dewey has it, "need remains a constant factor" though with its "quality" changed.[19] If it cannot quite "steam-roller" the insurgent opposition, it will at least make head as best it can. And the point I wish to press is that this process of composition of forces amounts on its intellectual side (which unhappily naturalism cannot quite read out of the story) to an appraisal or register of all the conflicting motivations in terms of the consequences (or their "values") expected to result from them. We have here what Professor Dewey calls a "dramatic rehearsal." The par-

[19] *Logic, loc. cit.*

ticipants, passing in review before a valuer of not-too-precisely indicated identity, are tagged (and likewise the drive itself) with a notation of what they have to offer. In such a case, all depends upon the standard of appraisal, no matter by whom applied. And the standard is the drive itself. The whole procedure is "rational" in the narrower sense of that term: the standpoint is that of adherence to the end originally in view and of approval or disapproval of intruding incentives according as their consequences in action promise to further or to hinder the endeavor. Uncertainty in such a case is factual only. The purposing individual (who insists on making indiscreet appearances) may be *disappointed* in the outcome; but it will only be because ignorance or miscalculation along the way may have misled him. If he has *regrets* it will be for having refused some small concession which, if shrewdly made, would have saved him much or all.

In the second, or ethical, type of situation the intruding incentive is not in this way held throughout in the position of an intruder. It is greeted with tolerance, at least—perhaps even with interest and hospitality. If it can qualify, it will be accepted as a contributor, coördinate in its own right with the ruling drive, towards the course of conduct which is to follow presently. And the essence of the matter as I see it is this. In the adaptive case just considered the incentives, ruling and intrusive, stand equated each to a more or less determinate series of consequences, experiences or "values" which are expected to result from it; and the net result will be—inevitably must be—approved or disapproved from the standpoint of the persistent drive. If the drive *and* its defeat or abatement or revision are, as Professor Dewey has said, often in reality only rival means to an end of greater generality more remote from the dust and heat of action, the case is for our present purpose in no way altered.[20] But in the distinctively ethical case there can be no such arbitrament of force or adjournment of the issue to a higher court. There can be no question of "rational" procedure in the narrower sense, in which already we quite dictatorially know what we want, *apart from* the direct consideration of particular moti-

[20] *Ethics* (1908), 209 (bottom).

vations in the present case. Distrusting, in our hospitality to the
intruding incentive, both our proximate and our more ultimate
previous notions of what we want, we cannot without new reflection allow our course in this instance and henceforth to be
determined by them. The method of comparing rival complexes
of values expected *de facto* to result is useless. Our procedure
must be of a different type, governed by a rationality or reasonableness conforming to a different logic—a logic not of sub-
sumption but of method. Our first need is not a factual study
of consequences which, when appraised by current standards,
may or may not pass muster. The very principle of our ethical
attitude is methodological distrust of these latter. First of all
must come, not a canvass of factual consequences for judgment in
detail but factual evidence upon the "trustworthiness" of the
incentives which may entitle them to be heard despite their odd
or daring or forbidding or even repellent promise. Have they
any measure of presumption in their favor which should incline
us, always critically, to heed them? Does this presumption serve
to any extent reasonably to offset the condemnation or the depre-
cation which, by the method of comparison of consequences, current standards must pronounce upon them?[21]

V

Toward an understanding of the method implicit in the conception of ethical incommensurability, Professor Dewey makes
an introductory contribution in the *Ethics* of 1908. This is to be
found in the chapter on "The Virtues." It is here held to be
impossible in theory and undesirable, except perhaps as an aid
to exhortation, to construct

a catalogued list of virtues with an exact definition of each. Virtues are
numberless. Every situation, not of a routine order, brings in some
special shading, some unique adaptation, of disposition. . . . Any virtuous
character exhibits, however, certain main traits, a consideration of which
will serve to review and summarize our analysis of the moral life. . . .
Bearing in mind that we are not attempting to classify various acts or

[21] I have elsewhere undertaken to suggest criteria of trustworthiness of the sort
here referred to and their place in ethical reflection. ("A Reversal of Perspective
in Ethical Theory," in *The Philosophical Review*, Vol. XXIX.)

habits, but only to state traits essential to all morality, we have the "cardinal virtues" of moral theory. As whole-hearted, as complete interest, any habit or attitude of character involves justice and love; as persistently active, it is courage, fortitude or vigor; as unmixed and single it is temperance—in its classic sense. And since no habitual interest can be integral, enduring, or sincere, save as it is reasonable, save, that is, as it is rooted in the deliberate habit of viewing the part in the light of the whole, the present in the light of the past and future, interest in the good is also wisdom or conscientiousness.[22]

The "cardinal" virtues, as the term implies, are virtues of method: upon their exercise issues hinge.

It is evident, I should say, that in this analysis we have to do with "traits" that are not simultaneous in their operation. They are coöperative but not coördinate in function. "Wisdom, or (in modern phrase) conscientiousness, is the nurse of all the virtues" and so has its place, in a sense, at the commencement, as a manifestation of the will to undertake a problem in incommensurability. Justice, as the fulfilment of conscientiousness, marks the solvent or harmonizing effect which should crown the work of reflection. Courage, as "the will to know the good and the fair by unflinching attention to the painful and disagreeable," and "temperance," as "that which checks the exorbitant pretensions of an appetite by insisting upon knowing it in its true proportions"—these two are definitely principles of a different order. They are simultaneous—at least in the sense that neither can be given precedence over the other or do its work without the other. They are principles of technique. Thus the process of reflection upon incommensurables not only takes place in time, but time is of its essence. It is a constructive and serial act in which one seeks not to bring to bear a sovereign principle or concept, ostensibly timeless though admittedly at the moment not quite perfectly known, but to formulate a plan of conduct meeting a situation dated in a personal career and observant of the temporal (as well as spatial) relations of the factors making up the situation.[23]

[22] Chap. XIX, 402-405.
[23] In the first part of the *Ethics* of 1908 and of 1932, reviewing "The Beginnings and Growth of Morality," Professor Tufts groups the various factors

In the *Ethics* of 1932, incommensurability is retained as the distinguishing characteristic of ethical situations. Associated with it, as in the *Ethics* of 1908, is the kindred conception of the virtues as correlative aspects of the attitude of the conscientious individual in facing a problem of incommensurables. The narrowing and rigidifying effects of thinking of the virtues moralistically, as separate and specific kinds of behavior each pertaining to a precisely definable type of juncture in experience, are set forth in the new edition as in the old. Although the word "cardinal" is not used, the interpretation of justice, wisdom, courage and temperance as distinguishable though not separable phases of an "interpenetrated whole" of "integrated interest" is reaffirmed.[24] However in 1922 had appeared *Human Nature and Conduct*, bearing the sub-title, "An Introduction to Social Psychology." One cannot read this expansion of a series of lectures

---

making for change at each transition-stage of development under the captions "psychological" and "sociological agencies." These terms comprise self-regarding and sympathetic tendencies of whatever sort and however initiated. Authoritative influences are mainly treated as making for the prevention or safeguarding of change rather than its initiation. Professor Tufts' whole account is methodological in emphasis. I have long thought it definitely superior in conception and insight to any of the other more extended surveys currently in use treating of the growth of morality and the slow emergence of ethics as a reflective interest. There is a famous remark of the economist Ricardo to the effect that "every transaction in commerce is an individual transaction." So also every change in moral norms must have had its beginning in the decisions of individuals confronting a situation of incommensurables in their experience. Consider such changes in moral opinion as have taken place in recent time regarding such matters as collective bargaining, workmen's compensation and the fellow-servant principle, divorce, birth-control, the equality of women, universal education, the reprobation of war. Such movements necessarily derive their momentum from the impact of "psychological" and "sociological agencies" upon the desires and feelings of nameless individuals whose heresies are frowned upon in the beginning by most of the accredited wise and good. The alleged sanction afforded such movements by eternal principles of morality is in large part a conscious or unconscious expedient of proponents to further their cause. It serves also as a merciful cover for the natural embarrassment of late converts. The "eternal," when all is said and done, must depend upon the sordid "temporal" for its elucidation.

[24] In this edition the virtues, instead of being given a chapter to themselves, are relegated to a closing section (pp. 280-286) of Chap. XIII, which comprises also a treatment of Approbation and The Standard. Temperance and Courage, to which nine pages are given in the earlier edition, receive only a bare mention to illustrate the general position (284).

intended for a general audience without a definite impression of enthusiasm and conviction on the author's part. The wealth of pointed illustration, the assurance evinced in meeting anticipated objections, the occasional flashes of irony and humor, join in suggesting a sense of release in being free to look at ethical issues and categories from a point of view somewhat removed from, and less exacting than, that of the ethical administration by the individual of his own personal affairs and social obligations. In the Prefatory Note to *The Study of Ethics: A Syllabus*[25] Professor Dewey had many years before recorded the belief that "amid the prevalence of pathological and moralistic ethics, there is room for a theory which conceives of conduct as the normal and free living of life as it is." Of all Professor Dewey's ethical writings, *Human Nature and Conduct* is perhaps the one most determinedly held to the elucidation and defense of this conception. It joins one side of his early ethical thought with the ethical parts of *The Quest for Certainty* and the *Logic*.

VI

This side is the naturalistic, which, in the very nature of the case (as I conceive the nature of the case) is overshadowed if not put out of the reckoning in both versions of the *Ethics*. *Human Nature and Conduct*, we read, has to do with the change that must come over ethics when we turn from moralistic suspicion and disparagement of human nature to positive respect for it. What human nature needs, to deserve and more surely command this positive respect is "association with scientific knowledge." Scientific knowledge acquaints the individual with the probable consequences of the lines of behavior which in their various ways and degrees attract and move him. He is no longer at the mercy of authority, which would coerce him to its own advantage, or of magic, which would entice him away

[25] The Inland Press: Ann Arbor, 1894, (out of print). In the ever-memorable early Chicago years, this little volume was a scripture—treasured in those years' dearth of systematic writing from Professor Dewey's hand—to be read, pondered, and interpreted. More than one eagerly contested argument was adjourned, to the confusion of a dissenter, with the not wholly humorous recital of the *logion* I here recall.

from the prosaic business of remaking the environment in detail at points where he encounters resistance.[26] "We compare life," writes Professor Dewey,

to a traveler faring forth. . . . Abruptly he is pulled up, arrested. . . . But a new impulse is stirred which becomes the starting point of an investigation, a looking into things, a trying to see them, to find out what is going on. . . . The momentum of the activity entered upon persists as a sense of direction, of aim; it is an anticipatory project. In short, he recollects, observes and plans.[27] . . . Then each habit, each impulse, involved in the temporary suspense of overt action takes its turn in being tried out. Deliberation is an experiment in finding out what the various lines of possible action are really like . . . carried on by tentative rehearsals in thought which do not affect physical facts outside the body. . . . In imagination as in fact we know a road only by what we see as we travel on it. In thought as well as in overt action, the objects experienced in following out a course of action attract, repel, satisfy, annoy, promote and retard. Thus deliberation proceeds. To say that at last it ceases is to say that choice, decision, takes place. What then is choice? Simply hitting in imagination upon an object which furnishes an adequate stimulus to the recovery of overt action. Choice is made as soon as some habit, or some combination of elements of habits and impulse, finds a way fully open. . . . The mind is made up, composed, unified. . . . Decision is reasonable [when] . . . to every shade of imagined circumstance there is a vibrating response; and to every complex situation a sensitiveness as to its integrity, a feeling of whether it does justice to all facts, or overrides some to the advantage of others.[28]

Introducing the sketch of "the psychology of thinking" thus summarized, there is a reminder that so far, in the main division of which this sketch forms a part, the course of exposition has lain "far afield from any direct moral issue."[29] But "the excursion must be continued" because "the problem of the place of knowledge and judgment in conduct depends upon getting the fundamental psychology of thought straightened out." Just where in the sketch that follows or in the subsequent discussions this necessary excursion ends and the transition is made from the

[26] *Human Nature and Conduct*, 1-13.
[27] *Ibid.*, 181-182.
[28] *Ibid.*, 190-194.
[29] *Ibid.*, 181.

general psychology of thinking to the special psychology of
ethical thinking is not apparent. The "deliberation" of which one
reads in the above account is, however, apparently ethical deliberation. The "rehearsals" carried on in "thought" or imagination are apparently rehearsals of possible courses of ethical (or
"moral") behavior. The "choice," which seems somewhat curtly
disposed of as a happy hit—since after all it might protest that it
emerges out of "vibrating responses" to every shade of imagined
circumstance, is sensitive as to the "integrity" of every complex
situation and heedful of the "just" claims of all the facts to their
share of consideration—this choice is certainly, patently, ethical.
And yet, if any statement has been given of what constitutes a
"moral issue," any suggestion of changes of method required
for the due conduct of deliberation upon a moral issue, I have
failed to find it. It may be that the difference Professor Dewey
had in mind was not a difference of method but only a descriptive difference in the alternative tentative actions presented for
deliberation. And this apparently is the explanation. Ethical
ends

are ends-in-view, or aims. They arise out of natural effects or consequences which in the beginning are hit upon, stumbled upon so far as
any purpose is concerned. Henceforth (or till attraction and repulsion
alter) attaining or averting similar consequences are aims or ends. These
consequences constitute the meaning and value of an activity as it comes
under deliberation.[30]

And accordingly "purposes or ends-in-view" ought not to be
regarded as "objects in themselves." They are, in truth, but
"means," in the last analysis, "to unification and liberation of
present conflicting, confused, habits and impulses."[31] However,
we must here be on our guard against an easy misapprehension.
Means we ordinarily think of as being used or not used as some
one pleases, in accordance with changing purposes. But any purpose, we are told, however general in character, is a purpose-in-
view and so only an aim, if it really signifies anything at all.
And an aim is only the projection into the future, in imagination,

[30] *Ibid.*, 225.
[31] *Ibid.*, 229.

of a habit formed in the past by hitting (once again) upon "natural effects or consequences" which one has liked, and will like so long as "attraction does not alter." In the end, therefore, it comes to this—that "concrete habits do all the perceiving, recognizing, imagining, recalling, judging, conceiving and reasoning that is done."[32]

VII

We are, however, here concerned with Professor Dewey's psychology of thinking only so far as is necessary for an understanding of its point of view. And its point of view, quite clearly as it seems to me, is that of an observer less directly interested, for the time being, in the actual solving of actual ethical problems than in safeguarding ethical theory and ethical procedure against certain supposed dangers. The good action is always a unique action. General rules are therefore intellectual and suggestive only, not imperative. Morality when we have it in definite form and prescription exists for man, not for its own sake or for the prestige and pleasure of any authority. It is for this life and not for a life to come. A purpose divorced from intention to achieve it or so irresponsibly conceived as to make its accomplishment impossible, is not merely futile (which might do no particular harm) but becomes very easily a poisonous narcotic. These and other like principles and counsels make up the

[32] *Ibid.*, 177. Nevertheless "habit does not *of itself* know." (my *italics*) It does all the knowing that is done but apparently there must be a provoking or enabling occasion, else it will not do *any*. "Habit incorporates, enacts or overrides objects, but it doesn't know them. . . . A certain delicate combination of habit and impulse is requisite for observation, memory and judgment." *(loc. cit.)* Here again one halts between two interpretations. Does this new statement mean (1) that observation, memory and judgment somehow identically *are* the "delicate balance" subsisting between habit and impulse as these components meet to combine, on the principle of the parallelogram of forces (192, middle); or does it mean (2) only that *without* the "delicate balance" of habit and impulse the functions of observation, memory and judgment do not get released or aroused and so cannot overtly occur? This latter interpretation would give us a situation like the one asserted in the first place for habit—"habit does not of itself know." The "delicate balance" would figure as an indispensable condition enabling, when present, knowledge to occur as the overt manifestation of some unnamed power or agency previously in restraint or in slumber. The regress might be continued, but perhaps we may forego this opportunity. I much prefer the latter of the two suggested interpretations, even though it may appear to envisage a transcendental ego.

preponderant burden of *Human Nature and Conduct* and of much of Professor Dewey's other writing, early and late. Conduct must be acknowledged frankly to be a function of human nature, or human nature sooner or later will have its revenge. With, I trust, all due recognition of the truth and the importance of these insights and principles, I question nevertheless whether the safeguarding they afford does not overrate the theoretical and even the practical dangers; whether the nature of the ethical interest itself is not misrepresented to a degree amounting almost to denial and whether the ethical interest and ethical procedure are not thereby endangered more than ever.

Human nature is known only as behaving and in terms of its behavior—as all other things are known. But the assumption is too easily made that the behavior of human nature can be fully known, and is best known, by observation of the individual by another, from without. I hold that deliberation cannot be adequately known unless we view it first of all as the act of a deliberator and, by putting ourselves as best we may at the deliberator's point of view, become aware of the act "from the inside" as the deliberator is aware of it. Deliberation proceeding in the mind of another person is undoubtedly suggested outwardly to an observer by bowed head, closed eyes, contracted brows, clenched hands and other "explicit" behavior of the body. A practiced observer, I suppose, might conceivably know in this way whether the problem troubling his subject was scientific or ethical. In the latter case (again, conceivably) there might be "implicit" behavior of a very recondite sort, accessible to the skilled physiologist alone, that would go still further. It might actually reveal, with at least the reliability of the "lie-detector," whether ethical deliberation was following the lines of Mandeville, of the philosopher Square, or of Anglo-Hegelian perfectionism. It would seem fairly obvious, however, that as an indispensable requisite for any such correlation of physiological behavior with the types and niceties of deliberative process, these latter must first have been "lived through" with interest, and known in essence and carefully distinguished in their proper and distinctive characters as immediate experiences—if not by the observer himself, then by someone else from whom the observer has chanced to hear of them. But for every purpose of ethical theory the direct and basic knowledge of all these matters is likely to remain the most instructive sort; for practical purposes exploration of the ethical experience of other persons by the methods of imaginative sympathy is likely to continue more useful than the methods of even the psychological laboratory.

VIII

Incommensurability of ends I take to be the basic and inclusive problem of ethics, within the scope of which all the procedures of ethical deliberation have their place. But incommensurability, as I have tried to show above, is a situation instituted, and kept from prematurely dissolving again, by responses of human nature to certain types of suggestive appeal. These responses (unless the term is found too archaic) may be comprised under the inclusive concept of the Good Will.[33] When Kant declares that nothing can possibly be conceived in the world which can be

[33] To speak of situations "instituted" by "the good will" is of course to invite from readers requests, ironical or otherwise, for metaphysical explanation. I can only say here that I should respond neither after naturalistic empiricism's method of solving metaphysical problems by the exorcism of explaining them away, nor in accordance with what seems to me the very different teaching of the following passage: "A philosophy which was conscious of its own business would . . . perceive that it was an intellectualized wish . . . a prophecy of the future, but one disciplined by serious thought and knowledge. [It would] deny that philosophy is in any sense whatever a form of knowledge." ("Philosophy and Democracy," 1918, in *Characters and Events;* II, 843)

William James' observation as to the elusiveness of choice will be recalled. (*Principles of Psychology,* II, 524) We painfully vacillate between the alternatives of getting up in the morning and lying in comfort a while longer. Then suddenly, says James, we find ourselves throwing back the covers and standing on our feet on the floor. We seem to have no direct awareness of decision and the voluntary initiation of bodily movement. This account accords with Professor Dewey's characterization of "choice" in *Human Nature and Conduct;* I think there can be no question of its accord with empirical fact. I have held, however, that the true location of choice is at the commencement of deliberation—at the end, if the process has been effectively carried on, a terminal act of choice would be superfluous even though it were possible. Freedom primarily is freedom to reflect, not to act—and this is not to suggest that reflection is a "mental" process disclaiming any purpose of shaping the course of personal behavior or of historic events. I should hold, however, that the election to reflect or deliberate, while we have awareness of it, can never, once taken, be recaptured and exhibited in the descriptive language of empirical psychology.

called good without qualification except a Good Will, I take him to be thinking of no empty abstraction or self-sufficient transcendental entity but of a human disposition responsive to the suggestive appeals of which I speak. Of these latter, modern analysis has given us a better understanding in detail than was available in Kant's day—doubtless for various reasons better than could have been achieved by Kant himself.[34] The appeals by deference to which the Good Will sets before itself problems of incommensurability are of course infinite in number and each one unique. We may, however, suggest a grouping of these under three general heads—the mutual exclusiveness of which I take to be for our present purpose unimportant and in any case very likely inexact. Suppose we say, accordingly, that there are (1) appeals of authority (in a great variety of forms) for compliance. (2) Other persons (overtly or by virtue of our imputation to them of a need they do not express in words) appeal to us for greater freedom and opportunity as members of the social order, for direct aid in particular situations, for a sympathetic and participating interest in their own views or hopes or undertakings. (3) Self-regarding impulses of one's own lay claim to some measure of new recognition in the approved scheme of life. No detailed analysis or illustration seems necessary in this connection.

I have spoken of these incentives as *appeals* in order to suggest that there is in human nature a native disposition to respond to them—to "appeal" to a court or to another person is to assume a legal duty of the one or a humane disposition of the other to hear and give relief—and as *suggestive* because, unlike the "perilous" eventualities that beset the path of life, they are received by us with affirmative interest if not cordiality, as indicators of possible betterment for all concerned. To call them "appeals" does not imply that they ask for more than justice: it means that their claim of justice asks for and awaits an ethical

---

[34] An important contribution which I wish personally to acknowledge was made to this better understanding by the series of studies by J. Mark Baldwin, published under the general caption of *Mental Development in the Child and in the Race.* These have the great merit of subordinating the observer's interest in problems of genesis and training to a primary endeavor to understand what the crucial stages in mental development mean to the mind in course of development.

determination in which they shall have a voice. Response to them is not persistence of need in the respondent but quest for new interests and orders of experience establishing and sustaining new needs as yet not predictable. Now because the new needs, toward which responses to these incentives look, transcend past and present experience, they must, in principle, suffer in competition with already established habitual needs whose congenial satisfactions are already familiarly known. If there is, in human affairs, to be progression in the types of motivation directing the private and social behavior of the individual (and I take it that the essential concern of ethics is with the mediation of just this advance) it is because the inevitable competitive disadvantage of new incentives as compared with old can be and is offset. There is possible a change of venue away from the plane of competition. There is a will in the individual to proceed on faith and on presumption—presumption that the incentives are by objective criteria deserving of trust, and faith that the new level or order of experience attained will require no comparison with the old, and from the old point of view, to substantiate it.[35]

[35] This is why I am unable to follow Professor Dewey in his view that the "hedonistic element is that which renders utilitarianism vulnerable in theory and unworkable in practice" (*Ethics* of 1932, 268). First of all, I do not myself believe it ultimately to be possible to eliminate hedonism from any ethical theory that can be called utilitarian in an exact sense of the term. Nothing seems to me less disputable than that much of the time, and quite rightly, individuals and communities decide for certain modes of behavior in preference to others because they have found the former more agreeable in the past and wish to repeat the pleasure. I do not hold that pleasure arouses or explains desire; undoubtedly without desire there would be no pleasure. But this truism seems to me to be irrelevant to the question of the basis of our frequent *preference* of *one* alternative action to *another*, both of which we have performed in the past. In fact, "Men *like* some of the consequences and *dislike* others. Henceforth (or till attraction and repulsion alter) attaining or averting similar consequences are aims or ends." (*Human Nature and Conduct*, 225). For the sake of the argument, however, let it be assumed that utilitarianism can be purged of hedonism. "Suppose we drop the hedonistic emphasis upon states of pleasure and pain and substitute the wider, *if vaguer*, ideal of well-being, welfare, happiness, as the proper standard of approval." (*Ethics* of 1932, 264; my *italics*). In that case, as Professor Dewey goes on to point out, "the more are we compelled to fall back on personal character as the only guarantee" that objective consequences rather than anticipated pleasures will operate as a standard. Just this, I should say, is the continuing and undiminished objection to utilitarianism which is no less "vulnerable in theory and unworkable in practice" than before the supposed change. "Per-

Intrusive incentives such as these are the actual realities which the "motives" of traditional ethical theories represent. In the particular situation in which it functions, such an incentive is a particular impulsion looking toward some particular but not necessarily as yet determined action. Intruding upon us, however, in the midst of "conditions wholly good," such incentives encounter an initial barrage of adverse criticism. For they are heedless of the way in which we have ordered the more immediate situation and its relations with the wider context of experience in which we have placed it. As seen from the point of view of the categories and values which have given the situation the general character it has for us, they are intellectually irrelevant and emotionally irresponsible. They demand recognition and influence without offering plan or method by which these can comfortably be accorded. And yet, partly because of these reasons and partly in spite of them, they may interest and attract us. If so, we fend off such criticism by invoking in their behalf the sanction of "universals," such as sympathy, loyalty, reverence, ambition, love, obedience, humility, self-respect, benevolence, self-sacrifice—conceptions which by more or less plausible analogy, carry over to new and suspect incentives some share of the credit and authority already attaching to approved modes of concrete conduct which they denote. From the point of view of incommensurability as the mark of an ethical situation, the intrusive incentive in any particular case is the "motive" to which the eventual action resolving the situation must be referred in retrospect. Without the new incentive there would have been no

sonal character" remains the standard, without provision of any method whereby personal character may subject itself to criticism in new junctures and keep itself, with temperance and courage, in the way of new enlightenment—waiving the point that, in an ostensible standard, vagueness is above all the one thing that ought to warn us that something is amiss. Utilitarianism no matter in what form, is essentially reliance on a standard. I fail to see wherein even a "de-hedonized" utilitarianism is more adequate as an ethical method than a "fundamentalist" perceptual intuitionism. The latter also comes, in the end, to reliance on one's personal character of the moment as a standard. As Professor Dewey wrote in 1908 (*Ethics*, 206-207): "The moral issue does not arise," so long as an end stands alone unquestioned; and again in 1932 (*Ethics*, 173): "Moral theory cannot emerge when there is positive belief as to what is right and what is wrong."

problem; without the problem no ethical solution and no new experience. Ethical theory however, with a partiality for names or universals over the realities for which these stand, takes the "motives" of conduct to be those real or fictitious general dispositions with the aid of which the actual motives—the intrusive incentives—are, in case of need, enabled to defend their place in our attention and exert their influence.

It is from this misplacement of the term that arises the familiar conception of conduct as a temporally circumscribed event— brought to pass by a "motive" pushing, as it were, from behind and followed by consequences which are its "intention." And from this conception arise (1) the problem as to whether "motive" or "intention" determines the moral quality of "conduct" and (2) the paradoxes of good motives prompting to bad conduct and of conduct good by every current criterion of results but prompted by evil or sordidly calculating motives. To enlarge upon these problems is surely unnecessary. It is tempting but, I think, far from satisfactory, to dispose of them by a short and easy answer: Simply remember that a motive is no longer good that persists in the face of unexpected evil consequences and that collateral and incidental evil consequences destroy or diminish the goodness of an intention otherwise deserving approval. The distinction of "motive" and "intention" is, in a word, an unreal one: a motive is no motive at all unless it have determinate consequences in view and therefore is intention; and again, our real intention is, in every case, our motive—that indivisible whole of foreseen consequences which actually we let move us.[36]

Dialectically this disposition of the problem is more or less effective; but effective only from the point of view of an observer—an observer who has a definite notion of his own as to what is good and what is bad in the situation he is watching and would have the reflecting individual take his word for it without more ado. But for the latter, it is of the essence of the situation that the rightness and wrongness of the motives and intentions which constitute it are precisely what he must deter-

[36] *The Study of Ethics: A Syllabus,* (1894), 50-56 (Sec. XXVI); *Ethics,* (1908), 246-254; *Human Nature and Conduct,* (1922), 118-124; *Ethics,* 1932), 184-188.

mine. And unless for the reflecting individual a presumption of rightness attach to the intrusive incentive in defiance of his customary valuation of its predictable consequences, the incentive, the motive, will cease to move him and reflection upon the problem summarily be quashed. To urge upon him that motives must move to some result in particular and are therefore intentions, that our only real intentions are those that in the end actually move us and are therefore motives—this telescoping annihilation of the reflective interval can only confuse him in the delicately critical moment of the first hesitant stirrings of the reflective interest. Such assertions as these are not, indeed, from every point of view untrue; from the reflective point of view they are irrelevant, which is worse. To press them at this critical moment in reflection is to divert attention from exploration of the concrete possibilities and promise of the new incentive to an anxious and premature reckoning of the incentive's worth—a reckoning which at this early stage can only be in terms of standards holding over from the past. It is to halt deliberation by a virtual denial of the first principle of all ethical deliberation—that in critical emergencies the values of the predictable consequences of the actions at issue shall be determined experimentally and afresh. With all its seeming dogmatism and rigidity, ethical intuitionism must be credited, paradoxically enough it may seem, with the historic service of keeping this principle from being quite lost to view in the strife of ethical theories. For in its total rejection of the teleological axiom of its more sophisticated and superficially more progressive opponents, intuitionism has comprised the less sweeping refusal to base judgment of the rightness and wrongness of general types of conduct or of particular acts upon a consideration of their *de facto* consequences *as currently understood and appraised*. I believe the latter to have been the true meaning and intent of intuitionism in the history of ethics, however misleadingly expressed. Intuitionism has had the all-important negative merit of expressing not stupidity or obscurantism but the individual's will towards freedom from the binding power of habit. This, as I believe, is the meaning of the "quest for certainty" in other fields as well of theoretical enquiry. In this way intuitionism has kept the possibility open for the more adequate expression of the will to freedom in an ethical theory of reflective reconstruction of moral norms. The actual aid and encouragement it has historically given to moral innovation and progress has probably on the whole more than offset its conservative tendency at particular times to confirm and consecrate modes of conduct that have become obsolete and restrictive.[37]

That actions cannot be judged without taking account of their concrete consequences of all significant kinds is a proposition having, as it stands, an altogether uncertain meaning for ethical theory.[38] Everything depends upon the manner of the taking into account. First of all, of course, any action that is ethically judged at all, already comprises much that, from a purely physical point of view, is consequent upon an initial physical act. No one, however, takes the trouble to condemn the initial act of fingers which trace marks on paper with a pen because they have as consequences a simulated signature and loss of money by a bank-depositor. Nor do we condemn the initial act of the crooking of a finger because it pulls a trigger, explodes a cartridge and so kills a man. We condemn instead the intentional acts of forgery and murder; question may then arise as to the significance for this judgment of the consequences which these kinds of total and meaningful action entail. How shall their consequences be taken into account?—meaning now by "consequences" the effects of forgery or murder upon the perpetrator's character, upon the victim, and upon the well-being of society at large. In the case of these particular sorts of behavior, however, it seems of course, to the general mind, not a little strained and artificial, apart from extenuating circumstances in a particular

[37] Cf. Professor Philip Wheelwright: *A Critical Introduction to Ethics*, 130-141. Discussions of motive and intention usually run in terms of cases so obviously cut and dried as altogether to remove the problem from its true setting of reflective procedure. We read, for example, of a prosecutor animated by desire for acclaim or political advancement who strives hard for the socially desirable result of convicting a dangerous criminal; or of a defense attorney who, from a motive of unselfish personal friendship, acquits an innocent man by the only possible expedient of procuring perjured testimony. Such examples are on a par with discoursing on the mortality of "all men" and of "Socrates" to elucidate the nature of inference.

[38] Cf. *Human Nature and Conduct*, 44 ff.

case, to consider such a question at all. Forgery and murder are crimes—for reasons moderns have forgotten, if, indeed, they ever were appreciated in their full extent and gravity. These crimes are at all events sins for us now: and of course we are all of us, like the clergyman in the now classic story, "against sin"—which is an end of the matter. Let us turn then to kinds of behavior more definitely problematical in this day and age— divorce, strikes, "work-relief," war, for example, upon which there is ethical judgment less prompt and unanimous than our moral judgment upon the kinds of action with which it seemed easier to begin this paragraph.

In deliberation upon such phenomena for ethical consideration as these, there are two ways in which "consequences" may be taken into account. One of these ways is to ascertain the proximate and long-range consequences of every kind, both of doing and of leaving undone the act in question—in order that we may know as fully and precisely as possible just what the alternatives factually are with which we have to do. Until this has been done (and I say *until* without wishing to suggest that the two procedures are separate in time or can go forward without interaction and mutual support) it must be utterly impossible to deliberate ethically to any useful purpose whatever. For ethical deliberation, we must surely know what the problem is upon which we are to deliberate. The other way of taking consequences into account is to carry forward our survey on all sides until "some habit or some combination of elements of habits finds a way fully open," until "energy is released" and "the mind is made up, composed, unified." The one way assumes that there is a logical distinction between (1) the completest possible definition of alternatives in terms of "consequences" in their far-reaching factual detail and (2) ethical deliberation upon them as they are thus defined—this, being an essentially social or democratic procedure in which the deliberator self-consciously keeps himself exposed to every type of environmental suggestion and appeal in the expectation of changes in his ruling principles and aims.[39] The other way seems to me simply to identify

[39] That Kant meant anything essentially at variance with this position by his insistence upon the ethical irrelevance of consequences, I do not in the least be-

ethical procedure with the full factual description of the alternatives and the progressive complexities of affective and emotional response to them which already established habits automatically record. This way, as it seems to me, amounts to denial of the ethical point of view. "Most conflicts of importance," writes Professor Dewey, "are conflicts between things which are or have been satisfying, not between good and evil."[40] We ought instead to say, I think, that ethical conflicts are between things, on the one hand, which are or have been found satisfying, and things, on the other hand, which have *never* been found satisfying, for the very excellent reason that they have never been known before. In the aspect which the precise juncture at hand puts upon them, these things as here and now suggested are found incommensurable with the congenial and the satisfying.[41]

There is, it seems to me, a certain danger to the cause of progress in such a statement as the following: "What is needed is intelligent examination of the consequences that are actually effected by inherited institutions and customs, in order that there may be intelligent consideration of the ways in which they are to be intentionally modified in behalf of generation of different consequences."[42] Intelligence is, of course, always more to be prized in its place than unintelligence. If we are to have examination of consequences, consideration of desirable modifications of institutions, and of the generation of different conse-

lieve. What he meant by his extensively caricatured formalism was simply the important truth that moral progress is possible only when the individual not only divorces himself from allegiance to old good but avoids the plausible mistake of *evaluating* proposed new good by the method of consequences. For the latter is to put on one's chains again after having put them off. Kant's primary concern with concrete moral progress, individual and social, seems to me evident throughout the *Critique of Practical Reason*—which I take to be, though perhaps seldom read today, the most penetrating and the truest analysis of our ethical experience ever set down in writing.

[40] *The Quest for Certainty*, Chapter X ("The Construction of Good"), 266.

[41] Things which have been found satisfying in the past may, indeed, be in conflict with each other in the present. Perhaps as a rule, however, they are dealt with as commensurable, in which happy case the conflict is not ethical. If they are treated as incommensurable, it is because one of them at least has, as reappearing in the present juncture, suggestive aspects or implications of novelty and promise.

[42] In *The Quest for Certainty*, Chapter just cited, 273.

quences, these ought all to be, at least in a certain sense, intelligent. But as I have argued above, perhaps at too great length, there is a sense of "intelligence" which is essentially conservative, not to say stationary. That any such meaning of the term is very far from Professor Dewey's intent is of course evident from the whole context of the passage quoted.

> Reflection upon what we have liked and have enjoyed . . . tells us nothing about the *value* of these things until enjoyments are themselves reflectively controlled. . . . We are not, then, to get away from enjoyments experienced in the past and from recall of them, but from the notion that they are the arbiters of things to be further enjoyed.

The statement could hardly be bettered as a warning against a supine bondage to the habitual past. But it is, I think, fair to urge that precisely what are the content and the method of the "intelligence" that *is* to be the "arbiter" requires clearer specification, if misconception of his meaning is not to vitiate Professor Dewey's intended teaching. And I think this is confirmed by two final passages which I shall cite, the one from the same chapter[43] and the other from the *Logic*. "Where will regulation come from," writes Professor Dewey,

> if we surrender familiar and traditionally prized values as our directive standards? Very largely from the findings of the natural sciences. . . . [Though of course] it would be too optimistic to say that we have as yet enough knowledge of the scientific type to regulate our judgment of value very extensively.

But the findings of the natural sciences are descriptive and interpretative of actions: they cannot possibly regulate conduct in the manner peculiar to values "prized" as "directive standards." And again:

> [Every] measure of social policy put into operation is, *logically*, and *should* be actually, of the nature of an experiment. For (1) it represents the adoption of one out of a number of alternative conceptions as possible plans of action, and (2) its execution is followed by consequences which, while not as capable of definite or exclusive differentiation as in the case of physical experimentation, are none the less observ-

[43] *The Quest for Certainty*, 273-274.

able within limits, so they may serve as tests of the validity of the conception acted upon.[44]

But consequences are, in the logic of ethics, incompetent to serve as tests of validity until they have themselves been weighed and measured and assigned their provisional degree of ethical significance.

IX

This discussion began with a brief reference to the status of method in experience. It was held that, unless ethics is an illusion due to a misleading "language-habit," there is in our experience a distinctive method of ethics and that this method is autonomous or constructive, not instrumental and subsidiary to the attainment of pre-determined ends. It was suggested that if the method of adaptive adjustment appropriate to "precarious" situations is regarded as instrumental and subsidiary in this way, then ethical method might be regarded, appropriating Professor Dewey's term (otherwise applied by him) as "supreme" in its province. In this application, the term would imply that ends-in-view, toward which the method of adaptation is instrumental, tend more and more, with the advancement of human society and the increasing sway of rational reflection over conduct, to be the outcome of prior ethical or constructive determination. This fact naturalism, from its point of view of external observation, loses sight of in a sweeping conception of distinguishable "situations" in experience as essentially "precarious" and of all deliberation as adaptive. It was suggested that ethical reflection and ethical theory could never have emerged from a nervous and shrinking dread of "disturbance" and the "precarious," and a yearning of the "organism" for the security of restored equilibrium or "integrated interaction" with the environment. These latter reactions of the "organism" when they occur represent a tacit commitment to what some naturalists are fond of calling "animal drive"—the urgent impulsion of the moment—whereas ethical reflection represents a type of constructive interplay of incommensurable interests which "animal drive" never institutes.

[44] *Logic*, 508-509.

This, however, was somewhat in the nature of a first approximation. If there really were, as Professor Dewey insists, a "natural continuity of inquiry with organic behavior,"[45] one might well begin to suspect argument about the status of methods as "instrumental" or "supreme" of being more than a little absurd. For if inquiry and organic behavior form a continuity, may not the same be true of inquiry and the method of inquiry? And according to Professor Dewey, just this is true. In art and in law, for example, "new formal properties accrue to subject-matter in virtue of its subjection to certain types of operation." The ordinary human activities of the dance, painting, sculpture, literature, music, in this way become fine arts; inevitable transactions between men begin to find their places in an ordered juristic system of crimes, torts, contracts, partnerships. The transformation in all such instances is accomplished by "subjection" of subject-matter to "certain types of operation" or "formal conceptions"—which latter, however, "are not imposed upon" the subject-matter "from on high or from any external *a priori* source. But when they are formed, they are also *formative;* they regulate the proper conduct of the activities out of which they develop." So "the way in which men *do* think" may legitimately be contrasted with "the ways in which they *ought* to think," provided the difference denoted is "like that between good and bad farming or good and bad medical practice." "Just as art forms and legal forms are capable of independent discussion and development, so are logical forms, even though the 'independence' in question is intermediate, not final and complete." The idea, to be sure, is unfamiliar in logic, but logical forms, like the forms of art or law or farming, "originate *out of* experiential material, and *when constituted* introduce new ways of operating with prior materials, which ways modify the material out of which they develop."[46]

---

[45] *Logic* (1938), 36.

[46] *Ibid.,* 101-103. The last italics in the above are mine. I call attention to the distinction between the actually occurring and authentic *subjection* of subject-matter to certain *types* of operation (under which formal properties *accrue*) and the *imposition* of formal conceptions "from on high," which is regarded as mythical: also to the *constituting* of logical forms after they have "developed" or "originated *out of*" the subject-matter—*operations upon which* they thereafter

I find this "metaphysical deduction" of the formal as dubious as the idealism for which Berkeley, to his embarrassment, found the common English idiom so unsuited; the difficulty, not to say impossibility, of achieving anything like consistency of statement seems to me as obvious and as significant in the one case as in the other. The assertion of a "natural continuity" of inquiry with organic behavior, while undoubtedly consistent naturalism, seems to me to be untrue to experience and unintelligible. In this matter as in very many others it is important to distinguish with some care the point of view of the observer of behavior from the "outside" from that of the individual within whose experience an idea or conception or function first makes its overt appearance. As Professor Dewey remarks, "The existence of inquiries is not a matter of doubt. They enter into every area of life and into every aspect of every area."[47] From which of these two points of view, however, is this statement made? From that of the human experience in which the existence of inquiry was first noted and observed, or from that of an observer, interested in the phenomenon or function of inquiry as a procedure, socially or privately advantageous the more actively it is carried on and everywhere needing protection and encouragement? I suggest, the latter. But for the purpose in hand, which is to determine the continuity or the discontinuity of inquiry with organic behavior this point of view seems to me to be irrelevant and misleading: the conclusion in which its adoption results is of a piece with the identification of thought with implicit bodily movements. The observer may well, and commendably, be concerned to promote the spread and vigor of inquiry as a human function or, as a logician, to "constitute" the due order of its successive stages. It would seem, however, that for the observer's embarkation on either enterprise some antecedent direct acquaintance with the function must be requisite. In his vocabulary, at least, there is certainly "a word for

---

keep true to form. Is it pertinent to ask why and by what natural impulsion the constituting is done? And by what natural impulsion the conformity of the new ways of operating with the newly constituted logical forms is maintained and a due tolerance of divergence allowed?

[47] *Ibid.*, 102.

it." But if there is a word, then on any theory of language, supplying the meaning of this word which his vocal mechanism utters, there must at some time and for some person have been an immediate and personal awareness of inquiry as a procedure then and there playing a vital part in that person's conduct of his own affairs. This awareness may have been an incident or episode in the experience of another person than the philanthropic observer, or of many others, from whom the observer has had report of it and has learned the word, or (perhaps to his deep confusion if he remembers) an episode in his own "past." Whether inquiry and organic behavior are continuous, "naturally" or otherwise, must be determined in direct experience like this, not in the observer's descriptive findings and, again, not by naturalistic dogma.

In our direct experience, inquiry is not "known as" naturally continuous with organic behavior. It is an interlude, an interrupting episode, whose continuity with "our common experience of free behavior, fluent discourse and direct and confident response to substantival meanings"[48] is on another basis and must be described in other terms than those of naturalism. With too little reluctance it may be, I excuse myself from attempting here this latter task, but the general lines on which I think it would have to be carried out may perhaps be indicated. The continuity in question is that of self-consciousness, not "nature." In our common or unreflective experience, organic responses are made not to "stimuli" categorially determinate which function as signs of natural or substantial realities over against us but to what are for us directly suggestive wholes of meaning—which, in nostalgic retrospect from the later point of view of inquiry may be termed substantives. Such responses follow upon the presentation of substantival meanings with the fluency of words and actions evoked by the familiar forms and phrases of one's native language.[49] When inquiry breaks in upon this natural

---

[48] *The Philosophical Review*, XLVI, 622-627, 632-633.

[49] I think "substantival meanings" to be an equivalent of James Ward's conception of "presentations" (*Psychological Principles*, Cambridge and New York, 1919; 46-51). Ward speaks of presentations as always "attended to" by a subject who, however, may be either "more or less aware" of them (46) and, in using the term attention, extends its denotation "so as to include even what we ordinarily call inattention." (49)

continuum of meaning and response, it is as an enterprise which one first becomes aware of as dull and tiresome or as mysteriously strange. Then comes more or less reflective knowledge of it as a rival for one's interest with the more congenial processes it contrasts with. First notice, scrutiny, analysis, constitution of its normal sequence, decision to prolong it, evaluation of it in particular cases as worth while or not, are, as I should maintain, attitudes toward inquiry which contrast it with the nature over against which the self has *pari passu* come to find itself set in problematic interaction.

We may, if we please, from the metaphysical or cosmical point of view of a glorified observer, describe the whole scheme of reality as one in which selves cope with the "nature" over against them with the weapon of inquiry. If we are to be true empiricists we must not, however, fancy that we can comprise the whole scheme of reality within any conceptual framework of the "nature" over against us, however prosperously employment of the latter may advance our undertakings. And finally, method is the perfecting of inquiry and in that sense continuous with it, if not inherent in it; but this continuity, like that of inquiry with fluent behavior, is not a "natural" one. It is a continuity of development within the purview and economy of self-consciousness. In this economy ethical method expresses more nearly the constructiveness, not to say spontaneity, of human nature than does the instrumental method of maintenance and adaptation.

HENRY W. STUART

DEPARTMENT OF PHILOSOPHY
STANFORD UNIVERSITY

11

George Raymond Geiger

DEWEY'S SOCIAL AND POLITICAL PHILOSOPHY

DEWEY'S SOCIAL AND POLITICAL
PHILOSOPHY

IT is not strange that men have come to be suspicious of professional philosophy. Has it not often given them resound-
ing phrases and tricky dialectic and moral opium when they
have approached with their tragically sincere questions? These
questions, it is true, have not been characteristically about the
dear delights of philosophy; perhaps that is why they have provoked patronizing stares. They have been questions more sordid, more earthly, downright inelegant, dealing with grubby
things like poverty and war, tyranny and ignorance, incompe-
tence and waste. Today these wonderments of man are likely
to be even more brutish and unphilosophical, for there is little
of epistemology or metaphysics—or even symbolic logic—in the
perplexing discussions about air raids and poison gas and the
liquidation of the opposition.

But, after all, what have these problems to do with philosophy? Philosophy is an august and privileged discipline; the
material it considers is refined, insulated, precious—so it has been
said. And further: These rather nasty inquiries men raise are
handled by social and political philosophy, which is an adjunct of
ethics, which is an adjunct of metaphysics—that core of all philosophic thinking. So philosophy can still remain aloof; its skirts
are clean. Yet, as Irwin Edman puts it, even from the ivory
tower bombs can be heard.

There is an overwhelming temptation to become oratorical
and preach a familiar sermon here. That temptation must be resisted, if for no other reason than that it would be completely
out of place in an introduction to the social and political philosophy of John Dewey. For no one is more impatient than Dewey
with moralizing. To rant at academic philosophy for its tradi-

tional indifference to specific social ills and specific political programs, for its sorry defeatism and glaring rationalizations, would be moralizing. But it is impossible to resist one small temptation. That is the urge, in this connection, to tilt at what is fervently hoped to be a man of straw. This hypothetical straw man is the modern philosopher who pays only lip service, if that, to "social problems"—(such a phrase of exquisite understatement). He is comfortably ensconced in some choice difficulty, deep and esoteric—preferably in a mathematical or symbolic sense—and watches the world pass by his window. The window is closed; no sound or smell reaches him. This is a caricature. But let us make believe it isn't. Is there any valid reason why this picture is, at least to some, a repellent one?

In a sense, of course, the whole Dewey philosophy is an answer to this question. But a more *ad hoc* reason for being profoundly suspicious of such an emancipated philosopher is that he seems singularly insensitive to the future of his trade. William James, writing at a time which might now be looked upon as almost the halcyon days, could still quote with warm approval those eloquent words of Morrison Swift: "The philosophers are dealing in shades, while those who live and feel know truth. And the mind of mankind—not yet the mind of philosophers and of the proprietary class—but of the great mass of the silently thinking men and feeling men, is coming to this view." How much more shadowy are the dear delights of philosophy today when one good push may bring about the collapse of everything that can be called civilized? How many more sabbatical years are due philosophic intelligence before it can be expected to go to work upon problems crying out so loudly for solution that they drown out the sirens warning of the bombers—problems, it should be added, grand, catholic, and possibly even unanswerable enough to attract the most courageous philosopher?

In turning, however, from rhetoric to John Dewey, it seems superfluous to call attention to the commanding position social philosophy occupies in his life and thought. Every essay in this volume must have made such a note. The attempt here must be rather to investigate the elements of that dominating sociopolitical strain in Dewey's work, starting with the very reasons why it has played a major rôle in his characteristic arguments.

I. The Challenge to Philosophy

It was William James who phrased one of the most poetic descriptions of philosophy when he termed it a name for unanswered questions. That phrasing well suggests the fascination which has been forever attached to the philosophic enterprise, the fascination of playing with profound riddles whose solutions are not waiting in the pages at the back of a book. But of much more weight in such a description of philosophy is the implied challenge. John Dewey has responded to that challenge as has no other philosopher. For what are the unanswered questions that today almost scream for attention? They no longer reside— if they ever did—in "sterile metaphysics and sterile epistemology;" neither are they inhabitants of some completely formal realm of sign-manipulation. In social relations and conflicts, in political and economic struggles, in a depressed ethics and a fumbling law and a struggling education—here are to be found the questions that demand answers. The failure to answer them, even to notice them, is the tragic and, it may well be, fatal indictment of human intelligence. This social orientation of Dewey's thinking is so familiar that documentation seems impertinent, although attention should be directed to the extraordinarily eloquent passages in his *Reconstruction in Philosophy*.[1] They show so graphically that even an orthodox definition of philosophy will provide a challenge for any thinker sensitive to questions which are really unanswered—and which demand answers.

But the social orientation of philosophy implies much more for Dewey than simply the opportunity of coming to grips with a stimulating enigma. It implies also something possibly less dramatic than the repeated warning that free philosophy itself has little place in the tortured and decadent brutalitarianism that looms ahead should these questions remain unanswered or be answered unintelligently. The social emphasis in Dewey's thought has been above all a function and an illustration of his entire experimental approach; for it is precisely the glaring failure of human intelligence in the social field that has cast the sharpest focus on the meaning and urgency of scientific method.

[1] Chap. V, 123 ff. and Chap. VIII.

This gloomy failure of reflective thinking is principally a methodological collapse, and it has impressed Dewey probably more than has any other human phenomenon. The incredible gap between technological advance and the application of that advance to the economic and political scene is nothing less than the almost deliberate abdication of intelligence from a whole area of human experience. After all, it is no secret why there have been fantastic revolutions in natural science; any history book will report the reasons. Man has finally learned to use experimental inquiry in the fields that have now been designated as "scientific." It is gratuitous to add that these fields were not indigenously "scientific," or that they indeed became "scientific" as they responded to the employment of a method. The point here is to lament the divorce of that same attitude of critical investigation from social questions. It would be but trite to proclaim that reflective thinking is used wholeheartedly by the mechanic in repairing an automobile, and that it is just as wholeheartedly absent when the United States Senate debates on confirming a Presidential appointee; that the physician employs diagnosis and hypothesis and application, which are conspicuously shunned by economic doctors and political practitioners. The unbelievable lag in referring the recognized methods of scientific techniques to disciplines other than the natural studies is so commonplace that it has become the occasion for good-natured humor. We are indeed confronted with what, in another setting, Lewis Mumford has called a pseudomorph—a cultural hang-over. It is exactly this fatal hesitation that has so profoundly disturbed a whole generation of thinkers of whom John Dewey is the most articulate and persistent representative. But it is not simply the humanism of Dewey that has been shocked by our social and political failures. His sense of the power of logic as a tool for inquiry has been correspondingly shocked—if there is any meaning in separating his logic from his humanism.

Social philosophy is thus an integral part of Dewey's thought. It is linked, first of all, with the very genesis of all philosophic enterprise—the concern with "questions of the most perplexing and significant sort." The task and meaning of philosophy itself, of human intelligence using reflective methods of inquiry to cope with relevant and unanswered problems, can in no way be dissociated from human (*i.e.*, social) life. By implication this is, of course, a challenge to the traditional philosophic traffic with irrelevant and unanswerable problems. In the second place, the extraordinary insolvency of social thinking testifies to an absence of fruitful method. The use of intelligence as revelatory instead of instrumental may go far in explaining this apparent scientific bankruptcy of much economic and political speculation. As illustrative, therefore, of that fundamental distortion in human intelligence which has called into action the entire instrumentalist attack, social philosophy is legitimately John Dewey's first and last love.

II. Method

It would be but tedious to launch into one more exposition of Dewey's instrumentalism, but, at the risk of repetition, the following points may be suggested. As fundamental to his entire reconstruction, Dewey has attacked, with all the weapons in his armory, the traditional elevation of knowledge over doing, of theory above practice. This elevation has inevitably taken the course of locating the object of knowledge in a realm of fixed Being, existing antecedently to the act of knowing, and being revealed to the knower by his act. Such a realm of Essence is, to be sure, a changeless and precious one: philosophy becomes "the quest for certainty." As a corrective for this—to him *the* philosophic fallacy—Dewey has insisted again and again that knowing is a form of doing, that it cannot exist apart from that which is known, that the objects of knowledge are the consequences of operations performed and are not mysterious entities existing sufficiently before the act of knowing, waiting, as it were, to be illuminated. These operations of knowing are decisive. They consist of experiments, instruments, methods, by which the very conditions that make knowing possible are created. This search for methods of control should be the philosophic quest as it is the scientific quest. "The heart of the experimental method," Dewey writes, "is determination of the significance of observed things by means of deliberate institution of modes of interaction."[2]

[2] *Logic: The Theory of Inquiry* (1938), 511.

There is nothing novel about this interpretation of knowledge. Dewey points out that knowing as operational is a commonplace in the activities of science. The conviction that method is more important than conclusion is the very essence of scientific experimentalism. It was indeed this concentration upon technique instead of upon final ends that provided the magic to transform out of a supernatural theology and philosophy what we now know as physical science. But this very lack of novelty is, for Dewey, the impressive element, for it indicates a stupendous failure of philosophy, above all of social philosophy, to avail itself of recognized approaches to problem solving. The paralysis of method is the fatal disease here. However, no worship of physical science is intended in this connection. Dewey has argued repeatedly that all aspects of experience are equally real—science has no vested claim upon it. Experimentalism means much more than the use of tricky machinery. In its widest sense it signifies opposition to fixed ends, system-making, and changelessness; it signifies a refusal to divorce thought from action. It stands for provisionalism and reconstruction, the reliance, that is, upon working hypotheses rather than upon immutable principles. Thus, science is in no wise limited to the professional scientist. It represents an attitude that can function in any area of experience, an attitude of free and effective intelligence. The extension of such a temper would be indeed the "unified science" that is being sought in many circles.[3]

And the installation of this experimental methodology would constitute a true Copernican revolution in social and political philosophy. For it would dislocate the orbit of social thinking which to so great an extent is now centered in fixed concepts and bound to them by what Dewey has termed "the logic of general notions." For example,

we need guidance in dealing with particular perplexities in domestic life, and are met by dissertations on the Family or by assertions of the sacredness of individual Personality. We want to know about the worth of the institution of private property as it operates under given conditions of time and place. We meet with the reply of Proudhon that property

[3] See Dewey's paper in the *International Encyclopedia of Unified Science* (University of Chicago Press, 1938), Vol. I, No. 1.

generally is theft, or with that of Hegel that the realization of will is the end of all institutions, and that private ownership as the expression of mastery of personality over physical nature is a necessary element in such realization.[4]

. . . The conceptions involved were not regarded as *hypotheses* to be employed in observation and ordering of phenomena, and hence to be tested by the consequences produced by acting upon them. They were regarded as *truths* already established and therefore unquestionable. Furthermore, it is evident that the conceptions were not framed with reference to the needs and tensions existing at a particular *time* and *place*, or as methods of resolving ills *then* and *there* existing, but as universal principles applicable anywhere and everywhere.[5]

Such pronouncements of universal principles end investigation instead of initiating it. (Especially do they end it in favor of the *status quo*.) The demand must be, however, for the specific formulation and diagnosis of problems, for data, for provisional multiple-working hypotheses, for the testing of beliefs by consequences, for empirical verification, where possible. But, more than anything else, the reconstruction of social philosophy requires that programs cannot be determined in advance. This is fundamental. It does not mean—as caricaturists would have us imagine—that the instrumentalist starts from a vacuum with no concepts or theories whatsoever. It does mean that such concepts and theories be used as tools of inquiry to advance investigation instead of to block it. It does mean that programs of action be regarded as working hypotheses to be supported or repudiated, as they are in the natural sciences, by the consequences which follow.

This may all sound plausible if dull. But the acceptance of such a policy would remove from social and political philosophy some of our most cherished playthings. It would make thinking in this field a matter of gathering prosaic facts and putting forward tentative and halting explanations, risking them to ridicule and collapse at every moment, accepting their collapse and trying other solutions—all of which would be considered by many thinkers as dreadfully dreary and grubby business, quite different from the warm and pleasing irrelevance of after-

[4] Dewey in *Reconstruction in Philosophy* (1920), 189.
[5] *Logic: The Theory of Inquiry*, 505-6.

dinner conversation. It would mean, in short, a revolution in thought just as middle-class and unspectacular, but just as stupendous, as the revolution in industry of a century ago.

Now, the experimental method in social philosophy does not mean—as, again, caricaturists paint it—"the carrying on of experiments like that of laboratories."[6] Each aspect of experience demands its own methods. For instance, one of the prime requirements for introducing a greater measure of reflective thinking into the social sciences is that freedom of inquiry and publication of results must be given much more than lip service. Whatever facts are discovered by experts must be "made known, and not simply be found out" (a phrase that Dewey uses often). This implies something quite other than platitudes about free speech. It is a positive, indeed a belligerent, qualification that is as vital in this whole region of investigation as are the conditions of precision and objectivity in the disciplines of science. Indeed, Dewey argues that the Great Society can turn into the democratic Great Community only when "free social inquiry is indissolubly wedded to the art of full and moving communication."[7] A glance at present world society will turn such a seemingly harmless statement of a necessary experimental condition into another revolutionary proclamation.

This insistence that identical methods are not everywhere applicable, that scientific control is not a term that can be lengthened and shortened, procrustean-like, to fit any situation, should illuminate the characteristic criticism that "science" (presumably scientific method) is responsible for the very world tragedy in which man today finds himself. The subject is a rich one for muralists. However, Dewey is unpoetic enough to regard "science" as impersonal. It can neither be debited nor credited. The indictment should be changed, its attention redirected to the unthinkable stupidity of using scientific method to extend interests which preceded its rise instead of to modify men's social acts and attitudes.[8] The benefits of science have not been spread

[6] See Dewey's *The Public and Its Problems* (1927), 202.

[7] *Ibid.*, 184.

[8] In this connection, note Dewey's *Philosophy and Civilization* (1931), 324. The last chapter in this book, "Science and Society," is very important for this whole point. See also the recent book by R. S. Lynd, *Knowledge for What?* (Princeton University Press, 1939).

out; and in this conflict between pre-scientific ideas and post-scientific realities has been nourished a "class struggle" more portentous than any in economic history. In fact, it is not simply democracy or capitalism that is on trial. That would be almost too simple a problem. Collective intelligence itself is at stake. The great scientific revolution is still to come.

If all this sounds academic and stilted, even—of all words—"theoretical," it must be remembered that John Dewey, in his long life, has been much more than a professional philosopher. He has been, among many other things, a publicist and editor, even a pamphleteer and propagandist. In a brief exposition such as this there is no opportunity to illustrate how he has actually applied his instrumentalist theories—although the following section will attempt to give some content to his method by referring it to some traditional problems in social and political thinking. Of course, even a casual reading of the newspapers over a period of years would draw the attention of the reader to Dewey's *specific* interests in social problems. No liberal movement of significance and weight has failed to enlist his ungrudging support, and no cause, however unorthodox, which proffers specific contributions and criticisms has gone unrecognized by him. Only a reading of a book like *Characters and Events: Popular Essays in Social and Political Philosophy* (1929), which is composed largely of articles written by Dewey for the *New Republic* during his long connection with that periodical, can show how the touch of his method gives an incandescence to what might otherwise be considered the most trivial of issues. But this whole question of technique requires illustration.

III. THE INDIVIDUAL AND SOCIETY

There is nothing quite so conducive to muddy thinking in the social sciences as the throwing about of grand generalizations. This is so commonplace an observation that it need hardly be made. The State, Society, The Individual *versus* the State, Individualism and Collectivism, Liberalism and Democracy, Fascism and Communism, Competition, Coöperation, Laissez-Faire—there are the concepts that we talk about when we discuss social and political problems. And so often we think the problem "solved" when our abstraction has so overcome our opponent's that, for the moment, he can think of no other abstraction with which to counter-attack. But no concept *qua* concept is of any real help here. The very abstractions of Individual and Society, for example, have done a work of untold mischief in deflecting the course of social thinking. When "individual" or "society" is looked upon as something in itself and factitiously separate; when the two are urged to coöperate or to remain opposed; when it is graciously admitted that "in reality" their interests are mutual—then we are in truth in the land of dialectic. We are using general ideas to solve particular problems. And that, for Dewey, is the mortal sin.

As soon as The Individual is regarded as a general idea, he becomes Something aloof, discrete, insulated; and, of course, there immediately arises a Problem. (An epistemological problem arises in the same way once the knower and the act of knowing are amputated from the mysterious that-which-is-known.) All amputations, especially when they are unnecessary, produce serious problems; it is so much easier not to cut in the first place. When the individual is severed from something which is called Society, to paste the two together again is indeed a task. Now, that isolating of the individual from the group has a certain measure of plausibility. No one, not even the most poetic subscriber to the organic theory of society, can ignore the elementary observation that single anatomical beings are the *loci* of action and desire and all else human.

But only intellectual laziness leads us to conclude that since the form of thought and decision is individual, their content, their subject-matter, is also something purely personal. . . . Association in the sense of connection and combination is a "law" of everything known to exist. Singular things act, but they act together. Nothing has been discovered which acts in entire isolation. The action of everything is along with the action of other things. The "along with" is of such a kind that the behavior of each is modified by its connection with others.[9]

This interaction is crucial. Joined by the vital element of communication, it forms the basis (in *Experience and Nature*) of Dewey's whole interpretation of social experience. But it is decidedly not an interaction between pre-existing individuals

---

[9] *The Public and Its Problems*, 22.

and some artificial creature like the state or society. The state, as shall be noted below, comes into being as an administrator of this very interaction, peculiarly when such interaction produces remote and indirect consequences. And "society is one word, but infinitely many things. It covers all the ways in which by associating together men share their experiences, and build up common interests and aims. . . . Society is the *process* of associating in such ways that experiences, ideas, emotions, values are transmitted and made common."[10] It stands above individuals no more than the alphabet stands over the letters composing it.

Dewey's point of view presupposes that *the* Social and *the* Individual are simply abstractions between which no clash can arise (although there are specific conflicts between *some* individuals and *some* actual social arrangements), and between which no "either-or" choice has to be made. The same focus also discloses that there is no fixed meaning to social and individual; they have changed as times and places have. In other words, when we talk of interaction, holding it to be a key word in this discussion, there vanish two ultra-imaginative pictures: (a) society is a *Ding-an-sich*, having its own value as over against that of the individual; and (b) individuality and selfhood exist essentially in splendid isolation, unmoved by what goes on without.

This approach to the individual and society is in no sense a rehashing of that hoary and fruitless business of heredity *versus* environment, for that, too, is another one of those notorious bloodless battles of the categories. Dewey's argument is instead an attempt to handle concepts like these in terms of the actual referents to which they can be attached. For instance, when the word individual is brought out into the open and thoroughly ventilated, it loses the halo of untouchableness with which "individualists" so often adorn it. True enough, the individual is indeed separate, discrete, and alone—from the viewpoint of physics and biology. But is it that bundle of electricity, of reflexes and bones and hair, which even the most incorrigible individualist has in mind when he warns against the domination

[10] *Reconstruction in Philosophy*, 200, 207.

of society? The individual, in this dimension, is at most an interesting biological specimen—perhaps more interesting when a cadaver. But an individual is more than a specimen or a caricature. He is a personality, a congeries of habits, with reflexes conditioned and operating, speaking a language and eating food—and loving or hating Hitler. This is what we mean by the term: any other referent would be as unreal and as unpleasant as the nub of a Frankenstein story. Even Robinson Crusoe, so dear to the hearts of economist and sociologist, wasn't a "real" Crusoe-individual. To be that he would have had to be born—alone—on his island, like a phenix, which is a rather difficult procedure for mammals.

The implications of all this should be clear. Upon everything that is legitimately characteristic of human personality society has laid a finger. This should not, however, provoke the threadbare complaints that (a) oh, the individual is nothing, society everything; or (b) so, biological factors are insignificant in determining individuality. Such naïve reactions could apply only to the very abstractions from which Dewey has always been trying to escape. The naïveté of the first is in erecting to an entity a symbol called "society." For society *is* individuals in their relations to each other. It is no more a separate structure than is the functioning individual. The ingenuousness of the second is in locating the concept of individuality within a watertight, non-social area. But individuals are always closely geared to other individuals, and biological factors—their influence in no way being depreciated—act by contributing to the normal or abnormal interaction between individuals. It is the interaction, however, that is vital in giving meaning to both individual and social. (In passing, it should be noted that even a eugenics program can function only as an adjunct of social control.)

These are only negative implications. The positive consequences of breaking down this fictitious and verbal barrier between individual and society are more substantial. For one thing, Dewey's method, as we have seen, insists on specificity. Thus, questions like these become relevant: *What* individuals will be aided or harmed by this or that act? Just how will these particular individuals be affected? Why are they in situations

SOCIAL AND POLITICAL PHILOSOPHY 349

which make their being harmed or aided a problem? What will happen to *other* individuals as a result of what happens to these? Questions of this type may not be easy to answer; in many cases they cannot possibly be answered with our present data. But unless this is the direction in which attention is turned, such questions can never be answered. For all relevant inquiries are blocked so long as there is no injunction against talking about The Individual. In a complementary fashion, Society must be particularized. Since society covers "street gangs, schools for burglary, clans, social cliques, trades unions, joint stock corporations, villages and international alliances,"[11] it has no meaning until, like individual, it is localized and, as it were, stained. *What* social groups should perform this or that task? In what way should a group approach its task? What other groups will be affected? Should specific groups expand or contract their control? Again, these may be the most perplexing of questions. Yet they translate into the most real of inquiries, inquiries with content. Problems about Society never can.

A second implication of this approach is the impetus it gives to control, which, like specificity, is fundamental to anything that claims affinity with scientific method. If individuality develops—is actually made—through a process of interaction, then the lever to move worlds is put into our hands. Social arrangements "are not means for obtaining something for individuals, not even happiness. They are means of *creating* individuals."[12] Thus, the fulcrum of control must rest upon the educational and social methods for *reaching* the individual. It is only when we turn our backs upon the preciously insulated Individual and his changeless nature that anything can be done. The myth of an adamant individual who has remained imperturbably immune to alteration ever since his paleolithic adventures has been an amusing, if vicious, fancy. It has placed a premium upon anatomy and physiology—not to say philosophic idealism—and a handicap upon personality. To assert that personality, which, after all, is what we know as the individual, has continued fundamentally the same for ages is downright

[11] *Ibid.*, 200.
[12] *Ibid.*, 194.

nonsense. *Potentially*, perhaps, man has remained more or less constant in certain gross features of his emotional make-up; that is the half-truth at the root of such a superstition. But *actually*, instead of being aloof, man has been the very creature of his surroundings, and his supposedly impregnable human nature has undergone fantastic acrobatics, not simply from one millennium to another, but from war to war, treaty to treaty, and even from one ruler (or election) to the next. The individual *can* be turned and directed and made over; but he can be controlled only when he can be reached. *The* Individual can be touched perhaps by metaphysics alone: specific individuals can be moved by specific social interactions. That way lies the hope (the danger, too) of anything that can be called a social science.

That way also lies the hope of ethics. Dewey's moral philosophy is being handled elsewhere, but a postscript can be added here to indicate how this approach to the individual, in fact, this whole interpretation of social philosophy, prepares a foundation for an instrumentalist ethics. For "morals is not a theme by itself because it is not an episode nor department by itself. It marks the issue of all the converging forces of life."[13] Yet traditional ethics has so often confined itself to much narrower forces, those which operate most effectively in metaphysical workshops, *e.g.*, a moral sense, will and motive, categorical imperatives and Absolute Goods. Undoubtedly these topics are significant (in any event, one would have to be endowed with remarkable philosophic courage to deny that they are), but how much consideration has ethical theory vouchsafed to education, poverty and social misery, law, culture, political structures and economic systems? These *social* phenomena form the great basis for the lives that morally judged creatures lead. To manipulate those conditions is to prepare a background for relevant ethical knowledge. This is no more or no less than the insistence that ethical theory and social theory must work together if moral philosophy is to become operative, that ends and means can never function as discontinuous entities, but must always act as a unit. There can be no divorce, as has been customary in moral theory, between ends which are intrinsic—or moral, and

<hr>

[13] Dewey in *Living Philosophies* (1931), 31-32.

those which are "merely" instrumental—that is, social. The effect of that divorce upon ethical concepts has been too often either to remove them from affairs here below and make them inhabitants of some other intellectual world of ends and goals, or to transform them into an elaborate system of apologetics. But ethics cannot permit itself to be emasculated. We must say of it what William James said of God—that in this world of sweat and dirt, God cannot be a gentleman. He cannot refuse to get his hands soiled. So with ethics.

Were ethics not so vital a part of Dewey's thought, an addendum such as this would be gratuitous. But ethics is vital: no other aspect of philosophy is so genuinely important. "Morals is as wide as everything which affects values of human living." Ethical theory is no mere matter of casuistry any more than it is one of apologetics. Its concern must be: How can individuals be *made* moral, *i.e.*, how can they achieve expression, and how can they realize their opportunities; in a word, how can they lead normal social lives? How can they be controlled? What conditions will enable them to develop to the utmost their capacities for well-rounded and individualized personalities? These questions require specific and objective answers; they require answers that must be supplied by social science. The burden of Dewey's entire social and political philosophy has been to indicate how such answers may be forthcoming.

IV. The State and Democracy

Another one of our grand concepts, The State, can be approached with as little respect for abstractions as greeted Society and The Individual. Of course, once we pronounce that magic phrase, The State, the temptation is to add immediately, "loud cheers." For it seems to be indeed a thing, an entity, a metaphysical essence; at the very least, a causal agency having power to produce action. Now, when we begin looking in this direction, almost anything may turn up, and so the state has come to mean the whole series of hypostatizations that parade regally through the history of political philosophy. It ranges from the Hegelian capstone of the universal processes to a wicked ogre which is waiting only to be pushed over. But we have been looking in the wrong place for the state.[14] It is not to be discovered in the land of essences or forms. If the method Dewey proposes is to be followed, the state must be sought in actual happenings and consequences.

Dewey finds the state in the need for regulation of activities. "The state is the organization of the public effected through officials for the protection of the interests shared by its members."[15] This seems to be a very pedestrian definition. We miss the flowing eloquence of the great political philosophers; for we have become accustomed to the rhetorical apostrophes made to the state, and we expect the warmth, the glow of great, meaningless periods. This kind of a state is much too bald. But what kind of a state is it, anyway? It derives clearly from the notion of a public, and a public comes into existence when the consequences of private actions are sufficiently extended to require control. Acts which are limited in their effects to the persons directly concerned with them are private; acts which have large and indirect effects reaching out to those persons not directly concerned become public. (The difference between private and public, however, is not equivalent to the difference between individual and social.) Public acts require officials and administration. This is the locus of the state.

Well, what is the value of such a definition—just its prosaicness? If prosaic can be tied up with specific, yes. For it is again, as with the individual and the social, the *specific* elements in such an approach that give it value. For one thing, the connection of the state with more elementary social organizations indicates that states come into existence as they are required; they grow and develop. They themselves are the consequences of specific needs. There is nothing here of some prepotent force which by fiat or nisus generates a mystical State. Neither is there any truck with changeless, permanent states. States—according to this hypothesis—are no more all-embracing than they are insignificant. They result from the projection of important consequences beyond the direct concern of persons and groups, con-

---

[14] Dewey's most detailed discussion of the state is in his *The Public and Its Problems*. The title of the book is worth noting.
[15] *Ibid.*, 33.

sequences which require the establishment of special agencies. Therefore, the formation of states becomes a series of (possibly unconscious) experiments. Publics differ; their needs and demands change. It is no more than reasonable to expect states to be flexible. By their very origin and nature they require constant scrutiny, revision, amendment. It is thus futile to talk about the "best state" in terms of some pious hope which waits at the end of a rainbow. Yet it is equally futile to rely simply upon improvisation. Instead, the *specific* search for the nature of the state directs its attention to problems that are real and soluble; it does not worry itself overmuch with the conceptual status or abstract justification of political activity. For example, included in this kind of an approach would be a deliberate accounting of the actual characteristics which states do possess, a type of inquiry which would be completely out of order were our attention fixed upon the traits which metaphysical states *ought* to have.[16]

Since the state is a functioning arm of public activity instead of some mystical power worthy of worship, it can be experimented with. In fact, as has already been emphasized, we should more correctly talk about *states* instead of *the state*. States are plural. They can be manipulated and directed. It is comic to set up some totalitarian political idol which is changeless, untouchable, and awe-provoking. It is scarcely less arbitrary to decide in advance upon the degree of state activity. As far as anything that can be called a qualitative character of the state is concerned, it must be regarded as neutral in predetermining the extension of powers. States expand when the indirect and far-reaching consequences of private action expand. They contract when intimate, face-to-face relations dominate. It goes without saying that the indirect and far-reaching consequences have expanded prodigiously since the industrial revolution; the inference as to

---

[16] These characteristics are worked out in Chapter II of *The Public and Its Problems*. They include such traits as localization of the state somewhere between associations which are narrow and intimate, and those which are remote and disconnected; concern of the state peculiarly with long-time interests which are channelized and standardized by means of law; functions of the state in dealing with irreparable conditions, *e.g.*, those of inferiority of age or capacity; and the like.

the powers of the state must be obvious. Yet to label the state collectivistic or total in its essence is as prejudicial to the understanding of political function as falling back upon *laissez-faire* or limited police powers.

However, the word "neutral" must not be misunderstood. Too often pragmatism, of whatever sort, has been decried as blind expediency or as resigned acceptance of whatever happens to be "working" at the moment. Ludicrously enough, it finds itself accused of being responsible at the same time for both the fumbling and pointless efforts of liberalism, and the ostensible efficiency of fascism. But neutral does not mean indifferent. It does mean refusal to allow concepts and symbols which have been obviously weighted one way or the other to determine antecedently what kind of state must be supported by political philosophy. Instead, the purpose of political philosophy is precisely "the creation of methods such that experimentation may go on less blindly, less at the mercy of accident, more intelligently, so that men may learn from their errors and profit by their successes."[17]

It seems unnecessary to add that the political set-up for such experimentation requires a democratic state—using "democratic" in the sense in which it was referred to some pages back, *i.e.*, as coterminous with freedom of inquiry. This mention of the democratic state will not be a stimulus for discussing historical or political democracy.[18] That would involve material which is both too familiar and too tricky; besides, it would not be exactly the point in question. For the connotations of Dewey here are those of method.

The prime condition of a democratically organized public is a kind of knowledge and insight which does not yet exist. In its absence, it would be the height of absurdity to try to tell what it would be like if it existed. But some of the conditions which must be fulfilled if it is to exist can be indicated. . . . An obvious requirement is freedom of social inquiry and of distribution of its conclusions.[19]

[17] *Op. cit.*, 34.

[18] Dewey discusses democracy historically in a number of places; perhaps his best treatment is in *The Public and Its Problems*, Chaps. III and V.

[19] *Ibid.*, 166.

Political, economic democracy is thus the setting for experimental method in social thinking. That alone is sufficient reason for cherishing it. Given that, and all the implications about democracy making possible the realization of individuality amid social coöperation will follow. Given that, liberalism assumes a new and richer significance.

V. LIBERALISM AND COLLECTIVISM

Perhaps no better illustration of the appropriateness of Dewey's criticism of current social and political philosophy can be found than the welter of discussion which has been rolling around the concepts of democracy and liberalism in these last tragic years—not to say months. It is not polite to say, "I told you so," but of any political philosopher Dewey should be granted that arid comfort. Democracy and liberalism have been so typically simply words, abstractions, functioning to inhibit investigation instead of to encourage it. They are battle-cries and shibboleths. They could be working hypotheses.

The historical fate of the liberal movement exemplifies, in too tragically neat a way, this bankruptcy of political concepts. This is a very trite observation and is the theme for too many current books. But Dewey has particularly addressed himself to this problem,[20] and has undertaken so complete a reformulation of neo-liberalism—and one that anticipated by a matter of years the rather febrile exhortations of so many writers today—that at least a mention of the liberal movement is necessary.

Legitimately liberal programs of any period must have, is Dewey's insistence, a similarity of purpose—a commitment to the principle that the mass of individuals should possess actual, not merely legal, liberty. (True, this is a "principle" that seems to be set up in advance; but it would prove to be a contradiction of Dewey's thesis only if it were looked upon as something more than a hypothesis.) Clearly, this "liberty" does not mean being let alone: it does mean that the individual be given full opportunity to develop the potentialities and talents that alone

[20] See particularly his *Individualism—Old and New* (1930); and *Liberalism and Social Action* (1935).

make him an individual. But that purpose will remain empty, and indeed as abstract as any platform that has only nobility to recommend it, unless it be elaborated with great particularity. Especially must anyone who claims (or rather admits to) the name of liberal be prepared to specify. Dewey's complaint arises at this point, for the liberal is so often found either to fall back upon the vaguest and most vicious abstractionism dealing with individualism, *laissez-faire*, free competition, and the rest; or to give his program content in terms of the historical liberalism of the eighteenth and nineteenth centuries, the liberalism, that is, of the commercial, the pre-industrial, revolution. (Possibly the latter alternative is less harmful, since at least it is particularized by way of Adam Smith and the Manchester School.)

Dewey's whole approach is introduced by his attack upon both of these brands of "latter-day" liberalism. His plea is that liberalism must become again the truly radical, the subversive, reform that once upon a time evoked energies directed to fundamental social change. To accomplish this it must undergo basic readjustment. Its principle of providing a soil for the complete growth of personality must be so adapted to economic and political life that direction and relevance can be achieved. And that requires recognition of the power of organized society, which alone can insure the conditions in which individuals may function fully. Here is where Dewey breaks cleanly with *laissez-faire* or individualistic liberalism—although that break was anticipated long since by liberals like Hobhouse and even John Stuart Mill in the closing years of his life when he changed his views so radically. Individualistic liberalism is bankrupt because it refuses to accept the corporate civilization which has made so many of its premises unreal and downright ghostly. It refuses to accept the need for coöperative control and organized social planning.

Now, these phrases are not simply words-of-the-month for Dewey. As abstractions with a modern and sophisticated ring they seduce him no more easily than do the old-fashioned slogans. Social progress cannot be trusted to words, even if they bear the magic talisman of "the collective state" or "dialectical materialism." They operate no more successfully than does "evolution," "Providence," or "manifest destiny." In fact, this trust in concepts is the real danger of a *laissez-faire* philosophy: let things alone and social problems will be solved by the prestige of great phrases. This is true even of "planning," the sorcery of which has captured all attention; no present writer on economics or politics could possibly ignore it. Yet, as a *word*, planning has no more power than any other word, except its vogue.[21] The concept will not solve anything. But *specific* plans can and must be accepted by a liberal philosophy. That is Dewey's constant and patient insistence. And every contribution he has made to social thought has illustrated his use of specific methods.

The study of particular social needs and the construction of special social machinery, the planned social employment of the resources of scientific knowledge and of the forces of production—these cannot be carried through by the uncoördinated acts of individuals, and they must not be stopped by platitudes of an older liberalism with its anarchy of natural laws and personal liberty. Traditional liberalism has lagged far behind the shattering consequences of the industrial revolution, just as the folklore of capitalism has lagged behind the transformation of a scarcity into an abundance economy. Both have been insufficiently impressed by the realization that economic insecurity is now institutional and not "natural," just as both have failed to appreciate that "socialism" must come—if it is not here already. Whether the socialistic, the corporate, state be public or capitalistic—that is the specific problem that must be met. But liberalism can never meet it by closing its eyes and wishing for the salad days.

Why then is Dewey a liberal instead of a socialist—if these labels really are of interest to anyone? Perhaps for the same reason that men like Max Lerner prefer the phrase "democratic collectivism." Socialism and communism are terms which are indissolubly connected with the name of Marx. Now, there

[21] As early as April, 1918, Dewey was talking of "planning." In an article, "Elements of Social Reorganization," reprinted in *Characters and Events* (Vol. II, 745-759), he argued for a program of planning instead of drifting to follow the war. Showing the importance of economic control in war-time, he presented specifically the problems of employment, industrial relations, production, and the like, demanding that they be approached in terms of intelligent, social foresight.

is much in Marxism of which Dewey not only approves, but which, in a real sense, he has actually helped put into operation. That is, the economic interpretation of history has been used by Dewey himself to explain many sections of the history of philosophy; and, in addition, through the work of his followers and students in political philosophy, history, and law—the work of Beard and Harry Elmer Barnes, Pound and Cardozo—the actual rewriting of much of American history and jurisprudence in terms of an economic appraisal of institutions has followed. Neither does Dewey quarrel with Marx over the very questionable intelligence and effectiveness of the capitalistic state, or over the values of a socialized society. Nor does the quarrel lie in any suspicion of the proletariat. "The world has suffered more from leaders and authorities than from the masses."[22] Dewey is definitely suspicious of an élite class, even of experts whose investigations he cherishes. Experts can discover and make known the facts, but it is only as an embodied intelligence raises the entire level of a society that fundamental social change has relevance.

Dewey's refusal to follow the philosophy of Marx (and, presumably, to accept the term socialist or communist) is, as might easily be expected, the refusal to accept metaphysical explanation for social and political problems. The Marxian dialectic, the class struggle, the labor theory of value—these are as abstract and, for Dewey, as essentially meaningless as any of the Hegelianisms or economic classicisms from which they derive. There is no cosmic reason why capitalism *must* give rise to communism *via* socialism, why collectivism *must* be achieved by means of a revolutionary technique, why surplus value *must* arise, why *any* abstract sequence *must* appear. Marxism is as much "a logic of general notions" as the individualistic liberalism it despises. Both rely on a metaphysic of general principles. What *does* happen, what *can* happen—these are realistic and instrumental problems; not what *must* happen. Once a philosophic concept is made supreme, then all apparent exceptions must be explained away. And despite its violent attacks upon traditional idealism and rationalism, that is just what Marxism proposes to do.[23]

---

[22] *The Public and Its Problems*, 208.

[23] To be sure, there have been "pragmatic" interpretations of Marx by a number of Dewey's own students—Sidney Hook's work being the most brilliant;

It seems to operate at the same old stand: witness the feverish explanations of why fascism has arisen, why the proletariat seems so weak, why communism began in Russia instead of in Germany where it *should* have begun (and therefore why Russian communism is not communism—or is the most realistic example of it). Intelligence cannot deal with inevitables. For example, Dewey cannot accept violence as an inevitable process in social change. Neither can he accept the inevitability of war or fascism or communism. This does not imply at all that fundamental reforms can come about painlessly. There is nothing mealy-mouthed or tepid in Dewey's challenges. But it is the *inevitability* of violence—as of anything else—that precludes the use of reflective methods. It is only when things are *not* final and once-for-all that thinking can function. Indeed, as with William James, Dewey has always been captured by the creationism of conscious intelligence: it can literally make and remake worlds. That is possible only when worlds—cosmic or social—are not yet completely made.

Thus, this approach to socialism and communism is one more example of Dewey's reliance upon techniques instead of concepts. It is perhaps the reason why he clings to the name of liberal, for liberalism still connotes "the mediation of social transition." This does not necessarily mean that liberalism is to provide a cushion for a shifting order; it is rather that the liberal philosophy seems elastic and tentative enough to supply the means to effect such transitions. It permits, indeed demands, an experimental method.

VI. Summary and Questions

For those of us who were undergraduates in the early twenties, the realization that the name of John Dewey no longer provokes the reverence it once did, is accepted with a feeling of more than simply wistfulness. There is an element of consternation, not to say foreboding, in that recognition. Especially is that the case in the field of social philosophy. To be sure, there are

but apparently Dewey has failed to be convinced, just as Hook himself is unconvinced that Marxist communism has been achieved in the Soviet Union (although Earl Browder—who certainly would yield to none in his Marxism—would hardly agree).

easy means of explaining away the admitted fact that in professional philosophy and, of much more importance, in so-called liberal and reform circles, Dewey's instrumentalism is not the touchstone of former years. We can show, for instance, that the ideas of Dewey are now unconsciously taken for granted. They have become commonplaces, and, as C. E. Ayres has recently remarked,[24] people don't get very excited about commonplaces. Instrumentalism, in performing the very task toward which it has directed itself, has been partially dissolved in the process. Again, we can argue that there are fashions in philosophy. The present vogue is mathematical logic and logical positivism. Today graduate students in philosophy talk about propositional functions, and syntactics, and protocol sentences, instead of about human nature, social conditioning, and moral reconstruction. The modes of thought change. (In fact, the argument might add: What graduate students talk about today appears suspiciously like a form of escapism.) So, Dewey is eclipsed by no permanent moon or cloud.

Are these explanations simply rationalizings? They do not seem to be egregiously so, at least when confined to the borders of technical philosophy. For it would be an arch-rebel indeed who would predict the long-time deflation of the pragmatic idea. But what about the lack of enthusiasm and the actual distrust which greet Dewey in the field of economics and politics where once his method of approach seemed almost unchallenged —unchallenged, at any rate, as far as protestations went?

This is the real problem, for it is not merely the experimentalist philosophy of a man that is obscured. That would be bearable—for those not his students. What is not so readily borne is the distrust of critical thinking, of provisional hypotheses, of the specific—and perhaps piecemeal—handling of specific problems, of patience which is truly reflective and exploratory—in a word, I suppose, the distrust of liberalism and democracy. This is not the place for one more excursion in defense of such ideas, especially since, if we are to be at all consistent, their defense would have to be in terms of methodology. And one can't drum up much of a peroration on methods. This is no place either for

[24] In the *New Republic*, January 18, 1939, where he discusses Dewey's *Logic*.

one more jeremiad. The apostles of pessimism are sufficiently eloquent, and almost they persuade us—witness the tenor of the few questions to be raised below. One cannot forebear noting, however, the almost too neat correlation between contemporary impatience with instrumentalism and contemporary seduction by dialectic. From neo-scholastic theories of education to neo-pagan worship of godlike leaders and god-created states, punctuated by—save the mark—dialectical materialism, there is the cry for soothing concepts. Let us, above all, be comfortable in our minds! Dewey is distinctly unsatisfying and discomforting, for he gives us nothing to which to hold fast except a dry-bones method, halting, tentative, vacillating. He is the typical liberal, and no more need be said. And if this be totalitarianism, let us make the most of it!

Thus, this apparent revolt against an experimentalist philosophy is something more than a problem involving any single thinker. It is part of a larger movement, a movement which is the current expression of the tender-minded retreat. That escape has taken many forms, all of them showing little stomach for the incorrigible toughness which refuses to succumb to formulas, all of them distrustful of criticism and analysis, in a word, of scientific method. The success or failure of that revolt can be predicted only in terms of our present mood. But unless we are blackly pessimistic, it is rather premature to foretell the permanent abdication of reflective thinking—even in international relations. It is just as premature to prophesy darkly about John Dewey. His power will vary directly as the power men accord to scientific inquiry in solving their social problems.

Many problems have been raised in these few pages, implicit ones for the most part. Some of them may be made explicit now. Perhaps that would be the best way to sharpen the focus on certain crucial issues, and, at the same time, to solicit possible comment from Professor Dewey. As was hinted some paragraphs back, the flavor of these questions is more pessimistic than critical. The questions are also definitely dated—as of the spring of 1939. For that reason they are more abrupt than should otherwise be permitted in a philosophic essay.

1. The experimental method has been emphasized in this exposition of Dewey's social thought. Of course, it has been qualified; that is, it does not necessarily mean "the carrying on of experiments like that of laboratories." But in just what way can it be employed? This is not simply the complaint that human beings and social structures cannot be put into test-tubes, although that complaint seems more than simply naïve. If laboratory technique of some sort is not implied by experimentalism, is the word completely relevant? Particularly is it relevant when specific and pressing demands confront us? For example, how can the present threat of world war (if it is no more than a threat when the present volume appears) be experimentally handled? What hypotheses can be tentatively put forward to be tested? Action must be taken (that's the tragedy); but what criterion is there for action? To insist that the criterion here, as elsewhere, must be one of provisionalism, workability, and operationalism seems almost a burlesque. In fact, in the political dimension, "experiments"—shall we cite the Chamberlain experiment of appeasement or the Hitler experiment of getting-away-with-it as "scientific" examples?—begin to appear absurd or tragic. Yet why is this the case? It would be entirely too ingenuous to say that the *right* experiments have not been tried—*e.g.*, first putting our own economic and political house in order, or revising the Treaty of Versailles to succor the "have-not" nations, or abolishing trade barriers. For, in the first place, these alternatives *at the present moment* are no more real than the ribald suggestion of inoculating the dictators with a "brooding" hormone that would infect them with the Golden Rule; and, in the second place, who is the judge of what the *right* experiments are? Where indeed does reflective thinking enter? Who is using intelligence—Hogben or Laski or Mumford at one extreme, or Bertrand Russell, Dewey, or Beard at the other?

This is not intended to be an oh-what-shall-we-do? type of query. It is rather a question about the very meaning and possibility of experimental techniques during crises like those staring at us now. Experimentalism must be more than merely a word which profits through the transfer of prestige. Likewise it must include more than simply an attitude. Actual experiments are never vague, whereas attitudes, even the most sound, usually are. The point of this first question therefore is to ask: In lieu of *actual* laboratory experimentation (which could be expanded to include statistical analysis), what can intelligence do when faced by the peremptory social problems that have turned the last years into a nightmare? Up to the present moment, the function of reflective thinking in this whole area seems to have been that of engendering controversial discussion, the kind of discussion which follows when doctors disagree. How can bickering—even pragmatic bickering—give way to action?

2. A similar gloominess about democracy also suggests itself. (Even Deweyites are becoming despondent—witness the latest yearbook of the John Dewey Society.)[25] If democracy is a necessary condition for the experimental method, and if the democratic state is being challenged today as never before, what are the prospects? How can experimentalism insure democratic conditions—particularly those of free inquiry—against attack, and, at the same time, rely upon such conditions for its very functioning? Of course, this business of preserving democracy can turn so easily into more example of the vicious circle. That is why some professed democrats look with dismay at men like Lewis Mumford whose recent *Men Must Act* begins the defense of democracy with the most rigorous curtailment of freedom of expression for dissenters—*i.e.*, fascists. And Dewey himself has become aligned with those who insist that any belligerent attempt to curb the fascist powers will immediately jettison the very democracy that is ostensibly being defended.[26] This approach has the strength and plausibility that accompany any concentration upon present means instead of upon final ends. That violent means can be transformed into pacific ends, that measures of repression will fade imperceptibly into goals of freedom, are delusions which call for constant therapeutic attention.

Yet this is only half of the vicious circle. It may well be that the argument which insists upon the sacrifice of democracy to save democracy is indeed self-refuting; or, if not self-refuting, it seems, at the very least, to be as paradoxical as the Christian

[25] *Democracy and the Curriculum* (1939), which concludes with a note of definite foreboding about the future of political democracy.

[26] See, for example, his contribution to a symposium on neutrality in the March, 1939, issue of *Common Sense*.

insistence upon losing a soul to save it. But can the alternative point of view, despite its apparent plausibility, promise us anything? Is it realistic to permit the evident weaknesses of democracy—even if they are only so-called short-term weaknesses—to bring about the collapse that seems to face us today in Europe, and perhaps tomorrow everywhere else? Is not the attitude which regards democracy as untouchable or as autonomic, which falls back upon clichés like "democracy has never been tried," and "the only cure for democracy is more democracy," guilty of the precise sins that have brought about the fall of *laissez-faire?* For specific problems of the here and now, the doctrinaire democrat proposes general formulas. In the meantime democracy itself, as a form of government and as the symbol standing for free thinking, sinks beneath the very forces which it is pledged to respect. And so a circularity as deadly as the overt sacrifice of democracy to democracy unrolls itself. It is no wonder that men are pessimistic.

Perhaps these last paragraphs are a dismal illustration of bickering, of a seeing-both-sides-of-the-question liberalism. Frankly, they are cathartic in purpose. For one who is committed to the kind of intellectual democracy that is so basic a part of Dewey's social and political philosophy, there are questions that can so easily fester. The chief one is: How can reflective thinking rest, as it must, upon "democracy" (which, in this connection, means specifically: conditions of free inquiry and free expression in the investigation of social affairs) and, at the same time, defend democracy from the bludgeoning to which it has been exposed?

3. In the program of liberalism, two questions may be raised. (a) Can the gradualness and tentativeness insisted upon by Dewey operate during crises? For that matter, can liberalism as "the program of social transition" adapt itself to that whole series of crises which stand for what we call our present social and political structure? It has been argued—and not simply by members of an extreme left wing—that economic conditions today are such that slow, moderate changes are self-defeating.[27]

[27] Possibly the best recent expression of this point of view is the paper by Oskar Lange in the short collection, *On the Economic Theory of Socialism* (University of Minnesota Press, 1938).

In any case, may not the experimental method sometimes demand abrupt if not actually violent social measures? This question is really part of a larger and more significant problem (one mentioned just a few sentences back), *i.e.*, does not the typically reflective and provisional character of liberalism inhibit action? This is, to be sure, an overly familiar, if not a banal, complaint these days, as trite as the story about the donkey who couldn't decide between his two bales of hay. But, commonplace or not, there does seem to be introduced a tragic blocking, an arrested development, as soon as the liberal is asked the question, what is to be done now, and how is it to be done? Seeing clearly both sides of a question is such a handicap at times. Fortunately or unfortunately, the alternatives to this reflective weighing of possibilities are even more unpalatable, for they can be nothing less than action based upon impulse, emotion, habit, or authority. Yet these unpleasant alternatives give only negative backing to liberal thinking; something more positive is demanded. In short, how can a liberal social philosophy, which develops from a type of thinking that compares and appreciates all the elements involved, get things done, especially in crisis periods?

   (b) As a corollary of this first question, it may be asked whether enthusiasm and loyalty can indeed be aroused for working hypotheses. Has not the accusation of fecklessness so often brought against liberalism resulted from its failure to capture the imagination and the emotions? Can motivation be found for a program of gradualness, or for a platform that recognizes its own limitations as well as the strength and partial soundness of the opposition? The problem of "getting things done" asks for tremendous energy and an almost frightening emotional drive. Fundamental economic and political change (the word "change" is inadequate and colorless, and "reform" is surrounded by the flabbiest of connotations: "revolution" is probably the most dependable term, but think of the shudders it provokes) depends upon a fanaticism and an abdication of reflective methods which can be termed only non-rational and non-liberal. To put it very crudely, it is not until men are aroused to an emotional seriousness for which even their lives may be sacrificed that anything happens. This is not intended to be a dramatic or spectacular interpretation of social processes, nor does it imply any fundamental retreat from reason. But there does appear to be so much in the liberal philosophy which is tied up with the eighteenth century age of reason, with a somewhat holy trust in man's rational nature. The reliance on coolness and calculation, on the inherent reasonableness of the conclusions resulting from reflective deliberation; faith in the illumination cast upon problems by the light of scientific techniques—these are the motives that are supposed to stir the liberal. But can they really move anything? That, at any rate, is the question proposed here. What motivation for action is to be found in the program of liberalism, and how is it to operate?

4. This opportunity for raising questions may be used to present one more, which, although not completely germane to the present issue, is characteristically suggested by any exposition involving pragmatism. It is a question that supposedly can be designated by the rather distasteful phrase, "ultimate values." That phrase is, of course, antipathetic to Dewey's instrumentalism, but nevertheless it connotes a difficulty which has always seemed a perplexing one in this dimension. That is to say, experiments in the natural sciences typically take certain ends for granted, e.g., efficiency, accuracy, objectivity, testifiability. Beyond that, "ultimate" ends or values—final causes—are taboo. But what, if any, are such ends in social experimentalism? Do they go further than methodological values? If so, how far and in what direction? By methodological values would be meant, above all, the assumption that reflective thinking itself is more valuable than any other end. This is a favorite statement of textbooks in logic and scientific method. It seems also to be implicit, at least by emphasis, even in the instrumental approach itself. For the instrumentalist concentrates almost entirely upon means, techniques, methods—upon the vital process of reflective thinking. Inevitably, then, this kind of question must arise: Do "thinking" techniques themselves constitute an ultimate value?—("value" being used here, in the accepted Deweyan sense, as the product of judgment, of comparison: the result of an act of evaluation which chooses between alternatives and

so, by preference, resolves a situation of doubt.) If so, is not such a tacit assumption that reflective thinking is more precious than any other value simply a modern reformulation of an Aristotelian or Spinozistic (or, in general, a "philosophic") worship of reason as the only characteristically human function? Would it not be a streamlined version of the good old body of rationalism? Now, these questions are not meant to be necessarily critical. The point is rather to discover whether Dewey, as an instrumentalist, is prepared to accept the values of method as final.

If they are not so accepted, then are we not pushed back to some other moral end, say, to happiness or to "the complete functioning of the individual," which appears to comprise the ethic of liberalism? And once that is admitted, aren't we already immersed in the most ancient of ultimates: Happiness for whom? For the individual or the group? Who is to be the judge? What criteria are to be employed? Why not something more noble and more worthy of respect than happiness? All the allegedly futile queries about moral goals crowd their way in. True, there is nothing illicit about falling back upon ultimates, but it seems occasionally that Dewey's social philosophy wavers between denying any reliance upon such moral purposes, and assuming unconsciously certain values, characteristically those either of reflective inquiry itself or of the processes of social reform.

It is perhaps very tedious if not impudent (at least, in a postscript such as this) to comment, in what passes for an impressive tone: Instrumentalism, yes; but instrumentalism for what? To take the next steps is important, but where are they going, in what direction? Yet that question raises a ghost which will not be laid except by making explicit and articulate whatever ultimate values may lie behind instrumentalism.

There is a strong possibility that these four basic questions—three of them anyway—are too closely tied to the hysterical demands of the immediate moment. Perhaps it is not fair to Dewey, or to anyone else, to place his social and political philosophy against the crazy background of a fugitive present. But if philosophy is to be of the here and now, no other course can be expected. In fact, it is just because Dewey's thinking is so adjusted to the dimensions of the present and the future that dated questions are at all in order. It would, of course, be too easy to say that the distorted picture society presents to us is a result of the failure to accept experimentalism. It would be more hopeful to suggest that when men are finally ready to apply the recognized techniques of inquiry to the solution of social riddles, the thought of John Dewey will be there, waiting to give them inspiration and guidance.

GEORGE RAYMOND GEIGER

DEPARTMENT OF PHILOSOPHY
ANTIOCH COLLEGE

12

Stephen C. Pepper

SOME QUESTIONS ON DEWEY'S ESTHETICS

SOME QUESTIONS ON DEWEY'S ESTHETICS

A PERSONAL item may more quickly reveal the grounds of certain issues I sense in Dewey's esthetic writings than anything else I could offer to the same end, and will also perhaps furnish him with a more direct focus for reply than the customary impersonal and more distant modes of statement. About 1932 I came to the point in a manuscript, which I was preparing on types of esthetic theory, where I wished to give an exposition of the pragmatic esthetics. I was not aware of any well considered work on the subject, and accordingly dug the matter out for myself, taking most of the details from scattered remarks on art and esthetic experience to be found in Dewey's writings up to that time, and for the rest following what I believed to be the implications of the general pragmatic attitude in the face of relevant facts. The section I tentatively prepared, therefore, amounted to a prediction of what I thought a pragmatist of importance would write if he undertook to make a carefully considered and extended statement. Accordingly, when Dewey's *Art as Experience* came out in 1934, I turned to it with avidity to see how nearly correct my predictions had been.

I was excited to discover that all of the features I had thought important were emphasized by Dewey, together with others along the same line revealing further insights that I had not previously noticed. But I was also amazed to find Dewey saying many things which I had deliberately excluded from my tentative pragmatic account, believing them to be contrary to the spirit of pragmatism—things which an organic idealist would have said, and which I should have thought Dewey would rather have bitten his tongue than to have said, implying as they did a view he has often vigorously repudiated. In fact,

Dewey said so much about the organic character of art that, when I had finished reading his book, this side of his work stood out for me more than the pragmatic. Was Dewey reverting to Hegelianism in his later years? Or had I so widely missed the character of pragmatism that I had seen only half of it, and that perhaps the lesser half?

The more I thought about the issue, the more convinced I became that I had been right in my predictions of the nature of pragmatic esthetics and that it was Dewey who had here gone astray. Accordingly, I set about myself to write what I thought a pragmatic esthetics should be. My *Aesthetic Quality*, of course, amply verifies my own predictions. But there is very little stated in *Aesthetic Quality* that is not also better stated in *Art as Experience*. The point is merely that many things are *not* stated in *Aesthetic Quality* which are said in *Art as Experience*, and which I believe should not be said by a pragmatist.

The criticisms to follow are now obvious. I shall try to show, first, that an organistic esthetics cannot be harmonized with a pragmatic esthetics. If one of these theories is unequivocally accepted, the other must be rejected. For even though the insights of the one can often be adjusted to the framework of the other, this can only be accomplished with considerable alterations or with loss of prestige to the insights in question.

I shall next try to show the presence of an almost fully developed organistic esthetics in *Art as Experience*. The presence of the pragmatic view I shall take for granted, assuming that it will be obvious enough to any reader.

I shall then point out certain unfortunate results that seem to me to arise from the mixture of the two views. Since my own solution of such a difficulty is to present the views separately (to use an old phrase, clearly and distinctly), I am virtually asking Dewey what objections he has to this solution, or why he prefers the mixture. This is a question of method which I believe reaches down into questions of fact, truth, and probability.

Finally, I shall hint that much of Dewey's polemic against Platonic and materialistic theories loses its force, unless he comes to terms with the criticisms that have preceded.

The characteristics of an organistic esthetics have, to my

mind, been ably and summarily presented by Bosanquet in his *Three Lectures on Aesthetics*. The basic traits seem to be the following: First, the general organistic principle that experience is intrinsically coherent or internally related, from which it follows, that the process of elucidating or of comprehending or of adequately seeing into experience consists in making explicit out of the fragments of experience as we originally find them the implicit coherence that lies there.

Second, the value of any sort of finite or relatively fragmentary experience is proportional to the degree of coherence that has been achieved in it.

Third, the differences among values are based solely on the materials organized. So truth is an organization of judgments in experience, ethical goodness an organization of acts in experience, beauty an organization of feelings in experience. It follows that the differences among values become less and less apparent the more organized the experience. Clear-cut classifications are accordingly signs of inadequate organization, comprehension, evaluation. All of our human experience, however, is, we note empirically, fragmentary in various degrees and incomplete. No *man* is the absolute, though men in different degrees according to their achievements approach the absolute or the real structure and coherence of the world. And relatively few men achieve coherent organizations of considerable stability.

Fourth, applying these principles to the field of art and esthetic appreciation, we find that this field is defined by the feelings (primitively mere pleasures) in materials which have trends, *nisuses*, demands for other feelings to enlarge and complete them. The man of taste or the artist of genuine creative capacity follows these trends, and in so doing constructs organizations of feelings having cumulative satisfaction. The process of constructing such esthetic organization has, after Coleridge, come to be called creative imagination. The greatness of a work of art is judged by the degree of imaginative construction it contains. A good appreciative critic is accordingly of the same nature as a good artist. The only difference between the two is that the latter actually draws the materials together out of experience and exhibits their coherence, whereas the former follows the coherence achieved by the latter. Both activities are active, and in a sense creative, because the organization achieved even by the appreciative critic is not precisely that achieved by the artist since every man or center of experience is different from every other and in the intimate organization of *his* feelings the appreciator draws upon *his* experience which is not precisely that of the artist. However, the firmer the organization, the greater the degree of communion or esthetic communication between artist and appreciator, since the two have come nearer to certain intrinsic structures of the world.

Fifth, just as differences among values in general are determined by differences of experience in general, so the specific practical criteria of esthetic judgments are determined by the materials of the arts. Every art in its selection of certain materials to work with determines its own detailed critical criteria. These criteria are intrinsic to the art, namely the potentialities and directions of coherent esthetic construction in those materials. The critical criteria are themselves discovered in the process of the development of the art. Hence painting cannot be judged by the criteria of literature, nor the painting of the impressionists by the criteria of the painting of the post-impressionists, though it may be fitting to say that the esthetic materials of the impressionists have less constructive potentiality than those of the post-impressionists.

The traits of an organistic esthetics, then, are: (1) coherence, (2) value as degrees of coherence, (3) differences of value as differences of cohering materials, the esthetic field being that of feelings rendered coherent, (4) creative imagination or the process of rendering feelings coherent, (5) potentialities for coherence in specific esthetic materials as the intimate criteria of value in the arts.

Now, turn to the traits of a pragmatic esthetics: First, experience is an enduring historical process with a past sloughing off, a central present, and a future coming in. For any man, his experience is embedded in an environment, which enters into his experience, and with which he is constantly interacting.

Second, there is a relational phase of experience with a web or texture-like nature, so that whatever experience one has is felt as interconnected with other experiences. The threads of these webs can be followed and their terminations to considerable degree predicted, or by means of instruments attained. But there are also frustrations, blockings, and downright novelties intrinsic to experience.

Third, there is a qualitative phase of experience, which may often be regarded as a 'fusing' or a 'funding' of certain of its relational phases resulting in an immediacy of perception of various degrees of vividness. The 'having' of a very vivid quality may be called a 'seizure.' In a broad sense (and perhaps in a final sense) the esthetic field can be identified with that of the qualitative phase of experience.

Fourth, it follows that the criteria of esthetic value are the extensity, depth, and degree of vividness of quality in experience.

Fifth, as secondary esthetic criteria, may be added those factors instrumental to the production of extensity, depth, and vividness of quality. Roughly speaking, organization is the chief instrument for increasing the extent and depth of an esthetic experience, and conflict the chief instrument for increasing vividness.

Sixth, a *physical* work of art is a continuant in the environment constructed so as to control esthetic values by acting as a stimulus to an organism whence an *esthetic* work of art is generated. This last is a qualitative experience partly contributed out of the organism and partly out of the environmental physical work of art (cf. 108-9).[1] It follows that the esthetic work of art is discontinuous, and that its quality will vary with the organism, with the amount of 'funded' experience available, and consequently with the culture or epoch. One cannot, therefore, legitimately speak of *the* value of a work of art in pragmatism as one can in organicism. A physical work of art has no absolute potentiality but only a potentiality relative to an epoch, for no man can develop beyond the limitations of his epoch. The esthetic value of a work of art, accordingly, changes with its epoch, and incidentally every epoch demands an art and a criticism of its own. The judgment of the value of a work of art

[1] All references are to *Art as Experience.*

should, accordingly, be distinguished from that of the esthetic value of an experience had. The latter is the genuine esthetic judgment; the former is an estimate of the potentiality of a certain continuant or set of continuants to produce the genuine esthetic judgment.

The traits of a pragmatic esthetic then are: (1) experience as historical duration, (2) relational texture of experience, (3) quality as the esthetic differentia of experience often unifying a texture of relations through 'fusing' and 'funding,' (4) extensity, depth, and vividness of quality as the basic criteria of esthetic judgment, (5) organization and conflict as secondary criteria, and (6) the work of art as an instrument for the control of esthetic values with its own (though related) criteria of evaluation.

That there are incompatibilities between these two theories must be evident from these summaries. For the moment, the question is not which is the more adequate theory (to me personally, they appear about equally adequate), but whether they are not definitely incompatible.

There is first a fundamental difference of emphasis on the defining feature of the esthetic field. For organicism the coherence of feelings is central, while for pragmatism it is secondary and instrumental. And for pragmatism quality is central, while for organicism, though quality is not actually neglected, it is only a sort of corollary, being the very concreteness of experience which is automatically attained with greater organization. But by this very fact, the quality envisaged by the organicist is not the same as that of the pragmatist, for the organicist disparages fusion as a limitation of finiteness and a species of confusion. The organicist recognizes 'funding' as part of the synthetic process of coherence, but in so far as 'funding' exhibits itself as a fused unity of quality it is incomplete and lacking in value. In other words, fusion, and therefore quality as the fused sense of the character of an experience, is appearance and not reality. Pragmatic quality is noticed by the organicist in finite experience and is preferable to singular and more abstract stages of experience; it is not, however, valuable in itself, but on the contrary a sign of disvalue. And for an organicist 'seizure' is little better than emotionalism. The organicist conceives *the* work of art as a complete clear whole in which every part or aspect implies every other and is implicit in it without blur or compromise or focus or fringe. That completely integrated whole is the individual thing, the character. Finite perceptions approximate it in various degrees, but in reality there is no fused quality of it. For the pragmatist, however, such a fused quality is as ultimate a reality as there is. The basis for this difference, of course, is that the organicist embeds his work of art in the absolute structure of the world, whereas the pragmatist finds the esthetic experience in historical processes as they come, and considers nothing more real or ultimate than an actually had experience.

A second major incompatibility is closely allied to the first. For the organicist there is really only one work of art, that integrated whole of feelings which has been achieved. Various finite centers enter into the work of art to the best of their abilities. If the work of art is really highly coherent, the variations of perceptions among the different perceivers only indicate men's own various limitations and failures to achieve the organization that is really there to be found. The value of the work is objectively there, the variations and incapacities to appreciate merely indicate a "weakness of the spectator" and his own lack of integration and reality.

For the pragmatist, there is no ground for belief in such a single real integrated whole, for he rejects the hypothesis of an absolute coherent structure of nature. He must therefore distinguish between immediate experiences had (the esthetic work of art), and the environmental instrument for the control of these experiences (the physical work of art). The pragmatist cannot adequately account for the facts of art without dividing the common sense 'work of art' into at least two factors. The result is a relativity of judgment about the value of a work of art. This relativity does not dissolve all objectivity of judgment, but it justifies differences of judgment in terms of inadequacy of experience and epochal changes in whole environments. For a pragmatist there is no absolute judgment of the value of a work of art, though the judgments about some works of art have a high degree of stability.

Thirdly, the organicist sees nothing in conflicts and frustra-

tions but appearance and illusion and disvalue. For a pragmatist
there is nothing more real or ultimate than a conflict had, and
under certain conditions a conflict is valuable in its own right.
The pragmatist notes that conflicts are actually sought after and
valued in games, in comedy, in tragedy, and, if he looks carefully, even throughout all art subtly in the minutest details.
He does not explain these away by suggesting that they are
transcended and thereby converted into harmonious integra-
tions in the organic wholes in which they appear. He stresses
and savors them and suggests that the organization sought in
works of art is mainly an organization of conflicts. For he finds
conflict a principal source of the vividness of quality, and thereby esthetically valuable in its own right, and to be sought after
up to that point where it cannot be endured and debouches into
practical action.

These three incompatibilities are sufficient, I think, to demonstrate that one cannot consistently have organicism and pragmatism present at once in the same theory. If coherence is
fundamental, then fused, had quality is not, and *vice versa*. If a
work of art is a single absolute entity, then it is not a multiple
relative entity, and *vice versa*. If conflict is always disvalue,
then it is not sometimes a positive value, and *vice versa*. I have
personally obtained esthetic insights from both of these theories,
and believe for the present we ought to keep them both separately and consistently in mind; but I think a mixture of the
two only blurs and damages both and adds nothing to general
esthetic understanding. My criticism of Dewey's *Art as Experience* is that it contains a mixture of these two theories, and
ccnsequently results not only in many implicit contradictions
and vacillations but also in mutual inhibitions such that some of
the important insights of both theories are concealed.

I wish now to show by some references that a fairly complete
organistic esthetics is present in *Art as Experience*. As for the
pragmatic esthetics, that, as I said, can be assumed to be there,
and is obvious in any ten pages of the book. The disturbing thing
is that the organistic theory is equally obvious to one who is
aware of what is going on, and that in large degree and at critical
points, notably in Chapter XIII, the chapter specially devoted

to esthetic criticism, it submerges the pragmatic view. Let us now consider Dewey's exposition of an organistic esthetics.

Let us follow *seriatim* the evidences for the five traits previously mentioned of an organistic esthetics.

(1) *Coherence.* That there is great emphasis on this principle will appear in the evidences for the other traits. It would be too much to expect of a deeply imbued pragmatist that he would ever slip into identifying reality with coherence. Had Dewey been aware that the evidences for the other traits went far towards committing him to this fundamental organistic principle, he would, I suspect, have drawn back and cleared his book of these implications.

(2) *Value as degrees of coherence.* This also is a general organistic principle which will exhibit itself so far as esthetics is concerned in the three remaining traits.

(3) *The esthetic field is that of the coherent organization of feelings.* Let us compare this with Dewey's definition of esthetic beauty.

In case the term [beauty] is used in theory to designate the total esthetic quality of an experience, it is surely better to deal with the experience itself and show whence and how the quality proceeds. In that case, beauty is the response to that which to reflection is the consummated movement of matter integrated through its inner relations into a single qualitative whole. (130)

Now, if Dewey had written, "Beauty is the consummated movement of feelings and their qualities integrated through their inner relations into a single individual whole," he would have given an orthodox organistic definition. What he did write is obviously far from a pragmatic definition as outlined recently. The emphasis is on integration, singleness, and wholeness, and quality comes out as the differentiating guide of the integrative process. There may be other kinds of integration, but the sort of integration that is esthetic is the sort that integrates quality. The question is how far Dewey conceived this quality in the organistic rather than the pragmatic sense. The two senses easily slip into one another but at extremes, as I have shown, they are very different. The quality of organicism (the individual, or the characteristic) is the coherent whole developed from the internal relations of the affective materials. The 'had' quality of pragmatism is the awareness of experience itself, and is not necessarily coherent, may even be indefeasibly incoherent. In Dewey's definition of beauty, which seems to me from its context to have been rather carefully considered, the meaning of 'quality' appears ambiguous. I am suggesting that it was so felt by Dewey—not, of course, with any intention to confuse, but possibly with an underlying (though I believe mistaken) intention to enrich. This same ambiguity runs through most of the book. I would even go so far as to say that the weight of significance for this and many other passages is predominantly organistic.

The definition quoted comes near the end of a chapter on "Substance and Form." Near the beginning of the chapter Dewey writes,

The *material* out of which a work of art is composed belongs to the common world rather than to the self, and yet there is self-expression in art because the self assimilates that material in a distinctive way to reissue it into the public world in a form that builds a new object. This new object may have as its consequence similar reconstructions, recreations, of old and common material on the part of those who perceive it, and thus in time come to be established as part of the acknowledged world—as "universal." The material expressed cannot be private; that is the state of the mad-house. But the *manner* of saying it is individual, and, if the product is to be a work of art, induplicable. Identity of mode of production defines the work of a machine, the esthetic counterpart of which is the academic. The quality of a work of *art* is *sui generis* because the manner in which general material is rendered transforms it into a substance that is fresh and vital. (107-8)

And immediately thereafter comes an approving reference to A. C. Bradley, the most consistent and illuminating organistic critic since Coleridge. The foregoing passage might very well have been written by A. C. Bradley, or F. H. Bradley, or B. Bosanquet, or any other imbued organicist. Coherence is the evaluating principle which assimilates, objectifies, universalizes material. Incoherence and privacy are "the state of the mad-house." The result of coherence embodying material is a concrete universal, to use the technical term, to be strictly contrasted with the repetitive abstract universal which develops academism, and is but another mode of incoherence. "The quality [value?] of a work of *art* is *sui generis*," a concrete universal, which is individual and common to every aspect, since every aspect is internally related with every other though a unique center in its own right.

Hence A. C. Bradley can be aptly quoted as saying: "Poetry being poems, we are to think of a poem as it actually exists; and an actual poem is a succession of experiences—sounds, images, thought—through which we pass when we read a poem. . . . A poem exists in unnumerable degrees." (108) That is, different finite individuals approximate the potential integration of the poem according to their capacities of integration in reference to the material at hand. It is true that immediately after this passage is another into which Dewey slips by imperceptible transitions and which stresses the absoluteness of pragmatic relativity as emphatically as anywhere in the whole book. But that, of course, is just my point. A passage like the preceding can grow only out of organistic modes of thought leading to the conception of *the* work of art as a 'public' object of the 'common world,' as 'universal,' 'individual' and 'induplicable' because it exhibits the necessary logic of the affective materials out of which it is made. And there is no justification in such a passage for an inalienable diversity of interpretations or for the idea that "it is absurd to ask what an artist 'really' meant by his product" (108), and that "if he could be articulate, he would say 'I meant just *that* and *that* means whatever you or any one can honestly, that is in virtue of your own vital experience, get out of it' " (109)—unless by "honestly, that is in virtue of your own vital experience" is meant precisely the inevitable logic of the affective materials themselves, "the inevitable self-movement of a poem" (70) which eventuates in "material completely and coherently formed" (116), *the* work of art "*sui generis.*" Just what weight and direction is given to "honestly" here? Is it the pragmatic relativistic honesty of "whatever anyone can get out of it?" Or is it the absolutistic organistic honesty of "vital experience" following "the inevitable self-movement of a poem?" Throughout *Art as Experience,* phrases are indecisive on this matter, as here in the midst of a typically pragmatic statement. But evidences for the interpretation of "honestly" in the organistic terms of "the inevitable self-movement of a poem" multiply in the passages dealing with the creative imagination.

(4) *Creative imagination.* This term owes its currency to Coleridge, who got the idea it contains from the purest early organistic sources and projected it into the literary world where, though generally half understood, it has still proved very effective. As Dewey says, "it is a *way* of seeing and feeling things as they compose an integral whole." (267) In the next paragraph,

Coleridge used the term 'esemplastic' to characterize the work of imagination in art. . . . But one may pass over his verbal mode, and find in what he says an intimation not that imagination is the power that does certain things, but that an imaginative experience is what happens when varied materials of sense quality, emotion, and meaning come together in a union that marks a new birth in the world. . . . Possibilities are embodied in works of art that are not elsewhere actualized; this *embodiment* is the best evidence that can be found of the true nature of imagination. (267-8)

The next paragraph is a quite orthodox organistic description of the processes of the creative artist:

There is a conflict artists themselves undergo that is instructive as to the nature of imaginative experience. . . . It concerns the opposition between inner and outer vision. There is a stage in which the inner vision seems much richer and finer than any outer manifestation. It has a vast, an enticing aura of implications that are lacking in the object of external vision. It seems to grasp much more than the latter conveys. Then there comes a reaction; the matter of the inner vision seems wraith-like compared with the solidity and energy of the presented scene. The object is felt to say something succinctly and forcibly that the inner vision reports vaguely, in diffuse feeling rather than organically. The artist is driven to submit himself in humility to the discipline of the objective vision. But the inner vision is not cast out. It remains as the organ by which outer vision is controlled, and it takes on structure as the latter is absorbed within it. The interaction of the two modes of vision is imagination; as imagination takes form the work of art is born. (268)

From the vague appearance to the clear reality; from the abstract and conflicting to the concrete and coherent; thesis, antithesis, synthesis; "enticing implications" becoming explicit in organic form and full "embodiment;" the internally constructive logic of the relations through which "the artist is given to submit himself in humility to the discipline of the objective vision." Is not this the very chorus voiced by Schelling, Hegel, Bradley, and Bosanquet? An "instructive" chorus, indeed, and to be well heeded, but where does it fit in or harmonize with the pragmatism of *Experience and Nature,* of *The Quest for Certainty,* and of the dominant message of Dewey?

Passages of this sort are not sporadic and unrepresentative. They constitute a theme that recurs with and without variations, and that is possibly (as I have suggested) the main theme of the book. It comes out most clearly and frequently in the form of the typical organistic principle that a work of art is the coherent embodiment of the esthetic implications of its materials.

(5) *Coherence of a work of art as the implications of its media.* This theme is the basis of Dewey's exposition of form, of the differences (or classification) of the arts, and of the critical esthetic judgment itself.

"*Form,*" he says, "*may be defined as the operation of forces that carry the experience of an event, object, scene, and situation to its own integral fulfillment.* The connection of form with substance is thus inherent, not imposed from without. It marks the matter of an experience that is carried to consummation." (137) It follows that "each medium has its own efficacy and value" (227), and that "we may safely start any discussion of the varied matter of the arts with this fact of the decisive importance of the medium: with the fact that different media have different potencies and are adapted to different ends." (226) The examination of the different arts (229-244) is carried through on this principle and he concludes,

I have been concerned with the various arts in but one respect. I have wished to indicate that, as we build bridges of stone, steel, or cement, so every medium has its own power, active and passive, outgoing and receptive, and that the basis for distinguishing the different traits of the arts is their exploitation of the energy that is characteristic of the material used as a medium. (243-4)

Moreover, "when the effect appropriate to one medium becomes too marked in the use of another medium, there is esthetic defect." (229)

The transition from this insight to the typical organistic theory of criticism is natural. Practically the whole of Chapter XIII on "Criticism and Perception" is occupied with this theory either in positive exposition or in polemic against rival theories. And this chapter as next to the last in the book comes to the reader as a sort of summary of the esthetic doctrine of the book, the last chapter being reserved for reaffirmation of the social implications. It is largely because of the location of this chapter and its strongly organistic trend, that one comes out of reading *Art as Experience* wondering if Dewey has not turned Hegelian.

After some pages of probing into the superficialities of what he calls "judicial criticism," what the orthodox organicist calls "abstract" criticism, in which "criticism is thought of as if its business were not explication of the content of an object as to substance and form, but a process of acquittal or condemnation on the basis of merits and demerits" (299), Dewey presents his constructive view of the critical judgment.

If there are no standards for works of art and hence none for criticism (in the sense in which there are standards of measurement), there are nevertheless criteria in judgment, so that criticism does not fall in the field of mere impressionism. The discussion of form in relation to matter, of the meaning of medium in art, of the nature of the expressive object, has been an attempt on the part of the writer to discover some of these criteria. But such criteria are not rules or prescriptions. They are the result of an endeavor to find out what a work of art is as an experience. . . . Criticism is judgment. The material out of which judgment grows is the work, the object, but it is this object as it enters into the experience of the critic by interaction with his own sensitivity and his knowledge and funded store from past experiences. As to their content, therefore, judgments will vary with the concrete material that evokes them and that must sustain them if criticism is pertinent and valid. Nevertheless, judgments have a common form because they all have certain functions to perform. These functions are discrimination and unification. Judgment has to evoke a clearer consciousness of constituent parts and to discover how consistently these parts are related to form a whole. (309-10)

The last sentences of the chapter are,

We lay hold of the full import of a work of art only as we go through in our own vital processes the processes the artist went through in producing the work. It is the critic's privilege to share in the promotion of this active process. His condemnation is that he so often arrests it. (325)

All of this with certain alterations of style might have been written by Bosanquet.

Well, what of it? If it is good doctrine, why shouldn't a pragmatist write it? What's in a label? A good deal, I think, if it is a significant label. 'Pragmatism' and 'organicism' I think are significant labels. Dewey's eclecticism in *Art as Experience* has damaged his pragmatism without adding anything we could not gather elsewhere concerning organicism. This damage is of two sorts: the pressure of organicism inhibited the full growth of a pragmatic esthetics in Dewey's hands, and the simultaneous presence of both theories produced a confused book. I will say nothing about the confusions, but let me show some of the effects of the inhibitions.

First, we have been deprived of a pragmatic theory of criticism. The germs of it are repeatedly stated—quality, fusion, seizure, realization, vivid perception, novelty, uniqueness, conflict—but they are toned down or suppressed to make way for the organistic theory. We get occasionally a few sentences that summarize the view:

I have had occasion to speak more than once of a quality of an intense esthetic experience that is so immediate as to be ineffable and mystical. . . . All direct experience is qualitative, and qualities are what make life-experience itself directly precious. . . . A work of art may certainly convey the essence of a multitude of experiences, and sometimes in a remarkably condensed and striking way. (293)

But such "directly precious" realization or "seizure" is elsewhere derogated to the vague confusion that precedes organistic integration: "Artist and perceiver alike begin with what may be called a total seizure, an inclusive qualitative whole not yet articulated, not distinguished into members." (191) This precious vital kernel of a new esthetic and a new criticism struggles to grow in three eloquent pages (192-4), but is finally mulched under a rich layer of organicism:

The undefined pervasive quality of an experience is that which binds together all the defined elements, the objects of which we are focally aware, making them a whole. The best evidence that such is the case is our constant sense of things as belonging or not belonging, of relevancy, a sense which is immediate. (194)

Second, we are deprived of a theory, or let us say a solution, of tragedy in art. Organicism is a theory of harmony culminating in the great cosmic harmony of the absolute. Pragmatism is a theory of conflict, celebrating struggle and vigorous life in which every solution is the beginning of a new problem, in which every social ideal is an hypothesis of action, in which values thrive on conflicts. The inference almost comes of itself that vital quality will thrive on tragedy, so that artists will seek out great conflicts for the esthetic values that directly sprout from them. Conflict is not something to be overbalanced or transcended in art, but something to be brought prominently forward and emphasized. What organization is required in art (and much is, of course, required) is instrumental to realization of the very quality of experience, of its conflicts. Yet Dewey gives us the conciliatory organistic theory of tragedy: "This sense of the including whole implicit in ordinary experiences is rendered intense within the frame of a painting or poem. It, rather than any special purgation, is that which reconciles us to the events of tragedy." (194) And again,

The peculiar power of tragedy to leave us at the end with a sense of reconciliation rather than with one of horror forms the theme of one of the oldest discussions of literary art. . . . The positive fact is that a particular subject matter in being removed from its practical context has entered into a new whole as an integral part of it. In its new relationships, it acquires a new expression. (96)

There is just a hint now and then of the pragmatic view, as in the reference to

Shakespeare's employing the comic in the midst of tragedy. . . . It does more than relieve strain on the part of the spectator. It has a more intrinsic office in that it punctuates tragic quality. Any product whose quality is not of the very 'easy' sort exhibits dislocations and dissociations of what is usually connected. The distortion found in paintings serves the need of some particular rhythm. But it does more. It brings to definite perception values that are concealed in ordinary experience because of habituation. Ordinary prepossession must be broken through if the degree of energy required for an esthetic experience is to be evoked. (173)

But this point of view is never developed further.

Third, we are deprived of a pragmatic theory of ugliness (or rather of its absence) and meet instead with statements that might have come out of Schasler, Hartmann, or Rosencrantz— for instance: "The explanation of the fact that things ugly in themselves may contribute to the esthetic effect of a whole is doubtless often due to the fact that they are so used as to contribute to individualization of parts within a whole." (204) The context indicates that Dewey is identifying dullness and conflict with ugliness. Why the problem obsesses orthodox organicists is easily understood. But though Dewey avoids the obsession, he does not escape the inhibition to look into the status of the concept in pragmatic terms. Unless I am mistaken, ugliness is a pseudo-concept in pragmatic terms, and some interesting consequences follow from this discovery.

Lastly, we are deprived of an intensive investigation into the nature of quality. Here is for pragmatists a fact correlative in importance with the fact of relations. The mutuality of the two was ably exhibited in *Experience and Nature*. In the *Quest for Certainty* the nature of relations in scientific procedures was intensively studied. In *Art as Experience*, we might have expected the corresponding intensive investigation into the nature of quality. We are not, to be sure, altogether disappointed. But there is so much to be said on this topic, and so much to be found out, that the spaces given up to the processes of integration in the book are a frustration to our hopes. Who more competent to tell us about the shades and discriminations and the scope and depth of quality, its fusions and its fundings, than Dewey? We are on the point of learning some new detail, our ears are pricked up, our heads turned to attend, and instead we are given another fragment of Hegelianism.

It is not that we should regret anything that Dewey writes, for his writing always has the glow of truth in it. These Hegelian insights are as valid, I think, as any. And Dewey presents them with his own personal flavor. But these insights are not new, and Dewey has insights that are. And those of us who feel what he might have given us, if he had not been drawn aside by the fascinations of the integrated whole, wish a little that he had not noticed these fascinations. Would he perhaps yet turn his eyes aside for a while, and give us what we are waiting for? There is no one else who can do it with his authority.

The comments I have made here on Dewey's esthetics come, it is clear, under two heads: comments on what I suggest to be shortcomings in the material and comments on shortcomings in the method. I believe the shortcomings in the material arise out of those in the method. Let me therefore summarize the preceding paragraphs in the following questions:

1. Is it not true that the method is eclectic—*i.e.*, employs two incompatible theories in the presentation of the relevant facts?

2. If so, would it not have been better to have given separate expositions of the two theories?

3. And if so, does not much of the polemic against certain other theories in terms of the pragmatic and organistic theories lose its force? By what criteria does Dewey justifiably distinguish between acceptable and unacceptable theories? Why, for instance, is a coherent whole to be accepted but a recurrent form of the Platonic type to be rejected?

4. But if not so, and if it is held that esthetic facts are obvious, indubitable, certified as such, and need no theories to assist their discrimination, how account for the inconsistencies suggested?

Of the social message in *Art as Experience*, its plea to break down the separation between art and life, to realize that there is beauty in the commonest and meanest things, and on Tuesdays and Wednesdays as well as on Sundays, I have said nothing. Possibly this message is the chief intention of the book. Dewey is ever a reformer. And here as elsewhere he has shown the contemporary evil and the direction to take for eliminating it. I have commented on the book only as on something that intends to be sound and true, and have only asked how far that intention has been realized.

Nor have I tried to bring out the reasons for the greatness of the book. I am personally convinced that *Art as Experience* is one of the four or five great books on esthetics, and is a classic though but five years old. I am assuming that any one who reads the book with understanding will see that. But even the greatest books are not flawless. The most elementary student in philosophy now sees the inconsistencies of Spinoza, and, if a reply could be expected, would like to write him about them. This is such a letter to Dewey.

STEPHEN C. PEPPER

DEPARTMENT OF PHILOSOPHY
UNIVERSITY OF CALIFORNIA

13

Edward L. Schaub

DEWEY'S INTERPRETATION OF RELIGION

DEWEY'S INTERPRETATION OF RELIGION

I

UNCERTAINTY, confusion and tension prevail in the religious life as well as in the religious and theological
thought of today, and they no less conspicuously characterize
the estimates currently passed on religion. On the one hand,
religion has quite generally lost its significance as the all-encom-
passing value or as that which when possessed makes negligible,
or at least tolerable, the deprivation of all else. During modern
times ever greater autonomy has been won by the theoretic,
political, economic, aesthetic and other interests, and thus by the
institutions in which these interests achieve organization and expression. This change has generated reflection on the specific
functions and values of the several institutions; and such reflection has in turn issued in modifications and enrichments of their
procedure, accompanied by an enhanced sense of the independence and recognition which should be accorded to them. In consequence religion has increasingly tended to be, and to be considered as, but one among numerous relatively distinct values.
The contention that it deserves rulership over the various interests distinguished as secular and temporal has encountered
an increasing scepticism. Rather has it come to be taken as but
one of several rival claimants for the attention and the allegiance
of men.[1] Indeed, even this status is not uncommonly denied to it.

[1] "When we take note of religion's attempts to stake out her claims in the realm
of human interests and values, the past centuries present a record of claims and
counterclaims. Conflicts in views and theory have been unintermittent." (Schaub,
Edward L., "Neo-Ptolemaism in Religion," *The Monist*, XL, No. 2, 288.) The
essay from which this quotation is taken includes a discussion of this issue more
specifically as concerns the relation of religion to the cognitive, the aesthetic and
the moral aspects of life. The conclusions reached will suggest the point of view
taken in the present paper and we will therefore indicate them by a citation of

In certain quarters doubts are entertained as to whether it is anything more than a survival of an antiquated culture, and thus it frequently suffers the ignominy of neglect. Numerous intellectually and morally earnest individuals and groups go so far as to attack it as an enemy of the good life. On the other hand, there are powerful currents and social forces of an opposite sort. Bitter disappointments experienced in connection with the pursuits of wealth, prestige, and power, have led to a Spinozistic realization that such goods cannot genuinely satisfy the spirit of man; that they are as elusive as illusory, and that even when clutched they rapidly turn to dust and ashes. Poignant dissatisfactions have reawakened yearnings that have given a powerful impetus to a fresh consideration of the possibilities of religion. Indeed, in extreme cases, they have issued, within theology, in the renaissance of radically supernaturalistic doc-

---

the following passages: "That one is living in such a wider world, *within* which fall such successes as human wit may achieve, inasmuch as *of* it the human individual is but a constituent, is an inevitable experience at the level of self-conscious reflection. With this experience comes a realization that in the interest of his own integrity, the individual must win an adjustment of his total self to this world, along with an increasing knowledge of its nature, appreciation of its beauty, and aspiration to express and enhance its life." (p. 306) "The concrete character of the reality which is the religious object depends in every given case upon the development of reflective knowledge. The relative strength of self-assurance may vary, as may that of other-reliance; such assurance and reliance, however, always dwell together. The call to moral effort and humanitarian devotion may be insistent and inescapable, but with it comes a realization that final issues are outside the reach of prediction and human determination, and comes also a confidence that these issues may be acquiesced in when judged, not by present hopes and values, but by the self which, through a rationally humble attitude towards reality and the religious object, through repentant realization of his own nature, and through spiritual effort, perpetually undergoes profound reconstruction." (pp. 307f.) "That feeling of oneness with the universe, reinforced by advancing science, experienced in the presence of beauty, and culminating the morally earnest life when this is serious and comprehensive, reconstructive of its values, and conscious of its matrix, is in one of its expressions religion itself. Religion has a cosmic reference. It reaches out beyond the world of realized knowledge and values to an encompassing whole. Science affords a large part of its creed and theology, though for religion, as for philosophy, this creed and theology are symbols and myths. Our purposes to reform our attitudes and practices, and to dedicate our powers to the specific requirements of that world which is expressed by and in ourselves, is the religious sacrifice. Our reverent wonder, our faith, and our unhesitating and unflinching submission are our worship." (309f.)

trines, and within life, in preoccupations with mysticism and even with the occult.

Then, also, religion has, on the one hand, been exposed to withering blasts from the side of the natural and historical sciences. These have been effective not simply in diverting attention to the world experienced by sense but, more than this, in casting grave doubts on the reality of any realm transcending it. They have seemed to leave to man but the status of a constituent or member of the order of nature, of a being who strives to maintain and magnify his life in an environment at least partially alien and not a little hostile to him; they have thrown into utter oblivion or at least into the dark shadows that which is superhistorical, absolute, or certain; they have made primal in efficacy and time, and frequently in significance whether as to truth or as to morals, the instinctive or sense perceptual as distinct from the value-seeking or rational aspects of human nature. On the other hand, man ever-recurringly manifests antipathy to such outlooks; deep within himself and his experience he finds incentives to take himself as more than an object among other objects, more than a being simply finite. He longs and feels himself to have the status of a mind seeking fulfillments universal in their significance, absolute in their value, and metaphysical in their import. Thus he is not without a certain sympathetic responsiveness to such assertions as those of Fichte when, in referring to doctrines unmindful of this character of egohood, he declared:

Empty, disagreeable and irresponsible babble has had ample time for utterance in all manner. It has expressed itself, we have heard it, and from this side nothing *new* will be said and nothing will be said *better* than it has been. We have had enough thereof; we feel its emptiness and the complete nullity which according to it characterizes us in reference to that sense for the eternal which after all may not be completely eradicated. This sense remains, and it urgently demands a business of its own.[2]

A bare glimpse at the historical backgrounds of contemporary life thus discloses vacillation and contradictory views and outlooks as respects both religion and religious philosophy. This

---

[2] *Johann Gottlieb Fichte's Sämmtliche Werke*, ed. by I. H. Fichte, VII, 230.

condition has continued unrelieved down to the present; indeed, it would even seem that it more than ever clouds the experience, impairs the life, and disturbs the thought of such individuals as are seriously in quest of the best that is attainable to them. Light and leading are here obviously as imperative as they are desiderated.

II

Dewey's devotion to the clarification and redirection of vital human concerns has been so outstanding throughout all the years covered by the memories of most living thinkers that his name at once comes to mind whenever one approaches a consideration of what has transpired during that period in any field of social activity or study. It is therefore not without a certain surprise, initial at any rate, to find no mention of him in any of the eleven essays included in the coöperative volume edited by Gerald Birney Smith and published in 1927 under the title *Religious Thought in the Last Quarter-Century*. A reference, however, to Dewey's writings up to that time would reveal that his central topics, wide as had been their range, had failed to include the problems of religion, and that his expressions on this subject had been but occasional and in part incidental. Not strange therefore that these statements seem to have attracted no especial attention on the part of religious thinkers.

Nevertheless we may now, in retrospect, discern in early expressions of Dewey much that was prophetic of the doctrines which he has since advanced and expounded in some detail. In one of his earliest statements concerning religion Dewey condemned its current forms as infected with a false and a morally dangerous supernaturalism and as "at war with the habits of mind congruous with democracy and with science."[3] Hence he earnestly cautioned against any action that might prolong the survival of traditional religion. Specifically he inveighed against the inclusion of religion within the curricula or objectives of public educational agencies. Of the latter he in so far demanded a strict *laissez faire* policy, motivated by neither "laziness nor

[3] "Religion and Our Schools," *The Hibbert Journal*, VI (1908), 800; on pages 808 and 809 may be found the other quotations in the above paragraph.

cynicism" but by "honesty, courage, sobriety, and faith." Hopefully he noted "decay of cohesion and influence among the religiously organized bodies of the familiar historic type" and the possibility that "their decadence is the fruit of a broader and more catholic principle of human intercourse and association which is too religious to tolerate . . . pretensions to monopolize truth and to make private possessions of spiritual insight and aspiration." What he believed desirable and what he thought might perhaps already be operative in destroying the roots of the old, is a religious mode of life "which will be the fine flower of the modern spirit's achievement." Now, when one considers Dewey's attitudes and thought as a whole, these ideas impress one as quite anomalous. He in general regards things as centers of possibilities; and even during that early period, when he envisaged the task of intelligence to be primarily, if not exclusively, that of liberating life from specific embarrassments and obstacles which constantly arise to keep it in check, he did not entirely overlook its more positive function of directly ministering to aspiration through the discovery of the possibilities of existing situations and their conversion into larger and more stable satisfactions. But in envisaging things and existences as possibilities, Dewey made an exception—and apparently the only one—in the case of the existing religions. As to them he bade us, in his earliest references to the subject, to eschew reformation and reconstruction, and to acquiesce cheerfully in an expected demise.

Writing of his personal experiences in Columbia University just prior to 1925, Walter Horton says:

. . . it was generally understood that there was but one true philosophy, and Dewey was its prophet. Dewey himself was less orthodox than his followers, and less outspokenly antireligious; but he was at that time still in the most positivistic and naturalistic phase of his thinking. . . . In the discussions among students majoring in philosophy, it was generally taken for granted that religion was no more than an interesting survival of an earlier period in mental evolution, a touching expression of the naïve longings and poetic imagination of primitive man. . . . "Religion used to say," was almost a hackneyed expression among these students.

Some of them grieved at the death of religion, others rejoiced; but all were practically unanimous in admitting the fact of her decease.[4]

That Dewey's own strictures bore on existing religious beliefs, organizations and institutions, however, rather than upon religion itself is a tenable inference from the statements quoted above. Somewhat later, in his *Human Nature and Conduct* (1922), he wrote (236f.):

It is the office of art and religion to evoke such appreciations and intimations; to enhance and steady them till they are wrought into the texture of our lives. . . . The religious experience is a reality in so far as in the midst of effort to foresee and regulate future objects we are sustained and expanded in feebleness and failure by the sense of an enveloping whole. Peace in action not after it is the contribution of the ideal to conduct.

Yet if this conception as to the function of religion and the reality of the religious experience is applied in passing judgment on the traditional religions, is it not unjust to declare that these must be buried and that a new birth must be awaited from the spirit of science and democracy? Again in the same volume (331f.) Dewey asserts:

There is a conceit fostered by perversion of religion which assimilates the universe to our personal desires; but there is also a conceit of carrying the load of the universe from which religion liberates us. Within the flickering inconsequential acts of separate selves dwells a sense of the whole which claims and dignifies them. In its presence we put off mortality and live in the universal.

Excellently said. Yet one cannot but feel astonished over the fact that in his concern for avoidance of both the conceits to which he refers, Dewey did not realize and acknowledge his essential kinship with the spirit of the high religions generally and with the message as well as experience which they have throughout the centuries sought to promulgate: unselfishness, such as has taken the form in extreme but therefore unusual cases of thorough-going selflessness and even of self-crucifixion; other-reliance and deep gratitude, such as have at times but by no means always been exaggerated to the point of a disregard of

[4] "Rough Sketch of A Half Formed Mind," *Contemporary American Theology: Theological Autobiographies*, ed. by Vergilius Ferm, I (1932), 182f.

the responsibilities and the successes devolving upon and claimable by the human individual. Normally that which religions have proclaimed and that to which the developed religious consciousness has testified is man's rôle in the creation of a more spiritual personal and social life and also his dependence upon a reality more ultimate, comprehensive, and worthy than any to which he may lay claim or hope ever to achieve. Hence again it seems strange that Dewey's hope was not in a piecemeal correction and improvement of many of the features characterizing existing religions, but rather in the supersession of the latter by something born from the womb of modernity.

Though, as we have noted, Dewey dealt but slightly with the subject of religion in his earlier writings, and his more or less incidental expressions on this particular topic would seem to have received but little attention, one cannot be less than amazed over the range and depth of the influence which his general logical and philosophical doctrines exerted upon the religious thought and publications of America. Even those thinkers, however, who were deeply indebted to Dewey for their intellectual stimulus and orientation, and who regarded themselves as essentially faithful to his point of view, did not all find it necessary to characterize historical religion as antiquated or as prejudicial to the cultivation of the high values of life. Their investigations, both historical and psychological, led them to conclude that religion exhibits a living nexus with social conditions and needs, and, secondarily, with the realm of ideas and beliefs; that it is definitely modifiable and tends to adapt itself to cultural changes as well as to assimilate new conceptions. Religion, they concluded, is the consciousness of the highest social values; and, as such, it undergoes changes in conformity with those factors of life which determine the values that acquire social preeminence. This makes for a more positive and sympathetic attitude toward existing religion than Dewey himself seems to have had.

Those who developed the implications for religion of Dewey's early philosophical doctrines traced the springs of religion to the disparity between human needs and prevailing circumstances. They described ceremonial as a mode of securing the satisfaction of basic social requirements; generated thereby were the feelings and the institutions distinguishable as religious, as well as the attendant myths, beliefs, and formulated creeds. Thus God was said to be not an object of meditation or of cognition but primarily a power invoked under the stress of necessity. In another reference He is found to be a symbol of that upon which the social group centers its most active interests. Now this general doctrine indeed proved suggestive and helpful, particularly in throwing light on such phenomena as taboo, magic, fetishism, the cruder ceremonial practices and the simpler religions generally. But, to quote from a previous essay by the present writer, this general doctrine

came far from giving adequate recognition to, or just appraisal of, mysticism, adoration, the theoretical, contemplative, and characteristically social (as distinct from the utilitarian) aspects of religion, particularly in its more advanced manifestations. The viewpoint, although allegedly genetic and functional, was not genuinely so. It failed to consider that even though conscious processes may in their beginnings be (largely, we would say) subservient to the demands of life, they in time win their emancipation and become ends in themselves, masters no less truly than servants. They develop along autonomous lines, under the guidance of self-critical reason and consciously evaluated norms. They initiate novel insights and values, besides conserving those attested in the past. Thus, in its characteristic manifestations, mind is not an instrument of adaptation, but a principle of conscious aspiration, a nisus toward more rational, social, universal, and thus perfect, selfhood. Defining a person as 'any reactor that approves or disapproves its own reactions, or that realizes consequences as successes or failures of its own,' Coe has utilized in the psychology of religion a functionalism that is at once more empirical and genetic, and more significant, than that of the earlier writers on this subject. Religion becomes a genuinely social experience in which self-conscious persons, through fellowship with their neighbors, devotion to the community, and worship of its indwelling spirit, seek for larger realization with increasing self-knowledge and a more delicate sense of ethical, aesthetic, cognitive, and social values.[5]

[5] "The Psychology of Religion in America," *Religious Thought in the Last Quarter-Century*, a coöperative volume edited by Gerald Birney Smith (1927), pp. 133f. In considerably greater detail, and with specific reference to individual thinkers and their writings, we have analyzed and evaluated this doctrine in a paper, "Functional Interpretations of Religion: A Critique" contributed to *Philosophical Essays in Honor of James Creighton* (1917).

Moreover, one may safely contend that of all human experiences none is more genuinely personal than is religion. So deeply imbedded is the latter in the life of the individual that many of its most penetrating students have described it in terms which quite conform to Whitehead's conclusion that "religion is what man does with his solitariness." Though this expresses a deep insight, a more complete view would doubtless reveal that religion likewise involves a conscious recognition of mutuality, wherefore it expresses itself in group ceremonial and in a language derived from the various forms of kinship and social life (as, for example, father, brother, children, bridegroom, elders, etc.) Religion therefore requires for its interpretation a psychology and a philosophy less impersonal than the standpoint of functionalism and instrumentalism. The latter permits of a concern with processes and functions, but scarcely of a recognition of a self characterized by self-knowledge and self-direction. Thus, for example, it describes thinking in relation to situations and to the formulation and execution of ideals, but it manifests at best but a bowing acquaintance with the thinking self. Obviously, at any rate, it fails to take into full account the inner, self-conscious life of a being who may not merely criticize his own desires and motivations but may come to desire a nature not yet possessed by him; who is capable of an immediate experience of his fellows and thus of a realization of his oneness with them; and who may be consciously, sometimes poignantly, alive to the fact of a cosmos upon which his destiny and that of mankind ultimately depend. Unless and until experience is recognized as essentially personal in character, neither the possibility nor the nature of that which has been called religion can be discerned.

In general one may say that the interpretations of religion offered during this earlier period by disciples of Dewey suffered from certain ambiguities and confusions, not to say contradictions, which seem traceable to the writings from which they derived their standpoint. Two frames of reference are in evidence: one which is rather naïvely naturalistic, objectivistic, and biological; another which makes central the specific practical needs and interests of the human individual, more especially as these are of a conscious character. In consequence the foundational principles are garnered now from science and now from a consideration of action; the conception of 'nature' is at times 'naturalistic' but then again 'idealistic' in character; and very different meanings are attached likewise to other basic terms, such as mind, mental life, and conation. Thus, for example, Ames in his *The Psychology of Religious Experience* (1910), says that the mental life is "an instrument of adaptation by which the organism adjusts itself to the environment" (15). But the function is described also as less general in character: "Mind is the means by which adaptations occur in novel and complex situations" (15). Again, "instinctive and perceptive processes as well as developed reasoning come within the conception of mind" (16)—indeed, "Psychology has discovered the great extent and dominance in all conscious life of instinct, desire, habit and emotion" (303); nevertheless, the instinctive processes are distinguished from intelligence, whose prime function is "accommodation to new and intricate environments" (16). In general, as in the case of the above quotations, mind is conceived as a function of the organism to whose needs it is instrumental; on occasion, however, the organism is made secondary, neural activities and various objective effects being said to express or register the adjusting activity. Similar confusions occur in accounts of "mind-body." The latter is first described in terms of a relation of "mental states and bodily states" (18); then we find that "mind-body" is taken as synonymous with "organism" (20), but almost at once are told that the question "What is the organism, the mind-body, doing" is "in other words" the question "What is the will, or purposeful activity, accomplishing, and what are the means, such as instinct, imitation, habit, attention, association, perception, and reasoning which it employs?" (20f.). Adjustment is described as that of organism to environment (15), but also as "adjustment in the psycho-physical organism" (18), and again as occurring "through the psycho-physical organism" (15).

In further consequence of ambiguities and shifts in meaning which are inherent in their fundamental doctrine, the disciples of Dewey who early attacked the problems of religion rather brusquely ruled metaphysical assertions out of court, and yet they on occasion manifested a disposition to entertain religious beliefs on the ground of their functional significance and the support which they offered to an aspiring life. Ames declares that "the philosophy of religion in its most ultimate problems and refined developments does not transcend the principles of psychology;" God thus is equated with the "idea of God" and this "central conception of theology" is made "subject to the same laws of the mental life as are all other ideas, and there is but one science of psychology applicable to it" (26f.). Obviously the ideational constituents of religious belief are here placed on precisely the same plane as those of the various physical sciences, and psychology is taken as the single organ of truth. It need scarcely be argued that this involves misconceptions of such a sort that theology and the philosophy of religion need not feel in the least disturbed; their freedom to develop tenable doctrines is as little in jeopardy as is that, for example, of astronomy, physics, chemistry, or biology. Irving King, in his *The Development of Religion*, (1910), likewise assigns one and the same status to all concepts. While insisting, however, that religious concepts (like all others) may not be construed "ontologically" but solely "functionally," he none the less holds that if "the question of the reality of the order of existence postulated by religion is raised, we should have to say that probably all the concepts of religion fall *short* of an adequate account of experience rather than that they attribute too *much* to it" (340f.). Even the concept of the supernatural he finds to be one which probably is necessary for the expression of higher valuations (*cf.* 352). "The concept of God," he writes, "is a legitimate way for the religious mind to symbolize its faith in the reality of life. In so far as such symbolism satisfies and helps, it represents a genuine aspect of reality" (353).

King apparently does not regard his contentions respecting the ideas of God and the supernatural as at odds with the general point of view which he owes in the main to Dewey. Not improbably, however, he arrived at them partly under the influence of his desire to reckon seriously with the facts which are revealed by a direct and empirical examination of the religions of mankind and of the religious experiences of individuals. That the latter present difficulties to one who endeavors to bring religion as a whole within the framework of instrumentalistic doctrine is frankly acknowledged by King himself when he deals with the subject of "mana," the "mysterious power" represented, for example, by "manitou," "wakonda," "orenda" and "kukini." The concept here in reference is one which, as King states, must be taken into account because it has "probably played a large part in the unfolding of human thought, and has consequently reacted in important ways upon behavior and custom." He himself, however, makes the following admission: "It is difficult to relate it exactly to what has thus far been said of the development of the value-consciousness, and yet it has had a part in that development which we trust will not seem to be altogether adventitious, even though we should stand firmly upon the theory as thus far outlined" (132).

The fact that the instrumentalism of the time tended to oscillate between mutually exclusive doctrines, along with the inability of instrumentalism to afford an adequate interpretation of religion as an empirical phenomenon of historical and personal life, doubtless accounts for the failure of its exponents to reach clear or consistent conclusions respecting the relation of morality and religion. Often the two are made to coalesce, though religion is none the less also described as a specific mode of experience, distinct from the moral even as it is, for example, from the aesthetic or the logical. In the volume to which we have already referred, Ames specifically equates religion and morality. "The attempt to delimit the field of natural morality from religion," he writes, "presupposes in the older writers a dualism between human and divine. . . . Without the definite assumption of this dualism the line between morality and religion becomes obscure and tends to vanish completely" (286f.); "the distinction between morality and religion is not real" (285). Non-religious persons are therefore described as such who "fail to enter vitally into a world of social activities and feelings" (359)—persons who are mentally defective or diseased, or who lead criminal lives, or whose "mental life is not organized in accordance with the scale of values which is recognized by the morally mature and efficient persons of the community" (360). Notwithstanding these contentions, Ames himself describes religion as a "specialized interest" (291), as distinguishable from science, art and "other interests" (296), and as "differentiated by the inclusiveness and ideality of the ends which belong to it" (302). Religion is conceived as something whose core is morality, though again it is described as a quality of the moral experience ("no genuinely moral consciousness can be without religious quality" (286)) and also as a "phase of all socialized human experience" (280).[6]

The difficulties which this theme presents to instrumentalists are discernible also in King's treatment of the subject. On the whole his examination of the facts of religious life and history constrained him to concede to religion an autonomous place in human experience. Thus, he wrote an essay on *The Differentiation of the Religious Consciousness* (1904); and in his subsequent work, *The Development of Religion,* he concludes that "there *is* such a thing as the religious attitude of mind" (340). religion being described in his final statement as "essentially a faith that the universe, in which we have our being, contains the elements that can satisfy in some way our deepest aspirations" (353). Yet it would appear that King's struggles to differentiate the religious consciousness were not entirely successful, more particularly in its relation to morality; and it would seem more than likely that his failures at this point, and the fact that his final statement regarding the nature of religion is but loosely connected with those of his discussions oriented by his instrumentalism, are evidence not of his inadequate grasp of the general point of view and method of instrumentalism but rather of the embarrassments suffered by one who would be faithful thereto and yet would likewise acknowledge the facts presented by religious phenomena.

III

The direct and personal contribution made by Dewey to the clarification of religious issues and to the redirection of religious thought and practice is to be found primarily in his *A Common*

---

[6] Some of the difficulties to which we have referred were escaped by Ames in his later book entitled *Religion,* in the preparation of which he apparently allowed his thought to move with considerable freedom instead of compressing it within the straight jacket of a psychology subordinated to the conception of an organism in functional relations with an external environment.

Faith of 1934. This book is an incisive and forceful expression of a fervid yet unsentimental, and carefully pondered concern for the highest interests of man. It cannot but enhance one's sense of the central importance of the theme discussed, as well as throw light on the precise nature of Dewey's most mature philosophical doctrine. That the views it presents are strikingly novel may, however, scarcely be claimed. Nor was this to be expected. Its topic is one that has long engaged leading minds characterized by very diverse outlooks upon life and the world. Moreover, it had previously been treated, psychologically, theologically, and philosophically, by thinkers whose intellectual commitment was primarily to a point of view explicitly derived or drawing support from the philosophy of Dewey. In so far one may say, in reminiscence of a remark once made by Mr. C. E. Ayres, that Dewey no longer seems remarkable because his thought has passed into the minds of so many that his own specific utterances can scarcely seem, either to them or to students of religion at large, as anything other than familiar.

Nevertheless it is worthy of note that in his own book on religion Dewey remained quite free from the dilemmas and theoretical embarrassments which we have noted in the earlier writings of his disciples Ames and King. On the other hand, he differs from the latter in giving to ideas and to the cognitive aspects of experience a wider rôle than one strictly functional in the rather narrowly utilitarian and biological sense of the term. Thus, for example, Dewey says: "Legends and myths grow up in part as decorative dressings, in response to the irrepressible human tendency toward story-telling, and in part as attempts to explain ritual practices" (59).[7] Moreover, Dewey has at no time, apparently, given serious attention to empirical investigations of the religions of history or of the varieties of religious experience. At any rate he has never indicated how he would construe the latter from the standpoint of a psychology connected with his instrumentalism. Indeed, such investigations on the part of others would seem to have concerned him but little, even as have, apparently, the studies of theologians and

---

[7] *A Common Faith;* all succeeding quotations are from this same volume, unless stated otherwise.

philosophers of religion generally. When, therefore, he came to present the outlines of his religious doctrine in his *A Common Faith* he remained content to set forth his conclusions in contrast with views which, while as frontally opposed as are a certain form of theism on the one hand, and atheistic humanism on the other, are nevertheless alike in that they have their orientation, by way either of acceptance or of rejection, in what may perhaps aptly be called "crass supernaturalism." Numerous other types of religious philosophy he thus left quite unregarded.

Those seeking to understand and estimate Dewey's *A Common Faith* would have been aided if a clearer and more specific description had been provided of the supernaturalism to which objection is raised. For the term has carried and continues to carry quite different meanings, and it is only by virtue of this fact that one may characterize the religions of the past as in general supernaturalistic. In illustration and confirmation hereof, one may even quote Dewey himself. Thus, he writes:

> In earlier times, what we now call the supernatural hardly meant anything more definite than the extraordinary, that which was striking and emotionally impressive because of its out-of-the-way character. Probably even today the commonest conception of the natural is that which is usual, customary and familiar. When there is no insight into the cause of unusual events, belief in the supernatural is itself 'natural'—in this sense of natural. (69)

Dewey's indictment of the doctrine which he generally calls supernaturalism includes several counts. Its wisdom, he insists, "consists in administration of the temporal, finite and human in its relation to the eternal and infinite, by means of dogma and cult, rather than in regulation of the events of life by understanding of actual conditions."[8] Dewey charges that supernaturalism is incompatible with the method and the spirit of scientific inquiry and with the relationships and institutions of democracy; he declares it philosophically untenable because of its belief in realities anteceding thought and practice, and its insistence on treating the ideal as more than the possibilities

[8] *Experience and Nature* (1925), 55.

discoverable in experience and in some measure capable of realization through the intelligent and devoted efforts of human
individuals; he insists that its attempts to inculcate through-
going assurance and a sense of absolute certainty and security are
alike hostile to the intellectual enterprise and subversive of socially and morally constructive action. In short, he makes the
charge that supernaturalism is intellectually false and morally
vicious.

But has the belief in question as a matter of historical fact
actually manifested itself as paralytic or otherwise harmful to
lives of strenuous and fruitful service in the realms of thought,
of art, or of social relationships? The affirmation that such has
been the case would seem to depend more upon an *a priori* argument that it must have been so since the logic of the doctrine
makes such a result inevitable, than to express an empirical
generalization from the scroll of history. Historical phenomena,
to be sure, are the outcomes of numerous interacting and counter-
acting forces; yet the evidence they offer certainly leaves this
count of Dewey's indictment without convincing grounds. When
one thinks of religion in general rather than merely of supernaturalism in Dewey's sense of the term, one cannot but be impressed by the magnitude of its contributions, in the way of incentive, inspiration or support, to all manner of revolutions
against conditions that have oppressed man, to constructive
movements of social reform, and to the general cause of human
enlightenment and refinement. Is it really true to the facts to
affirm, as Dewey does in his *Human Nature and Conduct* (5),
that "Protestantism, except in its most zealous forms, has accomplished the same result [namely, that of 'emphasizing those
qualities of human nature that are most commonplace and average, of exaggerating the herd instinct of conformity'] by a sharp
separation between religion and morality in which a higher
justification by faith disposes at one stroke of daily lapses into
the gregarious morals of average conduct?" Surely one may not
say of all supernaturalism "that it stands in the way of an effective realization of the sweep and depth of the implications of
natural human relations" (80); that the relations "of husband
and wife, parent and child, friend and friend, neighbor and

neighbor, of fellow workers in industry, science, and art, are neglected, passed over, not developed for all that is in them" —nay are not merely depreciated but are "regarded as dangerous rivals of higher values; as offering temptations to be resisted; as usurpations by flesh of the authority of the spirit; as revolts of the human against the divine" (71f.).

That the supernaturalism against which Dewey inveighs is philosophically defensible is denied even by numerous theologians and philosophers who find truth in organized religion and in the affirmations of the religious consciousness, most conspicuously, of course, in their more advanced expressions. The beliefs connected with the historical religions vary enormously, even as do the emotional constituents and manifestations of religion, and likewise its ceremonies and its cult practices. Religions, moreover, differ greatly in respect to the relative importance which they attach to ideas and creed. In general, however, it seems safe to say that for the religions, as distinguished from philosophies, and for the religious consciousness, the gods and God have not been aloof from man or remote from his world, but available and near at hand. They have not been conceived as purely transcendent but rather as factors in or features of the world of human experience, actually or potentially immanent in man and closer to him than "hands or feet." In so far it has been their concern to affirm a glorified naturalism and a strengthened—and, in the case of the high religions, a spiritualized— humanism, whether they have conceived the more than human power or powers of their belief as distinguishable constituents or features of the total order of being, or of Nature, or as the *natura naturans*, or as the sole and independent ultimate reality; and whether they have thought of the superhuman in terms of creativity or of logical ground.

Dewey's general philosophy, of course, precludes him from considering historical religion in its aspect of pastness, or religious experience from the standpoint of its actuality in distinction from its future possibilities and the challenge it presents to a reformatory interest. Hence his treatment of the religious problem is not "descriptive" in the sense in which this may be contrasted with the "normative;" rather is it "normative" with only such descriptive detail as is significant for an answer to the question as to what ought-to-be. He does not enter into the question of the right of or the pragmatic value of over-beliefs, but one is probably safe in concluding that he would deprecate the retention of over-beliefs on the part even of persons who have not entered into a philosophically reflective life. Doubtless, moreover, he would object to the practice of such as deliberately adhere to the forms and symbols associated with the religious institutions of their heritage, even when they do so on the ground of an aesthetic or other sort of emotional or sentimental or stabilizing value which they experience in them.

Dewey would seem to be somewhat suspicious of substantives; at any rate, he frequently shows a decided predilection for adjectives and adverbs. He writes:

It is a plausible prediction that if there were an interdict placed for a generation upon the use of mind, matter, consciousness as nouns, and we were obliged to employ adjectives and adverbs, conscious and unconsciously, mental and mentally, material and physically, we should find many of our problems much simplified (*Experience and Nature*, 75).

In conformity herewith he describes his proposal in *A Common Faith* as not "a religion, but rather the emancipation of elements and outlooks that may be called religious" (8). In its contrast with the substantive 'religion,' or rather 'a religion'—which alone is what we find, inasmuch as 'religion' is "a strictly collective term"—Dewey describes the 'religious' as follows:

The adjective 'religious' denotes nothing in the way of a specifiable entity, either institutional or as a system of beliefs. It does not denote anything to which one can specifically point as one can point to this and that historic religion or existing church. For it does not denote anything that can exist by itself or that can be organized into a particular and distinctive form of existence. It denotes attitudes that may be taken toward every object and every proposed end or ideal (9f.).

This and other passages may readily suggest an interpretation that is at odds with Dewey's real meaning. He indeed speaks of "a religious outlook and function" as well as of "religious attitudes;" and he says of a certain change that when it "takes place there is definitely religious attitude" (17). He is here, however, not referring to a distinctive kind of experience or a specific component of the mental life, such, for example, as the attitude described as religious by Pratt in his *The Religious Consciousness* (1920) or the sentiment in terms of which W. K. Wright, E. S. Conklin and others conceive religion. On the contrary he repudiates the view that there is "a definite kind of experience which is itself religious . . . as a kind of experience that is marked off from experience as aesthetic, scientific, moral, political; from experience as companionship and friendship" (10). 'Religious,' he holds, "as a quality of experience signifies something that may belong to all these experiences" (10), although, of course, it is as a matter of fact commonly absent from them. The experiences with which a "religious force" is connected, however, are deemed by him to be by no means infrequent; they comprise all such as have the "force of bringing about a better, deeper and enduring adjustment in life" (14).

For Dewey the quality or character of 'religious' appears when there are "changes in [or, of?] ourselves in relation to the world in which we live that are much more inclusive and deepseated" (16) than are the processes of 'adaptation,' changes "generic and enduring" and making for "that complete unification of the self which is called a whole" (19). Now, "The self is always directed toward something beyond itself and so its own unification depends upon the idea of the integration of the shifting scenes of the world into that imaginative totality we call the Universe" (19); and, since the "idea of a whole, whether of the whole personal being or of the world, is an imaginative, not a literal, idea" (18), "the idea of a thoroughgoing and deepseated harmonizing of the self with the Universe . . . operates only through imagination" (19).

The religious is 'morality touched by emotion' only when the ends of moral conviction arouse emotions that are not only intense but are actuated and supported by ends so inclusive that they unify the self. The inclusiveness of the end in relation to both self and the 'universe' to which an inclusive self is related is indispensable (22f.).

That religion may and should pervade the whole of life and express itself in even our most ordinary activities is by no means a novel or an uncommon contention. Has not Carlyle, for example, said that a carpenter may break the entire decalogue with a single stroke of his hammer? This thought recurs time and again in the sacred writings of the Hindus, and it is essentially that of Fichte when he writes:

Religiosity is not something that is isolated and exists by itself such that one might be very strong in piety but as for the rest very weak and deficient, and a bad man. He [Fichte is writing of the 'true Mason'] is not religious but he thinks and acts religiously; religion for him is not an object but solely the aether in which he sees all objects. He directs his entire strength exclusively to each and every task which here below confronts him, and an observer might think that he had no other concern than that of achieving his specific purpose, and that this purpose is exhaustive of his entire being and all his impulses.[9]

Nor can a claim to novelty be made for Dewey's view that religious emotions are "supported by ends so inclusive that they unify the self" or that the unification of the self "depends upon the idea of the interaction of the shifting scenes of the world into that imaginative totality we call the Universe" (19). Many there are who have identified religion with man's total response to that which for him is the regnant value or is the World in the deepest and most comprehensive meaning of this term. Thus one may cite the definition of Starbuck in the syllabus of his Oslo lectures: "Religion consists in one's complete response to That Which has supreme worth or value."

Dewey, then, singles out certain processes, functions, outlooks, and attitudes as religious in distinction from others which are said to lack this character; and he defines the religious attitudes in terms of their relation to the realization of a wholeness of selfhood such as is possible only in relation to "that imaginative totality which we call the Universe." The religious attitudes are apparently conceived to make a difference; they would seem to be thought of as productive of changes. Now, these religious attitudes are what the religions and the religious man have commonly meant by a person's religion. What then can be the point of the contrast which Dewey makes when he writes: "All re-

[9] *Briefe an Constant, Maurerische Klassiker,* I, *Fichte,* ed. by Albin Freiherr von Reitzenstein, 96f.

ligions, marked by elevated ideal quality, have dwelt upon the power of religion to introduce perspective into the piecemeal and shifting episodes of existence. Here too we need to reverse the ordinary statement and say that whatever introduces genuine perspective is religious, not that religion is something that introduces it" (24)? The contrast here made would acquire real point only if one were to substitute in these sentences the term 'God' for that of 'religion,' and if one meant by God a reality other than and completely external to the processes of nature and of human life, a conception quite unacceptable to many devout theists both within and without the ranks of theologians and philosophers.

For Dewey the 'religious' is a character or quality of certain processes and attitudes, and in so far it cannot be said to exist or occur as something isolated from experiences generally. On the other hand, it is not attributable to all processes and attitudes, and in so far it is set apart. Here the only difference discernible between Dewey and psychologists generally is the fact that in his predilection for adjectives the former speaks of *religious* described as a *quality* of (certain) attitudes, whereas the latter do not hesitate to retain the word *religion* which they then conceive as an *attitude* (or sentiment) *having a* (certain) *quality*. Alike they give to the religious attitude a function, and as to this Dewey is by no means alone when he thinks of it in terms of an integration of the self. Dewey, moreover, is not disposed to oppose the existence of churches as a specific form of social institution. Let them rather recover their vitality, he suggests, by celebrating and reinforcing the "fund of human values that are prized and that need to be cherished, values that are satisfied and rectified by *all* human concerns and arrangements" (82). To be sure he criticizes historic Christianity for its separation of "sheep and goats; the saved and the lost; the elect and the mass" (84). But would not Dewey himself be the first to distinguish between those who already are socially, morally, and religiously minded, and those who are only potentially so? And would he not insist that such religious-mindedness inevitably expresses itself in an endeavor to bring all within the fold?

Involved in religious experience, according to Dewey, is belief, not that some object or being exists but that "some end should be supreme over conduct" (20). What is requisite is moral conviction, the sense of "being conquered, vanquished, in our active nature by an ideal end" and an "acknowledgment of its rightful claim over our desires and purposes" (20). The religions of tradition, holding as they do that "the ideal in question is already embedded in the existent frame of things" and "is already the final reality at the heart of things that exist," really evince a lack of *moral* faith in that they convert "moral realities into matters of intellectual assent" (21). Thus, for the unseen power conceived to control our destiny, Dewey would substitute "the power of an idea" whose intrinsic nature is the basis of its claim upon our allegiance and devotion. Writes he:

The reality of ideal ends and values in their authority over us is an undoubted fact. The validity of justice, affection, and that intellectual correspondence of our ideas with realities that we call truth, is so assured in its hold upon humanity that it is unnecessary for the religious attitude to encumber itself with the apparatus of dogma and doctrine (44).

Without dwelling upon an obvious nodding on the part of Dewey in his reference to "intellectual correspondence" as "truth," we would ask precisely what it is that he declares "an undoubted fact." Is it merely some psychological or subjective experience or feeling associated with an individual's thought of "ideal ends and values?" Or are the ideal ends and values taken, and does morality require them to be taken, as objective in the sense of being metapsychological and overindividual in character, and ontological in significance? So far as he carried his argument, was not Fichte justified in repudiating the as-if doctrine of Forberg, with its dualism between dutiful conduct and theoretical beliefs, and in insisting that faithfulness to the requirements of morality is indissolubly connected with belief in an active principle making for the conservation and increase of values in the world? That some of Dewey's statements seem quite compatible herewith is evidenced by the interpretation which Wieman originally gave of *A Common Faith*; that Dewey's thought, however, was quite different, he then specifically declared; nevertheless, that one can stop short of admitting a *moralische Weltordnung*, in the Fichtean sense, if one would do full justice to what is involved in the experience whether of moral obligation or of compliance therewith, or would recognize the implications of the recognition, on the part of common man and philosopher alike, of the unique value possessed by the moral as distinct from other motives to conduct —this Dewey has certainly failed to establish. His grounds for rejecting the "antecedently given" here leave one quite unconvinced. It is difficult to think that he himself can escape the admission that Nature, in its distinction from experience and as that into which man is born, or that the characters Nature has acquired through the creative intelligence operative in the past, is antecedently given to both the thought and the action of the individual, and that they constitute that unity of being in vital relations with which alone man can achieve the genuine integrity which he desiderates and which he increasingly acquires through the "grace" of Nature as inciting, sustaining, and supplementing his moral endeavors. Dewey himself admits, even asserts, that an adjustment such as is religion "possesses the will rather than is its express product" (19), and that "the unification of the self throughout the ceaseless flux of what it does, suffers, and achieves, cannot be attained in terms of itself" (19). "Our successes are dependent upon the coöperation of nature," and thus the "essentially unreligious attitude is that which attributes human achievement and purpose to man in isolation from the world of physical nature and his fellows" (25).

Man's sense of dependence is indeed more profound than anything derivable from the experience of those precarious elements of the environment which Dewey stresses, or from the realization by an individual that his successes are conditioned by coöperating factors of his physical and social world. Man is a being who not merely succumbs to death but who knows that he will die, and this awareness makes poignantly vivid the absoluteness of Nature's control over him. Not strange then, that the phenomenon of death has played an important rôle in the genesis of religion, as was pointed out by Wundt in his *Völkerpsychologie*, or that its contemplation has ever tended to arouse religious feelings even in those who are otherwise but seldom consciously alive to the finitude of the human individual and to the awesomeness of Nature. But through other channels also man comes to experience what has aptly been called a creature-feeling and is claimed, quite properly, to derive from man's consciousness, however aroused, of the roots and of the limitations of his being. Here, then, he encounters Reality in the sense both of antecedent and of ultimate; and here, as the weight of the evidence would seem to prove, is the basis of an experience which may be distinguished as religious.

A full-orbed human life must include worship as well as wonder and work; and, though these moments are distinguishable, they yet play into one another in such a way that each may strengthen and enrich the others. Thus, from wonder work acquires goals and therefore significance, and worship an increasingly worthy object; from work wonder secures motivation and pointedness, and through it worship is saved from the perils of subjectivity and sentimentality; from worship comes wonder's deepest arousal, and that breadth of horizon, and confident, irrepressible zeal without which work is lacking in perspective and is eventually doomed to flag. Emphasis upon work, and upon wonder in connection therewith, is ever a needed gospel, and Dewey's message is perhaps peculiarly suited to the needs of our day. Yet what is also required, and probably even more deeply, is a corresponding stress upon the indispensability of worship and of that particular exercise of wonder to which worship gives rise and by which it is refined.

EDWARD L. SCHAUB

DEPARTMENT OF PHILOSOPHY
NORTHWESTERN UNIVERSITY

14

John L. Childs

THE EDUCATIONAL PHILOSOPHY OF
JOHN DEWEY

THE EDUCATIONAL PHILOSOPHY OF
JOHN DEWEY

I. Philosophy and Education

A CHILD, according to Dr. Dewey, is as evidential of the nature of reality as an electron or a star. For the purposes of philosophy the affairs of the nursery and the kindergarten seem to him as significant as those of the physical laboratory. This is in harmony with his general theory of existence which holds that no level of experience—physical, biological, or social —should be given superior metaphysical status.

The moral interest is also central in the philosophy of Dr. Dewey. Although resolute in the desire to understand and interpret the world solely on the basis of empirical findings, he is equally concerned to use these findings to *change* the world so that human goods may become more secure, more numerous, and more widely shared.

It is not surprising, therefore, that education in both its incidental and deliberate forms has always been a primary interest in his philosophy. Primary, not only in the amount of attention Dr. Dewey has given to it, but primary also in the part the practice and theory of education has played in the development of his own most basic ideas.

In an autobiographical essay, Dr. Dewey states that for many years *Democracy and Education* was the book in which his philosophy "was most fully expounded." In this essay he raises the question as to why so many philosophers, although themselves engaged in educational work, "have not taken education with sufficient seriousness for it to occur to them that any rational person could actually think it possible that philosophizing should focus about education as the supreme human interest in which, moreover, other problems, cosmological, moral, logical, come to a head."[1]

So intimate does Dr. Dewey consider this connection between education and philosophy that he proposes an educational extension of the pragmatic test of meaning. Building on the pragmatic notion that the meaning of ideas or conceptions is to be found in the definite practices to which they lead, he suggests that the actual significance of differences in philosophical outlook may be discovered by developing their implications and consequences for educational practice. He affirms, in *Democracy and Education*, that a difference in philosophy which makes no difference in the practice of education is an artificial, or verbal, difference. He adds that "unless a philosophy is to remain symbolic or verbal or a sentimental indulgence for a few, or else mere arbitrary dogma, its auditing of past experience and its program of values must take effect in conduct."[2]

It should be remembered in this connection that Dr. Dewey construes education very broadly. It includes schooling, but is by no means restricted to it. In its most inclusive meaning education denotes any change wrought in an individual as a result of experience. In its narrower, deliberate form education signifies conscious effort by some organized group to shape the conduct and the emotional and intellectual dispositions of its young.

All deliberate education is thus, in his opinion, a *moral* undertaking. Moral in the sense that it is a designed, controlled action concerned with the formation of fundamental attitudes of the individual toward nature and fellow human beings. It inescapably involves the manifestation of preference for some particular kind of social and individual life. We engage in deliberate education because we desire to make of the young something they would not become if left to their own unguided interactions with their natural and social environments. It is only when we view education from this broader standpoint that we are in a position to interpret Dr. Dewey's thesis that "edu-

[1] *Contemporary American Philosophy*, II, 23, "From Absolutism to Experimentalism," by John Dewey.
[2] *Democracy and Education*, 383.

cation offers a vantage ground from which to penetrate to the human, as distinct from the technical, significance of philosophical discussions."[3]

Accepting this suggestion, we shall explore some of the major conceptions of Dr. Dewey's philosophy by indicating their implications for the theory and practice of education. If we adhere to his own principle of analysis, we must begin our discussion with a consideration of method; for he has consistently maintained that the method of experience, often also designated as the method of experimental inquiry, is his supreme interest, criterion, reliance, and value.

Unquestionably, method is primary in the philosophy of Dr. Dewey. But the educator who pursues this method of experience whole-heartedly discovers eventually that philosophically he is committed to something more than a mere method. To be sure, the method as such does not automatically prescribe a complete set of metaphysical theses, but it does, nevertheless, define a principle of approach and analysis which clearly is not compatible with certain philosophical presuppositions. It inevitably cuts the ground, for example, from under the conception of supernaturalism—a conception which still permeates the philosophical outlook of the majority of the American people. From the standpoint of culture and education such a shift in general outlook carries consequences for human conduct and belief far too important to be subsumed under the category of method. A new world-view may be the necessary correlative of this empirical method, but desirable intellectual and moral reconstruction in the lives of individuals can be attained educationally only if the outlook itself be given independent consideration.

Apparently Dr. Dewey has recognized all along that his emphasis on experimental method has carried important implications for a life-outlook. His recent writings have been very definite and explicit on this point as the following statement from an article intended for popular consumption indicates:

Mankind has hardly inquired what would happen if the possibility of experience were seriously explored and exploited. Religions have been

[3] *Ibid.*, 383.

saturated with the supernatural—and the supernatural signifies precisely that which lies beyond experience. Moral codes have been allied to this religious supernaturalism and have sought their foundation and sanction in it. Contrast with such ideas, deeply imbedded in all Western culture, gives the philosophy of faith in experience a definite and profound meaning.[4]

As the above quotation makes quite definite, this emphasis on empirical method involves the acceptance of certain views as opposed to others which are still "deeply imbedded in all Western culture." To use the method of experience as Dr. Dewey himself uses it, is to make a naturalistic theory of existence the common presupposition of one's philosophical outlook and educational practice. In his philosophy the naturalistic outlook is as fundamental as the empirical method. Indeed, so intimate is the connection between the two, that the full import of his philosophy of education can be discerned only as we grasp that it is grounded in a naturalistic interpretation of human beings and their experiences. We turn now to the examination of some of the definite consequences for education involved in the experimental naturalism of Dr. Dewey.

II. MIND AND EDUCATION

Experimental naturalism signifies, in the first place, the unqualified acceptance of the principle of organic evolution. Organic evolution implies, for Dr. Dewey, that man's rational and moral attributes have had a natural genesis just as literally as have the structures of his body. He rejects, therefore, the dualistic presupposition of classical philosophy and theology "that experience centers in, or gathers about, or proceeds from a center or subject which is outside the course of natural existence, and set over against it."[5] The postulate of the continuity of the human, the organic, and the physical, is foundational in his approach to the problem of logic, psychology, politics, art, ethics and education. Indeed, it seems to him to be the necessary starting-point for the fruitful study of any aspect of human experience.

[4] *Living Philosophies*, 22-23, "A Credo," by John Dewey.
[5] *Creative Intelligence*, 30.

If biological developments be accepted, the human subject of experience is at least an animal, continuous with other organic forms in a process of more complex organization. An animal in turn is at least continuous with chemico-physical processes which, in living things, are so organized as really to constitute the activities of life with all their defining traits. And experience is not identical with brain action; it is the entire organic agent-patient in all its interaction with the environment, natural and social.[6]

What are the educational consequences of this naturalistic interpretation of human personality? This view of man's intellectual and moral nature certainly does not imply, as so many assume, that the education of human beings is to be reduced to a process of animal training.[7] No conception of education is farther from the thought of Dr. Dewey. Throughout his life he has protested against the notion that children should be subjected to a program of authoritarian, routine habituation. His educational aim has been the development and liberation of individual intelligence, not animal training in the form of mere mechanical conditioning of reflexes.

Neither does the rejection of this historic mind-body dualism involve approval of the notion that human interests are limited to those which make for creature comfort or for practical utility to the exclusion of those values which are often called cultural.[8] Man, a part of the natural world, cannot live without food, clothing, and shelter, but for a generation Dr. Dewey has pioneered in the demand that these means by which we make a living be transformed into ways of making a life that is worth the living.

Human traits, capacities, and interests, in the opinion of Dr. Dewey, are not less real or efficacious, because they have developed by a natural evolutionary process. Man is no less rational because his capacities for reflection have developed *from* organic acivities which are not consciously purposeful. Whatever creative abilities man has exhibited in his art, in his science,

[6] *Ibid.*, 36.
[7] See Mortimer Adler: "The Crisis in Contemporary Education," in *The Social Frontier*, Feb. 1939.
[8] President Hutchins: *The Higher Learning in America*, Chapter 1.

in his technology, and in his social relationships, these are the traits which define the distinctively human, and they are not to be eliminated by any theory about man's origin and psychological make-up. Dr. Dewey has consistently emphasized that conscious human association made possible by language-communication has added a new dimension to the natural order.

The naturalistic humanism of Dr. Dewey is no more compatible with the gross materialism which assimilates the human to the organic, and the organic to the physical, than it is with that species of mentalism, or spiritualistic monism, which goes to the opposite extreme and turns mind, an emergent function, into the ultimate ground and stuff of all existences. For Dr. Dewey evolution denotes emergence. Emergent events are not to be explained away by some metaphysical dogma; they are to be taken for whatever they are found to be. He says:

The term "naturalistic" has many meanings. As it is here employed it means, on the one side, that there is no breach of continuity between operations of inquiry and biological operations and physical operations. "Continuity," on the other side, means that rational operations grow out of organic activities, without being identical with that from which they emerge.[9]

Thus, in the philosophy of Dr. Dewey, to regard human beings as part of the natural evolutionary series does not strip them of their uniquely human traits. But this naturalistic principle of continuity, nevertheless, does carry important implications for both philosophy and education. It has profoundly conditioned, for example, Dr. Dewey's view of mind.

Mind is real; but its reality does not denote the presence of a transcendental reason or cosmic consciousness in the human form, which, in some mysterious manner, regulates the interactions of the organism with the environment thereby conferring rationality upon them. Neither is mind viewed as a complex of inherited faculties which unfolds when stimulated and trained by the so-called disciplinary subjects such as rhetoric, grammar, logic, and mathematics. In contrast to these dualistic notions Dr. Dewey regards mind as a quality of behavior—a

[9] *Logic; The Theory of Inquiry*, 18-19.

function. The organism "is part and parcel of the course of events."

It becomes a mind in virtue of a distinctive way of partaking in the course of events. The significant distinction is no longer between the knower *and* the world; it is between different ways of being in and of the movement of things; between a brute physical way and a purposive, intelligent way.[10]

In sum, mind appears in the conduct of the individual when outcomes are anticipated and thus become controlling factors in the present ordering of events and activities. To have mind, we must have knowledge which is grasp of the behavior of actual events. Meanings relate to behaviors. We may be said to have the meaning of events when we know what can be done with them, and how to behave with reference to them. This involves understanding of the conditions on which their occurrence depends, and also of the consequences to which they lead. Meaning, therefore, signifies that knowledge of operations, or of the behavior of events, which makes significant prediction and control possible.

This behavior which is mind, and which denotes freedom through control, is, to be sure, conditioned by the organic structures of the human form, but it is by no means the exclusive property of these inherited structures. In other words, mind is not an endowment given at birth. The child acquires mind— a rational nature—as he masters the meanings of affairs in his environment. These meanings are not primarily his own original creations. They have been developed by the long and painful experience of the race; they are funded in the habits, customs, traditions, tools, methods, techniques and institutions of his society. The child makes them his own through a learning process. It is through learning by participation in the ways of his community that he achieves mind—becomes a person.[11]

Important consequences for the practice of education follow from this view of mind. Reflection is linked with behavior. It is viewed as an indirect mode of response to the environment. The act of reflection begins in a situation of difficulty; it de-

[10] *Creative Intelligence,* 59.
[11] See Dewey: *The Public and Its Problems,* 154.

velops through observation, the gathering of data, the making of inferences, the tracing out of the implications of suggested meanings or ideas until such time as the nature of the problem is defined, and a promising plan for dealing with it has been projected in imagination; it ultimately leads to an action which puts the plan to the actual test.[12]

Deliberate education—including the work of the school—should therefore so arrange its program that it provides opportunity for the young to engage in activities which call for the exercise of this complete act of reflective thought. "The important thing is that thinking," according to Dr. Dewey, "is the method of an educative experience. The essentials of method are therefore identical with the essentials of reflection."[13]

Information as recorded in books is an indispensable resource for educative experiences of this kind. Dr. Dewey has vigorously condemned the notion that the child should deal with things, and not with words. He believes that it is a mistaken theory which opposes learning through activity to learning through language. Thinking, to be sure, is not identical with the manipulation of symbols, but it does involve the use of conceptions, terms, and principles of interpretation, the mastery of which is dependent upon the mastery of language. All of this Dr. Dewey has recognized and emphasized.

But he also contends that thinking in its pregnant form is experiencing, and experiencing in turn includes much more than the use of written and oral symbols. In its primary form experiencing denotes an active process of doing and undergoing, of acting on things in the environment and suffering or enjoying their reactions to our acts. We learn to think as we connect what we do with the consequences that follow from our doing. Ideas are valid or invalid to the extent that they define activities, which, as means, are appropriate to the ends the individual desires. The first principle of rationality is to learn "to think in terms of action and in terms of *those* acts whose consequences will expand, revise, test, your ideas and theories."[14]

[12] Dewey: *How We Think*, Revised Edition, Chapter 7.
[13] *Democracy and Education*, 192.
[14] Dewey: *The Educational Frontier* (W. H. Kilpatrick, editor), 305.

This kind of thinking cannot go on exclusively within the head of the child. It requires an environment in which whatever is projected in idea can be tested in deed. Nor is thinking a function of books alone. It is also an affair of the natural and social world. Holding this conception of the nature of thinking, and of the process by which mind develops, Dr. Dewey has sought two changes in the traditional school. He has desired that passive rote learning be supplanted by a form of active community life within the school. And, secondly, he has wanted the school to be in vital interaction with the surrounding natural and social environment.

An activity program is thus the legitimate off-spring of Dr. Dewey's naturalistic theory of mind. But it is an activity program which encourages that consecutive and cumulative ordering of experience which leads to the progressive enrichment of meaning and to added power of control over self and environment. Hence educational activity must not be confused with mere muscular movement, or busy work, much less with the indulgence of the momentary impulses and whims of children. Problems also are not to be construed narrowly. They are as wide as the range of human interests—æsthetic, and intellectual, as well as utilitarian.

Years ago Dr. Dewey offered the following criteria by which to judge the educational value of an activity:

We may say that the kind of experience to which the work of the schools should contribute is one marked by executive competency in the management of resources and obstacles encountered (efficiency); by sociability, or interest in the direct companionship of others; by æsthetic taste or capacity to appreciate artistic excellence in at least some of its classic forms; by trained intellectual method, of interest in some mode of scientific achievement; and by sensitiveness to the rights and claims of others—conscientiousness.[15]

Experimental schools would have been saved much waste, and much recent severe criticism, had they given greater heed to these criteria for the evaluation of the educational worth of an activity program.

[15] *Democracy and Education*, 285-286.

JOHN L. CHILDS

III. Nature and Education

Experimental naturalism calls not only for a reconstructed view of mind, it also calls for a reconstructed view of the nature of the world in which man lives, moves, and has his being. Dr. Dewey's empirical mode of thought demands that both philosophy and education take as their ultimate point of departure the world of ordinary experience.

This world as disclosed in common experience is qualitatively diversified. Indeed it is probable, according to Dr. Dewey, that "there would be no such thing as 'consciousness' if events did not have a phase of brute and unconditioned 'isness,' of being just what they irreducibly are."[16] In ordinary experience, "things are poignant, tragic, beautiful, humorous, settled, disturbed, comfortable, amazing, barren, harsh, consoling, splendid, fearful; are such immediately and in their own right and behalf."[17] "To the empirical thinker, immediate enjoyment and suffering are the conclusive exhibition and evidence that nature has its finalities as well as its relationships."[18] Indeed, "only if elements are more than just elements in a whole, only if they have something qualitatively of their own can a relational system be prevented from complete collapse."[19]

Fidelity to the method of experience requires that we take this world of uniquely diversified and interacting events at full face value. If we hold to the data of ordinary experience, and if we are disciplined enough not to make our preferences the measure of reality, Dr. Dewey believes we shall conclude: that our world is not one, but many; that it is a dynamic, changing world, not static and finished; that in this plural world from which individuality is not to be eliminated, the course of events is contingent, not predetermined by antecedent forces, either material or spiritual; that, although existence is characterized by recurring sequences and many relatively constant correlations between events, nature as a whole is "an affair of affairs" with no once and for all beginning of everything, and without

[16] *Experience and Nature*, 86.
[17] *Ibid.*, 96.
[18] *Ibid.*, 86.
[19] *Ibid.*, 87.

any final, all-embracing end toward which it trends; and, finally, that, although our world is such as to permit the emergence and continued existence of living forms, including human beings with all their distinctive intellectual and moral traits, "nature has no preference for good things over bad things, its mills turn out any kind of grist indifferently."[20]

This naturalistic view of a wide-open universe in which conflict and uncertainty are ultimate traits has its significant implications for human conduct and consequently for our view of the method, the content, and the aims of education. We shall first examine its implications for method.

Life is a process of experimental adjustment in a precarious world where man is confronted with a novel development of conditions. "The conjunction of problematic and determinate characters in nature renders every existence, as well as every idea and human act, an experiment in fact, even though not in design."[21] Since living is intrinsically a process of selective adjustment, Dr. Dewey believes that these adjustments should be made consciously. Impulsive behavior, blind trial and error, slavish reliance on custom and routine habit will not suffice in a world in which change and novelty are real. Hence the continuous exercise of intelligence is a necessity, not a luxury, for all who would live well in a precarious universe.

Thus an identical implication for education is inherent, on the one hand, in Dr. Dewey's naturalistic theory of existence, and, on the other, in his conception of the nature of mind and the processes by which mind develops in individuals. These two conceptions combine to underline the supremacy of method both in life and in education.

. . . Problems are solved only where they arise—namely in action, in the adjustments of behavior. But, for good or for evil, they can be solved only with method; and ultimately method is intelligence, and intelligence is method.[22]

Dr. Dewey believes that the method of experimental intelligence is man's ultimate resource for making adjustments in a

[20] *Ibid.*, 112.
[21] *Ibid.*, 70.
[22] *Influence of Darwin on Philosophy*, 44.

precarious world. In his studies in logic he has sought to identify the underlying pattern which he believes inherent in all experimental inquiry. He holds that inquiry—the conscious effort to resolve a problematical situation—defines the function and the structure of the act of reflection. The correlative aim for his work in education has been to construct a method for the school which would correspond to this logical pattern of experimental inquiry.

It should therefore be clear from the foregoing that Dr. Dewey's controversy with the rationalists in education does not stem from the fact that their regard for human thought is higher than his. The controversy really has to do with the nature of intelligence, its subject-matter, and the kind of educational experiences which are required if individuals are to grow in intellectual power.

In the naturalistic world outlook of Dr. Dewey, meanings, as we have seen, are of the world of ordinary experienced events; they do not constitute a realm apart. Principles and universals grow out of the subject-matters of the everyday world and are of the nature of means for ordering empirical affairs; they are not *a priori*, and they cannot be learned effectually apart from their use in social and natural contexts. Meaning, Dr. Dewey declares, "is primarily a property of behavior, and secondarily a property of objects," it "is not indeed a psychic existence."[23]

Nor is reasoning a self-contained autonomous process. It begins in a tensional situation, and its validity is tested by the pertinency of the plans it develops for the resolution of the conditions that create the tension, or problem.

Reasoning, as such, can provide means for effecting the change of conditions but by itself cannot effect it. Only execution of existential operations directed by an idea in which ratiocination terminates can bring about the reordering of environing conditions required to produce a settled and unified situation.[24]

The rationalists therefore cannot validate their educational views as opposed to those of Dr. Dewey merely by praising the

[23] *Experience and Nature*, 179.
[24] *Logic; The Theory of Inquiry*, 118.

intellectual virtues. If they want educators to take their theories seriously, they will have to show that their view of the nature of intelligence, of the actual world in which it operates, and of the means by which the young develop intelligence is superior to that outlined by Dr. Dewey. His respect for intelligence is so high that he has not been content merely to eulogize it; he has gone on to analyze its nature and to show the relations it sustains to other forms of experience. It is on the basis of these analyses that he has developed his theory of education. Therefore it is not surprising that the leaders of the schools have been influenced by his creative studies.

Dr. Dewey's naturalistic outlook has implications, in the second place, for what is to be considered worthy of a place in the curriculum. A world in which existence is precarious places a premium on control. From the naturalistic standpoint, man has gained this control as he has learned to abandon appeals to supernatural and magical powers, and has directed his attention instead t he construction of tools and techniques for the reshaping of natural materials and conditions. With the increase of his tools his personal powers have expanded, his ways of making a living have become more diversified, his needs and interests have multiplied, and his life in general has grown in significance. Man has prized his tools, not only for their utility, but also for the new dimensions they have added to his experience. He has regarded them as extensions of his own personality and he has striven to perfect and beautify them. Thus art, technique, and interest in the practical have been "dynamically continuous" in the course of civilization.

Scientific interests have also grown out of this invention and use of tools. For a tool "denotes a perception and acknowledgement of sequential bonds in nature."[25] Dr. Dewey believes that it is from the habits of observation and the experimental manipulation of materials which are involved in the making and use of tools, that science has developed both as technological invention, and as controlled method for the achievement of knowledge. The naturalistic notion of cause and effect is implicit in every invention and use of a tool. "That the sciences

[25] *Experience and Nature*, 123.

were born of the arts, the physical sciences of the crafts and technologies of healing, navigation, war and the working of wood,
metals, leather, flax and wool; the mental sciences from the art
of political management, is, I suppose, an admitted fact."[26]

These considerations carry important educational consequences for Dr. Dewey. He has been impatient with any view
of the curriculum which sought to omit the technological and
occupational phases of human experience. According to his view,
the intellectual and the practical, the cultural and the vocational, the consummatory and the instrumental—the means of
grace and the means of control—are so organically related in
any satisfactory community life that nothing but harm can come
from tearing them apart in the school. In one of his earliest
books, *School and Society,* he urges that both the practical and
the fine arts be given a fundamental place in the curriculum.
He has often suggested that the occupations of a well-ordered
society might provide the framework for the school curriculum.

All people at the outset, and the majority of people probably all their
lives, attain to some ordering of thought through ordering of action.
Adults normally carry on some occupation, profession, pursuit; and this
furnishes the stabilizing axis about which their knowledge, their beliefs,
and their habits of reaching and testing conclusions are organized.[27]

The liberal and the vocational are thus not opposed in Dr.
Dewey's educational thought. He has, however, consistently
opposed any program of vocational education which emphasized the achievement of mechanical skill to the neglect of
genuine intellectual and cultural interests.

Finally, experimental naturalism has implications for the way
in which the ultimate aims of education are to be conceived and
derived. Dr. Dewey even asserts "that the final issue of empirical method is whether the guide and standard of beliefs and
conduct lies within or without the *shareable* situations of life."[28]
His conception of the significance of education has been profoundly conditioned by the conviction that the ends and standards of life should be generated coöperatively from within the
process of experience.

[26] *Ibid.,* 128.
[27] *How We Think,* Revised Edition, 49.
[28] *Experience and Nature,* 38.

Experience, as already indicated, is viewed by Dr. Dewey as primarily a process of interaction between a living creature and its environment. The environment is the sole source of the energies and the means essential to the life and growth of the organism. But the surrounding conditions and energies are many and various: some signify food, health and growth for the living form; others threaten disease, injury and possible extinction. Hence the effort to maintain relations with environing affairs which sustain its functions is primary in the behavior of every living thing. Such selective adjustments as result in the attainment of these life-giving relations define what is meant by satisfaction, and human satisfaction is the basis for whatever is to be counted good.

With human beings this struggle is carried on by groups, and becomes consciously purposeful. Adjustment is no longer a one-way process; through coöperative effort the environment itself is deliberately re-constituted so as to provide more ample and secure means for the maintenance of the interests of the group. By this cumulative process human activities have become informed with meaning, but by meanings evolved from within the activities of the group, not from sources external to them.

Dr. Dewey believes that this logic of experimental behavior developed to deal with problems of practical adjustment is also competent to deal with problems of value. The ultimate source of values, he holds, lies within the concrete experiences of desire and satisfaction. But he also recognizes that "it is a matter of frequent experience that likings and enjoyments are of all kinds, and that many are such as reflective judgments condemn."[29]

Hence not all experiences of immediate satisfaction can be considered values—"using that word to designate whatever is taken to have rightful authority in the direction of conduct."[30] By what process can we distinguish which of those things that are immediately liked are also real objects of value? Dr. Dewey answers, by the process of judgment: "to call an object a value is to assert that it satisfies or fulfills certain conditions."[31] But

[29] *The Quest for Certainty*, 263.
[30] *Ibid.*, 256.
[31] *Ibid.*, 260.

how can we tell whether a desired activity or object is of the conditions which make for growth? By the study of its consequences in group and personal experience, not by the process of mystical intuition, nor by reliance on absolute standards alleged to be derived from some source beyond experience. An activity or a thing is to be judged a good—a value—if it makes for further all-round growth. By their fruits in everyday experience—personal and social—they are to be known and evaluated and by no other means. Dr. Dewey proposes the following tests:

Does this form of growth create conditions for further growth or does it set up conditions that shut off the person who has grown in this particular direction from the occasions, stimuli and opportunities for continuing growth in new directions? What is the effect of growth in a special direction upon the attitudes and habits which alone open up avenues for development in other lines? [32]

Thus life creates its own sanctions for conduct as it learns to judge consequences. That which makes for continued growth of flesh and blood human beings in their social relations is the end—the end for life and the end for education.

Our net conclusion is that life is development, and that developing, growing, is life. Translated into its educational equivalents, this means 1) that the educational process has no end beyond itself; it is its own end; and that 2) the educational process is one of continued reorganizing, reconstructing, transforming. [33]

Put to the test of actual educational experience this conception of education as its own end has been found to posssess a certain ambiguity. We may recognize with Dr. Dewey that experience is the ultimate criterion of both truth and value, and that education is all one with the process of growth, and still maintain that it is costly to let the immature derive their findings about truth and value exclusively from their own trial and error experiences. Put in this extreme form, the principle signifies the negation of adult guidance, and is thus contradictory to the very essence of deliberate education. Dr. Dewey himself,

[32] *Experience and Education*, 29.
[33] *Democracy and Education*, 59.

of course, has never supposed that desirable conditions for education of the young meant the absence of adult guidance. But, unfortunately, his conception of education as its own end has been used by some to support the notion that all guidance by adults is a form of "imposition" on the child, and is therefore contrary to the conception of education as a process of experiencing which generates its own standards and controls wholly from within itself. As Dr. Dewey has emphasized, it is one thing to say that the kingdom of meaning and value lies wholly within the realm of ordinary experience; it is another and quite different thing to assume that truths and values unfold spontaneously from within the unguided activities of children.

IV. Society and Education

Although Dr. Dewey's philosophy of education is consistently naturalistic, it is most widely known for its emphasis on the social. Many consider Dr. Dewey's social interpretation of education his most distinctive contribution to educational theory. This suggests that a thorough-going naturalistic point of view is wholly compatible with high regard for the distinctively human, or social. Indeed, Dr. Dewey's emphasis on the social is the correlative of his emphasis on the natural. His experimental naturalism requires, on the one hand, that he accept without reservation the principle of continuity between man and the rest of nature. It demands, on the other hand, that he also recognize "the extraordinary differences that mark off the activities and the achievements of human beings from those of other biological forms."[34] These "extraordinary differences" can be explained naturalistically only as consideration is given to the new properties behavior acquires at the social level. The social, according to Dr. Dewey, provides the natural bridge from behavior that is organic to behavior that is distinctively human. We can better appreciate the significance of his social theory of education when we view it as the natural out-growth of the empirical view of man and nature which has already been outlined.

First, he holds that education should be considered social

[34] *Logic; The Theory of Inquiry*, 43.

because meanings are properties of a kind of behavior which appears only in a society in which language has made deliberate communication possible. This process of communication transformed the natural environment into a cultural environment and in so doing "created the realm of meanings."[35] Meanings, therefore, are not mysterious intrusions in the natural order of events; they are not impotent, or illusory; and they do not denote an immutable, ideal structure, or grammar of existence subsisting apart from human discourse and those group activities which have reconstituted the natural environment for purposes of human control, use, and enjoyment. Meanings, on the contrary, emerge from within those coöperative human activities which culminate in consciousness of self and in significant communication.

When we turn to the social, we find communication to be an existential occurrence involved in all distinctively communal life, and we find that communication requires meaning and understanding as conditions of unity or agreement in conjoint behavior. We find, that is, meaning to be not an anomaly nor an accidentally supervening quality but a constituent ingredient of existential events.[36]

Now natural events acquire new properties when they are involved in the associated activities of human beings. When thus incorporated into purposeful human affairs, physical events function as signs of distant and future occurrences. They carry messages which can be read and utilized to guide human interactions with the environment. Natural occurrences are no longer merely physical things—they have become intellectual objects and carry implications by virtue of the rôles they now play in human activity.

When events have communicable meaning, they have marks, notations, and are capable of con-notation and de-notation. They are more than mere occurrences; they have implications. Hence inference and reasoning are possible; these operations are reading the message of things, which things utter because they are involved in human associations.[37]

Since the realm of meanings and values is created and con-

[35] *Experience and Nature*, 168.
[36] *Philosophy and Civilization*, 87.
[37] *Experience and Nature*, 174.

served by the organized life of society, the materials of education—its content and purposes—are social in nature.

Secondly, Dr. Dewey contends that education should be
viewed as a social process, because it is by participation in the
activities and meanings of society that the child learns the behaviors which are characteristic of person-hood. The infant at
birth is not a mind, nor would it achieve mind in any significant
sense apart from its nurture by a cultural environment. "Everything which is distinctively human is learned, not native, even
though it could not be learned without native structures which
mark man off from other animals."[38] Thus society with its
meanings stored in books, tools, techniques, occupations, customs, mores, and institutions, constitutes an objective realm of
mind. It is this society with its established modes of action and
thought which patterns the conduct of the child, and which,
therefore, functions as the great educator.

Every domesticated plant and animal, every tool, every utensil, every
appliance, every manufactured article, every æsthetic decoration, every
work of art means a transformation of conditions once hostile or indifferent to characteristic human activities into friendly and favoring conditions. Because the activities of children today are controlled by these
selected and charged stimuli, children are able to traverse in a short
lifetime what the race has needed slow tortured ages to attain.[39]

A cultural environment contains "charged stimuli" not
merely because it is an environment of persons, but also because
it is no longer an environment of bare physical things. By participating in the activities of their group, children early learn
to respond to things in terms of their connections with other
events, in terms of their rôles as human means, and in terms
of their potential consequences for human life. Meanings thus
become part of the very essence of things for the young and
operate as directing factors in their experience. Because he grows
up in a society "the occasions in which a human being responds
to things as merely physical in purely physical ways are comparatively rare."[40] The aim of education should be to help the

[38] *The Public and Its Problems*, 154.
[39] *Democracy and Education*, 44.
[40] *Logic; The Theory of Inquiry*, 42.

child act as a member of his group, and to be aware of the meanings inherent in his action.

Thirdly, education should be interpreted as a social process because the construction of the aims for education requires study of the child in connection with the conditions and institutions of his society. Taken in isolation from his society the individual is an abstraction. There is, to be sure, the important factor of organic individuality, and the human organism has its native needs and impulses. But these organic needs "are growing, not fixed; the needs for food, for protection, for reproduction, for example, are always the same in the abstract, but in the concrete they and the means of satisfying them change their content with every change in science, technology, and social institutions."[41]

The same considerations also hold for the powers of the child. We cannot discern these powers merely by an inspection of the individual human organism, no matter how thorough and objective that inspection may become. Powers, like functions, are relative to the culture as well as to the individual organism. So far as the inherited native equipment is concerned, it is almost indefinitely plastic in a normal child, and can be patterned into a wide variety of possible adult selves. Which of these potential selves shall become actual depends not only upon the child's organic equipment; it depends also upon what we see in our society in the form of activities, resources, limitations, possibilities and values.

Fourthly, Dr. Dewey believes that education should be interpreted from the social standpoint because each society insures its own continuance through the education of its young. No matter how superior its ways of life may be, the new-born are not disposed by organic constitution to prefer them. "What nutrition and reproduction are to physiological life, education is to social life."[42] By sharing its experience through a process of communication society transmits its ways to the young, and thus perpetuates itself.

There is more than a verbal tie between the words common, community, and communication. Men live in a community in virtue of the things

---

[41] Dewey: *The Social Frontier*, Vol. III, No. 21 (Dec. 1936), 71.
[42] *Democracy and Education*, 11.

which they have in common; and communication is the way in which they come to possess things in common. . . . The communication which insures participation in a common understanding is one which secures similar emotional and intellectual dispositions—like ways of responding to expectations and requirements.[43]

Much that the child learns is acquired incidentally in connection with his participation in the affairs of the community. In advanced cultures, however, the older members of the group provide special agencies such as the school for the deliberate induction of the young into their techniques, outlooks and values. In thus preparing its affairs for purposes of deliberate communication, a society is compelled to become more conscious of the principles and ideals implicit in its established practices. Thus education gives opportunity for re-examination and re-evaluation of a group's modes of life and thought. Unfortunately, most societies are so concerned to weave the patterns of their existing culture into the habits and dispositions of the young, "original modifiability has not been given a fair chance to act as a trustee for a better human life."[44]

Fifthly, education should be viewed as an affair of the ongoing life of society, because it is in society that the young will work out their careers after they leave school. To understand their society it is unconditionally important that they should see it against the background of the past from which it has come. But that past is the past of the present; nothing but disaster can come when education seeks to make the ways of the past a rival or substitute for the ways of today. As a naturalist, Dr. Dewey would endorse, I think, the following trenchant criticism of any attempt to make the classics the core of the curriculum.

The source of Greek intelligence and its products was not antiquity but nature. Those ancients drew from an inexhaustible source, one not located in the past or traditionally guarded, but one surrounding them and enfolding them with wonders daily new. The moment they forgot that source, they might still teach the wisdom of the fathers to the Romans; but they ceased to be productive. They could hold up examples to imitate, but they could produce no new models. Now, humanism in its educational program has interested itself in the past of man, in what

[43] *Ibid.*, 5.
[44] *Human Nature and Conduct*, 97.

he has accomplished rather than in the immediate sources of his inspiration. It has sedulously cultivated the classic tendency. By that I mean that it has placed the foundations of human excellence in the past achievements of certain men, and not in the experience of living persons. It has shut human life up in books, making these books authoritative and forgetting that the men who wrote them wrote, not out of contemplation of the past, but out of the richness of their own experience. That is why humanism was bound to exhaust itself.[45]

Dr. Dewey's philosophy of experience has too much respect for the findings of experience to slight the struggles and achievements of the past; it also has too much respect for experience as a present on-going affair to want to make devotion to the past a mode of escape from the problems and the possibilities of the present.

V. DEMOCRACY AND EDUCATION

The conception of education as a social process contributes an indispensable orientation for educational thought and practice, but it remains abstract and formal until factors of time and place are taken into account. Human beings act for different and conflicting ends, and the consequences of these differences in social purpose are critically important in education. For example, totalitarian, authoritarian, liberal-democratic, and laissez-faire-individualistic forms of group-life, all alike are social. Each of these types of human association, moreover, contains its distinctive patterns for the education of the young. Hence an expression of preference for some definite form of social life is inherent in every educational program. Dr. Dewey has emphasized this point: "The conception of education as a social process and function has no definite meaning until we define the kind of society we have in mind."[46]

His own philosophy of education is grounded in the democratic conception. Dr. Dewey believes that his preference for the democratic way of life is not arbitrary, and not merely due to the fact that he happens to be a member of a society which calls itself democratic, and which taught him in his early years "that democracy is the best of all social institutions."[47] Democ-

[45] Woodbridge: *Nature and Mind*, 89-90.
[46] *Democracy and Education*, 112.
[47] *Experience and Education*, 25.

racy, in his opinion, signifies the effort to conduct the affairs of society on an ethical basis. He is convinced that any society which is concerned to give its members the highest quality of experience, both materially and culturally, will be led to organize its affairs along democratic lines.

In this concluding section, some of the major meanings that Dr. Dewey finds in the democratic ideal will be examined from the standpoint of their implications for education.

First, democracy, according to Dr. Dewey, is an attempt to embody in our social relationships the principle which regards each individual as possessing intrinsic worth or dignity. He has urged that this principle be interpreted to include children as well as adults; for the child, he contends, is a developing person, and not merely a potential ideal self. The implication for education is that the child's present experience, uniqueness, and felt needs and interests are to play their part in the determination of the educational program. To meet this requirement of the democratic ideal, the school must be equipped to deal with each child as an individual, and not merely as an item in some class or age-group.

Secondly, the democratic conception implies a society in which individuals enjoy the status of ends, and institutions the status of means. Society has no good other than the good of its members. The concrete individual is the only center of experience, and hence the ultimate locus of all value. Dr. Dewey believes the growth of this actual individual is the supreme test of social arrangements, and the final end of all educational activity.

Democracy has many meanings, but if it has a moral meaning, it is found in resolving that the supreme test of all political institutions and industrial arrangements shall be the contribution they make to the all-round growth of every member of society.[48]

The social corollary of this democratic ideal is that a society must be ever alert to provide that equality of opportunity which permits each individual to develop his own unique capacities, and to make his own career. Among other things, this implies genuine educational opportunity for all. Adherence to this democratic ideal has made Dr. Dewey a vigorous champion of

[48] *Reconstruction in Philosophy*, 186.

public education. He has wanted every child, regardless of the race, or the religion, or the occupation of its parents, to have a chance to make the most of his possibilities.

Thirdly, the democratic principle that each individual be treated as an end signifies that the individual must be so educated that he shall be competent to judge of values. To be intelligent about values the individual must have knowledge of life-conditions and institutions—scientific, technological, economic, political, domestic, "cultural" and religious. If he is to perceive the possibilities and the limitations of institutionalized arrangements, he needs knowledge of the past from which they have come, knowledge of the actual conditions under which they now operate, and of the future which they prefigure. Only as he learns to view his own experience and that of his fellows in the matrix of these technological and social conditions can he be intelligent about his interests, and competent to share in the construction of purposes for himself and his society.

Fourthly, a democratic society which has respect for the individual will also prize individual differences and uniqueness. It will aim to provide maximum opportunity for individuals to initiate voluntary interest groups and associations. Since "diversity of stimulation means novelty, and novelty means challenge to thought,"[49] a democratic society will seek to encourage a healthy diversity, restricting it only where necessary to secure that coördination which is required for the maintenance of the welfare of all. Thus a democratic society implies a plurality of groups and a distribution of power: it is not compatible with a totalitarian state in which all forms of association and power are concentrated in one political party. "Since a democratic society repudiates the principle of external authority, it must find a substitute in voluntary disposition and interest; these can be created only by education."[50]

Fifthly, Dr. Dewey's interest in democracy also emphasizes the importance of method in education. A society composed of many diverse interest groups, and one in which power is distributed among all of its members, is a society in which conflicts of interest and value are bound to arise. These conflicts

[49] *Democracy and Education*, 98.
[50] *Ibid.*, 101.

will appear not only between groups, but also within the same group whenever new possibilities compete with older routines. Democracy, therefore, has great need for a method for the resolution of conflict. It cannot make adjustments by external authority, or by the application of fixed standards, and remain a democratic society. It seeks to make its adjustments by inquiry, discussion, conference, and the principle of majority rule. Dr. Dewey has sought to organize the school so as to give the young actual experience in this process of making adjustments by the method of conference and mutual give and take.

Finally, Dr. Dewey holds that present conditions in American society are such as to constitute a real threat to our democratic heritage. Existing economic and legal arrangements have so concentrated wealth in the hands of a small class that equality of opportunity has been destroyed in the economic sphere. This privileged class also seeks to maintain its position by restricting that free expression of thought, and that experimental use of intelligence which are foundational in a democratic society.

Dr. Dewey concludes that both democracy and education demand that the anarchy of the present competitive profit economy be supplanted by a planning society in which production is democratically controlled for the good of all.

An identity, an equation, exists between the urgent social need of the present and that of education. Society, in order to solve its own problems and remedy its own ills, needs to employ science and technology for social instead of merely private ends. This need for a society in which experimental inquiry and planning for social ends are organically contained is also the need for a new education.[51]

The supreme task of our generation is to bring about this social transformation. It is Dr. Dewey's faith that this transformation can be achieved by coöperative, peaceful economic and political means, provided education can be kept free to carry on its functions of criticism and construction.

JOHN L. CHILDS

TEACHERS COLLEGE
COLUMBIA UNIVERSITY

[51] Dewey: *The Educational Frontier* (W. H. Kilpatrick, editor), 64.

15

William H. Kilpatrick

DEWEY'S INFLUENCE ON EDUCATION

DEWEY'S INFLUENCE ON EDUCATION

NO one who is informed in the educational field can doubt for a moment the profound influence of John Dewey on both the theory and the practice of American education. And the more closely the matter is studied, the clearer appears the character of that influence. Nor is the effect confined to this country. Considering indirect as well as direct influences, one can safely assert that there are few countries in the world that show no effect of Dewey's thought. Rarely, if ever, has one man seen in his lifetime such widespread and defined effects flow from his teachings.

This chapter will contemplate, but of course not duplicate, the discussion of philosophy of education that appears in the preceding chapter. Here the effort is to trace the changes in the theory and practice of actual education brought about by the work of John Dewey. It goes without saying that it would be improper and unscientific to claim that Dewey has effected all the changes that now appear in line with his teachings. The same culture and historic influences that produced him had already been for some time more or less definitely at work not only in America but as well throughout the Western world. In consequence he found a world already largely disposed to consider favorably what he had to say. In this way, he is part of a larger movement. It is not without significance that he was born in the very year that saw the publication of Darwin's *Origin of Species*. His intellectual maturity came during the years when intelligent thought having accepted the evolutionary outlook was asking as to its second generation and deeper implications.

But if Dewey found a world in part congenial with his deepest vision, it is no less true that he found much to combat. It was then as now a world of many warring ideals. In education, which here concerns us, there was not only an old and discordant background to be evaluated and remade, but there were from the first, and have been during his whole career, many and diverse voices clamoring against each other for acceptance. It is not in peace that Dewey has eaten his bread nor given forth his ideas. From first to last he has felt called upon to oppose certain positions and defend others. Let us begin our inquiry by asking as to the background situation when John Dewey began to consider the problem of education. Only as we understand this can we understand his reactions, partly to oppose and correct, partly to clarify and strengthen, partly, and most significantly, to suggest new outlooks.

I. THE OLDEST BACKGROUND

The oldest defined strain in the American educational background was that brought by the colonists from Europe, chiefly of course from Great Britain. As far as Dewey was concerned this had, to be sure, been already remade in some measure during the Revolutionary era and much more so in the days of Horace Mann and Henry Barnard when the public free school was given its fixed place in American life. This oldest strain as thus modified was, however, still going strong in the seventies and eighties, and in fact forms much of the background of popular attitude today.

In origin this oldest strain was strongly Protestant, Puritan in New England, and mainly Scotch-Irish Presbyterian elsewhere. On the credit side of this we reckon a strong ethical outlook, the politico-religious doctrine of freedom of conscience, and a strong interest in universal education. On the debit side, as we now see it, we reckon the distrust of "human nature," the strong belief in vindictive punishment, and the theory that knowledge and proper conduct come authoritatively from the outside, specifically to youth from elders, who in their turn get what they know and have, ultimately, by divine revelation or by the trained intuition of self-evident absolute truths. Along with this same authoritarian theological philosophy went also a scholastic faith in a faculty psychology and formal discipline, and a schoolmaster faith in regimentation, drill, and memorizing.

From another angle this American background included a further potent element, probably inherited ultimately from Alexandria, that schooling is properly the acquisition of subject-matter-set-out-to-be-learned, study being the effort—mainly by drill and memorization—to acquire this set-out content, that learning is the successful acquisition of this subject matter, and that the proper and adequate test is whether the child can give back on demand precisely what had been originally so set out. It was on this theory of knowledge and learning, as Dewey well brings out in *The Educational Situation* (1902), that the graded school was built and its institutionalization effected. And it is because of this particular institutionalization, and its emotional acceptance in the popular mind, that the reformers have found it so difficult to introduce any real improvement into school procedures. The persistence of credit marks and of the promotion concept, for example, bear testimony to the strength of this subject matter theory in the educational tradition. When John Dewey first appeared on the scene, the old untrustworthiness of human nature with its harsh punishment and its domineering schoolmaster tyranny was disappearing into the past. Horace Mann's fight with the Boston schoolmasters over their 65 whippings a day in "a representative school of four hundred children" had won out, at least in principle. But in many parts the old practice lingered on for yet many years. In 1866, in the very year, we may suppose, when the youthful John began school in Vermont, an institute worker of New York state thus expressed a prevalent schoolmaster opinion:

The teacher's authority as absolute, must be imperative, rather than deliberative or demonstrative. His requirements and decisions, in whatever form presented, whether that of request, demand, or mandate, must be unargued. What he resolves upon and pronounces law, should be simply and steadily insisted upon as right *per se*, and should be promptly and fully accepted by the pupil as right, on the one ground that the teacher, as such, is governor.[1]

The faculty psychology, referred to above, deserves perhaps a further word. According to this, man had various faculties, for example memory, reasoning, accuracy, discrimination, imagina-

[1] Frederick S. Jewell, *School Government* (New York, 1866), 54.

tion, and the like. Such a faculty was an entity that had an existence of its own. In some way, now obscure, the faculty of memory, for example, did one's remembering for him. Not he, but
it remembered, or reasoned, or discriminated, or imagined, as
the case might be; and each such faculty being a thing in its own
right could be trained so that it thereafter did a better job of remembering or reasoning or discriminating, wherever it might
be applied, and this irrespective of the content on which it had
been trained or "disciplined," to use the older term. Such training was "formal," not "content," discipline.

Likely enough some who read these words will feel a certain
impatience at being asked to recall this dead past. To this two
answers may be returned, one that we must recall the actual
situation in which Dewey began his professional career, and the
other that varied treatments of certain of these old problems
help to show Dewey's answer and position in contrast with the
others given.

More specifically, these once prevalent psychological attitudes reinforced each other in a way to keep them all going
longer than their separate merits would warrant. Any wrong-
doing *ipso facto* required punishment to vindicate the authority
of law as well as uphold the personal authority of the master.
The child's depraved nature explained why he was not interested in his studies, which had been so ostentatiously arranged
for his good. Also as this life was a preparation and discipline
for the life to come, so was childhood a proper time of preparation and discipline for his future adulthood. Particularly was
the disciplining of the natural impulses important, because the
child was by nature averse to good and inclined to evil. If a child
did not like what was required of him, his very aversion was
perhaps sign that it was good for him. In disciplining his faculties, it was not at all necessary that the content of study have
any present meaning or bearing for the child in the child's life.
It was training that was sought, exercise of an already existent
faculty. Once the faculty had been properly disciplined it could
then be applied as needed to any required matter or content.
That the training did not otherwise enter into the child's life
or thought was quite beside the mark.

So much for the older and harsher element in our educational background. The writer himself recalls hearing in his younger days the positive advocacy of all that he has here written. Not that all believed it, nor that all practice was based on it, but that it definitely formed the background and foundational thinking of the people generally and might at any time be called up in support of some otherwise indefensible practice.[2]

But already two or three decades preceding John Dewey, Horace Mann, Henry Barnard and others had reached a new outlook of respect for childhood. Most of these better ideas were traceable directly or indirectly to Pestalozzi. A number of early mid-century studies of the Prussian schools had brought the best European thought to America and on this foundation the grading of schools, a more humane treatment of children, and the specific preparation of teachers in normal schools had been begun. By the eighties and nineties these reform ideas had been accepted in theory and to a considerable degree in practice, and a new set of European ideas were being brought forward as a further reform. These lead us directly to John Dewey's time.

II. The Educational Foreground at Dewey's Start

John Dewey, of course, began and has remained primarily a student of philosophy. In this interest, the psychological and ethical aspects were for him particularly strong from the beginning. Just when or how the young professor was led to a study of education is unknown to this writer except that his initial appointment at Chicago was (at his instance) to the headship of the Department of Philosophy, Psychology, and Education and that education was early felt to be inherent in the newer philosophy that was coming into being in his mind. For example, an idea was not an idea in any full sense until it was enacted in the actual situation to effect some purpose. On no other basis could its adequacy be tested and its deficiencies corrected. Moreover,

[2] It is perhaps pertinent, and at least interesting, that in the evening of the very day whose morning saw these words written, the writer heard a Balliol don defend "the classical curriculum" on exactly the lines sketched above, including specifically the faculty psychology and formal discipline. Theories, it is said, often live on—especially in sheltered places—long after their brains have been knocked out.

an idea could be initially conceived in any full sense only as the person concerned was himself involved in a situation which, on the one hand, called forth the idea and, on the other, called for the application of the idea so as to modify and control the situation.

This is to say, too briefly to be sure, that this philosophy properly required its own incarnation in order to be itself and to get itself adequately studied and criticized. And such an incarnation within the ongoing life of any personality would *ipso facto* be an educative experience which would of necessity change that person. In this way philosophy and education early became for Dewey two complementary phases of one ongoing intellectual process, each phase exhibiting and correcting the other.

While we lack any detailed contemporary account of how the philosophy-then-coming-into-being interacted with surrounding educational ideas, we have nevertheless a wealth of source material from which such a history could be written. How Dewey's early Hegelianism entered into his educational thinking will later appear. Let us now consider some of the principal educational movements of the eighties and nineties. For it was with these that John Dewey interacted in such a way as to redirect the current of American educational thought.

Among the most prominent educational influences of the time was Colonel Francis W. Parker, first prominent at Quincy, Mass., and later at the Cook County Normal School. No one who ever knew him can forget his wholesome enthusiasm for childhood and his faith in humanity. Every ounce of his 225 pounds exuded both enthusiasm and faith, and the effect was great. First at Quincy and later in Chicago he introduced life and spirit into the school, and freed teacher and pupil alike to live and experiment. If neither the Herbartians nor John Dewey had ever appeared on the scene, Parker himself would—save for one thing—have remade the schools of America. His schools anticipated in many vital respects the best modern practice. This writer recalls to this day, forty-five years later, the inspiration he got from *The Quincy Methods*, an account by Miss Lelia E. Patrick[3] of what went on in the Quincy schools.

[3] New York, 1885.

The one thing Colonel Parker lacked was theory, any really systematic philosophy of education. Well has it been said that theory is in the end the most practical of all things. Parker knew, as few others, how both children and teachers feel and act, and he provided both opportunity and encouragement for highly educative experiences. But, in spite of all this, he could not tell in any intellectually convincing way why he thus thought. His insight lacked inherent connection with any inclusive and fundamental outlook on life. That Dewey saw both the strengths of Parker's practice and the lack of adequate theory needs hardly be argued. It is impossible to believe that one so sensitive as Dewey was not influenced by one so magnetic as Parker, and equally impossible to suppose that he was not stirred to supply the lack of adequate theory, especially as his own growing philosophy inherently reached out in the direction of Parker's practice.

The kindergarten was a second line of influence in Dewey's early days. Once he had got started upon the study of education he would of necessity consider the kindergarten, that school without books, a school in which the teacher was explicitly expected to live with the children. Froebel, particularly in his *Education of Man*, had given the world no mean anticipation of Dewey's own school. There is, moreover, significance in the fact that Froebel founded his doctrine and practice on a conscious philosophy, the very thing Dewey was himself in process of doing. As we compare the two systems we see many similarities. Both stress child activity. Both find learning to be part and parcel of the process of actual living. Both subordinate books to life. That Dewey reacted to kindergarten we know from various references in his early writing. His rejection of Froebel's doctrine of development as the unfolding of latency is a case in point. In these and other respects it is easy to believe that Dewey found Froebel grist to his mill.*

* Since the above was written Professor Dewey has told the writer of his indebtedness to Miss Anna E. Bryan's reformed kindergarten for suggestions that influenced the experience provided for young children in his own Laboratory School. Miss Bryan had but recently come to Chicago from Louisville, Ky., where she had already stirred the creative imagination of Miss Patty S. Hill, who (as we shall later see) was powerfully to influence the education of the young child from two to eight.

W. T. Harris is another factor to be reckoned with. He presents an interesting and related instance of educational philosophy. As a strong Hegelian Harris would appeal to Dewey at least in the beginning of the latter's Hegelian period. But as Dewey moved away from Hegel, he moved specifically away from Harris's brand of education. It was said above of Parker that he lacked any deep-rooted and inclusive theory and therefore failed to spread in any vital degree his highly significant educational practice. Harris, too, in spite of great influence in his lifetime has failed to leave any especially lasting effects. Just why is not at once evident. He had at his disposal one of the outstanding philosophies of modern times and he built—so he thought—his education effectively thereon. As just said, he was in his own day one of the most outstanding leaders of American education, but where is he now? Who reads him or quotes him? His surviving influence is even less than Parker's. One ventures two reasons in explanation; one that his Hegelianism meets small response in the American mind; the other is that Dewey came just in time to supplant him. How this is so, we shall in part see in immediate connection with the Herbartians.

What appeared for a while the most promisingly fruitful of the educational groups that Dewey faced was that of the Herbartians, principally Charles De Garmo and Charles and Frank McMurry. These men began around 1890 to teach in America what they had learned, principally, at Jena. It concerns us here to present their doctrines only so far as John Dewey reacted to them. For this it perhaps will suffice to consider here only the doctrine of interest, leaving any others for further consideration.

By 1895 there had arisen a considerable dispute over the Herbartian doctrine of interest. This doctrine was the easy and perhaps necessary corollary of the Herbartian psychology, essentially that ideas and mind (and character) were to be built by the child under teacher direction—in fact almost in the child by the teacher; and that any suitably organized aggregate of ideas (called by Herbart the apperceptive mass) assumed therein a certain autonomy in the child's experience, favoring thereafter any ideas that fitted suitably with the apperceptive mass and opposing those that did not. This favorable attitude of the apperceptive mass for suitably related ideas—but not otherwise related to ends or aims—formed the basis of the Herbartian interest; so that the fact of present interest becomes the necessary condition for successful learning, but as intimated it was interest unrelated to purpose. And upon this principle the five formal steps of Herbartian pedagogy were based.

Such a conception of the educative process was clearly a schoolmaster's affair, as Dewey pointed out. It was based on the theory of subject-matter-set-out-to-be-learned. And the doctrine of interest became (especially in the hands of the less thoughtful) a process of sugar-coating so as to make the assigned learning more palatable. Against this, Dr. Harris and other stalwarts stoutly reacted. Sugar-coating, they said, meant humoring and spoiling the child so that serious effort was never called into play, with the result that a weak character must be expected. These opponents, on their part, would refuse all such sugar-coating and instead would institute a healthy regime of "effort," in which children were not asked what they wished but were told what they must do. To this the Herbartians (of the better sort) replied that interest was in fact the sole guarantee of attention and learning, and that the enforced "effort" of the Harris group must build either a dull and docile character or a rebellious one, neither of which was desirable.

III. Dewey's Interest as Related to Will

It was this dispute that called forth from John Dewey his *Interest as Related to Will*[4] (rewritten in 1913 as *Interest and Effort*). If the writer of these lines can judge at this distance, this article was epochmaking. Certainly it proved to be to this writer. This is the first of Dewey's distinctive contributions to education, and contains implicitly if not explicitly most of his significant doctrines.

The essay starts, most fundamentally perhaps of all, with a biological psychology. The organism (in this case the child) is of necessity, if life is to go on, in interaction with his environ-

---

[4] This appeared first in the *Second Supplement to the Herbart Year Book for 1895* (Bloomington, Ill., 1896), 209-255.

ment, and the whole discussion proceeds on this assumption. Life is exactly that sort of thing. We of today have become so familiar with this organismic conception, to use a recent phrase, that we can hardly conceive what a change it brought in the world's way of thinking. Dewey did not originate this psychologic outlook. For conceiving it—so he has told this writer— he was much indebted to William James, who in turn (we must believe) had built it by development out of Darwin. Next after this biological psychology (of which more later) came Dewey's explicit assumption that the child as a human is a self and not (as certain "behaviorists" would have us believe) simply the most intelligent animal. The fact of selfhood, while wholly natural, differentiates man from beast. This conception of self-hood Dewey got, no doubt, from his Hegelian studies. It forms for him the basis of human (as opposed to mere animal) intelligence and, specifically, of self-critical conduct. In the discussion immediately under consideration this selfhood is manifested in the ability to form conscious purposes out of otherwise animal impulses, and in the further ability to choose means in the light of foreseen consequences. When these things do happen, the self identifies itself—and this is no mere metaphor —primarily with the end in view, for only by so doing can the self be itself; and secondarily, derivedly, identifies itself with the means accepted as appropriate for attaining the end.

With these things before us we are ready to understand Deweys' solution to the alleged conflict between "interest" and "effort." And at this point, we may anticipate, the educational road forks. This doctrine is the crux. Those who see and accept Dewey's contention in this discussion become upholders of what is customarily called the "progressive" outlook. Those who do not, remain traditionalists. Except in ignorance, learned or otherwise, there seems no alternative.

Awake and alert the child is always in action. He is always already intent on something. If the stirring to act be sufficiently great and the surrounding conditions sufficiently novel and difficult, the child will "choose," after more or less of consideration, some object or end which he accepts for the time at least as his purpose and aim. With this, as we saw above, he identifies himself more or less fully. It is such a state of affairs that Dewey uses for defining both interest and effort. As Dewey sees it, we ascribe *interest* to this child so possessed of a purpose when we consider how he feels on the inside as he warms up to his desired end and as agent directs his attention to effecting his purpose. The word interest defines these aspects of such a situation. When we look again at the child, now rather from the "outside" as it were, we see movements in operation which not only tend, by actual observation, to bring the desired end but are, we believe, intended consciously so to serve and so intended as to withstand obstacles if such should arise. When we see and believe such things, we say the child is putting forth *efforts* to gain his end. Interest and effort are thus strict correlatives, not two opposed things but the same thing, the same on-going activity named now with one aspect in mind and now with the other.

The essence of the old opposition between "interest" and "effort" lay, said Dewey, in a common fallacy. Both sides agreed on one common error: they thought that the self is the kind of thing that has to be moved from the outside; that left to itself, it would stand inert. One side of the controversy, therefore, concluded that we should go ahead, as it were, and coax the child along by offering him pleasure, by making things interesting for him. The other side said no to this, that it would weaken the child. They would *make* him act, they would get behind him, as it were, and force him to put forth effort. Both sides are but partial and so are untrue to life and its lessons. The child is already active. He does not stand inert and unconcerned, waiting either to be interested or coerced. On the contrary, in his necessary interaction with the surrounding world he is stirred, at first organically, but later—after self-hood is established—by the conscious choice of what promises to answer to his want. From then on he is goal-seeking in the conscious sense and chooses, more or less critically, his means appropriate to his end.

So many things crowd forward at this point that one must doubt what is wisest to pursue. Possibly the effects of coercion should follow. Interest, as Dewey points out, is the state of affairs when the organism is unified within as it faces the outer world. Coercion is the exact negation of this. In interest one chooses his path as a good. In coercion he chooses what is to him the lesser of two evils. Some older person in control wishes a child to perform an act which the child, left to himself, would not do. Then the elder (if he believes in such) may present the child with a more disagreeable alternative: he must either learn the multiplication tables in school time or stay after school and learn them. Under such conditions, the child wisely decides to meet the teacher's demands. He is, however, not therefore directly interested in the tables, but only indirectly. His direct interest is in avoiding the "staying in" or the bad marks or the teacher's displeasure or (in the old days) the certain whipping. He therefore conforms, but principally on the outside. Inside, he still finds the tables uninteresting and gives himself but partially to them. Thus follows what Dewey calls the danger of a "divided self." If he works long enough under a regime of outward conformity but inward rejection, he will grow warped. Thus did Dewey anticipate what we now call "personality maladjustment."

IV. The Resulting School Procedure

If we followed up all the implications of this discussion of interest and effort, a whole book would not suffice. Accepting this solution as one's educational guide does not mean that there are thenceforth no problems. It does not even mean that there is henceforth no problem of interest and effort. Rather does it mean that the problem is shifted. We wish both interest and effort as truly as did the respective warring factions, but we no longer start with an assignment of set subject matter as an absolute and ask how to get it learned. We start with the child (wherever he may be, with his present stock of interests) and ask how we can help him start where he is and build himself up into an ever more adequate personality. Beginning at this place and working under this doctrine of interest we have enough problems and difficult enough problems to keep us busy for the rest of time. But we at least work with different orientation.

Specifically, we bring at once into play two other of Dewey's significant doctrines, the doctrine of democracy, and the theory of knowledge. To begin with the child and help him to build himself into an ever more adequate personality, respecting himself and considering others—this is democracy, especially as Dewey has helped to define it. To say that this is to spoil the child in that it proposes to "follow the interest of the moment" is, to use kindly words, a surprising misconception. Nothing could be farther from the truth. But this outlook does start with the child and his present interests and it does subordinate subject matter and its learned acquisition to the life and development of the child.

How the child will acquire subject matter, more of it and build it better into the warp and woof of his being than is possible in the old way, follows at once from Dewey's biological psychology (or the doctrine of interest) and his theory of knowledge. On the old theory, knowledge was somehow in existence before man appeared on the scene. It was out there perfect, absolute, and therefore authoritative; and man's business was to take it into his already waiting mind. On Dewey's theory knowledge results from man's effort to deal with the actual world of affairs. As man seeks to meet his wants, his past experience in the shape of accumulated habits and ideas will come forward to help him analyze the situation at hand and suggest promising ways of dealing with it. One who comes to think closely enough may formulate the criticized results of experience into usable form: Under such and such conditions, do thus and so. If one thought still more closely, he might say (with the scientist): When such and such conditions are present, such and such results may be expected to follow. When such formulations are used under varying conditions and still hold true, one naturally gains more confidence in them. As men came to learn, in what we call scientific method, to experiment more carefully and crucially, they could have not only more confidence but could more surely state the limits within which confidence seems justified. These scientifically drawn conclusions give man's most dependable knowledge, but they differ only in degree from man's early common sense conclusions drawn from practical experience. In other words, for Dewey, knowing is in degree, but it has always been present—in degree—since man achieved enough selfhood to criticize in common sense ways what he did and thought.

Now this is exactly the process by which the child learns. As he lives and tries to meet his wants, he learns from experience certain things to do, certain others not to do. The school exists to help him live this same life only better. On the one hand, the good school will, beginning where the child now is, so stir him through its shared life that he will conceive finer and better things to do. The school will then help him pursue the new vision in such way that he comes out of the experience further along, better developed—if possible—throughout his whole self. Nor does this overlook the stored up results of race experience, what Dewey once called "the funded capital of civilization." As the child lives amid his fellows in the school he finds, under the guidance of other pupils, teacher, and librarian, resources that help him do better what he is already concerned to do. Calling thus upon these resources he builds them into his mind, or better into his very being—mind, soul, and body—so that they become now his own, part and parcel of his very being, his because they meet his felt needs, his because he now holds them ready for use.

V. The Dewey School

As we look back we see three principal ways in which John Dewey gave his ideas to the world, through his university lectures, through his books and other writings, and through his school opened at the University of Chicago in 1896. It is not necessary to attempt the impossible of weighing these against each other. But the Laboratory School, as it came to be called, gave in its day a powerful impetus to attendance upon the lectures and even more to the study of the books. The bold daring of a school that could reject completely the ordinary course-of-study curriculum was bound to attract attention, especially because of its connection with so great an institution as the University of Chicago. Many a youthful spirit was stirred by the account of the school to new hopes and new vision. It is of course true that not all who saw it or heard about it were so stirred. Some there were who went to see and returned to scoff. One such rejecter, known to this writer, was so strategically placed in American education that his subsequent prejudice did damage (as the writer sees it) which even yet is positively active. But discussion is, in the long run, the hope of intelligent action, and this the school achieved as could no mere word of tongue or pen. Actual doing has stimulating effects beyond mere proposals. Unfortunately the school did not last, its life was snuffed out in tragedy. But the vision remained, until what was at first startling is by now—at least so far as concerns kindergarten and primary grades—an achieved actuality. The lower school of today that does not approximate the spirit of creative activity and free inquiry there upheld has to defend itself against a hostile profession. And the movement continually spreads upward.

Among the many things that might be said about this Laboratory School, two must here suffice. First, and in general, it was a school founded on experimental study, study by pupils, study by teachers. The pupils studied in the way already sketched in *Interest as Related to Will*, studied the pursuit of self-directed interests, interests that grew as they were pursued. These growing interests were pursued wherever they intelligently might lead, across conventional subject matter lines, across the threshold of the school house door. For these interests were life itself, and life knows no bounds of subject divisions or of buildings. Always does life reach out and across any lines that may in advance be drawn. In such ways did the pupils study, learning ever better how to direct their inquiries more penetratingly, more fruitfully. And the teachers studied, first we may say because they were pioneering, and pioneering in any true sense always requires creative thinking. Second, the teachers studied for the same reason that the pupils studied, because life when really lived calls inherently for study. Novelty continually emerges, the event is always precarious, of necessity we live experimentally. And third, if it be not tautology, this school was being run on a philosophy of experimentalism. Teachers, then as now, must be always learning ever better how to run such a school. There is no end to the experimenting, and so no end to the learning. Never can insight quite catch up with life's ever emerging problems. Life is like that. Study must go on forever. The Dewey school was alive with study.

Second, the Dewey Laboratory School differed from the conventional school in its use of subject matter. The old school as it thought of subject matter disregarded any present life of the learner save as this could be used in preparation for the future. It accordingly looked ahead primarily to adult life, asked what the adult needed to know and do, arranged what was thus needed into logically organized subjects as spelling, reading, writing, arithmetic, history, and the like, and proceeded to teach these by assigning daily quotas for learning. In it all the sole activity expected of the child was that of receiving, acquiring, chiefly by drill and memorizing. That he should exercise any choice—beyond choosing dutifully to do as he was told—was out of the question. That he should create was unthinkable, all that had been done for him; his but to accept. The whole process was one of taking in now for use at a later date.

For Dewey, on the contrary, as stated in *My Pedagogic Creed* (1897),[5] education "is a process of living and not a preparation for future living." "The school must" therefore "represent real life," and "as an institution, should simplify existing social life; should reduce it, as it were, to an embryonic form." "Existing life is so complex that the child cannot be brought into contact with it without either confusion or distraction." The school then as "simplified social life—should grow gradually out of the home life" and accordingly "take up and continue the activities with which the child is already familiar in the home." "The moral education centers upon this conception of the school as a mode of social life." "The best and deepest moral training is precisely that which one gets through

---

[5] Most recently reprinted by the National Education Association as *Personal Growth Leaflet* Number Nineteen. The quotations in this and the two following paragraphs all come from the relatively few pages of this *Creed*, where they can easily be located (between pages twelve and twenty-six).

having to enter into proper relations with others in a unity of work and thought." "The discipline of the school should" therefore "proceed from the life of the school as a whole and not directly from the teacher—the teacher's business is simply to determine, on the basis of larger experience and riper wisdom, how the discipline of life shall come to the child."

As regards curriculum, "the social life of the child" should be taken as "the basis of concentration or correlation—not science, nor literature, nor history, nor geography" as various ones (certain Herbartians, Colonel Parker, and others) had opposingly preferred. Then follows the crux of the Dewey School curriculum: "the only way to make the child conscious of his social heritage is to enable him to perform those fundamental types of activity which make civilization what it is." This provides "the place of cooking, sewing, manual training, etc. in the school." These are not to be thought of as special studies introduced in the way of relaxation or the like but "as types, fundamental forms of social activity." "There is, therefore, no succession of studies in the ideal school curriculum. If education is life, all life has, from the outset, a scientific aspect, an aspect of art and culture, and an aspect of communication. It cannot, therefore, be true that the proper studies of one grade are mere reading and writing, and that at a later grade, reading, or literature, or science, may be introduced. The progress is not in the succession of studies, but in the development of new attitudes towards, and new interests in, experience." "Education must be conceived as a continuing reconstruction of experience." In such a conception "the process and goal of education are one and the same thing."

One is tempted to continue indefinitely quoting from this *Creed*. Our task, however, is not exposition of doctrine, but to show the history of the influence. But because there has been from that day to this so persistent a misrepresentation of Dewey's doctrine of interest it may be well to quote a bit more. "Interests are the signs and symptoms of growing power." They show "the state of development which the child has reached . . . and prophesy the state which he is about to enter." "These interests are neither to be humored nor repressed. To repress interests is to substitute the adult for the child, and so to weaken intellectual curiosity and alertness, to suppress initiative, and to deaden interest. To humor the interests is to substitute the transient for the permanent. The interest is always the sign of some power below; the important thing is to discover the power. To humor the interest is to fail to penetrate below the surface, and its sure result is to substitute caprice and whim for genuine interest." As one relates this condemnation of humoring childish whims with even present-day attacks on Dewey for humoring childish whims, one hardly knows whether to laugh or to weep. Than Dewey himself no one has better stated why we should not exalt the transient nor humor whims. And he did more: he showed how to utilize child interests without doing either.

How much of what we have been reading constitutes abiding achievement? Is it true, as some critics urge, that the history of American education is an unending pendulum swinging from one slogan to another: object lessons, nature study as the center, interest, five formal steps, correlation, problem method, project method, measurement, I.Q. and standardized tests, activity movement, Progressive Education, and so on? Possibly the single answer, no, is too simple for so complex a world, but it comes fairly close to being the defensible truth. Taking a very long term view, say of two centuries, it is easy to see a very great change in educational procedures. Whereas once no picture of a school was complete without a bundle of switches, now no modern American school even thinks of such a thing. Then memorizing without understanding was the rule, now we make understanding a first consideration. Then the learning process was (as stated above) one of dutiful acceptance, now in our better schools it is predominantly one of creative and responsible self-activity.

It would of course be foolish to credit John Dewey with all the change, but it is not foolish, nay it is the solid truth, to say that he more than any other one person is responsible for changing the tone and temper of American education within the past three decades. The kindergarten was once fairly formal. While the children were treated pleasantly, nearly all activity was dictated by the kindergartner. Miss Patty S. Hill is the person who more than any one effected a complete change in the kindergarten. She got part of her original stimulus from Stanley Hall, who in the end of the nineteenth century and beginning of the twentieth was a power in American education, but she got her ideas from the philosophy of John Dewey. Stanley Hall is another instance, like Parker and Harris, of men who in their day exerted wide influence, but now are practically dead. His ideas, like theirs, seem now curiously indefensible. But Dewey's hold on.

And not only the kindergarten but the primary school has been almost completely remade on Dewey's theories. This does not mean that there is unanimity of opinion, and still less that the particular "occupations" work of the Dewey School is now standardized. Far from it. But the underlying doctrines, education as a process of living, the active child, interest (as above discussed), moral education, inherent subject matter—these are now practically for everybody—even critics of Dewey—the standard expectations of primary education.

When we come to the upper elementary grades, much the same thing holds with an added emphasis on the problem approach for which *How We Think* is largely responsible. In this field, especially as the normal schools undertook the preparation for it, Herbartianism once reigned nearly supreme, say from 1898 to 1910. Every good teacher was supposed to have a lesson plan for each class period, and the five formal steps were much in evidence. But with the publication of Dewey's *How We Think* and with McMurry's insistence on "the problem method," Herbartianism faded away. However, let it be emphasized, neither the coming nor the going of Herbartianism was a mere pendulum swing of slogans. In the closer study of the child's interests and in the almost complete change of the old time curriculum, Herbartianism was an improvement over what in general preceded and formed a preparation for better things to come. In the writer's opinion Colonel Parker led a more vital movement, but Herbartianism had a better stated theory and so was easier spread. Both worked together to break up the early tradition of harsh teaching and the slavish use of textbooks and in this way led to Dewey—not pendulum swing but an uneven process of progress.

In lesser degree the upper elementary school too is thus being remade, the country over, and it is John Dewey more than anyone else who has given the fundamental ideas on which the reconstruction is being effected. True enough, one hears criticisms of "fads and frills." Much of the criticism, however, is directed against caricatures that exist rather in the minds of the critics than in fact. Certain it is that on fundamental theory it is not the Dewey group that is giving ground. It is true that some theorists and many parents and laymen, possibly a majority, do not understand the doctrines of interest and of intrinsic subject matter; old ideas always yield slowly. But the doctrines themselves make continual progress in acceptance. The pendulum swing theory does not fit the facts.

The secondary school and college have hitherto been the bulwarks of the old position that subject matter as such must be set out to be learned. Even here a better day dawns. Almost everybody is dissatisfied with the old secondary school. The Aikin Committee, in persuading nearly all of American colleges to accept for eight years the recommended graduates of the thirty designated high schools, has broken down the wall. One dares to hope for better things on the secondary level. And even the colleges are changing. Bennington and Sarah Lawrence, to mention only two, are fairly clear exponents of the Dewey influence; Stephens somewhat less so. There are however, other and contrary movements in the college field, and the future is as yet undertermined.

VI. DEWEY'S SOCIAL OUTLOOK AND INFLUENCE

So far there has been no very explicit consideration of Dewey's social outlook for education; though this has of course all the while been obviously implicit. For Dewey, there were from the first the two sides of education, the psychological and the social, and these were "organically related," neither to be subordinated to the other. While the psychological furnished the starting point, it taken alone would be barren and formal.

The social is necessary to give direction and meaning to the psychological.

Along four lines Dewey has especially helped American education to more adequate social outlooks. First, the self is a social construct. There can be no such thing as a purely individualistic (solipsistic) outlook. All deliberative thinking is conditioned on the social nature of meaning. This position while abundantly evident in Dewey's writings is not specifically treated at any length in his educational works. So that his direct influence here is not as great as on some other points. Second, moral right and wrong get their definition from social consequences. Here Dewey's contribution is wider and more definite than with the preceding. Professor Frank McMurry has told the writer of the surprised incredulity with which the audience heard *Ethical Principles Underlying Education* presented in 1897. To place morals on a naturalistic basis came as a surprise and shock to many who heard him at that time. But it is not so now; and Dewey has been one main cause for the change of attitude.

A third line we have already seen in the discussion of the curriculum. Life is a social affair. To live is to live with others. To learn to live better one must learn to share more abundantly in the thoughts and feelings and interests of others. To do this with ethical regard for others is to give to democracy its best definition. For, according to Dewey, "democracy is more than a form of government; it is primarily a mode of associated living."[6] There may be a quotation from educational literature oftener brought forward than the one just given, but surely there are not many such in this country. Dewey is as truly the apostle of democracy for American education as is Thomas Jefferson for the political. How Dewey's conception of education as the reconstruction of experience gears in with his conception of democracy is probably as yet beyond most of the profession, but at any rate even for the many there is no conflict involved and the number who appreciate what is involved continually increase.

[6] *Democracy and Education* (1916), 101.

A fourth line is the relationship of education to social change. There are, of course, many conservatives who fear Dewey's social outlook, and not a few educators who look askance at his emphasis upon social change as a proper concern of American education. But an increasing number, it appears, share his outlook in this regard. It is interesting to read as far back as 1897 that "education is the fundamental method of social progress and reform," that all reforms resting "simply upon the enactment of law, or the threatening of certain penalties, or upon changes in mechanical or outward arrangements, are transitory and futile." As opposed to such external reform he held, on the one hand, that "education is a regulation of the process of coming to share in social consciousness" and, on the other, that therefore "the adjustment of individual activity on the basis of this social consciousness is the only sure method of social reconstruction." From this point of view "it is the business of every one interested in education to insist upon the school as the primary and most effective interest of social progress and reform." In a word, "the teacher is engaged, not simply in the training of individuals, but in the formation of the proper social life." "In this way the teacher always is the prophet of the true God and the usherer in of the true kingdom of God."[7]

The Dewey of the *Educational Frontier* (1933)[8] is much the same except that in the meantime consciousness of social-economic dislocation has become more definite, and possibly a greater emphasis needs to be placed upon institutional remaking. But even so the educational way remains the desirable way. While the Dewey of today customarily uses less theological sounding language, one may believe the meaning then and now is much the same. Perhaps it should be said that Dewey's education for social change is, of course, not an indoctrination of specific ways of change. His whole emphasis is to the contrary. And it may finally be added that Dewey's gradualism as here presented is stoutly opposed by the radical Marxians who confidently expect violence to prove the primary means

[7] *My Educational Creed.*
[8] William H. Kilpatrick (editor): *The Educational Frontier* (New York, 1933).

of effecting desired changes. It would be wrong to claim for Dewey all the current interest among educators in social change, but it is entirely just to claim for him a commanding position among the forces that along this line are today influencing American educational thought.

Before leaving this social side, attention must be called to Dewey's continual interest in bringing the principles and practice of democracy more effectually into school life and administration. There may be better statements extant on democracy in education than the one made by Dewey in 1903,[9] but this writer doesn't think so. Today, as then, it cuts to the heart of the matter. Possibly one reason it still remains so pertinent is that so little has been done to change the situation in the generation since the statement was issued. Democracy still remains a burning question, burning possibly a little more vitally now than in some of the intervening years. But Dewey's statement still stands to lead our thinking.

VII. From Uncritical to Scientific Thinking

Possibly no service of John Dewey to American education, in fact to American thinking in general, has been greater than his help in better methods of thinking. The America of his youth was on the whole content to think in terms of unexamined terms most of which meant entities where in fact there were no entities but processes. Will, consciousness, faculties as memory, reasoning and the like, instincts, intelligence, mind—these are but samples of processes masquerading as entities. James's pragmatism (following Peirce) and Dewey's experimentalism here joined hands with the rising army of scientific thinkers to question everything that could be questioned.

For teachers Dewey's *How We Think,* and particularly the seventh chapter (of the original edition) on "The Analysis of a Complete Act of Thought," has directly and indirectly brought great tonic effect. Through these, as stated earlier, American education discovered, so to speak, "the problem approach" as a teaching device. The effect has been very great. We cannot assert that all who read the book get out what

[9] *Elementary School Teacher,* 4:193-204 (Dec. 1903).

Dewey put in—some do not, we know from such sayings as "John Dewey may think that way, but no ordinary person does." These forget that thinking is simpler than adequate description of thinking. It is, however, easy to assert that this one book has brought a wide emphasis on problems and the conscious use of problems in school work.

That much remains to be done in improving such thinking is only too true. Many who denounce faculties still think in terms of them. There are even "scientific" writers on psychology who still treat I.Q., S—R bonds, and intelligence as faculties, not to mention the more unscientific who still talk as if instincts, mind, human nature, will, and emotion were separable things that work for man and move him around. That "mind" so far as it is persistent is something in process of building the whole waking time is a hard conception for the conventionally minded. In all these things and particularly in getting away from that old dualism of mind and body John Dewey has been a potent factor to better the thinking of American educators.

VIII. Dewey's Influence in Other Lands

In any movement it is, as we have seen, hard to separate the influence of any one man from the general trend of the *Zeitgeist*. If this is true with regard to John Dewey in America, much more is true of his influence abroad. Still some things can be said.

In the older countries of Europe there is little tendency to look to America for new ideas in the thought realm. Dewey's philosophy which seems so natural for us of this country is perhaps for that very reason the less welcome abroad. Our problem here, however, is not philosophy as such but education. It was J. J. Findlay, then head of the Manchester University school of education, who first brought Dewey to England. In 1906 he brought out a collection of Dewey's educational essays under the title *School and Child*[10] and in 1910 another volume called *Educational Essays*.[10] It seems, however, probable that Dewey's position was interpreted rather narrowly, more in keeping with Katherine Dopp's book on the *Place of*

---

[10] Blackie & Son, London.

Industries in Elementary Education (1902).[11] On the continent of Europe Georg Kerschensteiner (1854-1932) of Munich knew and admired Dewey. It seems rather probable that he chose the ambiguous name of *Arbeitsschule* to suggest the Dewey doctrine of child activity. But again did the interpretation turn out to be narrow. Adolphe Ferrière (b. 1879) of Geneva and Ovide Decroly (1871-1932) of Brussels and Peter Peterson (b. 1884) of Jena have each translated from Dewey. In the case of Ferrière and Decroly the effect on their respective systems is more than probable.

It has, however, been in certain new-old countries that Dewey's influence has been most observable, particularly in Russia, Turkey, Irak, India, Mexico, and China. In the USSR for the decade 1923-1933 Dewey's influence was very strong. Lunarcharsky was the head of education and an admirer of John Dewey. When at the beginning of the now widely discussed purging Lunarcharsky was dropped, the system changed, probably on grounds little connected with the merits of educational theory or practice. By special invitation of Turkey and Mexico Dewey visited those countries to advise on educational matters. Under the influence of Hu Shih, the foremost living thinker of China and present ambassador of his country to the United States, Dewey spent three years in that country, lecturing and advising. Men who have studied in America have carried Dewey's ideas to Irak and particularly to India.

IX. Summary and Conclusion

Four generalizations will perhaps sum up the principal contribution of John Dewey to American education. His influence, let it be said, has extended far beyond the range of any conscious alignment with any "Dewey movement." No one in position to judge would deny that he is the foremost leader in educational philosophy that America has produced. Professor William C. Bagley, known rather as critic than as disciple, speaking of Dewey's leadership in American education, said recently that it is "a leadership which he has now held for more than forty years with increasing prestige, and which long since

[11] University of Chicago Press (1st ed., 1902).

transcended national boundaries and became in a very real sense a world leadership in educational theory."[12]

First, Dewey has brought increased human interest into school life and work, interest in the pupil as a living person, and interest in current social affairs. It is doubtful that, outside of certain parochial schools and possibly a few others, there is to be found in this country a single child whose school life has not been made somewhat happier because John Dewey has lived. Certainly, most school children in what would be counted the better schools work very differently now because of the changes that Dewey's teachings have effected in school theory and practice.

Second, wherever the teacher works consciously to stir pupil initiative and aims consciously to encourage pupil responsibility, the probabilities are that such a teacher has directly or indirectly been influenced so to act and been guided in the process by the teachings of John Dewey. Wherever pupils and teachers talk things over together, there the Dewey interest probably is present in the degree that the teacher is conscious of the why and wherefore in what is done.

Third, wherever the community and the processes of society are matters of conscious study and concern, wherever education starts with present pupil or school or community problems and proceeds consciously to a wider and deeper social understanding of what is involved, wherever the aim is to start with present interests and deepen and extend these in their social implications, wherever the school is seen as a conscious agency to the intelligent improving of the culture, wherever the aim is to extend democracy farther and more consistently into school affairs—wherever any of these things thus go on, it seems fair to assert that in the degree that they are done consciously with the intent to affect the probable results of practice, in like degree is it probable that the teachers so acting have directly or indirectly profited by what John Dewey has taught.

Finally wherever the effort is made to get away in thought and practice from obscure and unscientific assumptions inherited

---

[12] Editor's introduction (p. xviii) to F. S. Breed, *Education and the New Realism* (New York, 1939).

from the past and *at the same time consider consciously the human values involved,* there also it is probable that the Dewey influence is at work. The italicized words in the statement just made are essential. There have been wide attempts to make scientific thinking prevail in education but do it in such way as in effect to disregard the most significant human values involved. In all such instances the effort has been rather consciously against John Dewey and his teachings and influence. But wherever the humaner concerns of personality, moral quality, and responsibility have been taken carefully into account along with the effort to think more adequately, there the chances are very great that John Dewey has been read and his teachings taken more or less adequately into account.

Are these things high praise? Yes, and they are so intended. But the statements are made only after deliberate consideration. There is no claim that John Dewey is the only begetter along the lines of the specific claims here made. As stated more than once, he is himself part and parcel of a much wider movement. But the claim is made that wherever in America today serious and conscious thought takes the lines indicated, the chances are very great that what is being done and thought will trace back more or less directly to the teachings of America's great leader in educational thinking, John Dewey.

WILLIAM H. KILPATRICK

TEACHERS COLLEGE
COLUMBIA UNIVERSITY

16

Alfred North Whitehead

JOHN DEWEY AND HIS INFLUENCE

JOHN DEWEY AND HIS INFLUENCE

I

PHILOSOPHY is a widespread, ill-defined discipline, performing many services for the upgrowth of humanity. John Dewey is to be classed among those men who have made philosophic thought relevant to the needs of their own day. In the performance of this function he is to be classed with the ancient stoics, with Augustine, with Aquinas, with Francis Bacon, with Descartes, with Locke, with Auguste Comte. The fame of these men is not primarily based on the special doctrines which are the subsequent delight of scholars. As the result of their activities the social systems of their times received an impulse of enlightenment, enabling them more fully to achieve such high purposes as were then possible.

By reason of the Stoics, the subsequent legal tradition of the Western World was securely founded in the Roman Empire; by reason of Augustine Western Christianity faced the Dark Ages with a stabilized intellectual tradition; Aquinas modernized, for the culmination of the Middle Ages, this ideal of a coördination of intimate sources of action, of feeling, and of understanding. The impress on modern life due to Bacon, Descartes, Locke, and Comte, is too recent to need even a sentence of reminder.

John Dewey has performed analogous services for American civilization. He has disclosed great ideas relevant to the functioning of the social system. The magnitude of this achievement is to be estimated by reference to the future. For many generations the North American Continent will be the living centre of human civilization. Thought and action will derive from it, and refer to it.

We are living in the midst of the period subject to Dewey's influence. For this reason there is difficulty in defining it. We cannot observe it from the outside in contrast to other periods also viewed in the same way. But knowledge outruns verbal analysis. John Dewey is the typical effective American thinker; and he is the chief intellectual force providing that environment with coherent purpose. Also wherever the influence of Dewey is explicitly felt, his personality is remembered with gratitude and affection.

II

The human race consists of a small group of animals which for a small time has barely differentiated itself from the mass of animal life on a small planet circling round a small sun. The Universe is vast. Nothing is more curious than the self-satisfied dogmatism with which mankind at each period of its history cherishes the delusion of the finality of its existing modes of knowledge. Sceptics and believers are all alike. At this moment scientists and sceptics are the leading dogmatists. Advance in detail is admitted: fundamental novelty is barred. This dogmatic common sense is the death of philosophic adventure. The Universe is vast.

Dewey has never been appalled by the novelty of an idea. But it is characteristic of all established schools of thought to throw themselves into self-defensive attitudes. Refutation has its legitimate place in philosophic discussion: it should never form the final chapter. Human beliefs constitute the evidence as to human experience of the nature of things. Every belief is to be approached with respectful enquiry. The final chapter of philosophy consists in the search for the unexpressed presuppositions which underlie the beliefs of every finite human intellect. In this way philosophy makes its slow advance by the introduction of new ideas, widening vision and adjusting clashes.

The excellence of Dewey's work in the expression of notions relevant to modern civilization increases the danger of sterilizing thought within the puny limitations of today. This danger, which attends the tradition derived from any great philosopher, is augmented by the existing success of modern science. Philosophy should aim at disclosure beyond explicit presuppositions. In this advance Dewey himself has done noble work.

ALFRED NORTH WHITEHEAD

DEPARTMENT OF PHILOSOPHY
HARVARD UNIVERSITY

17

William Savery

THE SIGNIFICANCE OF DEWEY'S PHILOSOPHY

THE SIGNIFICANCE OF DEWEY'S PHILOSOPHY

I T would be difficult in a brief essay to write a compact description of Dewey's entire system. I shall confine myself to what seems most important in it, and attempt to make an estimate of Dewey's place in American philosophy and in the philosophy of the Western world.

I. The Importance of American Philosophy

A subjective estimate of the value of a philosophy based upon one's own beliefs or likings is itself of little or no value. We must find, so far as possible, objective tests.

Windelband in his *History of Philosophy*[1] states two such tests: formal logical consistency and intellectual fruitfulness. In this classification originality is, perhaps, assumed although not stated. To this list of qualities comprehensiveness should be added. The adjective "formal" adds nothing to consistency, and I would not limit fruitfulness to intellectual consequences in too narrow a sense. With these suggested emendations the list stands as follows: (1) *originality*, (2) *consistency*, (3) *comprehensiveness*, and (4) *fruitfulness*.

Of these tests the first and the fourth are fundamental. If a philosophy is not consistent as a whole the parts may be important and the philosophy may be somewhat transformed by successors so that consistency is secured, and a doctrine of narrow range may still have great value; but without originality a philosophy is only a transmitter of more ancient wisdom, and without influence its value is entirely self-contained. In a word, an important philosophy is novel in itself and in its effects.

In my college days in the middle eighteen nineties Jonathan Edwards was still regarded as the greatest American philoso-

[1] English translation, 18.

pher. Recently Townsend in his excellent book, *Philosophical Ideas in the United States,* said that Peirce is perhaps the only American philosopher "worthy of ranking with Edwards for sweep of philosophical imagination and grasp of the deepest philosophical problems." I have never been able to find anything original in the philosophy of Edwards and he certainly produced no effects on Western philosophy. Höffding, for example, who stood outside the great philosophical countries and who treated modern philosophy with impartiality, does not mention Edwards in the index or, so far as I have been able to discover, in the text of his *History.* At the end of the nineteenth century some of us thought that Royce already exceeded Edwards in importance. He certainly saw the difficulties of absolute idealism better than any of the other classical or contemporary idealists and he made an heroic attempt to overcome them, particularly the difficulty of the experience of time. Except as a stimulus to Americans in logic, his importance does not seem so great now as it did then.

There is, however, a new philosophy in America of striking originality. Bertrand Russell has said,[2] "To my mind, the best work that has been done anywhere in philosophy and psychology during the present century has been done in America. Its merit is due not so much to the individual ability of the men concerned as to their freedom from certain hampering traditions which the European man of learning inherits from the Middle Ages . . . sophisticated America, wherever it has succeeded in shaking off slavery to Europe . . . has already developed a new outlook, mainly as a result of the work of James and Dewey." This new outlook is "embodied in the so-called instrumental theory of knowledge." I am not, I think, a philosophical patriot, but I would endorse this statement of Russell. I would carry the time back through the last quarter of the nineteenth century and include Peirce with James and Dewey.

During this period philosophy in Germany for the most part, with the notable exception of Mach[3] who was a forerunner of

---

[2] *Whither Mankind?,* edited by Charles A. Beard, Chap. III, 66f.

[3] Mach has been called a realist; he was actually a positivist, and an intermediary between Hume and James.

James, has been pouring water on the old tea-leaves of Kant and sometimes of Hegel. Even Husserl has not escaped from the subjectivity and the a priorism of Kant. The Italians have given us a thinned-out version of the romanticism of Hegel, and Bergson a most charming neo-Fichtean faery story. English realism has undergone a partly parallel development to that of America, and one must always make an exception of the stupendous achievement of the *Principia Mathematica* of Whitehead and of Russell himself.

It is not my intention however to depress the importance of European philosophy, but rather to exalt that of America. This philosophy has, I think, both novelty and fruitfulness. The originality of the American philosophy can be best exhibited in the systematic exposition of the next section of this paper. It is too early fully to estimate its fruitfulness. Although pragmatism or instrumentalism has been for the most part misunderstood in Europe and even by Russell himself, it has already given a concept of truth to the vigorous movement of logical positivism. Far more important, the operational theory of truth which is very much the fashion in such widely different fields as pure mathematics and experimental physics is nothing other than pragmatism or instrumentalism under another name. Brouwer, on the one hand, and Bridgman and Eddington, on the other, are followers, though perhaps unconsciously, of James and Dewey since for them truth is verifiability.

II. THE NATURE OF AMERICAN PHILOSOPHY

It will be necessary to limit our consideration to the main currents of American philosophy and this means, in effect, that we confine ourselves to Peirce, James and Dewey. Everything else in the main stream seems to be either derived from or a continuation of the work of these three men. We must not allow ourselves to explore so enchanting a side-stream as that of the philosophy of Santayana, overhung as it is with the magical beauty of essences.

I shall present a synthetic account of the thought of these three philosophers. This will be divided into two parts. The first deals with the contributions which are a continuation of

European philosophy although they are highly individual and important. The second part delineates the contributions that involve a break with Western philosophy. These form the American philosophy *par excellence.*

The first part comprises the logical discoveries of Charles Peirce. Little or nothing was added to these by James or Dewey and since their nature is well known a brief mention will suffice.

1. *The Logic of Relations.* That Aristotle's logic was a logic of attributes or of functions of one variable, that Boole turned this logic into mathematics, that De Morgan suggested a logic of relations, and that Peirce produced this logic in mathematical form, that Schröder recognized the importance of Peirce, that Peano and others developed the logic of relations further, and that Whitehead and Russell brought it to completion in their monumental *Principia Mathematica*—all this has been told many times. One might argue that Peirce is the greatest pioneer in deductive logic since Aristotle and that the work of Whitehead and Russell is the greatest culmination.

2. *The Theory of Induction.* (a) That inductive inference is the same as probable inference is the central thesis of Peirce's methodology; this carries with it a clarification of the entire problem of inductive logic. Since an inductive conclusion is never certain, it is either probable or it lacks entirely evidential value.[4] The other principal theses of Peirce's inductive logic are, perhaps, (b) that probability is the limit of a frequency series between classes of propositions and not of events; and (c) that the data of inductive inference are always statistical random samplings; and hence, (d) that the inductive method is fundamentally a method of enumeration as Mill also maintained.[5]

I come now to the second part, the distinctive features of American philosophy, features which made a break with the preceding philosophy of the Western world. I do not mean that this American thought had no roots in the past. This would have been impossible, and, if it had been actual, the thought

---

[4] Peirce also listed presumptive reasoning but only as suggestive of an hypothesis.

[5] Mill has been much misunderstood in this matter.

would have been well-nigh worthless. What I do mean is that some of these theories were of striking originality and that other theories which were more closely modeled upon the past were modified by their connection with the novel theories. The result was that the philosophy as a whole represented, to a considerable extent, a new departure in human thought.

There is one all-important connection with the past and that is with British empiricism. Peirce himself was a believer in universals (there was in him some sort of "exaggerated realism" as the scholastics would say) and there has been a strain of Platonic realism in American philosophy since, notably among some of "the new realists," but this strain does not appear in James or Dewey. The influence of Hume has been especially important. Hume might be said to be the first completely modern or post-medieval philosopher and, with the exception of the positivists, he perhaps had no important successor until the Americans appeared. The new departure of American philosophy is within the empiricistic tradition. I shall now briefly enumerate the principal theses of this philosophy, laying the greatest stress upon Peirce and James, since Dewey will be more fully considered in the later sections.

I. *Pragmatism.* In the latter part of the nineteenth century, after twenty-five centuries of Western philosophy, there were only two significant theories of truth: the correspondence theory of Aristotle and the scholastics, and the coherence theory of Spinoza and Kant and Hegel. The first is the theory of common sense. The second is essentially a deductive theory, a mathemetical deduction in Spinoza, a grotesque deduction in Hegel, a phenomenal consistency presided over by *a priori* categories in Kant. Modern science from the first had been both mathematical and experimental, but it was the mathematical method which most impressed the imagination of the philosophers and gave rise to the coherence theory. The inductive and experimental methods, although constantly used, were imperfectly formulated, and they remained without influence on theories of truth. It is, however, a curious thing that it was in unphilosophical America that an inductive theory of truth came into being. The inventors of this theory escaped from the European tradition, as Russell suggests, but this is hardly a *vera causa*. I attribute it to the genius of three men. There appeared in unaesthetic America the sporadic genius of three great pioneers in art— Whitman, Isadora Duncan and Frank Lloyd Wright, but each had no great successor in his own field.[6] But the three in philosophy were concatenated. Peirce led to James and James to Dewey and the result was an inductive and experimental theory of truth. It is the now famous theory of pragmatism or instrumentalism. According to this the original of truth is verification and its most extended meaning is verifiability. This theory may prove to be more acceptable than either of the older theories. It is, at any rate, a serious rival and it seems undeniably to be the most important contribution that America has made to philosophy. The rôles of the various thinkers in the development of pragmatism will be discussed in the next section.

II. *Neutralism.* The first half of the nineteenth century was characterized in general by the supremacy of idealism in European philosophy. The second half of the century was characterized by the supremacy of positivism. The present century thus far has been marked by the revival of realism. This revival has been mainly an Anglo-American phenomenon although the English influence has spread to Germany in the school of the Logical Positivists. Philosophy in Germany, Italy and France has been mainly the reverberation of the positivism of Kant and the romantic idealism of Hegel and Fichte to which have recently been added in Germany certain ingredients of the two late stray romanticisms of Nietzsche and Kierkegaard. Neo-scholasticism has also revived the realistic doctrine in the tradition of Aristotle and the scholastics. There has been considerable discussion of the order of events in England and the United States. English realism developed in good earnest after the publication of G. E. Moore's *The Refutation of Idealism* in 1903. Moore was preceded by Meinong in Germany. Hobhouse had written his *Theory of Knowledge* in 1895. The epochal paper of William James, on "The Function of Cognition," pub-

---

[6] Wright had an important predecessor in Louis Sullivan.

lished in 1885, which foreshadowed his pragmatism, was also the beginning of the revival of realism in America.

The important thing about the realism of William James is not that it is a revival but that it is a revival with a difference. James goes back to Hume not only in his denial of a pure self but also in his denial of consciousness. There is a stream of experience but it is not a stream of conscious experience since consciousness is not an entity. Hume, however, was essentially a positivist (in his own language a sceptic). Something like the hypothetical natural realism, which Hume suggested as an hypothesis only to reject it, was accepted by James as a part of his metaphysic. The same sort of entities enter both into our experience and also into the existential order of the physical world. Such entities in their essential nature are neither physical nor psychical. Sheffer called them neutral entities, and Holt put the phrase into his book, *The Concept of Consciousness*. James suggested that these entities might constitute the stuff of the universe, that matter might be one arrangement of them and that mind might be another arrangement. Broad coined the term *neutralism* for the theory that the basic constituents of the universe are neutral entities and Russell has called his own philosophy *neutral monism*, although he holds a representative theory of perception.

III. *Perspective Realism*. I have said in the previous discussion that a view similar to natural realism was accepted by James and he is commonly thought to be a believer in the selective view which passes under the name of *naïve* or *natural realism*. James himself seems in many places not at all clear on this point but in his essay, "A World of Pure Experience," there is one section entitled *The Conterminousness of Different Minds*[7] in which he is both clear and explicit. In this passage he points out that there are no logical difficulties involved in the overlapping of a portion of the physical world by our perceptions and hence in the conterminousness of two or more minds. The thing is logically possible and it is wholly a question of fact whether it

[7] William James, *Essays in Radical Empiricism* (1912), 76-86, and especially 82-86,

takes place. As a matter of fact, our perspectives (James actually uses the word *perspectives* which has figured so much in later discussion) are not the same. That is, James is fully aware of the so-called relativity of perception. The perspectives of two people have, however, one thing in common with the physical object and hence with each other, and that is their position in space; in other words, they attach themselves to the veritable physical object, and they form a series the limit of which (never reached) is the physical object itself. The perspectives are obviously outside the body of the percipient. We have here the prototype of the later views which have been called *Objective Relativism* by Murphy and *Perspective Realism* by McGilvary.

Recent realisms may be divided into (*a*) natural (Alexander and most of the Six), (*b*) representative (Russell, Broad and the Seven), and (*c*) perspective. In the latter view the perspectives are relative to the observers but they are outside their bodies, and are attached either (1) to the appropriate physical objects (Marhenke, Murphy and McGilvary) or (2) "projected" into space (Whitehead). Perspective realism is thus a *via media* between (selective) natural realism and representative realism in which latter the perspectives are either inside the body, or in a mind attached to a body, or (as with Santayana) in a realm of essences.

Perspective realism may be held along with a theory of the physicists' world which makes the latter quite different from the emergent perspectives. In James, however, perspective realism is in juxtaposition to neutralism although they can hardly be said to be combined in a unified theory.

IV. *Concatenism.* Either monism or pluralism must be true since these theories are exclusive and exhaustive. Either there is an all-inclusive being or there is not. If there is no all-inclusive being there are many entities (in the sense of more than one). Prior to the twentieth century in all the pluralisms that I am acquainted with, either Indian or Western, the entities are exclusive of each other and there are no clear ideas of how they can be related in the absence of an including whole. Leibniz alone had a clear idea that the monads cannot be related among themselves but he had an unclear idea as to how they could be related to God. At the end of the nineteenth century the intellectual triumph of monism over monadism seemed complete. In the first decade of the present century a new pluralism was born.

In 1890, in his famous chapter on "The Stream of Thought" in his *Principles of Psychology*, James had laid great stress upon the conjunctive relations of experience which Hume had left out, and later he called his philosophy *Radical Empiricism* in order to emphasize his difference from Hume. Charles Peirce coined the word *Synechism* in 1892 as a term for the continuity of experience. But it was James who developed the notion that experience consists of real units that overlap both successively and simultaneously. The world is a chain of interpenetrating links.[8] Entities are not exclusive as in the old pluralism. In the new pluralism they overlap.[9] It is this notion of overlapping that has been used by Russell to describe the universe as made up of events.

Concatenism is, then, a *via media* between monism and monadism. It is the only form of pluralism that is intellectually tenable. Hereafter, a philosopher must be either a monist or a concatenist. In my opinion, with the exception of pragmatism or instrumentalism, this hypothesis of a concatenated world is the most important invention of philosophy since the middle of the nineteenth century.

V. *Tychism*. The revival of the doctrine of a cosmic chance, so far as American philosophy is concerned, was the work of Charles Peirce. Naturally, there have always been in philosophy believers in ethical indeterminism, but the Epicurean doctrine of chance events in nature had come to be regarded as a philosophical curiosity and as an excrescence upon the more consistent determinism of Democritus. All modern naturalism or materialism was particularly committed to a strict determinism. Renouvier's disbelief in the possibility of infinite series led him to accept absolute beginnings in time and this had its effect upon

---

[8] The "great chain of being" of Neo-platonism is a continuity but not a chain.

[9] I have given the name *Concatenism* to this theory. See "Concatenism," *Journal of Philosophy*, vol. XXXIV (1937), 337-354.

James, but I do not know whether it influenced the philosophy of Peirce. Peirce made chance primordial and believed that laws were derived. The details of his theory may be unimportant; what is important is that he accepted the theory of absolute chance and gave it a name, *Tychism*.

James here, as elsewhere, followed Peirce and formulated the thesis that novelties continually appear in nature without cause.

This revival of the doctrine of chance events and its formulation as Tychism is especially interesting when we consider the present indeterministic formulas of physics in which statistical laws are substituted for causal laws. Physics has abandoned Democritus for Epicurus. The hypothesis of Lemaître of a beginning and subsequent generation of both time and space is an attempt to carry indeterminism still further into physics.

If we combine concatenism and tychism we see that the world of James is quite unlike the "block universe" which he disliked. The universe is not a block but a chain and the links exhibit frequent changes of pattern. Unlike the White Knight, there are all kinds of looseness in his design.

VI. *Naturalism* (and *Mysticism*). The only serious rival of a rationalistic philosophy is mysticism, since I understand by reason the use of both deductive and inductive inference working upon the material of experience.[10] And James became the champion of mysticism. Already in the 'Gay Nineties' James had published *The Will to Believe*, a defense of religious faith that had little or no philosophical influence but which bore some bitter theological fruit. In his *Varieties of Religious Experience*, in 1902, he put mysticism definitely on the philosophical map. His treatment of the subject was in character since it was empirical rather than speculative, and the facts were supplemented not by the will to believe but by a presumption elicited by the whole tenor of his own experience and study. Mysticism, however, has been only a side-stream in American philosophy. I have dealt with it because it is here that James and Dewey parted company and it is germane to our subject for its contrast

[10] I am in agreement with M. R. Cohen in this definition of reason.

effect. Dewey has been the most thorough-going and influential exponent of naturalism. This is the main current of recent American thought, a current which has been largely directed by Dewey himself. To this current belong Woodbridge and H. C. Brown and the writers of *The New Realism* who are not devotees of the Platonic Ideas. Especially important is the evolutionary naturalism of Sellars, a clear and comprehensive philosophy of emergence, of which he is the most important American creator.

Naturalism will be considered in the next section; here a brief description will suffice. Naturalism is realistic, as opposed to both idealism and positivism, and it is materialistic; or, at any rate, it follows the materialistic tradition as opposed to all forms of supernaturalism and the dualism of mind and body. In a very definite sense naturalism includes pragmatism or instrumentalism since the latter is the only naturalistic theory of truth that has thus far been devised.

III. Dewey's Contribution to American Philosophy

I. *Pragmatism or Instrumentalism.* Dewey's contribution to pragmatism can be best understood in its historical context. I shall give a sketch of the development of pragmatism. This may be divided into eight definite stages.

1. *The meaning of an hypothesis—the pragmatic method. Peirce.* The history begins, as is well known, with the famous statement of Charles Peirce, in 1878: "Consider what effects, that might conceivably have practical bearings, we conceive the object of our conception to have. Then, our conception of these effects is the whole of our conception of the object." It follows from this that if the experiential consequences of what appear to be two hypotheses are the same, the hypotheses are the same. It follows also that we can always, in principle, decide between two different hypotheses by a crucial experiment.

2. *The meaning of an idea. Knowledge. James.* Like his contemporary Royce, James was obsessed by the problem of objective reference, a problem which had been unsolved from Plato's *Theaetetus* up to his own time. He attempted a solution in two

articles,[11] published in 1885 and 1895. For the first time in the history of philosophical thought James put his finger upon an actual case of objective reference, the reference being to the future of one's stream of experience. The principal thesis, apparently, is that meaning is functional, that an experience means what it leads to; but it is a genuine reference beyond, since, as we proceed along the road to the terminus, we have "feelings of tendencies," the sense of "a more to come." (In this respect it differs from the theory of Dickinson Miller which was purely functional.)

James, however, was interested primarily in knowing, and a theory of knowledge was interwoven with his account of reference. In the early paper, in 1885, an idea *"knows whatever reality it resembles, and either directly or indirectly operates on."* In 1895 he reached the conclusion that *"To know an object is here to lead to it through a context which the world supplies."*

3. *The meaning of truth. James.* The meaning of truth was implicit in this description of knowledge, since truth and knowledge are correlative. The meaning of truth became explicit in James' famous lecture of 1898, "Philosophical Conceptions and Practical Results." In this lecture he brought Peirce's principle to the attention of the philosophical world, but he assimilated it to his own previous theory. He made it clear that the truth of a conception is to be determined by its prediction of future experiences.

The ultimate test for us of what a truth means is indeed the conduct it dictates or inspires. But it inspires that conduct because it first *foretells some particular turn to our experience* which shall call for just that conduct from us. And I should prefer to express Peirce's principle by saying that the *effective* meaning of any philosophic proposition can always be brought down to some particular consequence, in our future practical experience, whether active or passive; the point lying rather in the fact that the experience must be particular, than in the fact that it must be active.[12]

---

[11] "On the Function of Cognition," *Mind*, O.S., vol. X, 1885, and "The Knowing of Things Together," *Psychological Review*, vol. II, 1895; cf. *Principles of Psychology*, vol. I, 250-258, 463f.

[12] *Italics* mine.

4. *The experimental theory of knowledge. Verification. Dewey.* James' theory of objective reference to the future of the stream of experience was accepted by Dewey but he added that the meaning of an idea always contains a plan of action or operation. As early as 1903 in his *Studies in Logical Theory* he said that the test of the validity of an idea "is its functional or instrumental use in effecting the transition from a relatively conflicting experience to a relatively integrated one."[13] In his very important paper published in 1906, Dewey gives

the following definition: An experience is a knowledge, if in its quale there is an experienced distinction and connection of two elements of the following sort: *one means or intends the presence of the other in the same fashion in which itself is already present, while the other is that which, while not present in the same fashion, must become so present if the meaning or intention of its companion or yoke-fellow is to be fulfilled through the operation it sets up.*[14]

And in another paper, of 1907:

We call it "verification" when we regard it as process; when the development of the idea is strung out and exposed to view in all that makes it true. We call it "truth" when we take it as product, as process telescoped and condensed . . . an idea is made true; that which was a proposal or hypothesis is no longer merely a propounding or a guess. If I had not re- acted in a way appropriate to the idea it would have remained a mere idea; at most a candidate for truth. . . .[15]

Truth is definitely a verification and verification is definitely the realization of a prediction, brought about by an operation.

5. *The meaning of truth—satisfaction. Schiller and James.* In James' *Pragmatism*, in 1907, there was another view of truth, possibly derived from Schiller. It was the doctrine of Schiller and it was certainly disconnected with all of James' previous teaching. This is an ethical theory of truth, the thesis that truth consists in any useful consequences not only of an idea but also of a belief. Dewey's formulation of James' earlier

---

[13] 75.
[14] "The Experimental Theory of Knowledge," afterwards contained in *In- fluence of Darwin on Philosophy and Other Essays*, 90.
[15] Also in *Influence of Darwin . . .*, 140ff.

teaching is also accepted and there is one notable statement which adheres definitely to the verification view. The passage is this: ". . . but all roads lead to Rome, and in the end and eventually, all true processes must lead to the face of directly verifying sensible experiences *somewhere*, which somebody's ideas have copied."[16] (The copy is obviously prior to the experience copied.) These two views of truth were in juxtaposition in this book: Schiller's view in Lecture II; to some extent Schiller's view, but mostly James' old view, in Lecture VI.[17]

6. *Dewey's correction of James.* Soon after the publication of James' *Pragmatism* Dewey reviewed it in the *Journal of Philosophy.*[18] If he did not save pragmatism, since his own version of it needed no saving, he at least saved James from Schiller and from himself. Dewey is very explicit in recognizing the contradiction in James:

> Then arises the theory that ideas as ideas are always working hypotheses concerning the attaining of particular empirical results, and are tentative programs (or sketches of method) for attaining them. If we stick consistently to this notion of ideas, only *consequences which are actually produced by the working of the idea in co-operation with, or application to, prior existences are good consequences in the specific sense of good which is relevant to establishing the truth of an idea.* This is, at times, unequivocally recognized by Mr. James. (See, for example, the reference to veri-*fication*, on page 201; the acceptance of the idea that verification means the advent of the object intended, on page 205.)

> But at other times any good which flows from acceptance of a belief is treated as if it were an evidence, *in so far*, of the truth of the idea. This holds particularly when theological notions are under consideration. . . . Since Mr. James has referred to me as saying "truth is what gives satisfaction" (p. 234), I may remark (apart from the fact that I do not think I ever said that truth is what *gives* satisfaction) that I have never identified any satisfaction with the truth of an idea, save *that* satisfaction which arises when the idea as working hypothesis or tentative method is applied to prior existences in such a way as to fulfill what it intends.

These quotations, I think, need no comment.

---

[16] *Pragmatism*, 215.

[17] James generously attributed his new theory (in the singular) to Dewey and Schiller. This is a reason for thinking his new view was taken from Schiller, since he misunderstood Dewey.

[18] "What Pragmatism means by Practical," *Journal of Philosophy*, vol. V, 1908.

7. *Verification and verifiability. James.* Whether or not James was directly influenced by this criticism of Dewey, he returned in his later discussions of truth to his earlier views. "The pragmatist calls satisfactions indispensable for truth building, but I have everywhere called them insufficient unless reality be also incidentally led to . . . I remain an epistemological realist."[19]

. . . ideas *are* practically useful in the narrow sense, false ideas sometimes, but most often ideas which we can verify by the sum total of all their leadings, and the reality of whose objects may thus be considered established beyond doubt. That these ideas should be true in advance of and apart from their utility, that, in other words, their objects should be really there, is the very condition of their having that kind of utility. . . .[20]

The statement of James that ideas should be true in advance of their utility looks like a contradiction but it is not really one. James had distinguished in his *Pragmatism* between verification and verifiability and the word "truth" was applied to the latter as well as the former. This was made still clearer in *The Meaning of Truth.* Following the distinction between "saltatory" and "ambulatory" relations James says: "The logical relation stands to the psychological relation between idea and object only as saltatory abstractness stands to ambulatory concreteness. Both relations need a psychological vehicle; and the 'logical' one is simply the 'psychological' one disemboweled of its fulness, and reduced to a bare abstractional scheme."[21] And further: "Intellectualist truth is then only pragmatist truth *in posse.*"[22]

8. *Indirect verification. James and Dewey.* It had been objected to James' theory that he provided no truth about the past. He had, however, in his *Pragmatism* made provision for indirect verifications "by the present prolongations or effects of what the past harbored."[23] This was made more definite in his "Truth versus Truthfulness" in 1908: "Caesar *had,* and my statement *has,* effects; and if these effects in any way run together, a concrete medium and bottom is provided for the de-

[19] *The Meaning of Truth,* 195.
[20] *Ibid.,* 207f.
[21] *Ibid.,* 153.
[22] *Ibid.,* 205.
[23] *Pragmatism,* 214.

terminate cognitive relation."[24] Dewey said much the same thing the following year: "The past event has left effects, consequences, that are present and that will continue in the future. Our belief about it, if genuine, must also modify action in *some* way and so have objective effects. If these two sets of effects interlock harmoniously, then the judgment is true."[25] This implies that both James and Dewey had abandoned their earlier limitations of reference and knowledge to the future, although truth still consists in a future verification or verifiability.[26] Lewis in his *Mind and the World-Order* has treated the same situation as a partial verification of the entire process reaching from the past into the directly verified future.

We thus have a new gospel, although, like most new gospels, it was a formulation of (in James' words) "old ways of thinking." Peirce was the forerunner, James the creator, and Dewey the developer and the preserver.[27]

II. *Neutralism.* Dewey adheres to the neutralistic position although he does not call it by that name, but he has a more precise notion than James of the relation between matter and mind. The stuff of the world is natural events, in themselves neither physical nor mental. Both matter and mind are "functional characters." This view is best expressed in his *Experience and Nature:* "Nothing but unfamiliarity stands in the way of thinking of both mind and matter as different characters of natural events, in which matter expresses their sequential order, and mind the order of their meanings in their logical connections and dependencies."[28] Consciousness, for Dewey, is correlative with meanings: "consciousness in a being with language denotes awareness or perception of meanings;"[29] it has the same functional significance as with James.

[24] *Meaning of Truth*, 222.
[25] *Influence of Darwin . . .* , 160f.
[26] In the passage already quoted from "Philosophical Conceptions and Practical Results" (1898), James had amended Peirce's principle to read *"effective* meaning . . . can always be brought down to some particular consequences" (italics mine) ; but in "A World of Pure Experience," in 1904, he returned to his former limitation of reference and knowledge to the future.
[27] And Schiller was the tempter.
[28] 74.
[29] 303.

III. *Perspective Realism.* Dewey's most elaborate account of perspective realism is "A Naturalistic Theory of Sense Perception."[30] It is clear from this discussion that our perspectives are generated. Three theses are important in his theory. *First,* there is a sharp distinction between the physical cause and the perspective effects. For example, "Certain molecular disturbances in interaction with another set of molecular arrangements— empirically identified as the human organism—*cause* various phenomena of shape to appear. . . . 'Appearance' here has no other meaning than *effects.* . . ." *Second,* the empirical thing is the series of perspectives. It "is a series of phases, and physical conditions are such that the phases cannot occur simultaneously but only serially. . . ." *Third,* the place of the perspective is "literally an interaction field." In the case of the bent rays of light of the stick partly immersed in water this field

is not "in" the organism, nor is it "at" a highly delimited spot in the environment. The place where light rays impinge on the refracting thing . . . may form one focus in the field; the point where the refracted rays impinge on the molecular structures forming the optical apparatus may be another focus. But these, like foci of an ellipse, are determinations in a wider field. The sun—or other source of light—is a part of the "where" of the bent rays. . . .

IV. *Concatenism.* I can remember reading little or nothing in Dewey on overlapping events. He has, however, developed Peirce's synechism to a remarkable degree. Perhaps no other naturalistic philosophy (absolute idealism has internal relations) has so emphasized the connection of one thing with everything else. Professor Pepper has, I believe, characterized Dewey's entire philosophy as *contextualism.*

V. *Tychism.* Dewey accepted a certain measure of indeterminism, but this was subsidiary to his general theory that the entire universe is a history of unique events. He says "constancies, whether the larger ones termed laws or the lesser ones termed facts, are statistical in nature. . . . They are not descriptions of the exact structure and behavior of any *individual* thing. . . . No mechanically exact science of an individual

[30] *The Journal of Philosophy,* vol. XXII, (1925), 596-605.

is possible. An individual is a history unique in character."[31] This *historicism*, as it might be called, is allied to the romantic philosophies of Croce, Bergson and Spengler, which are influenced, perhaps respectively, by Hegel, Fichte, and Goethe or Schelling. It is possible that Dewey's view is a naturalistic version or inversion of Hegel.

VI. *Naturalism*. J. W. Krutch in *The Modern Temper* deplored the destructive nature of modern philosophy and contrasted it with the constructive systems of the Middle Ages. He was following in the footsteps of Henry Adams in the latter's autobiography and *Mont St. Michel and Chartres*. Krutch must have been acquainted with the philosophy of Dewey since he mentions one of his books (curiously, it is *Reconstruction in Philosophy*); but it never occurred to him that naturalism could be constructive. If supernaturalism is unsupported by evidence, it is obvious that some sort of naturalism in the widest sense of the word is the only valid philosophy. Positivism denies the possibility of all metaphysical construction, but idealism, dualism, and naturalism in the narrow sense remain as constructive systems.

Dewey is the most prominent spokesman of the new naturalistic philosophy. He rejects theological animism, the subsistentialism of ideas, and mysticism. He accepts realism and disbelieves in all forms of idealism and positivism. He rejects dualism with vehemence. For him the world consists of historical, natural events. He has no sympathy with a levelling-down naturalism. His philosophy is an emergent naturalism with a place for the emergent facts of life and mind. To coin a phrase patterned after a similar one of James, it may be called *Radical Naturalism*.

Dewey's entire philosophy may be designated *naturalism*, and all his other doctrines may be regarded as synthetically contained in it. His instrumentalism is the only naturalistic theory of truth; mind and matter are both functions of natural events (neutralism); our perspectives are emergent natural events; these events have a continuous flow (contextualism); events are unique, that is to say, historical (tychism).

[31] *The Quest for Certainty*, 248f.

His naturalism, however, includes much more than I have hitherto described as the American philosophy of Peirce and James. His ethics is a description of what men do when they are in perplexity, when they deliberate and when they choose harmonious ends and probable means to the realization of these ends. It is an instrumental theory of good as well as of truth. The two are closely connected, since what is good in conduct can only be experimentally determined. The whole of philosophy may be considered as a bridge between theory and practice. The experimental method has solved in principle the fundamental problems of technology and medicine. There remains the much harder task of arriving at solutions of social problems through similar scientific methods. The crown of Dewey's philosophy is his esthetic theory. *Art as Experience* is perhaps his most profound book. It is a consummatory theory of art, and it forms the natural complement to the instrumental theories of truth and goodness.

Dewey's naturalism possesses a massiveness which is perhaps found in no other recent naturalistic philosopher.[32] I have done scant justice to its concrete complexity.

IV. CRITICISM

There have been various philosophers who have criticized Dewey for both the ambiguities and the inconsistencies of his statements. I have come to the conclusion that most of the inconsistencies are of two types. First, Dewey's mature philosophy (leaving out his earliest writings) has been a gradual development so that we should not expect him to hold precisely the same views in 1929 that he held in 1906. In accordance with his own theory Dewey himself is an historical process. Second, Dewey, like James, in emphasizing now one phase and then another of the same philosophy, makes what seem to be verbally inconsistent statements. I suppose he might defend himself by saying, again in accordance with his theory, that the same words mean different things in different contexts. I believe that the supposed ambiguities are only another name for these incon-

---

[32] Alexander's orthogenetic *nisus* makes his universe too heaven-bent to be regarded as purely naturalistic. The *nisus* is an attenuated Jehovah.

sistencies and that the inconsistencies are superficial and are most troublesome to an indolent critic who does not try to penetrate beneath the surface.

Criticism may be textual or constructive. Textual criticism elicits the contradictions or inadequacies of the theory as it stands. Constructive criticism may content itself with the discrimination between imperfections of theory due to human frailty and those which are intrinsic to the theory, or it may also indicate how an imperfect theory can be modified or supplemented so that it will be consistent and adequate. I shall attempt the latter.

I. *Meanings of words.* One difficulty in understanding Dewey is caused by the fact that, like most original philosophers, he frequently uses old words with new meanings. Some of these words are:

1. *Acquaintance.* It "involves expectancy which is an extrinsic reference; it involves a judgment as to what the object of acquaintance will do in connection with other events."[33] This is a return to common-sense usage, but it is different from the meaning which has been popularized in philosophy by James and Russell.

2. *Knowledge.* This is limited to knowledge which is at least partly referential. If we divide what is ordinarily called knowledge into three kinds: first, intuition; second, description of what is intuited; and third, referential knowledge; we find that Bergson admits only the first kind, and that Dewey will admit nothing which does not have an ingredient of the third. Limitations such as these seem to me in general to be inadvisable.

3. *Ideas.* "Every idea originates as a suggestion, but not every suggestion is an idea. The suggestion becomes an idea when it is examined with reference to its functional fitness."[34] This is an unusual limitation.

4. *Meaning.* This is correlative to ideas; "their meaning is found in the modifications—the 'differences'—they make in this extra-mental situation"[35] (from which they arise).

[33] *Experience and Nature,* 329.
[34] *Logic,* 110.
[35] *Influence of Darwin . . .,* 155.

5. *Truth.* This is defined as the verification of an idea. This is obviously always future to the presence of the idea.

6. *Mind.* We have noted above Dewey's use of the word *mind.* Feelings of pleasantness and unpleasantness and emotions are ruled out by definition, as well as ideas, beliefs and desires considered as existential states.

> That there are certain existential qualities like emotions, which are referable to *persons* as a distinctive kind of existence (in the same sense in which stones, stars, oysters and monkeys, are kinds of existence with their own distinctive qualities), is a valid proposition. . . . A *person* is an object, not a "mind" nor consciousness, even though because of his capacity for inquiry he may be said to have mind.[36]

When we consider that the psychical has usually meant either (a) the whole of direct experience, including perspectives (the older definition), or (b) that part of direct experience, primarily attitudes, which is located within the body, we realize the startling change of meaning in Dewey's definition. In this nearly everything which is ordinarily called psychical is excluded.

7. *Epistemology.* This is described as a dualistic theory of knowledge, although the word *dualism* would hardly apply to the idealistic theory (either *Wissenschaftslehre* or *Erkenntnistheorie*) or to Dewey's own naturalistic theory. Epistemology I take to be a synonym of philosophical logic which includes analyses of the concepts of truth, evidence, certainty and probability. Such a logic must be both constitutive and epistemic, to use Johnson's terms; that is, it includes evidential materials, ordinarily called logical, and materials from the description of direct experience, ordinarily called psychological. Dewey thinks of his own theory of knowledge as logic and not as epistemology. Dewey's logic, however, contains little discussion of logical evidence. If epistemology is such a blend of logic and psychology, one might argue that Dewey's theory of knowledge is not epistemology, not because it is nearly all logic, but because it is nearly all psychology (in the ordinary meaning, and not in Dewey's meaning). The whole matter is one of definition.

[36] *Logic,* 525.

These unusual definitions lead to confusion on the part of the reader. If he attributes to Dewey the accepted meanings, Dewey's theses may be both extremely novel and plainly erroneous; whereas if he keeps Dewey's definitions in mind the theories are at least tenable and they are also less novel.

II. *Pragmatism.* We have seen that Dewey, like James, in his earlier formulation of pragmatism,[37] confined knowledge and truth to the experiential future. Later both James and Dewey[38] added knowledge of the past, attained by indirect verification.[39]

That there are many kinds of knowledge is most clearly expressed in *The Quest for Certainty.* In the following statements[40] we are said to know (1) sense-data, (2) mathematics and logic, (3) objects of common sense, and (4) objects of physical science. I have rearranged the order and inserted the numerals. [1] "It is only repeating what has been said to assert that no problem can be solved without a determination of the data which define and locate it and which furnish clews or evidence. In so far, when we secure dependable sense-data, we know truly." [2] "We develop operations, through symbols, which connect possible operations with one another; their outcome gives the *formal* objects of mathematics and logic. As consequences of suitable operations these two are truly known." [3] "When these operations, or some combination of them, are used to solve the problems which arise in connection with the things of ordinary perceived and enjoyed objects, the latter, as far as they are consequences of these operations, are themselves truly known." [4] "The systematic progress of inquiry in dealing with physical problems requires that we determine those metric properties by means of which correlations of changes are instituted so as to make predictions possible. These form the objects of physical science, and if our operations are adequate they are truly known." "We know whenever we do know; that is,

[37] "The Experimental Theory of Knowledge," 1906.
[38] "A Short Catechism Concerning Truth," (1909), included in *The Influence of Darwin.* . . .
[39] It was the earlier unmodified view that was so severely and ably attacked by Lovejoy in *Essays in Critical Realism.*
[40] 197f.

whenever our inquiry leads to conclusions which settle the problem out of which it grew. This truism is the end of the whole matter—upon the condition that we frame our theory of knowledge in accord with the pattern set by experimental methods."

Meanings (in the ordinary acceptation) now extend in both temporal directions, but past, present and future are not isolated but are co-implicated in a contextual whole. Not only is the past "of logical necessity, the past-of-the-present"[41] and the future presumably the future-of-the-present, but a proposition about the present means either the past or the future. " 'This is sour' means either that the actual performance of an operation of tasting has produced that quality in immediately experienced existence, or that it is predicted that if a certain operation is performed it will produce a sour quality."[42] " 'This is red' means, when it is analyzed from a logical point of view, that an object has changed from what it was, or is now changing into something else."[43] Even the part of a proposition about the present records a change.[44] Further, "There is no such thing as *judgment* about a past event, one now taking place, or one to take place in the future in its isolation."[45]

There is, moreover, no immediate knowledge; in the absence of tests we have only claims to knowledge or hypotheses. The tests are obviously in the future. Since all propositions about either past or present have also a future reference the test consists in the verification of the reference, brought about by an operation of experimentation (experiment being taken in the *Logic* comprehensively so as to include observation). Hence all

[41] *Logic*, 238.
[42] *Ibid.*, 289f.
[43] *Ibid.*, 308.
[44] Dewey is reluctant to say there are any propositions descriptive of presented data. Concerning something definitely qualified as sweet "a proposition may report it for purposes of record or communication of information." With reference to an enjoyment "The resulting linguistic expression will have the outward form of a proposition. But unless a question has arisen it is a social communication rather than a proposition, unless the communication is made to provide a datum in resolving a new situation." "The latter 'propositions' indeed record an occurrence" (*propositions* now in quotation marks). Such verbal contradiction is superficial. The foregoing quotations are from *Logic*, 128, 172, 173.
[45] *Logic*, 230.

knowledge is, in part, a knowledge of the future. I shall comment briefly on these theses.

It is true that we mean by the past what is earlier than the present, and we mean by the future what is later than the present; but although I relate the present to the past and future in a time-map I do not see that the meaning of the present entails their meanings. Neither does the meaning of the past entail the meaning of the future.

Further, only presented data are known with approximate certainty (in principle, certainty). We assume our memories of the past. Such memories are either crude or tested. Testing throws out some memories as probably false. Those that are indirectly verified are accepted. But—this is the important point —that the test has succeeded is only a memory. Further, we are never absolutely certain of our tested memories. Fortunately most of our original memories are left intact. So we say that our crude memories were probable. On this hypothesis our tested memories are more probable. The only thing that a verification of memories can ever do is to increase the probability. In other words, many of our untested memories were true, or none of our tested memories would be true. Verification increases the probability, if any; but it presupposes an immediate knowledge. That there is any knowledge is assumed.

On the basis of our knowledge of the past we extrapolate to the future and this is always hazardous.

We are spectators of the present and retrospectors of the past; on this basis alone we become prospectors of the future. When we verify we are again spectators, this time of new data, and retrospectors of the process of verification. Dewey, like a true American, is interested mainly in the future, but with all his concrete detail there is a certain abstractness in his interest and his treatment. Man looks in both temporal directions, but he knows better what was before. To call his previous verifications *funded knowledge* is a dodge. He may have verified before, but his memory that he has verified is not now verified but assumed.

The original pragmatism was based on Peirce's and James' account of an objective reference limited to the future. That was obviously an incomplete account of truth.[46] I shall make two generalizations of the developed pragmatism which includes indirect verification.[47]

1. Verification is a process which leads to a terminus where the object is compared with the meaning of the original idea. This comparison I shall call *confrontation*. This is the consummation of the process of verification. Strictly speaking, actual truth, truth *in actu*, is confrontation, because the proposition is not verified until, and it is verified when, confrontation takes place. *Hence the original of truth, truth in actu, is always in the present.* All other truths are derivative. Confrontation I shall now call *verification*. What James and Dewey call "verification," I shall call *the process leading to verification*. This is the first derivative. The second derivative is physical verifiability.

2. Propositions referring to inaccessible objects can only be verified indirectly by the supposed effects of these objects in the future. Such inaccessible objects include everything in the past, whether remembered or determined by historical investigations; spatial objects that we cannot observe, such as the other side of the moon, molecules, atoms and still smaller particles; and other minds. Now why is such an indirect process called verification? It is because it has given us assurance or probability that the past or other inaccessible events actually occurred or occur. There are two possible definitions of truth in such cases. First, we may define truth as the naturalistic process of indirect verification; or, second, we may extend the meaning of verifiability—we may (to use James' term) say that the process is physically "arrested," but that, if it could be carried out, a direct verification would take place. This we may call *logical verifiability*. The only truth *in actu* is the direct verification of confrontation; and the direct verification of a past fact can never be *in actu* but only *in posse*. Logical verifiability on this view would be the third derivative of truth. This is a consistent generalization of the pragmatic theory of James and Dewey.

[46] Cf. "On the Nature of Objective Reference," *Journal of Philosophy*, Vol. XXIII, (1926), 399ff.

[47] A more complete criticism is given by the writer in "The Synoptic Theory of Truth," *Philosophical Review*, Vol. XLVII (1938), 347ff.

In such cases, if we define truth as indirect verification, our procedure is *first*, arbitrary, since it is not what anyone has hitherto meant by truth; and, *second*, it makes a divorce between truth and knowledge, since the former is exclusively a process extending into the future, while the latter concerns the past (of course in its connection with the future).

Third, the crucial consideration, however, is our memories of the past. We have seen that, if there were no immediate knowledge, there would be no mediated knowledge, since verification merely increases the antecedent probability, which we must assume. Some of these memories cannot be verified at all, but we are practically certain that they are true. They would not be true according to pragmatism unless the remembered events actually took place, so that, if we did "remount the past" (James' expression), they would be verified.

According to my proposed generalizations true propositions would be classified as follows: (1) those that *are* verified, (2) those that *will be* verified, (3) those that *can be* (physically) verified, (4) those that *might be* (logically) verified. The truths are respectively:

(1) Verification. This is present and actual.

(2) The process leading to verification. This is an aggregate of concatenated entities. It is never actual as a whole.

(3) Physical verifiability. This is verification arrested but physically possible. Some conditions are actual and some are not.

(4) Logical verifiability. This is verification arrested, physically impossible, logically possible. Fewer conditions are actual than in the third.

According to this generalized theory, confrontation alone gives truth *in actu*, since all truth *in actu* is face-to-face contact where faith is consumed in sight. Verification as a process leads to truth *in actu*, but when we are on the way truth is still *in posse*. Physically verifiable truth is truth *in posse*. As James says, it is verification arrested. So in propositions about the past or other inaccesible regions we have verification permanently arrested, but the truth is still *in posse*. This is the logical completion of the ambulatory and saltatory scheme of James.

In order to substantiate this generalized pragmatism we

would need to show that the correspondence and coherence views can be analyzed or generalized into the same generalized theory.

Let us begin with correspondence. Unless we make the unwarranted presupposition of metaphysical monism, the relation of correspondence is existential only in actual confrontations. Other cases of correspondence are only *in posse*. So far as empirical truth is concerned, the correspondence theory when analyzed is confluent with our generalized pragmatism. Although the two theories differ in verbal formulation, they are precisely alike *in re*.

The coherence theory is usually formulated so as to entail, and that means to include, an absolute monism—all truth is *in actu*. If the coherence theory were generalized to include truth *in posse* it would be confluent with our generalized pragmatism for empirical truths. Mathematical truth is consistency. According to Dewey "Mathematical ideas are designations of possible operations . . . with respect *to one another*. This sense of possibility is *com*possibility of operations, not possibility of performance with respect to existence. Its test is non-incompatibility."[48] Incompatibility of two conceptions can only be discovered by their confrontation. Hence verification and coherence may be united in a confluent theory. In empirical truth there is an actual or possible agreement between meaning and fact, in mathematical truth between meaning and meaning. In mathematical truths we need the distinction between truth *in actu* and truth *in posse*, since mathematical inconsistency and entailment must usually be sought. Finally such truth is obtained by direct insight, but mathematical operations must be developed or the entailments and inconsistencies will not be apparent. Mathematical theorems, before they are proved, are verifiable; and, when they are proved, they are verified.

Such a generalized theory as I have briefly described is nearer to pragmatism than to either the correspondence or coherence theories. In the correspondence theory ordinary truth is potential; in the coherence theory all truth is actual; in pragmatism the original of truth is actual verification, but truth extends to

[48] *The Quest for Certainty*, 160.

physical verifiability. In the confluent theory, verifiability is further extended to include logical verifiability. Such a theory may well be called: *Generalized Pragmatism*.[49]

III. *Perspective Realism and Theories*. There is a very important problem in philosophy which Dewey leaves unsolved, and which, at times, he does not seem to regard as a problem at all. That is the problem of the nature of the external world. Dewey frequently writes as though he were a natural realist, disregarding the differences between our perspectives. This was the case through most of his recent *Logic*. He is, however, a perspective realist, and he holds that our perspectives are natural events which are added to, although continuous with events already existent. To use the language of Dewey's controversy with Santayana, the perspectives form the experiential foreground, but there is a massive background beyond. Two of us look at a chair. Our perspectives are different. What is the chair over and above these two perspectives? We both go out of the room. There are no perspectives of the chair. What is the chair now? Further, what is there in my physical organism in addition to my felt bodily attitudes? And what is my body during dreamless sleep? The answers to these questions depend upon the status of theory.

I have not been able to understand whether, in Dewey's view, theories are always operational or whether they are sometimes existential. In *The Quest for Certainty* he says "It is still questioned whether many of the objects of the most valuable and indispensable hypotheses in present use have actual existence; the existential status of the electron is still, for example, a matter of controversy." A little further on: "progress beyond the Newtonian scheme was made possible when the ascription of antecedently existing inherent properties was dropped out, and concepts were regarded as designations of operations to be performed."[50] In the *Logic*

The "problem" which occasions the epistemological interpretation arises when and because it is supposed that conceptions, in general and in particular, *ought.* to be in some fashion descriptive of existential material.

[49] This is a mere sketch. For a fuller statement see "The Synoptic Theory of Truth," referred to above.

[50] 191.

The idea that they should be descriptive is the only view possible when the strictly intermediate instrumental function, operatively realized of conceptions is ignored . . . unless conceptual subject-matter is interpreted solely and wholly on the ground of the function it performs in the conduct of inquiry, this difference in dimensions between the conceptual and the existential creates a basic philosophic problem. . . . From the standpoint of the *function* that conceptual subject-matters actually serve in inquiry, the problem does not need to be "solved;" it simply does not exist.[51]

These quotations would seem to indicate that theories are, properly, exclusively operational. Such a view would yield a pure positivism in which our knowledge would be confined to our perspectives and the operations by which we may pass from one to another.

On the other hand, we read in the *Logic* that popular positivism "has no recognized place for hypotheses which at a given time outrun the scope of already determined 'facts,' and which, indeed, may not be capable of verification at the time or of *direct* factual verification at any time."[52] This at least hints at a realistic view. A realistic standpoint was undoubtedly expressed in *Experience and Nature*.

If one is a positivist and accepts the view that we can know only perspectives and their connections, there is obviously no further realistic problem. If one is a realist the problem of the nature of the external world, that is, the massive background of our perspectives, cannot be ignored.

As a realist I would state the situation in this way: some of our theories, such as relativity, may be purely operational, expressed through mathematical equations; but other theories are existential, statements of entities indicated by possible operations which cannot be physically completed, such as the existence of the stars on astronomical evidence, and a granular structure of matter on the convergence of evidence of the Brownian movement, scintillations, condensation tracks, the actuation of Geiger counters and the determination of elementary electrical charges.[53]

[51] 466f.
[52] 519.
[53] Cf. Lenzen, *Procedures of Empirical Science*, 26f., 49f.

A scientific account of as much of the cosmos as we can know includes three things:

(1) Phenomenology. An empirical description of our direct experiences including their functional connections.

(2) A theory of the nature of the external world. By the external world I understand the stuff beyond our perspectives, including the connection or bridge between my direct experience now and that of yesterday, and between my direct experience and yours, and reaching back into the past before there were any perspectives and stretching out indefinitely in space.

(3) A theory of the joints between the external world and direct experience—not bifurcations but joints, or better, joinings.

These two theories are parts of an inclusive theory. Dewey thinks that the mind-body question is a pseudo-problem. But the problem of these joinings of direct experience and the external world takes the place of the pseudo-problem. There is a double connection: perspectives are joined to physical things (as the physicist describes them) and attitudes are joined to the human organism (as the physiologist describes it). The problem has shifted; it should be solved and not shelved.[54]

IV. *Naturalism.* In accordance with Dewey's definition of matter he would not call his philosophy *materialism*. Further, he believes in the emergence of life and mind from physical (inorganic) events. He says

while the theory that life, feeling and thought are never independent of physical events may be deemed materialism, it may also be considered just the opposite. . . . Historically speaking, materialism and mechanistic metaphysics—as distinct from mechanistic science—designate the doctrine that matter is the efficient cause of life and mind, and that "cause" occupies a position superior in reality to that of "effect." Both parts of this statement are contrary to fact. As far as the conception of causation is to be introduced at all, not matter but the natural events having matter as a character, "cause" life and mind. "Effects," since they mark the re-

---

[54] There are different species of perspective realism. The "multiple inherence" hypothesis of Whitehead is very different from what I may call the "multiple attachment" hypothesis of Marhenke, Murphy and McGilvary. Still another and different "multiple attachment" hypothesis is possible, but I cannot develop it here. With three hypotheses the problem presses for solution.

lease of potentialities, are more adequate indications of the nature of nature than are just "causes."[55]

What one calls his philosophy is a matter partly of taste and partly of utility. I have no desire to foist upon Dewey a name which he dislikes and it is quite possible that *naturalism* is better than *materialism* as a word to designate his philosophy, but it is, I think, quite certain (humanly speaking) that Dewey belongs to the materialistic tradition.

Materialism has been grossly misrepresented by historians of philosophy who stem, for the most part, from Hegelian idealism. The sins of the historians are many:

First. Absurd or preposterous materialism which either denies secondary and tertiary qualities (Leucippus and Democritus, as literally interpreted) or which reduces such qualities to motion (Hobbes in *De Corpore*) has been taken to be the only pure or consistent materialism, all other materialisms being adulterated. The other materialisms, however, which we may call sensible materialisms, are preponderant in number and in influence.

Second. The naïve materialisms of the early Greeks have been excluded under the name *hylozoism*. If we do exclude as hylozoistic the philosophers who regard either (a) all matter as animate (Xenophanes) or (b) basic matter as animate (Heracleitus, the Stoics) or (c) controlling matter as animate (Anaxagoras), we still have Thales, Anaximander and Anaximenes, the Pythagoreans and Empedocles at the beginning of the materialistic tradition.

Third. Epicurus and Lucretius have been represented as holding an absurd materialism when they explicitly say that a composite being (σύστημα or *consilium*) has properties which the elements lack. The Epicurean philosophy is implicitly emergent.

Fourth. There is the persistent misreading of La Mettrie and Diderot. In spite of the title of La Mettrie's book, *The Human Machine*, he is not a mechanist in the modern sense, since for him motion and feeling interact.

---

[55] *Experience and Nature*, 262.

Fifth. There is the neglect of Engels on the part of the academic philosophers. His philosophical importance consists in the fact that he holds an explicit emergence view.

Sixth. Because of the misconceptions that have been stated above, there is a misunderstanding of the continuity of the recent revival of materialism and its historical forms. Current materialism is critical and emergent (H. C. Brown and Sellars in America and Broad in England), but it is a further development of older forms.

The confusion is increased when several writers who are in the materialistic tradition refuse to classify themselves as materialists. Woodbridge seems clearly a materialist. Russell, whose world, like that of Dewey, consists of events, is, I should say, a materialist, since each event is extended in three dimensions and has a duration. As a concatenist he does not believe in an inclusive Space or Matter, but he believes in overlapping matter*s*. He is a materialist, but calls himself something else. Santayana calls himself a materialist but is something else, since he believes in eternal essences. I do not know that Dewey has ever said that each of the natural events of his world has extension. The fundamental tenet of the materialistic tradition is that nature is, for the most part, unconscious (in the widest meaning of that word) and that consciousness (in the narrow sense of objective reference), awareness, feelings, emotions and desires —in other words what are ordinarily called psychical states— are on a relatively small scale and are derived in some sense, emergent or other.

While I do not object to Dewey's preference for the word *naturalism* over *materialism*,[56] I do think that the meanings which he gives to "God" and "faith" in his book *A Common Faith* are apt to prove misleading.

Fundamentally, and in spite of his esthetic theory, Dewey exalts action above contemplation. He is a true disciple of Zarathustra rather than the Upanishads, Buddha or Plato, of Persia rather than India or Greece.

---

[56] I once read a paper to show that the word *naturalism* is better because of its utility.

When he does reflect he seems satisfied with the world. Bradley has said "if the main tendencies of our nature do not reach consummation in the Absolute, we cannot believe that we have attained to . . . truth."[57] My own reflection has led me to a different conclusion. Any philosophy which satisfies our main desires is probably false. Buddhism is not very useful for social reform, but perhaps the profoundest saying in all religion is the words attributed to Buddha: "So the world is afflicted with death and decay, therefore the wise do not grieve, knowing the terms of the world."[58] This states both the sorrow and its healing. Dewey, with his passion for social change and improvement, seems strangely silent about that feature of the world which finally sweeps all values away. Perhaps he is so completely cured of the sorrow that he forgets to dwell upon it in his philosophy.

However naturalistic one may be as he follows the scientific method in philosophy, he must bear in mind that his negative conclusions can never go beyond probability and that mysticism always remains as a possibility. I do not myself accept the presumptions of the cosmic mystics, but downright honesty compels us to admit that here as elsewhere we have no certainty. It is possible that in an ideal future, when all capitalists and all dictators have perished, there will always remain a small minority of intelligent mystics. "The opinion which is fated to be ultimately agreed to by all who investigate"[59] may never come.

WILLIAM SAVERY

DEPARTMENT OF PHILOSOPHY
UNIVERSITY OF WASHINGTON

[57] *Appearance and Reality*, 148.
[58] *Sutta-Nipâta*, (581) S. B. E., Vol. X.
[59] Peirce, *Collected Papers*, Vol. 5, section 407. Quoted with approval by Dewey as a "definition of *truth* from the logical standpoint." *Logic*, 345, n.

John Dewey

EXPERIENCE, KNOWLEDGE AND VALUE:
A REJOINDER

EXPERIENCE, KNOWLEDGE AND VALUE:
A REJOINDER

TO COMBINE acknowledgment of indebtedness to the
writers who have taken so much pains in expounding and
criticizing my views with reply to adverse criticisms is not an
easy task. I am confident I can count on their and the readers'
appreciation of this difficulty. I do not share, I confess, the
optimism expressed in the Announcement of the Series of which
this is one volume, regarding the possibility of terminating
controversy. As the history of philosophical discussion shows,
it is quite possible that what is said in answering one objection
and clearing away one misconception will give rise to others.
Yet, as the same Announcement also says, an undertaking of
this kind, providing as it does for interpretation on the part
of both friendly and adverse critics, should facilitate a "meeting of minds" so that whatever happens to the views and doctrines of a given writer on philosophy (in this case, mine), the
larger continuing cause of philosophic inquiry should be forwarded.

It may assist understanding of the comments and replies
found in the following pages if I say something about the
method adopted in arranging my remarks. The first idea that
occurred to me was to take up each contribution separately,
and reply *seriatim* to the several points made in each. But it
soon appeared that such a course would demand many quotations from both my own writings and those of my critics, with
the necessity for more or less extensive exegesis of passages
cited:—proverbially the source rather than close of controversy.
As Mr. Piatt says in his article, too frequently "clarifications
of meanings fail to clarify and merely repeat the initial difficulty." It is not easy at the best to move from a system of ideas

having one center and order into a system having a different
focus and arrangement. Neither a critic nor myself is responsible
for the fact that every philosophical word employed is charged,
in the degree of its importance, with ambiguities resulting from
centuries of controversial discussions. In addition, adoption of
the kind of procedure just mentioned may easily obscure the
matters at issue by covering them up with a multiplicity of
details so that the forest is not seen because of the trees. For
a time, then, I ·entertained the contrary hope that I might be
able to discuss a number of general issues, which the various
papers show are in need of clarification, with only incidental
reference to special criticisms. My experience in trying this
method proved however that there was danger that my reply
would be so very general as not to come to grips with specific
criticisms. Moreover, the variety of points touched upon and
the diversity of the philosophical perspectives in which they
are presented formed a serious practical obstacle. I have adopted
accordingly a sort of compromise procedure—in the not too
confident hope that it may not turn out in the end to combine
the worst features of the other two methods. I have selected
some main heads under which to restate my views in reference
to criticisms passed upon fundamental principles in my philosophy, and then under each head have attempted to meet with
specific comments a variety of special criticisms.[1]

In the hope that it may be of help in following what is said
and also in understanding the distribution of space given to
different contributors, I attempt a rough classification of the
papers which precede. Drs. Ratner, Geiger, Childs and Kilpatrick have at various times been members of classes taught
by me at Columbia University. Some of them have been colleagues as is the case with Dr. Randall. It would be a serious
reproach to me if my associates had not attained a juster understanding of what I had said in my written work than is likely
to exist in the case of those who have only the latter to con-
sult. Dr. Piatt was a student at the University of Chicago after

---

[1] In my rejoinders to some of the specific criticisms, I shall presuppose familiarity
with the text of the contributors' articles since space forbids reproduction of the
details of their argument.

I left there and had the great advantage of the teachings of Professors Tufts, Mead and Moore. Just because my obligations to these contributors are great I have said much less about their articles than about those in the third group mentioned below. In many respects a careful reading of their articles will serve as more effectual replies to some of the adverse criticisms than anything I can say. After all allowance is made for the loyalty of students to old teachers—a loyalty often carried to excess—I have to express my appreciation of the way in which these contributors have seen and reported the direction in which my thoughts have moved, of their sense of what it is I was doing and what it is I was after. In lieu of extended comments, I must ask them to accept my thanks, and with mine that of all readers who are concerned to know what my views actually are.

In the second group are a number of writers whose expositions of the topics with which they deal are essentially correct in some or many points, even though accompanied with disagreement with the conclusions I have reached. To these persons, comparative strangers, are due my thanks for the pains they have taken to become acquainted with my writings and to report faithfully their general tenor. Dr. Allport, an expert psychologist, has performed this service for one who long ago ceased to profess expertness in a highly specialized technical field. Dr. Parodi in his careful account of the relations of knowledge and action in my theory has lightened my task of reply by correcting in advance some misconceptions put forward by other contributors who touch upon the subject. Dr. Savery has provided a valuable supplement to the other contributions by placing my views in historic perspective in their relation to Peirce and James, while also correcting in advance, by his brief but pertinent remarks upon pluralism, continuity and contingency, some common misapprehensions. Professor Whitehead has written with his characteristic generosity of spirit.

In the third group fall the articles of a more definitely adverse kind—those of Drs. Reichenbach and Pepper in part, and of Russell, Murphy, Santayana, Stuart and Schaub in almost their entirety. It will readily be understood, then, why much more space is given to them than to the writers who are more sympathetic or more correct in their expositions of my views. My indebtedness to this third group is of a different kind. I am obliged to them for the stimulus of their challenges and for the opportunity to try and set myself right on some points where in the past I have obviously failed not only to carry conviction, but (a more important matter) to make clear my actual position.

A. INTRODUCTORY

As an introduction to the leading issues (Experience, Knowledge in its relation to experience, and Ethics) which constitute the main heads of my reply, I shall say something about the problems which have directed the course of my philosophical thinking—a procedure almost obligatory upon one who has emphasized the rôle of problems to the extent I have done. And in this particular connection I am especially grateful for the contributions of Drs. Ratner and Randall. I have been engaged by means of published writings in developing the essentials of my present philosophical views for at least thirty-five years, beginning with my essays in the *Studies in Logical Theory* in 1903. Inconsistencies and shifts have taken place; the most I can claim is that I have moved fairly steadily in one direction. Dr. Ratner has put his finger upon the main "shift" in my writings. It affects not only the special topic of philosophy but the more general one of knowledge. At various places in my writings I have said that, from the standpoint of empirical naturalism, the denotative reference of "mind" and "intelligence" is to funding of meanings and significances, a funding which is both a product of past inquiries or knowings and the means of enriching and controlling the subject-matters of subsequent experiences. The function of enrichment and control is exercised by incorporation of what was gained in past experience in attitudes and habits which, in their interaction with the environment, create the clearer, better ordered, "fuller" or richer materials of later experiences—a process capable of indefinite continuance. Dr. Ratner is quite right in indicating that the word "intelligence" represents what is essential in my view much

better than does the word *knowledge,* while it avoids that confusion of knowing—inquiry—and attained knowledge which has
led some of my critics astray in their accounts of my position.
At present, after reading criticisms of the kind of *instrumentalism* that is attributed to me, it is clear that I should,
from the start, have systematically distinguished between knowledge as the outcome of special inquiries (undertaken because of
the presence of problems) and *intelligence* as the product and
expression of cumulative funding of the meanings reached in
these special cases. Nevertheless, there are in my earlier writings
many indications of the distinction and of the rôle it plays,
as well as references to the principle of organic habit as the
physical agency by which the transition from one to the other
is effected. I cite two passages: "The function of knowledge is
to make one experience freely available in other experiences.
The word 'freely' marks the difference between the function of
knowledge and of habit," while sentences which follow show
that the difference is not ultimately one between habit and
intelligence but between routine habits and intelligent ones.[2]
From a later, though not latest, writing I cite the following
representative passage:

> The history of human progress is the story of the transformation
> of acts which, like the interactions of inanimate things, take place
> unknowingly to actions qualified by understanding of what they are
> about; from actions controlled by external conditions to actions having
> guidance through their intent:—their insight into their own consequences.
> Instruction, information, knowledge, is the only way in which this
> property of intelligence comes to qualify acts originally blind.[3]

I did not hit upon my position as a ready made and finished
doctrine. It developed in and through a series of reactions to a
number of philosophic problems and doctrines. During the
early nineties, practically all important philosophizing in the
English language was influenced by Neo-Kantian and Hegelian
idealism. Pragmatism and all versions of realism are of later
growth. In my own case change of residence from Chicago to

[2] *Democracy and Education* (1916), 395. The whole discussion of the topics of
Method, Subject-matter and Theories of Knowing is relevant.

[3] *Quest for Certainty* (1929), 245.

New York in 1905 brought me in direct contact with the Aristotelian realism of Woodbridge and the monistic realism of Montague. There was a new challenge and a new stimulus. It is
perhaps natural that I should not agree with the judgment expressed by Dr. Murphy that my discussion of certain important
issues "is not intelligible until we refer it back to the idealistic
and realistic philosophies in relation to which it was developed."
But I gladly admit that my philosophic views did not develop
in a vacuum and that I took seriously philosophic doctrines that
were current. Undoubtedly, study of the problems they presented played a part in the development of my own philosophic
method and doctrines. For I felt myself under an obligation to
develop my personal intellectual predilections in a way that
took cognizance of strong points in other teachings while trying
to avoid what appeared to me to be their weak points.

As, however, will be made evident later, it was not the issue
of idealism *versus* realism that constituted my problem, but the
bearing of these theories (as well as that of the older classic
tradition) upon two issues which chiefly preoccupied me. Personally, I do not feel that a defence of the habit of taking
seriously important historic systems is necessary. But it is important, even necessary, to appreciate what phases of historical
thought—past and present—enter deeply into determination
of the thinking of any philosopher. Consequently, I am deeply
grateful for two things that stand out in Dr. Randall's account.
One of them is the general and basic consideration that I regard the philosophy of any period as a reflex of larger and more
far-reaching cultural achievements, needs, conflicts and problems. The other as stated in his own words is the fact that there is
"one central conflict as the focus for understanding all Western
philosophies. It is the ever repeated struggle between the active
force of scientific knowledge and technical power and the deflecting force of the lag and inertia of institutionalized habits
and beliefs." Because of the centrality of this struggle and the
problem of readjustment set by it, I have approached (as
Randall says) our cultural "heritage as a critic and reconstructor
of tradition" so that "he is forever bringing men's past experience with ideas to the test of present experience." Whether I

am right or wrong in this attitude and whether or not I have exaggerated the extent to which vital cultural problems—which ultimately decide important philosophical problems—now centre about the reworking of traditions (institutions, customs, beliefs of all sorts), to bring them into harmony with the potentialities of present science and technology,—here is the setting in which my chief problems have arisen.

The form taken in my philosophical system by this underlying socio-cultural problem is seen in what I have said about the two issues which to my mind have controlled the main course of modern thought:[4] "The problem of restoring integration and coöperation between man's beliefs about the world in which he lives and his beliefs about values and purposes that should direct his conduct is the deepest problem of any philosophy that is not isolated from that life."[5] What is here designated by the phrase "beliefs about the world" is made explicit in a sentence of the next page: "Its [philosophy's] central problem is the relation that exists between the beliefs about the nature of things *due to natural science* to beliefs about *values*—using that word to designate whatever is taken to have rightful authority in the direction of conduct."[6] The other main problem has in verbal statement a more technical sound. It is "the problem of the relation of physical science to the things of ordinary experience."[7]

This latter problem is closely connected with the first in as far as things desired and enjoyed—and disenjoyed—are among the things of ordinary experience and also provide the material of valuation-judgments. It involves, however, a somewhat dis-

---

[4] There are also, it goes without saying, in the course of modern thought, a large number of questions of a more definitely technical sort, some of which are more closely connected with the main issue I state below and some more remotely. My *technique* has grown directly out of the problems and methods of historic philosophies. I hardly know any other way in which a competent technique can be formed; although it is possible that at times I have overdone the importance of obtaining technical skill. At least, were I to criticize my own writings, I should bring that charge rather than that of complete looseness which some critics find in what I have written.

[5] *Quest for Certainty*, 255.

[6] *Ibid.*, 256.

[7] *Ibid.*, 252.

tinctive set of problems, connected with the pre-experimental and pre-technological leisure class tradition, according to which the characteristic object of knowledge has a privileged position of correspondence with what is ultimately "real," in contrast to things of non-cognitive experiences, which form the great bulk of "ordinary experiences." Most of the dualisms forming the stock problems of modern epistemological theory have originated, as I have tried to show, out of the assumptions which generate these two problems. If, however, the philosophical theory of experience is brought up to date by acknowledgement of the standpoint and conclusions of scientific biology and cultural anthropology and of the import of the experimental method in knowing, these problems, I have argued, are "solved" by recognition that they depend upon premises inherited from traditions now shown to be false. Some of the gratuitous dualisms done away with, I have argued, are those of the objective and subjective, the real and apparent, the mental and physical, scientific physical objects and objects of perception, things of experience and things-in-themselves concealed behind experience, the latter being an impenetrable veil which prevents cognitive access to the things of nature.[8]

The source of these dualisms, I have contended, is isolation of cognitive experience and its subject-matter from other modes of experience and *their* subject-matters, this isolation leading inevitably to disparagement of the things of ordinary qualitative experiences, those which are esthetic, moral, practical; to "derogation of the things we experience by way of love, desire, hope, fear, purpose and the traits characterizing human individuality"[9]—or else in an effort to justify the latter by assertion of a super-scientific, supra-empirical transcendent *a priori* realm. Now I did not invent these problems; I found them controlling, often covertly rather than openly, the course of philosophic reflection and thereby determining conclusions reached. If the urgency of these problems is ignored or slighted (urgent in phi-

---

[8] Cf. the standpoint from which Santayana criticizes my view, a standpoint vitiated by its own uncritical assumption that the splits involved are matters of ordinary common sense acknowledged as such by every "candid" thinker.

[9] *Ibid.*, 219.

losophy because urgent in actual cultural life when the latter is submitted to analysis), the context of the larger part of what I have written will be so missed that what I have said will seem to be a strange, a gratuitously strange, intellectual adventure, redeemed—if at all—only by the presence of a certain technical skill. For what has governed my discussion of historical systems —at first idealistic and realistic theories of knowledge and later the classic tradition as it has come down to us from Greece —is the belief that the cultural causes, scientific, political and economic, which led to the doctrine of the supremacy of the cognitive experience and the consequent supposed necessity for relegating the things of all non-cognitive experiences to an inferior status, no longer apply. On the contrary, I believe that the factors of the existing cultural situation, scientific, technological, and "social," are such that philosophic theories which in effect, even if not in intent, are products of pre-scientific and pre-technological, dominantly leisure class conditions, are now as obstructive as they are unnecessary.

I do not find that my critics have much to say about my criticism of the virtual irresponsibility of theories produced by isolation of cognitive experience, and by assertion of the exclusively "real" character of its subject-matter in contrast with that of the things of ordinary, chiefly non-cognitive, experience. But these ideas when they govern philosophy (as a distinctive mode of knowledge) are the source of the notion that its business is to tell something about "ultimate reality" not told about in the natural sciences, so that in the end philosophy is separated from the sciences as well as set over against the things of ordinary experiences. I do not wish to intimate that no correct statements and valid criticisms of special points in my philosophic positions can be made unless their general setting is noted. But some of the accounts given of my ideas, together with the criticisms based on them, seem to me to have their source in the failure to take into consideration the contextual problems by which my statements have their import determined—a failure especially marked, as is shown later, in the case of Dr. Murphy, in spite of his professed respect for the principle of Contextualism.

Among the contemporary factors which enable us to get away from issues that lack present support and relevance is the influence of biology and cultural anthropology in transforming traditional psychological views. The point to be borne in mind in this connection is the respective bearings of the old "subjectivistic" psychology and the new behavioral one upon the philosophical conception of experience. It is to me a very curious fact that some of my critics take for granted a mentalistic view of experience; so that they cannot help attributing to me that view when I speak of experience. In addition they so largely ignore the difficulties inherent in their own subjectivism: —difficulties that are recognized by Santayana, and that drive him into complete scepticism, tempered by a sudden and unmediated practical jump of pure faith into the things of nature— a kind of arbitrary pragmatism from which I shrink. For it seems to me identical with the pragmatism sometimes attributed to Kant, although with the substitution of animal for moral faith on one side, and of a natural for the noumenal world on the other. The biological-anthropological method of approach to experience provides the way out of mentalistic into behavioral interpretation of experiencing, both in general and in its detailed manifestations. With equal necessity and pertinency, it points the way out of the belief that experience as such is inherently cognitional and that cognition is the sole path that leads into the natural world. Anybody who accepts the sociobiological point of view is bound, I think, to raise sooner or later the questions I put forward in *Studies in Logical Theory* about the relations between dominantly esthetic, moral and affectional modes and subject-matters of experience and the cognitional mode and its subject-matter. I can see how this issue can be considered without arriving at the idea of "Instrumentalism." But I believe the conclusion of any serious analysis will make the cognitional mode intermediate between an earlier, less organized, more confused and fragmentary sort of experienced subject-matter and one more ordered, clearer, freer, richer, and under better control as to its occurrence.

The other fundamental consideration is drawn from a study of modern scientific method in its contrast with Greek and medieval theory and practice of knowing. It is, of course, the importance of experimental method. If in this connection I have emphasized physical knowledge, it is not (as I have said many times) because the latter is the only kind of knowledge, but because its comparative maturity as a form of knowledge exemplifies so conspicuously the necessary place and function of experimentation; whereas, in contrast, beliefs in moral and social subjects are still reached and framed with minimum regard for experimental method.

I am aware that is is now not unusual to say that the value of experimental method is such a familiar commonplace that it is not necessary to dwell upon its implications; that putting it in antithesis to the theory of immediate knowing is but a case of slaying the dead. I wish this were so. If it were, I should feel that I had accomplished a large part of the purpose I set out to accomplish, and that philosophy would henceforth be free from this phase of epistemological doctrine. But I find the belief in immediate knowledge still flourishing, and I also find that a writer like Mr. Bertrand Russell can link my theory of knowledge and the place of experimentation (doing and making) in knowledge primarily with an age of industrialism and collective enterprise, so especially marked in this country as to make my philosophy peculiarly American. This view is a repetition of a position he took long ago. When, in 1922, he said that he found the "love of truth obscured in America by commercialism of which pragmatism is the philosophical expression," I remarked that the statement seemed to me to be "of that order of interpretation which would say that English neo-realism is a reflection of the snobbish aristocracy of the English and the tendency of French thought to dualism an expression of an alleged Gallic disposition to keep a mistress in addition to a wife."[10] And I still believe that Mr. Russell's confirmed habit of connecting the pragmatic theory of knowing with obnoxious aspects of American industrialism, instead of with the experimental method of attaining knowledge, is much as if I were to link his philosophy to the interests of English landed

[10] Reprinted in *Characters and Events*, Vol. II, 543.

aristocracy instead of with dominant interest in mathematics.

Similarly, when I read that I eschew discussion of a certain problem because "my *purpose* is practical," I am quite sure that all I have said—amounting first and last to a good deal—to the effect that my pragmatism affirms that action is involved in *knowledge,* not that knowledge is subordinated to action or "practice," has gone for naught—as it could hardly do if the emphasis upon experimental method were taken seriously. And I should not be obliged to devote to the topic of *truth* the space later given to it, if what I have said about *consequences* were put in the context of experiment. The outcome of the operations that are guided by a hypothesis is the only context in which consequences in my theory have anything to do with truth. Nor, were the point recognized, should I be compelled to repeat once more that, instead of holding that knowledge is instrumental to action and truth to personal satisfaction, what I have uniformly insisted upon is that knowledge when attained is the only medium to controlled enrichment and control of subsequent experiences of a qualitative non-cognitive type. As it is, however, I seem obliged to cite a passage like the following:

Many critics take an "instrumental" theory of knowledge to signify that the value of knowing is instrumental to the knower. This is a matter which is as it may be in particular cases; but certainly in many cases the pursuit of science is carried on, like other sports, for its own satisfaction. Instrumentalism is a theory not about personal disposition and satisfaction in knowing but about the proper objects of science, "proper" being defined in terms of physics.[11]

And again,

To say that knowledge as the fruit of intellectual discourse is an end in itself is to say what is esthetically and morally true for some persons, but it conveys nothing about the *structure* of knowledge; it does not even hint that its *objects* are not instrumental. These are questions that can be decided only by an examination of the things in question.

Earlier in the same paragraph, it is said to "be a priceless gain when it (gaining of knowledge) becomes an intrinsic de-

[11] *Experience and Nature,* 151.

light," while it is also pointed out that the more this possibility is emphasized, the more imperative becomes the social problem of discovering why it is that such a relatively small number of persons enjoy the privilege.[12] In short, I think I have lived up, with reasonable faithfulness, to the principle stated in the ensuing passage: "Genuine intellectual integrity is found in experimental knowing. Until this lesson is fully learned, it is not safe to dissociate knowledge from experiment nor experiment from experience."[13] I shall indeed be most happy when the day comes when all I have said on this topic becomes superfluous.

B. Experience and Empirical Method in Philosophy

After this introduction, intended to place some of my leading ideas in their proper context, I come to the first of the three chief subjects to be taken up in my reply. Dr. Piatt remarks in his paper that understanding my position would be facilitated if more attention were paid to my naturalism and less to my empiricism. I fully agree, with the proviso that my idea of experience and hence of empirical method is naturalistic. I have already mentioned the potential effect of biological and anthropological knowledge in transforming the older psychological and philosophical idea of experience. The modification thus effected is directly relevant to Mr. Russell's notions that my philosophy is holistic and that my empiricism leads to subjectivism; to the interpretation placed by Mr. Pepper upon my use of such words as coherence, integration, wholes, etc.; to Mr. Santayana's charge that my theory of experience commits me to a view that everything is "immediate foreground" so that there is no room left for nature as background; and, in a less direct way, to some of Mr. Reichenbach's criticisms. I shall accordingly discuss the criticisms which bear upon this point, concluding this section of my reply with a few remarks suggested by Mr. Allport's careful study of my psychological views.

[12] *Ibid.*, 203. The belief that a theory of knowing which in its origin was inherently a leisure class theory has influence in justifying the state of society in which only a few are thus privileged, hence in perpetuating the latter condition, *is* a part of my complete theory. If that be commercialism, I do not know what humanism would be.

[13] *Essays in Experimental Logic*, 74.

I. For many years I have consistently—and rather persistently—maintained that the key to a philosophic theory of
experience must proceed from initially linking it with the processes and functions of life as the latter are disclosed in biological
science. So viewed, I have held that experience is a matter or
an "affair" (*pace* Mr. Santayana) of interaction of living creatures with their environments; *human* experience being what
it is because human beings are subject to the influences of culture, including use of definite means of intercommunication, and
are what in anthropological jargon are called *acculturated* organisms. I am naturally somewhat surprised, accordingly, when I
find that Mr. Santayana sets forth as something he takes to be
in complete opposition to my position, the idea expressed in the
following sentence: "Every naturalist knows that this waking
dream [immediate experience of things] is dependent for its
existence, quality, intensity and duration on obscure processes
in the living body, in its interplay with the environment; processes which go back, through seeds, to the first beginnings of life
on earth." For in some fundamental respects this view of experience seems to be just that which I have consistently taken,
his word *interplay* being synonymous with my word *interaction*.
However, the phrase "waking dream" gives pause to complete
identification of our two views, where the advantage, from the
standpoint of common sense, seems to be on the side of my view.

However, there is a certain ambiguity in the sentence quoted
from Mr. Santayana, which possibly throws light upon why he
takes experience to be but a waking and specious dream. The
ambiguity is found in the phrase "obscure processes in the
living body;" for, if these obscure processes are isolated from
connection with organic activities which, in their interaction with
environment, constitute *life,* dependence of experience upon
obscure occurrences in the *inside* of the organism certainly
does cut experience off from intrinsic connection with environing conditions and render it a mere parasitic attachment to a
private body. However, this interpretation of the phrase as an
explanation of why Santayana regards experience as a dream,
as specious, as a veil drawn between us and nature, is speculative. It is safer to suppose that he starts from the traditional "mentalistic" view of British psychology; and yet he

takes sufficient cognizance of biological facts to connect *it* with the body in its interplay with environment. For the product of this combination—of Lockeian psychology with a reference to the organism—is a view in which an experience is a dream, while the dream is a product of interplay of a body with environing conditions.

Since, on the contrary, I begin with experience as the manifestation of interactions of organism and environment, it follows that the distinction between the things of a dream and of waking life is one to be itself stated in terms of different modes of interaction, so that it is pointless to call them both "dreams." At all events, it is only because he attributes to me the idea of experience which he himself holds—a view that seems to me to involve a complete abandonment of the professed naturalistic standpoint—that he draws the conclusions he sets forth from what he takes to be my view.[14]

Because of Mr. Santayana's own view of experience and his notion that no intelligent person can have any idea of "experience" save that put forth in orthodox British "mentalism," he attributes to me the monstrous position that "only the immediate is real;" a view that is obviously contradicted by the idea of experience as an interaction of organism and environment. Then when he finds that the implications of the latter view are in fact carried out in my writings, he decides that in addition to pure subjectivism I hold to an external behaviorism in which there is nothing immediate or consummatory and to identification of experience with conventions. Such a combination of contradictions, did it represent my philosophy, would confer a certain pre-eminence, although not an enviable one, upon my ideas. It is, however, Mr. Santayana's premises, not mine, which make experience merely immediate, specious and illusory, with Nature so completely screened by it that the only possible Naturalism is a gesture of genuflection aimed blindly in the direction of an object of pure faith.

[14] Mr. Santayana's paper is an almost literal reprint of an article published by him in 1926 in the *Journal of Philosophy*. As he makes no reference in reprinting it to my reply in the same *Journal* in February 1927, I am obliged to refer the reader to that article of mine for detailed discussion of many points in his contribution to this volume not here dealt with.

However, lest my reply here merely take the form of an *ad hominem* comparison of the respective merits of our two views, let me say a few words of a more general character. If the things of experience are produced, as they are according to my theory, by interaction of organism and environing conditions, then as Nature's own foreground they are not a barrier mysteriously set up between us and nature. Moreover the organism—the self, the "subject" of action,—is a factor *within* experience and not something outside of it to which experiences are attached as the self's private property. According to my view a characterization of any aspect, phase, or element of experience as *mine* is not a description of its direct existence but a description of experience with respect to some special problem for some special purpose, one which needs to be specified.[15] So much for alleged subjectivism, though I cannot refrain from once more asking how those who hold a purely "subjectivistic" idea of experience provide means for ever getting outside of its charmed circle. Mr. Santayana, at least, sees the need of some device and hence provides "animal faith" as the recourse of otherwise helpless "experience."

The account does not close here. I have repeatedly stated that an indispensable part of my theory is the fact that experience as an interaction consists of connections between doing-undergoing-doing . . . , and that the connections between the two, when they are noted and formulated, give rise to the distinctively cognitive experience; namely, a perception of relations which are mediated and mediating. I have pointed out the fallacy of supposing that because an experience is immediate in its existence—or is directly just what it is and nothing else— its *subject-matter* must be immediate. My theory of the relation of cognitive experiences to other modes of experience is based upon the fact that *connections* exist in the most immediate non-cognitive experience, and when the experienced situation becomes problematic, the connections are developed into

---

[15] Although the required specification is not particularly an issue here, I point out that I have several times suggested that reference of a specified experience to "me," like a reference to "you," arises in those social interactions in which there is need for assuming *responsibility*.

distinctive objects of knowledge, whether of common sense or of science.[16] The significance of experience as foreground is that the foreground is of such a nature as to contain material which, when operationally dealt with, provides the clews that guide us straight into Nature's background and into Nature *as* background. If philosophical writers would and could only forget their own dominating foreground of mentalistic psychological interpretation of experience, the historic course of the experiential development of the sciences out of experiences of the sort found among savage peoples would suffice to prove that experience is in fact of this sort. The proof would be reinforced by noting what happens whenever out of experiences previously had there develops a new experience based upon and containing juster and deeper cognitive insight into the world in which we live.

Some of my critics say that my philosophy does not tell much about the environing world which is discovered when experience takes on the cognitive phase. I hope this statement, though offered as an indictment, is correct. For, according to my view, the actual inquiries constituting the sciences of astronomy, archaeology, botany, down through the alphabet to the *zed* of zoology, are the procedures which tell us about the environing world; they tell because they follow out clews present in actually had experiences. The business of philosophy, in logic or the theory of knowledge, is not to provide a rival account of the natural environment, but to analyze and report how and to what effect inquiries actually proceed, genetically and functionally, in their experiential context. In this connection, I quote the following extraordinary passage from Santayana's essay: "Suppose I say that everything ideal emanates from something natural. Dewey agrees, *understanding that everything remote emanates from something immediate*. But what I meant was that everything immediate emanates from something biological." Eliminating the effect of an *aura* that clings to the word "emanates," the view stated in the last sentence is also mine. But

---

[16] Long ago I learned from William James that there are immediate experiences of the connections linguistically expressed by conjunctions and prepositions. My doctrinal position is but a generalization of what is involved in this fact.

I recognize frankly the circular movement involved, and that the experience which results from interaction with environing conditions contains within itself relations which when followed out tell us about the biological and about the further background—astronomical and geological. In other words, the proof of the fact that *knowledge* of nature, but not nature itself, "emanates" from immediate experience is simply that this is what has actually happened in the history or development of experience, animal or human on this earth—the only alternative to this conclusion being that in addition to experience as a source and test of beliefs, we possess some miraculous power of intuitive insight into remote stellar galaxies and remote geological eons. In the latter case, it is strange that astronomers and geologists have to work so hard to get first certain direct observational experiences and then to get those other experiences by whose aid they interpret and test the evidential value of what is observed. I am compelled to decide that the chief difference between myself and some of my critics is that I succeeded finally in freeing myself from observation of certain facts only through the medium of the traditional "subjective" view of experience, while these facts are still seen by my critics through the refracting medium of an uncriticized psychological doctrine.

II. When I turn to Mr. Reichenbach's paper, discussion finds itself in a context where there is agreement upon certain basic points. We have empiricism in common, and he also agrees with me—as against early logical positivists and Mr. Russell, at least in one of his periods—that experience as such cannot be reduced to sense data, since immediate reality in experience consists "of things, not of qualities." To a certain extent, I think, the further difference between us is lexicographical, due to different habitual associations with certain words, illustrated by the fact that he interprets "subjective" to mean—if I understand him aright—that which is influenced or affected by the action of the organism in that particular respect or capacity; whereas I give the word an objectionable metaphysical or epistemological meaning. However, since Mr. Reichenbach also makes the word synonymous with *apparent* and places what is designated by it in antithesis to the *objective* and *real*, the difference

between us is not wholly linguistic, even though Mr. Reichenbach expressly repudiates the traditional metaphysical meaning
of the words. In any case, since Mr. Reichenbach bases his justification for use of the words upon my idea about the relation
of the distinctive object of science to the subject-matter of perceptual experience, the need for special discussion of the latter
point is clearly indicated.

The foundation of his criticism is the belief that my identification of the scientific object with *relations*, instead of with some
kind of existing non-relational things, commits me to the doctrine of the *"non-reality"* of scientific objects. This point is so
fundamental that I am grateful to Dr. Reichenbach for the opportunity to discuss the matter. For I certainly have never
intended to say anything which could lead directly or indirectly
to a belief that I hold a "non-realistic interpretation of scientific
concepts." On the contrary—as is indicated in what I have said
in immediately preceding pages—the actual operative presence
of *connections* (which when formulated are *relational*) in the
subject-matter of direct experience is an intrinsic part of my
idea of experience. I am obliged, then, to conclude that Dr.
Reichenbach holds to that traditional particularistic empiricism
according to which "relations" have not the empirical reality
possessed by things and qualities, so that attribution of the
same view to me logically makes relational objects unreal. This
interpretation is borne out by Mr. Reichenbach's reference to
the "nominalistic reduction of abstracta to concreta," which
he assumes to be involved in the empiricism common to both
of us. But just here is where the view of experience as the manifestation of interactions of an acculturated organism—in the
case of human experience—with environment differs from
traditional empiricism. Mr. Reichenbach, as I see his position,
has advanced beyond traditional psychological empiricism to
the point of admitting *things* as material of direct experience
instead of just separate qualities. But he has not gone on to the
point of admitting that *actions* and modes of actions, ways of
operating, are also contained in what is directly experienced. Yet
if one starts with the biological-cultural approach to the theory
of experiencing, the presence of native and acquired (like habits)

general ways of behavior is an unescapable datum.[17]

Mr. Reichenbach, however, quotes from my writings a passage whose interpretation may seem to justify attribution to me of denial of the reality of scientific objects. The passage reads: "The physical object, as scientifically defined, is not a duplicated real object, but is a statement . . . of the relations between sets of changes the qualitative object sustains with changes in other things." Now the treachery of words is such that this sentence taken by itself may seem to read like an assertion that the scientific object is not "real," in spite of what is suggested by the word "duplicated." The context in which the passage is located has to do with one of the two problems mentioned in my Introduction as central in modern philosophy; namely, the relation of the "conceptual" objects of physical science to things of ordinary perception. I cannot be accused of inventing this problem. Moreover, one solution for it has been a doctrine which makes perceived and "conceived," or scientific, objects rival claimants for the position of being the "realities" knowledge is about. The sentence quoted is a denial of the validity of that view. What lies back of it is the belief that the qualitative traits of the things of ordinary common sense knowledge are not only legitimate but necessary in connection with one kind of problems, —those of use and enjoyment—, while the so-called "conceptual" objects of science are legitimate and necessary for the kind of problems with which scientific inquiry is concerned. Hence they are not rival claimants for occupancy of the seat of "real" knowing; and one does not duplicate in "true" or objective fashion what the other presents in a merely apparent and subjective fashion.[18] Or, as I have put the matter elsewhere, "The procedure of physics itself, not any metaphyical or epistemological theory, discloses that physical objects cannot be *individual* ex-

---

[17] Peirce's pragmatic empiricism is of course explicit on this point. James sometimes wavers, but his emphasis upon continuity and upon the motor factor are such as to take his theory definitely out of particularistic or nominalistic empiricism.

[18] That there is nothing peculiar to my form of pragmatism in the position taken about the scientific physical object may be seen in the fact that a writer like Broad can say "What really matters to science is not the inner nature of objects but their mutual relations." *Scientific Thought*, 39.

istential objects."[19] The phrase the "procedure of physics" is intended to point to the fact that the Newtonian-Lockeian supposed primary *qualities* of mass, solidity, extension, etc., are now treated in physical science *not* as qualities but as strictly relational.

What is meant by my statement that a scientific physical object is not a rival or duplicate of an object in the perceptual field may perhaps be made clearer if I mention a passage of mine which Mr. Reichenbach does not quote but which, I find, has been a stumbling-block to some readers in the past. The passage is the following: "The perceived and used table is the only table."[20] Now this passage, because of the use of the word *only*, might be taken to deny that a scientific physical object exists. If the passage had read: "The perceived and used table is the only *table*," the italics might have warded off misinterpretation. For it would have indicated that it was not the existence of a swarm of atoms (electrons, etc.) in rapid movement which was denied, but the notion that this swarm somehow constitutes a ghostly kind of *table*, instead of being just what it is in terms of electrons, deuterons, etc. One would hardly put books or dishes on the latter or sit down before it to eat. That the table *as* a perceived table is an object of knowledge in one context as truly as the physical atoms, molecules, etc., are in another situational context and with reference to another *problem* is a position I have given considerable space to developing.[21]

Pragmatic philosophers did not invent the idea of the nature of the scientific object here put forth. Long ago attention was called to the fact that English physicists tend to seek for literal models, while as a rule French physicists are content with interpreting physical objects symbolically rather than literally. Duhem, for example, many years ago presented a view which amounted in effect to saying that scientific objects are symbolic devices for connecting together the things of ordinary experi-

[19] *Quest for Certainty,* 241; a passage in which, I hope, the word "individual" protects the sentence from the misunderstanding the other sentence may give ground for—for *individual* is here contrasted with *relational* as general.

[20] *Quest for Certainty,* 240.

[21] The position that perceived objects are not as such cognitional is consistent with the position that *what* is perceived may be involved in inquiry.

ence. Others have held that they were devices for facilitating and directing predictions. Now my view does not go as far as these. Its import may be gathered from the following illustration. Suppose one of those persons of extraordinarily keen vision who abound in the Grimm fairy tales were in fact to *see*, sensibly to perceive, an object which had all the qualities a physicist attributes to the atom. He would surely see something. But would he see an atom in the definite sense of seeing that which is *an object of physical science?* I can find but one possible answer, namely: "It depends. If he himself has had a scientific training and if in sensibly perceiving this particular thing he explicitly *identifies* it as having all the *relational* properties required by the scientific theory of atomic structure and with no properties incompatible with the latter, the answer is Yes. But if he sees it merely as another man of lesser power of vision sees a rock, the answer is No." In other words, it is not just the thing as perceived, but the thing as and when it is placed in an extensive ideational or theoretical context *within which it exercises a special office* that constitutes a distinctively physical scientific object.

The exigencies of discussion have taken me beyond the topic of experience over into the topic of knowledge, discussed at greater length later in my reply. I return now to the connection that exists in my theory between the scientific physical object and the qualitative experienced situation. For, according to my view of the latter, the definitely relational objects of science are produced when *connections* existing in the immediate situation are noted and formulated, the latter process involving elaboration in discourse. If, however, the operational presence of *general* modes of activity (constituting *connections*) in the material of ordinary experience is ignored (if, in the sense in which "thing" is an equivalent of the Latin *res*, it is not noted that a *way* of behaving is a "thing"), then the general and relational character of scientific objects must be denied by a professed empiricist. Such a denial has been and will continue to be the occasion for the promulgation of transcendent aprioristic rationalism.[22]

[22] This is perhaps as good a place as any to say that in the sense in which Piatt uses the word *rationalism* my theory is rationalistic, though I much prefer the word *intelligence* to *reason* because of the long anti-empirical history back of the latter

I am sorry that I cannot give to the illustrations presented by Mr. Reichenbach the attention they deserve. About the alleged perceptual bent stick in water, let me say that the *ray of light is* bent—there is no illusion or "appearance" about *that*. It is not *scientific* knowledge which substitutes bending of light, as it passes from one medium to another, for bending of the stick. For "bent" and "crooked" in objects of perception are matters of *motor* adaptive responses. I doubt if any oarsman ever failed to make the correct response, the response being "correct" because it produces the consequences intended in the act of using the oar. The boatman, then, never supposed the *oar* was bent. A fisherman who catches fish by spearing them requires but a few trials, with no help from "science," to form a habit that is expressed in effective motor adjustments.[23] What science does is not to correct the thing of ordinary experience by substituting another thing but to *explain* the former. Moreover, the object as perceived can be explained only by giving the "appearance" full standing as it occurs; and explanation takes the form of a correlation, general in nature, between changes in the density of media and changes in the refractive index of light; the correlation being the scientific "physical object" in this case, so that the illustration would seem to prove my definition.[24]

Another instance cited by Mr. Reichenbach seems to me most naturally interpreted in my sense rather than in his—the instance namely of a needle on a dial, the motion of which is most

word. The kind of "*a priori*" which Mr. Piatt mentions (and which *is* involved in my theory) is so radically different from the fixed *a priori* located in and furnished by the inherent nature of Mind, *Intellectus, Purus,* Reason as *Nous*, figuring in the history of thought, that it seems to me the words rationalism and *a priori* should be either avoided, or else used only with explanatory qualification.

[23] It seems to me that the problem with which Mr. Reichenbach is concerned is of the same order as one that used to be discussed in psychological texts: How does it happen we see things upright when "images" on the retina are inverted? The problem arose only because the phenomena were placed in a cognitive context instead of in a stimulus-response context. We don't first see and "know" that the images are inverted, and then correct by appealing to scientific knowledge. We *learn* to make effective motor responses, and if and when *they* are acquired the nature of the stimulus is for perceptual experience a matter of no bearing or relevancy.

[24] The meaning of *explanation* as here used is functional—that of bringing a given set of cases into relation with sets that are of a different kind with respect to qualitative considerations so that free and systematic inference is possible.

regularly employed as a register of velocity or to serve as a speedometer. The index may, however, be moved by changes induced by a magnet without the occurrence of locomotion in space. I am unable to see the relevancy of distinctions of the *real* and apparent, the *objective* and *subjective* in cases like this. If a person who has formed the habit of making a motor response to the movement of an index hand as a sign of a rate of speed should apply that habit when the change of position of the index hand is a sign of something quite different, there is certainly a maladjustment in a stimulus-response situation. A habit formed under a given set of conditions, which have been constant in the past, does not work when the conditions in which that habit is effective are suddenly changed—and yet *as* a habit it will tend to operate. This is a very common source of mistakes—that is, of taking things amiss in action. Why it should be necessary to have recourse to the categories of "subjective" and "objective," "real" and "apparent," in connection with such cases I do not see;—save that the systematic neglect by traditional psychology of motor and active elements in the make-up of experiences has deprived those who accept such a psychology of the natural— and naturalistic—means of describing what happens.

III. There is some ground for thinking that my emphatic affirmation of the "reality" of the *qualities* of directly experienced things has had some effect in leading Reichenbach to suppose that I deny or am doubtful about the "reality" of scientific objects. In this respect, I agree with him that it would have been better to employ a more neutral word than "real," namely *existential*. But I fear that this linguistic change does not remove the actual difference between us. When I used the word *real* in the following passage (which he quotes from me), I used a word that is unfortunately highly ambiguous, so that I must accept partial responsibility for any misunderstanding occasioned: "Dreams, insanity, and fantasy are natural products, as 'real' as anything in the world." I now see that I should not have depended upon the use of quotation marks about *real* to protect the sentence from misconception, even in connection with the phrase "natural products." The meaning of the passage is less ambiguously conveyed in a sentence on the page previous to the one from which it is quoted, where all qualities, the tertiary and those usually called "subjective," are said to be "as much products of the *doings of nature* as are color, sound, pressure, perceived size and distance."[25] It means that as manifestations of interactions of a naturally existent organism and existent environing conditions all experienced materials stand on exactly the same level. But it does *not* mean that with respect to their *evidential* value, their function as dependable signs, they stand on the same level. On the contrary, I have repeatedly insisted that experiential control of what is directly given, a control which analyzes that material into simpler, more "elementary" data, is necessary for valid inference and hence whenever cognition comes into the picture. Hence I have held that any signification justifiably assignable to the words "real" and "apparent," "subjective" and "objective," has to do with experienced materials in their evidential, signifying function, and does *not* belong to them in their original and innocent occurrence. For this reason I do not see that my acceptance of the word *"existential"* in place of the ambiguous and hence objectionable word *"real"* would, in spite of its being an improvement in expression, remove the basic difference between us. For what to me is a difference arising *within* the reflective or cognitive use of primary experiential material, is to Mr. Reichenbach a difference between that primary material itself, which is inherently only "apparent," and the material of cognition as "real."[26]

Hence I agree fully with the statement that "the distinction between 'appearance' and 'reality' is a basic need for constructing a consistent picture of the everyday world, in particular the world of action." But (aside from wishing that less ambiguous words be found) I point out that the problem of forming a

---

[25] *Quest for Certainty*, 239.

[26] As a verbal matter, the words *apparent, real, subjective, objective* are so loaded with metaphysical and epistemological debris, that the force of the distinction would, it seems to me, be much better indicated by words like *dependable* and *unreliable* qua evidential; *relevant* and *irrelevant; effective* and *futile; directive* and *misleading*—all being used in a specified *functional* sense. That sometimes material is undependable in its evidential function because it is overloaded with qualities that are due to the organism's share in the organic-environment interaction is certainly true—as in the tendency to clothe natural occurrences with animistic properties. But elimination of this source of error does not involve, as far as I can see, any other principle than that involved in every experimental determination of data as appropriate and effective.

consistent picture of the world obviously falls within a definitely cognitive context, and is thus secondary and derived as compared with the materials of primary non-cognitive experiences. In leaving this phase of the matter, I may say that, so far as I am aware, there is nothing peculiarly pragmatic in this special phase of my general doctrine, but that the position I have taken follows directly from a thoroughly naturalistic treatment of experience in general, and of experiences in their plural occurrence. I am, however, more concerned here to make my own position clear, leaving its correctness or incorrectness to be judged after it has been made clear, than to engage in controversy with Mr. Reichenbach on this particular point.[27] So I conclude with saying that the plausibility of the contention that the qualitative objects of direct experience are *"replaced"* by other objects through the intervention of inferential processes, of the same type that lead to scientific objects, depends upon a confusion of the function performed by *adaptive motor responses* in things of ordinary experience with the function performed by controlled and systematic *inference* in cognitive experience of the scientific type.

By way of further clearing up my own position I would point out that I hold that the word "subject," if it is to be used at all, has the organism for its proper *designatum*. Hence it refers to an *agency of doing*, not to a knower, mind, consciousness or whatever. If the words "subject" and "object" are to be set over against each other, it should be in those situations in which a person, self, or organism as a *doer* sets up purposes, plans, to realize the execution of which is resisted by environing conditions as they exist. An *object*, as Professor Gildersleeve wittily suggested a good many years ago, is that which *objects:* that which gets in the way of the carrying out of some plan entertained by a person—where the word *person* has the denotative force of John Smith and Mary Jones. A *person* on this view is one

[27] Yet I cannot refrain from saying that (as Reichenbach's *Experience and Prediction* clearly shows) upon his view the existence of an "external world" is a *problem* for philosophy, whereas according to my view the problem is artificially generated by the kind of premises I call epistemological. When we *act* and find environing things in stubborn opposition to our desires and efforts, the externality of the environment to the *self* is a direct constituent of direct experience.

existing thing in the world—one "object" among other objects whose distinguishing traits are to be learned by inquiry, just as the difference between cats and dogs as things in the actual world is learned. I submit that if the words *personal* and *impersonal* were uniformly prefixed to things ("objects" in the sense in which they are linguistically identified with things) instead of the words "subjective" and "objective," an artificial, because gratuitously instituted, problem would be eliminated.

There remains in connection with this part of Mr. Reichenbach's paper, the matter of "tertiary qualities" in relation to valuation. It is of course an inherent part of the naturalistic view of experience that affective qualities are products of the doings of nature—of the interaction of an organism and environmental conditions. It also follows that as direct qualities their reference is primarily to the carrying on of life processes— I hardly need do more than allude to the qualities of things as loved and feared. *If* the object of science is something which is related as a real thing to a thing of direct experience as merely apparent, and if it has to be made, by means of inferential processes, to replace the latter, it is clear that no such scientific replacing object exists in the case of things of desire, affection and direct enjoyment. From this point of view the possibility of scientifically valid objects of valuation as a foim of knowledge is ruled out from the start. But if the scientific object is a generalized constant correlation of sets of changes, there is no insuperable object set up by premises laid down in advance. Correlations between changes that form *conditions* of desires, etc., and changes that form their *consequences* when acted upon, have the same standing and function in this field that physical objects have in their field.

There are many *practical* difficulties to be overcome in developing the methods of inquiry that will enable conclusions regarding such correlations to be reached. But as distinct from the position taken by Mr. Reichenbach there is no inherent theoretical bar on my view to some day succeeding.[28]

[28] I deal with this matter very briefly because a monograph on this topic, stating my views in detail, has recently been published: *Theory of Valuation*, in the *International Encyclopedia of Unified Science*, Vol. II, No. 4 (Chicago, 1939).

IV. Other criticisms of my theory of experience are connected
with the fact that I have called experiences *situations*, my use
of the word antedating, I suppose, the introduction of the *field*
idea in physical theory, but nevertheless employed, as far as I
can see, to meet pretty much the same need—a need imposed by
subject-matter not by theory. The need in both cases—though
with different subject-matters—is to find a viable alternative
to an atomism which logically involves a denial of connections and to an absolutistic block monism which, in behalf
of the reality of relations, leaves no place for the discrete, for
plurality, and for individuals. In philosophy there is also the
need to find an alternative for that combination of atomistic
particularism with respect to empirical material and Platonic
a priori realism with respect to universals which is professed,
for example, in the philosophy of Mr. Russell. According to the
naturalistic view, every experience in its direct occurrence is an
interaction of environing conditions and an organism. As such
it contains in a fused union some*what* experienc*ed* and some
processes of experienc*ing*. In its identity with a life-function, it
is temporally and spatially more extensive and more internally
complex than is a single thing like a stone, or a single quality
like red. For no living creature could survive, save by sheer
accident, if its experiences had no more reach, scope or content,
than traditional particularistic empiricism provides for. On the
other hand, it is impossible to imagine a living creature coping
with the entire universe all at once. In other words, the theory
of experiential situations which follows directly from the biological-anthropological approach is by its very nature a *via
media* between extreme atomistic pluralism and block universe
monisms. Which is but to say that it is genuinely empirical in a
naturalistic sense.

Mr. Russell, however, finds that what I write about situations
as the units of experience springs from and leads directly to
the Hegelian variety of absolutism. One indirect reason he
presents for this belief, when it is put in the form of an argument, runs somewhat as follows: Mr. Dewey admits not only
that he was once an Hegelian but that Hegel left a permanent
deposit in his thought; Hegel was a thoroughgoing holist;

therefore, Dewey uses "situation" in a holistic sense. I leave it to Mr. Russell as a formal logician to decide what he would say to anyone who presented this argument in any other context. The following argument answers perhaps more to Mr. Russell's idea of inductive reasoning. British philosophy is analytic; Dewey not only leans to the Continental synthetic tendency but has vigorously criticized British analytic thought; therefore, his identification of an experience with a situation commits him to "holism."

Coming to a more relevant matter, the interpretation put by Mr. Russell upon quotations of passages in which I have used the word *situation* contradicts what, according to my basic leading principle, is designated by it.[29] This position, however, is not just a necessary implication of that principle. The pluralistic and individualized character of situations is stated over and over again, and is stated moreover in direct connection with the principle of the experiential continuum. Take for instance the following passage:

> Situations are precarious and perilous because the persistence of life-activity depends upon the influence which present acts have upon future acts. The *continuity* of a life-process is secured only as acts performed render the environment favorable to subsequent organic acts. . . . All perceived objects are individualized. They are, as such, wholes complete in themselves. Everything directly experienced is qualitatively unique.[30]

I lay no claim to inventing an environment that is marked by both discreteness and continuity. Nor can I even make the more modest claim that I discovered it. What I have done is to interpret this duality of traits in terms of the identity of experience with life-functions. For in the process of living both absorption in a present situation and a response that takes account of its effect upon the conditions of later experiences are equally

---

[29] Mr. Savery has not had Mr. Russell's difficulty in understanding my point of view. Cf. his remark "Concatenism is, then, a *via media* between monism and monadism. It is the only form of pluralism that is intellectually tenable." There can be no genuine continuity unless an experience, no matter how unique or individualized in its own pervasive quality, contains within itself something that points to other experiences—or, in Mr. Savery's phrase, unless experiences *"overlap"* with respect to their subject-matters.

[30] *Quest for Certainty*, 234.

necessary for maintenance of life. From one angle, almost every-thing I have written is a commentary on the fact that situations are *immediate* in their direct occurrence, and mediating and mediated in the temporal continuum constituting life-experience.

I have pointed out that one person cannot communicate an experience as immediate to another person. He can only invite that other person to institute the conditions by which the person himself will *have* that kind of situation the *conditions* for which are stated in discourse. Even if this difficult condition is fulfilled, there is no assurance that any one will so act as to have the ex-perience. The horse led to water is not forced to drink. This pre-dicament has to be faced by the experimentalist in physical in-quiry. He, however, can describe the experimental set-up, the material involved, the apparatus employed, the series of acts performed, the observations which result and state the conclu-sions reached. But even so it is up to other inquirers to take this report as an invitation to *have* a certain experienced situation and as a direction as to how to obtain it. *This predicament is inherent, according to genuine empiricism, in the derived relationship of discourse to primary experience.* Any one who refuses to go outside the universe of discourse—as Mr. Russell apparently does—has of course shut himself off from understanding what a "situation," as directly experienced subject-matter, is.

An almost humorous instance of such refusal and its conse-quences is found when Mr. Russell writes: "We are told very little about the nature of things before they are inquired into." If I have said or tried to say the tiniest bit about the "nature of things" prior to inquiry into them, I have not only done some-thing completely contradictory to my own position but something that seems to me inherently absurd. Or if, as is possible, what the passage means is that, even after inquiry has been carried on, I still do not tell what things were like *before the time in which the inquiry* was undertaken, I can only say that I have always supposed that this sort of telling is the specific business of the inquiries themselves. I plead guilty to not having written into my philosophical writings an encyclopedia of the conclu-sions of all the sciences. Whatever Mr. Russell may have meant by the sentence quoted, my position is that *telling* is (i) a matter of discourse, and that (ii) all discourse is derived from and inherently referable to experiences of things in non-discursive experiential having;—so that, for example, although it is possible to tell a man blind from birth *about* color, we cannot by discourse confer upon him that which is had in the direct experience of color—my whole position on this matter being a generalization of this commonplace fact.

When Mr. Russell adds to the sentence just quoted from him, the phrase "we know, however, that, like dishonest politicians, things behave differently when observed from the way they behave when no one is paying attention to them," I do not suppose he is intending to say that, according to the Heisenberg principle, minute particles moving at high velocities behave like dishonest politicians. I take it he is referring to something he regards as a legitimate inference from my position. In the latter case, it is probably well for me to state once more what my view is. It is that scientific knowledge has an effect upon things *previously directly-experienced-but-not-known*. Now this I should have supposed to be a commonplace, although a commonplace which philosophers have mostly not deigned to notice. It is commonly believed, for example, that persons behave somewhat differently when they know they are mad than when they are mad without knowing it, and that a man who knows he is hungry will not behave in the identical way he behaves when he is hungry without being aware of it. Likewise with the knowledge of illness; the different kind of response engaged in is, *ipso facto,* a modification of the subject-matter of a previous non-cognitive experience. And, although the point involves trenching upon the topic of the second section of my reply, namely knowledge, I add here that I have not been guilty of the Irish bull with which I am occasionally charged. I have not held, as is intimated in Mr. Russell's allusion to knowledge of sun and planets, that knowing modifies the *object of knowledge.* That a planet *as known* is a very different thing from the speck of light that is found in direct experience, I should suppose to be obvious;—although, once more, one of those commonplaces of which philosophers engaged in pursuit of an artificial problem have failed to take proper note. The fact that critics so readily forget that the planet, rock (or whatever it is that is used, and which they imagine I hold to be modified by knowing), is *already* an object of knowledge indicates that they hold that the entire subject-matter of philosophical theory is exhaustively contained within the field of discourse. An empiricist will hold that subject-matter to be *philosophically* understood has to be placed in its reference to subject-matter of directly experienced situations.[31]

In this connection Mr. Russell's belief that I hold that the "raw material remains *unknowable*" is peculiarly indicative. For it affords final proof that Mr. Russell has not been able to follow the distinction I make between the immediately had material of non-cognitively experienced situations and the material of cognition—a distinction without which my view cannot be understood. A typical illustration of what I mean by such non-cognitive experiences is found in my not infrequent statements to the effect that the assumption of the ubiquity of cognitive experience inevitably results in disparagement of things experienced by way of love, desire, hope, fear and other traits characteristic of human individuality. Instead, however, of holding that this material is *unknowable*, my view is that when the situations in which such material exists become *problematic*, it provides precisely that which is *to be* known by being inquired into. But apparently Mr. Russell is so wedded to the idea that there is no experienced material outside the field of discourse that any intimation that there is such material relegates it, *ipso facto*, to the status of the "*unknowable.*"

Although the point now to be explicitly mentioned concerns my theory of knowledge rather than my theory of experience, it is so directly connected with the "holistic" meaning Mr. Russell reads into the word "situation" as used by me, that it is taken up here. Mr. Russell asserts that my use of the word "situation" commits me to the view that the entire universe is the only "real" object of knowledge, so that logically I am committed to the view expressed by Bradley. It so happens that I

---

[31] Stated in another way, the material of sensations, impressions, ideas as copies, etc., with which traditional empiricism has operated is material already taken out of the context of direct experience and placed in the context of material within discourse for the purpose of meeting the requirements of discourse.

have explicitly stated the fundamental difference between my view and that of the Bradleyan type. I quote the passage because it shows, unless I am mistaken, that the source of Russell's misconception of my view is his imperviousness to what I have said about the *problematic* quality of situations as giving both the occasion for and the control of inquiry.

The theory [that is, of the type just mentioned] thus radically misconstrues the unification towards which inquiry in its reflective mediate stage actually moves. In actual inquiry, movement toward a unified ordered situation exists. But it is always a unification of the subject-matter which constitutes an *individual problematic situation*. It is not unification at large.

If, however, "the feature of unification is generalized beyond the limits in which it takes place, namely *resolution of specific problematic situations*, knowledge is then supposed to consist of attainment of a final all-comprehensive Unity, equivalent to the Universe as an unconditioned whole."[32]

V. Mr. Pepper in his comments on my esthetic theory makes words like *coherence, whole, integration*, etc., the ground of his criticism, rather than *situation*. But since his charge of an "organicism" has something in common with Russell's charge of "holism," I shall deal with his criticism at this point. I have, however, to introduce my remarks by saying something about the topic of method in connection with esthetic theory. Mr. Pepper refers to an attempt on his part at one time to derive a theory of esthetics, at least in outline, from the "implications of the general pragmatic attitude in the face of relevant facts," and being led thereby to predict what a good pragmatist would say upon this subject. I cannot charge Mr. Pepper with trying to *deduce*, in a way opposed to pragmatic empiricism, esthetic theory from general premises in isolation from experienced subject-matter. His phrase "in the face of relevant facts" protects him from this charge. Nevertheless I think his adoption of that method is the source of the criticisms he brings against me. For when he finds in my *Art as Experience* ideas put forward and words used that were not predicted in his scheme, he assumes

[32] *Logic*, 531 (italics not in original text). The passage, however, is almost at the close of the book so that it may have escaped Mr. Russell's attention.

that I have combined an anti-pragmatic position with a genuinely pragmatic one, oscillating between the two. Now in my chapter in *Art as Experience,* I expressly objected to typical and to current philosophies of esthetics on the ground that they were not formed by examination of the subject-matter of esthetic and artistic experience but by deducing what the latter *must be* from antecedent preconceptions. The idea did not occur to me to employ myself the procedure I criticized when it was adopted by others.

These remarks, I hope, serve to clarify the issue, which is whether *words* I have used in describing and analyzing esthetic subject-matter apply to genuine traits of the subject-matter; so that, whether or not some of them have also been used by idealist (organicist) writers on esthetics, they have a meaning consistent with naturalistic and pragmatic empiricism.[33] With respect to these issues, I call attention to the fact that in earlier writings I pointed out that the very type of philosophy Mr. Pepper attributes to me arose historically precisely from the fact that Greek thinkers took categories which *are* applicable to works of art and to their enjoyed perception and then extended them to the whole universe where they are not applicable.[34] In other words, it *is* an integral part of my analysis of the material of esthetic experience that *it,* in distinction from the material of scientific and moral experience *as such,* has traits of qualitative wholeness, integration, etc., as genuinely characteristic of it. This point is the one to be critically appraised and objected to if my esthetic theory is erroneous. However, it is a point Mr. Pepper nowhere discusses. Apparently, my use of certain *words* suffices

[33] It may be pointed out that a large group of biologists have reached, on what they take to be experimental scientific grounds, conclusions they call *organismic,* as over against previous "cellular" conceptions comparable in biology to old views of atomism in physics. I do not know whether Mr. Pepper would bring against them the kind of charge he brings against me, since they also use with great freedom words like *whole, integration,* etc. There is, it seems to me, as much warrant in the one case as in the other.

[34] Cf., for example, in Chapter III of my *Experience and Nature* (and, quite explicitly, the last chapter of my recent *Logic,*) the following sentence. "Their thinkers [those of Greece] were as much dominated by the esthetic characters of experienced objects as modern thinkers are by their scientific and economic (or relational) traits."

to render unnecessary discussion of the subject-matter which is the only criterion for judging the applicability of theories.

In my *Quest for Certainty* I wrote as follows:

> There are situations in which self-enclosed, discrete, individualized characters dominate. They constitute the subject-matter of esthetic experience; and every experience is esthetic in so far as it is final, or arouses no search for some other experience. When this complete quality is conspicuous the experience is denominated esthetic.[35]

Were one to try to guess in advance what I would be likely to say in a more extended discussion of art and esthetics, this passage might form a point of departure. The question it raises is one of fact. Are there experiences of this kind? In the third chapter of my *Art as Experience,* this latter question is discussed at considerable length. The answer given is that every experience to which the name *an* experience emphatically applies is of this nature. Such experiences, of course, can only be *had* and be pointed towards by discourse. But several pages are spent in indicating the traits to be looked for in them, as against experiences that are tight and constricted on one side, and loose, slack, sprawling on the other side. Throughout all subsequent chapters the words *whole, complete, coherence,* refer exactly and exclusively to the materials of these experiences which are individualized and entire in the sense pointed out.[36]

The sole question at issue is then one of fact: Do or do not the objects of distinctively esthetic experiences have characteristics to which the words *whole, integration, complete* apply in that *special sense* which has been indicated?—a sense which is *special* just because it belongs to experiences as esthetic and *not* to experiences of other kinds, and certainly not to the world at large as objects of distinctively *cognitive* experience.

What I have just said exempts me, I believe, from responsibility of taking up one by one all the points made by Mr. Pepper,

[35] P. 235.

[36] For example it is pointed out that the subject-matter of an experience of knowing, while the knowing is in progress, is such as to arouse search for some other experience, but that every conclusion reached after active search is experienced as a finding of what has been searched for and in so far has esthetic quality.

since in each case I could only point to the special signification
given the words used in the context of having an esthetic experience, and raise the question of whether this subject-matter
justifies use of the words in the sense given them. I shall deal
briefly, however, with three of his points. (i) Instead of denying
the importance of *conflict* in esthetic experience, I have emphasized its indispensable function—see for example the references
under *Resistance* in the Index. What I have done is to distinguish
between the cases of conflict that lead to dispersion and disrup-
tion (of which for example modern psychiatry gives so many
examples), and those cases in which conflict and tension are converted into means of intensifying a consummatory appreciation
of material of an individual qualitative experience. The distance which separates such a view from a "theory of harmony
culminating in the great cosmic harmony of the absolute" is so
vast as to confirm the impression that Mr. Pepper was led
astray by ignoring what I said about the uniquely qualitative
individualized and discrete aspect of the situations which have
esthetic traits.

Then (ii) there is my distinction between the raw material of
a work of art which is said to belong to a "common world," and
not to be *private*—since it *is* common—, and the individual response of the personal and individualized vision and shaping
activity of the artist by which otherwise common material is
transformed into a work of art. Because I say—at least this is the
only reason I have discovered—that treating the antecedent
raw material as private, belonging merely to the artist's own
consciousness, takes us to "the state of the madhouse," Mr. Pepper finds something peculiarly organistic in this passage. The
context shows clearly that I am distinguishing between *pre-
artistic material*—which is common to the experience of many
human beings—and the material of the work of art *as such* in
which common material has been transformed into something
individual, unique, through the vision and creative procedures
of an artist.[37] The discussion in my text has for its context the

---

[37] I used, in single quotes, the word 'universal' as a synonym of "*common*." It
may be that Mr. Pepper was unable to distinguish the word thus used from the
"concrete universal" of idealistic philosophy.

old problem of the "representative" character of a work of art; my conclusion being that the material of the work of art as such is *not* representative of what existed before in experience since it represents a transformation of the material had in ordinary (common) experiences by transfusion through a *new* and individual mode of experience. If this view is wrong, *it* is the view to be criticized.[38]

Mr. Pepper is troubled (iii) by the fact that coherence of relations, even of inner relations, figures in my account of artistic form—for is not coherence a mark of the idealistic theory of knowledge, and "inner relations" the sign of its metaphysics? Let us, however, "look at the record"—in this case, my text. After defining form in terms of relations and esthetic form in terms of "completeness of relations in a given medium," I go on directly to say:

> But "relation" is an ambiguous word. In philosophical discourse it is used to designate a connection instituted in thought. It then signifies something indirect, something purely intellectual, even logical. But "relation" in its idiomatic usage denotes something direct and active, something dynamic and energetic. It fixes attention upon the way things bear upon one another, their clashes and unitings, the way they fulfill and frustrate, promote and retard, excite and inhibit one another.[39]

It hardly seems necessary to say any more about coherence and inner relations as they actually enter into my theory. I close by saying that I do not believe that any school of philosophy has a monopolistic hold upon the interpretation of such words as "whole, complete, coherence, integration," etc. I am also convinced that the school of objective idealism has borrowed these traits from esthetic experiences, where they do have application, and has then illegitimately extended them till they became categories of the universe at large, endowed with cosmic import.

[38] There is a touch of the humorous in the fact that Mr. Pepper reverses in this connection his previous dictum that for "organicism the coherence of feelings is central, while for pragmatism it is secondary and instrumental . . ., while for pragmatism quality is central and for organicism only a sort of corollary." It is a reversal because when I say that the private, the feelings, is not the subject-matter of a work of art, but things which, like qualities of color, sound, etc., are *common*, Mr. Pepper accuses me of deserting pragmatism for organicism.

[39] *Art as Experience*, 134.

I am not prepared to deny to writers of this school genuine esthetic insights; and in so far as these insights are genuine, it is the task of an empirical pragmatic esthetics to do justice to them without taking over the metaphysical accretions.

VI. What I have to say in connection with Dr. Allport's paper about my psychological view fits in here perhaps as well as anywhere else. First I want to say that I am gratefully appreciative of the painstaking study and faithful exposition an expert in this field has made of my scattered and, of late years, unprofessional writings. His criticisms are also just. Especially do I admit the truth of his remark that, although I have said that I regard psychology as indispensable for sound philosophizing at the present juncture, I have failed to develop in a systematic way my underlying psychological principles. Some at least of the criticisms of my theory of experience might have been averted if I had set forth my socio-biological psychology so as to show how and why, upon the negative side, many philosophical ideas still put forth as fundamental and as all but axiomatic represent uncritical acceptance of psychological theories formed two centuries ago; and, upon the positive side, so as to show how and why I believe a sound psychology provides the basis for a theory of the nature of experiencing, and of its different modes and their connections with one another. I have made the mistake of treating as incidental certain psychological matters which are central in the present state of philosophy. I had no right to assume that philosophical readers were sufficiently in touch with newer developments in psychology so that my references to the latter could be left with little elaboration. I now see how far contemporary philosophy as a whole is from having appropriated and digested the main principles set forth even in the psychology of William James.

The need for explicit statement is the greater because writers who proclaim the complete independence of philosophy from psychology are often the very ones who can be most seriously charged with uncritical use of outmoded psychological ideas, as if they were matters of course too assured to need examination. This statement is particularly applicable wherever the ideas of subjective-objective, mental-physical come into play, and wherever such a term as "sense-data" is employed as an objective or natural substitute for the older mentalistic word *sensations*. The influence of pre-biological psychology affects also the meanings attached to *ideas* and *conceptions*. As I remark from time to time in the course of my present reply, from the standpoint of a biological-cultural psychology the term "subject" (and related adjectival forms) has only the signification of a certain kind of actual existence; namely, a living creature which under the influence of language and other cultural agencies has become a person interacting with other persons (concrete human beings).

In my theory of experience and of the experiential continuum, this way of regarding the subject (or self, or personal being, or whatever name is employed) is fundamental. For, although the psychological theory involved is a form of Behaviorism, it differs basically from some theories bearing the same name. In the first place, behavior is not viewed as something taking place in the nervous system or under the skin of an organism but always, directly or indirectly, in obvious overtness or at a distance through a number of intervening links, an interaction with environing conditions. In the second place, other human beings who are also acculturated are involved in the interaction, including even persons at a great distance in space and time, because of what they have done in making the direct environment what it is. Were the presence of remote environmental influences, impersonal and personal, within direct experience recognized by my critics some of the objections brought would collapse, especially those which rest upon dialectical manipulation of the idea of "immediacy." For although distant conditions are not present *in persona propria*, they are present through their effects so that the latter provides matter usable as clews and evidential indications that conduct inquiry to knowledge of the indefinitely remote.

Returning now to specific criticisms of Dr. Allport, I am obliged to admit what he says about the absence of an adequate theory of personality. In a desire to cut loose from the influence of older "spiritualistic" theories about the nature of the unity and stability of the personal self (regarded as a peculiar kind of substantial-stuff), I failed to show how natural conditions provide support for integrated and potentially equilibrated personality-patterns. That this potentially often fails of realization is sufficiently proved by psychiatric evidence. But the same evidence shows that conditions which produce integrated personality-patterns are as natural as are those which produce pathological human beings, the differences being due to different kinds of *interactions*. The same evidence is equally convincing as to the rôle of interactions with other persons in determining unified or divided personality patterns. Dr. Allport criticizes my writings in the field where the psychology of persons in their social (inter-personal) relations is peculiarly weighty, on the ground that I have failed to show the compatibility of a community of integrated persons with the variety of segmental types of publics which are due to specialization of interests and divisions of labor. I certainly admit that at the present time the problem is unsolved, and would go so far as to say that as a practical problem it is *the* problem of our day and generation. Need for a theory that would point the way in which efforts at practical solution should be directed is manifested in the present widespread reaction from atomistic "liberal" theories to totalitarianism. But I cannot admit that the incompatibility between individual human beings integrated in themselves and a community life marked by diversity of voluntary groups representing different interests is *inherent*. It is an incompatibility which is historic and which is always changing its constituents so that the problems it sets have forever to be solved anew in construction of new forms of social relationships.

C. The Theory of Knowledge

I. In taking up the second of the main heads under which I am arranging my comments, I begin with Dr. Murphy's criticisms as they bear directly upon my theory of knowledge. In the case of his paper in particular, I have to remind readers of a caution, already given, about the need of keeping in close touch with the text of the original contributions. For although he quotes, in connection with his discussion of special topics, a number of passages from my writings, in his statement of my basic theory of knowledge he neither quotes passages nor gives references in support of his interpretation. Accordingly, although I quote his report of my supposed theory at some length, I must also ask readers to go directly to his paper. His general charge is that "the non-philosophical reader who studies the theory of inquiry in his [my] *Logic,* or the theory of Nature in *Experience and Nature* will not find what on the basis of the prospectus offered he had a right to expect." Now I do not know what criterion is implicit in the reference to a non-philosophical reader nor in the not infrequent references made to an "ordinary theory" of knowing. However, save perhaps as an indication of a certain undefined predilection on Mr. Murphy's part, these allusions are not important. For the sequel makes it clear that Mr. Murphy believes that a philosophical reader will be similarly frustrated. He restates as the ground of his criticisms the alleged fact that, in spite of my nominal opposition to what I call epistemology, my theory of inquiry-knowing is so entangled in the latter that I have come far short of presenting an intelligible theory of knowing.

What, then, acording to Mr. Murphy *is* my theory of inquiry? Instead of taking us, he says, "as it should to such specific sorts of inquiry as serve in practice as our means of finding out about the environment or the consequences of human behavior in it," my procedure, he claims, is as follows:

It [my theory of inquiry] refers us instead to a theory about the rôle of ideas as instruments to be used in so altering a present indeterminate situation that an enjoyed future experience, itself non-cognitive but worth while on its own account, will reliably ensue, through the use of procedures which have proved their instrumental value in this capacity.

At this point I regret all the more the complete absence of substantiating or verifying references because I have tried in my *Logic* to do exactly the thing Mr. Murphy says I have not done:—namely, go to specific sorts of inquiry and reach a generalized account of knowing through analyses of the features they present. Furthermore, I am so far from recognizing my theory of inquiry in the report Dr. Murphy makes of it, that, as presented, it seems to me quite as unintelligible as it does to Mr. Murphy, and, I presume, as it does to the reader. In lieu of verifying references, Murphy repeats twice his interpretation of my view on the nature of inquiry, saying that the "ordinary theory of knowing" (whatever that may be) is "replaced by a reference of ideas to future experience and to the means of so altering a present situation that a desired and anticipated future will reliably ensue;" and,

we have already seen [presumably in the passages just quoted] he regards it [knowing] as a use of ideas as signs of possible future experiences and means for effecting the transition to such experiences in a satisfactory manner. These future experiences, in so far as they terminate inquiry will not be cases of "knowing," that is of the use of given experiences as signs of something else.

I regret my inability to identify any part of my theory of knowing in the above passages. In fact I cannot identify any consistent and intelligible theory whatever by means of the sentences just quoted. If I found them advanced by any writer, my criticism would have to take the form of asking what in the world they are supposed to mean. However, since I cannot rewrite here my whole *Logic*, I shall point out in summary fashion a number of specific points in which the view attributed to me, so far as I can understand it, differs radically from that which I have placed on record in my writings. (1) Instead of saying that "*ideas* are signs of future experiences," I have denied their capacity to act as signs or evidence, pointing out that signifying capacity belongs *only* to observed facts or data. (2) Since Mr. Murphy makes no allusion to the latter in what purports to be an account of my theory of inquiry, I call attention to the fact that instead of saying that "given experiences are signs of something else," I have insisted that "given experiences" have to be experimentally analyzed in order to yield evidential signs. (3) Just what is meant by the statement that upon my view ideas ultimately refer to future experiences, I do not know. What I have said is that ideas are correlated, in strictly conjugate fashion, with discriminated material of observation, the former serving to indicate a possible mode of operative solution and the latter serving to locate and delimit a problem, so that a resolved situation is attained (if it *is* attained) by the operational interaction with each other of observed and ideational contents. If "ultimate reference" means that ideas *alone* do not determine an existential proposition, the statement is in accord with my view—just as I have also held that data alone do not constitute the object of a final and complete judgment. (4) The references in Mr. Murphy's account to future experiences as anticipated, desired and enjoyed are apparently intended to state the heart of my doctrine. But the references are so loose that I do not know what they mean sufficiently to be able to correct them. I shall, therefore, simply restate briefly the view that is repeated any number of times in my *Logic*.

The only kind of experience that is *anticipated or desired* is the operational production of that situation in which the specific problem under inquiry is solved, so that warranted assertion takes place. The only *enjoyment* that has any relevancy is that which a person may happen to obtain in appreciation of a resolved situation as consummatory of the inquiries that led up to it. This personal enjoyment has nothing to do with the logical or cognitive function of the attained resolved situation; yet the fact that solution of problems is capable of yielding keen enjoyment is a highly fortunate circumstance in promoting the disposition to inquire. (5) The statement that, according to my theory of inquiry-knowing, "future experiences as far as they terminate inquiry are not cases of knowing" is either the tautology that knowing-inquiry terminates when it does terminate, or, if it is taken to refer to *knowledge as attained* in distinction from knowing in process, is a flat contradiction of my actual position, according to which *only* the subject-matter in which inquiry terminates (in fulfilment of its own conditions) is knowledge. Nowhere in any of Murphy's statements about my theory of inquiry as knowing is there any reference, even an incidental one, to that which is the controlling factor in my entire view, namely the function of a *problematic* situation in regulating as well as evoking inquiry. Although the disastrous effect of this omission is most clearly in evidence in the cases of the third and fourth of the above mentioned points, leaving it out of account makes nonsense of my theory of ideas in themselves and in their reference to a terminal conclusion. If it were not that the same omission of this controlling factor of my whole logical doctrine is found in Mr. Russell's comments, I should have supposed that I had repeated so often the statement about its importance in determination of inquiry and of the adequacy of any conclusion reached that its regulative function could not be missed.

The failure on Mr. Murphy's part to refer to it is the more striking in his case because of his nominal acceptance of the principle of Contextualism. For the problematic situation is *the* context in which everything I say about knowing is placed and by reference to which it is to be understood. It controls the meaning of "ideas," the factor to which Mr. Murphy practically confines his account of my view. It controls my theory of the place and function of facts or data, about which he says nothing, although according to my view ideas are so related to observed facts that they can be understood only in this reference. It controls the nature and function of those "future experiences" which appear so mysteriously out of nowhere in Murphy's account of my position. Finally, it controls the meaning to be put upon the *operations* by means of which the terminal conclusion "reliably ensues." Since I have held that the relative defects of both the idealistic and realistic epistemologies is the result of their failure to set knowing in this context of problematic situations, it is quite possible that Murphy's notion that my theory of knowing is a product of preoccupation with these epistemologies springs from his failure to note the context which actually controls my theory, both in general and in all its constituent details.

This failure is responsible for Mr. Murphy's repeated statement that my theory neglects the fact that "the ideas used and analyses performed in the course of inquiry are instrumental to finding out whatever the particular inquiry was investigating." This truism is the starting point of my whole theory. More chapters of my *Logic* are devoted to stating what happens when one investigates, say, "some (hitherto) unperceived antecedent existence," or "the structure of some purely hypothetic logical system," or some past event like the "batting averages of all members of the New York Yankees in 1921," or "the cause of infantile paralysis"—(my own example being the cause of malaria)—than to all other topics put together. Consequently, I am at a loss to understand the point of view from which Mr.

Murphy's criticisms are made. Does he hold that there is no such thing as a theory of knowing beyond pointing to the *fact*[40] that when persons inquire, what they do is instrumental to finding out about whatever it is they are investigating? Does he hold that there exists only a multiplicity of special inquiries and that it is futile to search for any common logical pattern? Does he mean that there is some "ordinary theory of knowing" which is so satisfactory and so generally accepted that it serves as a criterion for judging every theory which is put forth? I do not know the correct answer to these questions. I had supposed that there are in existence a vast multitude of inquiries, investigations of quantities and qualities, of past events, of things that coexist, of mathematical topics, of social events, etc., which constitute the material of all the sciences; and that the business of logic is to investigate these different inquiries, in connection with the conclusions they arrive at, so as to frame a general theory of inquiry based upon and justified by what happens in these particular cases. If Mr. Murphy holds that no such generalized inquiry into inquiry is necessary or possible, I can see that he would regard my theory as superfluous. But I have difficulty in believing that he holds that a generalized logical theory is rendered unnecessary by the fact that one can point to a great number of cases of actual knowing. Moreover, there are in existence not only a large number of cases of inquiry or knowing, but also a considerable number of different *theories* about knowing and I supposed it was the business of one presenting another theory to take some notice of these. For, instead of holding, as Mr. Murphy intimates, that all of them, from Plato through Locke to the present, are of no value, I have held that *all* of them have laid hold of *some* actual constituent of knowing, but have failed to place it in the context in which it actually functions—a matter discussed at some length in the final chapter of my *Logic*.

There is some evidence that Mr. Murphy's failure to state my theory of knowing in its connection with the context which determines its meaning—both in general and in all its con-

[40] What Mr. Murphy regards as the "ordinary theory of knowing" does not seem to me to be a theory at all but one of the most obvious of the facts which the theory of knowledge is about.

stituent parts—is due to his carrying over into his report of my view about knowing-as-inquiry-in-process what I say about the function of knowledge as a mode of experiencing in its relation to other non-cognitive modes of experience. For example, he endorses what he finds Lovejoy to have said about my theory, namely, that according to it "I am about to have known is the pragmatic equivalent for I know." It is certainly true that with reference to know*ing*, as inquiry *in process*, I have held that its reference is to an object not as yet reached and hence future. To transfer to my view of knowledge when *attained* the reference to a future object involved in inquiry still *in process*, is much as if I were to say that, according to Mr. Murphy's view, "I am engaged in the process of trying to discover is an equivalent for: I already know what it is I am trying to discover." It is a truism that, while one is engaged in knowing, the things to be known are still future. This belief is not then a peculiarity of my view over against any other view. What *is* characteristic of my view is that it defines the conclusion for which inquiry is a search as that which resolves the problematic situation in which search occurs.

The transfer of what is said by me about the function of attained knowledge to an alleged account of knowing-inquiry-in-process may account for other errors in Mr. Murphy's statement. For example, right after the passage in which he speaks of the process of inquiry as instrumental to finding out about whatever a particular inquirer is investigating, he goes on to say something about "the worth of knowledge for improving man's estate being different from its worth as a conclusion based on evidence and proper method." Of course there is a difference, a difference in context and hence in kind. The first matter is a matter of know*ing*-inquiry in process. The distinctive thing in my theory of knowing, as set forth in the *Logic*, is its exposition of the *particular ways* in which various kinds of factual and ideational propositions function as instruments to attainment of conclusions resting on evidence and/or the use of a proper method. The instrumental worth claimed by me to exist in the functional relation of attained knowledge to non-cognitive forms of experience is another matter, having to do with another philosophical problem. I did not invent the problem of the possibility of controlling the occurrence or existence of consummatory experiences, of experiences that are marked by intrinsic values. I did not invent the problem of how such experiences can be enriched by clarifying and deepening their contained meanings, nor that of extending the range of persons and groups who enjoy such values.[41] For these are problems of every *moral* theory in its social aspects, of every social theory in its moral aspects. What is characteristic of my theory is simply the emphasis placed upon the knowledge mode of experience, defined in terms of the outcome of competent inquiry, as that which accomplishes these functions; an emphasis which goes so far as to say that intelligence, as the fruit of such knowledge, is the *only* available instrumentality for accomplishing them. The contrast is with those theories which hold that transcendent *a priori* principles, rational intuitions, revelations from on high, adherence to established authorities in state and church, inevitable social revolutions, etc., are the agencies by which experienced values are to be made more secure and more extensively enjoyed.

I had supposed that the contexts within which reference is made, on the one hand, to the instrumentality of propositions in the *process* of inquiry, to knowledge as warranted solution of a problem, and, on the other, to the instrumentality of *attained* knowledge, through development of intelligence, to enrichment of subsequent experiences, were such as to prevent transferring what is said about one kind of instrumentality to the other. It may be that I have not taken sufficient pains to make clear the transition from the discussion of one point to that of the other. There are, moreover, certain factors common to both kinds of instrumentality which may have induced confusion in the minds of some readers. Within the progress of inquiry, for example, intelligent action as the product of previously attained knowledge is constantly taking effect. The termination of inquiry, with respect to the procedures of inquiry that have led up to it, is a resolved situation whose *primary* status and value is

---

[41] "Improving man's estate" is but a vague name for the three specified things just mentioned: Extension of range of persons enjoying consummatory experience, enrichment of their contents, and increased control of their occurrence.

cognitional. But the terminal material is also a directly had situation, and hence is capable of treatment on its own account as an enriched experience. It is quite possible that I have not always made the particular universe of discourse which is the context of a given discussion as distinct as these overlappings demand it should be made. There is also the point made in Dr. Ratner's contribution about a shift from the use of the word "knowledge" in my earlier writings to the word "intelligence" in my later. If I had uniformly made it clear that attained knowledge produces *meanings* and that these meanings are capable of being separated from the special cases of knowledge in which they originally appear and of being incorporated and funded cumulatively in habits so as to constitute *mind,* and to constitute *intelligence* when actually applied in new experiences, it is quite likely my view would have been less exposed to misunderstanding. The function of knowledge-experience as the mode of experience which, through formation of intelligence in action, is the sole instrumentality for regulating the occurrence and distribution of consummatory experiences and for giving them increased depth of meaning, might then have stood out in a way which would not permit of misunderstanding.

I do not mean that this distinction of functions is not frequently clearly stated, but that it is possible that my mode of statement at times has put an undue tax upon the attention of readers in keeping track of transitions. Of my explicit statements the following passage is representative:

Experienced situations come about in two ways and are of two distinct types. Some take place with only a minimum of regulation, with little foresight, preparation and intent. Others occur, because, in part, of the prior occurrence of intelligent action. Both kinds are had. . . . The first are not known; they are not understood. . . . The second have, as they are experienced, meanings that present the funded outcome of operations that substitute definite continuity for experienced discontinuity and for the fragmentary quality due to isolation.[42]

[42] *Quest for Certainty,* 243; cf. 250, 259, 345 and 218-222. I quote a passage from p. 218, and another from the conclusion of the discussion: "Apart from knowledge the things of our ordinary experience are fragmentary, casual, unregulated by purpose, full of frustrations and barriers. . . . But we return from abstractive thought to experience of them with added meaning and with increased

I obtain a certain humorous enjoyment from reading criticisms which combine condemnation of my "pragmatism" for its alleged sacrifice of knowledge to practice with condemnation of my "instrumentalism" for greatly exaggerating the potential function of knowledge and of intelligence in direction and enrichment of everyday experiences. My position may be badly taken, but it is not so loose in its joints that the bones of the argument stick out at right angles to one another.

Mr. Murphy is not alone in being troubled by my denial that antecedent conditions constitute the object of knowledge. *If* I have written anything affirming that antecedent objects are not capable of being known and are not as matter of fact known, *if*, in Mr. Murphy's language, I have asserted their "inaccessibility," any one, myself included, ought to be troubled. But the trouble arises from confusion of the contexts in which certain statements are made. There is in a given practical and scientific inquiry the question as to what the objective of knowing is for that particular inquiry. There is the question in the form of inquiry constituting logical theory as to what the object of knowledge is and means—a problem I did not invent. Instead of denying that unperceived antecedent conditions are objectives of knowledge in the first context, I have very explicitly stated that no problem as to existential matters can be resolved except by inquiries which *ascertain antecedent conditions not previously observed.* I have also then pointed out that such objects do not fulfill the conditions which must be satisfied in a philosophical logical theory as to the *generalized* meaning of the category "object of knowledge." That is, as in a sentence quoted in Mr. Murphy's account but not discussed by him, I have said that such objects are not *final and complete* with respect to satisfying the conditions that must be satisfied, in philosophical in-

---

power to regulate our relations to them. Reflective knowledge is the *only* means of regulation. Its value as instrumental is unique." And, from the conclusion: "It is congenial to our idiom to call the reflective conclusions of competent methods by the name of science. But science thus conceived is not a final thing. The final thing is appreciation and use of things of direct experience. These are *known* in as far as their constituents and their form are the result of science. But they are also more than science. They are natural objects experienced in relations and continuities that are summed up in rich and definite individual forms."

quiry, by a candidate for the position of object-of-knowledge in this latter context.

From the time of my earlier essays, first printed in the *Studies in Logical Theory*, I have pointed out that material dealt with in inquiry passes through a series of temporal phases and that what is said of the material in one phase cannot be applied to material in another phase without production of confusion. There is the initial phase of a non-cognitive situation out of which knowing develops; there is the terminal stage of the attained knowledge; and there is the intermediate phase in which subject-matter is what it is *as* conditioned by inquiry (and hence is tentative, provisional, conditional, pending completion of inquiry). In my recent *Logic*, the words *subject-matter, object, and contents* are used technically to designate these different statuses of experienced material. Obviously such distinctions appertain to the logical-philosophical analysis of knowing; an investigation of a particular problem does not need to make them explicit because, as I pointed out in my early essay, the immediate exigencies of the conduct of his inquiry prevent an inquirer giving to the material of one phase the properties belonging to that of another phase. *Epistemological discussion, however, as I pointed out, is definitely marked by confusions arising from this source.* Hence the necessity for making clear what is the object-of-knowledge in its definitive sense. If the distinction between the particular object of a particular inquiry as such and the object of knowledge in its philosophical-logical sense is denied, then, as already indicated, there is *no* philosophical problem or theory of knowledge. It suffices to enumerate, without analysis, all the special cases of knowing for which one has time. As for myself, throwing out epistemological bathwater I had no intention of also throwing out the baby.

There are a few cases in which, in speaking of the object of knowledge in the sense it bears in philosophical discussion, I have prefixed the word "true." Two of these cases are quoted by Mr. Murphy and are interpreted by him as if "true" here refers to what is ascertained to be true in a particular inquiry. In speaking of certain controversies, I said: "They spring from the assumption that the true and valid object of knowledge is that which has being prior to and independent of the operations of knowing." This sentence, when isolated from its context, might be understood to refer to the object of a specific inquiry, instead of, as is intended, to the characteristic object of the *knowledge-function* as determined in philosophical theory.[43] Reference to its context shows that the expression "true object" is relevant to a philosophical issue—though not to that of idealism-realism. The issue to which the passage is relevant is stated as follows in a nearby paragraph:

The claim of physical objects, the objects in which the physical sciences terminate, to constitute the real nature of the world, places the objects of value with which our affections and choices are concerned at an invidious disadvantage. . . . The net practical effect is the creation of the belief that science exists only in the things which are most remote from any significant human concern, so that as we approach social and moral questions and interests we must either surrender hope of the guidance of genuine knowledge or else purchase scientific title and authority at the expense of all that is distinctly human. (*Quest for Certainty*, 195-196.)

There are contributors to this very volume who deny in a thoroughgoing way the possibility of any valid cognitive determination whatever of valuations, and who in consequence relegate all moral affairs, personal and social, to the status of private desires or else to the use of coercive force. It is a well known fact that others, perhaps not represented in this volume, deny the competency in moral inquiry of the methods used in practical and scientific knowing and in consequence insist upon the necessity of non-empirical validation for moral judgments. The existence of such theories gives pertinency to a theory which holds that the same methods of inquiry that yield ordinary practical and scientific conclusions are capable of application in reaching

[43] That I hold that a logical theory of knowledge can be formed only in terms of the *object* of knowledge as that is ascertained in critical analysis of actual cases of knowledge is not a matter for which I have any apologies to offer. To my mind, the framing of a theory of knowledge in terms of properties of its characteristic *object* is the only alternative to epistemological theories of knowledge that claim to decide its nature by analysis of "mind," "consciousness," mental states like "sensations and ideas," etc. To start from the fact that there are in fact objects of knowledge as distinct from objects of mere opinion or of fear and hope is the only way of avoiding the futile question as to how knowledge is possible.

moral judgments, so validated as to fall within the scope of verifiability. When it is said, therefore, that "the true object of knowledge lies in the consequences of directed action," the context is a philosophical logic of inquiry, *based upon what is found out in specific inquiries* as to the necessity for experimentation (directed action) if a valid conclusion is to be reached. If the context in which the passage occurs fails to make this point clear, I am glad of the opportunity to say (i) that I hold a philosophic logical theory of knowledge can be framed only in terms of properties that analysis finds to belong to attained objects of knowledge; and (ii) that physical scientific objects, when taken as models for framing such a theory, prove, through their dependence upon experiment (which is *ipso facto* a transformation of antecedently experienced materials), that existential consequences must be taken into account in forming the theory; (iii) that instead of denying that antecedent conditions are accessible to inquiry or knowing, I hold that all physical scientific objects are precisely generalizations, on a statistical basis, of such antecedent conditions, but (iv) that they nevertheless do not stand alone, or as "final and complete" fulfilments of the conditions involved in inquiry. To conclude this phase of my reply I quote, then, the following passage:

We know whenever we do know; that is, whenever our inquiry leads to conclusions which settle the problem out of which it grew. This truth is the end of the whole matter—*upon the condition that we frame our theory of knowledge in accord with the pattern set by experimental inquiry.*[44]

II. A close counterpart of Mr. Murphy's method of dealing with what I say about "ideas" is found in Mr. Russell's treatment of what I say about "apprehension." In both cases, there is neglect of the reference of "ideas" and "apprehensions" to a problematic situation and to their function in resolution of such a situation. If the reader will refer to Mr. Russell's paper he will find quotations from me in which I expressly recognize the

[44] *Quest for Certainty*, 198; italics not in original text. In view of the fact that nothing is said in what purports to be an account of my view about problematic situations and problems, it is perhaps not surprising that almost nothing is said about the rôle that *experimental* science plays in my theory.

existence of direct perception of objects and of direct apprehensions of meanings and of things. Mr. Russell also quotes in this connection what I said about the dependence of such cases upon causal conditions, *i.e.*, organic mechanisms formed by previous cases of mediated knowledge of the same objects. The point here is that we now *directly* grasp a book as a book and a typewriter as a typewriter, because of operation of organic mechanisms which were produced by a series of mediated inquiries by which at an earlier time we came to identify and discriminate these things as of the kinds in question. But Mr. Russell's remarks say nothing at all about the point made by me in the next sentences after the ones he quotes:

> But the important point for the purpose of the present topic is that either an immediate overt response occurs, like using the typewriter or picking up the book, or that the object directly noted is *part of an act of inquiry* directed toward knowledge as warranted assertion. In the latter case [the only cognitional one], the fact of immediate apprehension is no logical guarantee that the object or event directly apprehended is that part of the "facts of the case" it is *prima facie* taken to be. . . . It may be irrelevant in whole or part. . . . In other words, immediate *ap*prehension of an object or event is no more identical with knowledge in the logical sense required than is immediate understanding or *com*prehension of a meaning. (*Logic*, 143-144.)

It is possible that without taking still more of the context into account the force of the sentences just quoted will not be evident. So I add some further explanatory remarks, at the same time asking any interested reader to go to the complete original text. "But" in the passage just cited places the *important* point in opposition to one not important "for the purpose of the present topic," which purpose is the proper logical interpretation of direct apprehension. That which by contrast is said to be not important with respect to that problem is precisely the nature and action of the organic mechanisms to which Mr. Russell devotes his attention. That which is said to be important is the fact that if there is *knowing* involved—instead of direct motor response to a given stimulus—the thing apprehended is a means of knowing something else—in other words, is a mediating factor in arriving at knowledge of something else. The question involved is one of fact. Is there any case in which the occurrence of a directly apprehended object constitutes a *final* object terminating knowing? If not, to be a directly apprehended thing and to be *that* thing which provides the evidential data in a given case are not equivalents. The reference to the logical similarity between *ap*-prehension of a thing and *com*prehension of a meaning carries out the point. One may have, say, the direct comprehension of the meaning "sea serpent," but it does not warrant a proposition that sea serpents exist. Similarly one may directly apprehend a long thing gliding over the water, but its apprehension will not prove the object apprehended to be evidence warranting an existential proposition that a sea serpent exists. It is, I suppose, a familiar fact that more mistakes arise in scientific investigation from taking actually perceived things to be good evidential data in the inquiry at hand than from hallucinatory perceptions. One may see a lot of things and still be in doubt *what* seen things, if any of them, are relevant to reaching a sound conclusion.

Instead of discussing this point, which is said to be the *important* one with respect to the problem of immediate knowledge or of beliefs not mediated by inquiry, Mr. Russell discusses the point of causal production which is just the point which in contrast I take *not* to be important for the issue in question. Unless I am mistaken, Mr. Russell has himself upon occasion pointed out that causal issues should not be substituted for logical ones. As far as causal conditions are concerned, it makes no difference to my argument what they may be, as long as it is granted that habits are formed that enable us to spot familiar objects on sight. I have, therefore, no ground for quarreling with Mr. Russell's particular view on this point. *If* I held a holistic view, his reference to independent causal chains would be highly pertinent. But since I do not hold that position, and since in my own treatment, when I deal with the topic of causation, I expressly insist upon a plurality of sequences, I need only remark that Mr. Russell's considerations reinforce the point I have made about the logical aspect of the matter. For a given set of causal conditions, or the organic mechanism operating in a given case, may (as is obvious in the case of a hallucination) produce an object which is directly apprehended but which is just *not* the datum needed

EXPERIENCE, KNOWLEDGE AND VALUE 571

as evidence in the problem at hand, thereby proving it is not the "complete and final object of knowledge."

If I now cut somewhat short my discussion of the criticisms passed by Russell upon my theory of truth, it is partly because my discussion up to this point indicates the particular context— that of problematic situations—in which my view is set and which must be taken into account in discussing my view; and partly because former, rather extended, corrections of misconceptions on this point have indicated that nothing I can say will eliminate them from the minds of some of my critics. The rather elaborate exegesis of Mr. Russell of my presumed view as to truth would have been rendered unnecessary if Mr. Russell had only taken seriously the passage he, curiously enough, quotes from the Preface of my *Logic*—I say "curiously" because apparently he uses the passage only as a means of identifying me as a pragmatist, but not as a means of understanding what I mean by any pragmatic theory of "consequences" which I accept. The passage reads as follows:

The word "Pragmatism" does not, I think, occur in the text. Perhaps the word itself lends itself to misconception. At all events, so much misunderstanding and relatively futile controversy have gathered about the word that it seemed advisable to avoid its use. But in the proper interpretation of "pragmatic," namely, the function of consequences as necessary tests of the validity of propositions *provided* these consequences are operationally instituted and are such as to resolve the specific problem evoking the operations, the text is thoroughly pragmatic.

If I mention that the word *provided* is italicized in the original text it is because Mr. Russell, in spite of the reference in this very passage to "misunderstanding and relatively futile controversy" has paid no attention to what is stated in the proviso, and so repeats notions about pragmatism which he formed long ago and has frequently stated, despite my express repudiation of them at least as many as thirty years ago.

The proviso about the kind of consequences that operate as tests of validity was inserted as a caution against just the kind of interpretation which Mr. Russell gives to my use of consequences. For it explicitly states that it is necessary that they be *such as to resolve the specific problem* undergoing investigation.

The interpretation Mr. Russell gives to consequences relates them to personal desire. The net outcome is attribution to me of generalized wishful thinking as a definition of truth.[45] Mr. Russell proceeds first by converting a doubtful *situation* into a personal doubt, although the difference between the two things is repeatedly pointed out by me. I have even explicitly stated that a personal doubt is pathological unless it is a reflection of a *situation* which is problematic. Then by changing doubt into private discomfort, truth is identified with removal of this discomfort. The only desire that enters, according to my view, is desire to resolve as honestly and impartially as possible the problem involved in the situation. "Satisfaction" is satisfaction of the conditions prescribed by the problem. Personal satisfaction may enter in as it arises when any job is well done according to the requirements of the job itself; but it does not enter in any way into the determination of validity, because, on the contrary, it is conditioned by that determination.

There is a distinction made in my theory between validity and truth. The latter is defined, following Peirce, as the ideal limit of indefinitely continued inquiry. This definition is, of course, a definition of truth *as an abstract idea*. This definition gives Mr. Russell a surprising amount of trouble, due I think to the fact that he omits all reference to the part played in the theory of Peirce—which I follow—by the principle of the continuity of inquiry. Apparently Mr. Russell takes the statement to apply *here and now* to determination of the truth or falsity of a given proposition—a matter which, in the sense of validity as just stated, is determined, on my theory, by a resolved situation as the consequence of distinctive operations of inquiry. For Mr. Russell says: "I do not see how we can guess either what will be believed, or what would be believed by men much cleverer than

[45] The following lines from Parodi's contribution show that long before the *Logic* was written some readers were able to derive from what I wrote a correct idea: "Truth is not verified just by any kind of satisfaction, but only by that satisfaction which is born of the fact that a working hypothesis or experimental method applies to the facts which it concerns and effects a better ordering. No misconception concerning the instrumental logic of pragmatism has been more persistent than that one which would make of it merely a means for a practical end."

we are," as if something of the nature of that kind of guess at a future belief is so implied in the definition that the impossibility of making the guess is a refutation of the definition. The contrary is the case. The "truth" of any present proposition is, by the definition, subject to the outcome of continued inquiries; *its* "truth," if the word must be used, is provisional; as *near* the truth as inquiry has *as yet* come, a matter determined *not* by a guess at some future belief but by the care and pains with which inquiry has been conducted up to the present time.[46] Admission of the necessary subjection of every present proposition to the results to be obtained in future inquiry is the meaning of Peirce's reference to "confession of inaccuracy and one-sidedness" as an ingredient of the truth of a present proposition. In other words, a person who makes this admission is nearer the truth than any person is who dogmatically claims infallibility for the conclusion he entertains here and now.

Mr. Russell's inversion of what Peirce actually says upon occasion takes an amusing form. Peirce having, for example, defined truth in terms of the ideal limit *of inquiry*—ideal since not now actually attained—Mr. Russell says: "If the definition is interpreted strictly, every proposition investigated by no one is true;" from which it would appear that a *strict* interpretation consists in stating the contrary of a given proposition. The exclusive devotion of Mr. Russell to discourse is manifested in his assumption that *propositions* are the subject-matter of inquiry, a view assumed so unconsciously that it is taken for granted that Peirce and I likewise assume it. But according to our view—and according to that of any thoroughgoing empiricist—*things and events* are the material and objects of inquiry, and propositions are *means* in inquiry, so that as conclusions of a given inquiry they become means of carrying on further inquiries. Like other means they are modified and improved in the course of use. Given the beliefs (i) that propositions are from the start the objects of inquiry and (ii) that all propositions have either truth or falsity as their inherent property, and (iii) then read these two assumptions into theories—like Peirce's and mine—which

[46] The definition is directly connected of course with Peirce's principles of "fallibilism," and his emphasis upon the probability coefficient of all propositions.

deny both of them, and the product is just the doctrinal confusion that Russell finds in what we have said.

It does not follow of course that our views are the correct ones. But since they are after all the views which we hold, it is they, if anything, which should be criticized. It is hardly necessary to carry comment further. But Mr. Russell's allusion to the opinions of "the last man left alive," as if the reference had some relevance to Peirce's definition of truth *in terms of continued inquiry*, repeats his misunderstanding. His view that, according to our definition, the truth of the theory of relativity will be determined by Hitler's victory or defeat—the latter cutting inquiry off short—shows what can happen in the way of inversion of meaning when a critic declines to treat a view in its own terms, even as independent hypothesis, but insists upon translating it into terms of his own theory before considering it. For the technical purposes of strictly formal logic an assumption that every proposition is of itself, or intrinsically, either true or false may not do harm. But it is the last view an empiricist can possibly take who is concerned with truth and falsity as having *existential* application, and as something determined by means of inquiry into material existence. For in the latter case the question of truth or falsity is the very thing to be determined.

III. I regret that it is not possible within the limits of my reply to deal adequately with Mr. Reichenbach's comments on my theory of induction in connection with his presentation of his own view. I am, however, inclined to think that the difference between us is far from insuperable. When I criticized the theory of induction by simple enumeration I was criticizing that theory in its traditional formulation. The statement of that theory given by Reichenbach involves quite fundamental revision of it in its traditional form. If those who held it meant by it what Mr. Reichenbach finds in it, they failed to make their point clear. Now, my emphasis that the heart of the inductive process is the experimentally controlled analysis by means of which a given case is constituted to be a representative or exemplary instance (a sample or a specimen) admits the importance of *other* observed cases as means of the analysis which finally yields the representative instance. If I had treated the topic of probability in that immediate context, I should have been forced to recognize that an *indefinite number* of such other cases are, in theory, involved in determination of the representative case. If the theory of induction by simple enumeration *is understood in this particular sense*, I do not see that there are fundamental differences between Mr. Reichenbach's view and mine, though there are doubtless differences in detail. If there is such agreement, I should not allow what seems to me the inadequacy of the word "enumeration" for conveying the analytic function of enumerated cases to stand between us.

IV. I am so much indebted to Dr. Savery for his exposition of my main ideas in their historical perspective, together with his generous appreciation of the source of such inconsistencies as appear in successive writings, that I should gladly forego reply to his criticisms were it not that abstinence might seem to indicate lack of regard for them. I begin with the matter of verification. When a proposition about a thing in some specified respect is definitely in question, "confrontation" seems to me to be a good term by which to describe the nature of verification. If I doubt, for example, whether the outside walls of a certain house are colored white or brown, confrontation with the actual house settles the matter. It seems to me, however, that in the case of an *hypothesis* verification is of a more complex character than this; it *involves* confrontation, but only as one constituent. The point of this remark comes out most clearly when the hypothesis is a theory of considerable scope. A certain phase of Einstein's special theory of relativity was confirmed by observation of something that happened in the eclipse of Mercury. I doubt if any one could say more than that the confrontation which occurred tended toward confirmation. A negative result would have been a disproof of the theory *as previously stated*, but it would not have precluded a modification of it. I do not see how a theory can be said to be verified unless *a set of instances, positive and negative, inclusive and exclusive*, has been instituted. If this view is correct, it is the *function* of confrontations as experimentally determined consequences that confers upon them verifying power. In my *Logic* this function is said to be the "capacity of an idea or theory to order and organize particulars into a coherent whole"—it being understood, of course, that this organization is not "mental" but is existentially effected by suitable experimental operations. In the context in which the sentence just quoted occurs, it is put in opposition to the idea that hypotheses are capable of being "verified by particular objects in their particularity." (157) That is to say, I hold that confrontation is a necessary but not a sufficient condition for verification of an hypothesis. The remarks I make about ultra-positivistic views, while not identical in import with the point just made, have a similar bearing. For they indicate that the primary value of hypotheses and theories is found in their power to direct observation to discovery of newly observed facts and in their power to organize facts in such a way as to forward the solution of a problem. If I were to say that logical theory has exaggerated the importance of verification of ideas at the expense of some other uses of the latter, I should probably be understood by some persons to confirm their notion that I think rather lightly of truth. But as far as *scientific* hypotheses and theories are concerned, it is clear to me that the indubitable and supreme value of truth in its *moral* sense has often been uncritically carried over into the context of scientific inquiry and into the logical values of ideas and theories. What a scientist asks of his hypotheses is that they be fruitful in giving direction to his observations and reasonings. Confrontation with an observed fact which does not square with an hypothesis is consequently just as welcome as one which does—since it enables him to introduce modifications into his idea that renders the latter more efficient in future conduct of inquiry. Whereas if a liar is confronted with something which contradicts what he says, there is one hundred per cent nullification of what he has said, with no opportunity allowed for additional development because of the negative confrontation that has occurred. In science, discovery of an exception, of a fact that contradicts a theory in the form in which it has been previously held, is a positive means of advance. It is not only welcome when hit upon but is actively searched for.

This matter of verification is intimately connected, as Savery points out, with the more inclusive matter of the theory of knowledge. Accordingly I refer the reader to what he says on that point, especially about the matter of futurity in relation to knowledge. The point involved here as to futurity is not identical with that previously discussed. For example, in connection with the otherwise ambiguous phrase that "all knowledge is of the future," he cites my statement that the proposition "This is red" has for its logical equivalent "This has changed color from the quality it previously had." Obviously in this case what is known is something which *has* occurred. It may, then, help to clear up my theory if I point out three distinct contexts in which futurity appears in theoretical analysis of knowledge. One of them is the obvious case mentioned earlier. While inquiry is still in progress, its object, as the conclusion of inquiry, is, truistically, in the future. The second case is far from being truistic. It is exemplified in the case just cited regarding the color quality of a thing. Here the point is that the *material* subject-matter of an existential proposition is found to be *temporal* when the proposition is analyzed. As temporal it involves a change from what a thing was to something temporally future (but not to our knowing), *i.e.*, temporally future to what *it* was. In other words, any existential change is from a *past* into a present, something future to its past, so that "is," in an existential proposition, is just as temporal in its reference as "was" or "will be." Consequently it is dated and has no meaning when taken out of connection with the futurity, or "will be" of what was. The third distinction of futurity in connection with knowledge is that consequences still to be obtained as the outcome of experimental operations in inquiry serve to test ideas, hypotheses, theories, that are entertained. The immediate *reference* of an idea is not to these future consequences, but to facts, data of observation. But the *validity* of its reference to any given set of facts is determined by the consequences that result when the given idea and the given facts operationally interact in institution of a new experienced situation—a view clearly implying that the reference of the idea to facts is already there as a condition. These three kinds of connection with futurity are found in a theory of knowledge reached by analysis of what takes place in inquiry. The potential bearing of attained knowledge through the medium of intelligent action upon subsequent non-cognitive value-experiences belongs not in the theory of knowledge as such but in the theory of the relation of the knowledge function of experience to other modes of experience.

A further important question raised by Mr. Savery has to do with the existential character of scientific objects. One phase of this question was dealt with in connection with Reichenbach's criticism. Mr. Savery, however, raises the question in a somewhat different form so that it is possible that the answer already given—to the effect that scientific objects are statistically standardized correlations of existential changes—may not answer the question as he puts it. But that reply suggests that I cannot accept the problem in the form in which Mr. Savery phrases it, namely whether scientific objects are existential *or* operational. For in my view they are existential *because* they formulate operations which actually take place. The particular passage Savery quotes from me in this connection is concerned with "conceptual" subject-matters, and it is to them *as conceptual* that descriptive character is denied. Hence when he says that "such a view yields pure positivism"—in the sense, I take it, of pure phenomenalism—he unwittingly transfers to *knowledge* what is said about *theories*.

D. ETHICAL AND ALLIED TOPICS

Critics of my theory of knowledge have found the idea that qualitative transformation of antecedent conditions is required for its attainment to be a stumbling-block. It is accordingly interesting, if not surprising, that Dr. Stuart, a critic of my theory of moral judgment and action, comes close to finding that absence of this category—or something similar to it—is the source of the defects of my moral theory. For, being aware, and properly so, of the difference between operations that manipulate what is given or that merely adapt conditions to old ends and habits and operations that re-adapt habits to new ends, he thinks that my theory has thrown in its lot with the former. Now it is quite true that I hold there is a common logical pattern in scientific and moral knowing. But instead of first accepting the traditional theory of knowing according to which it is an accommodation of the self and its beliefs to conditions already fixed,

I have held that scientific knowing involves deliberate modification, through working ideas, of what previously existed—pointing to the necessary rôle of experiment in natural science as evidence. Since there seemed to be a certain similarity betwen this conclusion and the idealistic theory that mind constitutes the objective world, the commonest early interpretation of my view was that it consisted of a rather gratuitously devised, verbally novel, version of idealistic epistemology. The actual point of my theory may however be found in a transfer of traits which had been reserved for the function of moral judgment over to the processes of ordinary and scientific knowing. It is, accordingly, my belief that the difference between Dr. Stuart and myself is not where he puts it, but lies in the fact that his view of scientific knowing is such that it compels him to set up a rigid dualism between it and moral knowing, while I find the features which he reserves for the latter to be implicit, or involved, in all inquiry whatever. In any case, many of the criticisms of my theory of knowing have arisen from my insistence on the function of transformation, reconstruction, readjustment, of antecedent material in knowing, while an alleged absence of these categories seems to be the source and ground of Mr. Stuart's criticisms of my ethical views.

Mr. Reichenbach in his article makes a statement which shows an acute appreciation of an important, perhaps fundamental, "directive tendency" in my philosophy. He says: "In restoring the world of every-day life as the basis of knowledge, Dewey does not only want to establish knowledge in a better and more solid form. What he intends, and perhaps to a greater extent, is establishing the sphere of values, of human desires and aims, on the same basis and in an analogous form as the system of knowledge." This passage proves that Reichenbach grasps the direction in which my thoughts have moved. It marks a realization of the rôle played in development of my ideas by that problem which, in my introductory remarks, I said is the central problem of modern philosophy, because it is the central problem of modern life.

Were I anonymously to turn critic of my own philosophy, this is the place from which I should set out. I should indicate that after insisting upon the genuineness of affectional and other "tertiary" qualities as "doings of nature," Dewey then proceeds to emphasize in his theory of knowing, as that is manifested in both science and common sense, the operations of transformation, reconstruction, control, and union of theory and practice in experimental activity which are analogous to those involved in moral activity. Without continuing this line of criticism and then defending myself against it, I express my indebtedness to Dr. Stuart's paper for the opportunity to remove any doubts that may exist as to the direction in which I read the community of pattern which I find in physical and moral judgment.

Since apparently it is use of the word "Naturalism" to characterize my general position which has led Stuart off the track, I call attention again to the fact that instead of presenting that kind of mechanistic naturalism that is bound to deny the "reality" of the qualities which are the raw material of the values with which morals is concerned, I have repeatedly insisted that our theory of Nature be framed on the basis of giving full credence to these qualities just as they present themselves. No one philosophic theory has a monopoly on the meaning to be given Nature, and it is the meaning given Nature that is decisive as to the kind of Naturalism that is put forward. Naturalism is opposed to idealistic spiritualism, but it is also opposed to super-naturalism and to that mitigated version of the latter that appeals to transcendent *a priori* principles placed in a realm above Nature and beyond experience. That Nature is purely mechanistic is a particular metaphysical doctrine; it is not an idea implied of necessity in the meaning of the word. And in my *Experience and Nature* I tried to make it clear that while I believe Nature *has* a mechanism—for otherwise knowledge could not be an instrument for its control—I do not accept its *reduction* to a mechanism.

There are passages in Mr. Stuart's paper which seem to assume that I *must* give Nature and Naturalism a meaning that reduces it to a mechanism or something close to it. For he speaks as if I admitted a special field of morals only as "a grudgingly tolerated annex to biology," and he devotes considerable attention to a passage in my *Logic* which he takes to reduce all thinking to a merely biological phenomenon—in spite of the fact that the title of the chapter in which the passage quoted occurs is "The Biological Matrix of Inquiry" and that the next chapter on "The Cultural Matrix" deals expressly with the radical change wrought when biological conditions and activities are taken up into the distinctively human context of institutions and communication. Moreover, in close connection with the very passage he quotes, it is stated that, even on the biological plane, there is more than mere restoration of what previously existed, namely, production of *new* conditions in both *organism* and environment.[47] The most surprising venture of Mr. Stuart's in this line of interpretation is found in the view of deliberation he attributes to me. He holds I am capable of regarding it only from "without," thereby reducing it to a purely "muscular" phenomenon. At the outset of his paper, Mr. Stuart quotes a number of passages from me where I expressly differentiate modes of mental behavior from other forms on the ground that they are responses to the *doubtful* as such. It is surprising that within a few short pages Mr. Stuart completely forgets this differentia, since it is especially conspicuous in marking off deliberative from merely muscular behavior.

At all events, Mr. Stuart finds "implicit in the naturalism which is the dominant theme" of my later writings a conception of the nature of the "supremacy of method" which is as close to the opposite of my actual view (a view which in my inability to foresee all possible interpretations I had supposed to be clear) as is possible. For he believes that what is implicit in my naturalism is that my idea of the supremacy of method is in no way inconsistent with the view that method, considered as a procedure of the actual knower, engaged not in epistemological inquiry, but in the direct solution of a first-hand problem in his experience, is not and cannot be "supreme." The contrary is the

[47] The meaning of my insistence, as against Rignano, that it is the *relation* of organism and environment that is restored seems to have escaped Mr. Stuart. For without restoration of the relation of harmony or equilibration, life cannot continue while specific *conditions* constituting both organism and environment have to be made over in some degree in order that *this* relation may be re-instated. In other words, *trans*formation has a natural biological basis.

case. The whole point of my position is precisely that method *is* supreme in direct solution of every first-hand problem in experience, so that epistemological inquiry—*logical* inquiry in my terminology—has solely the business of pointing out the characteristic features of the method which is supreme in these first-hand investigations. From an inversion of what I intended and supposed I had clearly stated in my chapter upon "The Supremacy of Method" follow the further misconceptions of my ethical views upon which Dr. Stuart bases his criticisms.

The issue is perhaps made clearer by an earlier passage in which he says that methods are justified by their success, and "results derive none of their worth from the method by which they have been brought to pass." This view apparently he takes to be so axiomatic that I must also hold it as a matter of course:—even though I have repeatedly stated (as in the first chapter of my *Logic*) that conclusions owe their scientific worth to the method by which they are reached, while the only result an inquirer intends who observes the conditions which are set by inquiry itself is resolution of the problematic situation in question. How Stuart, or any observer of the procedures of the sciences, can say that for an individual inquirer "no method can be supreme," since "what is legislative is the result which he desires and intends," I cannot imagine. For if it means that attainment of some special result controls scientific inquiry, the remark is as good a description of violation of scientific method as can be found.[48]

In reducing what I say about method to an identification of it with "a formula of skill to be used as needed," the supremacy of method is so denied that I should have supposed Mr. Stuart would have been moved to wonder why I used such a totally inappropriate title. In any case what I hold, to repeat, is that method in knowing of physical objects is not a formula for conducting skilful manipulations, subordinating either the self to pre-existing material or the latter to some pre-existing impetus of the self, but is reconstructive of antecedent situations, a reconstruction in which the self as knower is changed as well as the environing conditions. The function of the chapter on

[48] The inversion of my view is marked in the last section of Stuart's paper, in which he refers to "*predetermined* ends."

"The Supremacy of Method" is thus quite literally to prepare for the discussions of the next chapter, which is entitled "The Construction of Good." That is to say, precisely because I hold that experimental method as union of theory and practice, of ideas and operations directed by them, has supremacy over an antecedent situation, I also hold that one and the same method is to be used in determination of physical judgment and the value-judgments of morals. In consequence I hold that enjoyments, objects of desires as they arise, are *not* values, but are problematic material for construction—for creation if you will— of values. The dualism between scientific and moral knowing arose, as I point out, before the rise of the experimental method in scientific knowing. The theory of scientific knowing that reflected this condition—pre-scientific in substance—limited knowing to ascertainment of antecedent reality, while a theory of knowing as *experimental* displays and proves the "supremacy of method." Thus once more the very point in my theory of knowing whose presence has called out the criticisms of other contributors is assumed by Mr. Stuart to be so utterly absent in my theory of scientific knowing as to vitiate my theory of morals. My assertion of the supremacy of method is identical with my assertion that "intelligent action is the sole ultimate recourse of mankind in every field whatever." For intelligent action, made manifest as it is in the experimental method of science, while it recognizes the necessity for discovering antecedent conditions, it employs them when discovered as *means* for construction of a new unified and ordered situation. Or as is stated in the very chapter under discussion: "Knowledge of special conditions and relations is instrumental to the action which is in turn an instrument of production of situations having qualities of added significance and order."[49] Almost at the end of the same chapter, there occurs the following passage, serving as a transition to the discussion in the next chapter of "The Construction of Good." "What possibilities of controlled transformation of

[49] *Quest for Certainty*, 250. The purport of the discussion is shown in a conclusion, drawn from the transformative power of the inferences of scientific method, to involve the elimination of the dualism between the categories of freedom and purpose which, upon the old theory, caused scientific and moral knowing to be thought of as two wholly separate kinds.

the content of present belief and practice in human institutions and associations are indicated by the control of natural energies which natural science has effected?"[50] In this passage is indicated a real difference between Mr. Stuart and myself. I hold that a philosophy of knowing based upon experimental method makes it possible to utilize the conclusions of science about natural energies so that the latter may become positive means of constructing values, of controlling (as I have said in previous pages) the occurrence of enriched values. Mr. Stuart seems to recur to the essentially Kantian dualism of scientific and moral knowing, a view which implies the complete indifference of what is found out about natural structures and events to formation and attainment of moral ends. This "splendid isolation" of moral values is bought at too high a price.

As far as I can make out, Mr. Stuart believes that I begin with two separate entities, those commonly called knowing-subject and object-to-be-known, and that I then think of knowing as some kind of transaction carried on between these two end-terms. This appears to be his view, and he further distinguishes knowledge of physical objects as involving subjection of the self, as knower, to conditions set by what is to be known, whereas in moral knowledge the reverse is the case— the self insisting upon subordination of existing material to an end *it*, in its very capacity as Self, sets up. At all events, he states my view as follows:

If conditions when encountered are found not "wholly good," it is because some *present end of the individual* finds itself adversely affected by them. In such a situation we have, according to the scheme of Professor Dewey's naturalism, the drive or inertia of the *"organism's"* disturbed or interrupted activity seeking to push forward. Pushing forward, it spreads out in continuously ramifying trains of attentive and *manipulative* behavior by which the *environment* is explored and reconstructed.[51]

---

[50] *Ibid.*, 252.

[51] Italics not in original text. They are emphasized to indicate how definitely Stuart reads into my theory an original separation of self and object, organism and environment, and regards that disturbance which initiates knowing to be something produced in the former by some change in the latter; as over against my actual theory in which the disturbance is of a *situation* in which organism and environment are functionally united. (Cf. passage on p. 305 above.)

The same point of view is found when he says, speaking of my supposed view, that "a situation presents itself *to the knower* as doubtful" or precarious, as if I held the situation to be *outside* the knower, and again when he says, nominally reporting my view, that "precariousness apprehended" is the "occasion for the *knower's* resort to *method.*" He also frequently speaks of some "intrusion" furnishing the occasion for the self's engaging in knowing. It is this background which leads him to suppose that I believe in the *supremacy* of method only in that rather trivial—or at least definitely secondary—sense in which, according to him, it does not apply to inquiry engaged in "direct solution of a first-hand problem in experience"—which is exactly where it does apply. From this attributed interpretation—and from it alone—follows the conclusion that to me knowing, even in the case of moral judgment, consists only in using a method of manipulative skill for getting rid of the external conditions which interfere with, disturb, intrude upon the self and the knower.

I can readily understand that Dr. Stuart may have worked out his own view of moral knowing in contrast to such a view as has just been stated, and I can certainly see how, if he takes such a view to be the correct statement and the "ordinary theory" of what takes place in scientific knowing, he should insist upon a rigid dualism between scientific and moral knowing. I do *not* see how he came to attribute this view to me since it is so nearly the opposite of the one I have set forth. Aside from his questionable deduction of what a naturalistic view must be, it is probable, judging from his quotations of passages found in the earlier part of the chapter on "The Supremacy of Method" that he was also misled by taking part of my view for the whole of it. For in the early part of that chapter I give a rather summary account of behavior, emotional, volitional, cognitive, from the *psychological* standpoint—that is from the standpoint of the organic factor in the total life-function. In this account psychological phenomena are interpreted as *behavioral responses to the doubtful as such.* However, this account is so far from being a statement of the *method* of knowing—that which has rightful supremacy—that it deliberately commences with conditions as they exist *after* a total qualitative existential situation has been disrupted from within and in consequence the self-organism—and environing conditions being no longer unified in that situation are set practically at odds. It then proceeds to describe the characteristic phenomena of the former from the standpoint just mentioned—behavioral responses to the doubtful—dealing, accordingly and deliberately so, only with a partial factor of method. So far is the account given in this connection from being the whole story, that this section of my discussion was occasioned by the need of advancing some theory of the phenomena ordinarily called mental or psychological in which the "self," "subject," "mind," "knower" is *not* (as I have held it is not) an original separate entity set over against objects and the world. Even from the standpoint of this intentionally partial account—partial because stated from a special angle—there is no justification for the introduction of the categories of "intrusions" and "manipulations." The doubtful is not an intrusion, and the last thing a behavioral response can do to or with the doubtful is to manipulate it. Only the definitely and mechanically settled can be manipulated by rules of skill. I believe that Francis Bacon did hold that rules of skill could be worked out so that all persons could be put by training on practically the same level, just as persons can learn proficiency in use of tools like a hammer or plane. But when a scientific inquirer is faced with a problematic situation rules of skill are just what are precluded by the very fact that the situation is so pervasively problematic.

In one passage, Mr. Stuart expressly points out that according to me determinations like *mind, body,* and the *outer world* emerge and function *within* "the situation taken as a whole in its problematic character." Taken by itself this passage might lead one to wonder how it was that he did not see that the distinction of *organism* and *environment, knower* and *that-to-be-known,* also arises and functions within the total problematic situation as a means to its resolution—a process by which *both* are in some degree modified or reconstituted. But his previous sentence explains why he did not grasp my actual view. For it reads "The precarious *environment* must accordingly be faced with such detachment and fortitude as the *agent* can muster and then grasped *as a whole* as problematic."[52] Not only does this passage prove that Mr. Stuart attributes to me from the very start a differentiation and opposition of "knower" and "the-to-be-known" but also supposes that it is the *environment* which is grasped as problematic—while according to my view a *situation* is problematic prior to any "grasping" or "apprehension" whatever, the first act of knowing being to locate *a problem* by selective or analytic discrimination of some of the observable constituents of the total situation.

It should then be clear that my view of the nature of knowing goes further than does that of Dr. Stuart in providing the groundwork and groundplan of a theory of moral knowing similar in general features to that he set forth in his article as if in opposition to mine. For his theory sets up an impassable dualism between the two kinds of judging, while mine asserts continuity, which, as I have said, involves difference as well as community. The formation of a self new in some respect or some degree is, then, involved in every genuine act of inquiry. In the cognitive situation as such the overt and explicit emphasis falls upon the resolution of the situation by means of change produced in environing conditions, whereas in the distinctively moral situation it falls upon the reconstruction of the self as the distinctively demanded means. But the difference is in any case one of *emphasis*. There are occasions when for the proper conduct of knowing as the controlling interest, the problem becomes that of reconstruction of the *self* engaged in inquiry. This happens when the pursuit of inquiry, according to conditions set by the need of following subject-matter where it leads, requires willingness to surrender a theory dear to the heart of an inquirer and willingness to forego reaching the conclusion he would have preferred to reach. On the other hand, the problem of reconstructing the self cannot be solved unless inquiry takes into account reconstitution of existing conditions, a matter which poses a problem in which scientific knowledge is indispensable for effecting an outcome satisfying the needs of the situation.

[52] See p. 294 above; italics mine.

In propounding a theory of knowing I have insisted that inquiry itself involves *in its own nature* conditions to be satisfied. The autonomy of inquiry is equivalent to demand for integrity of inquiry. It is this fact that leads to the definition of truth in its intellectual or cognitive sense in terms of fulfilment of condition intrinsic to inquiry. But the will, the disposition, to maintain the integrity intrinsic to inquiry is a moral matter. In this regard, the operations of valuation which I have affirmed to be involved in any case in knowing—in choice of data and hypotheses and experimental operations to be performed—pass into definitely moral valuations whenever the existing habits and character of an inquirer set up obstacles to maintenance of integral inquiry. Reconstitution into a self in some respects new is then not incidental but central. I suggested earlier that the current theory of verification and of the cognitive truth of propositions—validity as I call it—suffers from having read into it the moral meaning of truth. But whenever the immediate problem in conduct of inquiry for the sake of obtaining knowledge involves the will to search for evidence, to weigh it fairly, not to load the dice, to control a preference for one theory over another so that it does not affect the conclusion reached, the category of truth in its *moral* sense is supreme. This is a reason why denial of the possibility of validly grounded valuation propositions involves, as its logical consequence, suicide of scientific knowing, a logical destruction which is not averted by insisting that propositions are inherently true or false.

Perhaps I can illustrate my meaning by referring to an incidental remark of mine of which Mr. Stuart makes a great deal, the remark, namely, that "were existing conditions wholly good, the notion of possibilities to be realized would never arise." Now I think that common experience and the evidence of history testify that the occurrence of problematic situations, necessitating the putting forth of effort in thinking, was usually regarded as *bad*, as obnoxious, until the pursuit of inquiry was found to be a good on its own account. When inquiry is found to be a good, then the occurrence of problematic situations is welcomed as contributory to enjoyed possession of a good. I cannot find in the sentence quoted the ominous meaning it seems to bear to Mr. Stuart. "Were conditions *wholly* good" lays down a completely generalized and comprehensive condition. Its scope is not limited to conditions as they present themselves at a specified time. It applies to the total enduring experience of any person. Any one who has ever experienced conditions that are not wholly good will, in the degree of his capacity to learn, be aware that conditions may not be wholly good in situations where on the surface there seems to be nothing the matter. Just as the inquirer as such will be on the lookout for *problems*, so the conscientious person will be on the lookout for something better instead of being content with customary goods. There is, in other words, none of that incompatibility which Mr. Stuart seems to find between what I have said in my chapter in Dewey and Tufts' *Ethics* about the conscientious person and what I have said would happen if conditions "were wholly good." No one lives in a world in which he has found everything at all times perfect. If he understands the meaning of this fact he has learned to be alive to possibilities. The potential *better* will then be regarded as the good—and the only good— of any situation, a statement as applicable to scientific inquiry as to any moral matter. A disposition framed when conditions are overtly not wholly good is capable, like the experimental method itself, of exercise when, on the surface, they seem good.

It will be noted that I have given much more attention to Mr. Stuart's idea about my theory of knowing than to his special criticisms of what he takes to be my ethical position. The reason is that Mr. Stuart's belief that I deny the "incommensurability" and disparity of ends and values, and hence reduce what seem to be conflicts to a difference negotiable by "manipulation of intrusive" factors is the product of his misconception of my theory of inquiry. For according to this theory, the conflict which is involved in any problematic situation is such as to be resolvable only by qualitative transformations. I have indeed emphasized, in what I have said about morals, especially in their social aspect, the idea that production of new environing conditions is a prerequisite of the creation of an enduring new self. But that emphasis was not by way of disparaging the importance of a new self but by way of protest against the "subjectivistic" morals which identify "meaning well" with morality, and which thereby deny importance to active effort which always makes some change in previous conditions—exactly as does experiment in scientific inquiry.[53] If there is a difference between us as to the basic problem in the moral situation being the problem of what the self shall become and be (as the *end* at stake), it is in the fact that I treat the difference between this problem and that of adjusting means with reference to an accepted end as *relative,* not absolute. I quote the following passages from Dewey and Tufts' *Ethics:* "The person who completely ignored the connection of the great number of more or less routine acts with the small number in which there is a clear moral issue, would be an utterly undependable person;" and again, "Every act has potential moral significance because it is, through its consequences,[54] part of a larger whole of behavior;" and again,

Every choice sustains a double relation to the self. It reveals the existing self and it forms the future self . . . shapes the self, making it, in some degree, a new self. This fact is especially marked at critical junctures, but it marks every choice to some extent, however slight.[55]

And once more this position follows directly from the reconstructive function of inquiry in obtaining tested knowledge. Now I do not wish to infer that Dr. Stuart does in fact make a sharp separation between "economic" situations, in which the problem refers simply to conflict of *means* with respect to an accepted and unquestioned end, and "moral" situations where conflict of incommensurable ends sets the problem of determining what the self *shall* be. I only say that *if* he holds to such a separation, I go further in the direction he points out as necessary to genuine moral knowing than he does. For I do not admit anything but a strictly relative distinction between means and ends. Consequently when I have touched upon economic and political problems in writing upon social philosophy I have

[53] The trouble with the Kantian *Good Will* does not lie in its emphasis upon active disposition and resolute character, but in its separation of will from all empirical conditions of desire and purpose.

[54] Consequences, namely, upon formation of habits and hence formation of a self.

[55] *Ethics,* 178, 179, 317.

held that all such problems are problems of valuation in the moral sense. It is in *this* context that I have dwelt upon *intelligent action* as the sole and supreme method of dealing with economic and political issues, and have tried to take that statement out of the region of innocuous truisms by linking up the possibility of intelligence in action with that ascertained knowledge of conditions and consequences which is obtained by the use of the methods which stand out conspicuously in the physical sciences. We are thus brought back to that instrumental view of attained knowledge which has given so much trouble to some of my critics.[56]

II. Dr. Geiger's paper is welcome because of its recognition of the moral context of economic and political issues in my social philosophy, *moral* being here viewed as a matter of choice ensuing upon valuations. The importance of the practical questions he raises at the close of his exposition is not to be denied. To my mind they come to this: Is the disproportion between the application of the scientific experimental method to the physical conditions of human associations and its lack of application in direct social affairs such that, in the present state of the world, it is hopeless to expect a change? I know of no sweeping answer to this question. But the problem is one of degree, not of all or none. It cannot be denied that in our social life a great imbalance has resulted because the method of intelligent action has been used in determining the physical conditions that are causes of social effects, whereas it has hardly been tried in determination of social ends and values. One might point out that the use of other principles, custom, external authority, force, so-called absolute ideals and standards—out of the range of empirical adjudication because absolute—in lieu of intelligent action, has played the chief part in the production of the situa-

[56] I have said nothing here about Mr. Stuart's criticism of my view of the rôle of consequences. In principle, their rôle in morals is the same as in scientific inquiry. They are important not as such or by themselves but in their function as *tests* of ideas, principles, theories. It is possible that at times, in opposition to *ipse dixit* "intuitions" and dogmatic assertion of absolute standards, I have emphasized the importance of consequences so as to seem to make them supreme in and of themselves. If so, I have departed from my proper view, that of their use as tests of proposed ends and ideals.

tion which makes it so extremely difficult to use the method of intelligent action. While this fact does not modify the conditions which create the difficulty, application of the method, like charity, begins at home. The application is to the methods *we* are to apply in *our* economic and political predicaments, not as to what people on the other side of the world are going to do.[57] If, instead of letting our imagination roam abroad to dwell upon the difficulties other nations and persons experience in using the method, we fasten attention upon our own problems, the difficulties in the way of its use are much less. To consider the state of the world at large in this or any similar connection is itself a procedure that violates the supremacy of method. For we are here in a specific social and historic situation which compels a choice based on valuations, and it is we, with respect to our own specific problems, who have to form the valuations and to make a choice.

In any case, the question is not, as critics have sometimes put it, one of intelligence, or knowledge, versus action, but one of *intelligent* action versus some other kind of action—whether it relies on arbitrament by violence, or "dialectical materialistic inevitability," on dogmas of race, blood, nationality, or supernatural guidance. The method of intelligent experimental action is criticized on the ground that class interests are too strong to permit its use, so that the only alternative is the method of class war with victory to the strongest. It is not enough to counter this argument by saying that most of those who hold it are indulging in a dialectical game and have rarely faced what the concrete consequences of this appeal to violence would be. But when some dogma—called a "law"—of inevitable historic evolution is appealed to, it can be replied that the issue is not whether there will be clashes and conflicts of interests but how they are to be met and what *kind of action*, probably involving under certain conditions positive use of force, shall be under-

[57] I wish to take this opportunity to express my full agreement with what Dr. Randall says in his paper about the importance of developing the skills that, if they were produced, would constitute political technology. The fact—which he points out—that I have myself done little or nothing in this direction does not detract from my recognition that in the concrete the invention of such a technology is the heart of the problem of intelligent action in political matters.

taken. The alternative is not an extreme pacifism which makes a fetish of passivity. The basic difference is that one theory, that of inevitable class conflict and inevitable victory for one class, takes situations in a mechanical and wholesale manner, whereas the method of intelligent action insists upon analysis *at each step* of the concrete situation then and there existing, basing its hypothesis as to what should be done upon the results of that analysis, and testing moreover the adequacy of the hypothesis at every step by the consequences that result from acting upon it. The question is one of choice—choice between a procedure which is rigid because based on fixed dogma, and one which is flexible because based upon examination of problems actually experienced and because proposing policies as hypotheses to be experimentally tested and modified.

I return to Mr. Geiger's paper with a few words about the issue of the critical versus the gradual. I do not think the antithesis is well taken. There is something critical in every problematic situation; it marks a qualitative turn, a divergence; it is of the nature of a "mutation" rather than of a Darwinian "variation." Crises differ greatly of course, in the depth and range of the conflicting issues involved in them. But the critical quality remains in spite of differences of degree. The *execution* of any policy for directing change to one outcome rather than to another is nevertheless a gradual affair; the more critical the emergency, the more gradual will be the execution of the plans and policies by which it is finally resolved. The idea that the resolution of a crisis is of the same abrupt nature as is the occurrence of the crisis is a Utopian confusion. A revolutionary event is a crisis of high intensity. But the idea that the revolution in its immediate occurrence, as of a given date, 1789 or 1917/18, is anything more than the beginning of a gradual process is a case of Utopian self-delusion. The method of intelligent action has to be applied at every step of that process in which a revolution "runs its course." Its final outcome does not depend upon the original abrupt revolutionary occurrence but upon the way intelligent action intervenes at each step of its course—as all history shows in spite of *ex post facto* "inevitabilities" constructed *after* choice has manifested its effects. Perhaps the worst feature of social philosophies that substitute inevitabilities, materialistic in nature, for choices moral in nature because made after intelligent evaluation, is not that they get rid of choice, but that by eliminating intelligent valuation they put a premium on arbitrary choice.

I am glad to have an opportunity to say something about another question raised in Mr. Geiger's contribution. It concerns what he says about *ultimate* values. I have carried on a polemic against ultimates and finalities because I found them presented as things that are inherently absolute, like "ends-in-themselves" instead of ends-in-relationships. The reason they have been proferred as absolutes is that they have been taken out of any and all *temporal* context. A thing may be ultimate in the sense of coming last in a given temporal series, so that it is ultimate *for that series.* There are things that come last in reflective valuations and, as terminal, they are ultimate. Now Dr. Geiger is quite right in saying that for me the method of intelligent action is precisely such an ultimate value. It is the last, the final or closing, thing we come upon in inquiry into inquiry. But the place it occupies in the *temporal* manifestation of inquiry is what makes it such a value, not some property it possesses in and of itself, in the isolation of non-relatedness. It is ultimate in use and function; it does not claim to be ultimate because of an absolute "inherent nature" making it sacrosanct, a transcendent object of worship.

III. The topic of religion as presented by Dr. Schaub is not intimately connected with the subjects just discussed. But comments upon his paper seem to belong more properly here than at any other place. I shall follow Dr. Schaub's treatment in separating, for the most part, my view about religion from my larger and inclusive philosophical position, although if the latter approach had been chosen, I think something could be fruitfully said concerning my philosophic interpretation of experience in its religious aspect. As it is, Dr. Schaub finds an early article of mine prophetic of my later more explicit treatments of religion. While he mentions that the quotations he makes are from an article devoted to the question of giving religion a place in the subjects taught in our public schools he does not seem to have noted how directly and almost exclusively the passages he quotes have to do with that particular issue. An argument against the attempt to put instruction in religion into our public school curriculum (a movement that goes contrary to the whole American social and educational tradition), is not the place where I should look to find material regarding one's general attitude toward religion. Nor do I understand that Dr. Schaub is engaged in criticizing my views in that particular respect, or is himself arguing for making the teaching of religion a part of our tax-supported public school system. And yet I have some difficulty in judging just why he attaches so much importance to this particular article—written as it was so largely to explain to an English audience the difference between their and the American attitude in this matter. However, since Mr. Schaub selects it for special attention because of what he regards as its "prophetic" quality, I shall also deal with it in that aspect.

In the first place, it is true that I looked hopefully forward to a decay of the sectarian spirit that was, when I wrote, such a marked feature of the religion of the churches and to the emergence of a "broader and more catholic, and more genuinely religious spirit." I may have been unduly optimistic in entertaining these hopes; they are certainly still far from realization. But just how the fact that I had these particular hopes is a sign of an unsympathetic attitude on my part toward religion I do not see. I can hardly believe that Dr. Schaub is arguing by implication for a continuance of a narrow sectarian spirit. The alternative explanation is, I imagine, my belief that the association of religion with the *supernatural* tends by its own nature to breed the dogmatic and the divisive spirit. To this belief I plead guilty, and I do not find anything in what Mr. Schaub has to offer which contravenes what seems to be almost a commonplace of history. For, the greater the insistence by a given church body upon the supernatural, the more insistent is it bound to be upon certain tenets which must be accepted—at the peril of one's immortal soul. When Dr. Schaub quotes from me a passage about the possibility of "a religious mode of life which will be the fine flower of the modern spirit's achievement," he can hardly take that passage to be evidence of a coldly hostile attitude on my part to everything religious. So I imagine that the trouble he finds there also springs from my reference to the "modern spirit" as something which puts away the supernaturalism of the race's immaturity, and relies upon the resources of the scientific search for truth and upon a democratic way of life to generate a more humane, more liberal, and broader religious attitude.

In order that the reader may have before him the sort of thing which I was—in a spirit perhaps of too great hopefulness—"prophesying," I quote some additional remarks from the same article about the potential religious aspect of human experience when it is liberated from supernaturalism and dogmatism.

> That science has the same spiritual import as supernaturalism; that democracy translates into the same religious attitude as did feudalism; that it is only a matter of slight changes of phraseology, a development of old symbolisms into new shades of meaning—such beliefs testify to that torpor of imagination which is the uniform effect of dogmatic belief.

And again "It is the part of men to labor persistently and patiently for the clarification and development of the positive creed of life implicit in democracy and science." Again, "For all we know the integrity of mind which is loosening the hold of all these things [rites, symbols and ideas associated with dogmatic beliefs] is potentially much more religious than all it is displacing." And once more "So far as education is concerned, those who believe in religion as a natural expression of human experience must devote themselves to the development of the ideas of life which lie implicit in our still new science and our still newer democracy." I might quote other passages in the same vein. But these should suffice. I can understand why Dr. Schaub should object to the interpretation of the religious contained in these passages, for I can understand that his idea of religion may be radically different, more akin perhaps to the things to which I object in traditional religion. But he goes further than this. He finds in the article which includes such passages as those cited, signs of an attitude hostile to assigning any important significance and value to the religious phase of experience. To me, on the other hand, his interpretation is a fairly typical sign of that sectarian spirit which takes hostility to particular views about religion to be itself anti-religious.

About all I need to say accordingly about the later writings of which the passages I have quoted *are* prophetic, is that they are devoted to making explicit the religious values implicit in the spirit of science as undogmatic reverence for truth in whatever form it presents itself, and the religious values implicit in our common life, especially in the moral significance of democracy as a way of living together. Mr. Schaub prefers another kind of religion—which is his personal right. *A Common Faith* was not addressed to those who are content with traditions in which "metaphysical" is substantially identical with "supernatural." It was addressed to those who have abandoned supernaturalism, and who on that account are reproached by traditionalists for having turned their backs on everything religious. The book was an attempt to show such persons that they still have within their experience all the elements which give the religious attitude its value. The response from the persons to whom the book was especially addressed was so cordial as to more than make up for the disfavor that greeted it in other quarters.

E. SOME "METAPHYSICAL" QUESTIONS

There are certain issues—of the type usually referred to as "metaphysical"—touched upon in various criticisms; "metaphysical" in the sense in which an empirical naturalist may give that name to the more generalized statements about Nature which he finds to be justified. They are found in Mr. Parodi's article and in some of the criticisms passed by Messrs. Savery and Murphy. Before taking up the issue raised by Mr. Parodi, I want to thank him for his grasp of the main purpose of my philosophical writings: "To reintegrate human knowledge and activity in the general framework of reality and natural processes." For I doubt if another as brief a sentence can be found to express as well the problem which has most preoccupied me.

I. The special problem which Mr. Parodi's criticism raises is typical of my larger endeavor at reintegration. As stated by him, it has two sides. From one side, it is the problem of the possibility of bringing our conscious awareness into a frame of reference which also includes physical events; from the side of voluntary action, it is the problem of transition, within the same frame of reference, from conscious intent to physiological and physical movement. The first question is illustrated by the question of the relation of physical vibrations and nerve changes to sensations. Since the general problem is far too vast to be adequately considered here I shall select for discussion only the point that illustrates my position on the larger issue. Mr. Parodi says that in the sequence of physiological and nervous processes one nowhere finds "the color red, as something felt, as the sensation or the perception properly so called." This sentence suggests the difference between the problem as it presents itself to me and as it presents itself to Mr. Parodi. For in my theory, the problem is not that of the relation of the physical and external to the mental or internal. It is, as I hope some of my previous remarks have made clearer than it may have been before, the problem of the relation of immediate *qualities* to objects of science. According to my solution, the latter function as the existential causal conditions of the former, qualities being consummatory manifestations of these conditions. It is in this context, for example, that I have insisted that all qualities, even the tertiary ones and, *a fortiori*, those of color, like red, are "doings of natural conditions." If one accepts continuity as a natural category, then the problem of *how* specific transitions are made in the case of qualities is exactly the same sort of problem that is found in any case of temporal sequence where a later stage is qualitatively unlike an earlier one. The general fact that qualitative transitions occur—as, for example, in production of *water*—is something characterizing nature. It is something to be accepted rather than to be taken as posing a difficulty to be surmounted. These are problems of ascertaining the special conditions under which specific qualitative transitions take place, but not the problem of why the universe is as it is.

When I say then that Mr. Parodi states the difficulty in terms of his own philosophical premises, I mean that he takes a quality, say *red*, to be intrinsically something *felt*, a "sensation" in and of itself. My view is more realistically naïve. The *quality* occurs exactly, in principle, as any natural event, say a thunder-shower. There is no passage from the physical to the mental, from an external world to something felt or of the nature of a psychical consciousness, but from objects with one set of qual-ities to objects with other qualities. When, however, a quality is termed a "sensation," or is explicitly taken in connection with an act of perceiving, something additive has happened. It is now placed in a specially selected connection, that to the organism or self. Pending the outcome of an inquiry not yet completed, one may not know whether a quality, say red, belongs to *this* or *that* object in the environment,[58] nor indeed whether it may not be the product of intra-organic processes as in the case of "seeing stars" after a blow on the head. In other words, the occurrence of qualities upon my view is a purely natural event. Scientific physical objects in their relatively quality-less char-acter are selections of correlations between changes, in whose constitution qualities are irrelevant.

The final reference of qualities to intra-organic events is itself a reference to one kind of object *in* the natural world. Similarly, when we explain a curious superstition entertained by members of a savage tribe we do not do so, on my theory, by referring it to "consciousness," but to specifiable natural conditions—tradi-tions and institutions being included in this case among natural conditions. According to my position the problem as it is stated by Mr. Parodi is present only when what is secondary, because arising in a definitely cognitive situation, is taken to be pri-mary. When it is taken to be primary, all the difficulties that are found in epistemological theories—where controversy is never finally settled—present themselves: Namely, given a separate existential realm of consciousness or of the mental, how to get out of it over into a world that is "external" to it?

There is an issue closely connected with the view that qual-ities and individual and unrepeatable things are genuine natural

---

[58] It is in this connection that I identify certain forms of behavior, those de-nominated "psychological," as responses to the doubtful as such. Here, as in con-nection with Mr. Stuart's paper, they are derived, not original; secondary, not primary, occurring when an experienced *situation* becomes problematic.

existences. It is much too large to discuss here but it may be
mentioned. Were it not for ambiguities in the notion of "emergence" it might be connected with that idea. If scientific laws
and objects are of the kind I have said they are, the *connections*
which are involved in production of qualitative objects are necessary but not the qualities themselves. There is, then, room in
nature for contingency and novelty, for potentialities that are
actualized under conditions so complex as to occur only in the
course of processes of development that take a long time. *After*
the conditions have come about and the new qualities have appeared, it is possible to form generalizations about uniformities
and make predictions about the future occurrence of the qualities. But the first appearance of the qualities in question may
have been utterly unpredictable. In short, according to my view
of the relation between qualitative things and scientific objects
the natural world is itself marked by contingencies, instead of
being a closed box of tight necessities. Under specifiable conditions, these contingencies present themselves as indeterminates
that need to be determined if certain life-activities are to go on.
Then the kind of responsive behavior occurs that is marked by
qualities which, when they are abstracted, are called sensations,
images, ideas, etc., in a mentalistic sense. I do not of course offer
this remark as settling the problems raised by Parodi. But I think
it is clear that the problem of the relation of the "mental" to
the processes of the natural world must be stated differently if
that world is one of closed mechanical necessities than if it is
marked by contingencies that leave room for potentialities not
yet manifested. For in the former case, the terms of the problem are intrinsically opposed, whereas they are not in the latter
case.

II. According to Mr. Murphy certain things I have said
about the relation of experience to the world may be understood
in accordance with the principle of objective relativism, so that
the idea of bifurcation in nature is avoided. But, unfortunately,
that strain or aspect in my doctrine he finds to be brought to
nought by another and more persistent strain in my theory of
knowing—producing a veritable skeleton in my philosophical
closet. For

there is an unhappy discrepancy between experience as it ought to be if
its place in the natural world is to be made intelligible and experience as
it must be if Dewey's epistemology is correct. In the former capacity,
"experience" is the essential link between man and a world which antedates his appearance in it. In the latter, "experience" is the terminus of
all knowing, in the sense that our (*sic!*) cognitive claims refer ultimately
to what experience will show itself to be in a resolved state and nothing
else. If this latter account is true, all statements about a natural environment outside of these immediate experiences become on analysis simply
means of facilitating cognitive transitions to such enjoyed immediacies
and the world . . . collapses into immediacy.

The statement quoted is unfortunately not free from ambiguity. Does his reference to the fact that in *my* view knowing
terminates in *experience* signify that in *his* view cognitive reference to the world (say the world antedating the appearance of
human beings upon it), does not involve reference to *any* experience? Does it mean that knowledge of the world is not *in
any sense* whatever an experience? These questions suggest that
the problem Mr. Murphy raises as if it bore simply on my
theory is one which in some way must be met by any theory
whatever. If, for example, Mr. Murphy means that knowledge
of a world antedating experience is *not* in itself in any way whatever an experience of anybody, his view is certainly an extraordinary one. But if he does not mean this, he, too, must hold that
knowing in such a case has its terminus in experience—namely,
in an experience of the world as thus and so in time and space.
If he holds the latter view, then the fact that I also hold that
knowing terminates in an experience can hardly constitute a
peculiarly personal skeleton. *If* then his criticism is grounded,
it is not just because I hold that knowing terminates in experience, but because of the *kind* of experience in which he supposes knowing must terminate upon my theory—a view contained, I imagine, in his phrase "and nothing else." Since he
offers no evidence in support of his view that the resolved situation (which is the terminal of knowledge according to my
theory) cannot have as its subject-matter objects or events existing in the world independent of the knower, one hardly knows
how or where to lay hold of his argument. Apparently, however,

his point is somehow expressed in the clause "what experience will show itself to be in a resolved state and nothing else." I am unable, however, to derive an intelligible meaning from this phrase. For if experience is, as I have said, always *of* something, namely, of the environment (though not necessarily, according to my theory, of it, in a *cognitive* mode), it is impossible to see why the environing conditions that are involved should disappear or collapse when and because they are so ordered as to constitute a terminal resolved situation. Certainly Mr. Murphy offers no reason for concluding that such a disappearance is implied in my account of the transformation, through experimental operations of inquiry, of the existential material or an indeterminate situation into the ordered objects of a resolved situation. If the problem is how from experienced materials of the *present* environment we validly infer conditions of some temporally past environment—such as that of some long bygone geological age—the problem is one which any theory whatever has to face. And it is moreover a problem to which a chapter of my *Logic* is especially devoted.

Since one can only guess at what Mr. Murphy takes to be the logical core of his criticism, it may be that it is found in reference to the fact that, according to me, the terminal experience, that of the resolved situation, is "immediate." Now as has been said earlier in this reply—and not for the first time—every experience, every existence for that matter, is immediate in its occurrence. Calling it *immediate* signifies only that it is just what it is. There is, however, a sense of *immediate* in which it is opposed to *mediate*. Now by description or truistically, the resolved situation as terminal is not mediate. But immediateness in this sense has nothing whatever to do with the subject-matter and objective reference of the resolved situation. If final conclusions or terminals of inquiry because of their final, not mediating, character, render their *subject-matter* immediate, then, according to Mr. Murphy's implied logic, *every* conclusion would, on any theory, "collapse into immediacy." As they do not on other theories, so they do not on mine.

Since there is no possible interpretation from any point of view of the passage quoted from which the conclusion that Mr. Murphy draws really follows, one has good reason for supposing that his conclusion is derived from some other source. In view of his confusion of the two senses of the instrumental already discussed, one would look in that direction for an explanation, especially because of the otherwise superfluous mention of "enjoyed immediacies." One finds in an earlier page of Mr. Murphy's essay the following passage:

The essential fact is that where the distinction between the value of an idea as a means for discovering the truth has been confused with its value as a means for subserving interests felt on other grounds to be important, there is simply no ground left for an independent estimate of truth as such—

a statement no one can question. But as a practicing, and not just professed, contextualist I have distinguished the contexts in which ideas (in their correlation with facts of observation) serve as means for reaching knowledge as warranted assertion (or truth), and the context in which *attained* knowledge (*because* it has been attained by the foregoing process) serves as a potential means for control and enrichment of consummatory noncognitive experiences. I confess the idea that experiences of things in the latter capacity could possibly be controlled by anything *excepting* actual conditions of the actual world had never occurred to me, since I am not a believer in magic. The fact that external environing conditions are the causes—and the only causes—of the experiences that occur is just the reason why my theory has emphasized the fact that knowledge, through the intermediary of intelligent action, is the sole means of regulating the existence in experience of values or consummatory objects. It is also the reason why, in contrast to most social and moral theories, much importance is attached to the potential functions of the conclusions reached in the natural sciences. I quote once more a typical passage:

The final thing is appreciation and use of things of direct experience. These are *known* in as far as their constituents and their form (that of the constituents) are the result of science. *But they are also more than science.* They are natural objects experienced in relations and continuities that are summed up in rich and definite individual forms.

To be *known* natural objects and yet to be *more* than objects of sciences is hardly a way of saying that experience of a resolved situation cuts off, because of its terminal position, all links with the natural world.

III. The final "metaphysical" question upon which I shall touch has to do with a question raised by Savery—Naturalism or Materialism? I am aware that emotional causes often dictate preference for one word over another. It is then quite proper to ask whether dislike for associations with the word *materialism* have dictated my use of *naturalism* to describe my philosophic point of view. Since I hold that all the subject-matter of experience is dependent upon physical conditions, it may be asked why do I not come out frankly and use the word *materialism?* In my case, there are two main reasons. One of them is that there is involved in this view a metaphysical theory of *substance* which I do not accept; and I do not see how any view can be called materialism that does not take "matter" to be a substance and to be the *only* substance—in the traditional metaphysical sense of substance. The other reason is closely connected with this, being perhaps but a specific empirical version of what has just been said. The meaning of materialism and of matter in *philosophy* is determined by opposition to the psychical and mental as *spiritual*. When the antithetical position is completely abandoned, I fail to see what meaning "matter" and "materialism" have for philosophy. *Matter* has a definite assignable meaning in physical science. It designates something capable of being expressed in mathematical symbols which are distinguished from those defining *energy*. It is not possible to generalize the definite meaning "matter" has in this context of physical science into a philosophical view—which materialism most definitely is. This latter undertaking seems to me on an exact par with the enthusiasm displayed by a certain group whenever *energy* is regarded as an important scientific character; especially if, as is sometimes erroneously said, it is believed that science has resolved "matter," in the strictly technical sense it bears in physics, into energy. I see no inherent difference in principle between generalizing what is meant by matter in physics into materialism, and generalizing what is designated as energy in physics into spiritualistic metaphysics. Philosophy must, of course, accept what is ascertained in science as the proper *designatum* of "matter," as that which it denotatively stands for. But this acceptance instead of leading to metaphysical materialism will, if accepted at its full value, enable philosophy to free itself from associations that grew up about "matter" in the pre-scientific days when it acqured its meaning through alleged opposition to another and "higher" substance, the soul, mind, spirit or whatever.

If the term "matter" is given a philosophic interpretation, over and above its technical scientific meaning—*e.g.*, *mass* until recently—, this meaning, I believe, should be to name a *functional* relation rather than a substance. Thus, in case there is need for a name for existential conditions in their function *as* conditions of all special forms of socio-biotic activities and values, *matter* might well be an appropriate word. But recognition that all these activities and values are existentially conditioned—and do not arise out of the blue or out of a separate substance called spirit—is far from constituting materialism in its metaphysical sense. For it is only by setting out from the activities and values in experience just as they *are* experienced that inquiry can find the clues for discovery of their conditions. Denial that the former are just what they are thus destroys the possibility of ascertaining their conditions, so that "materialism" commits suicide. It is quite possible to recognize that everything experienced, no matter how "ideal" and lofty, has its own determinate conditions without getting into that generalization beyond limits which constitutes metaphysical materialism.

As I conclude my reply, I am aware how largely controversy has bulked in it. But the plan of the volume called, and very properly, for adverse criticism as well as for favorable exposition, and it is difficult to reply to the former, where they do not appear valid, except controversially. A more pertinent criticism of my reply might be that in claiming to have been misunderstood by my critics on a number of fundamental points, I have virtually admitted lack of clearness in my previous writings. That this is true in some of the cases where misconceptions have been the ground of criticisms, I am not concerned to deny. I wish, therefore, to express my indebtedness to these critics for having made it necessary for me to reconsider not only the language I have used—words, which for the reason stated at the outset, are peculiarly treacherous in any attempt at a philosophical formulation differing from those which have attained currency—but also the ideas back of the words. In this specific respect my obligation, although naturally not my human and personal gratitude, is greater to those who have disagreed than to those whose exposition has been favorable. If it be said that in selecting the points for reply and in apportioning space I have been guided by my own interests rather than by those of my critics, I can only say that it seems reasonable to believe that one main object of this back and forth discussion is to help make clear what points *are* central to my position and what are subsidiary. Under different circumstances I might well have given attention to criticisms I have passed over—because they have seemed to me to be negotiable differences, matters of degree rather than of central principles.[59]

In any case, it is congenial to believe that conflict of ideas, as distinct from that of force, is a necessary condition of advance in understanding, and that agreements which exist only because of lack of critical contact and comparison are superficial. It was, I believe, Jane Carlyle who said that mixing things which do not go together is the Great Bad. Confusion that comes from this evil mixture is bound to exist where criticism is not continually on the alert. Differences that proceed from clear perception of issues are a positive gain. They are conditions of further progress in indicating the direction in which thought should move. But they are also intrinsic gains since they enlarge the horizon of our vision. Although our knowledge is not *of* perspectives

[59] This remark applies particularly to the question raised by Dr. Randall at the close of his paper. I should not want it thought that I took advantage of what is favorable in his paper to my position to ignore what is adverse.

as its subject-matter, what is known falls into some perspective, and there is something to be learned from the perspectival arrangement of the ideas of any honest inquirer.

There is also, according to my own way of thinking, a close connection between the vital problems of philosophy and the conditions manifested in my living culture. It is for this reason I have held that, in the strictest sense, philosophy cannot solve important problems but only those that so arise from different linguistic habits that they can be straightened out by analysis. If basic problems can be settled only where they arise, namely, in the cultural conditions of our associated life; if philosophy is fundamentally a criticism which brings to light these problems and gives them the clarity that springs from definite formulation; and if after formulation philosophy can do no more than point the road *intelligent action* must take,—then the greatest service any particular philosophical theory can render is to sharpen and deepen the sense of these problems. Criticism by means of give-and-take of discussion is an indispensable agency in effecting this clarification. Discussion is communication, and it is by communication that ideas are shared and become a common possession.

Finally, in connection with the relation of philosophy and culture, we may felicitate ourselves that we live where free discussion and free criticism are still values which are not denied us by some power reaching out for a monopoly of cultural and spiritual life. The inability of human beings in so many parts of the world to engage in free exchange of ideas should make us aware, by force of contrast, of the privilege we still enjoy and of our duty of defending and extending it. It should make us aware that free thought itself, free inquiry, is crippled and finally paralyzed by suppression of free communication. Such communication includes the right and responsibility of submitting every idea and every belief to severest criticism. It is less important that we all believe alike than that we all alike inquire freely and put at the disposal of one another such glimpses as we may obtain of the truth for which we are in search. If there is one thing more than another which my participation in the discussions composing this volume has impressed upon me, it is the extent and depth of my indebtedness to ideas which others have expressed;—not only my teachers, students, colleagues and present fellow workers but the long succession of thinkers whose names are enrolled as the bearers of the ceaseless enterprise which is philosophy.

HUBBARDS, NOVA SCOTIA
AUGUST, 1939

BIBLIOGRAPHY OF THE WRITINGS
OF JOHN DEWEY

WRITINGS OF JOHN DEWEY

1882

THE METAPHYSICAL ASSUMPTIONS OF MATERIALISM. *Journal of Speculative Philosophy*, Apr. 1882, XVI, 208-213.

Abstracts in *Johns Hopkins University Circular*, Feb. 1883, II, 59; *Revue Philosophique*, Jan. 1883, XV, 109.

THE PANTHEISM OF SPINOZA. *Journal of Speculative Philosophy*, July 1882, XVI, 249-257.

Abstract in *Johns Hopkins University Circular*, Feb. 1883, II, 59.

1883

KNOWLEDGE AND THE RELATIVITY OF FEELING. *Journal of Speculative Philosophy*, Jan. 1883, XVII, 56-70.

1884

THE PSYCHOLOGY OF KANT.

Dissertation for the PH.D. degree at Johns Hopkins University. This was not published, and no copy is owned by the university.

KANT AND PHILOSOPHIC METHOD. *Journal of Speculative Philosophy*, Apr. 1884, XVIII, 162-174.

---

* EDITOR'S NOTE: Acknowledgment is hereby made to the Columbia University Press for the privilege of using their *The Bibliography of John Dewey*, edited by M. H. Thomas and H. W. Schneider, New York, 1929, which is the basis of this bibliography up until 1929. The editor is also happy to express his sincere gratitude and appreciation to several members of the staff of The Charles Deering Library of Northwestern University who, under the able direction of Miss Muriel Murray, compiled most of the material for the last decade of this bibliography.

Although every effort has been made to make this Bibliography exhaustive and complete (even reviews and translations having been included where known), it should be kept in mind that—in view of the great wealth of Professor Dewey's published work—it is probably too much to expect that our efforts have been completely successful. The editor hopes, therefore, that any discovered omissions or errors will be reported to him for future correction.

The New Psychology. *Andover Review*, Sept. 1884, II, 278-289.

1885

Education and the Health of Women. *Science*, 16 Oct. 1885, VI, 341-342.

1886

The Psychological Standpoint. *Mind*, Jan. 1886, XI, 1-19.
Abstract in *Revue Philosophique*, Apr. 1886, XXI, 436.

Health and Sex in Higher Education. *Popular Science Monthly*, Mar. 1886, XXVIII, 606-614.

Soul and Body. *Bibliotheca Sacra*, Apr. 1886, XLIII, 239-263.

Psychology as Philosophic Method. *Mind*, Apr. 1886, XI, 153-173.

Inventory of Philosophy Taught in American Colleges. *Science*, 16 Apr. 1886, VII, 353-355.

1887

Psychology. New York: Harper & Brothers, 1887 [°1886]. xii, 427 pp.
Abstract in *Johns Hopkins University Circular*, Aug. 1887, VI, 125.
See edition of 1891.

Illusory Psychology. *Mind*, Jan. 1887, XII, 83-88.

Ethics and Physical Science. *Andover Review*, June 1887, VII, 573-591.
Abstract in *Johns Hopkins University Circular*, Aug. 1887, VI, 125.

Review of George Trumbull Ladd, *Elements of Physiological Psychology*. *New Englander and Yale Review*, June 1887, XLVI, 528-537.

Knowledge as Idealisation. *Mind*, July 1887, XII, 382-396.

1888

Leibniz's New Essays Concerning the Human Understanding. A Critical Exposition. Chicago: S. C. Griggs and Company, 1888. xvii, 272 pp. (Griggs's Philosophical Classics, edited by George Sylvester Morris, No. 7.)
Reprinted in 1902 by Scott, Foresman & Co., Chicago.

THE ETHICS OF DEMOCRACY. Ann Arbor: Andrews & Company, 1888. 28 pp. (University of Michigan. Philosophical Papers. Second ser., No. 1.)

1889

APPLIED PSYCHOLOGY. An introduction to the Principles and Practice of Education. By J[ames] A[lexander] McLellan and John Dewey. Boston: Educational Publishing Company [n.d., pref. 1889]. xxxi, 317 pp.

THE PHILOSOPHY OF THOMAS HILL GREEN. *Andover Review*, Apr. 1889, XI, 337-355.

GALTON'S STATISTICAL METHODS. *Publications of the American Statistical Association*, Sept. 1889, n. s. I, 331-334.

ETHICS IN THE UNIVERSITY OF MICHIGAN. *Ethical Record*, Oct. 1889, II, 145-148.

1890

ON SOME CURRENT CONCEPTIONS OF THE TERM "SELF." *Mind*, Jan. 1890, XV, 58-74.

IS LOGIC A DUALISTIC SCIENCE? *Open Court*, 16 Jan. 1890, III, 2040-2043.

REVIEW of Edward Caird, *The Critical Philosophy of Immanuel Kant*. *Andover Review*, Mar. 1890, XIII, 325-327.

REVIEW of John Pentland Mahaffy and John Henry Bernard, *Kant's Critical Philosophy for English Readers*. *Andover Review*, Mar. 1890, XIII, 328.

REVIEW of Johann Eduard Erdmann, *A History of Philosophy* (English translation by Williston Samuel Hough). *Andover Review*, Apr. 1890, XIII, 453-454.

THE LOGIC OF VERIFICATION. *Open Court*, 24 Apr. 1890, IV, 2225-2228.

REVIEW of James MacBride Sterrett, *Studies in Hegel's Philosophy of Religion*. *Andover Review*, June 1890, XIII, 684-685.

PHILOSOPHICAL COURSES AT THE UNIVERSITY OF MICHIGAN. *Monist*, Oct. 1890, I, 150-151.

1891

OUTLINES OF A CRITICAL THEORY OF ETHICS. Ann Arbor: Register Publishing Company, 1891. viii, 253 pp.

PSYCHOLOGY. Third revised edition. New York: Harper & Brothers, 1891. xii, 427 pp.

Another issue of the third revised edition has the imprint: New York, American Book Company [c1891].

MORAL THEORY AND PRACTICE. *International Journal of Ethics*, Jan. 1891, I, 186-203.

REVIEW of James Hutchins Baker, *Elementary Psychology, with Practical Applications to Education and the Conduct of Life*. *Educational Review*, May 1891, I, 495-496.

POETRY AND PHILOSOPHY. *Andover Review*, Aug. 1891, XVI, 105-116.

Reprinted in *Characters and Events* (1929), I, 3-17, with the title "Matthew Arnold and Robert Browning."

THE PRESENT POSITION OF LOGICAL THEORY. *Monist*, Oct. 1891, II, 1-17.

Summarized in *Philosophical Review*, Jan. 1892, I, 112-113.

HOW DO CONCEPTS ARISE FROM PERCEPTS? *Public School Journal*, Nov. 1891, XI, 128-130.

1892

[THOMAS HILL] GREEN'S THEORY OF THE MORAL MOTIVE. *Philosophical Review*, Nov. 1892, I, 593-612.

TWO PHASES OF RENAN'S LIFE: THE FAITH OF 1850 AND THE DOUBT OF 1890. *Open Court*, 29 Dec. 1892, VI, 3505-3506.

Reprinted in *Characters and Events* (1929), I, 18-23, with the title "Ernest Renan."

1893

RENAN'S LOSS OF FAITH IN SCIENCE. *Open Court*, 5 Jan. 1893, VII, 3512-3515.

Reprinted in *Characters and Events* (1929), I, 23-30, with the title "Ernest Renan."

REVIEW of Bernard Bosanquet, *A History of Aesthetic*. *Philosophical Review*, Jan. 1893, II, 63-69.

THE SUPERSTITION OF NECESSITY. *Monist*, Apr. 1893, III, 362-379.
Summarized in *Philosophical Review*, July 1893, II, 488 (Albert Ross Hill).

TEACHING ETHICS IN THE HIGH SCHOOL. *Educational Review*, Nov. 1893, VI, 313-321.

SELF-REALIZATION AS THE MORAL IDEAL. *Philosophical Review*, Nov. 1893, II, 652-664.

1894

THE STUDY OF ETHICS: A SYLLABUS. Ann Arbor: Register Publishing Company, 1894. iv, 151 pp.
Reprinted in 1897 with the imprint: Ann Arbor, George Wahr.

THE PSYCHOLOGY OF INFANT LANGUAGE. *Psychological Review*, Jan. 1894, I, 63-66.

ETHICAL. *Psychological Review*, Jan. 1894, I, 109-111.
Review of Josiah Royce, "On Certain Psychological Aspects of Moral Training;" Georg Simmel, "Moral Deficiencies as Determining Intellectual Functions;" Josiah Royce, "The Knowledge of Good and Evil."

[JOHN] AUSTIN'S THEORY OF SOVEREIGNTY. *Political Science Quarterly*, Mar. 1894, IX, 31-52.

SOCIAL PSYCHOLOGY. *Psychological Review*, July 1894, I, 400-411.

SOCIAL PSYCHOLOGY. *Psychological Review*, July, 1894, I, 400-411.
Review of Lester Frank Ward, *The Psychic Factors of Civilization;* Benjamin Kidd, *Social Evolution;* George Burton Adams, *Civilization during the Middle Ages;* and Robert Flint, *History of the Philosophy of History*.

THE CHAOS IN MORAL TRAINING. *Popular Science Monthly*, Aug. 1894, XLV, 433-443.

THE THEORY OF EMOTION. I. Emotional Attitudes (*Psychological Review*, Nov. 1894, I, 553-569); II. The Significance of Emotions (*ib.*, Jan. 1895, II, 13-32).
Summarized in *Philosophical Review*, Mar. 1895, IV, 207-208 (David Irons); *Revue Philosophique*, Mar. 1895, XXXIX, 344.

REVIEW of James Bonar, *Philosophy and Political Economy in Some of Their Historical Relations*. *Political Science Quarterly*, Dec. 1894, IX, 741-744.

1895

THE PSYCHOLOGY OF NUMBER AND ITS APPLICATIONS TO METHODS OF TEACHING ARITHMETIC. By James A[lexander] McLellan and John Dewey. New York: D. Appleton and Company, 1895. xv, 309 pp. (International Education Series, edited by William Torrey Harris, Vol. XXXIII.)

Published in London by Edwin Arnold, 1895.

THE RESULTS OF CHILD-STUDY APPLIED TO EDUCATION. *Transactions of the Illinois Society for Child-Study*, Jan. 1895, Vol. I, No. 4, pp. 18-19.

THE PHILOSOPHIC RENASCENCE IN AMERICA. *Dial*, 1 Feb. 1895, XVIII, 80-82.

Review of Paul Deussen, *The Elements of Metaphysics*; Friedrich Max Müller, *Three Lectures on the Vedanta Philosophy*; David Jayne Hill, *Genetic Philosophy*; Georg Wilhelm Friedrich Hegel, *Philosophy of Mind*; Herbert Nichols and William E. Parsons, *Our Notions of Number and Space*; Théodule Ribot, *Diseases of the Will*; Charles Van Norden, *An Outline of Psychology*; Alexander Thomas Ormond, *Basal Concepts in Philosophy*; and Paul Carus, *A Primer of Philosophy*.

REVIEW of *Johnson's Universal Cyclopedia*, Vols. I-V. *Psychological Review*, Mar. 1895, II, 186-188.

1896

INTEREST AS RELATED TO [THE TRAINING OF THE] WILL. *In* National Herbart Society, *Second Supplement to the Herbart Year Book for 1895* (Bloomington, Ill., 1896), pp. 209-255.

Revised and republished in 1899.

Reprinted in *Educational Essays* (1910), pp. 73-132.

INTERPRETATION OF THE CULTURE-EPOCH THEORY. *In* National Herbart Society, *Second Yearbook* (Bloomington, Ill., 1896), pp. 89-95.

First published in the *Public School Journal*, Jan. 1896, XV, 233-236.

THE REFLEX ARC CONCEPT IN PSYCHOLOGY. *University of Chicago Contributions to Philosophy* (1896), [Vol. I] No. 1, pp. 39-52.

Reprinted from *Psychological Review*, July 1896, III, 357-370.

Summarized in *Philosophical Review*, Nov. 1896, V, 649-650 (James Edwin Creighton); *Revue de Métaphysique et de Morale*, V (Sup. to July 1897, p. 14); *Revue Philosophique*, June 1897, XLIII, 668 (Jean Philippe).

INFLUENCE OF THE HIGH SCHOOL UPON EDUCATIONAL METHODS. *School Review*, Jan. 1896, IV, 1-12.

PSYCHOLOGY OF NUMBER. Letter in *Science*, 21 Feb. 1896, N. s. III, 286-289.

THE METAPHYSICAL METHOD IN ETHICS. *Psychological Review*, Mar. 1896, III, 181-188.

REVIEW of Sophie Willock Bryant, *Studies in Character*, and John Watson, *Hedonistic Theories from Aristippus to Spencer*. *Psychological Review*, Mar. 1896, III, 218-222.

REVIEW of Hiram Miner Stanley, *Studies in the Evolutionary Psychology of Feeling*. *Philosophical Review*, May 1896, V, 292-299.

REVIEW of Levi Leonard Conant, *The Number Concept: Its Origin and Development*. *Psychological Review*, May 1896, III, 326-329.

[REMARKS ON THE STUDY OF HISTORY IN SCHOOLS.] *School Review*, May 1896, IV, 272.

A PEDAGOGICAL EXPERIMENT. *Kindergarten Magazine*, June 1896, VIII, 739-741.

IMAGINATION AND EXPRESSION. *Kindergarten Magazine*, Sept. 1896, IX, 61-69.

Reprinted in *Teachers College Bulletin*, 1 Mar. 1919, Ser. 10, No. 10, pp. 6-9; and in part in *Third Report of the Western Drawing Teachers' Association* (Chicago, 1896) pp. 136-138.

PEDAGOGY AS A UNIVERSITY DISCIPLINE. *University [of Chicago] Record*, 18 and 25 Sept. 1896, I, 353-355, 361-363.

REVIEW of James Sully, *Studies of Childhood*. *Science*, 2 Oct. 1896, N. s. IV, 500-502.

THE UNIVERSITY SCHOOL. *University [of Chicago] Record*, 6 Nov. 1896, I, 417-419.

1897

ETHICAL PRINCIPLES UNDERLYING EDUCATION. *In* National Herbart Society, *Third Yearbook* (Chicago, 1897), pp. 7-34.

Reprinted by the University of Chicago Press, 1908, 34 pp. and in *Educational Essays* (1910), pp. 19-72.
See *Moral Principles in Education* (1909).

THE SIGNIFICANCE OF THE PROBLEM OF KNOWLEDGE. Chicago: The University of Chicago Press, 1897. 20 pp. (University of Chicago Contributions to Philosophy, [Vol. I] No. III.)

"Reprinted with slight change" in *The influence of Darwin on Philosophy* (1910), pp. 271-304.

MY PEDAGOGIC CREED. New York: E. L. Kellogg & Co. [°1897]. 36 pp.

Published with Albion Woodbury Small, *The Demands of Sociology upon Pedagogy*.

Reprinted from *School Journal*, 16 Jan. 1897, LIV, 77-80; also published in Ossian Herbert Lang, *Educational Creeds of the Nineteenth Century* (New York: E. L. Kellogg & Co., 1898), pp. 5-20; also in *National Education Association Journal*, Dec. 1929, XVIII, 291-295; also in *National Education Association Journal*, Jan. 1935, XXIV, 13-16.

Republished at Chicago [1910?] by A. Flanagan Company with an introduction by Samuel Train Dutton. Republished also, with a preface by Joy Elmer Morgan, by the National Education Association. Washington, D.C. (1939?) (Personal Growth Leaflets, No. 9).

Translations. German by Rudolf Prantl, *Zeitschrift für christliche Erziehungswissenschaft*, XV (1925), 465-476; Italian by Luigi Oliva (Rome, 1913); Spanish in *Quaderns d'Estudi*; Spanish in *Revista de Pedagogia*, 1931, X, 1-5, 74-80; Polish by Josef Pieter (Warszawa, 1933).

THE AESTHETIC ELEMENT IN EDUCATION. *In* National Education Association, *Addresses and Proceedings*, 1897, pp. 329-330, and discussion, p. 346.

THE KINDERGARTEN AND CHILD-STUDY. *In* National Education Association, *Addresses and Proceedings*, 1897, pp. 585-586.

Extracts in *School Journal*, 14 Aug. 1897, LV, 112.

CRITICISMS, WISE AND OTHERWISE, ON MODERN CHILD-STUDY. *In* National Education Association, *Addresses and Proceedings*, 1897, pp. 867-868.

THE PSYCHOLOGY OF EFFORT. *Philosophical Review*, Jan. 1897, VI, 43-56.

Summarized in *Psychological Review*, July 1897, 437-438 (Harry Norman Gardiner); *Revue de Métaphysique et de Morale*, V (Sup. to Mar. 1897, p. 10); *Revue Philosophique*, Feb. 1898, XLV, 220.

THE PSYCHOLOGICAL ASPECT OF THE SCHOOL CURRICULUM. *Educational Review*, Apr. 1897, XIII, 356-369.

THE INTERPRETATION SIDE OF CHILD-STUDY. *Transactions of the Illinois Society for Child-Study*, July 1897, Vol. II, No. 2, pp. 17-27.

1898

[SYLLABUS] The University of Chicago. Pedagogy I B 19. Philosophy of Education. 1898-1899 Winter Quarter. [Chicago, 1898.] 11 pp.

REPORT OF THE COMMITTEE ON A DETAILED PLAN FOR A REPORT ON ELEMENTARY EDUCATION. *In* National Education Association, *Addresses and Proceedings*, 1898, pp. 335-343.

SOME REMARKS ON THE PSYCHOLOGY OF NUMBER. *Pedagogical Seminary*, Jan. 1898, V, 426-434.

EVOLUTION AND ETHICS. *Monist*, Apr. 1898, VIII, 321-341.
Summarized in *Philosophical Review*, July 1898, VII, 423-424.

THE PRIMARY EDUCATION FETICH. *Forum*, May 1898, XXV, 315-328.

REVIEW of William Torrey Harris, *Psychologic Foundations of Education*. *Educational Review*, June 1898, XVI, 1-14.

REVIEW of James Mark Baldwin, *Social and Ethical Interpretations in Mental Development*. *Philosophical Review*, July 1898, VII, 398-409; 629-630.

REVIEW of James Mark Baldwin, *Social and Ethical Interpretations in Mental Development*. *New World*, Sept. 1898, VII, 504-522.

THE SENSE OF SOLIDITY. Letter in *Science*, 11 Nov. 1898, N. S. VIII, 675.

1899

INTEREST AS RELATED TO [THE TRAINING OF THE] WILL. (Chicago: The Society, reprinted, 1899.) 40 pp.
Second supplement to the *Herbart Yearbook for 1895*; see 1896.

PSYCHOLOGY AND PHILOSOPHIC METHOD. Berkeley: The University Press, 1899. 23 pp.
Reprinted from the *University [of California] Chronicle*, Aug. 1899, II, 159-179; reprinted "with slight verbal changes" in *The Influence of Darwin on Philosophy* (1910), pp. 242-270, with the title "'Consciousness' and Experience."

THE METHOD OF THE RECITATION. A Partial Report of a Course of Lectures Given at the University of Chicago. Privately Printed for the Use of Classes in Theory at the Oshkosh [Wisconsin] Normal School, 1899. 62 pp.

THE SCHOOL AND SOCIETY; being Three Lectures by John Dewey, Supplemented by a Statement of the University Elementary School. Chicago: The University of Chicago Press, 1899. 125 pp. See under 1900.

PLAY AND IMAGINATION IN RELATION TO EARLY EDUCATION. *School Journal*, 27 May 1899, LVIII, 589; *Kindergarten Magazine*, June 1899, XI, 636-640.

PRINCIPLES OF MENTAL DEVELOPMENT AS ILLUSTRATED IN EARLY INFANCY. *Transactions of the Illinois Society for Child-Study*, Oct. 1899, IV, 65-83.

1900

THE ELEMENTARY SCHOOL RECORD. A Series of Nine Monographs. Nos. 1-9, Feb.-Dec. 1900. Chicago: The University of Chicago Press, 1900.

John Dewey, Editor; Laura Louisa Runyon, Managing Editor

The following articles are by Dewey: No. 1, Feb. 1900, General Principles of Work, Educationally Considered [Introduction to Group III], pp. 12-15; Historical Development of Inventions and Occupations, General Principles [Introduction to Group IV], pp. 21-23. No. 2, Mar. 1900, General Introduction to Groups V and VI, pp. 49-52. No. 3, Apr. 1900, Psychology of Occupations, pp. 82-85. No. 4, May 1900, Reflective Attention, pp. 111-113. No. 5, June 1900, Froebel's Educational Principles, pp. 143-151. No. 8, Nov. 1900, The Aim of History in Elementary Education, pp. 199-203. No. 9, Dec. 1900, The Psychology of the Elementary Curriculum, pp. 221-232.

Reprinted in part as *The "Dewey" School* (London: The Froebel Society [n.d.]), 80 pp.; revised edition, 1929, 119 pp.

See *The School and the Child* (1907); and *The School and Society* (1915).

THE SCHOOL AND SOCIETY; being Three Lectures by John Dewey, Supplemented by a Statement of the University Elementary School. Chicago: The University of Chicago Press, 1900. 129 pp.

Published also in London by P. S. King & Son, 1900.

Revised edition, 1915, *q.v.*

Translations. Bohemian by Ján Mrazík (Prague, 1914); French (in part, in *L'Education*, June 1909 and Dec. 1912); German by Elsie Gurlitt (1905); Japanese; Polish by Marja Lisowska (Lemberg, 1924); Russian; Spanish by

Domingo Barnés (Madrid, 1915); Turkish by B. Avni (1923); Arabic by Dimitri Kandaleft; Dutch by Tj. de Boer (Groningen, Den Haag, 1929); Polish by Roza Czaplinska-Mutermilchowa (Warszawa, 1933); Bulgarian by Dobroslav Miletic (1935); Servo-Croatian by M. Vanlic (1935).

INTUITIONALISM. In *The Universal Cyclopedia,* edited by Charles Kendall Adams (New York: D. Appleton and Company, 1900), VI, 321-323.

MORAL PHILOSOPHY. *Ib.,* VIII, 240-245.

PSYCHOLOGY AND SOCIAL PRACTICE. *Psychological Review,* Mar. 1900, VII, 105-124 (abstract, pp. 127-128); *Science,* 2 Mar. 1900, N. s. XI, 321-333.

Summarized in *Philosophical Review,* May 1900, IX, 340-341; *Revue Philosophique,* Sept. 1901, LII, 337.

Reprinted as University of Chicago Contributions to Education, No. II (Chicago: The University of Chicago Press, 1901), 42 pp.; also in *Educational Essays* (1910), pp. 133-167.

REVIEW of Josiah Royce, *The World and the Individual* (Gifford Lectures), First Series: The Four Historical Conceptions of Being (*Philosophical Review,* May 1900, IX, 311-324); Second Series: Nature, Man, and the Moral Order (*ib.,* July 1902, XI, 392-407).

SOME STAGES OF LOGICAL THOUGHT. *Philosophical Review,* Sept. 1900, IX, 465-489.

Summarized in *Revue de Métaphysique et de Morale,* VIII (Sup. to Nov. 1900, p. 11); *Revue Philosophique,* June 1901, LI, 674 (J. Segond).

Reprinted in *Essays in Experimental Logic* (1916), pp. 183-219.

1901

DICTIONARY OF PHILOSOPHY AND PSYCHOLOGY, Edited by James Mark Baldwin. Vol. I. New York: The Macmillan Company, 1901.

John Dewey, Consulting Editor.

The following article is by Dewey: History of Philosophy (with Josiah Royce), pp. 480-482.

THE SITUATION AS REGARDS THE COURSE OF STUDY. *In* National Education Association, *Addresses and Proceedings,* 1901, pp. 332-348.

Published also in *Educational Review,* June 1901, XXII, 26-49, and in *School Journal,* 20 and 27 Apr., and 4 May 1901, LXII, 421-423, 445-446, 454, 469-471.

Are the Schools Doing What the People Want Them to Do? *Educational Review,* May 1901, XXI, 459-474; *Review of Education,* June 1901, VII, 10-11.

The Place of Manual Training in the Elementary Course of Study. *Manual Training Magazine,* July 1901, II, 193-199. Summarized in *School Journal,* 31 Aug. 1901, LXIII, 182-183.

1902

Dictionary of Philosophy and Psychology. Vol. II. New York: The Macmillan Company, 1902.

The following articles are by Dewey: Mind, in Philosophy (with James Mark Baldwin), pp. 81-82—Natural Realism, p. 134—Naturalism, in Art (with James Hayden Tufts), p. 138—Nature, pp. 138-141—Nature, Philosophy of, p. 142—Necessity, pp. 143-145—Neo-Criticism, p. 149—Neo-Platonism, p. 150—Nescience, p. 167—Nexus, p. 176—Nisus, p. 178—Noetic, pp. 178-179—Nominalism, p. 180—Non-Being, pp. 180-181—Noölogy, pp. 181-182—Norm and Normative, in the Moral Sciences, p. 182—Noumenon and Noumenal, pp. 184-185—Nous, pp. 185-186—Nullibrists, p. 186—Number, in Metaphysics, p. 189—Object and Objective, General and Philosophical, pp. 191-192—Objectivism, p. 194—One, The, p. 201—Ontological Argument, pp. 202-203—Ontologism (2.), p. 203—Ontology, pp. 203-204—Opinion, p. 205—Optimism and Pessimism, pp. 210-212—Organic, p. 213—Organism, pp. 218-219—Outness, p. 251—Oversoul, p. 252—Palingenesis, p. 254—Panentheism, p. 255—Panlogism, p. 255—Panpneumatism, p. 256—Panpsychism, p. 256—Pantheism, pp. 256-257—Panthelism, pp. 257-258—Parousia, p. 263—Passion and Passive, pp. 266-267—Peripatetics, p. 280—Permanence, p. 280—Phase, p. 288—Phenomenalism, p. 288—Phenomenology, pp. 288-289—Phenomenon, p. 289—Philosophy, pp. 290-296—Phoronomy, p. 297—Pleroma, p. 305—Pluralism, p. 306—Plurality, p. 306—Pneuma, pp. 307-308—Pneumatology, p. 308—Posit, pp. 310-311—Positive (3. Philosophical), p. 311—Pre-established Harmony, pp. 329-330—Presentationism (2.), p. 333—Primary, Primitive, Primordial, p. 340—Primum Mobile, p. 341—Principle, pp. 341-342—Quietism, p. 412—Rationalism, pp. 415-416—Reals, p. 424—Relation, pp. 439-443—Same, The; and The Other, pp. 484-485—Scepticism, pp. 489-490—Schema, p. 490—Schematism, pp. 490-491—Scholasticism (The Schoolmen), pp. 491-495—Schopenhauerism (or Schopenhauereanism), p. 499—Scotism, p. 503—Sensationalism, pp. 515-517—Singularism, p. 533—Speculation, p. 568—Statue of Condillac, p. 601—Subject, Subjective, pp. 607-608—Subjectivism, p. 611—Substantiality Theory, or Substantialism, p. 614—Sui Generis, p. 620—Summists, pp. 620-621—Syncretism (1.), p. 655—System, p. 659—Tabula Rasa, p. 661—Transcendentalism, p. 711—Transient, p. 712—Ubication, p. 723—Understanding and Reason, pp. 725-726—Unity and Plurality, pp. 734-736—Universal and Universality (4. and 5.), pp. 737-739—Universal Postulate, p. 741—Universe, p. 742—Unthinkable, p. 743—Vacuum, pp. 747-748—World, p. 821.

THE CHILD AND THE CURRICULUM. Chicago: The University of Chicago Press, 1902. 40 pp. (University of Chicago Contributions to Education, No. V.)

Translations. Russian; Spanish, with an introduction by Lorenzo Luzuriaga (Madrid, 1925); 3. ed. (in: Publicaciones de la *Revista de Pedagogia*), 1934 (?); Swedish by Agnes Jacobsson-Undén (Lund, 1912); Chinese; Hungarian. Reprinted in *The School and the Child* (1907), pp. 17-47.

THE EDUCATIONAL SITUATION. Chicago: The University of Chicago Press, 1902. 104 pp. (University of Chicago Contributions to Education, No. III.)

DISCUSSION. *In* National Education Association, *Addresses and Proceedings,* 1902, pp. 719-720.

Discussion of Theodore B. Noss, "What Our Schools Owe to Child-Study."

THE SCHOOL AS SOCIAL CENTER. *In* National Education Association, *Addresses and Proceedings,* 1902, pp. 373-383.

Published also in *Elementary School Teacher,* Oct. 1902, III, 73-86.

ACADEMIC FREEDOM. *Educational Review,* Jan. 1902, XXIII, 1-14.

CURRENT PROBLEMS IN SECONDARY EDUCATION. *School Review,* Jan. 1902, X, 13-28.

THE EVOLUTIONARY METHOD AS APPLIED TO MORALITY. I. Its Scientific Necessity (*Philosophical Review,* Mar. 1902, XI, 107-124); II. Its Significance for Conduct (*ib.,* July 1902, XI, 353-371).

Abstract in *Revue Philosophique,* Nov. 1903, LVI, 553-554.

IN REMEMBRANCE: FRANCIS W. PARKER. *Journal of Education,* 27 Mar. 1902, LV, 199.

INTERPRETATION OF SAVAGE MIND. *Psychological Review,* May 1902, IX, 217-230.

Summarized by M. S. Macdonald, *Philosophical Review,* Sept. 1902, XI, 529-530; abstract in *Revue Philosophique,* Mar. 1903, LV, 348.

Reprinted in William Isaac Thomas, *Sourcebook for Social Origins* (Chicago, 1909), pp. 173-186.

REVIEW of Lightner Witmer, *Analytical Psychology. School Review,* May 1902, X, 412.

[In Memoriam: Colonel Francis Wayland Parker.] *Elementary School Teacher*, June 1902, II, 704-708.
Reprinted in *Characters and Events* (1929), I, 95-99.

The Battle for Progress. *Journal of Education*, 16 Oct. 1902, LVI, 249.

The University of Chicago School of Education. Editorial in *Elementary School Teacher*, Nov. 1902, III, 200-203.

1903

Studies in Logical Theory, by John Dewey, with the Co-operation of Members and Fellows of the Department of Philosophy. Chicago: The University of Chicago Press, 1903. xiii, 388 pp. (University of Chicago. The Decennial Publications, Second Series, Vol. XI.)
Published also in London by T. Fisher Unwin, 1909.

Logical Conditions of a Scientific Treatment of Morality. Chicago: The University of Chicago Press, 1903. 27 pp.
Reprinted from the Decennial Publications of the University of Chicago, First Series, Vol. III, pp. 113-139.

Ethics. In *The [Encyclopedia] Americana* (New York: Scientific American [ᶜ1903-1906]), Vol. VII [unpaged], *sub voce*.
Reprinted in the *Encyclopedia Americana*, New York [ᶜ1918], Vol. X, pp. 540-546.

Religious Education as Conditioned by Modern Psychology and Pedagogy. *Proceedings of the Religious Education Association*, 1903, pp. 60-66.

Introduction. *In* Irving Walter King, *The Psychology of Child Development* (Chicago: The University of Chicago Press, 1903), pp. xi-xx.

[Remarks on Frank Louis Soldan, "Shortening the Years of Elementary Schooling," *School Review*, Jan. 1903, XI, 4-17.] *Ib.*, pp. 17-20.

Psychological Method in Ethics. *Psychological Review*, Mar. 1903, X, 158-160.

The Psychological and the Logical in Teaching Geometry. *Educational Review*, Apr. 1903, XXV, 387-399.

THE ORGANIZATION AND CURRICULA OF THE [UNIVERSITY OF CHICAGO] COLLEGE OF EDUCATION. *Elementary School Teacher*, May 1903, III, 553-562.

METHOD OF THE RECITATION. *Elementary School Teacher*, May 1903, III, 563.

REVIEW of Katharine Elizabeth Dopp, *The Place of Industries in Elementary Education*. *Elementary School Teacher*, June 1903, III, 727-728.

EMERSON—THE PHILOSOPHER OF DEMOCRACY. *International Journal of Ethics*, July 1903, XIII, 405-413.

Summarized in *Philosophical Review*, Sept. 1903, XII, 574 (George Holland Sabine).

Reprinted in *Characters and Events* (1929), I, 69-77, with the title "Ralph Waldo Emerson."

THE ST. LOUIS CONGRESS OF THE ARTS AND SCIENCES. Letter in *Science*, 28 Aug. 1903, N. S. XVIII, 275-278.

Discussion of Hugo Münsterberg, "The St. Louis Congress. . . ."

DEMOCRACY IN EDUCATION. *Elementary School Teacher*, Dec. 1903, IV, 193-204.

TOTAL ISOLATION. *Journal of Education*, 24 Dec. 1903, LVIII, 433.

1904

EDUCATION, DIRECT AND INDIRECT. [Chicago] 1904. 10 pp.

Reprinted in *Progressive Journal of Education*, 15 Oct. 1909, II, 31-38.

THE RELATION OF THEORY TO PRACTICE IN EDUCATION. *In* National Society for the Scientific Study of Education, *Third Yearbook*, 1904, Part I, pp. 9-30.

NOTES UPON LOGICAL TOPICS. I. A Classification of Contemporary Tendencies (*Journal of Philosophy*, 4 Feb. 1904, I, 57-62); II. The Meanings of the Term "Idea" (*ib.*, 31 Mar. 1904, I, 175-178).

THE PSYCHOLOGY OF JUDGMENT. *Psychological Bulletin*, 10 Feb. 1904, I, 44-45.

SIGNIFICANCE OF THE SCHOOL OF EDUCATION. *Elementary School Teacher*, Mar. 1904, IV, 441-453.

THE PHILOSOPHICAL WORK OF HERBERT SPENCER. *Philosophical Review*, Mar. 1904, XIII, 159-175.

Abstracts in *Revue de Métaphysique et de Morale*, XIV (Sup. to May 1906, p. 13); *Revue Philosophique*, Apr. 1905, LIX, 439 (J. Segond).
Reprinted in *Characters and Events* (1929), I, 45-62.

REVIEW of Wayland Richardson Benedict, *World Views and Their Ethical Implications. International Journal of Ethics*, Apr. 1904, XIV, 389-390.

INTRODUCTION OF THE ORATOR [Nicholas Murray Butler]. *University [of Chicago] Record*, May 1904, IX, 12-13.

REVIEW of Ferdinand Canning Scott Schiller, *Humanism. Psychological Bulletin*, 15 Sept. 1904, I, 335-340.

1905

THE REALISM OF PRAGMATISM. *Journal of Philosophy*, 8 June 1905, II, 324-327.

THE POSTULATE OF IMMEDIATE EMPIRICISM. *Journal of Philosophy*, 20 July 1905, II, 393-399.

Summarized in *Philosophical Review*, May 1906, XV, 350 (Mattie Alexander Martin).
Reprinted in *The Influence of Darwin on Philosophy* (1910), pp. 226-241.

IMMEDIATE EMPIRICISM. *Journal of Philosophy*, 26 Oct. 1905, II, 597-599.

THE KNOWLEDGE EXPERIENCE AND ITS RELATIONSHIPS. *Journal of Philosophy*, 23 Nov. 1905, II, 652-657.

THE KNOWLEDGE EXPERIENCE AGAIN. *Journal of Philosophy*, 21 Dec. 1905, II, 707-711.

1906

CULTURE AND INDUSTRY IN EDUCATION. *Proceedings of the Joint Convention of the Eastern Art Teachers Association and the Eastern Manual Training Association*, 1906, pp. 21-30.

Reprinted in *Educational Bi-Monthly*, 1 Oct. 1908, I, 1-9; and in *Teachers College Bulletin*, Ser. 10, No. 1, 1 Mar. 1919, pp. 10-18.

THE TERMS "CONSCIOUS" AND "CONSCIOUSNESS." *Journal of Philosophy*, 18 Jan. 1906, III, 39-41.

REVIEW of George Santayana, *The Life of Reason* (Vols. I and II). *Science,* 9 Feb. 1906, N. S. XXIII, 223-225.

BELIEFS AND REALITIES. *Philosophical Review,* Mar. 1906, XV, 113-119.

Abstracts in *Revue de Métaphysique et de Morale,* XVI (Sup. to Nov. 1908, p. 18); *Revue Philosophique,* Apr. 1907, LXIII, 555.

Reprinted "with verbal revisions" in *The Influence of Darwin on Philosophy* (1910), pp. 169-197, under the title "Beliefs and Existences."

REALITY AS EXPERIENCE. *Journal of Philosophy,* 10 May 1906, III, 253-257.

THE EXPERIMENTAL THEORY OF KNOWLEGE. *Mind,* July 1906, N. S. XV, 293-307.

Summarized in *Philosophical Review,* Jan. 1907, XVI, 107-108 (M. W. Sprague); *Revue Philosophique,* Dec. 1906, LXII, 666.

Reprinted "with considerable change in the arrangement and in the matter of the latter portion" in *The Influence of Darwin on Philosophy* (1910), pp. 77-111.

EXPERIENCE AND OBJECTIVE IDEALISM. *Philosophical Review,* Sept. 1906, XV, 465-481.

Summarized in *Psychological Bulletin,* 15 July 1907, IV, 230-232 (Grace Bruce); *Revue Philosophique,* Apr. 1907, LXIII, 557-558 (J. Segond).

Reprinted "with slight verbal changes" in *The Influence of Darwin on Philosophy* (1910), pp. 198-225.

1907

THE SCHOOL AND THE CHILD; being Selections from the Educational Essays of John Dewey. Edited by J[oseph] J[ohn] Findlay. London: Blackie & Son, Ltd. [1907? pref. 1906]. 128 pp. (The Little Library of Pedagogics.)

Translation. Spanish. (Madrid, 1934.) (In: Ciencia y Educacion.)

REVIEW of A[rthur] S[idgwick] and E[leanor] M[ildred Balfour] S[idgwick], *Henry Sidgwick, A Memoir. Political Science Quarterly,* Mar. 1907, XXII, 133-135.

THE CONTROL OF IDEAS BY FACTS. I. (*Journal of Philosophy,* 11 Apr. 1907, IV, 197-203); II. (*Ib.,* 9 May 1907, pp. 253-259); III. (*Ib.,* 6 June 1907, pp. 309-319).

Summarized in *Philosophical Review,* Jan. 1908, XVII, 104-105 (C. H. Williams); *Psychological Bulletin,* Oct. 1908, V, 336-337 (Robert Morris Ogden).

Reprinted in *Essays in Experimental Logic* (1916), pp. 230-249.

REVIEW of *Studies in Philosophy and Psychology* by the Former Students of Charles Edward Garman. *Philosophical Review*, May 1907, XVI, 312-321.

EDUCATION AS A UNIVERSITY STUDY. *Columbia University Quarterly*, June 1907, IX, 284-290.

REALITY AND THE CRITERION FOR THE TRUTH OF IDEAS. *Mind*, July 1907, N. S. XVI, 317-342.

Summarized in *Philosophical Review*, Jan. 1908, XVII, 103-104 (Gustavus Watts Cunningham); *Psychological Bulletin*, May 1908, V, 166-167 (M. S. Case); *Revue Philosophique*, Dec. 1907, LXIV, 662.

Reprinted "with many changes" in *The Influence of Darwin on Philosophy* (1910), pp. 112-153 with the title "The Intellectualist Criterion for Truth."

PURE EXPERIENCE AND REALITY: A DISCLAIMER. *Philosophical Review*, July 1907, XVI, 419-422.

REVIEW of George Santayana, *The Life of Reason* (Vols. I-V). *Educational Review*, Sept. 1907, XXXIV, 116-129.

1908

ETHICS. New York: Columbia University Press, 1908. 26 pp.

Reprinted in *The Influence of Darwin on Philosophy* (1910), pp. 46-76 with the title "Intelligence and Morals."

ETHICS, by John Dewey and James H[ayden] Tufts. New York: Henry Holt and Company, 1908. xiii, 618 pp. (American Science Series.)

Published also in London by G. Bell and Sons, 1909.

Part I was written by Mr. Tufts, Part II by Mr. Dewey, and in Part III, Chapters XX [Social Organization and the Individual] and XXI [Civil Society and the Political State] are by Mr. Dewey, Chapters XXII-XXVI by Mr. Tufts.

Revised ed. New York: H. Holt & Co., 1932. 528 pp.

Reprinted in New York by H. Holt & Co., 1938.

Translations. Japanese by R. Nakashima (Tokyo, 1912); Chinese.

DOES REALITY POSSESS PRACTICAL CHARACTER? In *Essays, Philosophical and Psychological*, in Honor of William James, Professor in Harvard University, by his Colleagues at Columbia University (New York: Longmans, Green, and Company, 1908), pp. 53-80.

WHAT DOES PRAGMATISM MEAN BY PRACTICAL? *Journal of Philosophy*, 13 Feb. 1908, V, 85-99.

Review of William James, *Pragmatism.*
Summarized in *Revue de Métaphysique et de Morale,* XVI (Sup. to Nov. 1908, pp. 24-25).
Reprinted, except the last paragraph, as "What Pragmatism Means by Practical" in *Essays in Experimental Logic* (1916), pp. 303-329.

RELIGION AND OUR SCHOOLS. *Hibbert Journal,* July 1908, VI, 796-809.
Reprinted in *Characters and Events* (1929), II, 504-516.

THE LOGICAL CHARACTER OF IDEAS. *Journal of Philosophy,* 2 July 1908, V, 375-381.
Reprinted in *Essays in Experimental Logic* (1916), pp. 220-229.

THE BEARINGS OF PRAGMATISM UPON EDUCATION. I. (*Progressive Journal of Education,* Dec. 1908, Vol. I, No. 2, pp. 1-3); II. (*Ib.,* Jan. 1909, I, 3, 5-8); III. (*Ib.,* Feb. 1909, I, 4, 6-7).

1909

MORAL PRINCIPLES IN EDUCATION. Boston: Houghton Mifflin Company 1909. (Riverside Educational Monographs, edited by Henry Suzzallo.)
An elaboration of *Ethical Principles Underlying Education* (1897).
Translations. Bohemian by F. Pavlasch, with a preface by Miloslav Skorepa (Prague, 1934); Chinese.

THE PRAGMATIC MOVEMENT OF CONTEMPORARY THOUGHT: A SYLLABUS. New York, 1909. 11 pp.

OBJECTS, DATA, AND EXISTENCES. *Journal of Philosophy,* 7 Jan. 1909, VI, 13-21.
Summarized in *Revue de Philosophie,* May 1909, XIV, 735.

HISTORY FOR THE EDUCATOR. *Progressive Journal of Education,* Mar. 1909, Vol. I, No. 5, pp. 1-4.

DISCUSSION ON REALISM AND IDEALISM. *Philosophical Review,* Mar. 1909, XVIII, 182-183.

SYMPOSIUM ON THE PURPOSE AND ORGANIZATION OF PHYSICS TEACHING IN SECONDARY SCHOOLS, XIII. *School Science and Mathematics,* Mar. 1909, IX, 291-292.

[DISCUSSION ON THE CONCEPT OF A SENSATION.] *Journal of Philosophy,* 15 Apr. 1909, VI, 211-212.

TEACHING THAT DOES NOT EDUCATE. *Progressive Journal of Education*, June 1909, Vol. I, No. 8, pp. 1-3.

IS NATURE GOOD? A CONVERSATION. *Hibbert Journal*, July 1909, VII, 827-843.

Reprinted in *The Influence of Darwin on Philosophy* (1910), pp. 20-45, with the title "Nature and Its Good: a Conversation."

REVIEW of Albert Schinz, *Anti-pragmatisme. Philosophical Review*, July 1909, XVIII, 446-449.

DARWIN'S INFLUENCE UPON PHILOSOPHY. *Popular Science Monthly*, July 1909, LXXV, 90-98.

Reprinted in *The Influence of Darwin on Philosophy* (1910), pp. 1-19.

THE DILEMMA OF THE INTELLECTUALIST THEORY OF TRUTH. *Journal of Philosophy*, 5 Aug. 1909, VI, 433-434.

Summarized in *Revue Philosophique*, Sept. 1910, LXX, 322 (Guillaume L. Duprat).

1910

HOW WE THINK. Boston: D. C. Heath & Co., 1910. vi, 224 pp.

Published also in London by Harrap.

Rev. ed. (New York, Heath. 1933). 311 pp. Publ. in London by Heath. 311 pp.; and by Harrap.

Translations. French by O. Decroly (Paris, 1925); Russian; Spanish by Alejandro A. Jascalevich (Boston, [ᶜ1917]); Portugese by Godofredo Rangel (São Paulo, 1933); Polish by Zofja Bastgenówna (Warszawa, 1934); Chinese.

THE INFLUENCE OF DARWIN ON PHILOSOPHY AND OTHER ESSAYS IN CONTEMPORARY THOUGHT. New York: Henry Holt and Company, 1910. vi, 309 pp.

Published also in London by G. Bell & Sons, Ltd., 1910.

EDUCATIONAL ESSAYS BY JOHN DEWEY. Edited by J[oseph] J[ohn] Findlay. London: Blackie & Son, Ltd., 1910. 168 pp.

Translation. Swedish by Malte Jacobssen (Lund, 1912).

SCIENCE AS SUBJECT MATTER AND AS METHOD. *Science*, 28 Jan. 1910, N. S. XXXI, 121-127.

Reprinted in *Journal of Education*, 14, 21 and 28 Apr. 1910, LXXI, 395-396, 427-428, 454; and in *Characters and Events* (1929), II, 765-775, with the title "Science and the Education of Man."

REVIEW of Hugo Münsterberg, *The Eternal Values. Philosophical Review*, Mar. 1910, XIX, 188-192.

VALID KNOWLEDGE AND THE "SUBJECTIVITY OF EXPERIENCE."
Journal of Philosophy, 31 Mar. 1910, VII, 169-174.
Summarized in *Philosophical Review*, Sept. 1910, XIX, 563 (J. R. Tuttle).

SOME IMPLICATIONS OF ANTI-INTELLECTUALISM. *Journal of Philosophy*, 1 Sept. 1910, VII, 477-481.
Summarized in *Philosophical Review*, Mar. 1911, XX, 239 (J. Reese Lin);
Revue Philosophique, Apr. 1912, LXXIII, 439 (Guillaume L. Duprat).

WILLIAM JAMES. *Independent*, 8 Sept. 1910, LXIX, 533-536.
Reprinted in *Characters and Events* (1929), I, 111-117.

WILLIAM JAMES. *Journal of Philosophy*, 15 Sept. 1910, VII, 505-508.
Reprinted in *Characters and Events* (1929), I, 107-111.

THE SHORT-CUT TO REALISM EXAMINED. *Journal of Philosophy*, 29 Sept. 1910, VII, 553-557.

1911

A CYCLOPEDIA OF EDUCATION, Edited by Paul Monroe. Vol. I. New York: The Macmillan Company, 1911.
John Dewey, Departmental Editor for Philosophy of Education.
The following articles are by Dewey: Abstraction, p. 14—Accommodation, pp. 24-25—Activity, Logical Theory and Educational Implication of, pp. 33-34—Adaptation, p. 35—Adjustment, pp. 38-39—Altruism and Egoism, pp. 105-106—Analogy, Logic of, p. 116—Analysis and Synthesis, pp. 117-119—Art in Education, pp. 223-225—Causation, pp. 553-554—Character, pp. 569-572.

Ib., Vol. II, 1911.
The following articles are by Dewey: Comparison, p. 163—Conception, pp. 171-172—Concrete and Abstract, p. 173—Conduct, p. 175—Conflict, p. 175—Control, p. 196—Course of Study, Theory of, pp. 218-222—Culture and Culture Values, pp. 238-240—Culture Epoch Theory, pp. 240-242—Custom, pp. 243-244—Deduction, p. 275—Definition, pp. 280-281—Democracy and Education, pp. 293-294—Demonstration, p. 294—Determinism, p. 318—Development, pp. 319-320—Dialectic, pp. 321-322—Didactics, p. 327—Discipline, p. 336—Dualism, p. 374—Dynamic, p. 380—Education, pp. 398-401—Education and Instruction, p. 414—Effort, pp. 421-422—End in Education, p. 451—Environment and Organism, pp. 486-487—Epistemology, p. 491—Evidence, p. 528—Evolution: the Philosophical Concepts, pp. 528-529—Experience and the Empirical, pp. 546-549—Experiment in Education, pp. 550-551—Experimentation, Logic of, pp. 554-555—Explanation, p. 555—External Object, p. 559—Fact, pp. 567-568—Form and Content, pp. 641-642—Freedom, Academic, pp. 700-701—Freedom of Will, pp. 705-706—Function, pp. 723-724.

REJOINDER TO DR. SPAULDING. *Journal of Philosophy*, 3 Feb. 1911, VIII, 77-79.

JOINT DISCUSSION, with Articles of Agreement and Disagreement, by Dewey and Spaulding, *ib.*, pp. 574-579.

Summarized in *Revue de Métaphysique et de Morale*, XX (Sup. to Jan. 1912, pp. 22-24); XXI (Sup. to Mar. 1913, p. 23).

THE PROBLEM OF TRUTH. I. Why Is Truth a Problem? (*Old Penn, Weekly Review of the University of Pennsylvania*, 11 Feb. 1911, IX, 522-528); II. Truth and Consequences (*ib.*, 18 Feb. 1911, pp. 556-563); III. Objective Truths (*ib.*, 4 Mar. 1911, pp. 620-625).

IS CO-EDUCATION INJURIOUS TO GIRLS? *Ladies Home Journal*, June 1911, XXVIII, 22, 60-61.

MAETERLINCK'S PHILOSOPHY OF LIFE. *Hibbert Journal*, July 1911, IX, 765-778.

Reprinted in *Characters and Events* (1929), I, 31-44, with the title "Maurice Maeterlinck."

BRIEF STUDIES IN REALISM. I. Naïve Realism *vs.* Presentative Realism (*Journal of Philosophy*, 20 July 1911, VIII, 393-400); II. Epistemological Realism: the Alleged Ubiquity of the Knowledge Relation (*ib.*, 28 Sept. 1911, pp. 546-554).

Summarized in *Philosophical Review*, Jan. 1912, XXI, 120-121 (Elijah Jordan).

Reprinted in *Essays in Experimental Logic* (1916), pp. 250-280.

1912

A CYCLOPEDIA OF EDUCATION. Vol. III. New York: The Macmillan Company, 1912.

The following articles are by Dewey: Generalization, p. 15—Harmony, Harmonious Development, p. 217—Hedonism, pp. 242-243—Humanism and Naturalism, pp. 338-340—Humanities, The, p. 340—Hypothesis, pp. 363-364—Idea and Ideation, pp. 370-371—Idealism, pp. 371-373—Idealism and Realism in Education, pp. 373-375—Imitation in Education, pp. 389-390—Individuality, pp. 421-422—Induction and Deduction, pp. 422-424—Infancy, Theory of, in Education, pp. 445-446—Inference, p. 455—Information, pp. 455-456—Initiative, p. 457—Innate Idea, pp. 458-459—Interest, pp. 472-475—Intuition, p. 480—Isolation, p. 499—Judgment, pp. 571-572—Knowledge, pp. 611-613—Law, pp. 655-656.

REPLY TO PROFESSOR ROYCE'S CRITIQUE OF INSTRUMENTALISM. *Philosophical Review*, Jan. 1912, XXI, 69-81.

A Reply to Professor McGilvary's Questions. *Journal of Philosophy*, 4 Jan. 1912, IX, 19-21.

In Response to Professor McGilvary. *Journal of Philosophy*, 26 Sept. 1912, IX, 544-548.

Review of Hugh Samuel Roger Elliott, *Modern Science and the Illusions of Professor Bergson. Philosophical Review*, Nov. 1912, XXI, 705-707.

Perception and Organic Action. *Journal of Philosophy*, 21 Nov. 1912, IX, 645-668.
Summarized in *Revue de Métaphysique et de Morale*, XXII (Sup. to Mar. 1914, pp. 30-31); *Revue Philosophique*, July 1913, LXXVI, 107.

L'Ecôle et la vie de l'enfant (Translated by J. Desfeuille). *L'Education*, Dec. 1912, pp. 457-472.
See *The School and Society* (1900).

1913

L'Ecôle et l'enfant. Traduit par L. S. Pidoux, avec une Introduction par Edouard Claparède. Neuchâtel: Delachaux & Niestlé [1913]. xxxii, 136 pp. (Collection d'actualités pédagogiques, publiée sous les auspices de l'Institut J. J. Rousseau.)

L'Education au Point de Vue Social. *L'Année Pédagogique*, 1913, III, 32-48.

Interest and Effort in Education. Boston: Houghton Mifflin Company [^c1913]. ix, 101 pp. (Riverside Educational Monographs, edited by Henry Suzzallo.)
Translations. Portuguese by Anisio Taixeira (São Paulo, 1930); Servo-Croatian by M. Aersenijevic.

Should Michigan Have Vocational Education under "Unit" or "Dual" Control? *In* National Society for the Promotion of Industrial Education, *Bulletin 18* (Peoria, Ill. [1913]), pp. 27-34.

Introduction. *In* [Isadore Gilbert Mudge], *A Contribution to a Bibliography of Henri Bergson* (New York: Columbia University Press, 1913), pp. ix-xiii.

Introduction. *In* Henry Street Settlement, Committee on Vocational Scholarships, *Directory of the Trades and Occupations Taught at the Day and Evening Schools in Greater New York* (New York, 1913), pp. 2-3.

A Cyclopedia of Education. Vol. IV. New York: The Macmillan Company, 1913.

The following articles are by Dewey: Liberal Education, pp. 4-6—Many-Sided Interest, p. 129—Materialism, p. 158—Metaphysics, p. 202—Method, pp. 202-205—Monism, p. 296—Morality and Moral Sense, p. 314—Nativism, p. 386—Nature, pp. 387-389—Neo-Humanism, p. 408—Opinion, p. 552—Optimism, pp. 552-553—Pantheism, p. 598—Pedantry, pp. 622-623—Personality, pp. 649-650—Pessimism, pp. 654-655—Philosophy of Education, pp. 697-703—Plato, pp. 722-725—Play, pp. 725-727—Pluralism, p. 730.

Ib., Vol. V, 1913.

The following articles are by Dewey: Positivism, pp. 18-19—Pragmatism, pp. 22-24—Problem, p. 47—Process, p. 49—Progress, pp. 51-52—Proposition, p. 54—Rationalism, p. 109—Scientific Method, pp. 292-293—Self, pp. 317-319—Self-Consciousness, pp. 319-320—Sensationalism, pp. 324-325—Stimulus and Response, p. 422—Subject, pp. 446-447—Syllogism, 492-493—System, p. 496—Term, p. 566—Theism, p. 581—Theory and Practice, pp. 606-607—Tradition, p. 621—Transcendentalism, pp. 622-623—Truth, pp. 632-633—Universal, p. 651—Utilitarianism, p. 700—Validity, p. 703—Values, Educational, pp. 704-705.

An Undemocratic Proposal. *American Teacher*, Jan. 1913, II, 2-4; *Vocational Education*, May 1913, II, 374-377.

Some Dangers in the Present Movement for Industrial Education. *Child Labor Bulletin*, Feb. 1913, Vol. I, No. 4, pp. 69-74.

Reprint, with revisions, of "An Undemocratic Proposal," above; also printed as *Pamphlet No. 190* of the National Child Labor Committee, New York, 1913.

Industrial Education and Democracy. *Survey*, 22 Mar. 1913, XXIX, 870-871, 893.

Part II, Reprinted from *American Teacher*, Jan. 1913, above.

The Problem of Values. *Journal of Philosophy*, 8 May 1913, X, 268-269.

Cut-and-Try School Methods. *Survey*, 6 Sept. 1913, XXX, 691-692.

Professional Spirit among Teachers. *American Teacher*, Oct. 1913, II, 114-116.

1914

Reasoning in Early Childhood. *Teachers College Record*, Jan. 1914, XV, 9-15.

REPORTS OF LECTURES BY JOHN DEWEY. By Jenny B. Merrill. I. On Rousseau, Pestalozzi, Froebel and Montessori (*Kindergarten-Primary Magazine*, Mar. 1914, XXVI, 186); II. On Social Motives in School Life (*ib.*, Apr. 1914, p. 215); III. On Pestalozzi (*ib.*, May 1914, p. 251); IV. Comparison of Herbart and Froebel (*ib.*, pp. 255-256).

REPORT ON THE FAIRHOPE [ALABAMA] EXPERIMENT IN ORGANIC EDUCATION. *Survey*, 16 May 1914, XXXII, 199.

PSYCHOLOGICAL DOCTRINE AND PHILOSOPHICAL TEACHING. *Journal of Philosophy*, 10 Sept. 1914, XI, 505-511.
Summarized in *Philosophical Review*, Jan. 1915, XXIV, 120-121 (C. C. Church).

NATURE AND REASON IN LAW. *International Journal of Ethics*, Oct. 1914, XXV, 25-32.
Summarized in *Philosophical Review*, Jan. 1915, XXIV, 116 (A. J. Thomas). Reprinted in *Characters and Events* (1929), II, 790-797.

A POLICY OF INDUSTRIAL EDUCATION. *New Republic*, 19 Dec. 1914, I, 11-12; *Manual Training*, Mar. 1915, XVI, 393-397.

1915

GERMAN PHILOSOPHY AND POLITICS. New York: Henry Holt and Company, 1915. 134 pp.

THE SCHOOL AND SOCIETY. Revised edition. Chicago: The University of Chicago Press [1915]. xv, 164 pp.
Published also in England by the Cambridge University Press, 1915.
For translations, see edition of 1900.

SCHOOLS OF TOMORROW, by John Dewey and Evelyn Dewey. New York: E. P. Dutton & Company [ᶜ1915]. 316 pp.
Published in London by J. M. Dent & Sons, Ltd., 1915.
Translations. Spanish by Lorenzo Luzuriaga, 3. ed. (Madrid, 1930); French by R. Duthil (Paris, 1931); Roumanian by G. I. Simeon (Bucharest, 1937?); also Russian and Chinese translations.

INTRODUCTORY ADDRESS. *Science*, 29 Jan. 1915, N. s XLI, 147-151.

INDUSTRIAL EDUCATION—A WRONG KIND. *New Republic*, 20 Feb. 1915, II, 71-73.

STATE OR CITY CONTROL OF SCHOOLS? *New Republic*, 20 Mar. 1915, II, 178-180.

SPLITTING UP THE SCHOOL SYSTEM. *New Republic,* 17 Apr. 1915, II, 283-284.

CONDITIONS AT THE UNIVERSITY OF UTAH. Letter in *Nation,* 6 May 1915, C, 491-492, and in *Science,* 7 May 1915, N. S. XLI, 685.

EDUCATION *vs.* TRADE-TRAINING. Letter in *New Republic,* 15 May 1915, III, 42-43.

DR. DEWEY REPLIES. Letter in *New Republic,* 22 May 1915, III, 72.

THE SUBJECT-MATTER OF METAPHYSICAL INQUIRY. *Journal of Philosophy,* 24 June 1915, XII, 337-345.

THE EXISTENCE OF THE WORLD AS A PROBLEM. *Philosophical Review,* July 1915, XXIV, 357-370.
Reprinted in *Essays in Experimental Logic* (1916), pp. 281-302.

"TRAFFIC IN ABSOLUTES." An Extract from John Dewey, with a Review by F[rancis] H[ackett] and a Footnote by Walter Lippmann. *New Republic,* 17 July 1915, III, 281-285.
The extract is from *German Philosophy and Politics* (1915), pp. 123-132.

THE LOGIC OF JUDGMENTS OF PRACTICE. I. Their Nature; II. Judgments of Value (*Journal of Philosophy,* 16 Sept. 1915, XII, 505-523); III. Sense-Perception as Knowledge (*ib.,* 30 Sept. 1915, pp. 533-543).
Reprinted in *Essays in Experimental Logic* (1916), pp. 335-442.

IN REPLY. Letter in *New Republic,* 2 Oct. 1915, IV, 236.

PROFESSORIAL FREEDOM. Letter in *New York Times,* 22 Oct. 1915.
Reprinted in *School and Society,* 6 Nov. 1915, II, 673, with the title "The Control of Universities."

ANNUAL ADDRESS OF THE PRESIDENT. *Bulletin of the American Association of University Professors,* Dec. 1915, I, 9-13.

1916

DEMOCRACY AND EDUCATION. An Introduction to the Philosophy of Education. New York: The Macmillan Company, 1916. xii, 434 pp. (Text-Book Series in Education, edited by Paul Monroe.)
Reprinted. New York, 1929.
Translations. Japanese; Turkish by B. Avni with introduction by Mehmed Emin (1928); German by E. Hylla (Breslau, 1930); Czech by Dr. J. Hrusa

(Prague, 1932); Servo-Croatian by Dr. D. Ikonic (Belgrad, 1934); Russian; Portuguese by Godofredo Rangel and Anisio Taixeira (São Paulo, 1936); Chinese; Hungarian.

ESSAYS IN EXPERIMENTAL LOGIC. Chicago: The University of Chicago Press [ᶜ1916]. vii, 444 pp.
Published in England by the Cambridge University Press, 1916.
The introductory chapter was written especially for this volume; chapters 2-5 are reprinted (with editorial revisions) from the author's *Studies in Logical Theory* (1903); "the other essays are in part reprinted and in part rewritten, with additions, from various contributions to philosophical periodicals."

NATIONALIZING EDUCATION. *In* National Education Association, *Addresses and Proceedings*, 1916, pp. 183-189.
Reprinted in *Journal of Education*, 2 Nov. 1916, LXXXIV, 425-428.

METHOD IN SCIENCE-TEACHING. *In* National Education Association, *Addresses and Proceedings*, 1916, pp. 729-734.
Reprinted in *General Science Quarterly*, Nov. 1916, I, 3-9; *Journal of the National Education Association*, Mar. 1917, I, 725-730.

FORCE, VIOLENCE, AND LAW. *New Republic*, 22 Jan. 1916, V, 295-297.
Reprinted in *The New Republic Book* (1916), pp. 52-57, and in *Characters and Events* (1929), II, 636-641.

ON UNDERSTANDING THE MIND OF GERMANY. *Atlantic Monthly*, Feb. 1916, CXVII, 251-262.
Reprinted in *Characters and Events* (1929), I, 130-148, with the title "The Mind of Germany."

THE NEED OF AN INDUSTRIAL EDUCATION IN AN INDUSTRIAL DEMOCRACY. *Manual Training*, Feb. 1916, XVII, 409-414.
Reprinted in *Proceedings of the Second Pan-American Scientific Congress* (Washington, 1917), Vol. IV, pp. 222-225.

ORGANIZATION IN AMERICAN EDUCATION. *Teachers College Record*, Mar. 1916, XVII, 127-141.

VOCATIONAL EDUCATION. *New Republic*, 11 Mar. 1916, VI, 159-160.
Review of John Augustus Lapp and Carl Henry Mote, *Learning to Earn*.

AMERICAN ASSOCIATION OF UNIVERSITY PROFESSORS. Letter in *Nation*, 30 Mar. 1916, CII, 357.

PROGRESS. *International Journal of Ethics,* Apr. 1916, XXVI, 311-322.
> Summarized in *Current Opinion,* June 1916, LX, 419-420.
> Reprinted in *Characters and Events* (1929), II, 820-830.

FORCE AND COERCION. *International Journal of Ethics,* Apr. 1916, XXVI, 359-367.
> Reprinted in *Characters and Events* (1929), II, 782-789.

OUR EDUCATIONAL IDEAL IN WARTIME. *New Republic,* 15 Apr. 1916, VI, 283-284.
> Reprinted in *Characters and Events* (1929), II, 493-497, with the title "Our Educational Ideal."

UNIVERSAL SERVICE AS EDUCATION. *New Republic,* 22 and 29 Apr. 1916, VI, 309-310, 334-335.
> Reprinted in *Characters and Events* (1929), II, 465-473.

VOLUNTARISM IN THE ROYCEAN PHILOSOPHY. *Philosophical Review,* May 1916, XXV, 245-254.
> Reprinted in *Papers in Honor of Josiah Royce on His Sixtieth Birthday* [n.p., n.d.], pp. 17-26.

THE SCHOOLS AND SOCIAL PREPAREDNESS. *New Republic,* 6 May 1916, VII, 15-16.
> Reprinted in *Characters and Events* (1929), II, 474-478.

AMERICAN EDUCATION AND CULTURE. *New Republic,* 1 July 1916, VII, 215-216.
> Reprinted in *The New Republic Book* (1916), pp. 232-237; in *Essays Toward Truth: Studies in Orientation,* Selected by Kenneth Allan Robinson, William Benfield Pressey and James Dow McCallum (New York [°1924]), pp. 65-71; and in *Characters and Events* (1929), II, 498-503.

PROFESSIONAL ORGANIZATION OF TEACHERS. *American Teacher,* Sept. 1916, V, 99-101.

THE HUGHES CAMPAIGN. *New Republic,* 28 Oct. 1916, VIII, 319-321.

THE TRAGEDY OF THE GERMAN SOUL. *New Republic,* 9 Dec. 1916, IX, 155-156.
> Review of George Santayana, *Egotism in German Philosophy.*

THE PRAGMATISM OF PEIRCE. *Journal of Philosophy,* 21 Dec. 1916, XIII, 709-715.
> Reprinted in Charles Santiago Sanders Peirce, *Chance, Love and Logic,* edited by Morris Raphael Cohen (New York, 1923), pp. 301-308.

1917

ENLISTMENT FOR THE FARM. New York: Division of Intelligence and Publicity of Columbia University, 1917. 10 pp. (Columbia War Papers, Ser. I, No. 1.)

PROSPECTIVE ELEMENTARY EDUCATION. *In* Louis Win Rapeer, *Teaching Elementary School Subjects* (New York: Charles Scribner's Sons [ᶜ1917]), pp. 552-569.

THE NEED FOR A RECOVERY OF PHILOSOPHY. In *Creative Intelligence, Essays in the Pragmatic Attitude,* by John Dewey, Addison Webster Moore, Harold Chapman Brown, George Herbert Mead, Boyd Henry Bode, Henry Waldgrave Stuart, James Hayden Tufts, Horace Meyer Kallen (New York: Henry Holt and Company [ᶜ1917]), pp. 3-69.

ILL ADVISED. Letter in *American Teacher,* Feb. 1917, VI, 31.

EXPERIMENT IN EDUCATION. *New Republic,* 3 Feb. 1917, X, 15-16.

THE CONCEPT OF THE NEUTRAL IN RECENT EPISTEMOLOGY. *Journal of Philosophy,* 15 Mar. 1917, XIV, 161-163.

LEARNING TO EARN: THE PLACE OF VOCATIONAL EDUCATION IN A COMPREHENSIVE SCHEME OF PUBLIC EDUCATION. *School and Society,* 24 Mar. 1917, V, 331-335.

CURRENT TENDENCIES IN EDUCATION. *Dial,* 5 Apr. 1917, LXII, 287-289.

FEDERAL AID TO ELEMENTARY EDUCATION. *Child Labor Bulletin,* May 1917, VI, 61-66.

IN A TIME OF NATIONAL HESITATION. *Seven Arts Magazine,* May 1917, II, 3-7.
Reprinted in *Characters and Events* (1929), II, 443-446, with the title "The Emergence of a New World."

THE NEED FOR SOCIAL PSYCHOLOGY. *Psychological Review,* July 1917, XXIV, 266-277.
Reprinted in *Characters and Events* (1929), II, 709-720, with the title "Social Psychology and Social Progress."

H. G. WELLS, THEOLOGICAL ASSEMBLER. *Seven Arts Magazine,* July 1917, II, 334-339.
Comments on Herbert George Wells, *God, the Invisible King.* Reprinted in *Characters and Events* (1929), I, 78-82.

CONSCIENCE AND COMPULSION. *New Republic*, 14 July 1917, XI, 297-298.

Reprinted in *Characters and Events* (1929), II, 576-580.

THE FUTURE OF PACIFISM. *New Republic*, 28 July 1917, XI, 358-360.

Reprinted in *Characters and Events* (1929), II, 581-586.

WHAT AMERICA WILL FIGHT FOR. *New Republic*, 18 Aug. 1917, XII, 68-69.

Reprinted in *Characters and Events* (1929), II, 561-565, with the title "America and War."

DUALITY AND DUALISM. *Journal of Philosophy*, 30 Aug. 1917, XIV, 491-493.

CONSCRIPTION OF THOUGHT. *New Republic*, 1 Sept. 1917, XII, 128-130.

Reprinted in *Characters and Events* (1929), II, 566-570.

WAR ACTIVITIES FOR CIVILIANS. *New Republic*, 1 Sept. 1917, XII, 139-140.

Review of *National Service Handbook*.

FIAT JUSTITIA, RUAT COELUM. *New Republic*, 29 Sept. 1917, XII, 237-238.

Reprinted in *Characters and Events* (1929), II, 592-595.

THE PRINCIPLE OF NATIONALITY. *Menorah Journal*, Oct. 1917, III, 203-208.

[STATEMENT.] *New York Times*, 9 Oct. 1917.

On the resignation of Charles Austin Beard as Professor of Politics in Columbia University.

IN EXPLANATION OF OUR LAPSE. *New Republic*, 3 Nov. 1917, XIII, 17-18.

Reprinted in *Characters and Events* (1929), II, 571-575.

THE CASE OF THE PROFESSOR AND THE PUBLIC INTEREST. *Dial*, 8 Nov. 1917, LXIII, 435-437.

DEMOCRACY AND LOYALTY IN THE SCHOOLS. *New York Evening Post*, 19 Dec. 1917; *American Teacher*, Jan. 1918, VII, 8-10.

PUBLIC EDUCATION ON TRIAL. *New Republic,* 29 Dec. 1917, XIII, 245-247.

1918

EDUCATION FOR DEMOCRACY. [n. p., n. d.] 2 pp.

THE MOTIVATION OF HOBBES's POLITICAL PHILOSOPHY. In *Studies in the History of Ideas,* by the Department of Philosophy of Columbia University, Vol. I (New York: Columbia University Press, 1918), pp. 88-115.

VOCATIONAL EDUCATION IN THE LIGHT OF THE WORLD WAR. [Chicago, 1918.] 10 pp. (Vocational Education Association of the Middle West, *Bulletin No. 4,* Jan. 1918.)

INTRODUCTORY WORD. *In* Frederick Matthias Alexander, *Man's Supreme Inheritance* (New York: E. P. Dutton & Co. [ᶜ1918]), pp. xiii-xvii.

CONCERNING ALLEGED IMMEDIATE KKOWLEDGE OF MIND. *Journal of Philosophy,* 17 Jan. 1918, XV, 29-35.

AMERICA IN THE WORLD. *Nation,* 14 Mar. 1918, CVI, 287.
Reprinted in *Characters and Events* (1929), II, 642-644, with the title "America and the World."

MORALS AND THE CONDUCT OF STATESMEN. *New Republic,* 23 Mar. 1918, XIV, 232-234.
Reprinted in *Characters and Events* (1929), II, 645-649.

INTERNAL SOCIAL REORGANIZATION AFTER THE WAR. *Journal of Race Development,* Apr. 1918, VIII, 385-400.
Reprinted in *Characters and Events* (1929), II, 745-759, with the title "Elements of Social Reorganization."

A NEW SOCIAL SCIENCE. *New Republic,* 6 Apr. 1918, XIV, 292-294.
Reprinted in *Characters and Events* (1929), II, 733-738, with the title "The New Social Science."

EDUCATION AND SOCIAL DIRECTION. *Dial,* 11 Apr. 1918, LXIV, 333-335.

POLITICAL SCIENCE AS A RECLUSE. *New Republic,* 27 Apr. 1918, XIV, 383-384.
Reprinted in *Characters and Events* (1929), II, 728-732.

THE OBJECTS OF VALUATION. *Journal of Philosophy,* 9 May 1918, XV, 253-258.

REPLY TO A REVIEWER. Letter in *New Republic,* 11 May 1918, XV, 55.

WHAT ARE WE FIGHTING FOR? *Independent,* 22 June 1918, XCIV, 474, 480-483.

Reprinted in *Characters and Events* (1929), II, 551-560, with the title "The Social Possibilities of War."

AUTOCRACY UNDER COVER. *New Republic,* 24 Aug. 1918, XVI, 103-106.

THE APPROACH TO A LEAGUE OF NATIONS. *Dial,* 2 Nov. 1918, LXV, 341-342.

Reprinted in *Characters and Events* (1929), II, 602-605.

CREATIVE INDUSTRY. *New Republic,* 2 Nov. 1918, XVII, 20-23.

Review of Helen Marot, *Creative Impulse in Industry.*

THE CULT OF IRRATIONALITY. *New Republic,* 9 Nov. 1918, XVII, 34-35.

Reprinted in *Characters and Events* (1929), II, 587-591.

THE LEAGUE OF NATIONS AND THE NEW DIPLOMACY. *Dial,* 16 Nov. 1918, LXV, 401-403.

Reprinted in *Characters and Events* (1929), II, 606-609.

THE FOURTEEN POINTS AND THE LEAGUE OF NATIONS. *Dial,* 30 Nov. 1918, LXV, 463-464.

THE POST-WAR MIND. *New Republic,* 7 Dec. 1918, XVII, 157-159.

Reprinted in *Characters and Events* (1929), II, 596-601.

A LEAGUE OF NATIONS AND ECONOMIC FREEDOM. *Dial,* 14 Dec. 1918, LXV, 537-539.

Reprinted in *Characters and Events* (1929), II, 610-614.

THE NEW PATERNALISM. *New Republic,* 21 Dec. 1918, XVII, 216-217.

Reprinted in *Characters and Events* (1929), II, 517-521, with the title "Propaganda."

1919

THE PSYCHOLOGY OF DRAWING—IMAGINATION AND EXPRESSION— CULTURE AND INDUSTRY IN EDUCATION. New York: Teachers

College, Columbia University, 1919. 18 pp. (*Teachers College Bulletin*, Ser. *10*, No. *10*, 1 Mar. 1919.)

Reprints of three articles, collected by Professor Patty Smith Hill.

PHILOSOPHY AND DEMOCRACY. *University [of California] Chronicle*, Jan. 1919, XXI, 39-54.

Reprinted in *Characters and Events* (1929), II, 841-855.

THEODORE ROOSEVELT. *Dial*, 8 Feb. 1919, LXVI, 115-117.

Reprinted in *Characters and Events* (1929), I, 87-94.

REVIEW of Robert Mark Wenley, *Life and Work of George Sylvester Morris*. *Philosophical Review*, Mar. 1919, XXVIII, 212-213.

JAPAN AND AMERICA. *Dial*, 17 May 1919, LXVI, 501-503.

DEWEY'S LECTURES IN JAPAN. *Journal of Philosophy*, 19 June 1919, XVI, 357-364.

ON TWO SIDES OF THE EASTERN SEA. *New Republic*, 16 July 1919, XIX, 346-348.

Reprinted in *China, Japan and the U. S. A.* (1921), pp. 3-9, and in *Characters and Events* (1929), I, 170-176.

THE STUDENT REVOLT IN CHINA. *New Republic*, 6 Aug. 1919, XX, 16-18.

THE INTERNATIONAL DUEL IN CHINA. *New Republic*, 27 Aug. 1919, XX, 110-112.

MILITARISM IN CHINA. *New Republic*, 10 Sept. 1919, XX, 167-169.

LIBERALISM IN JAPAN. I. The Intellectual Preparation (*Dial*, 4 Oct. 1919, LXVII, 283-285); II. The Economic Factor (*ib.*, 18 Oct. 1919, pp. 333-337); III. The Chief Foe (*ib.*, 1 Nov. 1919, pp. 369-371).

Reprinted in *Characters and Events* (1929), I, 149-169.

THE DISCREDITING OF IDEALISM. *New Republic*, 8 Oct. 1919, XX, 285-287.

Reprinted in *Characters and Events* (1929), II, 629-635, with the title "Force and Ideals."

TRANSFORMING THE MIND OF CHINA. *Asia*, Nov. 1919, XIX, 1103-1108.

Reprinted in *Characters and Events* (1929), I, 285-295.

CHINESE NATIONAL SENTIMENT. *Asia*, Dec. 1919, XIX, 1237-1242.
Reprinted in *Characters and Events* (1929), I, 222-236, with the title "The Growth of Chinese National Sentiment."

THE AMERICAN OPPORTUNITY IN CHINA. *New Republic*, 3 Dec. 1919, XXI, 14-17.
Reprinted in *Characters and Events* (1929), I, 296-303, with the title "America and China."

OUR SHARE IN DRUGGING CHINA. *New Republic*, 24 Dec. 1919, XXI, 114-117.

1920

RECONSTRUCTION IN PHILOSOPHY. New York: Henry Holt and Company, 1920. vii, 224 pp.
Published in London by the University of London Press, 1921.
Translations. Bohemian by Josef Schützner (Prague, 1929); Chinese; Japanese; Spanish (Madrid, 1930); Italian, with an introd., by Guido de Ruggiero (Bari, 1931).

LETTERS FROM CHINA AND JAPAN, by John Dewey and Alice Chipman Dewey. Edited by Evelyn Dewey. New York: E. P. Dutton Company [°1920]. vi, 311 pp.
Published in London by J. M. Dent & Sons, Ltd. [1920].

[DEWEY'S SPEECHES IN FUKIEN. Fukien: Board of Education, 1920.] 126 pp. [In Chinese.]

[FIVE LECTURES OF DEWEY. Peking: *Morning Post*, 1920.] [In Chinese.]

THE SEQUEL OF THE STUDENT REVOLT. *New Republic*, 25 Feb. 1920, XXI, 380-382.

SHANTUNG, AS SEEN FROM WITHIN. *New Republic*, 3 Mar. 1920, XXII, 12-17.
Reprinted in *China, Japan and the U. S. A.* (1921), pp. 9-21.

OUR NATIONAL DILEMMA. *New Republic*, 24 Mar. 1920, XXII, 117-118.
Reprinted in *Characters and Events* (1929), II, 615-619.

THE NEW LEAVEN IN CHINESE POLITICS. *Asia*, Apr. 1920, XX, 267-272.
Reprinted in *Characters and Events* (1929), I, 244-254, with the title "Justice and Law in China."

WHAT HOLDS CHINA BACK. *Asia*, May 1920, XX, 373-377.

Reprinted in *Characters and Events* (1929), I, 211-221, with the title "Chinese
Social Habits."

FREEDOM OF THOUGHT AND WORK. *New Republic*, 5 May 1920,
XXII, 316-317.

Reprinted in *Characters and Events* (1929), II, 522-525.

AMERICANISM AND LOCALISM. *Dial*, June 1920, LXVIII, 684-688.

Reprinted in *Characters and Events* (1929), II, 537-541.

CHINA'S NIGHTMARE. *New Republic*, 30 June 1920, XXIII, 145-
147.

Reprinted in *Characters and Events* (1929), I, 193-198.

HOW REACTION HELPS. *New Republic*, 1 Sept. 1920, XXIV, 21-22.

Reprinted in *Characters and Events* (1929), II, 815-819.

A POLITICAL UPHEAVAL IN CHINA. *New Republic*, 6 Oct. 1920,
XXIV, 142-144.

Reprinted in *Millard's Review of the Far East*, 4 Dec. 1920, XV, 9-10, and
in *China, Japan and the U. S. A.* (1921), pp. 27-32.

INDUSTRIAL CHINA. *New Republic*, 8 Dec. 1920, XXV, 39-41.

Reprinted in *Impressions of Soviet Russia* (1929), pp. 237-251.

1921

AIMS AND IDEALS OF EDUCATION. I. [Nature of Aims and Ideals];
II. The Relation of Aims and Ideals to Existent Facts; III. Growth
as an Aim and Ideal. In *Encyclopedia and Dictionary of Education*,
edited by Foster Watson, Vol. I (London, 1921), pp. 32-34.

Reprinted in *Ideals, Aims and Methods of Education*, by John Dewey [and
others] (London, 1922), pp. 1-9.

CHINA, JAPAN AND THE U. S. A. Present-Day Conditions in the Far
East and Their Bearing on the Washington Conference. New York:
Republic Publishing Co., Inc., 1921, 64 pp. (New Republic
Pamphlet No. 1.)

Reprinted from the *New Republic*.

THE ALEXANDER-DEWEY ARITHMETIC, by Georgia Alexander.
Edited by John Dewey. New York: Longmans, Green and Co.,
1921. 3 vols.

VOL. I, Elementary Book—VOL. II, Intermediate Book—VOL. III, Advanced
Book.

FIRST INTRODUCTION. *In* Scudder Klyce, *Universe;* with three Introductions, by David Starr Jordan, John Dewey and Morris Llewellyn Cooke (Winchester, Mass.: S. Klyce, 1921), pp. iii-v.

RACIAL PREJUDICE AND FRICTION. *Chinese Social and Political Science Review,* VI [1921], 1-17.

IS CHINA A NATION? *New Republic,* 12 Jan. 1921, XXV, 187-190.
Reprinted in *Impressions of Soviet Russia* (1929), pp. 252-270; and in *Characters and Events* (1929), I, 237-243, with the title "Conditions for China's Nationhood."

THE SIBERIAN REPUBLIC. *New Republic,* 19 Jan. 1921, XXV, 220-223.
Reprinted in *Characters and Events* (1929), I, 185-192.

SOCIAL ABSOLUTISM. *New Republic,* 9 Feb. 1921, XXV, 315-318.
Reprinted in *Characters and Events* (1929), II, 721-727.

THE FAR EASTERN DEADLOCK. *New Republic,* 16 Mar. 1921, XXVI, 71-74.

THE CONSORTIUM IN CHINA. *New Republic,* 13 Apr. 1921, XXVI, 178-180.

OLD CHINA AND NEW. *Asia,* May 1921, XXI, 445-450, 454, 456.
Reprinted in *Characters and Events* (1929), I, 255-269, with the title "Young China and Old."

NEW CULTURE IN CHINA. *Asia,* July 1921, XXI, 581-586, 642.
Reprinted in *Characters and Events* (1929), I, 270-284.

HINTERLANDS IN CHINA. *New Republic,* 6 July 1921, XXVII, 162-165.
Reprinted in *China, Japan and the U. S. A.* (1921), pp. 21-27.

DIVIDED CHINA. I. (*New Republic,* 20 July 1921, XXVII, 212-215); II. (*Ib.,* 27 July 1921, pp. 235-237).
Reprinted in *China, Japan and the U. S. A.* (1921), pp. 33-44.

SHANTUNG AGAIN. *New Republic,* 28 Sept. 1921, XXVIII, 123-126.

TENTH ANNIVERSARY OF THE REPUBLIC OF CHINA, A MESSAGE. *China Review,* Oct. 1921, I, 171.

FEDERALISM IN CHINA. *New Republic,* 12 Oct. 1921, XXVIII, 176-178.

Reprinted in *China, Japan and the U. S. A.* (1921), pp. 44-50.

CHINA AND DISARMAMENT. *Chinese Students' Monthly,* Nov. 1921, XVII, 16-17.

THE PARTING OF THE WAYS FOR AMERICA. I. (*New Republic,* 2 Nov. 1921, XXVIII, 283-286); II. (*Ib.,* 9 Nov. 1921, pp. 315-317).

Reprinted in *China, Japan and the U. S. A.* (1921), pp. 51-64.

THE ISSUES AT WASHINGTON. I. Causes of International Friction (*Baltimore Sun,* 14 Nov. 1921); II. The Anglo-Japanese Alliance and the United States (*ib.,* 15 Nov. 1921); III. China's Interest (*ib.,* 16 Nov. 1921); IV. Suggested Measures (*ib.,* 17 Nov. 1921).

PUBLIC OPINION IN JAPAN. *New Republic,* 16 Nov. 1921, XXVIII (Sup. to No. 363, pp. 15-18).

Reprinted in *Characters and Events* (1929), I, 177-184, with the title "Japan Revisited: Two Years Later."

SHREWD TACTICS ARE SHOWN IN CHINESE PLEA. *Baltimore Sun,* 18 Nov. 1921.

FOUR PRINCIPLES FOR CHINA REGARDED AS BUT FRAMEWORK. *Baltimore Sun,* 23 Nov. 1921.

CLASSICISM AS AN EVANGEL. *Journal of Philosophy,* 24 Nov. 1921, XVIII, 664-666.

UNDERGROUND BURROWS MUST BE DUG OPEN. Success or Failure of U. S. Policies Depends on Adequate Demand for Publicity. *Baltimore Sun,* 29 Nov. 1921.

ANGLES OF SHANTUNG QUESTION. *Baltimore Sun,* 5 Dec. 1921.

THE CONFERENCE AND A HAPPY ENDING. *New Republic,* 7 Dec. 1921, XXIX, 37-39.

CHINESE RESIGNATION SEEMS UNSPORTESMANLIKE TO AMERICANS BUT A MATTER OF HABIT WITH THEM. *Baltimore Sun,* 9 Dec. 1921.

THREE RESULTS OF TREATY. *Baltimore Sun,* 11 Dec. 1921.

A FEW SECOND THOUGHTS ON FOUR-POWER PACT. *Baltimore Sun,* 17 Dec. 1921.

EDUCATION BY HENRY ADAMS. *New Republic,* 21 Dec. 1921, XXIX, 102-103.

1922

HUMAN NATURE AND CONDUCT. An Introduction to Social Psychology. New York: Henry Holt and Company, 1922. vii, 336 pp.
Published in London by G. Allen & Unwin, 1922.
Reprinted. With a new introduction (New York, 1930. Modern Library).
Translations. German by Paul Sakmann (Stuttgart, 1931); Swedish by Alf Ahlberg (Stockholm, 1936); Spanish.

IDEALS, AIMS, AND METHODS IN EDUCATION. By John Dewey [and others]. London: Sir Isaac Pitman & Sons, Ltd., 1922. 110 pp. (The New Educator's Library.)
Section I, "Aims and Ideals of Education," pp. 1-9, by Dewey.

SYLLABUS FOR PHILOSOPHY 191-192, Types of Philosophic Thought, Columbia University, 1922-1923. [New York, 1922?] 67 multigraphed leaves.
Copies in the Columbiana collection, Columbia University Library.

AS THE CHINESE THINK. *Asia,* Jan. 1922, XXII, 7-10, 78-79.
Reprinted in *Characters and Events* (1929), I, 199-210, with the title "The Chinese Philosophy of Life."

AN ANALYSIS OF REFLECTIVE THOUGHT. *Journal of Philosophy,* 19 Jan. 1922, XIX, 29-38.

AMERICA AND CHINESE EDUCATION. *New Republic,* 1 Mar. 1922, XXX, 15-17.
Reprinted in *Characters and Events* (1929), I, 303-309, with the title "America and China."

PRAGMATIC AMERICA. *New Republic,* 12 Apr. 1922, XXX, 185-187.
Reprinted in *Characters and Events* (1929), II, 542-547.

REVIEW of Walter Lippmann, *Public Opinion. New Republic,* 3 May 1922, XXX, 286-288.

THE AMERICAN INTELLECTUAL FRONTIER. *New Republic,* 10 May 1922, XXX, 303-305.
Reprinted in *Characters and Events* (1929), II, 447-452.

MIND IN THE MAKING. Letter in *New Republic*, 7 June 1922, XXXI, 48.

REALISM WITHOUT MONISM OR DUALISM. I. Knowledge Involving the Past (*Journal of Philosophy*, 8 June 1922, XIX, 309-317); II. (*Ib.*, 22 June 1922, pp. 351-361).

VALUATION AND EXPERIMENTAL KNOWLEDGE. *Philosophical Review*, July 1922, XXXI, 325-351.

NOTABLES AND COMMON PEOPLE. *New Republic*, 2 Aug. 1922, XXXI, 285-286.
Review of Charles Hitchcock Sherrill, *Prime Ministers and Presidents*, and Frazier Hunt, *The Rising Temper of the East.*

EVENTS AND MEANINGS. *New Republic*, 30 Aug. 1922, XXXII, 9-10.
Reprinted in *Characters and Events* (1929), I, 125-129.

EDUCATION AS A RELIGION. *New Republic*, 13 Sept. 1922, XXXII, 63-65.

EDUCATION AS ENGINEERING. *New Republic*, 20 Sept. 1922, XXXII, 89-91.

LE DÉVELOPPEMENT DU PRAGMATISME AMÉRICAIN. *Revue de Métaphysique et de Morale*, Oct. 1922, XXIX, 411-430.
Re-translated into English and published as "The Development of American Pragmatism" in *Studies in the History of Ideas*, Vol. II (1925), Supplement, pp. 353-377.

EDUCATION AS POLITICS. *New Republic*, 4 Oct. 1922, XXXII, 139-141.
Reprinted in *Characters and Events* (1929), II, 776-781.

KNOWLEDGE AND SPEECH REACTION. *Journal of Philosophy*, 12 Oct. 1922, XIX, 561-570.

INDUSTRY AND MOTIVES. *World Tomorrow*, Dec. 1922, V, 357-358.
Reprinted in *Characters and Events* (1929), II, 739-744.

MEDIOCRITY AND INDIVIDUALITY. *New Republic*, 6 Dec. 1922, XXXIII, 35-37.
Reprinted in *Characters and Events* (1929), II, 479-485.

INDIVIDUALITY, EQUALITY AND SUPERIORITY. *New Republic*, 13 Dec. 1922, XXXIII, 61-63.
Reprinted in *Characters and Events* (1929), II, 486-492.

1923

CULTURE AND PROFESSIONALISM IN EDUCATION. [New York, 1923.] 7 pp.
Published also in *Fortnightly Bulletin of the Institute of Arts and Sciences, Columbia University,* 9 Nov. 1923, Vol. XI, No. 3, pp. [iii-vi]; in *Journal of the National Education Association,* Dec. 1923, XII, 397-398; and in *School and Society,* 13 Oct. 1923, XVIII, 421-424.

SYLLABUS FOR PHILOSOPHY 131-132, Social Institutions and the Study of Morals, Columbia University, 1923-[1924]. [New York, 1923?] 57 multigraphed leaves.
Copies in the Columbiana collection, Columbia University Library.

FUTURE TRENDS IN THE DEVELOPMENT OF SOCIAL PROGRAMS THROUGH THE SCHOOLS. The School as a Means of Developing a Social Consciousness and Social Ideals in Children. In *Proceedings of the National Conference of Social Work, Washington, May 16-23, 1923* (Chicago [1923]), pp. 449-453.
Reprinted in *Journal of Social Forces,* Sept. 1923, I, 513-517.

INTRODUCTION. In Frederick Matthias Alexander, *Constructive Conscious Control of the Individual* (New York: E. P. Dutton & Co. [ᶜ1923]), pp. xxi-xxxiii.

SOCIAL PURPOSES IN EDUCATION. *General Science Quarterly,* Jan. 1923, VII, 79-91.

A SICK WORLD. *New Republic,* 24 Jan. 1923, XXXIII, 217-218.
Reprinted in *Characters and Events* (1929), II, 760-764.

CHINA AND THE WEST. *Dial,* Feb. 1923, LXXIV, 193-196.
Review of Bertrand Russell, *The Problems of China.*

INDIVIDUALITY IN EDUCATION. *General Science Quarterly,* Mar. 1923, VII, 157-166.

SHALL WE JOIN THE LEAGUE? *New Republic,* 7 Mar. 1923, XXXIV, 36-37.
Reprinted in *Characters and Events* (1929), II, 620-624, and Dewey's reply, pp. 625-628.

ETHICS AND INTERNATIONAL RELATIONS. *Foreign Affairs*, 15 Mar. 1923, I, 85-95.

Reprinted in *Characters and Events* (1929), II, 804-814.

"WHAT IS A SCHOOL FOR?" *New York Times*, 18 Mar. 1923.

POLITICAL COMBINATION OR LEGAL COÖPERATION? *New Republic*, 21 Mar. 1923, XXXIV, 89-91.

Reprinted in *Characters and Events* (1929), II, 666-671, with the title "Why Not Outlaw War?"

IF WAR WERE OUTLAWED. *New Republic*, 25 Apr. 1923, XXXIV, 234-235.

Reprinted in *Characters and Events* (1929), II, 672-676.

REVIEW of George Santayana, *Scepticism and Animal Faith*. *New Republic*, 8 Aug. 1923, XXXV, 294-296.

WHAT OUTLAWRY OF WAR IS NOT. *New Republic*, 3 Oct. 1923, XXXVI, 149-152.

This article and "War and a Code of Law" were reprinted in pamphlet form with the title *Outlawry of War: What It Is and Is Not* (Chicago: American Committee for the Outlawry of War [1923]). 16 pp.

Extract in *Congressional Digest*, Mar. 1928, VII, 94.

Reprinted in *Characters and Events* (1929), II, 677-684.

SHALL THE UNITED STATES JOIN THE WORLD COURT? *Christian Century*, 18 Oct. 1923, XL, 1329-1334.

Reprinted in *Characters and Events* (1929), II, 650-655, with the title "Which World Court Shall We Join?"

WAR AND A CODE OF LAW. *New Republic*, 24 Oct. 1923, XXXVI, 224-226.

Reprinted in *Characters and Events* (1929), II, 685-690.

VALUES, LIKING, AND THOUGHT. *Journal of Philosophy*, 8 Nov. 1923, XX, 617-622.

1924

FUNDAMENTALS. *New Republic*, 6 Feb. 1924, XXXVII, 275-276.

Reprinted in *Characters and Events* (1929), II, 453-458.

THE CLASS ROOM TEACHER. *General Science Quarterly*, Mar. 1924, VII, 463-472.

SCIENCE, BELIEF AND THE PUBLIC. *New Republic*, 2 Apr. 1924 XXXVIII, 143-145.

Reprinted in *Characters and Events* (1929), II, 459-464.

SOME COMMENTS ON PHILOSOPHICAL DISCUSSION. *Journal of Philosophy*, 10 Apr. 1924, XXI, 197-209.

KANT AFTER TWO HUNDRED YEARS. *New Republic*, 30 Apr. 1924, XXXVIII, 254-256.

Reprinted in *Characters and Events* (1929), I, 63-68, with the title "Immanuel Kant."

THE LIBERAL COLLEGE AND ITS ENEMIES. *Independent*, 24 May 1924, CXII, 280-282.

REVIEW of Charles Kay Ogden and Ivor Armstrong Richards, *The Meaning of Meaning*. *New Republic*, 11 June 1924, XXXIX, 77-78.

REVIEW of Charles Santiago Sanders Peirce, *Chance, Love, and Logic*. *New Republic*, 25 June 1924, XXXIX, 136-137.

SECULARIZING A THEOCRACY: YOUNG TURKEY AND THE CALIPHATE. *New Republic*, 17 Sept. 1924, XL, 69-71.

Reprinted in *Characters and Events* (1929), I, 324-329, and in *Impressions of Soviet Russia* (1929), pp. 220-234.

ANGORA, THE NEW. *New Republic*, 15 Oct. 1924, XL, 169-170.

Reprinted in *Characters and Events* (1929), I, 330-334, and in *Impressions of Soviet Russia* (1929), pp. 208-219.

DEWEY AIDS LA FOLLETTE. *New York Times*, 23 Oct. 1924.

LOGICAL METHOD AND LAW. *Philosophical Review*, Nov. 1924, XXXIII, 560-572; *Cornell Law Quarterly*, Dec. 1924, X, 17-27.

THE TURKISH TRAGEDY. *New Republic*, 12 Nov. 1924, XL, 268-269.

Reprinted in *Characters and Events* (1929), I, 335-339, and in *Impressions of Soviet Russia* (1929), 197-207.

FOREIGN SCHOOLS IN TURKEY. *New Republic*, 3 Dec. 1924, XLI, 40-42.

Reprinted in *Characters and Events* (1929), I, 346-351, with the title "America and Turkey."

EXPERIENCE AND NATURE. Chicago, London: Open Court Publishing Company, 1925. xi, 443 pp. (Lectures upon the Paul Carus Foundation, First Series.)
See edition of 1929.

THE "SOCRATIC DIALOGUES" OF PLATO. In *Studies in the History of Ideas*, by the Department of Philosophy of Columbia University, Vol. II (New York: Columbia University Press, 1925), pp. 1-23.

THE DEVELOPMENT OF AMERICAN PRAGMATISM. In *Studies in the History of Ideas*, by the Department of Philosophy of Columbia University, Vol. II (New York: Columbia University Press, 1925), Supplement, pp. 353-377.
Retranslated from the French, "Le Développement du pragmatisme américain," in *Revue de Métaphysique et de Morale*, Oct. 1922, XXIX, 411-430 [by Herbert Wallace Schneider].
Reprinted in Daniel Sommer Robinson, *An Anthology of Recent Philosophy* (New York [°1929]), pp. 431-445.

THE PROBLEM OF TURKEY. *New Republic*, 7 Jan. 1925, XLI, 162-163.
Reprinted in *Characters and Events* (1929), I, 340-345.

THE MEANING OF VALUE. *Journal of Philosophy*, 26 Feb. 1925, XXII, 126-133.

HIGHLY-COLORED WHITE LIES. *New Republic*, 22 Apr. 1925, XLII, 229-230.
Reprinted in *Characters and Events* (1929), I, 312-316, with the title "The White Peril."

DEDICATION ADDRESS. *Journal of the Barnes Foundation*, May 1925, Vol. I, No. 2, pp. 3-6.

LITERATURE OR MATHEMATICS? *School and Society*, 27 June 1925, XXI, 786.

VALUE, OBJECTIVE REFERENCE, AND CRITICISM. *Philosophical Review*, July 1925, XXXIV, 313-332.

WHAT IS THE MATTER WITH TEACHING? *Delineator*, Oct. 1925, Vol. CVII, No. 4, pp. 5-6, 78.

EXPERIENCE AND NATURE AND ART. *Journal of the Barnes Foundation*, Oct. 1925, Vol. I, No. 3, pp. 4-10.

"Adapted from *Experience and Nature*."

Reprinted in *Art and Education,* by John Dewey [and others] ([Merion, Pa.] Barnes Foundation Press [°1929]), pp. 3-12.

THE NATURALISTIC THEORY OF PERCEPTION BY THE SENSES. *Journal of Philosophy*, 22 Oct. 1925, XXII, 596-605.

IS CHINA A NATION OR A MARKET? *New Republic*, 11 Nov. 1925, XLIV, 298-299.

Reprinted in *Characters and Events* (1929), I, 316-321, with the title "The White Peril."

PRACTICAL DEMOCRACY. *New Republic*, 2 Dec. 1925, XLV, 52-54.

Review of Walter Lippmann, *The Phantom Public.*

1926

FOREWORD. *In* William James Durant, *The Story of Philosophy* (New York: Simon & Schuster, 1926), p. v.

After the first printing, this was taken out and thereafter printed on the jacket.

INDIVIDUALITY AND EXPERIENCE. *Journal of the Barnes Foundation*, Jan. 1926, Vol. II, No. 1, pp. 1-6.

Reprinted in *Art in Education,* by John Dewey [and others] ([Merion, Pa.] Barnes Foundation Press [°1929]), pp. 175-183.

SUBSTANCE, POWER, AND QUALITY IN LOCKE. *Philosophical Review*, Jan. 1926, XXXV, 22-38.

Summarized in *Revue d'Histoire de la Philosophie*, Jan.-Mar. 1927, I, 122-123.

THE CHANGING INTELLECTUAL CLIMATE. *New Republic*, 17 Feb. 1926, XLV, 360-361.

Review of Alfred North Whitehead, *Science and the Modern World.*

ART IN EDUCATION—AND EDUCATION IN ART. *New Republic*, 24 Feb. 1926, XLVI, 11-13.

Further considerations of Whitehead's *Science and the Modern World.*

AFFECTIVE THOUGHT IN LOGIC AND PAINTING. *Journal of the Barnes Foundation*, Apr. 1926, Vol. II, No. 2, pp. 3-9.

THE HISTORIC BACKGROUND OF CORPORATE LEGAL PERSONALITY. *Yale Law Journal*, Apr. 1926, XXXV, 655-673.

WE SHOULD DEAL WITH CHINA AS NATION TO NATION. *Chinese Students' Monthly*, May 1926, XXI, 52-54.

AMERICA AND THE FAR EAST. *Survey*, 1 May 1926, LVI, 188.

Reprinted in *Characters and Events* (1929), I, 309-311, with the title "America and China."

EVENTS AND THE FUTURE. *Journal of Philosophy*, 13 May 1926, XXIII, 253-258.

A KEY TO THE NEW WORLD. *New Republic*, 19 May 1926, XLVI, 410-411.

Review of Bertrand Russell, *Education and the Good Life*.

WILLIAM JAMES IN 1926. *New Republic*, 30 June 1926, XLVII, 163-165.

Review of *The Philosophy of William James*, edited by Horace Meyer Kallen. Reprinted in *Characters and Events* (1929), I, 117-122.

REVIEW of Graham Wallas, *The Art of Thought*. *New Republic*, 16 June 1926, XLVII, 118-119.

CHURCH AND STATE IN MEXICO. *New Republic*, 25 Aug. 1926, XLVIII, 9-10.

Reprinted in *Characters and Events* (1929), I, 352-357, and in *Impressions of Soviet Russia* (1929), pp. 137-149.

ETHICS OF ANIMAL EXPERIMENTATION. *Atlantic Monthly*, Sept. 1926, CXXXVIII, 343-346.

MEXICO'S EDUCATIONAL RENAISSANCE. *New Republic*, 22 Sept. 1926, XLVIII, 116-118.

Reprinted in *Characters and Events* (1929), I, 364-371, and in *Impressions of Soviet Russia* (1929), pp. 150-167.

FROM A MEXICAN NOTE-BOOK. *New Republic*, 20 Oct. 1926, XLVIII, 239-241.

Reprinted in *Characters and Events* (1929), I, 358-363, with the title "The New and Old in Mexico," and in *Impressions of Soviet Russia* (1929), pp. 168-180.

BISHOP BROWN: A FUNDAMENTAL MODERNIST. *New Republic*, 17 Nov. 1926, XLVIII, 371-372.

Reprinted in *Characters and Events* (1929), I, 83-86.

AMERICA'S RESPONSIBILITY. *Christian Century*, 23 Dec. 1926, XLIII, 1583-1584.

Reprinted in *Characters and Events* (1929), II, 691-696.

1927

THE PUBLIC AND ITS PROBLEMS.   New York: Henry Holt and Company [ᶜ1927].   vi, 224 pp.
Published also in London by G. Allen & Unwin, Ltd.

THE RÔLE OF PHILOSOPHY IN THE HISTORY OF CIVILIZATION.   In *Proceedings of the Sixth International Congress of Philosophy*, edited by Edgar Sheffield Brightman (New York: Longmans, Green & Co., 1927), pp. 536-542.
Reprinted in *Philosophical Review*, Jan. 1927, XXXVI, 1-9; also published in Daniel Sommer Robinson, *An Anthology of Recent Philosophy* (New York [ᶜ1929]), pp. 47-54. Summarized in *Journal of Philosophical Studies*, Apr. 1927, II, 270-271.

ANTHROPOLOGY AND ETHICS.   In *The Social Sciences and Their Interrelations*, edited by William Fielding Ogburn and Alexander Goldenweiser (Boston: Houghton Mifflin Company [ᶜ1927]), pp. 24-36.

INTRODUCTION.   *In* Roswell P. Barnes, *Militarizing Our Youth: the Significance of the Reserve Officers' Training Corps in Our Schools and Colleges* (New York: Committee on Militarism in Education, 1927), pp. 3-4.

INTRODUCTORY NOTE.   *In* Joseph Kinmont Hart, *Inside Experience: a Naturalistic Philosophy of Life and the Modern World* (New York: Longmans, Green and Co., 1927), pp. xxi-xxvi.

INTRODUCTORY WORD.   *In* Sidney Hook, *The Metaphysics of Pragmatism* (Chicago: Open Court Publishing Co., 1927), pp. 1-5.

FOREWORD.   *In* Charles Clayton Morrison, *The Outlawry of War: a Constructive Policy for World Peace* (Chicago: Willett, Clark & Colby, 1927), pp. vii-xxv.

FOREWORD.   *In* Paul Radin, *Primitive Man as Philosopher* (New York: D. Appleton and Company, 1927), pp. xv-xviii.

THE PRAGMATIC ACQUIESCENCE.   *New Republic*, 5 Jan. 1927, XLIX, 186-189.
Reprinted in *Characters and Events* (1929), II, 435-442, with the title "Philosophy and the Social Order."

"HALF-HEARTED NATURALISM."   *Journal of Philosophy*, 3 Feb. 1927, XXIV, 57-64.

POLITICS AND HUMAN BEINGS. *New Republic,* 16 Mar. 1927, L, 114-115.

Review of William Ernest Hocking, *Man and the State;* and George Edward Gordon Catlin, *The Science and Method of Politics.*

IMPERIALISM IS EASY. *New Republic,* 23 Mar. 1927, L, 133-134.

Reprinted in *Characters and Events* (1929), I, 372-377, with the title "Mexico and the Monroe Doctrine," and in *Impressions of Soviet Russia* (1929), pp. 181-194.

THE REAL CHINESE CRISIS. *New Republic,* 27 Apr. 1927, L, 269-270.

THE INTEGRATION OF A MOVING WORLD. *New Republic,* 25 May 1927, LI, 22-24.

Review of Edmund Noble, *Purposive Evolution: the Link between Science and Religion.*

BANKRUPTCY OF MODERN EDUCATION. *Modern Quarterly,* June-Sept. 1927, IV, 102-104.

Review of John Ervin Kirkpatrick, *The American College and Its Rulers.*

Reprinted in part in *School and Society,* 7 Jan. 1928, XXVII, 21-23.

AN EMPIRICAL ACCOUNT OF APPEARANCE. *Journal of Philosophy,* 18 Aug. 1927, XXIV, 449-463.

Summarized in *Journal of Philosophical Studies,* Oct. 1927, II, 592-593.

THE FRUITS OF NATIONALISM. *World Tomorrow,* Nov. 1927, X, 454-456.

Reprinted in *Characters and Events* (1929), II, 798-803, with the title "Nationalism and Its Fruits."

SCIENCE, FOLK-LORE, AND THE CONTROL OF FOLKWAYS. *New Republic,* 9 Nov. 1927, LII, 316-317.

Review of Clarence Edwin Ayres, *Science, the False Messiah.*

PSYCHOLOGY AND JUSTICE. *New Republic,* 23 Nov. 1927, LIII, 9-12.

Reprinted in *Characters and Events* (1929), II, 526-536.

1928

THE PHILOSOPHY OF JOHN DEWEY. Selected and edited by Joseph Ratner. New York: Henry Holt and Company [°1928]. xii, 560 pp.

Published in London by Allen and Unwin, 1929. 230 pp.

Translation. Spanish by J. Mendez Herrera. (Madrid, 1930).

PROGRESSIVE EDUCATION AND THE SCIENCE OF EDUCATION. [Washington, D.C.: Progressive Education Association, °1928.] 14 pp.
Reprinted from *Progressive Education*, July-Aug.-Sept. 1928, V, 197-204.

A CRITIQUE OF AMERICAN CIVILIZATION. In *Recent Gains in American Civilization*, edited by Kirby Page (New York: Harcourt, Brace and Co. [°1928]), pp. 253-276.
Reprinted, with additions, from *World Tomorrow*, Oct. 1928, XI, 391-395.

PHILOSOPHY. In *Whither Mankind: a Panorama of Modern Civilization*, edited by Charles Austin Beard (New York: Longmans, Green and Co., 1928), pp. 313-331.

PHILOSOPHIES OF FREEDOM. In *Freedom in the Modern World*, edited by Horace Meyer Kallen (New York: Coward-McCann, 1928), pp. 236-271.

AN EMPIRICAL ACCOUNT OF APPEARANCE. *Journal of Philosophy*, *from Henry George's* Progress and Poverty, edited by Harry Gunnison Brown (Garden City, N.Y.: Published for the Robert Schalkenbach Foundation by Doubleday, Doran & Co., Inc., 1928), pp. v, 1-3.

[ADDRESS.] In *A Tribute to Professor Morris Raphael Cohen, Teacher and Philosopher* (New York, 1928), pp. 17-20.

WHY I AM A MEMBER OF THE TEACHERS' UNION. *American Teacher*, Jan. 1928, Vol. XII, No. 5, pp. 3-6.

BODY AND MIND. *Bulletin of the New York Academy of Medicine*, Jan. 1928, IV, 3-19; *Mental Hygiene*, Jan. 1928, XII, 1-17.
Reprinted in Dewey, *Philosophy and Civilization*, 1931.

JUSTICE HOLMES AND THE LIBERAL MIND. *New Republic*, 11 Jan. 1928, LIII, 210-212.
Reprinted in *Characters and Events* (1929), I, 100-106, with the title "Oliver Wendell Holmes."

REVIEW of Robert Harry Lowie, *The Origin of the State*. *Columbia Law Review*, Feb. 1928, XXVIII, 255.

THE MANUFACTURERS' ASSOCIATION AND THE PUBLIC SCHOOLS. *Journal of the National Education Association*, Feb. 1928, XVII, 61-62.

PHILOSOPHY AS A FINE ART. *New Republic*, 15 Feb. 1928, LIII, 352-354.
Review of George Santayana, *The Realm of Essence*.

TO THE CHINESE FRIENDS IN THE UNITED STATES. *Chinese Student Bulletin,* Mar. 1928, I, 4.

"AS AN EXAMPLE TO OTHER NATIONS." *New Republic,* 7 Mar. 1928, LIV, 88-89; 194-196.
Reprinted in *Characters and Events* (1929), II, 697-702.

SOCIAL AS A CATEGORY. *Monist,* Apr. 1928, XXXVIII, 161-177.

PERSONAL IMMORTALITY: WHAT I BELIEVE. *New York Times,* 8 Apr. 1928.

THINGS, THOUGHT, CONVERSATION. *Nation,* 18 Apr. 1928, CXXVI, 449-450.
Review of Scott Buchanan, *Possibility;* and Mortimer Adler, *Dialectic.*

THE DIRECTION OF EDUCATION. *School and Society,* 28 Apr. 1928, XXVII, 493-497; *Teachers College Record,* Oct. 1928, XXX, 7-12.

CHINA AND THE POWERS: II. Intervention a Challenge to Nationalism. *Current History,* May 1928, XXVIII, 212-213.
Reprinted in *Characters and Events* (1929), I, 321-323, with the title "The White Peril."

OUTLAWING PEACE BY DISCUSSING WAR. *New Republic,* 16 May 1928, LIV, 370-371.
Reprinted in *Characters and Events* (1929), II, 703-706.

MEANING AND EXISTENCE. *Journal of Philosophy,* 21 June 1928, XXV, 345-353.

BRAVE GOSPEL. *Saturday Review of Literature,* 7 July 1928, IV, 1016.
Review of Mary Hammett Lewis, *An Adventure with Children.*

WHY I AM FOR SMITH. *New Republic,* 7 Nov. 1928 [published 1 Nov.], LVI, 320-321.

IMPRESSIONS OF SOVIET RUSSIA. I. Leningrad Gives the Clue (*New Republic,* 14 Nov. 1928, LVI, 343-344); II. A Country in a State of Flux (*ib.,* 21 Nov. 1928, LVII, 11-14); III. A New World in the Making (*ib.,* 28 Nov. 1928, pp. 38-42); IV. What Are the Russian Schools Doing? (*ib.,* 5 Dec. 1928, pp. 64-67); V. New Schools for a New Era (*ib.,* 12 Dec. 1928, pp. 91-94); VI. The Great Experiment and the Future (*ib.,* 19 Dec. 1928, pp. 134-137).

Reprinted in *Impressions of Soviet Russia* (1929), pp. 3-133; and in *Characters and Events* (1929), I, 378-431.

THE WAY TO THINK. *Saturday Review of Literature*, 1 Dec. 1928, V, 423.
Review of Ernest Dimnet, *The Art of Thinking*.

1929

CHARACTERS AND EVENTS. Popular Essays in Social and Political Philosophy. Edited by Joseph Ratner. New York: Henry Holt and Company [ᶜ1929]. 2 vols.

EXPERIENCE AND NATURE. New York: W. W. Norton & Co., Inc. [ᶜ1929]. ix, 1a-4a, 1-443 pp.
Published also in London by G. Allen & Unwin, 1929.
Another issue of this edition has the imprint: Chicago, Open Court Publishing Co., 1926 [ᶜ1929].
This edition contains a new preface; the first chapter has been completely re-written, and a few minor corrections have been made throughout the volume.

IMPRESSIONS OF SOVIET RUSSIA AND THE REVOLUTIONARY WORLD, MEXICO—CHINA—TURKEY. New York: New Republic, Inc., 1929. 270 pp. (The New Republic's Dollar Books.)
Reprinted from the *New Republic*.
Translation. Japanese by Tokuji Yashamita (1935).

ART AND EDUCATION. By John Dewey, Albert C. Barnes, Laurence Buermeyer, Thomas Munro, Paul Guillaume, Mary Mullen, Violette de Mazia. [Merion, Pa.], Barnes Foundation Press [ᶜ1929]. x, 349 pp.
The following articles in this volume are by Dewey: Experience and Nature and Art, pp. 3-12; and Individuality and Experience, pp. 175-183.

THE QUEST FOR CERTAINTY. New York: Minton, Balch & Co. [1929]. 318 pp.
Published in London by Kegan Paul, 1930. 302 pp.
Translation. Japanese by Seizi Uyeada (Tokyo).

PHILOSOPHY. In *Research in the Social Sciences*, edited by Wilson Gee (New York: The Macmillan Company, 1929), pp. 241-265.

FOREWORD. *In* Helen Edna Davis, *Tolstoi and Nietzsche, a Problem in Biographical Ethics* (New York: New Republic, Inc., 1929), pp. ix-xiv.

SOVIET EDUCATION. In *Am I Getting an Education?* edited by Sherwood Eddy (Garden City, N.Y.: Doubleday, Doran & Co. [ᶜ1929]), pp. 39-46.

FOREWORD. *In* Eastern Commercial Teachers Association, *First Yearbook,* 1929, pp. xiii-xiv.

FOREWORD. In Feiwel Schneersohn, *Studies in Psycho-Expedition* (New York: The Science of Man Press, 1929), pp. vii-viii.

LABOR POLITICS AND EDUCATION. *New Republic,* 9 Jan. 1929, LVII, 211-214; LVIII, 20.
Excerpts in *School and Society,* 19 Jan. 1929, XXIX, 92-93.

GENERAL PRINCIPLES OF EDUCATIONAL ARTICULATION. *School and Society,* 30 Mar. 1929, XXIX, 399-406.

REVIEW of George Sylvester Counts, *School and Society in Chicago. New Republic,* 10 Apr. 1929, LVIII, 231-232.

THE HOUSE DIVIDED AGAINST ITSELF. *New Republic,* 24 Apr. 1929, LVIII, 270-271.
Comments on Robert Staughton Lynd and Helen Merrell Lynd, *Middletown.*

ETHICS. *Encyclopedia Americana.* New York: Americana Corporation. Vol. X, 540-546.

SOURCES OF A SCIENCE OF EDUCATION. New York: Liveright. 77 pp. *Translation.* Chinese.

CONTRASTS IN EDUCATION. New York: Teachers College, Columbia University. 50 pp.

AMERICA, BY FORMULA. *New Republic,* 18 Sept. 1929, LX, 117-119.

WHAT DO LIBERALS WANT? *Outlook,* 16 Oct. 1929, CLIII, 261.

THE MARSH LECTURE. A lecture delivered at the University of Vermont in Commemoration of the Centenary of the Publication of James Marsh's *Introduction* to Samuel Taylor Coleridge's *Aids to Reflection.* Burlington, Vermont, November 26, 1929. (Bound in typewritten form at the University of Vermont Library.) 32 pp.

DEMOCRACY IN EDUCATION. *National Education Association Journal,* Dec. 1929, XVIII, 287-290.

THE SPHERE OF APPLICATION OF THE EXCLUDED MIDDLE. *Journal of Philosophy*, 19 Dec. 1929, XXVI, 701-705.

SPEECH AT THE SEMI-CENTENNIAL BANQUET OF "THE AMERICAN HEBREW." *American Hebrew*, 29 Nov. 1929.

1930

INDIVIDUALISM, OLD AND NEW. A series of 6 articles first printed in *New Republic*, LXI (1930), 239-241, 294-296 and LXII (1930), 13-16, 64-67, 123-126, 184-188.
Published in New York by Minton, Balch & Co., 1930. 171 pp.
Published in London by Allen and Unwin, 1931. 160 pp.

THE UNITED STATES, INCORPORATED. (*Individualism, Old and New I.*) *New Republic*, 22 Jan. 1930, LXI, 239-241.
Reprinted in *Essays in Contemporary Civilization*. Ed. by C. W. Thomas. New York: Macmillan. 1931. Pp. 5-13.

THE LOST INDIVIDUAL. (*Individualism, Old and New II.*) *New Republic*, 5 Feb. 1930, LXI, 294-296.

TOWARD A NEW INDIVIDUALISM. (*Individualism, Old and New III.*) *New Republic*, 19 Feb. 1930, LXII, 13-16.
Reprinted in *Essays in Contemporary Civilization*. Ed. by C. W. Thomas. New York: Macmillan. 1931. Pp. 598-612.

CAPITALISTIC OR PUBLIC SOCIALISM? (*Individualism, Old and New IV.*) *New Republic*, 5 March 1930, LXII, 64-67.

THE CRISIS IN CULTURE. (*Individualism, Old and New V.*) *New Republic*, 19 March 1930, LXII, 123-126.

INDIVIDUALITY IN OUR DAY. (*Individualism, Old and New VI.*) *New Republic*, 8 April 1930, LXII, 184-188.
Translation. German by O. Knopf. *Internationale Zeitschrift für Individualpsychologie*, 1930, VIII, 567-576.

PSYCHOLOGY AND WORK. *Personnel Journal*, Feb. 1930, VIII, 337-341.

CREDO. *Forum*, March 1930, LXXXIII, 176-182.
Reprinted in *Living Philosophies*, by A. Einstein and others. New York: Simon and Schuster, 1931, pp. 21-35.

PHILOSOPHY AND EDUCATION. In *Addresses delivered at the Dedication of the New Campus of the University of California at Los An-*

geles, March 27th and 28th, 1930. The University of California Press, Berkeley, Calif., 1930, pp. 46-56.

Reprinted in *Higher Education Faces the Future.* Ed. by Paul A. Schilpp. New York: Liveright, 1930. Pp. 273-283.

OUR ILLITERACY PROBLEM. *Pictorial Review,* March 1930, XXXI, 28.

RELIGION IN THE SOVIET UNION. *Current History,* April 1930, XXXII, 31-36.

THE APPLICABILITY OF LOGIC TO EXISTENCE. *Journal of Philosophy,* 27 March 1930, XXVII, 174-179.

HOW MUCH FREEDOM IN NEW SCHOOLS? *New Republic,* 9 July 1930, LXIII, 204-206.

DUTIES AND RESPONSIBILITIES OF THE TEACHING PROFESSION. *School and Society,* 9 Aug. 1930, XXXII, 188-191.

LETTER TO HOOVER ON CUBAN SUGAR LOAN. *New York Times,* 24 Nov. 1930, 10:2.

CONDUCT AND EXPERIENCE. In *Psychologies of 1930.* Worcester, Mass.: Clark University Press. Pp. 409-422.

CONSTRUCTION AND CRITICISM. New York: Columbia University Press. 25 pp.

Published in London by Oxford University Press, 1930.

FROM ABSOLUTISM TO EXPERIMENTALISM. In *Contemporary American Philosophy.* Edited by G. P. Adams and W. P. Montague. New York: Macmillan. Vol. II, 13-27.

Translation. Italian by Carlo Coardi. (Milan, 1939.)

1931

AMERICAN EDUCATION PAST AND FUTURE. Chicago: University of Chicago Press. 14 pp. Excerpts in *Ohio Schools,* Jan. 1932, X, 15.

JUSTICE HOLMES AND THE LIBERAL MIND. In *Mr. Justice Holmes.* Edited by Felix Frankfurter. New York: Coward McCann. 241 pp.

PHILOSOPHY AND CIVILIZATION. New York: Minton, Balch & Co. 341 pp.

Published in London by Putnam, 1933.

THE WAY OUT OF EDUCATIONAL CONFUSION. Cambridge, Mass.: Harvard University Press. 41 pp.
Published in London by Oxford University Press.

SPEECH AT THE CURRICULUM CONFERENCE, WINTER PARK, FLORIDA, JAN. 19-24, 1931. *Proceedings,* pp. 49-54. (Typewritten.) John Dewey, Chairman.

COLLEGE SONS—AND PARENTS. Review of Christian Gauss, *Life in College. New Republic,* 4 Feb. 1931, LXV, 332-333.

ETHICS OF ANIMAL EXPERIMENTATION. *Hygeia,* Feb. 1931, IX, 118-120.

LETTER ON SUGGESTION THAT PEOPLE SHOULD VOTE FOR MAN RATHER THAN PARTY. *New York Times,* 15 Feb. 1931, III, 2:8.

DEMOCRACY FOR THE TEACHER. *Progressive Education,* March 1931, VIII, 216-218.

THE NEED FOR A NEW PARTY. A series of 4 articles. *New Republic,* LXVI, 115-117, 150-152, 177-179, 202-205.

THE PRESENT CRISIS. (*Need for a New Party I.*) *New Republic,* 18 March 1931, LXVI, 115-117.

THE BREAKDOWN OF THE OLD ORDER. (*Need for a New Party II.*) *New Republic,* 25 March 1931, LXVI, 150-152.

WHO MIGHT MAKE A NEW PARTY? (*Need for a New Party III.*) *New Republic,* 1 April 1931, LXVI, 177-179.

POLICIES FOR A NEW PARTY. (*Need for a New Party IV.*) *New Republic,* 8 April 1931, LXVI, 202-205.

"SURPASSING AMERICA." Reviews of Sherwood Eddy, *The Challenge of Russia,* George S. Counts, *The Soviet Challenge to America,* and William C. White, *These Russians. New Republic,* 15 April 1931, LXVI, 241-243.

A PHILOSOPHY OF SCIENTIFIC METHOD. Review of M. R. Cohen, *Reason and Nature. New Republic,* 29 April 1931, LXVI, 306-307. (s. also letter by Dewey in *New Republic,* 17 June 1931, LXVII, 127.)

SCIENCE AND SOCIETY. *Lehigh Alumni Bulletin,* July 1931, XVIII, 10, 6-7.

Is There Hope for Politics? *Scribner's Magazine*, May 1931, LXXXIX, 483-487.

George Herbert Mead. *Journal of Philosophy*, 4 June 1931, XXVIII, 309-314.

On War Debts; Letter to Senator Borah. *New York Times*, 15 July 1931, 17:3.

Social Science and Social Control. *New Republic*, 29 July 1931, LXVII, 276-277.

The People's Lobby. (Letter.) *New Republic*, 26 Aug. 1931, LXVIII, 48.

Should America Adopt a System of Compulsory Unemployment Insurance? *Congressional Digest*, August 1931, X, 212.

Teachers as Citizens. *American Teacher*, Oct. 1931, XVI, 7.

Some Aspects of Modern Education. *School and Society*, 31 Oct. 1931, XXXIV, 579-584.
Condensed in *School Management*, March 1932, I, 12-15.
Excerpts in *Educational Review* (China), Jan. 1932, XXIV, 6-8.
Translation. Spanish in *Revista de Pedagogia*, 1931, X, 554-560.

Context and Thought. *University of California Publications in Philosophy*, 1931, XII, 203-224.
Published in London by Cambridge University Press, 1932.

1932

Encyclopedia of the Social Sciences. New York: Macmillan, 1932-35. 15 vols. *The following articles are by John Dewey:* Human Nature, vol. 7, 531-537;—Logic, vol. 9, 598-603;—Outlawry of War, vol. 11, 508-510;—Philosophy, vol. 12, 118-129.

Introduction. To *The Use of the Self: Its Conscious Direction in Relation to Diagnosis, Functioning and the Control of Reaction*, by F. M. Alexander. New York: Dutton.

Are Sanctions Necessary to International Organizations? Yes, Raymond Leslie Buell; No, John Dewey. New York: Foreign Policy Association. (*Foreign Policy Association Pamphlet No. 82-83.*) 39 pp.

A Résumé of Four Lectures on Common Sense, Science and Philosophy. In *Bulletin of the Wagner Free Institute of Science of Philadelphia*, May 1932, VII, no. 2, 12-16.

Charles Sanders Peirce. Review of Charles Sanders Peirce, *Collected Papers, Vol. I*, ed. by Charles Hartshorne and Paul Weiss. *New Republic*, 6 Jan. 1932, LXIX, 220-221.

Education and Birth Control. *The Nation*, 27 Jan. 1932, CXXXIV, 112.

Place of Minor Parties in the American Scene. Chicago: The University of Chicago Press.

Monastery, Bargain Counter, or Laboratory? In *The Barnwell Bulletin*. Philadelphia, Feb. 1932, IX, no. 40, 51-62.

Political Interference in Higher Education and Research. *School and Society*, 20 Feb. 1932, XXXV, 243-246.

A Third Party Program. (Letter.) *New Republic*, 24 Feb. 1932, LXX, 48-49.

Marx Inverted. Review of Gerald Heard, *The Emergence of Man*. *New Republic*, 24 Feb. 1932, LXX, 52.

Schools and the White House Conference. *American Teacher*, Feb., March 1932, XVI, 3-4, 15.

To Replace Judge Cardozo. (Letter.) *New Republic*, 9 March 1932, LXX, 102.

Self-Saver or Frankenstein? *Saturday Review of Literature*, 12 March 1932, VIII, 581-582.

Peace, By Pact or Covenant? *New Republic*, 23 March 1932, LXX, 145-147.

Bending the Twig. Review of Albert Jay Nock, *The Theory of Education in the United States*. *New Republic*, 13 April 1932, LXX, 242-244.

The Collapse of a Romance. *New Republic*, 27 April 1932, LXX, 292-294.
Reprinted in *New Republic Anthology 1915-1935*. Ed. by G. Conklin. New York: Dodge, 1936. Pp. 418-423.

ADDRESS. Delivered before the Twenty-third Annual Conference of the National Association for the Advancement of Colored People, Washington, D.C., May 19, 1932. (Typewritten, from stenographic notes. Never published.)

THE ECONOMIC SITUATION: A CHALLENGE TO EDUCATION. *Journal of Home Economics*, June 1932, XXIV, 495-501.

MAKING SOVIET CITIZENS. Review of Thomas Woody, *New Minds: New Men*, and Nicholas Hans, *History of Russian Educational Policy*. *New Republic*, 8 June 1932, LXXI, 104.

INTERVIEW ON NATIONAL PROBLEMS. *New York Times*, 10 July 1932, VI, 9.

PROSPECTS FOR A THIRD PARTY. *New Republic*, 27 July 1932, LXXI, 278-280.

THE MEIKLEJOHN EXPERIMENT. Review of Alexander Meiklejohn, *The Experimental College*. *New Republic*, 17 August 1932, LXXII, 23.

FUNDS FOR BROOKWOOD LABOR COLLEGE. (A Letter.) *New Republic*, 7 Dec. 1932, LXXIII, 701.

1933

NEW YORK AND THE SEABURY INVESTIGATION; A DIGEST AND INTERPRETATION OF THE REPORTS BY SAMUEL SEABURY. Edited by John Dewey. New York: City Affairs Commission of New York. 48. pp.

PROGRESS. In *Types of Writing*. Ed. by C. H. Slover and D. W. T. Starnes. Boston: Houghton Mifflin. Pp. 357-366.

THE FUTURE OF RADICAL POLITICAL ACTION. *Nation*, 4 Jan. 1933, CXXXVI, 8-9.

A GOD OR THE GOD? *Christian Century*, 8 Feb. 1933, L, 193-196; and 22 March 1933, L, 394-395.

UNITY AND PROGRESS. *World Tomorrow*, 8 March 1933, XVI, 232-233.

OPINIONS REGARDING THE SIX-YEAR HIGH SCHOOL. *Junior College Journal*, March 1933, VIII, 320.

EDUCATION AND OUR PRESENT SOCIAL PROBLEMS. *School and Society*, 15 April 1933, XXXVII, 473-478.
Also in *Educational Methods*, April 1933, XII, 385-390.
Excerpts in *National Education Association Proceedings*, 1933, pp. 687-689.
Translation. Spanish in *Revista de Pedagogia*, 1933, XII, 337-344.

THE ADVENTURE OF PERSUASION. Review of Alfred North Whitehead, *Adventures of Ideas*. *New Republic*, 19 April 1933, LXXIV, 285-286.

ON SCHOOLS OF UTOPIA. *New York Times*, 23 April 1933, IV, 7:3.

CRISIS IN EDUCATION. *American Teacher*, April 1933, XVII, 5-9.
Excerpts in *Bulletin of the American Association of University Professors*, May 1938, XIX, 318-319.

SHALL WE ABOLISH SCHOOL FRILLS? No. *School Management*, June 1933, II, 5.

WHY HAVE PROGRESSIVE SCHOOLS? *Current History*, July 1933, XXXVIII, 441-448.

A CHALLENGE TO CRITICISM. Review of Martin Schuetze, *Academic Illusions in the Field of Letters and the Arts*. *New Republic*, 16 Aug. 1933, LXXVI, 24-25.

PLENTY VS. SCARCITY. *Commerce and Finance*, 30 Aug. 1933, XXII, 751-752.

IMPERATIVE NEED FOR A NEW RADICAL PARTY. *Common Sense*, Sept. 1933, II, 6-7.

1934

ART AS EXPERIENCE. New York: Minton, Balch & Co. 353 pp.
Published in London by Allen and Unwin, 1934.
Excerpts in *Progressive Education*, May 1938, XV, 375, 379.

A COMMON FAITH. New Haven: Yale University Press. 87 pp.
Published in London by Oxford University Press, 1934.
Published in Toronto by Ryerson Press, 1934.
(Cf. RELIGIONS AND THE 'RELIGIOUS.'—(Letter.) *New Republic*, 13 March 1935, LXXXII, 132.)

EDUCATION AND THE SOCIAL ORDER. New York: League for Industrial Democracy. 14 pp.

IMPERATIVE NEED: A NEW RADICAL PARTY. In *Challenge to the New Deal*. Ed. by Alfred M. Bingham and Seldom Rodman. New York: Falcon Press. Pp. 269-273.

INTRODUCTION. To *Challenge to the New Deal*. Ed. by Alfred M. Bingham and Selden Rodman. New York: Falcon Press.

WHY I AM NOT A COMMUNIST: (A.) Bertrand Russell. (B.) John Dewey. In *The Meaning of Marx, a Symposium*, by Bertrand Russell, John Dewey (and others). New York: Farrar & Rinehart. 144 pp.

SUPREME INTELLECTUAL OBLIGATION; ADDRESS AT DINNER IN HONOR OF DR. CATTELL. *Science Education*, Feb. 1934, XVIII, 1-4.
Also in *Science*, 16 March 1934, n. s. LXXIX, 240-243.
Condensed in *Bulletin of the American Association of University Professors*, May 1934, XX, 306-309.

ART IN A VACUUM. *Saturday Review of Literature*, 24 Feb. 1934, X, 501-503.

SANTAYANA'S ORTHODOXY. Review of George Santayana, *Some Turns of Thought in Modern Philosophy*. *New Republic*, 28 Feb. 1934, LXXVIII, 79-80.

TOMORROW MAY BE TOO LATE. A Talk with K. Glover. *Good Housekeeping*, March 1934, XCVIII, 20-21.
Summary in *School Management*, April 1934, III, 13.

INTELLIGENCE AND POWER. *New Republic*, 25 April 1934, LXXVIII, 306-307.

LETTER TO ROOSEVELT ON UNEMPLOYMENT PROGRAM. *New York Times*, 11 June 1934, 2:6.

LETTER ON CHAPTER OF "PLAY OF IDEAS." *New York Times*, 8 July 1934, IX, 7:7.

LETTER ON PHILOSOPHY OF EXPRESSION. *New York Times*, 15 July 1934, X, 7:7.

CHARACTER TRAINING FOR YOUTH. *Rotarian*, Sept. 1934, XLV, 8.
Also in *Recreation*, June 1935, XXIX, 139-142.
Condensed in *Kansas Teacher*, Oct. 1934, XXXIX, 6.
Abstracted in *School Management*, Sept. 1934, IV, 6.

CAN EDUCATION SHARE IN SOCIAL RECONSTRUCTION? *Social Frontier*, Oct. 1934, I, 11-12.

NEED FOR A PHILOSOPHY OF EDUCATION. *New Era*, Nov. 1934, XV, 211-214.

RADIO'S INFLUENCE ON THE MIND; SUMMARY. *School and Society*, 15 Dec. 1934, XL, 805.
Also in *Educational Review* (China), March 1935, XXVII, 178.

EDUCATION FOR A CHANGING SOCIAL ORDER. In *American Association of Teachers Colleges. Thirteenth Yearbook.* Pp. 60-68.
Also in *National Education Association Proceedings*, 1934, pp. 744-752.

LIBERATION OF MODERN RELIGION. *Yale Review*, 1934, N. S. XXIII, 751-770.

1935

THE FOUNDER OF PRAGMATISM. Review of the *Collected Papers of Charles Sanders Peirce*, ed. by Charles Hartshorne and Paul Weiss. Vol. V. *New Republic*, 30 Jan. 1935, LXXXI, 338-339.

INTIMATIONS OF MORTALITY. Review of Corliss Lamont, *The Illusion of Immortality*. *New Republic*, 24 April 1935, LXXXII, 318.

BERGSON ON INSTINCT. Review of Henri Bergson, *The Two Sources of Morality and Religion*. *New Republic*, 26 June 1935, LXXXIII, 200-201.

NEEDED A NEW POLITICS. In *World Fellowship*. Addresses and Messages. Edited by C. F. Weller. New York. Pp. 119-125.

EMPIRICAL SURVEY OF EMPIRICISM. In *Studies in the History of Ideas*. Edited by the Department of Philosophy of Columbia University. New York: Columbia University Press. Vol. III, 3-22.

FOREWORD. In *Education in the Soviet Union, an Exhibition under the Auspices of the American Russian Institute for Cultural Relations with the Soviet Union*. Edited by W. A. Neilson. New York: American Russian Institute.

LIBERALISM AND SOCIAL ACTION. New York: Putnam. 93 pp.

SCIENCE AND SOCIETY. In *Leadership in a Changing World*. Edited by M. David Hoffman and Ruth Wanger. New York: Harpers. Pp. 266-276.

THE FUTURE OF LIBERALISM. *School and Society*, 19 Jan. 1935, XLI, 73-77.
Also in *American Association of University Professors Bulletin*, May 1935, XXI, 415-417; and in *Journal of Philosophy*, 25 April 1935, XXXII, 225-230.

THE TEACHER AND THE PUBLIC. *Vital Speeches*, 28 Jan. 1935, I, 278-279.
Also in *American Teacher*, March 1935, XIX, 3-4.

THE TEACHER AND HIS WORLD. *Social Frontier*, Jan. 1935, I, no. 4, p. 7.

THE CRUCIAL RÔLE OF INTELLIGENCE. *Social Frontier*, Feb. 1935, I, no. 5, 9-10.

TOWARD ADMINISTRATIVE STATESMANSHIP. *Social Frontier*, March 1935, I, no. 6, 9-10.

UNITED, WE SHALL STAND. *Social Frontier*, April 1935, I, no. 7, 11-12.
Also in *School and Community*, April 1935, XXI, 143-145.

GOVERNMENT AND CHILDREN. *American Teacher*, May 1935, XIX, 20.

YOUTH IN A CONFUSED WORLD. *Social Frontier*, May 1935, I, no. 8, 9-10.

EDUCATION AND OUR SOCIETY; THE NEED FOR ORIENTATION. *Forum and Century*, June 1935, XCIII, 333-335.

EDUCATORS URGED TO JOIN WITH OTHER WORKERS. *School Management*, June 1935, IV, 207.

TOWARD A NATIONAL SYSTEM OF EDUCATION. *Social Frontier*, June 1935, I, no. 9, 9-10.

LIBERTY AND SOCIAL CONTROL. *Social Frontier*, Nov. 1935, II, 41-42.

THE MEANING OF LIBERALISM. *Social Frontier*, Dec. 1935, II, 74-75.

PEIRCE'S THEORY OF QUALITY. *Journal of Philosophy*, 19 Dec. 1935, XXXII, 701-708.

1936

GOVERNMENT IN THE MACHINE AGE. In *Modern Reader*. Edited by W. Lippmann and A. Nevins. New York: Heath. Pp. 25-36.

LIBERALISM AND EQUALITY. *Social Frontier*, Jan. 1936, II, 105-106.

THE JAMESES. Review of Ralph Barton Perry, *The Thought and Character of William James*. *New Republic*, 12 Feb. 1936, LXXXVI, 24-25.

EDUCATION AND NEW SOCIAL IDEALS. *Vital Speeches*, 24 Feb. 1936, II, 327-328.

LIBERALISM AND CIVIL LIBERTIES. *Social Frontier*, Feb. 1936, II, 137-138.

SOCIAL SIGNIFICANCE OF ACADEMIC FREEDOM. *Social Frontier*, March 1936, II, 165-166.

CHARACTERISTICS AND CHARACTERS: KINDS AND CLASSES. *Journal of Philosophy*, 7 May 1936, XXXIII, 253-261.

CLASS STRUGGLE AND THE DEMOCRATIC WAY. *Social Frantier*, May 1936, II, 241-242.

WHAT ARE UNIVERSALS? *Journal of Philosophy*, 21 May 1936, XXXIII, 281-288.

ONE CURRENT RELIGIOUS PROBLEM. *Journal of Philosophy*, 4 June 1936, XXXIII, 324-326.

THE WORK OF GEORGE MEAD. Review of George H. Mead, *Mind, Self and Society*, and of *Movements of Thought in the 19th Century*. *New Republic*, 22 July 1936, LXXXVII, 329-330.

HOW THEY ARE VOTING. (Letters by John Dewey and others.) *New Republic*, 7 Oct. 1936, LXXXVIII, 249.

AUTHORITY AND RESISTANCE TO SOCIAL CHANGE. *School and Society*, 10 Oct. 1936, XLIV, 457-466.
Abridged in *Survey Graphic*, under title: "Authority and Freedom." Nov. 1936, XXV, 603-606.

HORACE MANN TODAY. *Social Frontier*, Nov. 1936, III, 41-42.
Also in *Educational Digest*, Jan. 1937, II, 12-14.

INTEGRITY OF EDUCATION. *Educational Digest*, Nov. 1936, II, 1-3.
Reprinted in *Internationale Zeitschrift für Erziehung*, 1937, VI, 57.

GENERAL PROPOSITIONS, KINDS AND CLASSES. *Journal of Philosophy*, 3 Dec. 1936, XXXIII, 673-680.

RATIONALITY IN EDUCATION. *Social Frontier*, Dec. 1936, III, 71-73.

RELIGION, SCIENCE AND PHILOSOPHY. *Southern Review*, 1936, 2d ser., I, 53-62.

1937

THE TEACHER AND SOCIETY. Written by John Dewey, in collaboration with William H. Kilpatrick, and others. New York: Appleton-Century. 360 pp. (First Yearbook of the John Dewey Society.)

AUTHORITY AND SOCIAL CHANGE. In *Authority and the Individual*. Cambridge, Mass.: Harvard University Press. Pp. 170-190.

THE CASE OF LEON TROTSKY; REPORT OF HEARINGS ON THE CHARGES MADE AGAINST HIM IN THE MOSCOW TRIALS. By the Preliminary Commission of Inquiry, John Dewey, Chairman. New York: Harper & Brothers. 617 pp.

EDUCATION, THE FOUNDATION FOR SOCIAL ORGANIZATION. In *Educating for Democracy, a Symposium*. Yellow Springs, Ohio: Antioch Press. pp. 37-54.
Excerpts in *National Education Association Journal*, Dec. 1936, XXV, 275; also in *School and Community*, May 1937, XXIII, 186. Condensed in *Educational Digest*, March 1937, II, 32-34.

THE FORWARD VIEW: A FREE TEACHER IN A FREE SOCIETY. By John Dewey and Goodwin Watson. In *The Teacher and Society*. First Yearbook of the John Dewey Society. New York: Appleton-Century. Pp. 330-345.

TRUTH IS ON THE MARCH: REPORT AND REMARKS ON THE TROTSKY HEARINGS IN MEXICO. New York: American Committee for the Defense of Leon Trotsky. 15 pp.

PRESIDENT HUTCHINS' PROPOSALS TO REMAKE HIGHER EDUCATION. *Social Frontier*, Jan. 1937, III, 103-104.

CHARLES SANDERS PEIRCE. Review of the *Collected Papers of Charles Sanders Peirce*, ed. by Charles Hartshorne and Paul Weiss. 6 vols. *New Republic*, 3 Feb. 1937, LXXXIX, 415-416.

CHALLENGE OF DEMOCRACY TO EDUCATION. *Progressive Education*, Feb. 1937, XIV, 79-85.

HIGHER LEARNING IN AMERICA. *Social Frontier*, March 1937, III, 167-169.

WHITEHEAD'S PHILOSOPHY. *Philosophical Review*, March 1937, XLVI, 170-177.

PRAVDA ON TROTSKY. (A letter.) *New Republic*, 24 March 1937, XC, 212-213.

RIGHTING AN ACADEMIC WRONG. (Letter in Kraus case.) *New Republic*, 31 March 1937, XC, 242.

DEMOCRACY AND EDUCATIONAL ADMINISTRATION. *School and Society*, 3 April 1937, XLV, 457-462.
Reprinted in *Official Report of the American Association of School Administrators*, 1937, pp. 48-55.
Excerpts in *Educational Digest*, April 1937, II, 1-3.

SUBJECT MATTER IN ART. Review of Walter Abell, *Representation and Form*. *New Republic*, 21 April 1937, XC, 335.

THE FUTURE OF DEMOCRACY. *New Republic*, 28 April 1937, XC, 351.

EDUCATION AND SOCIAL CHANGE. *Social Frontier*, May 1937, III, 235-238.
Reprinted in *New Trends in Group Work*. Edited by Joshua Lieberman. New York: Association Press, 1938, pp. 15-27.
Excerpts in *Bulletin of the American Association of University Professors*, Oct. 1937, XXIII, 472-474.

THE PHILOSOPHY OF WILLIAM JAMES. *Southern Review*, 1937, 2d ser., III, 447-461.

SIGNIFICANCE OF THE TROTSKY TRIAL. Interview with John Dewey. By Agnes E. Meyer. *International Conciliation*, Feb. 1938, no. 337, pp. 53-60. (Reprinted by permission from *The Washington Post*, Dec. 19, 1937.)

1938

EXPERIENCE AND EDUCATION. New York: Macmillan. 116 pp.
Published in London by Macmillan, 1938.

LOGIC: THE THEORY OF INQUIRY. New York: Holt. 546 pp.
Published in London by G. Allen, 1939.

FOREWORD. *In* David Lindsay Watson, *Scientists Are Human* (London: Watts, 1938; 249 pp. Toronto: Ryerson Press, 1938).

NOT GUILTY: Report of the Commission of Inquiry into the Charges Made against Leon Trotsky in the Moscow Trials. New York, 1937. John Dewey, Chairman. New York: Harpers. 422 pp.
Published in London by Secker and Warburg, 1938.
Published in Toronto by Musson, 1938.

UNITY OF SCIENCE AS A SOCIAL PROBLEM. *International Encyclopedia of Unified Science.* Edited by Otto Neurath and others. Chicago: University of Chicago Press. Vol. I, no. 1, 29-38.

TO THOSE WHO ASPIRE TO THE PROFESSION OF TEACHING. In *My Vocation,* by eminent Americans. Compiled by Earl Granger Lockhart. New York: Wilson. Pp. 325-334.

RELATION OF SCIENCE AND PHILOSOPHY AS THE BASIS OF EDUCATION. *School and Society,* 9 April 1938, XLVII, 470-473.

WHAT IS SOCIAL STUDY? *Progressive Education,* May 1938, XV, 367-369.
Excerpts in *Educational Digest,* Sept. 1938, IV, 52-53.

EDUCATION, DEMOCRACY, AND SOCIALIZED ECONOMY. *Social Frontier,* Dec. 1938, V, 71-72.

DETERMINATION OF ULTIMATE VALUES OR AIMS THROUGH ANTECEDENT OR A PRIORI SPECULATION OR THROUGH PRAGMATIC OR EMPIRICAL INQUIRY. In *National Society for the Study of Education. Thirty-Seventh Yearbook.* Chicago. Part 2, pp. 471-485.

DOES HUMAN NATURE CHANGE? *Rotarian,* LII, 8-11, 58-59.

DEMOCRACY AND EDUCATION IN THE WORLD OF TODAY. New York: Society for Ethical Culture. 15 pp.

1939

INTELLIGENCE IN THE MODERN WORLD. John Dewey's Philosophy. Ed. by Joseph Ratner. New York: Modern Library. 1077 pp.

Published in Toronto by Macmillan, 1939.

Selections reprinted from earlier publications with the following new material: THE ECONOMIC BASIS OF A NEW SOCIETY. Pp. 416-433. THE UNITY OF THE HUMAN BEING. Pp. 817-835.

FREEDOM AND CULTURE. New York: G. P. Putnam's Sons (1939), 176 pp.

Translation. Spanish, by Angela Romera Vera. (Rosario, 1946).

TURKIYE MAARIFI HAKKINDA RAPOR. (Istanbul, Devlet Basmevi, 1939.)

On education in Turkey.

THEORY OF VALUATION. *International Encyclopedia of Unified Science.* Chicago: The University of Chicago Press. Vol. II, no. 4. 67 pp.

WHAT IS DEMOCRACY? ITS CONFLICTS, ENDS AND MEANS. By John Dewey and others. Norman, Oklahoma: Cooperative Books. 35 pp.

INTRODUCTION. By John Dewey and William H. Kilpatrick. To *Talks to Teachers,* by William James. New Ed. New York: Holt. 283 pp.

INTRODUCTION. To *Problems of Ageing.* Ed. by Edmund Vincent COWDRY. (Baltimore: William and Wilkins. 788 pp.)

CREDO. Revision of, in Clifton Fadiman, ed., *I Believe* (New York: Simon and Schuster, 1939) pp. 347-354.

First published in 1930.

(Published separately, New York: Simon and Schuster (1931).

IF WAR COMES, SHALL WE PARTICIPATE OR BE NEUTRAL? A Symposium. John Dewey: "No Matter What Happens—Stay Out!" *Common Sense,* March 1939, VIII no. 3, 11.

EDUCATION: 1800-1939. Founder's Day Lecture at the University of Vermont, May 1, 1939. In *The Vermont Alumnus,* Vol. XVIII, No. 8 (May 1939), pp. 169-170 and 188-189.

COLLEGE YOUTH BETTER MANNERED. *Vermont Alumnus.* June 1939, XVIII, 196-197.

REVIEW of *America in Midpassage* by Charles A. Beard and Mary R. Beard. "Atlantic Bookshelf," *Atlantic Monthly,* July 1939, CLXIV, preliminary pages.

EXPERIENCE, KNOWLEDGE AND VALUE: A REJOINDER. In *The Philosophy of John Dewey.* (Vol. 1 of *The Library of Living Philoso-*

phers), ed. by Paul Arthur Schilpp, 517-608.

1st edition, Evanston and Chicago: Northwestern University, 1939 The Library of Living Philosophers, Inc., Evanston, Illinois, and 2nd edition, Tudor Publishing Company, New York, 1951.

A PHILOSOPHER'S PHILOSOPHY. New York Times, October 15, 1939, 5.

CREATIVE DEMOCRACY—THE TASK BEFORE US. In *John Dewey and the Promise of America*. Columbus, American Education Press, 1939. (Progressive Education Booklet, no. 14, pp. 12-17.)

Same. In *The Philosopher of the Common Man; Essays in Honor of John Dewey*. New York, G. P. Putnam's Sons (1940), 228 pp.

Same. *Bulletin of the Association of American Colleges*, May 1940. XXVI, 198-203.

Excerpts. *Childhood Education*, December 1939, XVI, 153.

HIGHER LEARNING AND WAR. *Bulletin of the American Association of University Professors*, XXV, 1939, 613f.

REPLY, to discussion of his philosophy by W. E. Hocking and M. Cohen. *New York Times*, December 29, 1939, 17:4.

1940

EDUCATION TODAY, edited and with a foreword by Joseph Ratner. New York, G. P. Putnam's Sons (1940), xix and 376 pp. Abridged English ed., London, Allen & Unwin, 1941.

THE LIVING THOUGHTS OF THOMAS JEFFERSON, presented by John Dewey. New York, Longmans, Green and Co., 1940; "Presenting Thomas Jefferson," 1-30. (Vol. 14 in *The Living Thoughts Library*, ed. by A. O. Mendel.)

THOMAS JEFFERSON AND THE DEMOCRATIC FAITH. *Virginia Quarterly Review, XVI*, January 1940, 1-13.

MEANING OF THE TERM: LIBERALISM. *Frontiers of Democracy*, February 1940, VI, 135.

LETTER TO C.C.N.Y. HEAD, defending Bertrand Russell's appointment. *New York Times*, March 12, 1940, 27:5.

NATURE IN EXPERIENCE. *Philosophical Review*, XLIX, March 1940, 244-258.

Reprinted in *Problems of Men*, 1946.

LETTERS on educational inquiries, U. S. *New York Times*, May 6, 1940, 16:5, and May 14, 1940, 22:6.

CONTRARY TO HUMAN NATURE. *Frontiers of Democracy*, May 1940, VI, 234f.

CASE FOR BERTRAND RUSSELL. *Nation*, CL, June 15, 1940, 732f.

VANISHING SUBJECT IN THE PSYCHOLOGY OF JAMES. *Journal of Philosophy*, XXXVII, October 24, 1940, 589-599.
Reprinted in *Problems of Men*, 1946.

1941

THE BERTRAND RUSSELL CASE, edited by John Dewey and Horace M. Kallen. New York, The Viking Press, 1941, 227 pp.
Introduction and *Social Realities Versus Police Court Fictions*, by John Dewey.

SCIENCE AND DEMOCRACY. *Scientific Monthly*, LII, January 1941, 52-55.

PROPOSITIONS, WARRANTED ASSERTIBILITY, AND TRUTH. *Journal of Philosophy*, XXXVIII, March 27, 1941, 169-186.
Reprinted in *Problems of Men*, 1946.

BASIC VALUES AND LOYALTIES OF DEMOCRACY. *American Teacher*, May 1941, XXV, 8f.

FOR A NEW EDUCATION. *New Era*, June 1941, XXII, 134.

MESSAGE TO AMERICAN FEDERATION OF TEACHERS. *New York Times*, August 24, 1941, 18:2.

OBJECTIVISM-SUBJECTIVISM OF MODERN PHILOSOPHY. *Journal of Philosophy*, XXXVIII, September 25, 1941, 533-542.
Reprinted in *Problems of Men*, 1946.

REVIEW. *Philosophy of George Santayana*, ed. by P. A. Schilpp. *Mind*, L. October 1941, 374-385.

1942

GERMAN PHILOSOPHY AND POLITICS. Revised edition, New York, G. P. Putnam's Sons (1942).
First published in 1915.

HOW IS MIND TO BE KNOWN? *Journal of Philosophy*, XXXIX, January 15, 1942, 29-35.
Reprinted in *Problems of Men*, 1946.

CAN WE WORK WITH RUSSIA? A LETTER TO THE NEW YORK TIMES. *Frontiers of Democracy*, March 1942, VIII, 179f.

INQUIRY AND INDETERMINATENESS OF SITUATIONS. *Journal of Philosophy*, XXXIX, May 21, 1942, 290-296.
Reprinted in *Problems of Men*, 1946.

AMBIGUITY OF "INTRINSIC GOOD." *Journal of Philosophy*, XXXIX, June 4, 1942, 328-330.
Reprinted in *Problems of Men*, 1946.

1943

THE DEVELOPMENT OF AMERICAN PRAGMATISM, in Runes, D.D., ed., *Twentieth Century Philosophy*, 1943, pp. 451-468.
First published as *Developpement du Pragmatisme*, 1922 (cf. pp. 649 and 653 *supra*).

REPLY to letter on his educational principles. *New York Times*, January 8, 1943, 18:7.

THE PRINCIPLES. *Psychological Review*, L, January 1943, 121.

LETTER ON FILM, MISSION TO MOSCOW. *New York Times*, May 9, 1943, IV, 8:5.

REPLIES to responses to his letter, *New York Times*, May 24, 1943, 14:6, and June 19, 1943, 12:7.

VALUATION JUDGMENTS AND IMMEDIATE QUALITY. *Journal of Philosophy*, XL, June 10, 1943, 309-317.
Reprinted in *Problems of Men*, 1946.

FURTHER AS TO VALUATION AS JUDGMENT. *Journal of Philosophy*, XL, September 30, 1943, 543-552.
Reprinted in *Problems of Men*, 1946.

1944

ANTINATURALISM IN EXTREMIS. In Krikorian, Y. H., ed., *Naturalism and the Human Spirit*. New York, Columbia University Press, 1944, pp. 1-16 (Columbia Studies in Philosophy, no. 85).

MY PEDOGOGIC CREED. In *Future Teachers of America, Fourth Yearbook*, 1944, pp. 8-23.
First published in 1897. (Cf. p. 618 *supra*.)
Also in *Education Today*, 1940.

BY NATURE AND BY ART. *Journal of Philosophy*, XLI, May 25, 1944, 281-292.
Reprinted in *Problems of Men*, 1946.

HUMAN NATURE AND CONDUCT. Reprinted in War Dept. *Education Manual* E M 618, (1944).

First published in 1922. (Cf. p. 648 *supra*.)

Instructor's Course Outline, Ethics. College Course. War Dept. *Education Manual* E M 618 a, (1944).

Excerpt in Thorp, W. and Thorp, M. F., ed., *Modern Writing*, 1944, pp. 323-331.

Excerpt entitled MORALS AND CONDUCT in Commins, S. and Linscott, R. N., eds., *Man and Man: The Social Philosophers*, (Vol. II of *The World's Great Thinkers*), Random House, 1947, pp. 449-485.

Excerpt entitled INTRODUCTION TO SOCIAL PSYCHOLOGY in Mayberry, G., ed., *Little Treasury of American Prose*, 1949, pp. 353-358.

STATEMENT opposing R. M. Hutchins' educational theories. *New York Times*, May 28, 1944, 35:4.

DEMOCRATIC FAITH AND EDUCATION. *Antioch Review*, June 1944, IV, 274-283.

Reprinted in *Problems of Men*, 1946.

SOME QUESTIONS ABOUT VALUE. *Journal of Philosophy*, XLI, August 17, 1944, 449-455.

Reprinted in *Problems of Men*, 1946.

CHALLENGE TO LIBERAL THOUGHT. *Fortune*, XXX, August 1944, 154; XXXI, March 1945, 10.

Also in *Time*, XLIV, August 21, 1944, 48.

Also in *Education Digest*, X, September 1944, 1.

Reprinted in *Problems of Men*, 1946.

PROBLEM OF THE LIBERAL ARTS COLLEGE. *American Scholar*, October 1944, XIII, 391-393.

Reprinted in *Problems of Men*, 1946.

85TH BIRTHDAY: STATEMENT CHIDING N. M. BUTLER AND R. M. HUTCHINS, INTERVIEW. *New York Times*, October 20, 1944, 32:1.

1945

DEMOCRATIC FAITH AND EDUCATION. In *Conference on the Scientific Spirit and Democratic Faith*, 2nd, Columbia University Press, 1945, pp. 1-12.

DEMOCRATIC VERSUS COERCIVE INTERNATIONAL ORGANIZATION: THE REALISM OF JANE ADDAMS. In Addams, Jane, *Peace and Bread in Time of War*, Anniversary edition, 1915-1945. New York, Kings Crown Press, 1945, ix-xx.

SEARCH FOR FIRM NAMES. *Journal of Philosophy*, XLII, January 4, 1945, 5f.
With A. F. Bentley.

METHOD IN SCIENCE TEACHING. *Science Education*, April 1945, XXIX, 119-123.

PEACE AND BREAD. *Survey Graphic*, XXXIV, April 1945, 116-118+.

TERMINOLOGY FOR KNOWINGS AND KNOWNS. *Journal of Philosophy*, XLII, April 26, 1945, 225-247.
With A. F. Bentley.

ARE NATURALISTS MATERIALISTS? *Journal of Philosophy*, XLII, September 13, 1945, 515-530.
With others.

POSTULATIONS. *Journal of Philosophy*, XLII, November 22, 1945, 645-662.
With A. F. Bentley.

ETHICAL SUBJECT-MATTER AND LANGUAGE. *Journal of Philosophy*, XLII, December 20, 1945, 701-712.

1946

THE PUBLIC AND ITS PROBLEMS. Second edition, Chicago, Gateway Books, 1946.
First Published in 1927. (Cf. p. 656 *supra*.)
Excerpt entitled STATE AS AN ORGANIZED PUBLIC in Snyder, R. C. and Wilson, H. H., eds., *Roots of Political Behavior*, 1949, pp. 90-97.

PROBLEMS OF MEN. New York, Philosophical Library (1946), 424 pp.

DISCOVERY OF THE STATE. In Browne, W. R., ed., *Leviathan in Crisis*, 1946, 3-13.

PEIRCE'S THEORY OF LINGUISTIC SIGNS, THOUGHT AND MEANING. *Journal of Philosophy*, XLIII, February 1946, 85-95.

CRISIS IN HUMAN HISTORY. *Commentary*, I, March 1946, 1-19.

INTERACTION AND TRANSACTION. *Journal of Philosophy*, XLIII, September 1946, 505-517.
With A. F. Bentley.

TRANSACTIONS AS KNOWN AND NAMED. *Journal of Philosophy*, XLIII
September 1946, 533-551.
With A. F. Bentley.

SPECIFICATION. *Journal of Philosophy*, XLIII, November 1946, 645-
663.
With A. F. Bentley.

1947

ART AND EDUCATION. Second edition revised and enlarged, 1947.
First published in 1929. (Cf. p. 660 *supra*.) With others.

SUBSTANCE, POWER AND QUALITY IN LOCKE. In *Freedom and Experience; Essays Presented to Horace M. Kallen*. Ithaca, Cornell
University Press, 1947, pp. 205-220.

WHAT IS THOUGHT? In Bader, Arno Lehman and Wells, C. F., eds.
Essays for Our Time. New York, Harper, 1947, pp. 3-7.
First published in Smith, C. A., ed., *Essays on Current Themes*, 1923, pp. 12-23.
Reprinted in Michigan University, Department of Rhetoric and Journalism,
Adventures in Essay Reading, 1924, pp. 377-382.

S. 2499; ITS ANTIDEMOCRATIC IMPLICATIONS. *Nation's Schools*, March
1947, XXXIX, 20-21.
Same. *Progressive Education*, April, 1947, XXIV, 206-207+.

DEFINITION. *Journal of Philosophy*, XLIV, May 1947, 281-305.
With A. F. Bentley.

CONCERNING A VOCABULARY FOR INQUIRY INTO KNOWLEDGE. *Journal of Philosophy*, XLIV, July 1947, 421-433.
With A. F. Bentley.

LIBERATING THE SOCIAL SCIENTIST. *Commentary*, IV, October 1947,
378-385.

1948

RECONSTRUCTION IN PHILOSOPHY. Enlarged edition with a new introduction, Boston, Beacon Press, (1948). (Cf. p. 644 *supra*.)
First published in 1920.

WHAT IS DEMOCRACY? In Bishop, H. M., and Hendel, S., eds. *Basic
Issues of American Democracy*, 1948, pp. 20-23.

WILLIAM JAMES' MORALS AND JULIEN BENDA'S. *Commentary*, V.
January, 1948, 46-50.

DEMOKRATIE ALS AUFGABE UNSERER ZEIT. *Bildung und Erziehung,* Stuttgart, I, 1948, Heft 2, 1-6.

COMMON SENSE AND SCIENCE: THEIR RESPECTIVE FRAMES OF REFERENCE. *Journal of Philosophy,* XLV, April 8, 1948, 197-208.

1949

KNOWING AND THE KNOWN. *Boston,* The Beacon Press, 1949. xiii and 334 pp.
With A. F. Bentley.

THE WIT AND WISDOM OF JOHN DEWEY; edited, with an introduction, by A. H. Johnson. Boston, Beacon Press, 1949; 47-111.

THE FIELD OF "VALUE." In Lepley, Ray, *Value: A Cooperative Inquiry.* New York, Columbia University Press, 1949; 64-77.

LANGUAGE AND THE TRAINING OF THOUGHT, excerpt from HOW WE THINK (1910) in Briggs, H. E., ed., *Language, Man, Society,* 1949, pp. 55-65.

EDUCATION AND THE SOCIAL ORDER. New York, League for Industrial Democracy, *Pamphlet Series,* 1949. 14 pp.

PHILOSOPHY'S FUTURE IN OUR SCIENTIFIC AGE. Commentary, VIII, October 1949, 388-394.

PHILOSOPHER-IN-THE MAKING: AUTOBIOGRAPHY. Saturday Review of Literature, XXXII, October 22, 1949, 9-10+. (Cf. p.663 *supra.*)
First published in 1930, under the title, "From Absolutism to Experimentalism."

1950

JOHN DEWEY AT NINETY, addresses and greetings on the occasion of Professor Dewey's ninetieth birthday dinner, October 20, 1949, at the Hotel Commodore, New York, by John Dewey and others. Edited by Harry W. Laidler. New York, League for Industrial Democracy (1950).

ADDENDA TO THE
WRITINGS OF JOHN DEWEY

1900

MENTAL DEVELOPMENT. (Chicago) c1900. 12 leaves, mimeographed.
At head of title: University of Chicago, Department of Philosophy and Pedagogy. Copy in University of Chicago Library.

1909

THE MORAL SIGNIFICANCE OF THE COMMON SCHOOL STUDIES. Northern Illinois Teachers' Association, *Program of Meeting,* November 5th and 6th, 1909, pp. 21-27.

1928

DEWEY'S SUPPRESSED PSYCHOLOGY: a psychological study of John Dewey . . . being correspondence between John Dewey and Scudder Klyce, Winchester, Mass., S. Klyce, 1928. 294 pp.

1930

QUALITATIVE THOUGHT. *The Symposium,* January 1930, I, 5-32.
Reprinted in *Philosophy and Civilization* (1931), pp. 93-116.

1931

APPRECIATION AND CULTIVATION. *Harvard Teachers Record,* April 1931, I, 73-76.

PEOPLE'S LOBBY BULLETIN, Washington, D. C., 1931-5. Many articles contributed by John Dewey.

1932

EDUCATION IN ACTION. In Devere Allen, *Adventurous Americans,* New York: Farrar and Rinehart (c1932), pp. 130-140.

POLITICS AND CULTURE. *Modern Thinker,* May 1932, I, 168-174, 238.

1933

ENCYCLOPEDIA OF THE SOCIAL SCIENCES, IX. (New York: The MacMillan Company, 1933).
Dewey contributed articles on *Logic, Outlawry of War,* and *Philosophy.*

1934

INDIVIDUAL PSYCHOLOGY AND EDUCATION. *The Philosopher*, April 1934, XII, 56-62.

1935

WHEN AMERICA GOES TO WAR. *Modern Monthly*, June 1935, IX, 200.

NATURE AND HUMANITY. *The New Humanist*, Autumn 1935, VIII, 153-157.

DER PROJEKT-PLAN. Weimar, 1935. In German. 213 pp.
With William Kilpatrick.

1936

A LIBERAL SPEAKS OUT FOR LIBERALISM. *New York Times*, February 23, 1936, 3.

1937

THE EDUCATIONAL FUNCTION OF A MUSEUM OF DECORATIVE ARTS. *Chronicle of the Museum for the Arts of Decoration of Cooper Union* (New York), April 1937, I, 93-99.

INDEX

(Not including Bibliography)

687